Dear R+R, We need much more R+R!

GLOBALIZATION AND SOVEREIGNTY

Thanks for your support & inspiration — & friendship I Am so happy about & best | best)

Sovereignty and the sovereign state are often seen as anachronisms; *Globalization and Sovereignty* challenges this view. Jean L. Cohen analyzes the new sovereignty regime emergent since the 1990s evidenced by the discourses and practice of human rights, humanitarian intervention, transformative occupation, and the UN targeted sanctions regime that blacklists alleged terrorists. Presenting a systematic theory of sovereignty and its transformation in international law and politics, Cohen argues for the continued importance of sovereign equality. She offers a theory of a dualistic world order comprised of an international society of states, and a global political community in which human rights and global governance institutions affect the law, policies, and political culture of sovereign states. She advocates the constitutionalization of these institutions, within the framework of constitutional pluralism. This book will appeal to students of international political theory and law, political scientists, sociologists, legal historians, and theorists of constitutionalism.

JEAN L. COHEN is Nell and Herbert Singer Professor of Contemporary Civilization and Political Theory in the Department of Political Science at Columbia University where she has been teaching political theory for over twenty-five years. She has taught courses on sovereignty, the state, global constitutionalism, and global justice for the past ten years. She is the author of *Class and Civil Society: The Limits of Marxian Critical Theory* (1982); *Civil Society and Political Theory* (co-authored with Andrew Arato, 1992); and *Regulating Intimacy: A New Legal Paradigm* (2002).

D1256918

GLOBALIZATION AND SOVEREIGNTY

Rethinking Legality, Legitimacy, and Constitutionalism

JEAN L. COHEN

CAMBRIDGE
UNIVERSITY PRESS

CAMBRIDGE UNIVERSITY PRESS

Cambridge, New York, Melbourne, Madrid, Cape Town,
Singapore, São Paulo, Delhi, Mexico City

Cambridge University Press
The Edinburgh Building, Cambridge CB2 8RU, UK

Published in the United States of America by Cambridge University Press, New York

www.cambridge.org
Information on this title: www.cambridge.org/9780521148450

First published 2012

Printed and Bound in the United Kingdom by the MPG Books Group

A catalogue record for this publication is available from the British Library

Library of Congress Cataloguing in Publication data

Cohen, Jean L.
Globalization and sovereignty : rethinking legality, legitimacy
and constitutionalism / Jean L. Cohen.
pages cm
Includes bibliographical references.
ISBN 978-0-521-76585-5 (Hardback) – ISBN 978-0-521-14845-0 (Paperback)
1. Sovereignty. 2. International relations. 3. International law.
4. Globalization–Political aspects. I. Title.
JZ4034.C63 2012
320.1′5–dc23
2012012601

ISBN 978-0-521-76585-5 Hardback
ISBN 978-0-521-14845-0 Paperback

CONTENTS

PREFACE

I was motivated to write this book by two contradictory trends beginning in the second half of the twentieth century. The first is the growing importance of the discourses of human rights, cosmopolitanism, global constitutionalism, and democracy, along with the proliferation of international covenants, United Nations (UN) resolutions and international courts focused on promoting and enforcing them. The second is the use of these discourses and institutions to legitimate (or spur) the development of novel forms of hegemonic international law, new imperial formations, global hierarchies, and transgressions of existing international law by the powerful. Since the early 1990s the Janus-faced nature of humanitarian and "democratic" interventions, transformative occupations, and increasingly activist, intrusive, legislative, and at times rights-violating resolutions of the United Nations Security Council (UNSC) in the "war on terror," has become evident. The intervention in Kosovo and the American war in Iraq are the two most obvious early examples. These events triggered my interest in international political and legal theory along with my determination to decode the ideological discourses on both sides of the conundrum just described.

It is striking that irrespective of whether one's focus is on the first or the second trend, many analysts of legal and political globalization assume that the rules of international law based on the principles of sovereign equality, non-intervention, self-determination, and domestic jurisdiction are anachronistic today, as is the frame of an international society of sovereign states. Indeed it is claimed that both the concept of sovereignty and the ideal of the sovereign state should be abandoned. The task today, apparently, is to constitutionalize or fight institutional expressions of global right depending on one's diagnosis and point of view, not to defend rules and concepts that allegedly no longer fit the contemporary constellation.

Such claims are useful to those seeking to do an end-run around restrictions on the international use of force. But they are also invoked by people deeply concerned with human rights, the rule of law, constitutionalism, and with what is now called the state's and the international community's "responsibility to protect." Indeed, juridification and "constitutionalization" in the international/global domain are also Janus-faced processes and discourses: both enabling (by helping constitute) and limiting new and older global powers and new freedoms and counter-powers. At the heart of these conflicting and ambiguous trends and projects lies a paradox: the sovereign state form has been globalized, but the international organizations (IOs) states have created in part to secure non-aggression and sovereign equality are morphing into global governance institutions (GGIs) whose expanding scope and reach, in conjunction with human rights discourses and law, seem to place the very ideal of the sovereign state and the principles of sovereign equality, self-determination, and non-intervention into question. So do the geopolitical and socio-economic imperatives of size facing twenty-first-century polities. The international legal rules and principles devised to minimize the aggressive use of force and ensure domestic political autonomy are under threat while global decision-makers and the new forms of collectively authorized intervention in the name of humanitarian justice do not seem to be under any legal restraints or democratic controls. These developments spurred the emergence of the discourse and project of the constitutionalization of international law. But if constitutionalism entails hierarchy of norms, legal sources, and institutional authority, then the constitutionalization of international law and international organizations seems incompatible with state sovereignty. This is the conundrum my book addresses.

I try to move between ideological and infeasible utopian positions on both sides of the statist/cosmopolitan divide. I do so by rethinking the concepts of sovereignty and constitutionalism so as to come up with a workable conception of each, and by reflecting on the issues of legality and legitimacy that sovereignty, global governance, and human rights claims pose in the epoch of globalization. Thus this book does not fall neatly into any camp, be it statist or cosmopolitan, pluralist or monist, sovereigntist or global-constitutionalist. I turn to the more basic questions that these divides gloss over. Are human rights and sovereign equality really antithetical? Should the discourse of sovereignty (popular or state) be abandoned and replaced by global governance talk? Or is the latter simply the new hegemonic discourse of emergent imperial formations? Must the project of global constitutionalism entail the demise of the sovereign state, replacing a pluralist international system with a monistic, cosmopolitan world order? Or is there a coherent way to understand our epoch as permanently and productively dualistic: as undergoing a transition to a new sovereignty regime in which sovereign states (in a plural international society) and global governance institutions (referencing the international community) coexist, and in which constitutionalism and democracy on both domestic and international levels have an important role to play? And why does this matter?

This book tries to answer these questions by developing a theoretical framework based on the core intuition that human rights and sovereign equality are two key principles of our current dualistic international political system and that both are needed for a better, more just, and more effective version of that system. The hope is that with an adequate conception of sovereignty, constitutionalism, and of international human rights discourses and practices, we can develop feasible projects to render global governance institutions and all states more rights-respecting, democratic, and fair. The discourse of constitutionalization is, in my view, appropriate to this context. But it is time to soften the rigid hierarchical Kelsenian approach, and to develop a conception that acknowledges constitutionalism's inherently pluralistic dimensions as well as its requirement of unity and coherence: both are needed for any legal system to merit the label "constitutionalist." I thus embrace the novel idea of constitutional pluralism but see it as quite compatible with the principle of political autonomy of self-governing political communities at the heart of sovereignty, and with the principle of sovereign equality that still structures our international order. I argue that ours is a dualistic world order, comprised of an international society of sovereign states and a globalizing political system referencing an international community populated by global governance institutions, transnational actors, and courts as well as states. The question facing us is how to order and reform this dualistic system so that the achievements of democracy, constitutionalism, and justice are not lost, but rather, made available to everyone. The focus of this book is the conundrum of legality and legitimacy facing the premier GGI in the world today: the UN Charter system.

Thus the shift from civil society (the focus of my first two books), and privacy and equality law in the domain of intimacy (the focus of the third) to issues surrounding sovereignty and the state is not so terribly odd. One has to follow the path that new forms of power and injustice and new possibilities for freedom and fairness take, in order to intervene productively in the important debates and conflicts of our time. No one book can do everything, however, so this book leaves to the side the issues and injustices generated by contemporary forms of capitalist globalization as well as the challenges posed by increasingly powerful transnational and domestic religious organizations, to the secular liberal-democratic constitutional welfare state. Domestic legal and political sovereignty is certainly at stake in both, and I have already begun to work on the latter problematic. But this book lays the groundwork by focusing on rethinking the concept of sovereignty in analytic and normative terms, and assessing the fate of the sovereign state in the context of globalization.

Like all of my books, this one, too, was long in the making. I began working on sovereignty at the turn of this century, teaching courses on related topics at Columbia University and abroad. I thank my graduate students in those early seminars, for being wonderful and inspiring interlocutors and for their insights and questions, which helped me develop my ideas. Among those who participated and whose patience and intelligence are well worth commending are Adam Branch, Axel Domeyer, Alex Gourevitch, Jennifer Hudson, Ronald Jennings, Hanna Lerner, Raider Maliks, Bajeera McCorkle, Christian Rostboll, and Ian Zuckerman.

My first article on the topic, "Whose Sovereignty? Empire Versus International Law," appeared in *Ethics and International Affairs* in 2004, and I thank Christian Barry, at the time the editor of the journal, for encouraging me and for featuring the piece so centrally. I am also grateful for the terrific response I received from so many readers. This inspired me to pursue my interest in the field. But many colleagues and friends heard me present or commented on earlier drafts of various chapters whom I want very much to thank. Among these are Jose Alvarez, Eyal Benvenisti, Samantha Besson, Nehal Bhuta, Hauke Brunkhorst, Hubertus Buchstein, Mary Dietz, Andreas Fischer-Lescano, Rainer Forst, Robert Howse, Andreas Kalyvas, Regina Kreide, Claude Lefort, Frank Michelman, Terry Nardin, Yoav Peled, Pierre Rosanvallon, Michel Rosenfeld, Kim Scheppele, Ann Stoler, John Tasioulas, Ruti Teitel, Gunther Teubner, and Alain Touraine.

Many conferences (too many to provide a full list) and institutional affiliations helped me to refine and develop my ideas. I presented versions of various chapters at several American Political Science Association meetings, at three sessions of the yearly conference, "Philosophy and the Social Sciences," held in Prague, the Czech Republic, and at various conferences on sovereignty at Columbia University, including two organized by myself: "Rethinking Sovereignty" in 2003, and "Republic and Empire" in 2009, where the discussions with the conference participants were truly first-rate and enormously helpful. I benefited greatly by participating in a conference organized by Ruti Teitel on "Post Conflict Constitution-Making" at New York Law School in 2006, where I presented an early version of Chapter 4 on occupation law. I presented a very early version of the first part of Chapter 5 at the 2007 workshop of the journal *Constellations*, and another version at the international workshop on "Democratic Citizenship and War" organized by Noah Lewin-Epstein, Guy Mundlak, and Yoav Peled at Tel Aviv University in 2007. I presented the second part of Chapter 5, on the Kadi case, at a subsequent conference on "Constitution-Making in Deeply Divided Societies" organized by Amal Jamal and Hanna Lerner, also at Tel Aviv University and also at Sciences Po in Paris, France. I thank the organizers of these conferences for the opportunity to present and discuss my ideas with first-rate international scholars. The feedback by Eyal Benvenisti at the latter conference was invaluable. I wish also to mention the RECON working group in Norway for inviting me to give the plenary lecture at its conference on "Constitutionalism Beyond the State" in October, 2010, where I engaged in fruitful conversations with John Erik Fossum and Erik Eriksen, among others, on yet another version of portions of Chapter 5. I presented versions of

Chapter 3 on human rights at the President's Conference of the American University in Paris to which Richard Beardsworth invited me, in spring 2009; to the Istanbul Seminars organized by Reset Dialogues also in spring 2009; and at the Carnegie Council in fall 2009. On all of these occasions the discussion was first-rate and very helpful.

Without Columbia University's generous leave program and supportive atmosphere it would not have been possible for me to write this book. My thanks to the Reid Hall Faculty in Residence program in Paris, France, a Columbia University affiliate, for institutional support during the summer of 2003 and the fall semester of 2004 for providing me the time, the space, and the support to work on my project. I also thank the University of Sciences Po in Paris, France for twice hosting me (2004, 2009) as a Visiting Professor and enabling me to interact with French colleagues in a productive way in discussions about international political theory. My time as a Visiting Distinguished Professor at the Johann Wolfgang Goethe Universität in Frankfurt during the winter of 2008 was very helpful in affording me the opportunity to discuss my work with German and other international colleagues and students and I thank Rainer Forst for making this possible. Finally I am most grateful for the invaluable opportunity I was given to present a version of all the chapters in the book, with the exception of Chapter 2, at the Collège de France in Paris, France. I was honored by the invitation to give a distinguished lecture series there during the month of May 2008. This was an invaluable occasion as it helped me systematize my work and my ideas and thus to develop this book project. I want to thank Pierre Rosanvallon for this wonderful opportunity. Finally I am also grateful to the University of Toronto Law School where I was a Visiting Distinguished Professor in January 2009. I received wonderful feedback from very excellent students and colleagues in a mini-seminar on related topics. I thank Nehal Bhuta and David Dyzenhaus for this.

Portions of Chapter 1 appeared as "Sovereignty in the Context of Globalization: A Constitutional Pluralist Perspective," in S. Besson and J. Tasioulas (eds.), *The Philosophy of International Law* (Oxford University Press, 2010), pp. 261–282. An early and rather different version of Chapter 3, titled "Rethinking Human Rights, Democracy and Sovereignty in the Age of Globalization," appeared in *Political Theory*, 36 (August 2008), 578–606. The basic argument of Chapter 4 appeared as "The Role of International Law in Post-Conflict Constitution-Making: Toward a *Jus Post Bellum* for 'Interim Occupations,'" in the *New York Law Review*, 51 (2006–7), 497–532. Chapter 5 is a revision and composite of three separate publications, one of which appeared in *Constellations*, 15 (2008), 456–484, under the title, "A Global State of Emergency or the Further Constitutionalisation of International Law: A Pluralist Approach"; another, "Security Council Activism in the Age of the War on Terror: Implications for Human Rights, Democracy and

Constitutionalism," appeared in Y. Peled, N. Lewin-Epstein, G. Mundlak, and J. Cohen (eds.), *Democratic Citizenship and War* (New York: Routledge, 2011, pp. 31–53); and a third, "Constitutionalism Beyond the State: Myth or Necessity?" in *Humanity*, 2 (Spring 2011), 127–158. A very small piece of Chapter 2, "Rethinking Federation," appeared in the online journal *Political Concepts: A Critical Lexicon* (Fall 2011).

Most of all, and as always, I thank my husband and my colleague Andrew Arato. Without his support, patience, advice, and brilliant insights, this book would not have been written. And now, to my great delight, I have the pleasure of thanking another family member who has become a peer and a colleague: Julian Arato. His help and advice regarding the legal material in this book has been invaluable.

The love and encouragement given to me by my husband and my son has been indispensable to me. I dedicate this book to them.

Jean L. Cohen

~

Introduction

Developments associated with globalization challenge the way we think about sovereignty, rights, legitimacy, and international law. We have been told for quite some time that state sovereignty is being undermined. The transnational character of risks from ecological problems, economic interdependence, burgeoning illegal immigration, and terrorism, highlight the apparent loss of control by the state over its territory, borders, population, and the dangers its citizens face. The proliferation of new threats to peace and security seem increasingly to come from civil wars, failing states, grave domestic human rights violations, and the risk that private actors will acquire weapons of mass destruction (WMD). Today belligerency and violent aggression requiring international regulation appears to be caused by anarchy and tyranny within states rather than anarchy between them.[1] Global governance and global law seem to be the necessary response to the problems generated by but not resolvable within the old framework of an anarchical international society of sovereign states.[2]

Indeed, key political and legal decisions are being made beyond the purview of national legislatures. Alongside other globalizing systems, we seem to be witnessing the emergence of a global political system in which multiple supranational actors bypass the state in the generation of hard and soft law. The apparent decoupling of law from the territorial state and the proliferation of new, non-state transnational and supranational legal orders and sources of law suggest that the former has lost legal as well as political sovereignty. The general claim is that the world is witnessing a move to global (for some, cosmopolitan) law, which we will not perceive or be able to influence adequately if we do not abandon the discourse of sovereignty.[3] Apparently a new world order is emerging, in which global law based on consensus is, in key domains, replacing international law based on state consent.[4] In the twenty-first century, the very category "international" appears outdated.

Viewed from a geopolitical perspective, the imperative of size, which first triggered the emergence and expansion of the international state system, has apparently re-emerged. It seems that the nation-state, as the city-state before it, is now too small to provide security and welfare. It is ironic that as soon as the international system of sovereign nation-states was universalized in the

1

aftermath of decolonization and the collapse of the Soviet Empire it apparently became an anachronism. Hence, in response to geopolitical and economy-related pressures, the effort to form ever more integrated regional polities and hence the tendency of international organizations to become global governance institutions (GGIs) making binding decisions and global law that intrude deeply into what was once deemed the "domaine reserve" of states, in order to provide collective security, peace, and welfare and solve collective action problems generated by interdependence.[5] The UNSC is the key global governance institution in the global political system, and it now invokes the norms of the "international community" while drawing on its pre-existing public authority to engage in new and unanticipated forms of legislation and administration of populations and territory that directly (and at times, adversely) affect individuals and their rights yet which claim supremacy over domestic constitutional laws and other treaties.

Accordingly, the organizing principle of international society entrenched in public international law and in the UN Charter system – the sovereign equality of states – with its correlative concepts of non-intervention, domestic jurisdiction, self-determination, and so forth, seems outdated. It is alleged that the concept of sovereignty is useless as an epistemological tool for understanding the contemporary world order and that it is normatively pernicious. Indeed more than a few legal cosmopolitans argue that we are witnessing a constitutionalization of the international legal system in tandem with the replacement of the "statist" model of international society by a cosmopolitan, global political and legal community.[6] They point to the key changes in the international system mentioned above to ground their claim of a fundamental shift in its underlying principles. Cosmopolitan legal and moral theorists invoke human rights discourse as the basis for arguing that "sovereignty" as an international legal entitlement and the legitimacy of governments should be contingent on their being both non-aggressive and minimally just. A radical idea is at stake: that the international community may articulate and enforce moral principles and legal rules regulating the conduct of governments toward their own citizens (when their human rights are at stake). By implication, the neutrality of international law toward domestic principles of political legitimacy is being (or should be so the argument goes) abandoned.

Although much debated, some view the transformation of the aspirational discourse of human rights into hard international law, its apparent merger with humanitarian law, and its deployment as justification for departures from the hitherto entrenched norm of non-intervention (except as a response to aggression or threat to international peace), as an indication of the constitutionalization of international law. Similarly, the discourse of constitutionalization is being applied to the expanding reach of GGIs.[7] Since the end of the Cold War, the global political system centered in an increasingly activist UN Security Council now identifies and responds to the proliferation of the "new" threats mentioned above. The dangers these threats pose to "human security" – the term of art meant to displace the old focus on state security – also seem to indicate the necessity to transcend the state-centric, sovereignty-oriented paradigm of international relations and international law. Indeed there are now impressive global measures backing up the increased juridification of the "international" system including UN-sponsored "humanitarian interventions," UN-authorized transformative "humanitarian" occupation regimes, UNSC terrorist blacklists and targeted sanctions against individuals whose names appear on them, among other global security measures made or authorized by an increasingly activist and legislative Security Council.[8] These developments also seem to render the idea of unitary autonomous state sovereignty in a system of sovereign states useless for understanding the new world order characterized by global risks, global politics, and global law. In its place, we are offered a functionalist conception that disaggregates "sovereignty" into a set of competences and legal prerogatives which can be granted serially by the international community, conditioned on the willingness of states to meet cosmopolitan moral standards of justice, comport with human rights law, as well as demonstrating administrative capability (control).[9] This disaggregated functionalist approach underlies the cosmopolitan notion of the international community's "responsibility to protect."[10] It also informs attempts to replace the organizing principle of the post-World War Two international legal order – the sovereign equality of states and international law based on state consent – with a new international "grundnorm" – human dignity – allegedly informing the new types of consensual global law-making by the organs of the international community.

There is, however, another way of interpreting the changes in the international system since 1989. From a more disenchanted and critical political perspective, it seems that the organizing principle of sovereign equality with its correlatives of non-intervention, self-determination, domestic jurisdiction, consent-based customary and treaty law, is being replaced not by justice-oriented cosmopolitan law, but rather by a different bid, based on power politics, to restructure the international system. Relentless attacks on the principle of sovereign equality coupled with the discourse about "rogue" and "failed" states, "preventive war," the "war on terror," "unlawful enemy combatants," etc., are useful for neo-imperial projects of great- or superpowers interested in weakening the principles that constrain the use of force and deny them legal cover or political legitimacy when they violate existing international law.[11] From this optic, the discourses and practices of humanitarian or democratic intervention, transformative occupations, targeted sanctions, terrorist blacklists, and the dramatic expansion of its directive and legislative powers by the Security Council in its fight against global terrorism (all driven by the US since 1989), are mechanisms which foster the deformalization of existing international law, and enable the very powerful (the US predominant among others) and/or those states aspiring to become twenty-first-century great powers (Russia, China), to create self-serving global rules and principles of legitimacy, instead of being new ways to limit and orient power by law.[12]

Accordingly, the morphing of international organizations into global governance institutions does not herald a global rule of law or a global constitutionalism that tames sovereignty. Rather it involves the instrumentalization of the legal medium and of the authority of existing international organizations for new power-political purposes. "Global governance" and "global law" tend, on this reading, to authorize new hierarchies and gradations of sovereignty, and to legitimate depredations of political autonomy and self-determination in ways that are distinct from but disturbingly reminiscent of those created in the heyday of nineteenth-century imperialism.[13] Sovereignty in the classic, absolutist (predatory) sense remains alive and well, but only for very powerful states – including those controlling global governance institutions (the P5: the permanent members of the UNSC) – while new technologies and practices of control are created through the innovative use of unaccountable and legally unconstrained power accumulating in those institutions – something the functionalist discourse of gradations of sovereignty and neo-trusteeship plays into. The direction of the new world order is, in other words, toward hierarchy not sovereign equality, and the appropriate concepts are not cosmopolitan constitutionalism but "grossraum," regional hegemony, neo-imperialism, or empire.

This book is meant as an intervention in the debates and politics over the nature and possible future of the current world order. The stakes are quite high and the need to rethink the concept of the sovereign state and its relation to the globalizing international legal and political system has become pressing. Although I acknowledge that there are important changes wrought by globalization, this book rejects the notion that we have entered a cosmopolitan world order without the sovereign state. I argue that we are in the presence of something new but that we should not abandon the discourse of sovereignty or the ideal of sovereign equality in order to conceptualize these changes. Yet I do not thereby embrace a "state-centric," sovereigntist or power-political reductionist conception of the shifts in the international system. Nor do I accept the futility of devising normatively compelling projects for the legal regulation of (and constitutionalization that limits) new global powers. I seek instead a middle way appropriate to the unavoidable dualisms between norms and facts, principle and power in this domain. I am critical of approaches that too quickly characterize our current world order as cosmopolitan and constitutionalist thanks to their anti-sovereigntist enthusiasm about international human rights, international juridification, and global governance. Such analyses overlook the ways global legal and political institutions can be the creatures of imperial ambitions of powerful states. But I am also critical of those motivated solely by the hermeneutics of suspicion, and focused exclusively on providing genealogical analyses which always and only portray law as an instrument or medium of power technologies, and which aim always and only to unmask new constellations as new power relations. For these approaches overlook the ways in which law and normative order fashions and constrains power, and the ways in which new political formations, in conjunction with political struggle, can enhance and not only restrict freedom.

In contrast to both approaches, this book will defend three theses. The first is that it is empirically more accurate and normatively preferable to construe the changes in the international system as involving the emergence of a *dualistic world order*. Its core remains the pluralistic segmentally differentiated international society of sovereign states creating consent-based international law (via custom and treaties). Superimposed on this are the legal and political regimes and GGIs of the functionally differentiated global subsystems of world society, whose institutional structures, decision-making bodies, and binding rules have acquired an impressive autonomy with respect to their member states and one another.[14] My focus is the relation of the international society of sovereign states to the global political and legal subsystem with its referent, the "international community," of which states are, along with the UN, the key organs. My second thesis is that within this dualistic structure, a *new sovereignty regime* is emerging, redefining the legal prerogatives of sovereign states.[15] It is true that states no longer have the monopoly of the production of international/global law, and consensus operates on key levels of this system (regarding *jus cogens* norms in international society and within key global governance institutions such as the UN Charter organs, based on forms of majority voting). But states continue to play the key role in the production of international law. Moreover, the jury is still out on the nature and legal source of sovereign prerogatives and on the appropriate way to reconceive sovereignty, not to mention the prerogatives GGIs ascribe to themselves. On the one hand, the post-World War Two commitment of the international legal order to sovereign equality, territorial integrity, self-determination, and the non-use of force, is still very powerful. On the other hand, the increased commitment to human rights, and since the 1990s, to their global enforcement, as well as to the creation of global law and global governance informed by cosmopolitan principles, is also striking. I argue that the concept of changing sovereignty regimes is preferable to the discourse of a cosmopolitan world order for the former allows one to see the complexity, messiness, power relations, and contested character of the contemporary dualistic system. But I also argue that it is time to reflect anew on the concept of sovereignty itself. The functionalist approach to reconceptualizing (disaggregating) sovereignty is only one highly contested political alternative and I shall present another one in the first chapter of this book.

My third thesis is that the "further constitutionalization" of international law and global governance is the right approach but much depends on how this project is construed. The idea of the progressive constitutionalization of international law gained a foothold in theoretical discussions thanks to the new willingness of the Security Council to sanction grave domestic human rights breaches and the development of supranational courts to enforce the "values of the international community" regarding international criminal law – thus apparently indicating that the basic rights of all individuals would be protected even if their own states fail to do so. But the somewhat arbitrary and selective framing of certain domestic rights violations as threats to international peace and security meriting outside intervention, and the self-ascription by the UNSC of deeply intrusive legislative and quasi-judicial "global" governance functions unforeseen by the Charter and apparently not subject to judicial oversight or legal restrictions (some of which can themselves be rights violating such as the SC's terrorist blacklists), have created a new legitimation problematic. Loose talk about "constitutional moments" is irresponsible in such a context.

The assumption of certain "global governance" functions by the UN, the premier GGI in the global political system, is unavoidable. Its further constitutionalization must be guided in part by cosmopolitan principles. In this book I will restrict my discussion of global constitutionalism to the UN Charter system. However, and this is crucial, unlike most theorists of global constitutionalism I argue that this project must be conceived on the basis of a *constitutional pluralist* rather than a legal monist perspective. Indeed, I will argue for the constitutional pluralist approach as the theoretical analogue of the sociological concept of a dualistic sovereignty regime. There now exists alongside the domestic constitutional law of each sovereign state an increasingly autonomous legal order coupled to the global political system. The constitutionalist character of the global political system in general, and of the UN Charter system in particular, however, is rudimentary, to say the least. It is a vérité à faire rather than a fait accompli. But given the heterogeneous character of a still pluralist and deeply divided international society of sovereign states, a monistic conception of the project of constitutionalization of the global legal order, whether one locates it in the UN Charter or not, is a bad idea. The risk is "symbolic constitutionalism" – the invocation of the core values and legal discourse of the international community to dress up self-serving regulations, strategic geopolitical power plays, and morally ambivalent military interventions and impositions, in universalistic garb.

This does not mean we must abandon the concept of global constitutionalism in favor of a disordered global pluralism of normative, legal, and political orders. I will argue instead, that the concept of a dualistic sovereignty regime based on the principles of sovereign equality and human rights, and the stance of constitutional pluralism given an appropriately reformed UN Charter system could be an important barrier to symbolic constitutionalism. I will, in addition, reconsider the theory of federation, on the intuition that a federal frame might be helpful for thinking through the puzzles of legal and political supranationalism. As the book will show, taken together these concepts may provide for legal, political, normative, and institutional bulwarks against the proliferation of neo-imperial projects and regional attempts at "grossraum" ordering (annexation or direct control of neighboring polities by a local great power) that invoke human rights, democracy, or human security concerns and global law while de facto undermining them. Chapters 1 and 5 will take up these theoretical and empirical issues.

If there are to be humanitarian interventions, transformative occupations, and Security Council legislation, these must be regulated and constrained by clear legal rules, appropriate, representative decision-making procedures adequate to the principles of sovereign equality and human rights, and there must be global bodies able to police constitutional limits. Ever since 1945, sovereign equality and human rights have become the two core legal principles of the dualistic international system, and both are needed in order to construct a more just version of that system. Given their global governance functions, it is now necessary to bring powerful international institutions and not only sovereign states under the rule or law, through political, institutional, and legal reform. They too must become legally and politically accountable in order to remain legitimate. Given the Janus face of law we must be aware that juridification can entail the authorization of new power hierarchies as well as normatively desirable constructions and limits of public power. But we cannot simply transpose domestic conceptions of legitimacy, democracy, or constitutionalism, to the global political system. We must maintain the distinction between internal and external principles of legitimacy when speaking of human rights and political legitimacy even while searching for acceptable and effective functional equivalents for ordering GGIs.[16] The constitutional pluralist approach and the federal frame are crucial for preserving the principles of political autonomy expressed in the still compelling idea of sovereign equality while addressing the plural levels of the globalizing legal and political international order and their interrelation. Political institutional and legal reform along the lines of further constitutionalization is thus part of the counter-project to empire, neo-imperialist, and/or grossraum ordering.

This book is thus an exercise in international political theory. It will operate on two levels: empirical-diagnostic and normative-prescriptive. By bringing together normative political theory, legal analysis, constitutional theory, and a critical diagnostic approach toward shifts in the international political system since 1989, I will attempt to clarify the dilemmas and propose some solutions to the paradoxes generated by the astonishing pace of regulation and juridification on the global level. I do so in three case studies framed by two theoretical first chapters and a conclusion.

Overview

Chapter 1 addresses the theoretical issues involved in the reconceptualization of sovereignty and its relation to international law in the context of globalization. I begin with a brief reconstruction of the traditional absolutist conception presupposed by many global constitutionalists as well as legal pluralists who argue for abandoning the concept. Doing so will enable me to dispense with the distractions of the old canard of the incompatibility of sovereignty with international law. I will distinguish between the *concept* of sovereignty and various *conceptions*, to lay the conceptual groundwork for the idea of changing sovereignty regimes.

Briefly, the concept of sovereignty involves a claim to supremacy of the authority and exclusive jurisdiction of the state within a territory and over a population, signifying the coherence, unity, and independence of a territorially based legal system and political community. The correlative of domestic supremacy is external independence, i.e. the political autonomy and self-determination of the domestic constitutional order and political regime vis-à-vis outsiders (foreign powers). However, the absolutist conception linked the analytic concept of sovereignty to a positive set of competences including the competence to decide its own competence; to the necessity of organ sovereignty (i.e. the locus of unified sovereign powers within a specific organ of the state); and to the command theory of law (the notion that positive law and the unity of a legal system depends on tracing it back to the will of an uncommanded commander: a legislator whose legislative and constituent power is by definition *legibus solutus*: legally illimitable).[17] The dilemma that a sovereign state cannot be bound or bind itself yet must be able to act as a legal person in international law in order to be recognized as sovereign and hence to bind itself and be bound by that law followed from this absolutist conception. This led to the assumption of the incompatibility of sovereignty with international law (and indeed with constitutionalism domestically).

The next section of the chapter discusses the challenges to this version by theorists in the early twentieth century focusing on Hans Kelsen's reconceptualization of sovereignty as legal concept, instead of as a fact of power or as a set of material competences. This will allow us to see that the real dilemma of sovereignty is not that it cannot be self-binding, but that it seems to entail the impossibility of two autonomous valid legal orders operative within the same territory, or regulating the same subject matters and persons. Kelsen believed that the existence of a mature international legal system requires abandonment of the doctrine of sovereignty. I will present the Kelsenian argument, and some criticisms of it.

The third section of Chapter 1 addresses the re-emergence of this idea in the current context. The significant changes in the substantive rules and sources of positive international law that have been characterized by some as constitutional moments, apparently confirm the Kelsenian approach – i.e. the monist interpretation of the increasingly autonomous global legal order seen as post-sovereign. But this view is deeply contested. Against those who mobilize the discourse of constitutionalization to characterize the increased juridification and regulatory reach of regimes of international law and governance, legal pluralists insist on the multiplicity of sites of law-making and rule. They point out that there is no overarching meta-rule for regulating interaction or conflicts among or within these globalizing legal and political orders. The hierarchy of authority among global, international, and domestic law is and should remain unresolved. But they too reject state sovereignty as a relevant discourse or as an answer to this question.

What are the stakes of this dispute? The former see the constitutionalization of public international law as the way to tame the bellicose power politics and imperialist tendencies of nation-state sovereignty by constraining actors to solve their disputes through law while protecting human rights. The latter insist that the heterogeneity of international society and the pluralism of the international political system (along with the proliferation of international legal regimes within it) is a desirable antidote to hegemonic imposition that too often occurs in the name of "universalist" global law. This assessment expresses sensitivity to the asymmetry among global powers and to the emergence of new types of hegemony or imperial formations, not to mention the diversity of a still deeply divided international society. From this perspective, global constitutionalist discourse appears naive if not apologetic. The discourse and project of constitutionalism with respect to the emergent global political system is rejected out of hostility to the leveling (*gleichschaltung*) of the autonomy of the multiple legal and political orders that would apparently have to go with it. It is seen as a strategy of power aiming at putting claims to final authority beyond contestation and at suppressing alternative policies or ways of ordering. Legal pluralists argue that the diversity of legal-political orders increases the avenues of contestation and protects domestic autonomy and local democracy, while also making the legitimacy of global law a question rather than a given. But the constitutionalists counter that accepting the multiplicity of orders as is leaves the issue of coordination, authority, and hierarchy for the powerful to resolve.

As just indicated, the really hard question today concerns the compatibility of sovereignty not with international law (long resolved) but with autonomous supranational legal orders that allegedly have constitutional quality and claim supremacy and jurisdictional reach that penetrates the black box of the territorial state. How can we conceptualize state sovereignty within the framework of a supranational polity like the European Union (EU) or a globalizing political and legal order like the UN Charter system? Is the concept of state sovereignty useless for understanding the globalizing world order? Or are the principles of sovereignty and sovereign equality, along with human rights, as I argue, central to such a project?

I take up the theoretical debates surrounding these issues in the fourth and fifth sections of Chapter 1. I follow a different route in reconceptualizing sovereignty than that of the global constitutionalists many of whom either abandon it altogether or opt for the functionalist disaggregation of the concept (ultimately another way to abandon it). I adopt Kelsen's insight that the concept of sovereignty is ultimately a negative one that must entail the unity, supremacy, and autonomy of a legal system although very few specific positive competences follow from this.[18] Conceptions of sovereignty along with the content (prerogatives) entailed by it are various depending in part on the nature and structure of the international order and the existing sovereignty regime. But sovereignty is not only a legal concept; it is also a political one: autonomy of a sovereign state has to mean internal political self-determination of the political community. These aspects of the "negative" concept of sovereignty cannot be "disaggregated." It is true, however, that international/global law and legal conceptions of sovereign prerogatives are, in part, the expression of a concrete political order, of a nomos.[19] The shape of the new "nomos of the earth" is at stake in the contestation over the way to rethink sovereignty, rights, global governance, and the constitutionalization of globalizing international law.

In the subsequent two sections I challenge the monist theoretical basis of the neo-Kelsenian assumption that global constitutionalism involves the abandonment of sovereignty, by presenting and defending the competing conceptual approach of constitutional pluralism. This approach was first developed in order to theorize the changing sovereignty regime in the EU, once the latter developed an autonomous legal system claiming supremacy over and direct effect within domestic legal orders of sovereign member states which also claim autonomy and supremacy.[20] I reflect on its theoretical coherence with a view toward its relevance to the changes that have occurred and should occur in the global political system. As already indicated, I see the constitutional pluralist approach as an alternative, based on my reconception of sovereignty and my idea of a dualistic world order, to the false choice between monistic hierarchical constitutionalization and pluralist disorder.

Any discussion of constitutionalism beyond the state, however, must perforce confront the question of whether there exists at the supranational level an object capable of being constitutionalized. It must, in short, confront the issue of political form. This is especially pressing with respect to global governance institutions. I take up these issues in Chapter 2. I do so because I share the discomfort expressed by some analysts with the contemporary discourse of constitutionalization that seems to equate it with juridification on the supranational level, thereby severing it completely from politics, from any coherent conception of a polity, and from any connection with issues of democratic legitimacy. Constitutionalism, although it involves the coupling of public power to public law, is not identical with or reducible to legalization, at least not from the qualitative normative perspective. To put this differently, constitutionalism is a discourse that carries a normative and symbolic surplus over mere juridification and we must be careful not to trade on that surplus by applying the term to inappropriate contexts. That is why the issue of political form matters. However, this does not mean that we must restrict the discourse of constitutionalization to the state alone. Instead we have to imagine and reflect on the new types of polities to which the discourse is appropriate.

In Chapter 2 I try to reflect on and imagine a type of polity or polities in formation that are not states, but which are, arguably, adequate objects for constitutionalism and constitutionalization. This is in part an exercise in retrieval of a concept that has been relegated to the dustbin of history and deemed an anachronism ever since the system of sovereign states triumphed in Europe, but which in my view has become apposite once more, namely federal unions of states that are not themselves states.[21] I focus on what is now called in the literature "coming-together federalism," and in the first section raise the question of why sovereign states would choose to federate and what the alternatives are.[22] I discuss in detail the dynamics of size that motivates such a response, among others. But my goal is to retrieve a concept of federal union that escapes the statist paradigm in which most discussions of federation are trapped, i.e. which construes federating (whether "coming together" or "holding together") as a process of state-making or as a way of dividing competences and powers within a federal state so that it endures.[23] I then consider various approaches to federal unions. The first, the "continuum model" exemplified in Hans Kelsen's work, denies that there is anything importantly distinctive about federations as a political form, insisting that a federal union or federal state and for that matter, international organizations and international law all can be understood as points along a single axis, namely the degree of centralization and decentralization characteristic of the relevant legal order. This approach insists that formulae such as shared rule and self-rule, independence and interdependence, contractual voluntary beginnings, and so forth are not only not specific to federal polities but also that there is no single criterion or organizational principle that yields sharp distinctions among the various political formations. Accordingly the better approach is to analyze all polities and all public legal orders along the axis of centralization/decentralization such that a continuum can be established on which different political formations are placed. While a wealth of useful distinctions follow from this approach, the continuum model seems to throw out the baby with the bathwater for it screens out precisely those, in my view, quite distinctive features of the federal political and constitutional form. I argue that the juridical perspective is too one-sided and misses the problem (geopolitical issues and issues of legitimacy) to which a federal union provides one important political solution.

The other approach breaks with the state-centric paradigm, insisting, however, on the distinctiveness of federation as a political form. It comes in two versions and in the next two sections I address each of these. Both versions abandon the standard dichotomies that follow from the statist paradigm: confederation (construed as an international treaty organization) versus federal states; federal versus unitary states, thereby allowing a different conceptual spectrum of ideal types to come into view. The idea is to develop a conception of federal unions of states (and peoples) that are not themselves states.[24] The first version uses a sovereignty-oriented perspective to indicate the distinctiveness of federal unions of states as a constitutional and political form. It reasons from the standpoint of political legitimacy rather than from a juridical perspective. This approach is associated with Carl Schmitt and his contemporary followers.[25] The second version abandons the sovereignty concept as irrelevant to the analysis of federal unions. It construes federations as a genus (with subtypes) of political formations with a distinctive (ideal-typical) set of political, structural, and constitutional features to which no "statist" categories pertain. This approach allows for a new assessment of the genesis and structure of previous federal unions while providing a theoretical perspective for analyzing contemporary unions of states that are not themselves states. It informs some of the most exciting recent theory of federation to date.[26] I discuss the strengths and drawbacks of each approach and try in the final section of this chapter to offer a synthetic approach of my own. I wish to combine a juridical perspective liberated from monistic dogmatism with a political perspective on federation freed from political theological myths regarding sovereignty – in short to think federation with respect to legality and legitimacy. This theoretical exercise will open the terrain for reflecting on the mode of legitimacy specific to federal polities that are not states and for posing the question as to the relevance of such a framework for rethinking the constitutionalization of global as well as regional international organizations. As we shall see, federal unions that are not themselves states are the ideal-typical analogue of the discourse and practice of constitutional pluralism.

The next three chapters shift to empirical/diagnostic analyses of the changes in the international political system that impinge on the core elements of traditional state sovereignty: immunity from outside military intervention, self determination by a political community of its political form of life, its internal principle of legitimacy and constitutional regime, and supremacy of one's own constitutional laws along with control over one's own security apparatus. The three new domains and forms of global governance that these chapters focus on put all of this into question while simultaneously causing legitimation problems for GGIs.

I see the changing legal norms of the international system as indicative of a new and salutary political culture of sovereignty that has shifted from one of impunity to one of responsibility and accountability. From this perspective, sovereign equality and human rights are the new interrelated principles of the dualistic global political system, indicative of the existence of a new sovereignty regime. The relation between these principles has changed, but sovereign equality and the correlative principles of non-intervention, domestic jurisdiction, and self-determination remain the legitimating basis and default position of the international order. But as already indicated above, it is incorrect and ideological to describe the important shifts regarding sovereignty, rights or security as constitutional moments. The post-1989 discursive practices of humanitarian intervention, of "transformative" occupations, and the post 9/11 coupling of the discourse of human security to the new legislative practice of the Security Council in the war on terror are political facts. They should be normed in terms of the concept of a shifting sovereignty regime and not seen as constitutional moments that take us beyond sovereignty. Indeed, the UN reform project aimed at legally articulating and steering these shifts was a failed constitutional moment rather than a successful example of regulating power by law.[27] The danger is that these shifts further the deformalization of international law instead of being normatively desirable adjustments in the interrelation between sovereignty and human rights.

I will thus argue in my next three chapters that the further constitutionalization of the UN Charter system is an important political project and that formal legal rules should be devised and agreed upon to regulate these new practices and understandings of jurisdiction. Such rules have to be widely discussed, negotiated, and shaped in a representative political process in which all member states of the international community have a voice. Legitimacy is required on both levels of the dualistic sovereignty regime: regarding changes in what is deemed to be in the domestic jurisdiction of sovereign states in light of human rights considerations, and regarding the new procedures and substantive rules of GGIs. This requires institutional mechanisms based on the principle of sovereign equality, providing for voice and continuous participation of national political communities in shaping the norms and rules of the global political community particularly in the most important global governance institution, the UN. It also requires that global political institutions are regulated by and comport with the rule of law.

Chapter 3 takes up the question of how to think about the relation between human rights and sovereign equality in the epoch of humanitarian intervention, construed as the enforcement by the international community of human rights. In the aftermath of the Cold War, human rights violations have been invoked as justification for debilitating sanctions and military invasions by multilateral organizations or states acting unilaterally under the rubric of humanitarian intervention. Indeed there has been a partial merger between humanitarian and human rights law.[28] Cosmopolitan liberals argued for redefining sovereignty as the responsibility to protect rather than as state autonomy.[29] But the heady rhetoric of human rights fundamentalism also played into the hands of powerful states eager to loosen the rules regulating the use of force in order to pursue their own geopolitical agendas. This, and the problem of mixed motives in any military intervention, led some to come up with a new "political" conception of human rights, aimed at toning down the moralism and avoiding some of these dilemmas. I discuss this problematic, defend my own version of a political conception, and argue that it must be understood against the backdrop of a normative conception of sovereignty and in the context of the dualistic framework discussed above. In the process I address the International Commission on Intervention and State Sovereignty (ICISS) Report and the UN High Commission proposals in this regard and argue for formal legal rules regulating "enforcement" of human rights. I do this in the following steps.

After a brief historical overview of the revival of international human rights discourses in the post-World War One context, which situates the emergence of the enforcement model, I present an ideal-typical version of the traditional conception. The traditional approach construes human rights as universal moral rights all people have due to some basic feature or interests deemed intrinsically valuable and is concerned with identifying and justifying such rights.[30] This approach comported well with the revival of the discourse of human rights in the wake of atrocities committed during World War Two. It served as a useful referent for local struggles against foreign rule and domestic dictatorship in the 1970s and 1980s. Since 1989, human rights discourse acquired a new function: the justification of sanctions, military invasions, and transformative occupation administrations by outsiders, framed as enforcement of international law against violators. In short, since the 1990s, human rights discourses serve to disable the sovereignty argument against political sanctions and military interference by outsiders in the affairs of a state. The traditional approach does not quite fit this new function. The shift from aspirational declarations of human rights to the notion that international human rights documents constitute hard, globally enforceable international law raises a new set of issues regarding which subset of human rights among the long lists in the international documents should play such a role and who is to decide upon violations and enforcement. Hence, there arose efforts to develop a "political" conception.

The chapter then analyzes several recent versions of the political conception. But in order to understand their purpose it is necessary to reconstruct the normative dimensions and new meaning of the concepts of sovereignty and sovereign equality that are entailed by a cogent "political conception" of human rights. I do so before turning to my own version of a political conception. If we see state sovereignty not only as a fact of power but as a normative concept and as an international legal entitlement to political auton-omy, we can view the discourse of international human rights in a new way: as a mechanism to prevent and correct injustices that may follow from the international legal ascription and distribution of sovereign equality to states.[31] The thesis that will be defended from this perspective is that sovereign equality and human rights are both normative principles of our dualist international system and both are needed to construct a more just version of that system. Respect for sovereignty and sovereign equality entails, as will become clear, careful distinction between internal and external principles of legitimacy. By protecting the autonomy and plurality of polities and their legal systems, sovereign equality helps constitute the space in which political freedom, dem-ocracy, human rights, and the rule of law can mutually reinforce each other

The principles of self-determination and public autonomy (non-domination of a political community by outsiders) implicit in this respect for sovereign equality do not, however, entail immunity from international concern or jurisdiction regarding an agreed-upon subset of inviolable human rights that the sovereignty argument does not alter. The idea of a changing sovereignty regime means that prerogatives associated with sovereignty and sovereign power can shift. I thus argue that international enforcement models of human rights must be construed and indeed legally regulated so as not to impinge on the key principle associated with sovereign equality, namely the idea of self-determination by a political community of its own internal political forms and legitimating principles, and non-domination by outsiders. But I also argue that insofar as sovereignty must be understood as a political relation among members of a political community and their government, the norms of membership preclude certain kinds of rights violations. The current sovereignty regime involves an important shift in the conception of what should be in the "domaine reserve" of any sovereign state. In short, when a state (or its proxies) indulges in what I call the four E's – (mass) extermin-ation, expulsion, ethnic cleansing, enslavement (virtual or formal) – it forfeits the claim to be standing for a self-determining political community and thus to be sovereign over the groups it oppresses in these radical ways. These practices violate individual moral and human rights but they must also be understood as a politics of exclusion and of denial of membership of the relevant group in the political community that the sovereign state is supposed to represent internationally. By denying not a particular set of rights such as freedom of speech or assembly, but the very right to have rights within the state, the government forfeits the claim to speak for and the "right to coercively rule" the groups it excludes and oppresses in these radical ways. In other words, the government itself has abolished the political and legal relationship between the state and the targeted group that sovereignty establishes.

On my version of the political conception, however, "the proper subset" of human rights whose violation might suspend the sovereignty argument against international sanctions and intervention should thus be restricted to what have been called the "new human security rights" indicative of a partial merger between humanitarian and human rights regimes. But apart from this subset, I also argue for the disaggregation conceptually, discursively, and normatively of the international humanitarian and international human rights regimes. Indeed I conclude by arguing for two political conceptions, one referring to those human security rights violations, specified by the international community, that can legitimately and legally suspend the sovereignty argument against forceful intervention and other forms of international enforcement, the other referring to international human rights that function as public standards of critique to which citizens and denizens, domestic rights activists, and social movement actors can refer in their political struggles against domestic oppression, injustice, and arbitrariness, and in order to make their own governments more democratic, more rights respecting, and more accountable to the citizenry. None of this, as we shall see, denies the independent importance of moral justification of human rights.

The fourth chapter follows logically from the third. This chapter addresses the paradoxes involved in the transformative occupations that follow upon humanitarian intervention and the dilemmas posed by legalization proposals. The need to replace the "sovereign," or rather, ruler who has been involved in grave rights violations and to change domestic laws that contribute to such violations is undeniable in such contexts. But transformative occupation regimes that legislate their favorite conceptions of rights and democracy, by changing laws and imposing constitutions, violate the principles of self-determination and popular sovereignty even if they maintain territorial integrity and only temporarily "suspend' international legal sovereignty. These paradoxes pertain to belligerent as well as UN-sponsored "humanitarian" occupations.

The relevant international law is the law of belligerent occupation codified in two key treaties: the 1907 Hague Regulations and the 1949 Fourth Geneva Convention and the Additional Protocols I and II 1977. The concepts of belligerent occupation and the related "conservation principle" delimit the authority of the occupier administering a territory the occupier controls by virtue of the purely factual nature of the occupier's power – which is assumed to be temporary and provisional. Indeed, the foundation of the entire law of occupation is the principle of inalienability of sovereignty through the actual or threatened use of force.[32] We thus face a paradox: if the conservation principle intrinsic to the law of occupation rules out fundamental change in political, legal, and socio-economic structure by occupying powers, do not the imperatives of contemporary occupations, be they unilateral and belligerent or UN-sponsored and "humanitarian," render it an anachronism today?

If what is at stake in an occupation is the protection of human rights, regime change, democracy, and "post-conflict constitution-making," if the quality of governance is now a matter of international concern, should not the conservationist principle and the law of belligerent occupation be abandoned?

On the other hand, how can they avoid the charge of liberal imperialism if occupiers have a free hand to impose their preferred form of "liberal-democratic" institutions on a subject population? Are not "transformative occupations" more akin to a modern form of indirect colonialism than the liberation they pose as? Would not new legal rules simply enable the resuscitation of a type of mandate or trustee system that once again condones prolonged occupation administrations, foreign control, and, in the name of the "civilized values" of the international community – this time, democracy and human rights – treats the occupied as wards, incapable or unwilling to govern themselves responsibly? Should we not resist giving a legal imprimatur to any (non-consensual) foreign project of transformative occupation and leave the burden of proof on the occupier?

I take these dilemmas seriously. Nevertheless, this chapter will argue, first, that the conservation principle if not the letter of the law of belligerent occupation remains relevant today and that it is well worth the effort to articulate its normative thrust in light of contemporary conditions. In particular, the principle of the "inalienability of sovereignty by force" remains compelling, although the understanding of who the ultimate bearer of national sovereignty is, and of what prerogatives sovereignty entails have undergone important shifts. Second, while the Hague and Geneva Conventions remain relevant international law, it is nonetheless important to update them and to make rules with respect to UN-sponsored humanitarian occupations, adequate to contemporary conditions and expectations. I acknowledge the paradoxes of legalization due to the Janus face of law – as a medium of power and as an institution that regulates and delimits power – and try to think through both its enabling and constraining aspects in this domain. The issue here is not "law or no law" but rather, which kind of legal regulation and in light of what principles.

After an opening discussion of the existing legal framework, I analyze the two major contemporary approaches to the law of occupation: the moral humanitarian and the realist/Schmittian, both of which suggest that the conservation principle is irrelevant today albeit for different reasons. The first interprets the development of occupation law as a process of humanization guided by the salutary influence of human rights on humanitarian law and justifying the expansion of the scope of the legislative and institutional change on the part of occupying powers. The law of belligerent occupation and the newer Chapter VII, UN-sponsored humanitarian occupations are interpreted in that light. The second insists that the concept of belligerent occupation and the conservation principle are anachronisms because the international order and social structural conditions to which they were functional no longer exist.

It also rejects legalization of transformative occupations, belligerent or humanitarian, as playing into imperialist hands. After critically discussing both approaches, I suggest a third that grants that we are in an epoch of transformative occupation and claims that this is precisely why clear principles and updated legal rules that remain true to the conservation principle are so necessary. It is possible to square the circle if we look more closely at what is at stake in the law of occupation today in light of other relevant principles of international law. Our epoch is regulated not only by human rights norms, but also by the normative legal principles of sovereign equality, self-determination, territorial integrity, and strictures against annexation – these provide the basis on which to reconstruct the conservation principle in a non-anachronistic way. If we replace organ and ruler sovereignty with state and popular sovereignty in interpreting that principle, it can then balance "humanity law" in this domain. In the last section I confront the debates over legalization and conclude by arguing that all occupations should be regulated by international law, based on the principles these norms embody. Once again we shall see that the dualistic world order involves two distinct levels of relations: international relations among sovereign states in international society to which the law of belligerent occupation, appropriately reinterpreted, certainly still does and should apply; and global governance institutions whose newly expanded legislative functions and highly intrusive, dictatorial interventions in domestic legal and constitutional processes during humanitarian occupations are sorely in need of legal regulation, normative guidance, and limits.

Chapter 5 addresses head-on the new legitimation problems generated by the transformation of international organizations into global governance institutions by focusing on the UNSC. Two features of GGIs are at issue: the expansive interpretation of their powers and their extension in unanticipated domains and, as in the case of the UNSC, the claim to supremacy and the direct impact of their regulations and resolutions on member states and increasingly on their individual citizens. Such developments burst the traditional principal–agent models extant at the time of their creation as IOs and undermine the thesis of indirect delegation by member states and thus legitimacy for their subsequent decisions. Legislative initiatives of GGIs and regulations that directly and at times negatively impact individuals, challenge traditional ways of conceptualizing how public international law is made, and alter the relation between international and domestic public law.

This is clearly so in the case of the Security Council's expansion of its role and powers since the 1990s. In addition to determining internal human rights abuses or maltreatment of domestic populations to be threats to international peace and security and authorizing "humanitarian" interventions, and in addition to sponsoring highly transformative occupation regimes in territories that it directly administers, the Council now blacklists individuals allegedly involved in terrorism and imposes severe sanctions on them, requiring all states to implement these sanctions, thereby assuming quasi-judicial functions but without affording due process guarantees. It has begun to legislate in this domain, i.e. to adopt legal norms and rules via Chapter VII resolutions, which are to be treated as binding global law affecting whole classes of persons and pertaining to general rather than specified situations. Thanks to Article 103 of the Charter and the binding nature of Chapter VII resolutions, these new governance functions enjoy the aura of legality and trade on the authority of the UN even when they have rights-violating effects and tend to undermine domestic constitutionalism, and even though they entail a quasi-dictatorial expansion and use of Council powers without accountability or apparent legal or institutional checks and balances. My first thesis in this chapter is that the Council's radical expansion of its discretionary powers, especially its recent assumption of legislative capacity in pursuit of the war on terror, indicates its embrace of a new security paradigm that can threaten not only civil liberties and constitutionalism everywhere, but also the legitimacy of the UN Charter system itself.

I begin by showing how the linkage of human rights discourses to the concepts of human security and the responsibility to protect (R2P) doctrine in the "enforcement model" paved the way for the discursive shift to the current security regime. I then describe this regime by analyzing the three key SC resolutions that have constituted it – in order to pinpoint what is radically new and dangerous here. Part three of Chapter 5 analyzes the structural features of the UN Charter system that are the enabling conditions of this transformation. I argue that it is rooted in the flawed hybrid structure of the UN constituted by the veto power of the five permanent members (P5) on the Council and in the amendment rule. Obviously the veto gives them unequal powers, privileges, and immunities. But the veto in the Council and, more crucially, in the amendment rule also places the P5 in a unique structural relationship within the UN that differs from the position of all other member states. In short, they remain external to the treaty. Hierarchy instead of sovereign equality is the appropriate characterization of the internal relations this entails. The second thesis of the chapter is that this structural position enables the P5 to usurp the constituent authority of the international community and to hide the constituent activity under the guise of a more ordinary exercise of its decision-making powers. This is at the heart of the Council's current legitimacy problems.

While this structural design has been in place since the beginning, the expansive interpretation by the Council of its competence and the recent self-ascription of legislative and constituent capacity renders it increasingly threatening to the rule of law domestically and internationally. I demonstrate this by examining the high-profile and controversial "Kadi case" that recently came before the European Court of Justice (ECJ).[33] This case raised all the issues pertaining to the conundrum of global (and regional) "governance," sovereignty, human rights, and the discourse of constitutionalization. My third thesis in the chapter is that the much-discussed project of the further constitutionalization of public international law is the right remedy, but a great deal depends on how it is understood. As already indicated, the UN is now at the center of the global political system and certain global governance functions are unavoidable. These must be guided in part by cosmopolitan principles and the rule of law. A project for correcting the flawed hybrid design of the Charter is crucial, but it must aim at a different type of dualism: a new sovereignty regime that places all the members of the UN in the same structural relationship to the organization (inside it), formalizing the principle of sovereign equality of states in relation to the UN itself. Such a "further" constitutionalization in the sense of political and institutional reform of the UN Charter system must, however, be understood in the framework of constitutional pluralism.[34] I thus conclude the chapter by returning to the theoretical issues regarding sovereignty, sovereign equality, and constitutionalization with which I open the book. I distinguish between internal and external pluralism and raise once more the issue of political form, in order to see in what respects the discourse of constitutionalization in general and constitutional pluralism in particular could become apposite to a reformed GGI like the UN given the dualist nature of our world order. I close with a renewed reflection on the relevance of federal theory to this reform project.

In short, I argue in this book for a form of "low-intensity" constitutionalization that would articulate a new sovereignty regime able to steer the evolution of the dualist structure of the international political system (a system of sovereign states and of increasingly important GGIs) in a normatively attractive direction.[35] As already indicated, I see the project of constitutionalization as an alternative to new forms of global rule-making – hegemonic international law – and new forms of hierarchical rule – neo-imperial formations and new types of regional grossraum. This is a political project, contingent on the political will to transform institutions in a way that fosters instead of undermining constitutionalism and democracy on every level of the global political system. I conclude the book with a brief reflection on the relation between my version of pluralistic constitutionalization and democratic legitimacy. With respect to this issue as well, I argue that a new sovereignty regime that respects the principles of political autonomy for all polities inherent in the idea of sovereign equality and applies these principles to all institutions, can be seen as a democratizing move. Such a move is also crucial for protecting human rights and constitutionalism against depredations by states and by global governance institutions. This project may not measure up to utopian aspirations for a democratic cosmopolitan world order but it will be hard enough to muster the political will even for low-intensity constitutionalization. This for now may be as good as we can get.

1

Sovereignty in the context of globalization: a constitutional pluralist approach

It is an understatement to say that the contemporary international society of states is deeply divided. Despite the happy consciousness of those who believed in the worldwide triumph of liberal democracy in the early 1990s, the legitimating principles for domestic polities around the globe remain diverse.[1] True, the sovereign state form was globalized in the second half of the twentieth century.[2] Yet we still inhabit a global pluri-verse of 192 sovereign states whose political cultures, organizational principles, and conceptions of justice and legitimacy are diverse and at times in conflict with one another.

Superimposed on this segmentally differentiated, pluralistic international society of sovereign states are the legal and political regimes of the functionally differentiated global subsystems of world society, whose institutional structures, decision-making bodies, and binding rules have acquired impressive autonomy with respect to their member states and one another.[3] These "regimes" or "subsystems," of which the global political system is one, engage in new forms of global governance and law-making that reach beyond and penetrate within states. Individuals are increasingly ascribed rights and responsibilities under globalizing international law. This expanding individuation of international law seems to mark an important difference from the pre-World War Two international legal system and from stereotypes of "Westphalian" sovereignty. Although states remain the main subjects that make international law, they no longer have the monopoly of the production of that law. Indeed the international organizations they have spawned seem to be transforming into global governance institutions, which, like the sorcerer's apprentice, tend to invert the principal–agent relationship extant at the time of their creation.[4] These GGIs now regulate states and individuals, including the treatment by states of their own citizens, in the name of the "international community," importantly redefining (some would say abolishing) state sovereignty. As a result, states are bound by rules and regulations that make the old images of international society and the consent-based production of international law appear anachronistic.

As indicated in the introduction, these developments have given the discourse of global constitutionalism a foothold in theoretical discussions.[5] Advocates cite the individualization of the subjects of international law (undermining principles of state immunity in international criminal and human rights law), the dramatic increase in juridification since 1945, the emergence of "higher law" – *jus cogens* norms – based on "consensus" which can void international treaties violating the relevant norms,[6] the proliferation of *erga omnes* rules (which obligate all states whether or not they signed a treaty), the pervasive discourse and expanding reach of international human rights, and the development of global remedies in the form of supranational and hybrid courts, as indications of the constitutionalization of new forms of public international law.[7] International/global and hybrid courts (International Criminal Court (ICC), International Criminal Tribunal for Rwanda (ICTR), International Criminal Tribunal for the former Yugoslavia (ICTY), etc.) decide on violations of *jus cogens* norms and the relevant rights and duties of individuals and settle disputes about legal validity in the global legal system.[8] There now appear to be rules for rule-making in this system, and national courts increasingly double as its organs insofar as they participate in interpretation of what amounts to a violation of the norms of the world community and in their enforcement.[9] At the heart of these norms, according to cosmopolitan thinkers, is the individual, who is replacing the state in the globalizing international system, as the ultimate unit of moral concern. These shifts away from the state-centric model of international law are seen as indicative of the irrelevance of sovereignty talk.

Accordingly, we are in a transitional phase away from an international toward a global public legal order coupled to the globalizing political system. The international society of sovereign states is apparently being replaced by world society.[10] If states are to be part of a global constitutional political order, in which disputes are settled by binding law, they can no longer be sovereign. Whatever their differences, legal cosmopolitans view the globalization of public international law and politics as a presenting a welcome opportunity to finally get beyond the bellicose power politics allegedly inherent in the sovereignty paradigm of international relations and law. Indeed, global constitutionalists argue that we should finally dispense with that paradigm and replace it with appropriate cosmopolitan and constitutionalist principles of justice, human rights, and, institutionally, subsidiarity.[11] The further constitutionalization of international law appears as a desirable and feasible alternative both to anachronistic sovereignty discourses and to the risk of disorder attached to unregulated global governance.

Other legal theorists, however, are suspicious of the discourse and project of constitutionalism and indeed of legalization generally as regards the globalizing political system. From the perspective of the counter-discourse of global legal pluralism, the constitutionalization of the global political system is neither a feasible nor a desirable response to the new forms of (and bids for) global power, for it would threaten the diversity, autonomy, and legitimacy of competing normative and political orders and projects.[12]

Insofar as constitutionalization requires hierarchy and legal monism, it would entail leveling of the existing plurality among political and legal systems. Ascription of constitutional quality to the emergent global political system and its new forms of governance, intervention, regulation, and control, would give it an undeserved normative dignity and discursive edge – a symbolic plus – enabling rather than limiting the powers that control it by allowing them to appear as defenders of constitutionalism, law, and human rights (apparently neutral non-political principles) against would-be critics. The risk is a new form of global hegemony that undermines the legitimacy of contestation and politics as antithetical to the global rule of law.

As we shall see, however, the new global legal pluralists also abandon the discourse of sovereignty as anachronistic and authoritarian insofar as it has always been used to deny the legal quality of non-state domestic normative orders and of non-sovereign polities. What the new global legal pluralists object to in the current discourse of global constitutionalism is its tendency to transpose the hierarchical unitary and monist sovereigntist mindset formerly linked to the state, to the global domain. They defend diversity, plurality, multiplicity, negotiation, and contestation among multiple normative orders, against the impulse toward (imposed) order, regulation, juridification, and hierarchy (associated with the discourse of constitutionalization) as the best bet for attaining voice, fairness, and some justice in the shifting, dynamic, globalizing political system. However, for them, too, the sovereignty-based model of international law and of the state is part of the problem, rather than a component of the solution.

The above notwithstanding, sovereignty remains a frequently invoked, if now essentially contested concept both in reference to the state and to the people (popular sovereignty).[13] Is the twenty-first century witnessing the demise of the concept of sovereignty and the disaggregation of the state or do the transformations and shifts that are occurring involve instead the transition from one sovereignty regime to another? Should we at last dispense with outmoded frames for thinking about global political and legal ordering or are we perhaps too quick and too eager to leap into a new paradigm, heedlessly throwing out the baby with the bathwater in our anxiety to be au courant and post-modern? I defend the latter proposition. As already indicated in the introduction, I believe it is more cogent to construe the changes in the international system in terms of the emergence of a dualistic sovereignty regime, not as portending the irrelevance of state sovereignty or the decomposition of the state. A new but highly contested sovereignty regime is emerging that is redefining the legal prerogatives of sovereign states thanks partly to the increased salience of cosmopolitan principles and institutional elements and legal transformations within this dualistic system. But bids for empire or efforts to establish new imperial formations are also contesting the definition of sovereignty and the principle of sovereign equality. It is true that states no longer have the monopoly of the production of international/global law, and consensus operates on key levels of this system (regarding *jus cogens* norms and within the organs of GGIs based on forms of majority voting). And it is worth noting that while individuals have in certain key respects become the direct subjects of international law, they have not become its authors.[14] States, however, continue to play the key role in the production and enforcement of international law although GGIs (whose members are states) are moving into this domain. Moreover, sovereignty talk – whether to insist on the autonomy of one's polity against foreign imposition or on the input of the citizenry (popular sovereignty) via democratic representation and voice in government at all levels – is still quite salient on the part of actors (elites and ordinary citizens) although it is also invoked against outside judgment regarding human rights abuses. What sovereignty entails is being renegotiated, but the discourse of sovereignty and its epistemic function as an ordering principle, although it is not the only one, is still relevant today.

The conceptual dispute turns in part on the image one has of the direction in which globalization is pushing our polities and our international institutions – and the appropriate response. We should avoid simplistic dichotomous and naive evolutionary thinking when we reflect on what is new and try to refine our analytic tools. New forms of global interrelations stand on what has been created before. We should not be too quick to abandon our concepts. In this regard Joseph Weiler's geological metaphor is wise, for we have to avoid both infeasible utopias and unimaginative realism.[15] The expanding regulatory role of GGIs, the increased importance of the discourse of international human rights and of human rights law, and increased juridification and integration of the international community (and of regional communities), do not amount to the end of sovereign territorial states. Yet the universalization of the international society of states or global functional differentiation and the emergence of "world society" and "international community" has not left sovereignty or international law unchanged.

I do not believe one should abandon the discourse of sovereignty in order to perceive and conceptualize the shifts described above. I am not convinced that the step from an international to a global cosmopolitan world order without the sovereign state has been or should be taken. The two doubts are connected: I will argue that if we (prematurely) drop the concept of sovereignty and buy into the idea that the state (and sovereignty) has been disaggregated, we will misconstrue the nature of contemporary international society and the political choices (and stakes of struggle) facing us. If we assume that a constitutional cosmopolitan legal order already exists which has or should replace international law and its core principles of sovereign equality, territorial integrity, non-intervention, and domestic jurisdiction with "global (cosmopolitan) right" we risk becoming apologists for neo-imperial projects. We will also miss what is normatively important about, worth defending, and reconstructing in the discourse of sovereignty.[16] I argue we should instead opt for strengthening existing international law by updating it, making explicit the particular conception of sovereignty on which it is now based, and showing that this is compatible with cosmopolitan principles inherent in human rights norms and with necessary forms of global governance and cooperation, so that appropriate reform and feasible constitutionalist projects can come into view.

This project entails acknowledging the existence and value of a dualistic world order whose core remains the (now universalized) international society of states embedded within a (still to be suitably reformed and adequately constitutionalized) global, political system that also has important cosmopolitan elements. What is required is formal legal reform and the creation of a global rule of law that protects both the sovereign equality of states based on a revised conception of sovereignty, and human rights. As I indicated in the introduction, I think that the project of "constitutionalization" is the right approach. Unlike most theorists and critics of global constitutionalism, however, I argue that this political project must be conceived on the basis of a constitutional pluralist rather than a hierarchical legal monist perspective. In addition, in this book, I address the project of further constitutionalization or constitutional reform to the premier global governance institution in the international order today, namely, the UN Charter system.[17]

This chapter will lay the conceptual ground for these claims. I do so in the following steps. First, in order to grasp the animus against what I take to be a misunderstanding of the current sovereignty regime we must revisit the conception of sovereignty in its classical form. I will distinguish between the *concept* of sovereignty and various *conceptions*, the theoretical basis for the idea of changing sovereignty regimes. I briefly reconstruct the traditional absolutist conception presupposed by many who argue for abandoning the concept (Section 1.1). Section 1.2 discusses challenges to this version by theorists in the early twentieth century, focusing on Hans Kelsen's reconceptualization of sovereignty as legal concept, instead of as a fact of power or set of competences. Kelsen believed that the existence of an autonomous international legal system would require that sovereignty be radically suppressed. I present Kelsen's reasons for this along with the relevant criticisms. Section 1.3 addresses the revival of this idea in the current context. I turn to what have been characterized as the key contemporary "constitutional moments" in the transformation of international law and politics: the construction of the UN Charter system, its new post-1989 efficacy especially regarding human rights, humanitarian intervention and occupation, the creation of an International Criminal Court, and the "human" security regime erected by the Security Council in the aftermath of 9/11. The radical changes in the substantive rules and sources of positive international law, especially its "centralization," seem to vindicate the Kelsenian approach.[18] Hence the resurrection of the monist interpretation of the increasingly autonomous global legal system coupled to the global political system as a post-sovereign legal order of constitutional quality. The debate between global constitutionalists and legal pluralists operates within this problematic and presents us with a choice: either the further constitutionalization of the global political system that has to dispense with the concept of sovereignty, or acceptance of a disorderly (indeed, order-less) global legal pluralism that acknowledges the multiplicity of overlapping legal, normative, and political orders and sources of international law but renounces attempts to devise legal rules to regulate their interrelations or to constitutionalize the emergent global political system, for that is deemed antithetical (and therefore undesirable) to that very plurality. I will take up these debates (Sections 1.4 and 1.5), and conclude by challenging its terms, in particular, the monist theoretical basis of the neo-Kelsenian assumption (shared by constitutionalists and legal pluralists alike) that constitutionaliza-tion on the global level must involve relations among legal orders that require the abandonment of sovereignty. I will present and defend the competing conceptual approach of constitutional pluralism (Section 1.6) indicating why it is preferable and under what conditions it would be feasible.

1.1   The absolutist conception: organ sovereignty and the impossibility of international law

Cosmopolitan legal theorists are eager to discard the concept of sovereignty because it signifies to them a claim to (or a fact of) power unrestrained by law, and a bulwark against international action necessary to enforce human rights. Yet the absolutist and "Westphalian" conception of sovereignty that corres-ponds to this negative assessment has long since been abandoned. It is thus important to distinguish between the concept of sovereignty and differing historical conceptions, in order to see that there can be different sovereignty regimes and that the relation between sovereignty and law can shift.

The concept of sovereignty involves a claim to supreme authority and control within a territory signifying the coherence, unity, and independence of a territorially based political and legal community. It thus has an internal and external dimension. Internally, sovereignty involves supremacy: a claim to unified, indivisible, comprehensive, and direct authority within a territory over its inhabitants construed as members of a polity. Internally the sover-eignty of the state means that there are no equal or autonomous powers within the polity with independent claims to jurisdiction or political rule. The correlative external dimension involves a claim to autonomy from outside powers. External sovereignty entails independence and, presumably, imper-meability and non-subordination of the territorial state to jurisdictional claims or political control by foreign authorities. There are accordingly no higher powers of jurisdiction or control externally whose rulings stand above (or penetrate) those of the sovereign states. Sovereignty implies political and legal self-determination.

So conceived, sovereignty is a negative concept: ultimately internal supremacy and external autonomy are two sides of the same coin: meaning the absence of other equal or independent jurisdictions or powers within, and the absence of hierarchical subordination to external legal or political orders controlling or determining the nature of the political and legal order of a sovereign state.

The modern discourse of sovereignty was associated from the beginning with two initially interdependent processes: the development of absolute monarchy and the making of the modern state. The absolutist conception emerged when the discourse of sovereignty was deployed in favor of the Prince, in polemical opposition to and struggles with the feudal estates, and the universalisms of church and empire.[19] As a polemical political concept, sovereignty was tied to the assertion of royal power – the carrier of state-making – in the context of the struggle for political control and unity against internal and external forces. The concept of sovereignty was thus linked by the contemporary theorists to a positive conception of powers, ascribed to the legislative head of state.[20] A positive set of powers – specific competences and functions – were deemed essential attributes of sovereignty on the absolutist conception.[21] Moreover, it was assumed that internal sovereignty had to be located in a unified organ at the head of the state (apex or organ sovereignty). The absolutist conception also involved the command theory of law: to ensure the unity of a legal and political system all posited law had to be traced back to the will of a sovereign that is, moreover, *legibus solutus*.[22] Hierarchy was thus deemed essential to the concept of a legal order: the ultimate decision of what is law had to rest in one institutional locus: the head of state. Sovereignty was deemed a matter of the will, of the organ, personified in the legislator whose laws are coercive orders backed up by threats (sanctions). The absolutist conception links the command theory of law to organ sovereignty, assuming that where there is law there must be a sovereign organ with these attributes.[23] Limited, shared, blended, divided sovereignty thus seemed an oxymoron. Because it was also assumed that sovereignty entails what the Germans call "Kompetenz-Kompetenz" – the unrestricted competence to decide the extent of jurisdiction and competences – sovereignty and constitutionalism were deemed incompatible.

Indeed, on the absolutist conception, the sovereign will is the source of all law, inherently endowed with the capacity to change the law, including the constitution. The sovereign organ (easily identifiable in this conception as the Prince) thus has not only the highest legislative or juridical competence but also the "constituent power" – the capacity to make or remake the constitution – a capacity, which must be above and prior to posited law and delimited competences. In this capacity the sovereign power does not derive from the legal order established by the law of the state but is its source.[24] This and other prerogatives, especially the right to make law and the *jus belli*, were assumed to flow directly from the fact of sovereign power. Indeed, it was assumed that these among other competences such as the right to make treaties, coin money, and so forth are the marks of sovereignty, and that sovereignty had to be located in a unified organ, at the head of state.[25] The right to war, the right to decide whether the state's rights and national interests have been violated or threatened, and the right to decide the enemy were deemed inherent in the very concept of sovereignty.

The external claim to autonomy was directed against the universalisms of emperor and pope. This implied the existence of a plurality of sovereign states, and an international society that attributed sovereignty to polities on a coherent basis. The same is true of a third idea constitutive of external sovereignty: the equality of sovereign states in respect of their legal status and basic rights. Equal sovereignty provided a basic rule of coexistence within the states system; it made the practice of mutual recognition and the regulation of interactions among sovereign states possible. Accordingly a state is sovereign if it exercises effective control over its territorial boundaries and population through a governing apparatus able to maintain law and order. In theory, recognition as a sovereign state followed from these empirical political facts.

On the "Westphalian" absolutist model, however, the sole subjects and sources of international law are sovereign states, bound only by those rules to which they consent. Individuals could not be subjects at international law. Hence another meaning of impermeability: international law did not have direct effect on individuals: its norms regulated external relations between sovereign states, primarily via bilateral agreements.[26] Accordingly, international law was deemed to be a body of norms exclusively regulating relations between sovereign states based on their consent. The two key prerogatives (positive powers) tied to external sovereignty, on this conception, were the *jus belli* and the "right" of sovereign states to be subjects of and to make international law through treaties and custom. However, all this seemed to reduce international law to an instrumentally useful medium of coordination reflecting underlying power relations, without effectively constraining or transforming them. Hence, the "incompatibility" of sovereignty and international law, if the latter is understood as an autonomous system of effective, binding, "hard" law.[27] The dilemma that neither a sovereign will nor a sovereign state can be bound or permanently bind itself yet must be able to act as a legal person in international law and hence to bind itself and be bound by that law flows, as indicated in the introduction, from this absolutist conception.

Until the late nineteenth century the system of sovereign states was part of a political arrangement called "international society" that gave equal recognition only to European member states through *jus publicum Europaeum*.[28]

The principles of non-intervention and domestic jurisdiction, the rules of war, and the obligation to respect treaties applied only to European member states, not between them and the rest of the world – no equal sovereignty was ascribed to non-European states no matter how much effective control or competent governance they exhibited. Hence the argument that this sovereignty order was predicated on the domination and exploitation of non-sovereign territories (the rest of the world).[29]

Indeed, by the second half of the nineteenth century, sovereignty appeared as a claim to power unrestrained by law within as well as outside of Europe.[30] Once the ideas of sovereignty, the nation-state, and imperialism had joined together, fierce competition among sovereign states construed as self-contained, self-interested entities, undermined the rudimentary mechanisms enabling coexistence within European international society. Sovereignty has been associated with arbitrary and rapacious power politics ever since.

1.2   The legalist challenge

This is the context in which major attempts to reinterpret the concept of sovereignty took shape. Four assumptions of the absolutist conception were contested: that sovereignty must be apex sovereignty located in an organ of the state, that this entails a supreme will which must be *legibus solutus*, that the coherence and unity of a legal system must be traced back to the will of such a sovereign, and that key prerogatives of the ruler or the state derive from the essence of sovereignty, are indivisible, and include the *jus belli* which renders it ultimately incompatible with autonomous international law. The work of jurists like Georg Jellinek, Hans Kelsen, Carré de Malberg, and later H. L. A. Hart all challenged this conception.[31]

Since my focus is on the external dimension I note in passing that the claim that internal sovereignty must be located in a single body (organ) whose will is *legibus solutus* has been belied ever since the first modern constitutional democracy emerged in the US in the eighteenth century based on the separation of powers, checks and balances, and the idea of popular sovereignty, not to mention the division of powers entailed by federalism.[32] The theory and practice of modern constitutional states demonstrates that sovereignty, constitutionalism, and the rule of law are not incompatible.[33] The separation and division of powers within a constitutional legal and political order based on the principles of popular sovereignty, democratic legitimacy, representative government, and basic rights certainly does not mean that sovereignty is banished from the system: if the legal order remains internally coherent and supreme and external actors do not impose their rules or claims on the polity and hence do not subordinate it to their own legal or political systems, the state is sovereign. It is perfectly conceivable for a sovereign state to be a constitutional democracy in which no institutional instance is designated as the final hierarchical locus of legal and political decision.[34] Nor does sovereignty require economic autarky, a misleading assumption that ignores the interdependence of all sovereign states with capitalist economies.

The conceptual error behind these claims identified by all the legal theorists is the assumption that sovereignty is a matter of fact, will, and power which law merely registers. But sovereignty, according to them, is a juridical concept, a concept of public law.[35] A state is sovereign when its legal order is unified, supreme, and thus recognized as autonomous. However, as a legal concept, sovereignty is not tied to any particular form of the state.[36] The state's political structure and its government's prerogatives derive from the legal rules of its constitutional order rather than the reverse.[37] While organ sovereignty is one possible rare form of the sovereign state, it is not the only one.[38] The markers of sovereignty, that is, the positive competences associated with it by the classical theorists, can be divided and exercised by different state organs without undermining the unity of the state or its legal system.[39] Indeed, as Jellinek argued, sovereignty is a negative concept pertaining to internal supremacy (no internal competitors) and external autonomy (non-subordination): it is not a matter of a laundry list of positive competences. The only "positive" competence or dimension that he associates with it is the capacity for self-determination of the legal rules that articulate and delimit a polity's own internal sovereign powers. By implication, sovereignty does not involve unlimited power (or will); rather, the capacity of self-limitation, delegation, and constitutional delimitation of sovereign competences is a feature of sovereign statehood. It is perfectly possible to have a legal system in which legal limits on the supreme legislative authority are legal disabilities contained in the very rules that qualify the ruler to legislate, and constitute the organ as a legal power in the first place.[40] The same holds for executive power within a state. Thus sovereign power under law is not an oxymoron. Moreover, as we shall see, a similar point was made regarding the prerogatives of "sovereign" states in the international legal system although, for reasons that will become clear, Kelsen at least assumed that an autonomous (and hence primary) international legal system spelled the end of the concept of the sovereign state.

Indeed it was Hans Kelsen who developed the strongest, most coherent, and influential theoretical reconstruction of sovereignty as a legal concept. He famously asserted that sovereignty is the essential characteristic of the state.[41] Yet Kelsen also famously argued that the concept of sovereignty should be "radically suppressed."[42] Why? In order to answer this question and to understand the influence of Kelsen's legal theory on the contemporary debates over the constitutionalization of international law, it is necessary to briefly reconstruct his conception of sovereignty and of law.

Kelsen radicalized the move that others had already taken from organ to state (or national) sovereignty by reconceptualizing sovereignty as a legal condition – as a pure concept of public law – and by defining the state as a legal order.[43] The concept of sovereignty does entail internal supremacy and external autonomy, but this has to do with the highest binding (authoritative) power and refers to a structure of obligation, not to the empirical facts of power, competences, institutional instances, force, or even control. Sovereignty pertains to a normative order: that of the national legal community. But for Kelsen the state is equivalent to its objective normative legal order whose referent (and product) is a legal community.[44] The state does not have a legal order, it is not subordinated to or regulated by a legal order or constitution; it is a legal order. From this perspective, the state is the supreme authority, but since authority is a normative concept, only a normative order can be sovereign. Authority is a characteristic of a normative order involving the right to issue obligating commands. There can, accordingly, be no such thing as a non-sovereign state. The sovereign state has (or is) a monopoly of force but the "monopoly," too, refers not to a physical power or means of violence but to a normatively mediated chain of command in which the "force" that accounts for the monopoly of force is the legal system itself – construed as a normative hierarchical coercive order.[45] In other words, the monopoly of force simply means that law enforcers appeal to norms authorizing the coercive acts (sanctions) that belong to the same legal system. To be sure, the legal order of the state must be efficacious in order to exist but the internal structure of validity does not derive from such efficacy and is irreducible to it. Accordingly the state is equivalent to the legal order, all its organs are legally constructed and legally delimited, and sovereignty is the essential quality of a state signifying its supremacy and autonomy as a legal order. Kelsen thus severs the concept of sovereignty from any particular set of governmental functions, factual powers, or competences, and from its attachment to a specific organ.

He also severs it from the command theory of law. Unlike other legal positivists such as John Austin, Kelsen's legal positivism does not trace legal validity back to a source construed in terms of a sovereign will or identifiable by tracing out de facto obedience.[46] Indeed given his attempt to construct a "pure" theory of law, recourse to the will or to tradition or natural law to vindicate the binding character and validity of posited law is unacceptable and unnecessary. Indeed, Kelsen's conception of the legal norm leads to a reversal of previous positivist legal theory; instead of tracing the validity of law back to the will of the law-giver, he maintained that it is the normative quality of the legal norm that allows the will to enforce it.[47] How can we make sense of this?

The legal norm for Kelsen has two elements: the delict or the description of an unlawful act and the sanction, the consequence to be imposed in case of such action. Thus the norms which form a legal order must be norms stipulating a coercive act, a sanction. However, the conception of the legal order as a coercive normative hierarchal system does not require the notion of a sovereign will; instead it requires the notion of authorization, for what makes a coercive act a sanction is that its commission is authorized by the legal system. It is the normative, not the voluntaristic aspect (imposition of a sanction is an act of will by an enforcer) or effectiveness (compliance) of any particular legal norm that matters here – that is, it must be possible to see sanctions as the authorized reaction of the legal community against the delict.[48] Moreover, the delict is not a contradiction to law or a negation of law, it is a condition determined by law – an act that is sanctionable.[49] This implies that one must be able to construe the legal order as a hierarchical system of norms and authorizations (legal rights) that articulates delicts and imposes sanctions.[50]

Accordingly, the legal order is a system of norms and what makes it a system is the reference by legal actors to the validity of the norm and the normative order in which it is situated and their authority to enforce it. However, norms are not statements about reality and in Kelsen's neo-Kantian perspective, this means that norms cannot be true or false but only valid or invalid.[51] It is the dynamic aspect of norm creation that is central here. Only a norm can be the basis of validity of another norm. Thus if one reasons in the context of a national legal order, the chain of justifications of validity and authority leads back to the constitution of the state, the ultimate positive legal "source" for validity of norms lower down the norm hierarchy. The question why the fundamental constitutional norms are valid leads to the concept of an ultimate norm, whose validity the jurist does not question but must presuppose.[52] This is the famous concept of the "grundnorm," understood as a transcendental postulate, not a substantive legal principle.[53] A legal *system* must be characterized by strict unity and hierarchy in the structure of validity claims – all norms whose validity may be traced back to one and the same basic norm form a legal system.[54] The basic norm constitutes the common source and bond between all the different norms of the order. However, this "source" is not a will or a principle of legitimacy extrinsic to the legal system, it is simply the fundamental rule according to which the various norms of the order are to be created. "The ultimate hypothesis of positivism is the norm authorizing the historically first legislator. The key function of this basic norm is to confer law-creating power on the act of the first legislator and on all other acts based on the first act."[55] The basic norm itself, however, is not valid because it too is created in a certain way (this would lead to infinite regress) but rather because it is presupposed to be valid, a necessary presupposition without which there could be no legal order whatsoever.[56] The basic norm thus pertains to the domain of validity, not facticity. From this juristic perspective of legal validity, law regulates its own creation and determines its own validity through its internal hierarchy of norm-regulated norm creation.

To be a sovereign state thus means that the ultimate reason for the validity of the system of norms constituting the domestic legal order has to be traceable back to the constitutional order of that state, "grounded" in the grundnorm. As already indicated, the legal order must be effective as a whole in order to exist. This is the only concession Kelsen makes to the domain of facticity but this requirement does not pertain to issues of the validity of legal norms.[57] The constitutional order of a sovereign state is, accordingly, the highest underived legal authority above which there can be no higher authority that is its source of validity, regulating and determining its conduct. Sovereignty as supremacy is, as we saw, a negative legal concept. The state as sovereign, as the "supreme authority," refers to the ultimate reason for the validity of norms which are issued as commands and deemed obligatory. But this means that international law as an autonomous legal system that authorizes and obligates states must be denied on the sovereignty thesis.

Indeed Kelsen famously makes two claims regarding the sovereignty thesis: first that it precludes viewing international law as a valid autonomous legal system, and second that it blocks viewing other states as equally sovereign. Ironically the principle of equal sovereignty constitutive of the "Westphalian" system of international law is undermined by the very concept of sovereignty that subtends it. Let us look at both claims.

The sovereignty thesis means that from the perspective of a domestic legal order, international law is law only if it is consented to or "recognized" by that state. Its principle of validity lies in the domestic constitution. There are two versions of the relation between domestic and international law on this thesis, one "dualist," the other "monist."[58] The dualist approach (or if one considers also numerous national legal orders, pluralist) construes international and domestic law as two autonomous legal systems, regulating different subject matters and having different legal sources.[59] The autonomous system and specific rules of international law are binding on a state, on this view, only if the latter consents to them. Kelsen, for reasons that will become clear below, rejects this approach as incoherent. The second, monist approach links the recognition theory to an understanding of the relationship between the domestic legal order and international law that construes them as a unity, as the same legal system, in which the sovereign state is primary. International law on the state-monist conception is a binding albeit subordinate part of the national legal order. International law is able to determine the sphere and validity of national law only if international law has validity, but it has legal validity only on the basis of the principle of validity of the domestic constitutional order recognizing it. The recognition theory of international law thus entails the primacy of national over international law as well as the monist interpretation of the unity of these legal systems.[60]

But this also means that equal sovereignty of a plurality of states is impossible. The sovereign state cannot, from its internal perspective, acknowledge the simultaneous autonomous validity of any other legal order. The necessary relationship of equal autonomy between sovereign states can be established only by positive international law and only if it is granted that international law determines the spheres of validity of the legal orders of these states.[61] Under the monist thesis of the primacy of national law, however, the solipsistic sovereign state can recognize only its own sovereignty, which it assumes to be independent of the recognition by international law or by any other state. This stance is likened by Kelsen to subjectivist philosophy that proceeds from the sovereignty of the ego, interprets the world as the will and idea of the subject, and is incapable of comprehending another subject as an equal being.[62] As a consequence of the thesis of the primacy of national law, the recognition theory, and the monist interpretation, the absolute sovereignty of one state excludes the sovereignty of every other.[63] Insofar as supremacy and validity are concerned, the logic of absolute sovereignty as a juristic hypothesis also invites abuse or misleading "idealizations" such as the false deduction that the sovereignty of the state implies that it is not always bound by treaties it has concluded or that it cannot be subjected to the compulsory jurisdiction of an international court or be obliged against its will by majority resolutions of collegiate international organs.[64] Kelsen insists that these questions cannot be analyzed deductively from the concept of sovereignty, even absolute sovereignty in the above sense, but only from an analysis of positive law to which a sovereign state can of course consent with no such restrictions. It is also misleading to assume that the thesis of the primacy of national law of a sovereign state, given the construal of its legal order as the universal legal order, conceptually entails empire, although Kelsen himself did seem to think there is an elective affinity between at least the discourse of absolute state sovereignty, nationalism, and imperialism.[65]

The alternative hypothesis is a monist interpretation that accepts the unity of national and international law, but construes the international legal system as the autonomous and supreme legal order whose basic norm is the principle of validity for national legal orders. This would enable one to account for the autonomy of binding rules of international law and its constitutive principle: equal sovereignty. Accordingly, it is the essential function of the international legal order to delimit the spheres of validity and guarantee the equal sovereignty of each territorial state.[66] International law enables states to coexist as equal legal subjects. The normative delimitation of the spheres of jurisdiction cannot be achieved by norms belonging to the legal order of one state since every such order is limited in its validity to the territory and people of that state. Instead equal sovereignty is a legal principle of the international legal order whose validity must comprise the territorial and personal spheres of validity of all national legal orders. Thus international law enables states to coexist side by side as equal legal subjects.[67] The state as a subject of international law is a juristic person, recognized by that law according to the principle of effectiveness and is in this sense constituted by it.[68] Kelsen resolves the paradox that public international law is constituted by states but sovereign states are constituted by public international law by arguing that when states make treaties or customary law they function as "organs" of the international legal community. Indeed the recognition theory is unable to account for the validity of positive international law for the latter does not make its validity for a state dependent upon recognition by that state. Kelsen gives the example of a new state, which, upon coming into existence immediately receives all the rights and duties conferred on states by the international legal order whether or not it independently recognizes them.[69] It is not necessary to prove that a new state consented to a norm in order to hold it liable for infringing it.

On the monist interpretation of the primacy of international law, every national legal order is connected with the international legal order and through this with every other national legal order so that there is one integrated legal system. But, and this is the key move, from this perspective the international legal order by means of the principle of effectiveness not only determines the spheres of validity of the national legal orders, making possible the coexistence of a multitude of states, it also provides the reason of validity of the national legal orders. The international legal system has its own basic norm, and Kelsen even offers a clue as to what this authorizing principle formally speaking must be, namely the principle that countenances custom as a norm-creating fact – for example: "states ought to behave as they have customarily behaved" – and a principle which also authorizes the validity of norms created by international treaties (e.g. *pacta sunt servanda*), both of which belong to the first, ultimate stage of general international law and which is presupposed by, rather than being derivable from, the "consent" involved in the development of customary law or treaty-making.[70] Accordingly, the "grundnorms" of national legal orders are basic norms only in a "relative sense."[71] It also means that state powers and prerogatives are, in the specific Kelsenian sense, delegated by the international legal order – the latter as it were empowers an authority to create norms at its own discretion for a certain sphere (domestic jurisdiction).[72]

To be sure, the idea of a relative grundnorm is quite meaningless in Kelsen's framework. What he is actually saying is that the equality of all states is a legal principle that can be maintained only on the basis of the primacy of public international law, monistically and hierarchically interpreted. Under the monist hypothesis of the primacy of international law, "the state could be pronounced sovereign only in the relative sense that no other order but the international legal order is superior to the national legal order, so that the State is subjected directly to international law only."[73] But this means, that "states can be considered equal only if they are not presupposed to be sovereign."[74]

Tertium non datur. Kelsen denies that there is another cogent way to conceive the relation of national and international law. The dualist/pluralist approach which construes national and international law as two autonomous and independent legal systems is, to Kelsen, incoherent. Why? From the internal legal perspective, according to Kelsen, it is simply not possible for there to exist two valid legal norms that are not part of the same legal system, yet which regulate the same issues or actors. International and national law cannot be different and mutually independent equal systems of norms for the same space at the same time. "A jurist who accepts both as sets of valid norms must try to comprehend them as parts of one harmonious system."[75] This epistemological postulate of unity pertains to the entirety of national and international law. Since there is no subject matter that due to its essence can only be regulated by national and not by international law the pluralist thesis cannot make its stand on that ground.[76] Indeed Kelsen was one of the first to argue that individuals can be the direct subjects of international duties and rights and that there is nothing intrinsic or essential about international law that restricts it to obligating states or regulating "foreign relations" only.[77] On the contrary, international law always addresses individuals but for the most part does so indirectly, through incomplete norms that stipulate only the material element, delegating to states the task of determining by whom something is to be done or forborne, and of directly obligating individuals and ensuring compliance. Citing the examples of international labor law, piracy, and anti-slave trade laws, he argued that there is no subject matter that is essentially off limits to international law and that nothing systemic prevents it from directly addressing individuals.[78] Increased direct effect on individuals and expansion of the scope of international law is simply a matter of overcoming its existing primitive state through centralization and the strengthening of individual responsibility: something Kelsen strongly advocated.[79] To be sure, he did note that it is only in exceptional cases that international law directly obligates or authorizes individuals and he did state that, "If this should become the rule, the borderline between international and national law would disappear."[80]

Kelsen rejects the pluralist thesis on logical grounds as well, insisting that two legal norms that contradict each other could not both be valid. Indeed he denies the possibility of a logical contradiction between a norm of international and a norm of domestic law. Conflicts of norms can of course occur, but this does not affect the unity of the legal order or entail a contradiction in the emphatic sense.[81] Indeed conflicts between legal norms must be construed as conflicts between higher and lower norms, which can be dealt with by legal means: by either deeming the lower norm illegal via abrogation as in legal systems with constitutional review or by deeming the framing of the norm-violating norm as a delict to which the legal order attaches a sanction (as in international law). Just as an unconstitutional law in a domestic legal order does not affect the unity of that order, so the possibility of a national law "violating" international law does not affect the unity of the legal system comprising both. Indeed the use of the term "contradiction" to describe such conflicts is misleading: valid legal norms cannot contradict one another.[82] To posit such a thing, given the need to decide which norm or order is supreme and to enforce the law, would lead to irresolvable conflicts. Absent an impartial adjudicator, the pluralist thesis would lead to the fragmentation and loss of efficacy of the legal system.[83] Jurists who are concerned with the question what is the law, need not and should not entertain the pluralist epistemology. The pluralist thesis would be self-defeating since it would, perforce in case of conflict, lead to the treatment of one of the legal systems (or contradictory norms) as non-law, i.e. as an order or norm with a different type of validity than that of compulsory law. The validity of law is one and indivisible. If it were not, then the question of what, in light of apparently conflicting considerations, the law requires would not be answerable.[84] In short, as one commentator aptly puts it, Kelsen is not a conventionalist.[85] The monist hypothesis pertains to legal validity, and it is legal validity that must guide adjudication. But for the neo-Kantian legal theorist, a law is valid (or a rule is a legal rule) not because a judge applies it, or happens to consider it valid; rather judges must apply the law because it is valid.

We thus face a choice between the two monistic postulates: the primacy of the domestic legal system linked to subjectivist philosophy or that of the international legal system linked to an objectivistic approach. Kelsen frames this as an ethical political choice, the former allegedly having an elective affinity to nationalism and imperialism, the latter with internationalism and pacifism.[86] Clearly his preferences lay with the latter.

The premise of my argument is that this is a false choice, based on misleading reasoning that flows from Kelsen's overly rigorist neo-Kantian epistemology. Due to the latter, Kelsen failed to see that it is the dynamics of mutual recognition and intersubjectivity that create and subtend the relationships between two or more subjects and thus it is not necessary to have recourse to an objectivistic theoretical stance that reasons from the "objective world" in order to see both *ego* and *tu* as parts of a whole – the internal, interactive communicative "we" perspective permits this as well. Kelsen assumed that equality can be guaranteed only from the objectivistic (identitarian) stance that requires the primacy of international law. Indeed, because he insisted on a pure theory of law, reasoning exclusively from the internal perspective of validity, he ignored the relevance of the political context of law (legitimacy) and screened out the intersubjective political dynamics of recognition that can subtend the mutual ascription of equal sovereignty. Political legitimacy is not deemed relevant to the positivist theorist focused on internal legal validity.[87] But insofar as sovereignty is concerned, the failure to transcend Kantian subject philosophy led to a misunderstanding of the relational dimensions of legal and political sovereignty.[88] Moreover, his insistence on a pure theory of law independent of any considerations (or practices) of legitimacy, and his anti-conventionalism, led him to ignore the importance of "social facts" in the sense of a shared and communicative practice that includes action-orienting norms (what Hart called the "internal attitude"), shared reference points, and modes of apprehending the world that structure the way in which validity can be convincingly ascertained, asserted, and accepted by the relevant legal actors qua participants in a legal/political community.[89] To be sure, the validity of a norm does not turn on whether any particular judge believes it to be so – its validity has to be established, so that it can be recognized by a judge. But who, if not the legal community – i.e. adjudicating and norm-creating bodies – establishes legal validity? And on what basis – i.e. with reference to which legal/political community, and what legitimate authority or normative source – do legal actors do so? In other words, the understanding of their common practice, world-view, "object-language," and conception of the respective community whose law is being adjudicated (and of which they are members), on the part of those involved in ascertaining the law, matters even if they must appeal to its universal validity in so doing. I will return to this issue.

Not surprisingly, the most famous rebuttal of the necessity of monism came from a conventionalist – H. L. A. Hart – a legal theorist also concerned with the pragmatic function of validity in informing practitioners what the law is.[90] As is well known, Hart embraced a system-relative (methodological nationalist) and conventionalist conception of validity substituting the concept of the "rule of recognition" for the Kelsenian grundnorm.[91] But he also replaced Kelsen's neo-Kantianism with a reliance on Wittgenstein's philosophical framework, following the linguistic turn in philosophy, thereby drawing on the concept of language-game for his analysis of the pragmatics of legal practice including the assessment of validity, and introducing intersubjectivity into his theoretical framework. To be sure, he was not strictly speaking a pluralist when it came to the relation between national and international law, for he denied the quality of legal system to the sets of laws he believed comprised the latter field in his day.[92] Nevertheless the mix of conventionalism and the concept of the pragmatics of law as a rule-governed intersubjective practice led to several important insights that are useful for vindicating a constitutional pluralist perspective (not Hart's own), in case one does try, as I do, to construe international law as a coherent system, advocating its further constitutionalization. These include Hart's distinction between "validation proper" and "the relation of validating purport," the concept of the internal attitude regarding rules, and the rejection of the sanction theory of law all of which lay the ground for a more complex approach to the role of reflexivity and legitimacy in law creation and conflict resolution or avoidance.[93]

As for the first: Hart argued that while it is true that an essential function of international law is to delimit the spheres of validity of national legal orders and that efficacy is a criterion of recognition of a state as a state, this does not mean that the latter's principle of validity therefore derives from the international legal order or that the former is only a relative grundnorm, an oxymoron in any case. Efficacy is a necessary but insufficient condition of validity of a legal system. The principle of effectiveness is a positive rule of international law that conditions recognition as a sovereign state in the international legal system on a fact: that the state has a governing apparatus and an intact legal system, and that it is in control of its territory and population and capable of being a subject of international law.[94] These are the agreed-upon criteria for ascribing equal legal standing to states in the international system – a fact of positive international law. But while a fact such as this may be a rule of international law it does not mean that the domestic legal system of sovereign states thereby must be deemed a subordinate component part of a hierarchically superior international one. As Hart argued in his critique of the Kelsenian monistic hypothesis, from the point of view of a domestic legal order of a sovereign state, efficacy is a presupposition, not a reason of validity of that order. The relation of the rule of international law regarding efficacy and delimiting the domestic jurisdictions of sovereign states amounts to what Hart called a relation of "validating purport," not validation proper.[95]

This distinction is important. It allows one to distinguish between an internal and an external perspective. While it is correct that an essential function of international law is to delimit the territorial, personal, and temporal spheres of validity of distinct municipal orders, and that the norms regulating this subject matter must be international legal norms, this is not sufficient to establish that the rules of each form part of a single system or to show that one (international) provides the reason of validity for the other (domestic) and that the state is thereby to be construed as an organ of the international legal order.[96] From the perspective of international law construed as an autonomous legal system with its own grundnorm, it may be logically coherent, given the principle of effectiveness, to treat municipal law as a subordinate part of a single system, construing the authority of states, including their prerogative to determine which individuals are obligated to comply with international legal norms (to do or forbear), as 'delegated'. However, the fact that international law must view national legal systems in this way does not, on its own, establish the reality of subordination especially if the relevant domestic constitutional jurists reject this hypothesis. The theoretical requirements of the science of jurisprudence for coherence in construing its object domain, and valid laws, as a unity and thus all law as comprising a single hierarchically structured system, are not enough to make it so.[97] Hart gives the example of two types of relations between distinct domestic legal orders to make his point. If the British parliament adopts a law according to the appropriate British constitutional principles (or rule of recognition), this is an example of validation proper. Given the rule of recognition in Britain, legal practitioners can agree as to the law's validity and invoke the same justification for it. However, if that same parliament declares that all laws it has adopted are valid for another state, say the Soviet Union (Hart's example), or if it declares the latter's laws valid for that state because it, the British parliament, says so, or if it declares the latter's laws are valid for Britain: these would be instances of the relation of validating purport. Certainly the legal practitioners in the Soviet Union would consider their own laws valid regardless of this relation of validating purport: validation proper for them would come from reference to their domestic rule of recognition.[98] The same holds for the relation of national and international law and the principle of effectiveness, which is, accordingly, an expression of the relation of principle of validating purport.

For Hart what matters is whether the relevant official actors, practitioners, or members of a legal community actually reason in that manner and justify their authority to decide in such a way that would lead back implicitly to an international "grundnorm" or, in Hart's terms, rule of recognition. According to Hart, it is recognition by law-identifying and law-enforcing agencies that establishes a law as part of a specific legal system along with the individuation of different legal systems, and one would first have to know the "rule of recognition" of the relevant legal orders, i.e. the criterion of membership of laws within a single system, in order to ascertain whether the validity of a law derives from the same or from a different legal system.[99] For this, however, one would have to adopt what Hart calls the "internal attitude" of the practitioners in the legal game: i.e. one would have to know what are the standards, reasons, or justification they invoke as the basis of their authority and as guiding their decision-making (the domestic constitution or international law) and what they reference as the relevant legal (and I would add political) community. The issue of validity (and obligation) has to be understood from the internal and participant perspective, while the efficacy of a legal order can be assessed from the external, observer perspective.[100]

This insight, I contend, does not bind one to a relativistic conventionalism – rather it invites reflexivity regarding legal practice. In other words, it does matter what authority legal practitioners in a legal community invoke for determining validity and how they understand the legal (and ultimately political) community whose laws, ground rules, and constitutional principles they are enforcing. But they do and must – Kelsen is right – argue in terms of what the law requires.[101] The reflexivity involved is the following: the legal practitioner must apply or identify a certain rule as the law because it is valid but knows or presupposes that she or he is acting in the name of a particular legal community whose criteria of validity are being enforced. The distinction between the internal and external attitude thus invites reflexivity regarding the question: is a rule valid and part of the same legal system because we say so or do we say so because the rule is valid law and therefore part of one system? Because he ignores this distinction, Kelsen fails to develop a reflexive theoretical standpoint vis-à-vis the internal participant perspectives of multiple legal orders and instead relies on a legal theory that is "too pure."

Of course Hart's own approach rests on a position Kelsen does not share, namely the existence of different rules of recognition for different legal systems. Hart assumes this to be a descriptively accurate fact of the international system of states, one, to be sure, that could change. Against this stance, Kelsen seems to make a coherent logical claim: the "epistemological postulate" that if conflicting norms of international and national legal orders are both to be considered valid simultaneously, then the pluralistic construction is untenable.[102] This point ultimately boils down to what Kelsenians call "the harshness of the legal code," namely that at the end of the day legal conflicts require resolution and only one or the other norm is going to be lawfully applied.[103] The other competing legal norms are, in the end, non-law. Indeed even if a political choice is made regarding the precedence of one of the conflicting legal norms, there must be a legal rule in place explaining why such a resolution of the conflict is legally binding.[104] But a Hartian answer could be that it is only theoreticist reasons, and the peculiarities of Kelsen's legal theory, that make the monist position appear to follow logically from this – the legally binding character of the "political" choice could have other explanations. Kelsen's insistence on a pure theory of law independent of any considerations (or practices) of legitimacy, coupled with the sanction theory of law according to which every legal norm must have a sanction attached to it for the legal system to be efficacious, is what led to the monist position. Kelsen had to reject the dualist (pluralism) position as incoherent because two conflicting legal norms could not both be valid and *enforced*. But, as Hart argued, there are constitutional norms that are not attached to sanctions.[105] Moreover, as I will argue below, from the perspective of legitimacy and the practice of mutual recognition, the idea of constitutional tolerance between independent yet interdependent legal systems that compete for but do not have to resolve the question of the final locus of authority (because practitioners can take a doubly reflexive internal and external stance) is at least conceivable.[106]

1.3   Global "constitutional moments": cosmopolitan monism revived

While Kelsen's political choice for the primacy of international law is understandable, given his assumptions, it made little practical sense prior to 1945. States certainly deemed themselves sovereign, in possession of the *jus belli* and acted accordingly. Moreover, as Kelsen himself admitted, dualism and the recognition theory have been the reigning jurisprudential approach.[107] Domestic legal practitioners did not invoke the "basic norm" or authority of an international legal community to justify their legal decisions, and the discourse of a global political community with its autonomous legal system was, if it existed at all, marginal and an abstraction, an ineffective legal fiction given the minimal institutionalization of public power on the global level.[108] The relevant debates in jurisprudence thus had a limited scope and seemed rather scholastic. However, some have interpreted changes in the international political system since then as "constitutional moments" – steps in the systematization, integration, autonomy, and even constitutionalization of international law, apparently vindicating the overall thrust of Kelsen's approach.[109]

Accordingly, the erection of the UN Charter system in 1945, its subsequent and other related developments, is (retrospectively) construed as the first step in the construction of an autonomous, increasingly integrated and institutionalized global legal order of constitutional quality coupled to the global political system and claiming supremacy that has profoundly modified state sovereignty.[110] Indeed the discourse of an international (or global) community has begun to replace the old discourse of international society.[111] Membership in the UN is practically universal and commitment to its goals of peace, human rights, and legal resolution of disputes (by the International Court of Justice (ICJ)) is a condition of membership. The changes in the positive rules of international law this entails are well known: the most important being the principle of collective security eliminating the *jus belli* except for self-defense. This is now seen as an unprecedented attempt to legally regulate the use of force. The legal principles of sovereign equality, non-intervention, territorial integrity, domestic jurisdiction, and self-determination were enunciated and eventually universalized. Since the 1960s colonialism was dismantled, annexation in the aftermath of war became illegal, political autonomy and territorial integrity of borders affirmed. These principles apply to all states: international legal recognition and inclusion in the international community as sovereign, now really is presumably based on the principle of effectiveness, not on being European or western.[112]

Moreover, human rights principles were enunciated in the Charter and codified in important subsequent international Covenants.[113] Genocide, ethnic cleansing, and enslavement are not considered to be within the domestic jurisdiction of any state and no treaty will be deemed valid that involves an agreement to engage in or tolerate such action. These *jus cogens* principles are deemed by some to be constitutional, auxiliary to the UN Charter system.[114] Since 1989, it is considered the responsibility of the sovereign state to protect its civilian population against grave rights violations and in case of default, this responsibility (R2P) devolves on the international community.[115] Some have referred to this post-1989 expectation as a second "constitutional moment" involving the emergence of a new basic norm in the international system, described as a principle of civilian inviolability.[116] Indeed, the elevation of human as distinct from state security to a central concern of the

Security Council, its practice of transformative "humanitarian occupation," and its recent assumption of the power to list and sanction individual terrorists and to legislate for the rest of the United Nations membership regarding transnational terrorism indicate to some that a third international constitutional moment has occurred.[117] To be sure, in principle, the equal standing of states is now backed up by the global coercive legal order of the international community. Yet some speak of a new model of the state, whereby recognition, political autonomy, and non-intervention are increasingly made contingent on the state being non-aggressive and minimally just.[118] As indicated in the introduction to this book, a radical idea is at stake: that the international community may articulate and enforce moral principles and legal rules regulating the conduct of governments toward their own citizens (when their human rights are at stake).

Finally, the international order has become more legalized than ever before.[119] The proliferation of global and transnational (or hybrid) and regional courts to enunciate and enforce the values and law of the "international community," and in an increasing number of cases, to act as constitutional courts exercising constitutional review, is quite striking.[120] So is the emergence of new sources of international law, including the organs of international organizations morphing into GGIs which presumably rest on consensus, rather than state consent. From this perspective, it does seem as if Kelsen's hopes for centralization of the once primitive international legal system are coming to fruition. By centralization Kelsen meant two things: increased individuation of the subjects of international law and the emergence of a hierarchy among legal norms which legal adjudicators invoke, and which is backed up by international courts acting as organs of the international community, preferably with compulsory jurisdiction. To greater or lesser degrees, the new substantive rules, global remedies, sources, and discourses of international law seem to indicate progress in Kelsenian terms.[121] Hence, within global constitutionalist discourse there is a revival of the monist interpretation of the increasingly autonomous, and post-sovereign, global legal order coupled to the global political system, which is deemed primary and, on some interpretations, hierarchically superior vis-à-vis the legal orders of states.

However, others have challenged this interpretation. The discourse of legal pluralism and not only a neo-Kelsenian international legal monism is also experiencing a renaissance. Indeed many see the globalizing international political system as increasingly fragmented, and cite the proliferation of international legal regimes and the apparent absence of any meta-norms, overarching grundnorm, or general "rule of recognition" to mediate conflicts among them, as reason enough to revive the discourse of legal pluralism, now on the global register.[122] Moreover, for some the plurality of cross-cutting overlapping legal orders is deemed normatively desirable. This empirical and normative assessment, together with sensitivity to the asymmetry among global powers and the emergence of new forms of hegemony or imperial formations, not to mention the diversity of a still deeply divided world society, lead to the rejection of global constitutionalist discourse as apologetic, or even neo-imperial.

The challenges the above-mentioned changes pose to traditional ways of apprehending the relation between international and national law and to the classical sovereignty paradigm of international relations are deep, and it is unsurprising that they have led to an intense, widespread debate with quite serious potential political ramifications. The question is how to characterize these shifts and what kind of global political and legal order they constitute. Because much of the literature on global constitutionalism operates within the Kelsenian problematic and because legal pluralists reject Kelsenian monism in whatever form, yet also assume that the constitutionalist project requires it, we are presented with the following choice: either the further integration/constitutionalization of the global political system which entails taking the step to a monist global legal order based on cosmopolitan principles, that has to dispense with the concept of sovereignty (replacing it with subsidiarity), or acceptance of a disorderly (indeed, order-less) global legal pluralism that acknowledges the multiplicity of political orders and sources of international law but renounces any attempt to construct an order of orders or to constitutionalize the emergent global political system, rejecting the Kelsenian-type hierarchy and the leveling (*gleichschaltung*) of the autonomy of domestic polities and their legal orders that goes with it. On the other hand, the constitutionalists level a similar charge against the legal pluralists: by accepting the multiplicity of orders simply because they are there, and renouncing the constitutionalist project, and by attaching the label "law" indiscriminately to any form of coordinated rule-making, legal pluralists tend to collapse the distinction between law and regulation, dissolve the legal code into one among many normative-regulatory regimes, reduce legal decisions to policy choices, and thereby lose sight of the critical point of the exercise.[123] There are nuances among the positions in each camp but this is the basic divide.

As one cogent analyst puts it, the revival of both discourses can be seen as responses to three disturbing features of the globalizing world: fragmentation, deformalization, and empire.[124] Fragmentation refers to the splitting of international law into functionally defined "regimes" such as "human rights law," "security law," and "trade law," each geared to further particular types of interests and managed by narrowly defined expert competence. Deformalization is the process whereby the law retreats to the provision of procedures or broad directives to experts and decision-makers for the purpose of administering (or coordinating) international problems by means of functionally effective solutions and balancing interests. By empire is meant the emergence of patterns of constraint intended to advance the objectives of a single dominant actor (or a few imperial-minded ones) through the law or irrespective of it.[125] Given the morphing of international organizations into global governance institutions with vastly expanded competences, the absence of accountability mechanisms, and the resultant enhancement and concentration of the power of executives on the national and global level, which tends to undermine domestic constitutionalism, the stakes are high.[126] The advocates of global constitutionalism and of global legal pluralism both make empirical, analytical, and normative claims for their projects as the solution to the problems these phenomena generate.

Nevertheless, in what follows I will challenge the terms in which this debate is framed.[127] I argue that the dichotomy erected between constitutionalization and pluralism screens out the most interesting alternative – constitutional pluralism – as if it were an oxymoron. It misses the dualistic character of the contemporary (to be sure, contested, shifting, evolving) sovereignty regime and thus fails to perceive the possibility of a conception and a politics (project) that could vindicate much of what is valued by both sides. I turn now to the main arguments and counter-arguments for each side of this debate and then indicate how and why it is necessary to alter its terms. My focus is on the analytic grounds for each approach but I will include the normative and empirical arguments when relevant. As will become clear, my understanding of constitutional pluralism is different from both the UN-centered and the various de-centered versions of global constitutionalism, alternatively labeled "cosmopolitan pluralism" and "societal constitutionalism" insofar as they both assume away the segmental pluralism of international society, and reject the relevance of the concept of sovereignty.[128] My focus throughout the book will be on constitutionalization of the premier GGI in the world political system today, namely, the UN. But I differ from the legal pluralists insofar as they too tend to reject the relevance of sovereignty talk as well as the possibility of a legal way to resolve conflicts among the various autonomous legal orders in the world system.

1.4 Constitutionalist approaches: centered and de-centered

Legal theorists and advocates of global constitutionalization reasoning from a neo-Kelsenian perspective agree that the ascription of autonomy and constitutional quality to the legal order regulating the global political system would have to entail monism regarding validity and supremacy claims. The debates from this perspective are over whether to conceptualize the juridification (and/or constitutionalization) of the global political system via centered or de-centered institutional models. Before turning to their differences, I will indicate the main assumptions shared by the global constitutionalists. But first, a caveat. The literature on constitutionalist approaches to international law is vast, and I do not pretend to provide an overview of it.[129] My focus will be on the neo-Kelsenian juridical versions, all of which link the discourse of constitutionalization to a Kelsenian conception of the legal medium – i.e. the requirement of unity and internal normative hierarchy in the legal system. Constitutionalist discourse of this sort nonetheless has a descriptive and prescriptive dimension to it. From this perspective, the increased legalization of the globalizing international system invites its description as an autonomous and however inadequately, constitutional, domain and spurs projects for its further integration and constitutionalization. The idea is that the coupling of new forms of globalizing public power(s) to public law can be power limiting, efficiency fostering, and rights enhancing.

The global constitutionalists share three key assumptions, their differences regarding the institutional implications of constitutionalization notwithstanding. The first is that the autonomy and constitutional quality of the global legal system spells the end of sovereignty. Accordingly, the changes in the positive rules of international law described above are indicative of a step away from sovereignty in the direction of the constitutionalization of the global political system. In one prominent interpretation, the principle of "sovereign equality" enunciated in the UN Charter and deemed a general principle of international law, is not a principle of sovereignty at all.[130] The grammatical shift from noun to adjective in the term that appears in the Charter, "sovereign equality," expresses this transformation.[131] Instead of being the supreme power of a state, existing apart from and prior to international law, or as indicative of the self-referential autonomy and supremacy of the domestic constitutional legal order, "sovereignty" is now seen as a set of rights and a legal status ascribed conditionally by positive public international law to states. "Sovereign equality" is the core legal principle (along with human rights) established by the Charter of the new, autonomous constitutional legal system of the reconstituted international community. To quote Hans Kelsen's path-breaking 1944 article, "The Principle of Sovereign Equality of States as a Basis for International Organization," written with respect to the nascent UN:

> Therefore the sovereignty of the states, as subjects of international law, is the legal authority of the states under the authority of international law ... If sovereignty means "supreme" authority the sovereignty of States as subjects of international law can mean, not an absolutely but only a relatively supreme authority ... Sovereignty in the sense of international law can mean only the legal authority or competence of a state limited and limitable only by international law and not by the national law of another state.[132]

As one neo-Kelsenian commentator put it, "in other words, sovereignty is a collective or umbrella term denoting the rights which at a given time a state is accorded by international law and the duties imposed upon it by that same law. These specific rights and duties constitute 'sovereignty'; they do not flow from it."[133]

Equality, the noun in the phrase "sovereign equality," means equality of capacity for duties and rights – it is nothing other than the principle of legality – a formal legal principle indicating that under the same conditions states have the same duties and the same rights. As such, legal equality is of course compatible with actual inequality.[134] Moreover, and this is more to the point, the legal principle of sovereign equality does not entail the idea that a state cannot be bound against its will: on the contrary, since the sovereign equality of states is itself a positive rule of public international law, all states are bound by all international legal obligations regardless of their will and even against it.[135]

The second assumption shared by neo-Kelsenian global constitutionalists is that an international community now exists, although they differ as to its institutional structure and membership.[136] What is crucial here is the notion that the traditional concepts of sovereignty and equality of states (equal sovereignty) focused on national interest are replaced by the new principle of sovereign equality, with "community-oriented" content. The shift from the concept of "international society" to "international community" allegedly expresses this change.[137] The autonomous international legal and political community is an entity committed to "human kind" as a whole with its own (common) purposes and at least in the case of the version of global constitutionalism centered in the UN, its own legal personality enforceable against recalcitrant states.[138] Let us not forget that to a Kelsenian, law regulates its own creation and reference in legal discourse to (and compliance with) the norms of one and the same legal order is what creates a legal community.[139] The unity of appeal is all it takes (assuming efficacy) and any invocation of law involves legal unity.[140] Kelsen-inspired constitutionalists thus presuppose the existence of a global legal community. Some invoke a global community of values allegedly underpinning all communities and embedded in all the various legal structures in national, regional, and functional regimes, some are content with pointing to the new organs, especially courts, that articulate global law, others to the more centralized institutions but all assume that such an institutionalized international community now exists and is the basis of the shift beyond the sovereignty paradigm.[141]

The third shared assumption regards the unity, universality, and supremacy of the global constitutional legal order vis-à-vis domestic legal orders. On the Kelsenian monist approach as we have seen, in order for a legal order to be autonomous and of constitutional quality, it is not enough that it be supreme. The subordinate legal orders have to be construed as belonging to the same legal system, otherwise subordination would be meaningless: supremacy and hierarchy require unity. This entails far more than the idea that states are "sovereign" insofar as they are subordinate "only" to international law but not to one another. It means that they are no longer sovereign at all: their legal orders are not supreme or autonomous, their constitutions do not derive their validity from their own grundnorm, nor can their constitutional legal orders be imputed to their own autonomous demos (the idea of popular sovereignty) as the highest source. Rather, states, in the relevant respects, are now construed as organs of the constitutional globalizing international legal system. This legal order grants (delegates to) them a wide range of political and legal autonomy although the intrusions on domestic jurisdiction are not trivial. More serious, on the global constitutionalist reading their legal systems have their condition of validity not in themselves but in the higher, supreme, autonomous international legal order. The cosmopolitan constitutionalist approach thus revives the formalist Kelsenian argument to the effect that as a matter of international law, the limits of sovereignty are defined by international law.[142]

This is why on the monist reading of the primacy and supremacy of the autonomous global legal system with constitutional quality, sovereign equality means that states are no longer sovereign. Strictly speaking, the rules of this legal system do not depend on the consent of all the independently sovereign states but rather bind all states as members of a constitutional order whose validity references the grundnorm of the global legal system, however construed.[143] The latter is supreme over the domestic constitutional orders of states and trumps any agreement they make. "Autonomy" in this framework does not describe the self-referential nature of the sovereign states' legal system, it now merely refers to some set of prerogatives accorded to states (equally) by the global constitutional legal order – a matter of degree. It is the supreme international constitutional order that decides the competence of domestic legal orders, and this order cannot be altered by traditional treaty methods. Clearly, then, subsidiarity and multilevel governance are not equivalent to sovereignty. Indeed global cosmopolitan constitutionalists argue that subsidiarity has/should replace sovereignty as the principle for governing the allocation of competences, decision-making authority, and jurisdiction among the subunits of world society – i.e. in a context of different levels of public authority.[144]

Moreover, the assumption of unity and hierarchy in the global constitutional legal system implies that there is a legal way to address conflict among norms and jurisdictions. Legal principles of communication are possible and desirable to protect coherence and resolve conflicts. Since system and hierarchy are allegedly intrinsic to juristic thought in order for there to be legal normativity, it is apparently incumbent upon legal practitioners to reason in terms of the global constitutional legal order and its supremacy and to act as if there are no legal regimes outside general, now global and constitutional, international law.[145]

As already indicated there are centered and de-centered versions of this type of global constitutional discourse and the meaning of constitution/constitutionalism varies accordingly. The best-known exemplar of the first construes the UN Charter as *the* (substantive and formal) constitution of the international community.[146] Accordingly, it is the UN Charter system that now constitutes and is at the center of an autonomous legal order referencing a global legal and political community. The inclusive world political organization, constructed via the Charter, is the institutional representative of this community. States and their citizens must understand themselves as the constituent parts of a politically constituted world society with the Charter as the constitutional document – the higher law – regulating its global governance – the prime example of a non-state "supranational" constitution.[147] Although formally created as a treaty, the Charter has a "constitutional quality" which has been confirmed and strengthened over the years. This means that the governance of the international community must now be construed as a "multilevel system" characterized by universality (inclusiveness) of membership and unity, in which the allocation of competences is based on the principle of subsidiarity, rather than sovereignty. Ascribing constitutional quality to the Charter means construing it as the supporting frame of all international law and the highest layer in a hierarchy of legal norms.[148]

According to one analyst, there is thus now a hierarchy of rules and sources of international (global) law: those with constitutional quality enjoy the highest rank.[149] There can be no higher norms above the global constitution: neither general nor customary international law, nor the constitutions of member states qualify. In short, the monist "view dissolves the dualism of 'general international law' and the law of the Charter."[150] The Charter is supreme over international treaty law as per Article 103, and it "incorporates" prior customary international law. "World order treaties" like the two human rights covenants and the genocide convention are seen as "constitutional by-laws" of the international community, adding to and implementing the objectives and law of the Charter.[151] The UN Charter system, and the associated supranational and/or hybrid courts and *jus cogens* rules, is construed as the pinnacle of a global monist constitutional legal order. Moreover, via the Charter system it is now equipped with its own organs: it can articulate community law, adjudicate, and enforce it.[152] Indeed, it provides the global community's supreme enforcement organ: the Security Council.

Indeed, the Charter is deemed supreme not only vis-à-vis other treaties and treaty organizations, but also over the constitutional orders of the member states themselves. As we have seen, on the monist neo-Kelsenian reading on which this analysis depends, this means that domestic legal systems have their condition of validity not in themselves but in the higher, supreme, autonomous international legal order of the UN Charter system. However, in a departure from Kelsen, this reading is linked to what is known in the literature as the "foundationalist" conception of constitutionalism. Accordingly a constitution is construed not only as a way to limit and render calculable public power by coupling it to public law and legal rules, but as a constitutive process in which the founding moment(s) overturns established structures or powers, institutes a new political authority, and creates a new framework and design of governance, outside of which public power can no longer be legitimately exercised.[153] Moreover, the founding act is understood in a legislative frame, in which the constitutional form and all public power is traceable back (imputed) to the constituent power and thus can be construed as a form of self-government. Thus despite the fact that the UN Charter was established as an international treaty by the diplomatic representatives of the governments of the relevant states – the only legal method available under the conditions in 1945 – the reference in the preamble to "we the peoples of the United Nations," together with the super-majoritarian amendment rule (as distinct from unanimity typical of a treaty) is taken to indicate that it was not only established on behalf of but also by the peoples of the United Nations through their representatives. It is, in short, ascribed to the peoples (demoi) of the member states of the United Nations as their respective constituent power(s).[154] Accordingly, it can only be altered through following the amendment procedure or through a new exercise of constituent power of the peoples of the United Nations in joint action even to replace, if they wish, the Charter.[155] In other words, the claim is not only that the Charter articulates an autonomous legal order of constitutional quality, but that as a constitution (process) it has to be understood in the foundational legislative sense such that it can be ascribed to a constituent power(s). As a material constitution, the Charter clearly involves a set of substantive norms, purposes, and procedures that establish organs and articulate their powers, including primary and secondary rules. As a formal constitution, the Charter is a written document that may be changed only through the stipulated amendment procedure requiring a two-thirds majority of the members of the General Assembly including all of the five permanent members of the Security Council (ratified in accordance with the respective domestic constitutional processes of the member states).[156] The supermajority requirement for amendment establishes its formal character, its relative rigidity, and its superior rank with respect to the rules its organs make. By implication, the constituent units – states – are legally subordinated to their new creation: its rules apply to them irrespective of their continuing individual consent.

This is a strong claim that Hans Kelsen himself explicitly rejected, as late as 1950, insisting that the Charter is an international treaty constituting a treaty organization.[157] Nevertheless from the more contemporary (1998) retrospective standpoint and in light of other "constitutional moments" alluded to above, the above analysis insists that the treaty reading is inadequate and invokes instead the model of federation through which new political orders equipped with constitutions are created by states acting as representatives of their peoples, although they do not thereby constitute a federal state, or in this case a global federal state.[158] Accordingly, the "functional equivalent" of the people in the case of a domestic republican constituent process, is "we the peoples" of the United Nations.

> in the international community the constituent power lies with the "Peoples of the United Nations", who today are virtually all peoples of the world, and who normally act through their governments. The use of that constituent power in 1945 resulted in the UN Charter as a formal framework of rule (constitutional form).[159]

This centered monist version of the global constitutionalist approach is clearly overdrawn. As I will argue below and extensively in Chapter 5, the complex hybrid structure of the UN Charter (as a constitutional treaty – a treaty and a constitution), actually matches the dualistic (and asymmetrical) structure of international society/community. The federalist project for the UN clearly failed in the 1940s and it is misleading and even ideological to read the quasi-federal dimensions of the Charter system even today as indicating that a global political federation is a fait accompli, rather than a vérité à faire. There is a gap between the object-language of participants in this organization and the theorist's meta-language, i.e. between the self-understanding of the actors/participants and some theorists.[160] A federal and constitutional construction of the global political system would require a political project, perhaps on the agenda in the twenty-first century, but, as Hart already objected to Kelsen, neither legalist reasoning nor the coherence demands of theory can make it so either for the original Charter or for its present status despite formal analogies. The same is true regarding the legitimation problems of the current system – something which the foundational constitutionalist reading finesses to the point of ideology.[161] Moreover, as I will argue throughout this book, the appropriate ideal-typical conception of constitutionalism for a federal polity that is not a state is constitutional pluralism, not constitutional monism.[162]

The de-centered understanding of global constitutionalism is also based on the claim that new forms of global governance and law have emerged that render the discourse of sovereignty irrelevant.[163] There is much variety among the de-centered versions of global constitutionalist theory, ranging from approaches centered on the idea of an international community with shared values and solidarity, to the power-limiting versions stressing judicially enforceable global constitutional law that can protect economic freedom and human rights. One of the most coherent and interesting for our purposes is the systems-theoretic approach, which merges a Kelsenian understanding of the legal medium with a Luhmannian concept of constitution. To the theorists who elaborate this approach, the key development is the emergence of world society out of the old international order.[164] The idea is that international society has gone global, shifting from a segmental form of differentiation to a set of relations between many functionally differentiated global subsystems of which the political subsystem is only one. Functional differentiation has also occurred within that subsystem, overlaying and undermining the previous order of "international society" composed of sovereign territorial states. Accordingly, this order is composed not of states but of components of states, of networks of executives, adjudicators, along with non-governmental civil actors that make key policy decisions and legal rules.[165]

From this perspective as well, there is a proliferation of law-making in world society independent of state consent or control. Although the systems theorists of world society are legal pluralists regarding the relations among "subsystems" or international legal regimes, they argue that each subsystem is internally constitutionalized to a greater or lesser degree, and the furthest along this road is the global political system.[166] Thus there is a plurality of global constitutions in world society that are structurally coupled with each functional subsystem but there is no single world constitution or legal order coupled to world society as a whole capable of legally regulating the relations among or legally resolving the conflicts between the subsystems. This approach to global constitutionalism is thus monistic regarding the legal order of each subsystem and pluralist vis-à-vis the relations among the global subsystems.

However, in good Kelsenian fashion, they insist that it is the legal system itself and not external political, administrative, or corporate economic actors which determines what the law is. A legal system cannot be understood in terms of the implementation of political programs or sovereign will, it must be seen as autonomous and in charge of the codification of the code: legal/ illegal. Courts, in short, are the core of any legal system, and they must decide whether or not the law has been violated in any particular instance and resolve any controversy over the legal status (validity) of norms. Accordingly legality is not a matter of more or less: legalization cannot be understood in terms of a continuum. From the internal perspective concerned with validity, oriented by the code, legal/illegal, a legal order must be construed as a closed, gapless normative system.

Under the conditions of globalization, the legal system and its courts escape the bounds of states and no longer require reference to the political or legal concept of sovereignty.[167] Globalization undermines the traditional legal doctrine that traces the distinction between law and non-law back to the constitution (higher law) of the nation-state and to legislation imputable to a demos or constituent power (sovereignty).[168] The global political constitution is not produced by legislation but through de-centered legal self-reflection and through a global community of courts (domestic, transnational, supranational, global) which ascertain legal validity and legal violations. In other words, the emphasis here is on the emergence of a global political constitution and a global legal system through *polycentric*, plural, autological processes that produce valid legal norms which regulate actors connected through complex networks bounded not by territory but by function, communicative codes, and particular practices.[169]

Why does it matter that we perceive and help to institutionalize de-centered, cosmopolitan constitutional law? For the systems theorist, a constitution is a matter of "structural coupling" between subsystemic structures and legal norms. Its function is to guarantee the multiplicity of social differentiation and to liberate the internal dynamism of each subsystem while also institutionalizing mechanisms of self-restraint against their society-wide expansion. This is a systems-theoretical version of "power-limiting" as distinct from foundational constitutionalization.[170] This problem emerged first for the political system within the nation-state: mechanisms that could block the political instrumentalization of civil society, of the economy, of law, and so forth, had to be found and legally institutionalized. The structural coupling of law and political power was the solution.[171] Accordingly, constitutional rights in the form of negative civil liberties are mechanisms that preserve the autonomy of spheres of action in a counter-movement to the expansionist logic of the state. Structural coupling reduces the harm that politics and law can cause each other. The theory of global constitutionalism generalizes this idea to the global political subsystem: human rights (negative and positive) are the functional equivalents of civil liberties. I restrict my analysis to the systems-theoretical version of the constitutionalized global political subsystem, leaving to the side their approach to the interrelations among the various global legal orders.[172]

This approach points to several indicia of global political constitutionalism. The transnational judicial networks that have emerged are construed as a "heterarchical" organization of courts which provide global remedies and are at the center of global political constitutionalism. These involve various levels of communication, ranging from the citation of decisions of foreign courts by national courts, to organized meetings of supreme court justices such as those held triennially (since 1995) by the Organization of the Supreme Courts of the Americas, to the most advanced forms of judicial cooperation involving partnership between national courts and a supranational tribunal such as the European Court of Justice and more recently, the ICC.[173] The proliferation of supranational courts must be seen as providing global remedies for violations of cosmopolitan law despite the fact that they originate in treaty organizations. Even national courts can double as elements of this cosmopolitan legal system, insofar as they participate in the interpretation and judgment of violations of global law. Thus despite the fact that states are the primary agents responsible for delivering on individual rights, they are also the key violators; what their judicial organs enforce are cosmopolitan constitutional legal norms and their failure to do so may expose them to penalties by the enforcers of "global justice."[174]

Indeed innovation of *jus cogens* which signals the obligatory character of key global legal norms based on consensus, not state consent, as per the Vienna Convention on the Law of Treaties (VCLT) means that formal constitutional law exists and functions as higher law vis-à-vis the will of states.[175] *Jus cogens* rules are deemed higher law insofar as they place certain norms beyond the reach of states and thus are superior to ordinary rules of international law. No treaty will be considered valid that violates these pre-emptory norms. Included in this category are the prohibition against torture, genocide, slavery, torture, extralegal killing and disappearances, crimes against humanity, and so on. The proliferation of *erga omnes* rules (rules obligating all states whether or not they signed a treaty and thus giving states a legal interest in their protection even if they are not affected by a particular breach of rules) is another sign of constitutional cosmopolitanism indicating transcendence of the old international legal order: unaffected states are on this doctrine the enforcers of the constitutional values of the international community.[176] The fact that the individual is now a key subject at international law, as evidenced by human rights law, also confirms the cosmopolitan character of the global legal system.

Finally, courts decide what amounts to violations of *jus cogens* norms, and they settle disputes about legal validity in the global legal system. There are now norms in that system designating the sources by which norms become law. This ultimate indication of a global political constitution means that there is legal law-making (a rule of recognition, higher law regulating lower law). Whenever a question arises about the source of law, it immediately becomes a question about whether a law invoked really is law and only the legal system (courts) can resolve such a question. Thus, there exists a closed, autopoetic global legal system coupled to the global political subsystem. Ultimately this de-centered approach (vis-à-vis world society and its various societal constitutions) weds the Kelsenian concept of a legal system as monist, internally hierarchical in terms of norms (without necessitating hierarchy of legislative organs or an institutional legislative center), and key features of Kelsen's conception of centralization – individualization and normative hierarchy – to Hartian criteria (or lingo) for indicia of a systemic legal order. Each constitutionalized global subsystem is understood in Kelsenian terms internally as monist while the multiplicity of autonomous, indeed hermetically sealed systems reveals a pluralist approach on the part of the systems theorist and something akin to state monism from the perspective of the participants reasoning from within the logic of the respective subsystem.[177]

These developments in the global political system are indeed impressive and certainly transcend traditional international law principles. Other de-centered versions of cosmopolitan constitutionalism invoke the same *formal* (a hierarchy of norms including *jus cogens* and Article 103 of the UN Charter), *functional* (multilateral treaties creating regime-specific constitutional charters for complex transnational governance practices), and *substantive* (human rights obligations piercing the veil of sovereignty in relations between states and their citizenry) features of the globalizing international legal order to make their case.[178] These "constitutional elements" transcend the traditional statist paradigm. However, to claim that they already amount to a global political constitution is premature and dangerous. The risk is that of "symbolic constitutionalism," i.e. the invocation of the core values and legal discourse of the international community to dress up strategic power plays, self-interested regulations, and interventions in universalistic garb. For example, the invocation of the values of the international community to justify unilateral military intervention in "rogue" states as the enforcement of global right, allows the violator of international law to appear as the upholder of global constitutional legal norms. Some systems theorists are aware of this risk, but they attribute it to the incompleteness of the transition from international to cosmopolitan law insisting nonetheless on the constitutional and systemic character of the global legal system.[179] The problem from their perspective is the restricted reach of global remedies: the ICJ lacks compulsory jurisdiction, the ICC lacks a definition for the crime of aggression or of torture, or terrorism, the Security Council of the UN is legally unrestrained, and escapes subjection to separation of powers principles, there is no global human rights court with contemporary jurisdiction, and so on. When these restrictions are overcome, the global constitution will be complete.

These are serious problems and I will return to them in Chapter 5. But I argue that there is a basic flaw in this overall approach, which renders it defenseless against political instrumentalization despite its intentions. To be sure the de-centered approach does not suffer from the counterintuitive claims of the strong centered version: it does not need to find one formal constitutional document (the Charter) or a single "sovereign," legislative or constituent power to argue for the constitutional quality of the global political system thanks to the idea of structural coupling. Nonetheless, there is something forced and overdrawn about the analysis. The systems-theoretical analysis of the global political constitution is neo-Kelsenian insofar as it deems the legal order of the global political system to be monist and inclusive vis-à-vis the legal orders of member states: from this perspective domestic regional and international courts all reference and enforce the global constitutional legal order although the latter is not (yet) fully centralized or hierarchical institutionally insofar as no global court has compulsory jurisdiction for human rights or international crimes or the power of constitutional review. Hierarchy may not even be necessary institutionally. Even so, to articulate what a de-centered cosmopolitan global legal system must involve

conceptually, by reasoning from the standpoint of legal validity, is not enough
to demonstrate the sociological claim that it in fact exists. The problem
(here as with Kelsen) lies in a specific kind of legalism: generalizing from a
purely internal juridical-theoretical perspective, coupled with an overly
narrow concept of constitutionalism and an indefensible evolutionary bias.
Constitutional elements and some structural coupling do not amount to
constitutional*ism* and the presence of some global remedies, pre-emptory
norms, judicial transnational communication, etc. does not mean that an
autonomous cosmopolitan legal system already exists whose supremacy
renders the discourse of sovereignty anachronistic, or that the functional
differentiation of "world society" makes segmental pluralism of the international society of states irrelevant. Moreover, severing the concept of constitutionalism entirely from considerations of democratic legitimacy seems to
regress behind achievements of the democratic-constitutional state, repeating
the Kelsenian error of construing sovereignty, the state, and the international
or global world order from a one-sided internal purely legal-theoretical
perspective thereby eliding important political-theoretical considerations.[180]
I will return to these issues in Chapter 5.

Similar criticisms apply to the other key version of de-centered constitutionalism dubbed "cosmopolitan pluralism."[181] This approach tries to square
the circle of global constitutionalism and the plurality of legal orders in a
different way than the systems theorist. The "cosmopolitan pluralist"
approach purports to be both empirically and normatively compelling.
It claims to describe the deep structure of public law as it now is (international and domestic constitutional law practices) *and* to offer a coherent
normative standard for ascribing supremacy among institutions (courts)
within the global cosmopolitan legal order in a principled way.[182] The idea
is to replace the discourses of sovereignty and democratic legitimacy that
ascribe the ultimate authority of a constitutional order to the constituent
power construed as "we the people," or "we the peoples," with a complex
standard of public reason that refers to jurisdictional and procedural principles for the construction of legal and political authority.[183] Unlike the
centered version of global constitutionalism, this approach refrains from
projecting the forms and principles of constitutional democracy developed
on the level of the nation-state onto the global order. It does not look for
founding moments, constituent powers, we the people(s), a fundamental text,
or institutional hierarchy and it does not locate supremacy in global institutions or in a global constitution. In short, this approach abandons all the
discourses that are bound up with the allegedly anachronistic "statist paradigm." The legal cosmopolitan cognitive frame abandons "statism," substituting a focus on the abstract principled moral grounds for legitimate
constitutional authority for the older (and statist) idea of a collective will or
democracy as the basic referent.[184] It replaces sovereignty with the principle of

subsidiarity and just background norms (due process, respect for human rights, and reasonableness) as the starting point for reflecting on the criteria that should be invoked to resolve conflicts of law and the appropriate locus of institutional authority.[185] The constitutional frame for global politics and global law, in short, rests on a set of ideal principles of constitutionalism that provide the ultimate criteria and source of authority of the political and legal order. The latter's constitutional quality depends on the degree to which it lives up to the ideal of constitutionalism arrived at through the exercise of public reason.

Despite its claims of finding an alternative to the dualist/monist divide, however, this approach has been described by critics as covertly monist.[186] The principle of subsidiarity it advocates in place of sovereignty presupposes a unified global legal order in which an appropriate authority ascribes competence to the various units comprising it. The moral "just" background norms that are to guide this ascription, embodied in the global constitutional order, also presuppose the unity of the legal system and not only the integrity of the principle of legality or the legal medium. What is at issue for the legal cosmopolitan is the allocation of competences within a coherent and unified, if institutionally plural constitutionalized legal order. As the most talented proponent of this paradigm puts it, "Cosmopolitan constitutionalism establishes an integrative basic conceptual framework for a general theory of public law that integrates national and international law."[187] The pluralist dimension in this cognitive frame does not pertain to the distinct and separate existence of autonomous constitutional orders and their possible modes of interrelation (as per the constitutional pluralist approach I will discuss below) but rather to the multiple sources of laws, possible conflicts, and criteria for resolving them and for allocating competences based on, as already indicated, the "complex standard of public reason." Yet clearly the cosmopolitan legal order imagined here is a single coherent one, albeit quite institutionally decentralized. The absence of institutional hierarchy (the alleged pluralist feature) does not, however, mean the absence of monism (unity of legal orders and hierarchy of norms).

Certainly the subsidiarity idea is attractive if it is taken to mean that the institutional instance best able to solve a problem efficiently and with the fewest normative costs should have the power to do so and/or that local actors should not be able to undermine solutions to international global problems or violate basic human rights by invoking sovereignty. But these considerations are what inspire international organization generally and changing public opinion regarding sovereign prerogatives and can be analyzed through the cognitive frame of changing sovereignty regimes and international law – they do not require the cosmopolitan constitutionalist stance. Cosmopolitan pluralists are perhaps too quick to generalize a cognitive frame devised to settle legal conflicts and contested issues of ultra vires control within the

European Union to the globalizing international legal system. Indeed it is contested whether the imagined legal and political order of cosmopolitan pluralism with its implicit monist assumptions obtains even in this regional context.[188] Be that as it may, I am not at all convinced that the discourse of sovereignty is irrelevant even in this most integrated of regional legal and political orders.

But the cosmopolitan pluralist paradigm generates normative doubts as well. Indeed, one wonders whose account of public reason should or would prevail in such a system. Once one replaces the principle of democratic legitimacy with the "complex standard of public reason" we lose the reference to "we the people" or "we the peoples" and all the institutional forms this entails, as mechanisms for limiting our representatives (legal or political) and as the referent for constitutional legitimacy. Political equality, accountability, indeed democracy all drop out of the legitimacy equation, disclaimers notwithstanding. Here too a concept of constitutionalism is at work (constraining the exercise of public authority by public law) coupled with a purely moral, justice-based account of legitimacy that omits entirely the power-political and political-normative dimensions of legitimacy and legality. Instead of citizens and their representatives checking the public use of power and legalistic discourse through the appropriate institutional mechanisms, we end up risking a global "juristocracy," to borrow Ran Hirschel's phrase, in which judges and courts communicating with one another allegedly guided solely by justice instead of power-political considerations decide the allocation of competences and the general rules of the game.[189] To be sure, cosmopolitan pluralism is a normative project with the aim of spurring real world approximation (in the EU and in the global legal system) of institutional arrangements to universal, substantive, and structural constitutional principles and values.[190] Despite the appropriation of the term, "constitutional pluralism," however, this approach is cosmopolitan and ultimately monist regarding the legal order, insofar as it imagines the world legal system in the singular even if it is "institutionally" pluralist with respect to loci of competence and legal sources. It too quickly assumes away the discourse of sovereignty as it pertains both to the state and to the people as if the only serious issue is the allocation of competences and jurisdictions within a single legal order rather than, additionally, issues of democratic legitimacy and political community.[191] One need not embrace a Schmittian conception of constituent power in order to make this point.[192]

1.5   The legal pluralist alternative

Legal pluralists have adduced these and additional arguments against the constitutionalist approach to the changing nature and scope of international law and global governance. Pluralists tend to see the discourse of constitutionalization (which for them as well entails normative hierarchy and monism) as Kelsenian wishful thinking or worse as apologetic of hegemonic projects. Nevertheless, their purpose is not to defend the unified sovereignty of the state.[193] Rather, they apply insights drawn from an older (critical anthropological) tradition of legal pluralist thinking that was focused on independent if overlapping local, infra-state normative and/or legal orders coexisting within the same national (or imperial) space and the politics of their interaction, to the analysis of supra- or transnational global legal orders coexisting in the world system along with state and infra-state legal orders.[194] For them, the disorderly relationship between multiple legal and normative orders, cross-cutting jurisdictions, and competing claims to supremacy that is now characteristic of the global constellation cannot and should not be resolved through the legal means involving normative or institutional hierarchy.[195] There is a descriptive/diagnostic and normative set of assumptions at work here that many legal pluralists share despite their differences. Nevertheless, as with the global constitutionalists, there are a variety of positions within the overall pluralist approach: in this case the range is between strong and softer accounts. I will briefly summarize what they all have in common and then address the stronger and weaker versions.

Legal pluralists share the following assumptions, their differences notwithstanding: first, that sovereignty is not necessary to the concept of a legal order; second, that the existence of multiple, overlapping, and diverse legal orders belies the necessity of a unitary, logically ordered, and hierarchically differentiated conception of a legal system; and third, that conflicts of legal norms, clashes of claims of supremacy, and competition for primacy are unavoidable but not necessarily destructive of healthy political ordering. Indeed such conflicts and clashes can be seen as mechanisms for managing hybridity, enhancing voice and choice, and fostering accountability.[196]

First, like the global constitutionalists, legal pluralists also challenge the view that law must be identified with the uniform, comprehensive, exclusive legal order of the modern sovereign state. The prevalence of the idea of the monopoly of law by the state merely attests to the success of the state-building project in the West in the post-medieval period and of its ideological discourses.[197] Sovereignty – or supremacy (and unity) of the state's legal order – is neither necessary for there to be functioning legal systems (the empirical claim) nor is it desirable either on the level of the state or on any other level of governance since its imposition tends to involve leveling, homogenizing, and other oppressive practices (the normative claim).[198] This stance reveals the difference between the modern (and post-modern) legal pluralist and classical dualist insofar as the latter did deem the legal order of the state to be sovereign, exclusive, and impermeable.

However, second, unlike the constitutionalists, pluralists contest not only the indispensability of the concept (and practices) of sovereignty to law, but also the need for a unitary, hierarchical concept of law. They point to the multiplicity of coexisting, overlapping bodies of law and institutionalized systems of varied geographical reach (the medieval period) and to the emergence of new forms of legal pluralism afterwards (in the contexts of empire, imperialism, and colonialism and now in the domain of global governance) as a challenge to the descriptive cogency of the "identitarian" "modernist" concept of law. The plural legal regimes produced in the epoch of imperial colonization via the simultaneous transplanting/superimposition of western legal codes abroad and the codification of local legal codes and practices (as "customary," "religious," or "personal" law) into systems of "indigenous" norms and institutions alongside state law (whether or not officially recognized) is adduced as empirical proof of the cogency of descriptive legal pluralism in the modern context.[199] Similarly, the current post-national or global phenomena of multiple forms of legalization – the fragmentation of once unified sovereign legal orders and the emergence of a multiplicity of trans- and/or supernational legal regimes – indicates the cogency of the legal pluralist analysis vis-à-vis the contemporary, "post-modern" context.[200] The point is that dual, or rather plural normative/legal systems can exist simultaneously in the same space and time with complex mixtures and combinations prior to and in the aftermath of the success of the emergence of the modern nation-state and despite the discourse of unified sovereignty.[201]

Drawing on discoveries of legal anthropologists, contemporary legal pluralists argue that modern (state-organized) societies also have multiple normative systems made by a variety of social actors other than legal officials. Hence the idea of a central legislative and/or unified coherent hierarchy of legal sources is a myth for them as well. Indeed, they deny the meaningfulness of the sharp distinction between legal and other normative orders (religious, moral, customary) given the efficacy of the latter within society and their input into the only apparently autonomous official legal system.[202] As Boaventura de Sousa Santos put it, "Rather than being ordered by a single legal order, modern societies are ordered by a plurality of legal orders interrelated and socially distributed in different ways."[203]

Third, the absence of legal unity or agreed upon legal rules or meta-norms to govern the relation among domestic, transnational, and global legal regimes, so as to settle the issue of supremacy is, for the legal pluralist, nothing new. Rather, it should remind us of what has always been true: that between different yet overlapping legal and normative systems conflicts emerge, and are resolved through political negotiation, compromise, and mutual adjustment or legal rules of thumb ("inter-legality"), without thereby undermining the existence or functioning of the plurality of the extant normative orders.[204] It is the positivist concept of the necessity of one overarching legal system that is logically ordered and hierarchically differentiated that is the myth whether this is associated with the impermeable legal order of the sovereign state or with the global legal system.[205] Instead, the legal pluralist insists that we have entered the epoch of "inter-legality" wherein multiple legal networks overlap, intersect, are porous to one other, subject to constant trespassing and interaction.[206] It is worth noting another distinction between this legal pluralist and the classical dualist approach to the relation of domestic and international law: the latter presupposes, as already indicated, entirely distinct legal orders that regulate different subjects, have different content, and are valid in different spaces while the former assumes distinct legal orders that nonetheless can overlap along all these axes.

Strong legal pluralists make a virtue out of the necessity of managing hybridity through ad hoc forms of mutual accommodation.[207] They add to the apparently undeniable descriptive fact of global legal pluralism – the diversity among different overlapping national and international normative systems and levels of governance – the claim that it is neither possible nor normatively desirable to come up with legal rules or meta-norms for regulating the interaction among them.[208] It is assumed that in order to govern the relation among local, domestic, regional, international, and global legal systems legally, by legal rules, one would have to buy into the constitutionalist project, understood in neo-Kelsenian terms. In other words, not only shared norms, but also a shared conception of a legal hierarchy of norms, and unity would have to be the common regulative ideal. But this would not only contradict the descriptive, analytical claims of pluralism regarding its adequacy to the contemporary global constellation. The very search for or effort to create a common legal frame is allegedly burdened with authoritarian hegemonic implications. Hence the alleged normative advantages of the pluralist approach.

According to one advocate, pluralism does follow reality descriptively, but, pace the critics, it also makes demands on it insofar as it seeks to foster a reasoned, justifiable (plural) structure of governance.[209] Strong pluralists make three normative claims for pluralism vis-à-vis the constitutionalist approach: first, pluralism acknowledges and accommodates the diversity and hybridity of normative orders in the world today; second, it fosters the accountability of global governance institutions insofar as it entails counterpowers able to criticize and challenge them; and third, it allows for contestation of established power structures and new power bids thus helping actors resist the solidification of hegemonic or imperial formations (and their legitimation via symbolic constitutionalism). Whatever constitutionalist methods exist for recognizing and managing diversity on the domestic level cannot be transposed to the supranational domain because the social and political preconditions for this are lacking: neither regional nor supranational orders are federal, con-federal, or consociational states or likely to become so in the near future.[210] By resisting the attempt to subject the interaction among the multiplicity of distinct, or hybrid and permeable sub-orders, to common legal rules, an overarching framework, harmonization, and ultimately hierarchy, through "constitutionalization," by opting instead for more open *political* forms of accommodation, pluralism allegedly does justice to legitimate diversity. As one advocate puts it, with its acceptance of heterarchy and of political rather than legally determined joints between the different sub-orders, pluralism opens up space for adaptation and acknowledgment of differences in what remains a deeply divided international community.[211] Global constitutionalism talk on the other hand risks de-politicization and premature imposition of an alleged moral "consensus."

Pluralism might also better achieve accountability than implausible constitutionalist approaches because it allows for mutual influence and pressure (politics) among sites of governance without ceding supremacy to any one of them.[212] Given the unsettled nature of post-national space, global governance, and its relation to other levels of normative ordering, and given the fact that global governance institutions and the law they produce often follow from an unjust distribution of power outside and within GGIs, establishing legal relations among these levels through constitutionalization could undermine accountability to the less powerful rather than enhancing it. Ascribing the qualifier "legal" to regulations imposed by the powerful allegedly enhances their hegemony, by legitimating their rule while casting those who resist or challenge power-enabling rules in the name of greater responsiveness, equality, justice, or accountability, as law-breakers. Instead, and this is the third point, the normative stance of legal pluralism opens the discursive space for alternative legalities and subaltern politics and voices to challenge mainstream forms of global governance sustained by dominant powers. By keeping legitimacy in question and opening spaces for contestation and mutual challenge, the ad hoc forms of mutual accommodation advocated by the strong versions of legal pluralism can foster creative adaptation, tolerance, dialogue, and mutual adjustment.

Soft pluralists agree with much of the above but are uneasy with leaving the resolution of normative conflicts to political processes or ad hoc forms of interaction.[213] Taking the risk of fragmentation and destructive conflict seriously, they advocate various legal mechanisms of harmonization and coordination (legal inter-legality), and propose some general legal principles for deciding competing authority claims without embracing hierarchy or centralization. Coupling techniques that indicate how plural yet overlapping legal systems might interact are adduced by several "soft pluralists," while others advocate the principle of subsidiarity as a substitute for sovereignty (variously interpreted) for allocating competence, jurisdiction, and deciding or avoiding normative conflict in the global political "system."[214] The assumption underlying this approach is that judges, local, national, and international, consider themselves part of a common enterprise of legal adjudication and law enforcement, share at least the core legal values, and thus can through dialogue settle conflicts in legal ways. Legal principles of communication are deemed possible and desirable to protect coherence, resolve conflicts, and enforce law, without resurrecting sovereigntist or unitary hierarchical tropes. Inter-judicial dialogue through transnational networks is allegedly evidence of the former while the emergence of hybrid national/international tribunals are examples of the latter.[215]

We thus face something of a standoff. Pluralists of whatever stripe are certainly right in resisting the "constitutionalist" assumption of monist hierarchy and supremacy of global law as descriptive of the contemporary constellation and in raising the legitimacy question regarding the discourse of an institutionalized, integrated international community on which it rests. They are also right to insist that insofar as constitutionalist methods for handling diversity *within states* – federalism, consociationalism, multicultural jurisdictions, local autonomy, rights and so forth – invariably locate supremacy at the center, even if the latter delegates quite a lot of competences, they presuppose hierarchy. In the global context in which there is no definitive acceptable meta-framework for the attribution and/or the devolution of powers and competences and in which neither the political nor social conditions for locating supremacy at the center exist, these techniques are not directly applicable. If these methods presuppose a world federal state and a unitary monistic global legal system, the pluralist critics are right.[216] Moreover, if the discourse of global constitutionalism serves primarily to take certain issues off the political table, then the pluralist suspicion of it as covering over hegemonic power projects is compelling

On the other hand, the constitutionalists are also right against strong and even soft pluralists: they offer no way to differentiate between legitimate and illegitimate normative diversity, no antidote to the upward drift of political authority to increasingly intrusive and disturbingly unaccountable global governance institutions that already claim legality and legitimacy, no alternative to the tendency of GGIs to enhance executive power at the center of the global political system and domestically, at the expense of national constitutionalist and democratic procedures, and no mechanisms to foster accountability other than conflict. "Constitutional" may not be a description of the current constellation, but at least its advocates can be understood as pursuing a political project seeking to limit power by law, to protect basic rights through courts, and to enhance accountability. Indeed constitutions do not necessarily de-politicize; rather, they provide a shared framework within which political conflicts among actors in diverse pluralistic societies, national or global, can take place. Strong pluralists resist such projects on mistaken conceptual grounds, largely shared by the strong constitutionalists, as I will show below, but they do not offer another way to limit power by law, settling rather for "politics" whatever that means. *More serious, even soft pluralists who do seek "legal" mechanisms to manage conflict between normative systems pull the conceptual rug out from under their enterprise because they are unable to provide a coherent concept of law or to distinguish "law" from other forms of normative order.* While they avoid "essentialist" accounts, post-modern legal pluralists tend to collapse law with any form of normative regulation – morality, religion, self-regulation by networks of actors, and so forth. Law gets placed on a continuum of descriptions of regulations of social life running from state law to vague forms of informal social control, "soft law," to self-regulation of autonomous regimes and now to global "governance."[217] As indicated, to the legal pluralist, the "constitutionalist" model of a legal system as a unified hierarchy of norms, clearly distinguished from other kinds of social norms, and in which there is a differentiation between primary and secondary rules, and identifiable "legislative" legal sources is a phantasm of jurists. But, legal pluralists face an equally serious problem:

> When the distinction between law and other social norms disappears, when every social actor who is creating social norms and who has the power to execute them is treated as a legislator, when the validity of positive law goes side by side with other types of legitimate validity … and finally, when negotiating processes between various social actors make valid law – then it makes no more sense to speak of the law and one has to give up on the principles of equal adjudication.[218]

In other words, the integrity and distinctiveness of the legal medium as an institution and not only as a vehicle to coordinate or administer – and its internal rule-of-law principles – impartiality, equality before the law, fairness, legal justice – is lost with such a move.[219] Indeed, loss of the law/non-law distinction leads one to query what role the word "legal" plays in the legal pluralist discourse.

As Klaus Günther rightly notes, the theoretical heart of the problem is the fact that legal pluralists interpret law and the relation of transnational or global legal orders to domestic systems and to one another, from the external point of view only.[220] But, and here Günther repeats the Kelsenian point, if there is to be transnational legal communication among legal actors (judges, advocates, arbitrators) then they must perforce treat legal materials under the hypothesis of unity, coherence, and internal normative integrity otherwise they would not be dealing with or applying law.[221] Even if one insists that legal validity is "system-relative," and even if one embraces a strong pluralist position and does not seek inter-legality, the legal pluralist would have to reference a legal rule to explain why a resolution of a conflict brought about on political grounds is also legally binding or why a conflict cannot be adjudicated on legal grounds.[222] They must, to draw on Hart's language, adopt the internal attitude, and the pragmatics of this entails operating with a legal meta-language, what Günther calls a universal code of legality, however indeterminate, involving ideas of fair procedures, the concept of a sanction, a competence, rights, legal sources, and so on.[223] The question then becomes whether one can render legal pluralism as a description from an external point of view complementary with the requirement of subscribing to the universal code of legality – from an internal point of view.[224]

Indeed. That I submit is the project/stance of constitutional pluralism. However, for this to be possible conceptually, one would have to revise the monist hierarchical conception of global *constitutionalism*, and of monist state sovereigntism and reconceive legal *pluralism* as referring to the multiplicity of autonomous public legal systems that operate according to the universal code of legality, attain constitutional quality, interact and overlap without impugning the integrity of any one of them. Legal actors would have to be able to take the internal attitude toward the legal resolution of conflicting norms in deciding cases coupled with reflexivity regarding the political community's relations with others in a broader political community and cooperative setting without settling the matter of ultimate supremacy. I will argue that this need not entail replacing the concept of sovereignty with subsidiarity.[225] Yet the relation among the autonomous legal and political orders of constitutional quality would have to be re-imagined, and a willingness of the relevant legal *and political* actors to defer resolving the ultimate question of which constitutional order is sovereign and which institutional instance is supreme (sovereignty would not thereby disappear from the systems at issue) thereby displaying "constitutional tolerance" would be indispensable. For this, reflexivity on the part of legal actors and theorists regarding the internal and external standpoints would be required.[226] But all this would also have to entail reflection on the political preconditions for the constitutional pluralist perspective to be convincing and successful: i.e. *reflection about what political context, relations, commitments, and political forms enable and require the adoption of the internal attitude among actors attached to distinct yet interrelated and in some instances embedded or nested legal/political communities.*[227] Indeed vis-à-vis the global political system, as I will argue in Chapter 5, constitutional pluralism would have to be seen as linked to a *political project* – of legal and institutional reform that binds global public power to public law (constitutionalization) and helps reconstruct (re-found?) the global political system such that sovereign equality and human rights are respected, and accountability and representativeness of the relevant institutions and hence their legitimacy are enhanced.[228] I will turn to the issue of institutional arrangements in Chapter 5. First it is necessary to construct an ideal type and working definition of constitutional pluralism as a distinctive way of imagining legal and political ordering in the supranational context of a regional or global governance institution. Before proceeding let me reiterate that I restrict my analysis of a conceivable constitutional pluralist project on the global level to the global political subsystem and its premier global governance institution: the UN.

1.6   Constitutional pluralism

The concept of "constitutional pluralism" is not an oxymoron.[229] Rather, it involves a distinctive theoretical (and political) perspective that entails an ingenious way to break out of an unhelpful dichotomy. The dichotomy between global (or regional) constitutionalism construed in monist hierarchical terms and a descriptive and/or normative legal pluralism that loses the distinctiveness of the legal medium, both of which entail the irrelevance of the concept of sovereignty, is inadequate for the reasons described above. Neither side of this either/or is compelling: the first fails on descriptive and pragmatic grounds, the second on conceptual ones.

In this book I will argue for the cogency of the constitutional pluralist conception and project vis-à-vis the global political system, linked to the concepts of a dualistic world order and changing sovereignty regime. To do so, however, requires rethinking of the concept of sovereignty outside the box of the absolutist and Westphalian conception as I try to do in this chapter and throughout the book. Once this is done, it is possible to see that despite the expanding regulatory role of supranational institutions (GGIs), the increased integration of the international community (and its constitutionalization) does entail the end of sovereign territorial states. Segmental pluralism still exists although it is overlaid by global functional differentiation. The global political system is dualistic, composed of sovereign states and the international law they make, alongside new legal subjects with new functions and global cosmopolitan legal elements. The sociological thesis of the disaggregation of state sovereignty is unconvincing. Certain competences once associated with the sovereign state can and have been delegated to other supranational actors. Indeed this is a key premise of the concept of changing sovereignty regimes. But sovereignty as the autonomy and supremacy of a legal order cannot be divided, pooled, or shared.[230] Sovereignty is a legal, normative, epistemological as well as a political concept, but it is not reducible to a bundle of rights or prerogatives.[231] Instead, sovereignty is the unifying and self-identifying claim of a polity regarding the supremacy and autonomy of its legal order, the self-determination of its political system, and its status as the ultimate authority in its respective domain of jurisdiction and as an equal, recognized under international law with a hand in making that law. State sovereignty remains, as will become clear in the next chapter, a crucial referent of popular sovereignty as well. Nevertheless, the "positive" competences and jurisdictions typically associated with "sovereignty" can be disaggregated from any particular organ of a state, or from the state itself, and jurisdictions, competences, and functions can be delegated, shared, or pooled. This has been clear since the famous discussion by Jay and Madison in *The Federalist Papers*, and is obvious in the institutional practice of the EU and with the creation of the UN Charter system.

It is certainly still the case that even in the twenty-first century, national states are deemed by the relevant domestic actors (judges, civil servants, politicians, their publics) to be sovereign: supreme domestically and autonomous internationally.[232] The discourse of sovereignty is, in other words, still prevalent in the "object-language" of actors and retains its epistemological function as an explanatory ordering principle of international society, although it is not the only one.[233] The principle of "sovereign equality" articulated in the UN Charter is a legal principle, but it is still a principle of sovereignty from the internal perspective of member states – the core members and participants – who continue to invoke it as a discursive claim and an institutional "fact." In other words, the legal principle of sovereign equality both registers and constitutes the autonomy and self-determination of states and it expresses this through the related Charter principles of non-intervention, domestic jurisdiction, self-determination, and the right to self-defense. Sovereign states certainly do not deem their sovereignty as delegated by international law or as derivative from an internal or global "grundnorm." Nevertheless the state monist solipsistic perspective regarding sovereignty and international law was always misleading: sovereignty is a relational concept involving mutual construction and containment within a system (and international society) of sovereign states, which acknowledges claims to ultimate authority within a territory, as the international legal and political recognition of a state as sovereign indicates. The complex relations between law and power, fact and norm, validity and efficacy in sovereignty discourses and practices should not be elided either by an exclusive legalistic or by a power-political approach.[234]

Nonetheless, my claims that we are not in a "post-sovereignty" system and that sovereignty as the autonomy and self-determination of a polity's constitutional order (legal and political) cannot be disaggregated, do not bring us back to a Westphalian model, nor need it entail the denial of the autonomy of the legal order of the global political system or its (potential) constitutional quality. It would be as wrong to see the UN Charter system's legal order today as simply delegated authority on the treaty model as it is to see the validity of state constitutions as derivative of the "grundnorm" of the global legal system. The non-derivative character of legal supranationalism is as important to grasp as the non-derivative character of domestic constitutions. Taking sovereignty discourse seriously does not mean that one can ignore shifts in the substantive international legal rules of sovereignty and acknowledged sovereign prerogatives, structural changes in the international system, or the emergence of a functionally differentiated autonomous global legal order referencing the international community. The transformative developments associated with globalization, including the emergence of supranational orders (of and regulating GGIs) that are distinct, overlap with, but which cannot easily be regarded as simply derivative of states and their consent, is what informs the "meta-language" of those who want to dispense with the language of sovereignty be they monists or pluralists.[235] However, it is important to avoid a total disconnect between concepts used in object-language and those used in meta-language. Thus, Neil Walker is right to insist that "a concept that retains significant discursive currency in the real world, such as sovereignty, must also continue to be taken seriously at the meta-level."[236]

Indeed, it is perfectly conceivable that a state can give up the *jus belli*, accept that all states are bound by enforceable human rights norms, and open up its territory to jurisdiction by a functionally delimited supranational legal order, and still be sovereign. A sovereign state need not exercise all public authority within its territory. It may delegate and transfer the exercise of public power to other bodies. From the internal perspective, the state is sovereign so long as it is politically self-determining, so long as there is an autonomous relationship between the government and the citizenry, and so long as its legal order is supreme domestically.[237] As indicated above, sovereignty is in this sense a negative concept: it is not tied to a specific set of positive competences. Accordingly, sovereignty requires political self-determination in the negative sense of the non-imposition of a constitutional order or regime by outsiders – hence more is involved here than the general principle of subsidiarity regarding competences. The sovereign state can indeed delegate competences, and even accept the primacy of certain rules made by a supranational organization (or polity) in certain domains, since it is the capacity of the sovereign domestic legal order to make such delegations and to accept such decisions. From its internal perspective, the domestic legal order remains supreme and retains interpretive autonomy over jurisdiction and over issues of compatibility of external decisions with its internal constitutional legal order. Indeed "a sovereign order must assume its own continuing or self-amending sovereignty within its sphere of authority (rules of recognition and change) and must retain interpretive autonomy (rules of adjudication) deciding the boundaries of that sphere of authority."[238] For these are polity-identifying rules, that describe a normative context that the sovereignty claim disposes over.

However, internal supremacy need not be tightly coupled to exclusivity of jurisdiction.[239] On the "Westphalian" model, overlapping jurisdictions within the territory of a state meant that the latter was not sovereign: a non-exclusive authority was typically a dependent one – i.e. a colony, or a dependent and unequal component of an imperial order or a form of social order that need not be respected as a sovereign entity. Autarky was imagined as the ideal of a sovereign state.[240] In today's sovereignty regime, these two dimensions have been decoupled. It is possible to conceive of supremacy without territorial exclusivity and to imagine jurisdictional overlap without subsumption.[241] The development of functionally delimited supranational jurisdictional claims in the global political system can thus supplement and overlap without abolishing the autonomy of territorial sovereign states.

On the other hand, from *its* internal perspective, the global legal order of the UN Charter system coupled to the global political system would also have to be construed as autonomous.[242] Even though it can be seen as a functional not a territorial system, it too makes the claim of supremacy and interpretive autonomy over the precise extent of the functional mandate. Functions and purposes like "international peace and security" and "respecting human rights" and guaranteeing the sovereign equality of states can be interpreted very broadly. Yet, no one could claim under current conditions that the global political system and its autonomous legal order are equivalent to that of a sovereign federal state or even a federation of states. The status of the constitutive legal orders of international organizations that are morphing into global governance institutions including the UN in international law remains contested. The latter's Charter is a "constitutional treaty," and it is still left to member states to define its international legal position, even though the UN's legal order has, as the centered version of global constitutionalism correctly contends, become autonomous.[243] But what that version elides is that the UN itself has a dualist structure reflecting the sociological dualism of the world system: its member states are sovereign but they are also bound by the legal system of the Charter which is now increasingly autonomous vis-à-vis their ongoing individual consent.[244] As the constitutional treaty of the global political system, the Charter changes the status of the parties and the nature of their relationships, and is protected against unilateral interpretation and alteration via its amendment rule.[245] Indeed UN membership today is deemed crucial to full international recognition as a sovereign state. UN Security Council decisions obligate all states and withdrawal from the UN is not an option. Yet the efficacy of the binding obligations imposed by the Council as well as the supremacy claims made by the Security Council still depends very much on acceptance of its legitimacy and compliance by sovereign member states, and not only because the Charter is not self-executing. The understanding of the Charter as a constitutional treaty expresses this dualism. Indeed given the flaws in the Charter's constitutional design, from a normative constitutionalist perspective (the rudimentary character of the separation of powers, the absence of a court with compulsory jurisdiction or powers of judicial review, the structural inequalities among members' prerogatives), its constitutionalist character is aspirational. I will return to this issue in Chapter 5.

The key point here is that even its further constitutionalization should not be conceived as entailing a monistic relation to sovereign states within the global political system. Indeed, constitutional monism should be avoided on the level of meta-language. But the legal pluralist approach would screen out new forms of legal ordering among member states and the supranational political communities they are involved in and refuse a constitutionalist project. What Kelsen called the dualist position would be of no help here either because it is ultimately wed to a form of state monism and solipsism or because it would be identical to the global constitutionalist position. I argue that the concept of "constitutional pluralism" is analytically, empirically, pragmatically, and normatively far more helpful as a frame for addressing the complex structure and competing discourses in the globalizing international political system and for imagining its "further" constitutionalization, than the alternatives.[246] In my view, this approach could do justice to the continuing importance of sovereignty and to the need to legally regulate and reform the new forms of global governance and global law. The constitutional pluralist approach was developed to address the shifting relations among sovereign states and the autonomous European legal order in the European Union.[247] As a concept and project it could, under the right circumstances, suit dimensions of the global political system as well.

Here I can only summarize a complex argument, the details of which will have to wait until Chapter 5. As we have seen, *legal pluralism* refers generally to a multiplicity of competing jurisdictional, public, and private normative orders deemed independent of one another (although they may overlap and be hybrid) and without a hierarchical relationship among them. Porosity, non-closure, and political bargaining characterize their interrelationships, not legal or hierarchical ordering. *Constitutional pluralism* refers to a plurality of constitutional sources of authority and competing claims to jurisdictional supremacy by autonomous, interacting, and overlapping public (state and supranational) legal orders, whose relationship must be also characterized as heterarchical and which creates a potential for constitutional conflicts that have to be solved in a non-hierarchical manner.[248] What is involved here is a complex of political communities *within an overarching political association of communities* each of which has its own legal order of constitutional quality. The core claim is that interrelations between the constitutional legal orders of states with that of the overarching political community of which they are members, can be characterized as legal, even constitutional, without pre-emptive closure, imposition of hierarchy, leveling unity, or final resolution of ultimate supremacy claims.

The EU, on this analysis, is the prime example of constitutional pluralism.[249] Accordingly, its multiple autonomous constitutional orders, sites of norm creation and power coexist within an overarching order of orders; these are mutually recognized and yet are organized in a heterarchical and horizontal, rather than in a hierarchical and vertical manner. The internal constitutional pluralism of the EU thus involves a plurality of constitutional sources whose interrelation cannot be analyzed in classical monist or dualist terms. The practices of its legal actors and the structure of its legal order escape that binary. EU law has direct effect on individuals and often regulates the same subject matters as member states, it thus is not dualist; it claims supremacy but this is granted conditionally by other putatively supreme and autonomous constitutional orders (sovereign states), thus their interrelation is not monist. The autonomy of the domestic constitutional orders of the member states is acknowledged and the autonomy, constitutional quality, and supremacy of EU rules over national constitutional rules are asserted and (conditionally) accepted, even though it is clear that the legal orders at each level are profoundly influenced by each other.[250] On the constitutional pluralist analysis, the coordination among the distinct autonomous, at times competitive yet interrelated and integrated legal orders proceeds through dialogue and mutual accommodation: EU law has a "negotiated" yet binding, supreme yet sometimes contested normative authority.

However, constitutional pluralism as originally formulated with respect to the EU was taken to mean two things: (a) that conflicts across constitutional legal orders within an overarching legal and political order are not resolvable legally because of a surfeit of legal answers and (b) that sovereignty is no longer a continuing property of any member state nor an attribute of the Union's organs.[251] Conflict avoidance, circumspection, and political judgment are thus deemed crucial for the ongoing project of the European political and legal community to succeed. Circumspection means that courts, both national and European, should reach interpretive judgments keeping in mind their potential impact on one another's legal orders and commitments.[252] Political judgment (phronesis) means that sovereignty assertions should be toned down and reduced to a minimum. Indeed, sovereignty, according to this analysis, is utterly residual in the sense of an ability of a state to renounce membership of the Union and return to its former independence but otherwise it is merely symbolic.[253] This version thus seems indistinguishable from the new legal pluralist approach described above.

Later formulations of the concept of constitutional pluralism are more distinctive and more sociologically realistic in that they do not dispense with the discourse of sovereignty or belittle the self-understanding of member states within the EU as sovereign.[254] This is important because member states certainly consider themselves sovereign and their international recognition as sovereign states does not depend on withdrawal from the EU. The idea behind the later versions of the concept of constitutional pluralism is that it does justice to the constitutive power of sovereignty claims on the part of member states *and* to the autonomy and constitutional quality of the legal order of the supranational polity of which they are members (the EU) – i.e. to the object-language of participants and the meta-language of analysts. Moreover, constitutional pluralism involves more than strategic interaction among the relevant juridical and political bodies – it entails a legal and normative relationship among them.

This empirical and epistemological account is wed to a normative one: the idea that such a configuration need lead neither to the imposition of a new monist unity with a fixed internal hierarchy of centered constitutional authority (for, given state sovereignty claims, it would indeed be an imposition) nor to a fragmentation of authority such that the sense is lost of there being distinctive units of constitutional authority interacting with one another in a cooperative way and that their interrelations are legal as well as political. In the case of the EU, the provisions for direct effect of its legal decisions, direct domestic applicability in member states of regulations, compulsory transposition (in the case of directives) of supranational legislation and its judicial enforcement, unmediated implementation of supranational administration, and obligatory (preliminary) reference of questions of the authoritative interpretation of supranational law from national to supranational courts, are all indicative of close structural linkage among national and supranational constitutional sites of legal (and political) authority.[255] Given the now common constitutional understandings and traditions of member states and the high degree of integration of the distinctive polity that is the EU, given the composite and iterative nature of its constitutionalism, based on a convergence of horizons from different systemic starting points, the thesis of constitutional pluralism seems to offer a compelling account of internal legal processes.[256] It captures the distinctive mode of interrelation among the legal and political orders of a non-state polity in the making that strong legal pluralists and hierarchical constitutionalists both miss.

I will argue in this book that this conceptual toolkit can become useful also for addressing the complexities and projects for the dualistic international system because it is not tied to the "end of sovereignty" thesis. Accordingly, constitutional pluralism involves an external perspective – of the legal or political theorist – but it can also inform that of the internal legal practitioner. The stance of constitutional pluralism is linked to the unavoidable political problematic and dynamics of mutual recognition regarding the construction and interrelation of legal orders. The basic idea is to acknowledge the existence of distinct autonomous legal orders – of sovereign states and of the relevant regional or global political community – and that the latter's claims to autonomy, supremacy, and constitutional quality can exist alongside the continuing claims of states. As indicated, the relation between these orders must be seen as heterarchical. As distinct from monist globalism and monist sovereigntism, neither of which are compelling descriptions or interpretations of supranationalism today, constitutional pluralism involves the normative idea that what is required for acknowledging and dealing with competing claims to authority coming from national and supranational constitutional sites is an ethic of political responsibility, premised on mutual recognition and respect and commitment to the overarching legal and political order.

Constitutional pluralism thus ideal-typically involves the normative commitment of taking seriously both sovereignty and monism in the internal perspective of an autonomous legal order and pluralism on the meta-level.[257] Autonomous legal systems, by their nature, each assume the role of higher law. For example, from the internal perspective of its globalizing international legal order as autonomous (and of its constitutionalization as an ongoing project), the UN Charter is primary, supreme, and higher law in the global political system. From the internal perspective of a national constitution, globalizing Charter law, including Article 103, owes its supremacy to recognition by the national legal order and thus the ultimate power of legal adjudication belongs to national constitutional courts. After all, from this perspective the Charter is a treaty signed on to by sovereign states with no intention of relinquishing their sovereignty. The stance of constitutional pluralism entails acknowledging these competitive claims to independent political and legal ultimate authority.[258] But insofar as the UN is turning into a global governance institution, to be a feasible project, constitutionalization of the public powers its organs assert must be understood in the frame of constitutional pluralism, not monism. This could lead to collisions and conflict since the question of who decides has initially different answers in the domestic and supranational context. There is no neutral higher "third" to decide this question.

But it can also lead to reflexivity, communication, and cooperation and it need not end in fragmentation of either legal system, *given sufficient commitment to a common enterprise, i.e. to the overarching political community created by member states and peoples.* The unity of a legal system requires that each new legal decision is coherent with the previous legal decisions. But pace Kelsen, this does not require a single monist hierarchy: it is possible to have a coherent legal order in a context of initially conflicting determinations of the law (and competing claims to ultimate authority) so long as all the participants share the same commitment to a coherent legal and political supranational order and adjust their competing claims accordingly and consider the final decision to be "law."[259] What is required is indeed political and juridical phronesis – the willingness to make the effort to avoid ultimate conflicts by anticipating them and trying to resolve them cooperatively.[260]

A non-hierarchical conception of the relationship between norms and courts and informal cooperation could and should prevail given the appropriate level of reflexivity on the part of the relevant actors. But reflexivity requires communication, the internal attitude toward supranational as well as domestic law, and willingness to justify interpretations of regional, global, or relevant domestic law in general rather than parochial terms.[261] Such "constitutional tolerance" is a political normative stance, predicated on belief in the *legitimacy* of the project of developing and maintaining a supranational legal and political order, a political community of political communities, of which sovereign states are members (and of the desirability of the project of a regional and global rule of law). Given the legitimacy of such a project, i.e. assuming the relevant actors value it, devising legal and institutional mechanisms to facilitate adjustments to respective claims over capacity, competence, jurisdiction, and authority, in order to avoid collision, is certainly not impossible.

Indeed, the status of claims to legal autonomy and supremacy is inseparable from the political question of legitimacy. It is not the role of the political theorist to come up with specific mechanisms for "ordering pluralism" from the internal validity perspective, but to reflect on the conditions of political legitimacy that legal systems ultimately depend on. One problem with Kelsenian monism is that it ignores this dimension entirely. Nevertheless, it is important to make the general point that what distinguishes constitutional pluralism from the more general concept of legal pluralism (and as we shall see in Chapter 5, external constitutional pluralism), is the claim that it offers a way to invoke the universal code of legality in addressing conflicts of norms or jurisdictions without impugning the autonomy claims of the relevant interacting, indeed interrelated, legal systems. There are several versions of the theory of constitutional pluralism but they all involve taking a theoretical and normative political stance that relates the legal question of internal validity to the political question of legitimacy and they all pertain to dynamic, evolving systems in respect to which reflexivity is crucial for the key actors. Construed as an ideal type of relation among domestic and supranational legal order, constitutional pluralism admits of several variants or degrees of approximation and thus is useful as a frame for evaluating new polities in formation like the EU and IOs as they morph into GGIs.

As already indicated, the constitutional pluralist approach was developed to address the shifting nature of state sovereignty in the European Union. But it could come to fit the evolving logic of the global political system as well. The point is that disputes need not lead to disintegration so long as political legitimacy is maintained and prudence is practiced by supranational institutions and by member states. Given the heterogeneity of political regimes of member states in the UN Charter system and the low degree of integration of the globalizing international legal order compared with the EU, the legitimacy of the latter turns on whether it respects the principles of sovereign equality and human rights. It is not appropriate at this point to try to make it contingent on the principle of "democratic" subsidiarity as some try to do generalizing from a conception of the model of the EU.[262] Before the discourse of constitutional pluralism could become descriptively apposite for that key GGI, instead of being simply a project, institutional reform of the UN and commitment to its new role and legal order by member states would be required.[263] It is quite appropriate, moreover, to insist on the fair inclusion of all affected states in generating the new global rules and in demanding equal standing and treatment under global law.

Accordingly, the centered constitutional reading of the UN Charter system is premature to say the least. So is the de-centered constitutionalist reading of the global political system despite evidence of structural coupling. The constitutional quality of the global political system is a vérité à faire not a fait accompli. Of course, in an increasingly interdependent world, different legal orders will have to try to accommodate each other's jurisdictional claims. There is no going back to the dualist billiard ball model of Westphalian sovereignty. Whether a legitimate legal path can be found for ascertaining validity and responding to conflicts between competing global and domestic legal orders remains to be seen. I contend it depends on political commitment, and certain political transformations, not legal theory.

Under current conditions, the monist cosmopolitan approach to the global legal order would lead to irresolvable conflict, undermining the legitimacy of the entire project. This is true because its "constitutionalist" character is so underdeveloped. Legal autonomy and constitutional quality are not, after all, the same thing, and the further constitutionalization of international law of the UN Charter system must be seen as a project within the conceptual field of constitutional pluralism. It must target not only states but also international organizations and their foundational charters. The absence of an international human rights court with compulsory jurisdiction, the fact that the ICJ, also lacking compulsory jurisdiction does not engage in judicial review, the various restrictions on the ICC, the lack of adequate checks and balances or a clear separation of powers in the UN Charter system coupled with the supremacy claims of an increasingly active UNSC, and the difficulty of applying human rights norms to the UN or legal limits to the Security Council, in view of its new role in the world means that its further constitutionalization is now a pressing need.[264] Bringing the latter under the rule of law is indispensable to claims to constitutional quality and political legitimacy. This, however, would have to entail political and institutional reform. The monist model of national constitutions is inapposite here. Since the primary means of enforcement (courts and armed forces) remain in the hands of states, their cooperation and willingness to adopt the internal point of view regarding global law will depend on the perceived legitimacy of that law and of global governance institutions. And that will depend on an approach that protects the sovereign equality of states, as well as human rights and global peace and security. The same holds for international or global courts.

That is why it makes sense to interpret the principle of "sovereign equality" in the framework of constitutional pluralism. The changing rules of positive international law are indeed indicative of a new political culture of sovereignty that has shifted from one of impunity to one of responsibility and accountability. From this perspective, sovereign equality and human rights are the interrelated principles of the dualistic global political system, indicative of the existence of a new sovereignty regime. The relation between these principles has changed, but sovereign equality and the correlative principles of non-intervention, domestic jurisdiction, and self-determination remain the legitimating basis and default position of the international order. As should now be clear, it is conceptually meaningless and ideological to redefine sovereignty as a duty or function – the responsibility to protect – and to "disaggregate" it so that other instances could take on this responsibility should the state default. The issue is when the sovereignty argument should be suspended and outside intervention legally permitted.[265] Chapter 3 will address this question and argue that when a state engages in genocide, ethnic cleansing, or crimes against humanity it forfeits the claim to stand for and coercively rule the groups it oppresses in these radical ways. In other words, the government itself has abolished the political relationship between the rulers and the targeted group that sovereignty establishes.

It is also incorrect and ideological to describe the important shifts regarding sovereignty, rights, or security as "constitutional moments." The post-1989 discursive practices of humanitarian intervention, transformative occupations, and the post-9/11 coupling of the discourse of human security to the listing and legislative practices of the Security Council in the war on terror are political facts. They should be analyzed, and when appropriate, normed in terms of the concept of a shifting sovereignty regime and not seen as constitutional moments that take us into a cosmopolitan world order beyond sovereignty.[266] That is the task of the third, fourth, and fifth chapters. Indeed, the UN reform project aimed at legally articulating and steering these shifts was a *failed constitutional moment* rather than a successful example of regulating power by law.[267] The danger is that these shifts further the de-formalization of international law and weaken limits on the use of force by the powerful, instead of being normatively desirable adjustments in the interrelation between sovereignty and human rights.

1.7   Conclusion

Formal legal rules should be devised to regulate these new practices and understandings of competences and jurisdiction. Such rules have to be widely discussed, negotiated, and shaped in a representative political process in which all member states of the international community have a voice. Two things are at stake here: establishing thresholds and procedures for suspending the strictures against forceful intervention into a sovereign state, and the application of constitutionalist principles and the rule of law to global governance institutions.

The discourse of constitutionalism involves framing, constituting, regulating, and limiting power, but an autonomous global order could also centralize it and undermine the rule of law, domestic democracy, and self-determination. Constitutional pluralism (acknowledging state sovereignty as well as autonomous regional or global legal orders) can serve as a bulwark against concentration and abuse of power on the global level. This is the correct intuition of the legal pluralist school. On the other hand, the further constitutionalization of a global legal and political system could enhance rights and justice by checking abuses in domestic legal and political orders and forcing them to take into account possible negative externalities and the external interests of the global community and of other members. Here the cosmopolitan constitutionalists are right. For this to be a virtuous circle, legitimacy is needed on both levels of the dualistic sovereignty regime: regarding changes in what is deemed to be in the domestic jurisdiction of sovereign states and regarding the new procedures and substantive rules of public international/global law. Both require institutional mechanisms providing for fair participation of political communities (states and perhaps others in other capacities) in shaping the norms and rules (the further constitutionalism) of the global political community. Today it is increasingly the case that for states to realize their sovereignty (as international lawmakers, as exercisers of international political influence, and as having a say in decisions that affect their citizens) they need the status of member with the right to participate in the decision-making processes of the various international organizations, GGIs, and networks that regulate the international system, on fair terms. Unlike some, however, I argue that this new dimension of sovereignty as status and inclusion in coercive global governance institutions supplements but does not replace sovereignty as autonomy.[268] Both the constitutionalists and the legal pluralists are wrong in their eagerness to abandon the discourse of sovereignty as somehow antithetical to constitutionalism or legitimate diversity.

It also requires that global political institutions, especially the UN, are regulated by and comport with constitutionalist principles, the rule of law, and human rights. This is why a UN reform project, however difficult, is so important today. But this involves a political project that blends new forms of power-limiting and foundational constitutionalism as we shall see.[269] A dimension of re-founding may be unavoidable.[270] Otherwise, the invocation of cosmopolitan right or global constitutional law to justify radical innovations (and interventions) on the part of unilateral or multilateral actors (GGIs) will play into the hands of the imperial or great-power projects and/or culminate in the loss of legitimacy.

Finally the question arises, even if constitutional pluralism as an ideal type would enable the theorist and practitioner to articulate and help secure the sovereignty of states along with the autonomy and legitimacy of globalizing legal orders, why is this desirable? Why not just abandon sovereignty talk for a multileveled cosmopolitan world order? Apart from the obvious fact that such a system is hardly a feasible utopia at present, I will argue throughout this book that sovereignty protects moral values and has normative value itself. We should understand sovereignty not as a set of competences, but as a concept involving the supremacy of a domestic legal order and external autonomy in the political sense of self-determination (non-imposition by foreigners).[271] Accordingly, sovereignty protects the special relationship between a citizenry and its government that may involve domestic constitutionalism and democracy. Sovereignty secures the normatively special status of members and their prerogative to assess the legitimacy of their domestic system, and to struggle to make it more just, more democratic, more inclusive.[272] The principle of sovereign equality accords this to all political communities organized as states. On the global level functional equivalents for democracy are possible (accountability, avenues of influence for civil society, non-decisional parliaments, communication about best practices, subsidiarity, etc.) but they could never duplicate the kind of representative democracy and effective electoral participation possible on the level of the modern state or even a regional polity. For those embracing constitutionalist principles and democratic aspirations, the constitutional pluralist approach is a feasible utopia and the best way to protect their normative bases.

What sort of institutional arrangements or which form of political association is most appropriate for facilitating the practice of constitutional pluralism remains an important question. We cannot generalize to the global international system institutional arrangements that have been devised for a highly integrated regional polity like the EU for obvious reasons. Although debates still rage over the nature of the political association that is the EU, clearly the degree of political homogeneity of its member states (all are and are required to be constitutional democracies) and the general acceptance of its legal order, its well-developed autonomous Court, direct effect of its laws, and so forth are characteristics that make possible a level of constitutionalization, and a kind of "internal" constitutional pluralism that turns on the sense of belonging and commitment to the political project that is the Union that does not yet obtain in the international political system.[273] It is thus important to keep the institutional level of analysis distinct from the theoretical level when it comes to sovereignty, constitutional pluralism, and issues of political form. Again, I refer to constitutional pluralism as an ideal type: empirical supranational institutional arrangements, be it on the regional or global level, are perforce hybrids and approximations. The main point of this chapter is to indicate that this ideal type could suit the dualistic nature of our international political system. The next chapter will address an ideal-typical conception of a political formation – a federation of states that is not itself a state – that is the appropriate institutional analogue of the practice and theory of constitutional pluralism. But in respect to this concept as well, we must remember that all empirical political forms are hybrids: ideal types are never realized, only approximated in varying degrees in practice. They are heuristic devices, not meant to be taken as descriptions of actual states of affairs. I turn to the idea of federation because the issue of political form has to be taken seriously especially if we are not willing either to abandon the discourse of sovereignty and sovereign equality or to ignore important changes in the global political system and in the current sovereignty regime. In other words, the issue of political form must be addressed so as to enable one to clarify the range of possible transformations that could be aimed at by reform projects seeking to rectify legitimation deficits on the regional as well as on the global level. The subsequent chapters will address those deficits insofar as they pertain to the global political system. It will become clear, however, that it is not the case that the theory and practice of constitutional pluralism requires the same institutional arrangements or political form on the regional and global level, as we shall see in Chapter 2.

Constitutionalism and political form: rethinking federation

Two apparently contradictory trends since the mid-1970s, call for creative thinking regarding constitutional and political forms. The first is the striking "contagion of sovereignty" as a discourse and claim, culminating in the universalization of the legal and political form of the sovereign national state – initially in the context of decolonization (the 1970s) and subsequently in the aftermath of the decomposition of the great land-based empire of the Soviet Union (post-1989).[1] The strong norms against conquest and forced annexation imposed post-1945, but especially in the post-colonial epoch, and the remarkable decline of violent state death seem to indicate that the ideal of the self-determining sovereign national state with internationally recognized borders, autonomous constitutional and political structures, and international legal standing has become the norm today.[2] There are now approximately 192 sovereign states recognized by international law and enjoying UN membership, each of which clings tenaciously to its sovereignty. New polities continue to aspire to recognition as sovereign states and to join the UN. Nevertheless the legitimacy and efficacy of state sovereignty seem to be undermined by undeniable ideological transformations, global legal developments, and structural trends.

Indeed, and second, the nation-state and the traditional conception of sovereignty that went with it came under great stress in the same period as its universalization and remain so today for a number of reasons. The ideal (myth?) of "one nation–one state" linked to the principle of self-determination was already unobtainable for the newly emerging polities particularly in South Asia and Africa in the period of decolonization. The "cleansing" of ethnic/religious/linguistic plurality that would be required to instantiate this ideal is now considered unacceptable.[3] Instead of nation-states there are sovereign "state-nations": multinational, multiethnic states are the norm today.[4] The homogeneous *nation*-state, always a myth, is deemed an anachronistic and destructive ideal.

From another quarter, the economic and geopolitical imperatives of globalization and the pressures of size they generate seem to render the idea of *sovereign* states (except for great powers or very large polities) as anachronistic today as the city-state became in an earlier period of globalization (and state-making), at the end of the sixteenth century.[5] The realities of international interdependence, of transnational risks requiring regional or global "governance" (from immigration, ecological, and economic issues, to transnational crime networks and terrorism), and the emergence of ideological challenges to the classic "Westphalian" conception of absolute state sovereignty (arguments from global justice, world peace, and human rights) are just a few of the forces one could mention. None of the innovative modes of governance on regional, global, or transnational levels fit the model of the sovereign state "writ large," and many of them seem to undermine it. From this perspective too, the classic ideal of the sovereign state is deemed a problematic, anachronistic and for most states, unrealizable idea. Contemporary geopolitical and economic pressures of size imply that for a polity to remain autonomous and efficacious it must grow larger or merge with others. However, the idea of creating a world of sovereign regional mega-states ("grossraume"), or a world state is objectionable for normative and/or pragmatic reasons. Yet the proliferation of concepts like "post-," "supra-," or "trans"national to refer to emergent political formations and talk of regional and global "governance" indicate a lack of political-theoretical precision. These terms give few clues regarding the question of political and constitutional form for the new political communities and/or proliferating regulatory regimes that are neither states nor simply their creatures.

Three conceptual responses to this conundrum have dominated contemporary debates. One resurrects the discourse of empire or new imperial formations as an analytic, a descriptor, or prognosis,[6] a second weds the discourse of global governance to the concept of a cosmopolitan multileveled world order and a normative ideal of a cosmopolitan constitution,[7] and a third involves a revival of the federal vision.[8] All three approaches try to conceptualize important shifts in constitutional and political form in light of structural, geopolitical, and economic transformations (globalization of capitalism) and all three involve frameworks of public law that regulate government and governance. Whatever their differences, however, the first two share the view that the concept, discourses, and aspirations of state sovereignty are irrelevant today. I find the thesis of post-modern empire in the influential form presented by Hardt and Negri confused and premature.[9] But I also find the idea of a cosmopolitan multileveled world order of constitutional quality (assuming this is not the same as post-modern empire) to be incorrect as an empirical description and weirdly apolitical as a project. Both are too quick to relegate the ideal of a plurality of autonomous self-determining and self-governing (sovereign) political communities and international relations among them to the dustbin of history. In the first, a new form of imperial polity (which at least for Hardt and Negri and their followers ultimately turns into the "sovereignty" of capital) comes to replace that of the nation-state whereas in the second international law cedes its pride of place to cosmopolitan law and global right. Both responses to the geopolitical problematic of size and to economic globalization are also too totalizing: there is no outside to world empire, or to the global cosmopolitan world order, and despite disclaimers, both are ultimately monist conceptions.

According to idealistic advocates of world federalism, the federal principle is also deemed to be the opposite of the sovereignty principle. Accordingly, federalism connotes mutuality, reciprocity, voluntary association, and plurality, and is thus one of the two great organizing principles of social and political life, the other being hierarchy, rule, unity, uniformity, homogeneity, and dominance from the center, all associated with sovereignty.[10] From this perspective the federal principle can be applied to many social and political groupings. Accordingly it connotes a distinctive way for groups to grow larger and to structure their organization – voluntary association and non-centralized internal relations among members versus rule by a centralized mega-sovereign state and/or the center–periphery relations typical of empire. There is something to this idea and I shall return to it. Throughout much of the nineteenth and twentieth centuries, however, federalism has for the most part been studied as a type of state structure.[11] Even sophisticated analyses of the distinctive constitutional and political features of federal versus unitary states screen out the issue with which this chapter is concerned, namely the structure and dynamics of non-state polities based on the federal principle, because they focus on types of states. Most analyses of federalism, in other words, operate with two dichotomous frameworks: federal versus unitary states, and confederations construed as contractual international associations of sovereign states versus federal states. A confederation is, from the international law perspective, merely a treaty organization in which states remain sovereign. A federal polity, from the same perspective, is a sovereign state, a legal subject with its own autonomous constitutional order that is sovereign domestically as well as internationally. Neither of these versions of federalism helps much with the issue of political and legal form for non-state composite polities that bridge the domestic/international divide without renouncing the discourse of sovereignty for member states and which are not imperial formations.

It is time perhaps to recuperate insights of the federal vision while freeing it from infeasible utopianism and from the statist paradigm. I believe it can offer a distinctive approach to the problems of size and legitimacy raised by regional and/or global governance institutions. Here is how to think about the conundrum we now face: If the political and personal freedoms we associate with constitutional democracies are at risk the greater the size of the polity, then what chance is there for liberal-democratic republics, already enlarged through the device of representation, to avoid being eviscerated by centralizing distant executives and administrations of the proliferating regional and global governance institutions? Is there a way to theorize a mode of political integration (growing larger) and a type(s) of polity or political formation(s) that is normatively attractive and feasible on the regional or global level, to which the legal *and political* discourse of constitutionalization would be analytically adequate? I suggest that there is and that we should proceed by rethinking the concept of federation as a type of union of states and peoples, a type of constitutional polity that is not itself a state.

In this chapter I try to do just that. I argue that a reconsideration of the concept of federation, of the federating process and the structure and dynamics of federal unions of states is well worth the effort. If appropriately formulated, an ideal-typical concept of federal union (federation) can provide a way to conceptualize a range of political formations (polities – legal and political orders) that have a distinctive constitutional and political form, a structure and set of internal relations different from that of a state, an empire, an international alliance and/or an international organization. I will argue, however, that the discourse of sovereignty is neither irrelevant to nor absent in federations. Federation as a type of union of states that is not itself a state, if thought together with the non-absolutist non-Westphalian conception of sovereignty discussed in the previous chapter, may provide the missing concepts needed to theorize a mode of political integration (via extension) that is normatively attractive and analytically necessary to make the discourse of the constitutionalization of international law and of regional or global "governance institutions" meaningful. Referring to a process or set of political and legal acts (federating) and a distinctive type of political formation, the concept (or rather the ideal type) of federal union can (like constitutionalization itself) be deployed in a normative and descriptive sense. Conceptualizing a range of subtypes of federal unions that are not states may allow us to construct the appropriate political referent and process of the constitutionalization of international law and thus to address the legitimacy problematic of regional and global "governance" in a creative way. Moreover, the federal vision, appropriately analyzed, can do justice to the dual trends mentioned above. In other words, as we shall see, the concept of a federal union of states (and peoples) involves a way of making the external (international relations) internal, and allows one to conceive a political structure that enables both self-rule and shared rule, autonomy and participation of discrete (even sovereign) political entities coexisting within an overall union under its public constitutional law, without positing the federation itself as a (large, federal) state or as an empire.[12]

Indeed, the federal political form as a community composed of political communities is, *ideal-typically*, the analogue of the concept and practice of constitutional pluralism. I argue that the discourse of the constitutionalization of regional, or global governance institutions must ultimately have some type of quasi-federal political formation and process as its referent, if it is to avoid being simply metaphorical, legalistic, naive, or, worse, ideological. This should not be read as an argument that a single federal political form or institutional arrangement is suitable for every supra-state order or organization. The process of federating (what is called in the literature "coming-together federalism") and the concept of a federal union of states that is not itself a state, can be constructed ideal-typically, as a genus with several subspecies, whose relevance to particular regions or global institutions will vary for no one model will fit all.[13] Indeed there will remain many international organizations or regional regimes to which the federal vision is irrelevant. My purpose is to rethink the federal vision in ways that allow the question at least to be posed.

The same is true for the project of the democratization of global governance institutions aimed at solving their legitimation deficits.[14] Democratization on regional or global levels of governance must be seen as a complex and long process and need not involve the identical modes of participation and accountability that exist on the level of the democratic national state.[15] At the very least, however, constitutionalism and democratization on supranational levels must involve the subjection of governance institutions to regulation by public law and ensure accountability of public officials and of the institutions wielding public power, involving the regulation of self-regulation.[16] Here too issues of political form and legitimacy are unavoidable. Here too the concept of federation may be of help regarding the institutional structure of public power on the regional or global level, the process by which a political community of community gains legitimacy and gets (re-) formed, and the question of to whom accountability is owed. We have perhaps reached the point where constitutionalism in the sense of curbing the arbitrary exercise of power and institutionalizing accountability by bringing those ascribed the "right to rule" (to govern, i.e. to make collectively binding decisions and publicly enforceable law) under the rule of public law within a public structure devised or reformed for that purpose is a conceivable next step.[17] Instead of neo-medievalism, or multileveled governance, unhelpful metaphors for such a process, I argue that the non-statist version of the concept of federation is the right frame for thinking about the further constitutionalization and democratization of international law on the regional level and perhaps for some functionally differentiated global governance institutions such as the UN Charter system.[18] I suggest that taking a step in that direction is in the twenty-first century not an infeasible utopia. Constitutionalization is not only a matter of the legal entrenchment of fundamental values by courts, it is not only about power limitation but also about power creation and generation and it always involves questions of political processes, political form, and political legitimacy of the constitution-making power(s) – i.e. who this must involve (to whom a constitution can be ascribed) and how to conceptualize it. Serious theoretical analysis of federal union may provide some answers, particularly with respect to new forms of sovereignty (understood as involving participation in global governance regimes) and changing sovereignty regimes. But the type of federal union and constitutional order would vary with the type of political formation and degree of integration deemed feasible and desirable. The modes of legitimacy and democratic credentials of more or less integrated, more or less comprehensive federal unions would also vary accordingly and, I believe, would be distinct from those appropriate to even very large states.

In this chapter, I develop the non-statist ideal type of the genus, federation as a union of states and peoples, in order to screen in what statist, cosmopolitan, and imperial approaches to political forms generally screen out, namely the idea of a political and legal community, that is neither a state nor a classic international organization yet which has international legal personality, its own public legal order of constitutional quality, internal legislative capacity and legal autonomy, and which is composed of member states with similar characteristics. All mentions of an international community (as distinct from the international society) of states, of a global legal community, of the constitutionalization of international law, of de-centered coordinate or composite constitutionalism and/or constitutional pluralism have as their implicit referent some conception of political form. I will argue that both the concept of federation and the concept of sovereignty as reconceived along the lines of the preceding chapter are relevant to the conceptualization of political unions that are not states. Federations understood as unions of states (and peoples) are dualistic political formations which bridge the international and the national, the foreign and the domestic, treaty organizations and constitutional polities in ways that require careful conceptual (and normative) analysis. Sovereignty does not describe their internal relations if by sovereign one means hierarchical, centralized absolute supremacy and rule. But sovereign states are members of such federations and can remain sovereign with respect to the outside if they retain international legal standing, and even without this they can resort to the discourse of sovereignty regarding actual or potential conflicts of jurisdiction and competences or over the ultimate locus of constitution-making power inside the federation. In some types of federations the locus of sovereignty is left unresolved, the ultimate resolution of this question permanently deferred. But this does not mean, as we shall see, that there is no sovereignty in the system. Disputes over the internal locus of sovereignty, and indeed the relevance of sovereignty discourse, remain one of the key issues in conceptualizing federal unions, as we shall see. A nuanced analysis is called for here. It is my thesis that the discourse of constitutionalization (and democratization) of non-state legal and political "international" orders raises the question of political form for which the concept of federation provides a helpful referent.[19] As will become clear, federal thinking and federal forms of participation in decision-making can be of use in addressing the legitimacy problematic plaguing regional and global governance institutions in which the principal–agent model of the old consent-based international law is no longer adequate but for which statist concepts of electoral democratic legitimacy based on one person–one vote and the idea of the self-determination of a single homogeneous sovereign people, are inappropriate.

In what follows I address the question of why states federate, and what the federal principle entails, from a pragmatic and normative perspective (Section 2.1). I then turn to questions of taxonomy (Section 2.2). Insofar as the issue is the applicability of the federation concept to non-state political formations, it would seem that classifying them on a continuum of central-ization/decentralization would make more sense than analyzing them as discrete ideal types. Indeed for those who deem the concept of sovereignty to be anathema, there is no fundamental difference between federalist polities and highly decentralized legal/political orders whether or not one is speaking of federal states. Kelsen's analysis of federalism is the locus classicus of this approach.[20] But as I shall show, this approach screens out precisely what is distinctive politically and legally about federations and loses much of what is conceptually useful for our problematic.[21]

An alternative taxonomic approach develops ideal types of discrete consti-tutional forms and political structures distinguishing federations from states and from international organizations, operating with a non-statist model of federal union. There are two important variants of this approach: one which is sovereignty centered, exemplified by Carl Schmitt's theory of federation (Section 2.3), and another which rejects sovereignty as the organizing principle of the ideal types it constructs but builds on some of Schmitt's key insights regarding constitutional form while incorporating many of the insti-tutional criteria discussed by Kelsen to come up with a richer set of ideal types than what Schmitt offers (Section 2.4).[22] As we shall see, both approaches locate federal unions and their model of political integration on an entirely different axis than the centralization–decentralization approach and both are able to render visible the form, structure, and principle of organization and of legitimacy of federal unions of states that are not themselves states. Indeed both break with the classic statist paradigm based on the dichotomies men-tioned above: confederation as an international treaty organization of states or federal polities as a type of state differentiated from unitary states, however decentralized they may be. I will present and critically assess these approaches. I will try to show that it is not necessary to choose between them. I combine these perspectives to create a taxonomy of ideal types of federations involving a spectrum ranging from weakly to highly consolidated unions. Ideal types, however, are heuristic concepts, not descriptions of actual constitutions, institutions, practices, or political formations – the latter are always hybrids.[23] One can make use of ideal types as constructs to see in what way existing political formations are hybrids and whether the hybridity they entail is legitimate and effective or whether it has become unjustifiable and dysfunc-tional. I will close the chapter by indicating what is gained by using a synthetic non-statist conception of federal union with respect to the discourse of the constitutionalization and democratization of regional and global governance institutions (Section 2.5). The next chapters will address the legitimacy problems specific to global institutions (the UN Charter system is my main case) as they assume more tasks of global governance with direct effects on individuals: in the domains of human rights and humanitarian intervention (Chapter 3), humanitarian occupation (Chapter 4), and global security law (Chapter 5). The question is whether some version of federation and constitutional pluralism can provide a normatively attractive way of reconstructing and reforming the increasingly contested relations among domestic, regional, and global legal and political orders.

2.1 Why federate?

The question, "why federate?" implies analyzing a political form in terms of its purpose – an approach abandoned through much of the twentieth century ever since Georg Jellinek and Max Weber banned it from the political theory of the modern state.[24] Any attempt to theorize federation that seeks to avoid state-centrism – i.e. the reduction of a federal polity to a type of state – must perforce address this question. Most analysts agree that the point of creating or joining a federal union is to establish a structure in which the independence and political existence of member states of the federation is maintained yet which serves their shared or common goals.[25] Indeed what is distinctive about federal union is that it seeks to create a political structure that is appropriate to this duality of particular and general (community) purposes.[26] The idea is to find a form of political association that defends, indeed guarantees, the political existence and autonomous status of member states (the particular purpose) by federal law while creating a political entity, a federal union, that is able to secure the collective goals of the union, purposes that are imputable to the community as a whole, i.e. to its members in their status as members of a community of communities.[27] Accordingly the autonomy of the federation in relation to the member states must also be institutionalized to a greater or lesser extent. The structure of "shared rule and self-rule" that ensues thus involves complex relationships of independence and interdependence of political and legal orders.[28]

Indeed federal unions of states are typically based on a consensual foedus – a pact or covenant – that articulates the purposes of federating, and establishes a totality, a polity, that has its own distinct representation (some form of assembly at the very least) and within which each of the member states is represented.[29] This enables the federation to present a common face to the outside, in modern parlance to acquire a legal personality, but in so doing a transformation of the external into the internal occurs. In creating or joining a federal union, international relations among foreign states become internal relations between member states at least with respect to the relevant purposes of the association.[30] This does not obviate the fact that the purview of a polity that is constructed via union is not comprehensive: the purpose is not to create a mega-state but, as already indicated, to create a legal and political order that is structured and delimited so as to preserve the integrity of all the parties while being able energetically to pursue collective goals.

2.1.1   Pragmatic arguments

There is little mystery surrounding the *pragmatic* reasons for federating on the part of independent polities: historical analysis of the practice and theory of federal unions shows that the main incentives have to do with issues of security, defense, peace, and welfare.[31] The first two and arguably the third relate to the imperatives and dynamics of size that all polities face, regardless of regime type, in a competitive geopolitical context. As is well known, at the onset of the modern epoch in Europe, federation originally appeared as an alternative to the state-making logic carried out by centralizing monarchies seeking territorial conquest and dominion.[32] The latter involved the expansion of power radiating out from a center and coercively incorporating territories, cities, peoples, estates (*stande*), and all formerly independent authorities into its structure and annihilating their political and legal autonomy. The classic state-making logic carried by absolute centralizing monarchies in Europe proceeded via mobilization for war as Tilly has argued and it seemed to require absolute sovereignty as its theorists from Bodin to Hobbes insisted, preferably in the form of monarchy.[33] The expansionist logic of this process unleashed the imperative of size and control that had to be faced for all those in proximity or in any relation with the new leviathans, providing a strong incentive to reproduce the political form and regime of the absolutist sovereign state.[34] Once one polity succeeds in state-making others apparently have to follow suit, simply in order to survive geopolitically and to compete economically. This logic of expansion, annexation, hierarchy, and rule over subject populations was projected outward by each state in their imperialist quest for colonies and rule over overseas subject populations once the system of states established itself on the continent and no one of them could gain imperial control over the others.[35]

   This logic, however, did not go unchallenged. One alternative was to federate: small polities could defend themselves if they pooled their resources, acted together for collective security and welfare, created common institutions for that purpose, and were willing to cooperate economically (through suspending internal trade barriers and the like) and to come to the defense of one another and of their federal union if attacked.[36] Federations did emerge as an alternative to state-making in the post-medieval period as exemplified by the United Provinces of the Netherlands (1759–1795), the old Swiss Confederation (from the later medieval period until 1789 and renewed 1815–1848), and of course, the best-known example of the United States at the very least between 1781 and 1787 and arguably 1787–1865.[37] Moreover, federation had its own political theorists: Althusias countered Bodin, Pufendorf answered Hobbes, opposing the "sovereignty" of "the people" – the conglomerate of the varied and stratified population of the cities and provinces of the compound polity – to that of the monarch or state and insisting on the possibility of a complex, heterarchical, and freedom-preserving union as an alternative to leveling centralized administrative and political forms and to monarchical absolutism.[38] These thinkers were constitutionalists who argued against absolutism and ruler sovereignty by finding an alternative to state formation to which these political regimes seemed wed. Montesquieu proposed federation as a way for republics to grow larger that is superior to imperial expansion because it does not involve the sacrifice of the freedom of the citizenry.[39] Of course the context and debates surrounding the most enduring experiment in federal union – the American – generated the most innovative theorizing of federation culminating in *The Federalist Papers* and later, the work of J. C. Calhoun.[40]

Nevertheless, the overwhelming success of the state-making project, first in Europe and then ultimately worldwide, is undeniable. The federal alternative seemed to lose out to its statist competitor due to intrinsic weaknesses (especially the problem of credible commitments mentioned by Spruyt) and the apparently inexorable dynamic of either centralization or dissolution.[41] Non-state federations of states until very recently have been judged to be either anachronisms, or as unstable, conflict-ridden, and transitional political forms – way stations en route to consolidated federal and/or centralized statehood. Federations, according to the standard assessment, may exist as tolerated exceptions within an international society of states but federal union is not as such a viable alternative to that system.

Moreover, as already indicated, a highly influential recent theory of contemporary geopolitical and economic globalization explicitly challenges the idea that federation ever was a distinct alternative to empire either at the onset or now at the end of the modern period. According to the famous thesis of Hardt and Negri, the imperative of size has re-emerged in the context of a new stage of politically enabled economic globalization of capitalism, but they deem it illusory to construe federation as an autonomous political form or as an adequate response to the contemporary constellation.[42] While it makes sense to devote serious attention today to the federal constitutional form in their view, that is because they construe it in terms of network theory, as the vehicle and core structure of post-modern empire. Let us look into this claim.

On their analysis, the effective response then (in the modern period) and now to imperatives of size and capitalist globalization has always been some sort of imperialism. Borrowing from but altering Arendt they distinguish two imperial logics: the *imperialism* of modern western sovereign nation-states characterized by *expansion*, annexation, hierarchy, centralized control, and domination over subject indigenous colonial populations deemed inherently unequal; and the late twentieth- and twenty-first-century revival of the logic of *universal* (now post-modern) *empire* which allegedly involves the *extension* of the federal (and republican) constitutional form through a process of inclusion without annexation, that renders the external internal, yet without formal hierarchy or leveling, to the entire globe.[43] *Imperialist* states erect a secondary structure of state organisms designed for conquest, pillage, geno-cide, colonization, and slavery (a sort of dual state); the latter involves extension of the model of *network power* Hardt and Negri deem constitutive of the imperial and federal form.[44] Accordingly there is an intrinsic connec-tion between federation and empire, and the republican constitutional form when connected to this structure is apparently very well suited to adapt to today's imperatives of size and to global capitalism. Hardt and Negri's para-digmatic cases are Rome and America. The globalization of the federal and republican constitutional form – construed as the combined division (for the former) and separation (for the latter) of powers within a de-centered net-work architecture – is indeed possible, in their view, but it takes the shape of empire. To put it another way, the American constitutional form, which successfully developed the network model of federation on a large scale in the modern period, was imperial from the beginning, and has now been globalized.[45] This construal is not restricted to Hardt and Negri, as the recent work of Lauren Benton drawing on that of Anthony Anghie reveals.[46] For her too, American federalism is seen in terms of one solution to the conundrums of imperial sovereignty, namely how to characterize a dependent sub-polity that was "outside the scope of [international] law yet within it, lacking international [sovereign] capacity yet necessarily possessing it."[47] She con-strues federalism as a solution to this conundrum that places states along an imperial continuum stretching, at one end, from the American federal model in which dependent states retain significant jurisdictional prerogatives but could not engage in foreign policy, to at the other end, polities with some measure of control over external sovereignty such as the German states under the Holy Roman Empire, Tunis in relation to France, and the tributary polities of the Mughal and Chinese empires, etc.[48] Her point, like that of Hardt and Negri, is to reveal the conundrums of quasi-sovereignty accorded such states as inherent in the strategies of imperial rule.[49]

But this sort of analysis, however much it seeks to make distinctions, elides the most crucial one. For a federation of states, and the federal constitutional form, is not by definition an empire or imperial. Indeed as Montesquieu pointed out long ago, republican states voluntarily federate precisely in order to preserve their republican constitutional forms and in order to avoid the imperial alternative for themselves. This surely holds true for the forma-tion of the US as for the Roman Republic.[50] Pace Hardt and Negri, Benton, et al., the federal principle and the imperial one are as much at odds with each other as the imperialist and imperial ones are with the republican constitutional form. To be sure, a federation can also be imperialist, imperial, or become an empire, but this does not mean that conceptually these are identical. Let me briefly look at these three ideal-typical logics and then turn to the normative arguments for federation that are well worth reviving and expanding upon.

Nation-state imperialism is an aggressive response to the dynamic intrinsic to the plural inter-state and capitalist world system, whereby each state seeks security and competitive advantage by having large standing armies and acquiring colonies. In so doing, the nation-state develops a secondary structure of state organisms (alongside and in tension with national republican political forms) designed for conquest, annexation, administrative rule, exploitation, and control over subject populations, as already indicated.[51] In one respect this continues the logic of absolutist state-making (itself, caught up in the dynamic of size in a plural system) which has an intrinsically imperialist centralizing leveling dynamic – expansion as already indicated, proceeds from a center and fans out through the imposition of coercive control and rule over larger territory and populations.[52] This expansionist, centralizing, homogenizing, imperialist logic was adopted by the nation-state for rule in its overseas colonial dominions. However, once the absolute monarchical state became the constitutional-democratic national state, the differences between rule over citizens and rule over mere subjects intensified.[53] The key features of nation-state imperialism, insofar as it extended neither its republican political forms nor the rule of law to the colonies, are its differential and unequal categories of citizenship, status-based legal pluralism and police state, and executive/administrative modes of rule in its possessions often justified by racialized, civilizational categories.[54] War and conquest are the mechanism; annexation, boundaries, hierarchical rule, assimilation, together with the construction and maintenance of difference and inferiority between full citizens in or from the metropolis and subject indigenous populations overseas, the outcome.[55]

The logic of *universal empire* is different. Hardt and Negri are right: empire is a political form that has a universalist organizational structure: it constitutes a world in which there are no borders, only frontiers, it is inclusive, boundless, oriented to global peace and security and to the incorporation of all encountered polities or groups.[56] It does not require assimilation, or homogenization, but rather is designed to manage diversity. In their model, a republican empire (Rome, the US) expands by making alliances or via conquest. But it allegedly does not destroy the powers which join or which it conquers; it opens itself to them by incorporating them in its de-centered "network" constitutional architecture.[57] An empire thus also renders the external internal and aims to establish peace within its domain. To be sure, an empire recognizes no autonomous political equals, no legal order equivalent to its own or with the competence to decide its own competence, but renders all polities it allies with or conquers parts of the whole – the external becomes incorporated as internal. Global right is imperial right, there is no law but its law and the legal jurisdictions it is willing to co-opt, construct, delegate, tolerate, and ascribe to the religious and political and juridical elites judging local populations within it. All of this is well known.

However, contrary to Hardt and Negri, even a republican empire is a political system *with a center and peripheries* regardless of the fact that authority of rule is not premised on territorial delimitation.[58] It is political centralization and military presence that guarantees economic flows from the periphery (tribute, taxes). Rome is the paradigmatic example of an empire with a republican core, and it did initially extend and expand this core and the constitutional protections and rights of citizenship to Latins through a mix of conquest and alliance and in response to violent struggles.

But it is a myth that subject populations in its peripheries enjoyed equal citizenship when it mattered, i.e. when citizenship entailed participation in republican political institutions. Montesquieu puts it well: liberty prevailed in the center, tyranny in the extreme parts.[59] Republican constitutionalism characterized by the separation of powers with representation for the people, equal citizenship, and the rule of law prevailed in the center, *pro-consuls and praetors* with plenary powers in the periphery. As Montesquieu states:

> While Rome extended her dominions no farther than Italy, the people were governed as confederates, and the laws of each republic were preserved. But when she enlarged her *conquests*, and the senate had no longer an immediate inspection over the provinces, nor the magistrates residing at Rome were any longer capable of governing the empire, they were obliged to send prætors and proconsuls. Then it was that the harmony of the three powers was lost. The persons appointed to that office were entrusted with a power which comprehended that of all the Roman magistracies; nay, even that of the people.[60] (my emphasis)

Indeed, the administrative/military forms of rule there as well as the standing armies needed to maintain it ultimately came back to the metropolis and destroyed its republican constitution.[61] *Pace Hardt and Negri, the empire that destroyed Roman republicanism (for Montesquieu based on a separation of powers) was not governed by a genuine federal structure.* Rule of law and republican constitutional principles prevailed at home but the enlargement into the peripheries did not follow the *logic of iteration* but rather of coercion. Only once the republic was destroyed was citizenship extended to all those ruled by the empire. As Montesquieu and Hintze after him correctly argued, it is easy for a monarchy but impossible for a conquering republic to rule the conquered according to its own constitution.[62] Accordingly the implication seems to be that once a republican federation engages in an imperial project, replacing the egalitarian federative logic of consensual extension and iteration of its political form, law, and mode of integration into the union with coercion, arbitrariness, differential statuses for citizen/subjects, and hierarchy, the republican form of the federation itself comes under great stress. The Roman federal republic, in other words, morphed from being a Federation with an imperialist relation to conquered peoples outside Italy to becoming an empire internally and losing both its republican and its federal forms.

The old argument of Polybius and Machiavelli (and Turner for the US) is repeated by Hardt and Negri: to wit that republics with democratic foundations seek to resolve internal conflicts through the appropriation of new territories and thereby avoid the cycle of corruption they would otherwise invariably fall prey to.[63] But while insisting on the distinction between colonialist imperialist expansion and the imperial way of responding to the pressure of size, they elide the distinctiveness of the federative logic by collapsing it with the imperial one. They confuse analytic distinctions (or ideal types), with hybrid empirical historical formations. They thus lose the insight articulated by many whom they cite, from Montesquieu, Madison, and Tocqueville, to Otto Hintze and Hannah Arendt, namely that federating involves a distinctive logic of extension – one that involves iteration of its republican constitutional form to new members – that was explicitly conceived of as an alternative to the centered, dominating, coercive, leveling, homogenizing sovereigntist-imperialist model of the absolutist monarchical and later national sovereign state but also to the expansionist logic of empire just described which manufactures differences, internal status-based legal pluralisms, internal quasi-sovereignty, and so forth in contradistinction to the egalitarian structure of federal political forms and citizenship principles.[64]

Indeed, much of what Hardt and Negri deem to be distinctive about the constitution of the American republic pertains to its federal, not its imperial dimensions. *To be sure, the formation of the US federation originally and throughout its continental expansion did mix imperial and federal principles, conquest and free alliance.* The appropriation of land, the expulsion, extermination, and sequestering onto reservations of native-Americans under the direct centralized rule of the Bureau of Indian Affairs, an administrative agency of the Federal government, is an exemplar of the former along with the mendacious discourse of quasi-sovereignty that sought to justify this.[65] But the free associational logic of acquiring statehood and equal membership within and under the US federal constitution, offered to territories controlled by white colonists on the condition they establish republican constitutions, is an example of the latter. The superficial analogy to Rome notwithstanding, the federated member states were never provinces. The extension of the republican constitutional form and the guarantee of the autonomy and equality of the newly federated member states with other members of the federation was the consensual basis of inclusion within the federation. While federations like empires do not have rigid borders (as does a territorial nation-state) insofar as new members bring with them new territory, at any given point in time its boundaries are clear and inclusion is ideal-typically voluntary on both sides.[66] In the late nineteenth century the American Federation did become imperialist, like the European nation-states – acquiring territories through conquest and ruling (formally or informally) over these and other territories and populations never intended to become equal members of the federation or to enjoy the protections of the federal constitution.[67] From the second half of the twentieth to the early twenty-first century an imperial project is indeed also discernible. Today the mix and tension between the federal, imperialist, and imperial logics remains with us. But it does not help our understanding of historical dynamics or future possibilities, here or elsewhere, to collapse these logics into one another or to confuse empirical with theoretical analysis. We know that the three logics – federal, imperialist, and imperial – can come together also on the global level: Otto Hinzte already described the League of Nations as an instrument of federal imperialism, and the collective status of the veto-wielding members of the UN Security Council established by the UN Charter (and the rules they produce) has been analyzed through the concept of hegemonic international law.[68] The point is to struggle to transform and abolish the imperialist/imperial side of this equation domestically and internationally. Instead of reasoning from empirical hybrids and collapsing our categories into one another on the basis of superficial analogies, the better route is to attain analytical clarity by reflecting on the distinctive logics of and normative arguments for the respective political and constitutional forms.[69]

The pragmatic arguments for federating include, as indicated, increasing the security and welfare for small states in the framework of a union of states. But collective defense vis-à-vis the outside is only one side of the security dimension: peace on the inside, i.e. among the member states, and their common welfare is also a key goal and product of a successful federal union of states. As we shall see, this need not be directly linked to an alliance for external defense although that is usually the case. The maintenance of peace and overcoming of the destructive antagonism and competition between contiguous states is a strong enough motive (pragmatic and normative) for federating. It is time for democratic and republican theorists to recuperate insights of the federal vision as pertinent to the post-modern condition insofar as it provides a newly relevant and distinctive answer to the problems of size facing states under pressures of globalization and to legitimacy problems created by regional and/or global governance institutions.[70]

2.1.2 Normative arguments for federation

To see what is distinctive about the federal logic, we must thus abandon the superficial analogy between empire and the federal form, and between a vague notion of "de-centered networks" and federal constitutional structure.[71] The normative arguments for federation are illuminating in this regard. There are three main justifications for federation as a constitutional form: the argument from freedom (republican/democratic), the argument from peace, and the argument from diversity. Let us look briefly at each of these before turning to the issue of taxonomy.

The argument that federation is a device for preserving republican freedom on the part of small republics facing the imperatives of size is as old as Montesquieu.[72] Indeed the phrase later adopted by Madison in the federalist papers was his:

> "It is very probable" (says he) that mankind would have been obliged at length to live constantly under the government of a SINGLE PERSON, had they not contrived a kind of constitution that has all the internal advantages of a republican, together with the external force of a monarchical, government. I mean a CONFEDERATE REPUBLIC.[73]

By this Montesquieu meant not that a federation (a confederate republic in his terms) is republican on the inside, and expansive in the imperial manner vis-à-vis the outside. Rather, pace Hardt and Negri, he meant that as an association of associations, a community of communities, this political form, once it reaches the appropriate dimensions, is able to withstand external force without internal corruption. While preserving the autonomy of member states, federating allows them to maintain their republican form of government and the freedom and security of their citizenry. Indeed Montesquieu seems to imply that member states retain their sovereignty within a confederate republic for although it constitutes a polity with a distinctive constitutional form a federation involves a mode of unification that preserves rather than annihilating or merging the constitutional and political autonomy of its members:[74]

> This form of government is a convention by which several petty states agree to become members of a larger one, which they intend to establish. It is a kind of assemblage of societies that constitutes a new one, capable of increasing by means of further associations, till they arrive at such a degree of power as to be able to provide for the security of the whole body.[75]

To be sure by republican freedom Montesquieu did not mean democracy: he had in mind something more along the lines of the rule of law and the security enjoyed by a citizenry that is free to obey the law and knows others will be constrained to do so including those in government.[76] In contemporary parlance republican forms of participation and constitutional structures (the separation of powers) and republican liberty are understood as non-domination, i.e. security against arbitrariness and the abuse of power.[77] But the link between republican freedom and confederation constituted the main normative argument for the latter and thus Montesquieu argued that the confederate government ought to be composed of states of the same nature, especially of the republican kind.[78] Of course, he was well aware of the existence of confederations that consisted of states with heterogeneous polit-ical regimes, as in the case of the confederate republic of Germany with its free towns and princes, but such combinations were not ideal from a normative point of view. The reason Montesquieu gives is worth quoting: "The spirit of monarchy is war and enlargement of dominion: peace and moderation are the spirit of a republic. These two kinds of government cannot naturally subsist in a confederate republic."[79] In other words, by federating, small republican states can maintain their autonomy, render their citizens' free-doms secure, enjoy peace in their internal relations, and yet can expand when necessary through consensual and iterative means, thereby becoming large and powerful enough to deter external aggression.[80] This, of course, assumes that a (con)federation will not become more aggressive than each state separately. Indeed Montesquieu believed that the federal principle provides the means for preserving republican moderation and that federations are ultimately defensive in purpose and logic. A federal union maintains the peace internally insofar as members will have the authority to act together against a usurper who tries to undermine *the equal standing of member states* within the confederation, and to quell insurrections and other abuses of power in a member state that would threaten the republican and/or federal principles. The elective affinity between republican and federal structures is due to the similarity in constitutional logic: both establish, separate, and divide power; both set up counter-powers so as to expand the power of the whole while preserving liberty of the parts. At the same time federation serves the general welfare as member states develop common interests in internal trade and commerce, lifting the barriers to these while fostering mutual peace and security.

Similar normative justifications of federation can be found in all the major theorists of federal union. Madison's anti-tyranny argument in Federalist No. 51 is the classic restatement of this position for modern federal republican constitutions. There, Madison famously stated that:

> In the compound republic of America, the power surrendered by the people is first divided between two distinct governments, and then the portion allotted to each subdivided among distinct and separate depart-ments. Hence a double security arises to the rights of the people. The different governments will control each other at the same time that each will be controlled itself.[81]

Madison thereby wed the discourse of popular sovereignty to republican and federal government using the anti-tyranny argument to quell fears that a centralized mega-state and/or a tyrannical empire would be the outcome of his project for the further consolidation of the confederacy of the American states.

The argument from democracy is related to but distinct from the republican thesis. By federating, small democratic states also seek to preserve the freedom inherent in their form of government in the context of a competitive and threatening political environment. By facilitating coordination, participation within a sufficiently powerful federation enhances the political weight of small democratic states internally by giving them influence or even a veto over policy-making on the federal level and externally by making their voice, combined with others, matter more than it otherwise would on the world scene. Moreover, the well-known argument from size – the smaller the polity the more vital the democracy – seems even more pertinent in this case.[82] To be sure much depends on how one understands the ideal of democracy and its correlative concept of freedom, but it is striking that the argument in favor of federation as opposed to formation of a centralized state has been invoked regarding both direct and representative models.[83] If the democratic ideal requires conformity between the general will expressed in the legal order and the will of the individuals subject to that order (Rousseau, Kelsen) and thus that the addressees of the law can see themselves as its authors (Habermas), then self-government is at risk the larger the polity. Federation is one way to preserve democracy as self-government insofar as it diminishes the possible contradiction between the contents of the legal order and the will of individuals subject to it.[84] Because federation preserves the constitutional autonomy along with the political existence and territorial integrity of member states, insofar as it involves shared rule and self-rule, it diminishes the danger of autocratic or unaccountable rule by a distant center, inherent in large centralized states, so the argument goes.[85] The guarantees of territorial division of powers, the delimited and non-comprehensive nature of the government typical of a federation, and voice and participation for member states within the central structure are deemed democratic mechanisms to prevent unaccountable and unresponsive distant government. Otherwise the chain of delegation and accountability becomes too long and the opportunities for meaningful political representation and participation by citizens along with the weight of their votes, shrinks the larger the polity. Federal polities, moreover, so the democratic argument goes, increase opportunities for citizen participation in public decision-making by combining electoral representation with participation through deliberation and opportunities to hold office on both levels.[86] In other words, if democracy presupposes political equality – self-government together with the idea that the legal order and legislation generally are created by the individuals bound by it according to the principle of majority – the normative argument for federation as opposed to the creation of large centralized hierarchical mega-states seems compelling.[87] As Halberstam recently argued, federalism enhances voice. Since the number of local officials is large compared to few central office holders, "... this translates into greater citizen access to representatives at the local level as well as a more realistic opportunity for citizens to become involved in local politics (either as elected representatives or as activists) than in politics at the center."[88] Federalism multiplies the loci of decision-making and so increases the avenues through which citizens can attempt to realize their preferences, try out new ideas, protect their interests and their rights, and foster the common good or general welfare. This is a version of the legal pluralist argument described in Chapter 1. The "democratic experimentalism" aspect of this argument stresses the progressive possibilities federalism proffers: the plurality of state governments in a federation can create "laboratories of democracy" which, in the best case scenario, foster creative local and diverse solutions to economic and social problems and the possibility of adopting "best practices" on the part of other states and the federal government. To be sure, this is more of a pragmatic argument from the standpoint of profes- sional policy-makers who view member states of a federation as laboratories for testing new policies than it is a democratic argument focused on political laboratories for new forms of participation.[89] But the two can be wed. They can also be linked to a liberal argument. If the federation and the member states both protect fundamental individual rights and personal and political equality, accountability can be secured via iteration of constitutionalist and democratic forms of representation and participation at all the levels of government through each level checking every other level.[90]

To be sure, the counter-argument is obvious, namely that it is precisely the principle of equality at the heart of democracy and its institutional corollary – one person–one vote – that seem to undermine the democratic justification of the federal principle. The democratic norms of equal citizenship, decision rules by simple majority so that no vote counts more than any other, and the requirement of legal uniformity seem to fit the model of the unitary sovereign democratic state far better than any federal arrangement. Simple majority rule is certainly not the principle that regulates ordinary or extraordinary (legisla- tion or constitutional change) decision-making within a federation. Indeed equal representation of states means overrepresentation of populations of small units within the federal representative body. The right of federal units to be involved in amending the federal constitutional treaty typically on a qualified majority basis (while they can change their own constitutions unilat- erally) seems to undermine the democratic justification of federation by enhancing the weight of the votes of small states and minorities. This seems to violate the principle of political equality and the institution of majority rule, allegedly the only fair way of realizing equal concern and respect for all citizens.

There is, however, a democratic-theoretical response to this argument, one which becomes quite compelling once it is linked up to the second normative justification for federation, namely, the argument from diversity or pluralism. The democratic counter-argument to the above is that there are no simple majorities or minorities: all majorities are compounded of congeries of groups, and federalism first emerged and is resurfacing as a political force today because it acknowledges this basic fact.[91] By federating, polities protect the possibility for minorities to preserve themselves but also the possibility for majorities to be compounded.[92] Federal arrangements may also protect minorities' basic rights against member unit authorities insofar as the center has the authority to intervene in them and if the federal constitution includes basic individual rights.[93] This is so because federal principles and structures provide for consensus-building and militate against the tyranny of the (simple) majority (local or federal). The federal principle of self-rule and shared rule acknowledges the importance of non-imposition on fundamental matters by a simple electoral majority. Federalism thus perforce institutionalizes mechanisms for deliberation and decision-making predicated on the assumption of a starting point of a plurality of views and even deep disagreement or conflicts between political projects. Its aim is to build broader consensus without abolishing or disparaging heterogeneity within. The federal principle of legitimacy is based on the idea of compound majorities, *sovereign equality among the member states* and their equal representation on the federal level. Modern federalism emerged first, as an alternative to the absolutist centralizing homogenizing and hierarchical statist model of political integration premised on the assumption that sovereignty had to be located in a single center, and then as an alternative to the myth of the modern homogeneous nation-state which when based on the ideal of popular sovereignty, seems to entail the Jacobin logic that assumes that democracy entails the self-government of one homogeneous demos.[94]

The argument from diversity reinforces this reasoning. Just as the notion of absolute national sovereignty is undermined in the face of interdependence and global or regional governance in the "post-modern" era, so too, as already indicated, the myth of the homogeneous nation-state gives way to the reality of the near universality of multiethnic, multireligious, multicultural (and so on) polities.[95] This realization opens the conceptual and operational space for a federal revival in order to accommodate diversity within polities and for a rethinking of what is entailed by federation, so as to come to grips with new conceptions and new emerging forms.[96] It is worth quoting Kelsen in this context:

> The fact that the majority of the total community belongs to a certain political party, nationality, race, language, or religion does not exclude the possibility that within certain partial territories the majority of the

individuals belong to another party, nationality, race, language or religion . . .
In order to diminish the possible contradiction between the contents of
the legal order and the will of the individuals subject to it, it may be
necessary, under certain circumstances, that certain norms of the legal
order be valid only for certain partial territories *and be created only by
majority vote of the individuals living in these territories*."[97] (my emphasis)

Thus, Kelsen concludes, federalism as a way to accommodate diversity in
deeply divided societies may be a democratic postulate.[98] This argument from
diversity has its contemporary formulations. If citizens' interests or policy
preferences vary locally or regionally, tracking political subunits, then a
diverse array of local regulation will meet these interests and track citizens'
voice by allowing regionally or locally varying preferences to have some
efficacy alongside one another without however reifying the cleavages that
may involve language, culture, or ethnicity because in a federal system
individuals can vote with their feet.[99]

Indeed the argument that its democratic credentials are superior to the two
standard contemporary alternatives for managing and accommodating diversity – consociational democracy or status-based legal pluralism (typical of
empire) – seems compelling. Consociational democracy, like federalism, is
based on "compound majorities," and both involve devices to build more
substantial consensus than simple majority systems. But the latter involves
concurrent majorities that are based on personal status.[100] Federalism refers
to the form of a polity that is polycentric, composed of legally autonomous
territorial units, which are typically constitutionally anchored. The diversity
and plurality it institutionalizes may map onto substantive divisions (ethnic,
linguistic, religious, etc.) but conceptually it has to do with political and
legal institutional diversity at the subunit level – the groups, majorities,
and minorities it articulates or generates are not fixed: they can shift over
time. In short ideal-typically democratic federalism permits institutional,
constitutional, legislative, and policy diversity across member states with the
proviso that their political form of regime remains republican and/or democratic.[101] This facilitates *democratic* experimentalism, choice of laws, domicile
shopping, and so forth for citizens seeking the most appealing bundle of local
laws, customs, and attitudes as well as creativity.[102] It permits subgroups
of citizens to live together under their own local laws but it does not reify
the groups or render the substantive identities or cleavages permanently
politically salient, as does consociational democracy and status-based legal
pluralism. Consociational arrangements pertain to a polity's regime (a way to
structure the exercise of public power, particularly among political parties)
not to constitutional/political form. It is, classically, characterized by grand
coalitions and segmental autonomy, and usually also involves principles of
proportionality and minority veto.[103] Two features of these arrangements are
distinctive: they emphasize (and reify) the existence of apparently permanent

religious, ethnic, or cultural groups and cleavages on the assumption that the society is so deeply divided that their consent can be won no other way, and the power-sharing among political leaders of the segmentally differentiated autonomous groups is typically linked with elite control and hierarchy within them.[104] Status-group legal pluralism (or "multicultural jurisdiction"), like consociationalism, involves the granting of legal autonomy on the basis of personal status instead of territorial division.[105] However, this way of accommodating (and reifying) diversity usually entails ceding public control of personal and/or religious, tribal or "customary" law (particularly over family, education, religion, and personal property) to non-public authorities within the overall polity and exempting their community members from the general laws of the polity (civil codes and human rights) that relate to these domains. This ultimately combines the reification of identities with the reification of communities and their internal hierarchies (usually of religious and/or tribal male authorities and traditional elites) and the loss of equal protection of the civil law, of the constitution and of human rights for members of subordinate groups (usually women) within the relevant communities. The authority structure within the jurisdictions granted legal autonomy and enforcement are typically not required to be congruent with the republican or liberal-democratic principles that structure the overarching constitutional democracy in which they are situated. It is not surprising that from a democratic, rule of law, liberal constitutionalist standpoint, consociationalism and multicultural jurisdiction are seen as *faute de mieux* techniques for the pragmatic purpose of managing diversity within deeply divided societies, involving serious tradeoffs between democratic and liberal constitutionalist principles and unity.[106]

Advocates of federation as a public political form maintain that it has no such intrinsic drawbacks. In other words, while a key purpose of federating is to preserve the political autonomy of member states, the minorities and majorities within these states are not reified, traditional elites are not necessarily entrenched, and the federal compact can entail the "regulation of self-regulation" such that basic human rights of individuals within the territorial units are guaranteed by the federal constitution much the same way that a republican or democratic form for the constitutions of member states may be required. The reverse is also true: member states can insist on iteration of basic rights protections and republican institutions on the federal level in exchange for compliance. Monitoring can and should be mutual. Agreement that both the federal and domestic constitutions secure such basic rights is perfectly possible as a core proviso for membership and equal status in a federal union of states.[107]

To be sure, it would be absurd to argue that federations are intrinsically liberal, democratic, republican, tolerant of diversity, and respectful of rights or that all of these must go together.[108] There have been monarchical federations, imperial federations, illiberal and undemocratic republican federations, hegemonic federations, asymmetrical federations, and polities that are federal in form only such as "grossraume" or empires with a paper federal constitution. Elites in member states may choose to federate and create institutional rules of the federation in order to preserve their local power, hegemony, and local tyrannies or they may use federal principles and structures for that purpose. The point is not that federal unions of states are *necessarily* superior to large centralized states along these normative dimensions. Rather it is that they *can* involve a mode of growing larger; of structuring institutions and power relations among the parts that avoid the problems of top down hierarchical rule and reified group identities while creating a federal constitutional treaty that hews to democratic and liberal constitutional principles and insists on these as conditions for membership in the effort to preserve diversity and plurality while creating or enabling commonalities and transnational solidarities to emerge.

2.2   Federation as decentralization

2.2.1   Taxonomic issues

Whether or not the normative arguments for federation are convincing they certainly turn on its distinctiveness as a political form. Given the immense variety of federal arrangements it is obvious that there is more than one way to institutionalize federal principles.[109] Variety on the empirical level raises taxonomic questions: What if anything is distinctive, structurally or normatively, about federal unions when compared with highly decentralized unitary polities and/or those with autonomous provinces? What distinguishes the organizational principle of a federation of states from an international organization? Is there a systematic difference between a federal union of states and a federal state?

There are two basic approaches to these issues and to federal unions in the literature that I would like to discuss. One maintains that formulae such as shared rule and self-rule, independence and interdependence, contractual voluntary beginnings, and so forth are not only not specific to federal polities but also that there is no single criterion or organizational principle that yields sharp distinctions among the various political formations. Accordingly the better approach is to analyze all polities and all public legal orders along the axis of centralization/decentralization such that a continuum can be established on which different political formations may be placed. The locus classicus of this "continuum" model is the work of Hans Kelsen.[110] While many useful distinctions follow from this approach, the centralization/decentralization continuum throws out the baby with the bathwater for it screens out precisely those distinctive features of the federal political and constitutional form.[111] Denying any fundamental distinction between federal and unitary states, or between federal unions, international organizations, and federal states, apart from degree of centralization, this approach ultimately reasons from the perspective of a monist view of international law. Accordingly, there is no qualitative break between the intra-state and the inter-state worlds in the Kelsenian juridical analytic for everything is a matter of greater or lesser centralization of law-making, adjudication, and enforcement. In this regard, the decentralization continuum model is cosmopolitan.

The other basic approach breaks with the state-centric paradigm while insisting on the distinctiveness of federation as a political form.[112] There are two versions of this: one spurred by the emergence of the League of Nations and the revival of utopian talk of federal union between the two world wars, the other developed to analyze the type of polity and legal arrangements that is apparently emerging in the European Union and possibly elsewhere in the twenty-first century.[113] Both versions abandon the standard dichotomies that follow from the statist paradigm – confederation (construed as an international treaty organization) versus federal states; federal versus unitary states – thereby allowing a different conceptual spectrum to come into view. The idea is to construct a conception of federal unions of states (and peoples) that are not themselves states.[114] The first version uses a sovereignty-oriented perspective to indicate the distinctiveness of federal unions of states as a constitutional and political form. It reasons from political legitimacy rather than from a juridical perspective. But it ultimately falls prey to a misleading teleology and normative assessment that follow from the anachronistic perspective tied to the very nineteenth-century state theory it sought to avoid insofar as it embraces a "Westphalian" and political theological/existentialist conception of sovereignty and constituent power. Non-state federations perforce appear as temporary, unstable, and inferior second cousins to "real" polities, i.e. sovereign states.

The second version abandons the sovereignty concept as irrelevant to the analysis of federal unions. It construes federations as a genus (with subtypes) of political formations with a distinctive (ideal-typical) set of political, structural, and constitutional features to which no "statist" categories pertain.[115] This approach allows for a new assessment of the genesis and structure of previous federal unions while providing a theoretical perspective for analyzing contemporary unions of states like the EU. Instead of insisting on the sui generis character of the latter (i.e. as unprecedented and unique – itself an artifact of the state-centric perspective), however, this non-Kelsenian juridical theory of federal union opens the conceptual horizon for analyzing other empirical political formations, past and present, from that optic.[116] The conceptual shift involved in the construal of federation as a genus which can have a variety of subspecies, or a plurality of subtypes, yields a new taxonomy within which the (non-state) federal formations can be constructed.[117] In other words, from this perspective, just as modern states vary in their institutional make-up and organizational structure, so too do federations of states.[118] Accordingly this model allows one to conceive of contemporary forms of non-state polities in their own terms – i.e. as unions that are other than ordinary international organizations, states, or empires. A new set of public, political forms gets screened in freeing us to imagine and theorize a range of types of polities and constitutional legal orders that may well be on the horizon in the twenty-first century without having to fit them into the statist straitjacket. Nevertheless the abandonment of the sovereignty problematic is premature and has the disadvantage of excluding important subtypes within the genus it constructs.[119]

While I am convinced that federal unions of states and peoples are a distinctive political form, there is much to be learned from the Kelsenian centralization/decentralization optic and from both versions of the non-statist approach. In what follows, I first discuss the continuum model in its cosmopolitan variant (the Kelsenian model), and turn in the next two sections to discuss the main versions of the alternative approach (the one sovereignty-centered, the other not). I will propose a synthesis of all three approaches. I wish to combine a juridical perspective liberated from monistic dogmatism with a political perspective on federation freed from political theological myths regarding sovereignty – in short to think federation with respect to legality and legitimacy. This theoretical exercise will open the terrain for reflecting on the mode of legitimacy specific to federal polities that are not states and for posing the question as to the relevance of such a framework for rethinking the constitutionalization of international law with respect to global as well as regional international organizations.

2.2.2   The decentralization model

In his seminal work on the *General Theory of Law and the State*, Kelsen states the following:

> Only the degree of decentralization distinguishes a unitary State divided into autonomous provinces from a federal State. And as the federal State is distinguished from a unitary State, so is an international confederacy of States distinguished from a federal State by a higher degree of decentralization only. On the scale of decentralization, the federal State stands between the unitary State and an international union of States.[120]

There is not much original here with respect to the three main possibilities discussed: federal state, unitary state, international confederation of states construed as an international alliance/organization. This was standard fare for late nineteenth- and early twentieth-century state theory. What then is the point of this approach and what does it accomplish?

By placing the distinction among state forms and international organizations along the centralization–decentralization continuum, Kelsen is able to remain true to his juridical monism and to hold on to his concept of a legal system as a hierarchal order of norms, while accounting for the existence of federal states, and avoiding what appears to be an oxymoron, namely the existence of two sovereignties within one polity: a problem that plagued theorists of federal states from the beginning.[121] The conundrum is the following. If sovereignty is the essential characteristic of a state, and if sovereignty cannot be divided, pooled, or shared, then it seems contradictory to speak of a federal state composed of member states. Either the federal state is sovereign and is the only real state in the federal union or the member states are sovereign and the union they belong to is not a state or real polity at all but only some sort of international alliance/organization. Recall that for Kelsen, the state is equivalent to the legal order. Recall also that for Kelsen sovereignty does not refer to the allocation of competences but rather to the supremacy, unity, and autonomy of a legal order and the coercive force of its internal hierarchy of valid legal norms. Thus Kelsen cannot accept the idea of dual or shared sovereignty.[122] These terms usually refer to a positive or material conception of a division of "sovereign" powers (competences or jurisdiction along functional lines or on the basis of the principle of subsidiarity) but that means that those who speak in this way are operating on a different level of analysis and avoiding the key conceptual problem. For how can there be more than one autonomous constitutional legal (and political) order within a single polity?

Kelsen gets around this dilemma by analyzing federal polities along the quantitative axis of centralization and decentralization in a way that sidelines the sovereignty problematic and downplays the distinction between federal and non-federal polities. In order to do so, he distinguishes between two forms of centralization and decentralization: static and dynamic. The former refers to the territorial sphere of validity of a legal order: in a centralized legal order its norms are valid throughout the whole territory over which it extends while in a decentralized legal order, there are norms that have different territorial spheres of validity: some for the entire territory (otherwise it would not be the territory of a single legal order), some only for different parts thereof.[123] The dynamic dimension refers to the methods of creating and executing valid norms. Dynamic decentralization means that there is a plurality of norm-creating organs, and this is analytically distinct from the territorial locus or spheres of validity of the norms they create. It can refer to the separation of powers within the center or to a vertical plurality of norm-creating organs on the local and central levels. The point is that static and dynamic centralization need not co-vary. Decentralization that is both static and dynamic can indicate the existence of a federal state in which statutes valid for the territory of a member state only, must have been passed by the local legislature elected by the citizens of that state.[124] On the other hand, static decentralization can go together with dynamic centralization as in the case of a hereditary monarchy which enacts different statutes, say, on religion for different provinces of the realm.[125]

Kelsen proceeds to construct a taxonomy that places political communities, be they unitary states, federal states, unitary states with autonomous provinces, confederacies of states, or the international legal community as a whole, on a continuum structured in terms of the degree of centralization and decentralization of legislation and execution (judicial and administrative) and in light of a range of other relevant variables.[126] I will turn to this taxonomy below. The upshot of this approach is the denial of any systematic difference between a highly centralized federal state and a highly decentralized unitary state when it comes to legislation: "On this point a federal state differs from a unitary state with autonomous provinces only by the fact that the matters subject to the legislation of the component states are more numerous and important than those subject to the legislation of autonomous provinces."[127] Moreover, it makes little difference whether the federal polity was created through a federal pact or through a process of internal decentralization.[128] Indeed Kelsen contends that member states of a federal polity are ultimately not really states at all, for the reasons suggested above: thus the difference between them and relatively autonomous provinces is diminished from this perspective as well.[129] Finally, although he does acknowledge that the component states in federal polity are typically characterized by constitutional autonomy whereas autonomous provinces in a unitary state typically have their constitutions prescribed for them by the constitution of the state as a whole, the importance of this distinction is minimized, by placing it too on the decentralization/centralization axis.[130] Constitutional autonomy for the former means nothing more than that changes in the constitutions of the component states must be accomplished by statutes of the component states themselves. This amounts only to a relative autonomy vis-à-vis the center, however, insofar as member state constitutions are limited (typically) in a federal state by constitutional principles of the federal constitution.[131] Kelsen gives the example that the component states may be obliged to have a democratic-republican constitution.[132]

As Olivier Beaud correctly points out, this overall approach allows Kelsen to hold on to his hierarchical and monistic conception of legal order for all polities including federal ones.[133] But it is fruitful for other reasons as well. It also enables him to come up with an innovative tripartite conception of federal polities and to resolve certain conceptual difficulties inherent in dualistic models.[134] Instead of double or shared sovereignty, Kelsen conceives the relation among constitutional orders within a federal state in the following way: the legal orders of the component states and the legal order of the center (the federation) are construed as two partial legal orders: decentralized legal norms constitute the partial legal community of the former, centralized legal norms constitute the partial legal community of the latter. Every individual in a federal state belongs simultaneously to a component state and to the federation: i.e. to two legal communities. However, and this is key, both legal orders are partial insofar as they form only a part of the "total Federal state," the total legal community that consists of the federation, the central legal community and the component states, several local legal communities, each resting on its own constitution. The federal constitution is simultaneously the constitution of the whole Federal state.[135] In other words in place of the binary relation between member states and federal state, there are in Kelsen's conception three elements: the "total" state, the federal state, and the member states. Kelsen asserts that traditional theory erroneously identifies the federation with the total Federal state.

This tripartite conception solves several conceptual problems at once. First with respect to the inside, it allows Kelsen to acknowledge the egalitarian relationship unifying member states in a federation along with the non-comprehensive character of the "partial" legal order (constitution) of the federation vis-à-vis its members. However, Kelsen does not thereby give up his hierarchical conception of a legal order or his monism. Rather he maintains that it is thanks to the supremacy of the global Federal legal order that the equality among component states and between these and the partial federal legal order is made possible and maintained. The global federation is the legal order (state) that authorizes, ascribes, and maintains the equality and integrity of the partial legal orders within this legal arrangement.

Moreover, the tripartite approach provides a solution to the conundrum addressed by Hardt and Negri: namely, how to conceptualize an imperialist or imperial federation from a juridical point of view, without conflating the concepts. The tripartite conception indicates that the egalitarian coordinate relation among federal member states can exist alongside a hierarchical relationship of the global Federal polity as a whole toward territories and populations that are not members of the federal union but are ruled by and subject to the law of the Federal polity or state. The latter are under its legal order, ruled directly by the global Federal order but are not members of the partial federal order. In other words the Federal legal order (state for Kelsen) can acquire territory through treaty, conquest, or other means ("discovery") and rule over people directly who are not ever meant to become members of the partial federal constitutional legal order: they are governed by laws created by the central organ(s) of the Federal order and administered through special agencies but need not be granted the privileges and immunities of citizenship that members of the federated states enjoy. As Forsyth reminds us this was true of the earliest modern federations: both the old Swiss Confederation (1291–1798) as well as the United Provinces of the Netherlands (the Dutch Federation: 1579–1795) held subject possessions over which they ruled.[136] It is also true of the American Federal polity created with the ratification of the constitution. Accordingly an imperial Federation is not an oxymoron – it is a hybrid – however undesirable and corrosive it might be for domestic republican, democratic, and/or liberal constitutionalist and egalitarian federal principles. To be sure questions can be posed as to the constitutionality of acquiring territories and populations never intended to become member states of the federation and never to be granted equally the privileges and immunities of federal citizenship.[137] The answer depends partly on the constitution of the particular Federal polity at issue but also raises conceptual issues: if the Federal constitution doubles as the constitution of the federated states and of the global federation, and if the latter grants certain basic rights and privileges, on what basis can a Federal polity deny these to those subject to its rule and its laws? We come up once more against the tension between imperial(ist) and federal logics: once these are differentiated, and once the possibility of imperial expansion as distinct from federal extension (growing larger by iterating its constitutional form to new members) is accounted for (i.e. territorial possessions of the Federal polity directly ruled by it) the question of their interrelation analytically, normatively, and empirically returns. I am persuaded that these logics are distinct and that imperial rule is corrosive of and violates the core principles of liberal federal constitutionalism.[138] However, the tripartite approach accounts for its possibility theoretically.

The tripartite approach to federation should sound familiar to any student of Kelsen's theory of international law: for he makes exactly the same argument using the logic of centralization/decentralization with regard to the relation of international law, states, and the sovereign equality of states.[139] Indeed the two are linked in his mind and it is no accident that the section on federal state and confederacy in his magnum opus *General Theory of Law and the State* ends with a discussion of the international legal community, and the assertion that there is no absolute borderline between national and international law. This is immediately followed by his theory of the international legal system as a decentralized global legal order.[140] Kelsen elsewhere insists that a juridical concept of a federal union of states signifies nothing else than the fact that such collectivities have been constituted by the intermediary of a superior legal order: either the universal international legal order or a partial legal order (the global Federal one) which is in turn authorized by the international legal order.[141] In short, the Kelsenian theory of the federal polity rests on a double presupposition: first that the federal order exists thanks to it being authorized by the international order and second that the Federal order of a federal state is supreme over its two other components which it in turn authorizes.[142]

This double presupposition may be required by Kelsen's hierarchical and monist conception of legal order but this does not in itself make it convincing. Indeed it seems to undermine the conceptual gains of the tripartite framework insofar as it insinuates hierarchy back into the structure overall, thereby rendering the egalitarian relations among member states insignificant. Indeed if the authority and constitutional autonomy of member states in a federal union is delegated by the global Federal state's legal order (constitution) along the lines of decentralization, then the distinctiveness of the federal structure as a political form from an empire is lost. Nor is there any conceptual space here for differentiating a federal union of states that is other than an international alliance, but whose internal legal and political relations are not hierarchical, from a consolidated federal state in which legal hierarchy obtains. This approach, in other words, prejudges the question of the relation among legal and political forms in a federation in a dogmatic way – these relations must, in order to fit the monist conception, be hierarchical and the member states can only be relatively autonomous, their prerogative to construct constitutional legal orders delegated by the overall federal constitutional legal order. But this is no more conceptually necessary or convincing than it is to construe the constitutions of sovereign states as delegated by global international legal order or as "relatively autonomous."[143] Such an approach also unhelpfully relegates issues of political legitimacy to the background insofar as it renders the mode of creation of a federal union and the dynamics of its transformation normatively irrelevant. Moreover, and ironically, although he strenuously seeks to avoid the sovereignty problematic by expelling it from his classificatory scheme, Kelsen nevertheless remains prisoner of the classical statist paradigm insofar as he narrows the conceptual alternatives down to two types of political structures: states (centralized or decentralized, unitary or federal) and confederacies of states construed as international organizations governed by international law. To be sure the decentralization/centralization frame is linked by Kelsen to a range of institutional criteria that would allow for a wide variety of empirical forms to be placed on the continuum between unitary and federal states, and international organizations but this ultimately involves the same conceptual binary, the same either/or that the classical statist approach yields.

I reproduce below the list of variables, because, although incomplete, it is useful for whatever conceptual taxonomic framework one deploys. The variables Kelsen mentions are the degree of centralization of legislation, of execution, of the distribution of competences, the nature of citizenship, direct or indirect obligation and authorizing, and the degree of centralization regarding foreign policy.[144] Accordingly a *confederation of states* is construed as an international association, which has as its *legal basis* a *treaty* among states. It is an international alliance or organization that is not necessarily imagined to be *permanent*. The *legislative body* is typically a *board* (or congress) composed of representatives (delegates) of the member states appointed by their governments. It enacts norms valid for all member states typically on the basis of *unanimity* but also typically it has specific competences ascribed to it. In contemporary parlance the member states thus remain masters of the treaty, thus *supremacy* remains with the domestic legal orders and courts especially regarding constitutional issues. *Jurisdiction* and *execution* can involve a central court and a central administration. But the court is normally competent to settle conflicts between member states and only exceptionally may private persons be plaintiffs and defendants. *Administrative competence* (execution) of the central governing organ also has the character of a board and typically functions according to the rule of *unanimity*. As for competence generally, an international confederacy is usually limited to settlement of disputes between member states and defense against external aggression. But the competence of member states in external politics and military affairs remains unrestricted; there is *no centralization of executive power*, no confederate police, army, navy, air force, etc. Typically a confederacy cannot impose direct *taxes* on individuals or states: rather member states have to contribute funds or troops for specific purposes and thus have to enact the required laws by which the individuals are obligated to military service or to the payment of taxes to the confederacy.[145] Nor is there any *citizenship* for individuals in the confederation: individuals are citizens of the member states only and belong legally to the international community only indirectly. A confederacy is an alliance of states, not individuals. There is no *direct effect* within a confederacy: the central norms of the legal order constituting the confederation obligate and authorize directly only states – affecting their courts and individuals only indirectly by the medium of the legal orders of the states to which they belong. This is a typical technique of international law. The *constitutional autonomy* of the member states is usually intact insofar as there is no provision typically in an international union in regard to their constitutions. However, a league could require members to have democratic-republican constitutions.[146] Accordingly the *relations* among members of a league although regulated by a *treaty* that can be called a constitution, ultimately remain *international* and member states remain *subjects of international law*. They, in short, are sovereign. Although, curiously, Kelsen does not mention it, one should add that typically the amendment rule of a confederation or league's constitution would require unanimity and a right to exit.

By contrast, a *federal legal order (state)* in Kelsen's taxonomy "presents a degree of decentralization that is still compatible with a legal community constituted by national law, that is, with a State and a degree of centralization that is no longer compatible with an international legal community constituted by international law."[147] This certainly involves making the external internal: the law of the federal state is national and domestic not international and foreign. Although sometimes founded on the basis of a treaty, the *legal basis* of a federal state is its own constitution and it is an autonomous legal subject with international legal personality. It is sovereign, member states are not. It develops competences from its own constitution; these are not derived from or delegated by the member states' legal orders. *Legislation* in a federal state differs as we have seen from a unitary state only in terms of the degree of centralization. The *legislative body* typically consists of *two houses*, one directly elected by all the people of the federal state, the second chosen either by the people or by the legislative organ of each component state. Thus both states and individuals are represented in the central legislative organ. The fact that each component state typically is represented in an upper house indicates the ideal-typical origin of a federal state through an international treaty concluded by independent states indicating their aim to be dealt with according to the international law principle of equality of states.[148] But since legislation even in the "upper" house typically proceeds by the *majority principle*, this element of decentralization is almost completely neutralized and the legislative organ is divested of its international character.[149] Constitutional change also proceeds via (qualified) majority. *Jurisdiction* in a federal state typically involves a system of *federal courts* alongside the courts of the component states. Crucially a supreme court is competent not only to settle conflicts between the component states but also for the settlement of certain conflicts and the punishment of certain crimes of private individuals. Moreover the federal government can *execute sanctions* against individuals and against component states if their organs violate the constitution of the federation (which doubles as the constitution of the whole). Typically member states in a federal state have nothing to do with foreign affairs. Instead there is an *executive centralization of all foreign affairs*. The relevant armed forces are organs of the federation under command of the head of the federal state. It is exclusively the latter that makes treaties. Typically there is also centralized competence with respect to economic matters including the establishment of a single customs and currency unit and levying of taxes, and obligations to military service directly onto individuals. Indeed, *citizenship* in a federal state is federal (national) such that each individual is a citizen of a certain component by virtue of being a citizen of the Federation. The federal polity is thus composed of member states and of individuals. Federal laws obligate and authorize individuals directly without any mediation of local norms and thus have what is today called *direct effect*. It is this especially that proves for Kelsen that the legal order of a federal state is national and not international.[150] Member states of a federal state are typically not subjects at international law. The constitution of the Federation is, moreover, *supreme* and there is no right to exit from a federal state.

Kelsen concludes his analysis with a brief discussion of the forces pushing federal states to become ever more centralized and to morph into unitary states: Once the entire foreign policy is in the hands of the central organs, and given the fact that international treaties can relate to any subject matter, enforcement of treaties leads federations to interfere ever more frequently into the competence of member states. This together with the centralization of state control over economic life fosters political centralization and a leveling of cultural differences among member states. To be sure Kelsen also notes that unitary states can turn into federal ones, as in the case of Austria. But this does not seem to him to be the dominant trend.

The spartan elegance of this taxonomic approach notwithstanding, it has two serious drawbacks. First, as already indicated, the decentralization/centralization axis screens out what is distinctive normatively and structurally to the federal organizational principle, and second, it leaves us with an impoverished range of ideal types at the cost of analytic clarity with respect to new (and old) political formations and their distinctive legitimation issues, something irrelevant to the juridical perspective of Kelsen in any case. To be sure it would be possible to fit every relevant empirical political formation on the spectrum confederation–federal–unitary state, if one tweaked the variables sufficiently with most appearing as hybrids. But the conceptual apparatus is still too constraining and leads to aporia.[151] While Kelsen's approach is distinctive it nonetheless operates with the classic statist model that sees only states (federal or unitary) or international organizations (alliances, confederations, etc.) with nothing in between. Let me briefly discuss these drawbacks and then turn to the alternatives.

2.2.3 Critique of the decentralization model

The heart of the problem with attempts (not only of Kelsen's but of much of twentieth-century political science) to understand federalism in terms of the decentralization/centralization axis is that its three constitutive principles – non-hierarchy (normative), associative polycentricity (structural), shared rule and self-rule (normative and structural) – are located on an entirely different axis and thus hidden from view in this taxonomic approach.[152] The center–periphery model underlying the latter is ultimately hierarchical and monist. Implicitly or explicitly, decentralization is understood along the lines of delegation. Accordingly the central government or legal order can centralize or decentralize at will and the diffusion of power and local norm-making capacity is a matter of grace, not of right. By contrast the federal idea involves the mutual recognition of the integrity of each partner, and a special form of unity among them that is regulated by the federal pact.[153] Indeed to most theorists of federation the concept of "foedus" from which the term "federal" derives and which means pact or covenant, is not incidental but constitutive of a federal polity.[154] This is because it entails and institutes a special form of agreement (a constitutional contract) that involves contractual, constitutional, and institutional relationships that permeate the whole structure.[155] The federal principle involves the constitutional diffusion of power in a way that secures the existence and authority of both the general and constituent governing bodies. This perforce entails participation in the decision-making of the common government while its activity is conducted in such a way as to maintain the respective autonomy and integrity of the component or member states.[156] Hence, the ongoing negotiation over competences and constitutional issues that is typical in federal polities.

The polycentric matrix model of federalism developed by defenders of the uniqueness of federal as contrasted with unitary states makes sense of this principle. According to one eminent analyst, the correct way to think about the federal polity is in terms of *non-centralization*, not decentralization.[157] In other words, unlike a hierarchical normative or power pyramid, in a matrix there are multiple centers and power is structurally diffused such that it *cannot be legitimately* centralized or concentrated without breaking the structure and spirit of the constitution.[158] The relation among the component entities is not hierarchically fixed: rather it is, in principle, heterarchical. However, this does not mean that unity should be counter-posed to diversity; indeed from this perspective it makes little sense to classify states as unitary versus federal, as per the classical approach. For what gets lost is the fact that federal polities combine unity with plurality and/or diversity. The unity, however, is de-centered and non-hierarchical while the plurality is political (and territorial) and constitutionally entrenched. As one analyst aptly put it, this is why

> federalism is not to be located on the centralization–decentralization continuum but on a different continuum altogether, one that is predicated on non-centralization, or the effective combination of unity and diversity ... Unity should be contrasted with disunity and diversity with homogeneity.[159]

As already indicated federalism is deemed a device to accommodate diversity as a legitimate element in a polity although the question remains open as to what kinds of diversity are compatible with federal unity and which are not.[160] Instead of construing diversity as a disadvantage and political integration as a matter of building a strong center to which the more closely tied the peripheries the better; instead of viewing federal arrangements as unimportant or as a way station toward full integration, as per the decentralization–centralization continuum; instead of viewing competences and capacities as delegated either from the center to the periphery (federal state) or the reverse (con-federal international association) – one should take the federal principles, structures, and purposes seriously, in their own terms. Doing so would enable one to grasp the legitimacy problematic specific to federations and to assess at what point a federal legal form masks a centralized concentration of power or governmental processes that contradict it; and at what point the federal principle of association – a polycentric union of a plurality of discrete "relatively autonomous" polities – is hidden but operative and/or called for in a given organizational and political framework. This approach also allows one to screen in the legitimacy principles distinctive to federal unions.

Until very recently, however, even those who rejected the centralization/decentralization paradigm continued to associate a federal polity with a state and to counter-pose this particular state form to non-federal states on the one side, and to confederations understood as loose international linkages of polities that retain their sovereignty even within a permanent league, on the other.[161] Indeed that is why they too ultimately assume that to get round the problematic "para-logism" of dual sovereignty within a federal state, one has to drop the discourse of state sovereignty altogether. In other words, it is assumed that so long as one operates with the concept of sovereignty, it is impossible to grasp the federal principle or to account for a federal polity/state. Accordingly, and typically, sovereignty is understood as a particular type of "statist" discourse, entailing a hierarchical centralized structure of rule- and law-making that locates authority in a single center (the central government and unitary legal system).[162] The paradigmatic case is, of course, France and the Jacobin-republican model of integration and assimilation. In order to understand a distribution of powers that is not a matter of decentralization from such a center, it is assumed that the concept of state sovereignty as such has to go. The alternative to this "seventeenth-century" European view of the sovereign state, so the argument goes, apparently was discovered and implemented first by the Americans who understood sovereignty to be vested in the people.

> Thus it was possible for the sovereign people to delegate powers to the general and constituent governments without normally running into the problem of which possesses sovereignty except in matters of international relations or the like. In matters of internal or domestic governance it was possible to avoid the issue except when political capital could be made out of it.[163]

In this way one could have one's cake and eat it too; i.e. by removing sovereignty from the state as such and lodging it with the people one could arrange for power sharing, and set limits on governmental authority while aspiring to the same goals of political unification and integration as the Jacobin state.[164] Popular sovereignty vests authority in the people who may delegate governmental powers to whichever level and in whatever form they choose.

The flaw in this analysis is rather obvious as soon as one notes that the Jacobins also located sovereignty in the people. Thus the issue of sovereignty in a federal state is in no way resolved by switching to the discourse of popular sovereignty, it is merely displaced. To put this another way, the solution first adumbrated in the *Federalist Papers* and recently reproduced by Elazar that shifts sovereignty from the state to the people, who can allocate or delegate sovereign powers (competences) among the various instances of government in their polity as they wish only resolves the problem of organ sovereignty. As every analyst of American debates over federalism until at least 1865 knows, however, the crucial issue in the shift to the discourse of popular sovereignty as per the opening phrase in the American constitution that ascribes it to "we the people," is which people? Does "the people" refer to the peoples of the several states or does it refer to a national demos composed of individual citizens or to a combination thereof?[165] While it is true that it was possible to avoid a definitive resolution to this issue for some time, as is well known, a great deal of ink was spilled and finally, blood shed over it in the US. At issue is not only an empirical conundrum of a deeply divided society unable to remain together on terms acceptable to each side (i.e. the wrong kind of internal diversity). Rather the point is that the shift to a discourse of popular sovereignty does not resolve the conceptual problem. As is obvious in the case of France, a republican state based on the legitimation principle of popular sovereignty and the separation of powers is nonetheless a sovereign state: its legal order is autonomous on the outside, supreme and hierarchical on the inside. In the case of a federal polity, the discourse of popular sovereignty finesses but does not resolve questions regarding the sovereignty of the member state(s) or of the center. It does not supply an answer to questions about the autonomy and supremacy of the constitutional legal/political orders within a federal polity, or about the structural nature of their relationship. Only by virtue of an ultimately anachronistic reading from the perspective of the twentieth-century American federal *state* in which the issue of *the locus of sovereignty is basically resolved*, thanks in part to the nationalization of citizenship and of the demos in the aftermath of the Civil War, can one claim that the sovereignty of the people refers to the individualized national demos.[166] But such a state-centric mode of reasoning, despite its insights into the distinctiveness of the federal principle, is too quick. For the claim that popular sovereignty is located in an individualized national demos reintroduces monism on the most basic level – that of the "constituent power" – along with the logic of delegation that the structural polycentric matrix model sought to avoid in the first place. The problem stems from an exclusive analytic focus on the distinction between federal and non-federal *states* and the effort to develop a comparative taxonomy of *state* federalisms. The phenomenon (and concept) of a union of states that is not equivalent to a federal state but is other than an ordinary alliance or international organization raises conceptual and normative issues that escape both this and the centralization/decentralization approaches.[167] Indeed as we shall see, in federal unions that are not states, but which are unions of states and peoples (in the political-theoretical sense) the issue of the locus of constituent power remains quite pressing.

2.3 Federal union as a distinctive political form: the sovereignty-centered approach

As indicated above, there are two "non-statist" approaches to the theory of federation: one for which the sovereignty problematic is central, and one for which it is deemed irrelevant. Both build their ideal types of political formations along an axis distinct from the centralization/decentralization approach. Both reject Kelsenian monism and insist on the distinctiveness of the federal organizational principle particularly insofar as it is not based on a hierarchical relation between the legal and political orders of member states and that of the federal union. Yet in distinction from statist-centric federalists, both develop a taxonomy of ideal types that takes seriously the concept of a federal union of states as a distinctive type of political formation and response to the pressures of size. I begin with the sovereignty-oriented approach and turn in the next section to the alternative, discussing the strengths and weaknesses of each. I will argue that both models are flawed because both operate with a "Westphalian" conception of sovereignty – the first embraces the concept as the key to the political dynamics (and instability) of federal unions, the second rejects it because it is deemed irrelevant to the (non-hierarchical) organizational structure of such polities. I want to square the circle. I argue that if one abandons the absolutist and political-theological conception of sovereignty one can account for the object-language of actors within federal unions (that indeed involves sovereignty claims) while maintaining a sophisticated meta-framework able to theorize the non-hierarchical organizational, legal, and political structure of federal unions that is not a prisoner of, yet is responsive to, that language. I conclude by arguing for a more nuanced and flexible approach that does not throw out the sovereignty baby with the statist bathwater.

The most original attempt in the early twentieth century to develop a constitutional theory of federal unions of states as a distinct political form is that of Carl Schmitt.[168] Schmitt's interest was triggered by the emergence of the League of Nations, which he deemed to be a "misleading and sham enterprise," insofar as it purported to be more than an international alliance – i.e. a "volkerbund" (the German term for the League) akin to a federal union committed to cosmopolitan values such as world peace and minority rights. The League in his view was not a genuine federation given its composition of ultimately self-interested sovereign states with heterogeneous political regimes despite the unconvincing universal moral pretensions of the imperialist great powers controlling it. Schmitt's analysis of federations of states that are not themselves states was obviously intended to show the impossibility of a universal, cosmopolitan "bund" (federation) and to deny that status to the League of Nations.[169] Nevertheless he saw that claims regarding the League raised fundamental questions as to the core features, conditions of possibility, and legitimacy of a "real" bund (Schmitt's word for a federation of states that is distinct from a federal state).[170] These are what interest us here.

Anyone who has read *The Concept of the Political* or *The* Nomos *of the Earth* knows Schmitt's views on international law, the discourse of human rights, the League of Nations, the United Nations, and the, to him, purely ideological notion of universalistic impartial international or global law able to bind political power (states, the great powers) to legally valid norms. Regarding human rights: "he who says humanity wants to cheat" was his well-known dictum.[171] Treaties among sovereign states are discrete strategic particular acts in his view, not evidence of an international community based on shared universal values, or a cosmopolitan constitution. To be sure, Schmitt did think that the nineteenth-century European international society of sovereign states ascribing one another equal rights to make international law, wage war, and to acquire colonies constituted a "nomos," an international political order centered in Europe, that regulated its affairs through conferences and through European common law, the *jus publicum Europaeum* – which was supposedly binding upon sovereigns.[172] Nevertheless, whatever international laws, norms, or rules such an order generated could not be abstracted from a concrete power-political arrangement. As he insists in the opening pages of the fourth section of *Constitutional Theory*, the customary or conventional rules comprising international law ordered relations of mere coexistence: they did not establish a deep connection between all states.[173] The twentieth-century concept of international legal community or family of nations is to Schmitt only the logical cognate of these relations of coexistence:

> The international legal community is not a contract nor is it based on a contract. It is also not an alliance and still less a federation. It does not have a constitution in the distinctive sense. It is, instead, the reflex of the politically plural universe.[174]

Accordingly, no constitutional issues are raised by ordinary treaty-making, or by observance of customary international law, on this account.

One would think upon a cursory reading of *Constitutional Theory*, given the tight link of the positive concept of constitution (Schmitt's own) to the state, to the concept of constituent power and ultimately to sovereignty, that Schmitt gives us even more reasons to avoid constitutional discourse or the application of the moniker "political" for the inter-state associations, regional or global. The positive concept of constitution involves a concrete political decision, not a norm; it is the choice by the constituent power (monarch or more relevant for our purposes, a politically united people) of the political form of its own existence.[175] Accordingly a *state* is the political unity of a people, both of which precede and are presupposed by the legalistic concept of constitution in the sense of legal norms, higher law, or constitutionalism.[176] The validity of the constitution as a legal order – as a system of higher legal norms – derives from the legitimacy of the fundamental political form embodied in but irreducible to that legal order. The state is understood existentially, with reference to the political will of a people to exist politically and to determine its political form of existence. The positive concept of constitution refers to this political decision over political form. Given Schmitt's political-existential concept of sovereignty – "sovereign means that a foreigner cannot decide the question of political existence" – a sovereign state must be construed as self-determining regarding its constitutional order and political form, impermeable, and impenetrable, standing apart from others and bearing alone the decision regarding its political existence (form) (ascribable to the constituent power of a politically united demos or people) including the all-important autonomous determination of the friend/enemy distinction.[177]

Indeed Schmitt challenged the legalistic redefinition of sovereignty described in Chapter 1 and ridiculed the Kelsenian reduction of the state to the domestic legal system.[178] He sought to replace the anachronistic absolutist model based on the omnipotence of the embodiment of organ sovereignty and constituent power (the monarch), the "wrong political theology," not with legalisms, but with another, better political theology, focused on the exception and the sovereign as he who decides the exception, analogized with the miracle in theology. Understood as the capacity to decide (a) that an exception exists, i.e. that there is an existential conflict facing the state and (b) who the enemy of the political community is, sovereignty accordingly pertains to existential issues that are not amenable to legal resolution. Schmitt grants that sovereignty, constitutionalism, and the rule of law are not incompatible in the ordinary functioning of the state and that the latter's constitution can distribute competences among various organs and separate powers, with no loss of sovereignty. For such jurisdictional disputes even over the locus of the competence to decide the competences of state organs ("Kompetenz-Kompetenz" in German) are, normally, in normal times, not at the heart of the sovereignty problematic. Sovereignty and constitutionalism, the rule of law, and the separation and division of powers are perfectly compatible in the ordinary functioning of a sovereign state.

Nevertheless, on Schmitt's redefinition of sovereignty, even if a constitutional order is based on the separation of powers and does not assign any single agent sovereign authority to make an unconstrained "decision," this does not mean that no such agent exists. Rather, it means that the identity of the sovereign will be revealed in a crisis, in the context of an exceptional situation. Indeed, Schmitt's version of the shift from the absolutist monarchical model to popular sovereignty, unlike earlier anti-absolutist constitutionalists, resurrects the core of the idea of organ sovereignty with respect to the people and turns democratic legitimacy into a new political theology.[179] Popular sovereignty is construed in a populist way that constructs "the people" (the constituent power) as a homogeneous macro-subject, a unity based on shared substantive characteristics (ascribed to and embraced by them) and endowed with a will that can and indeed must be embodied in a single sovereign representative (insofar as the people cannot act), in cases of exceptional emergency. Democracy entails equality for equals understood as sameness and homogeneity such that fundamental politically salient social divisions among the people are not tolerable in a sovereign democratic state. Democratic legitimacy of the sovereign representative means that the latter has been able to attain an identity, or identification with the people, and to embody its will.[180] The people as constituent power are postulated as unified and with a will, but unlike monarchy: on the old principle of legitimacy in which sovereignty and constituent power were merged into one figure (organ), the people cannot act. The people can, however, acclaim their sovereign representative who can take decisive action including the determination that an emergency or an exception exists.

This plebiscitary model at the heart of Schmitt's theory of popular sovereignty and sovereign dictatorship is ultimately a unitary embodiment model that posits sovereignty as indivisible and *legibus solutus* on two levels: the constituent power and the power of the sovereign dictator. When necessary, the sovereign representative of the sovereign people can use the latter's *legibus solutus* prerogative to recreate unity when he or she determines that internal division has become existentially threatening or in light of grave outside threats. A constitution may or may not contain laws stipulating emergency powers or ascribing them to an organ of the state to preserve the constitution in cases of crisis. Schmitt's existential conception of sovereignty does not pertain to this level of constitutional law, be it implicit or explicit. It revives the idea of organ sovereignty with respect to exceptions, linking it to the concept of sovereign dictatorship, which may not only suspend constitutional laws, but also radically transform the constitution in the name of the constituent power, the "sovereign" people. Thus, in *Constitutional Theory*, the discussion of internal sovereignty became quite nuanced, splitting into the theory of the constituent power and its sovereign representative.[181] But it remains the case that the constitution is construed as the product of the act and will of the constituent power, the people, that gives the state its political form and that the people is understood under the sign of unity: i.e. the will to live together in a political way as a unified political community. The sovereign representative embodies this will and acts so as to preserve that unity, political existence, and political form. Finally let us recall that for Schmitt, a sovereign state by definition is a territorial state that has the *jus belli*. Sovereignty entails the "right" to self-defense, which if conclusively renounced by a state, means that it does not have its own political existence.[182]

How, then, given all this, is it possible for Schmitt to apply the concept of political form to a union of states as well as to its members which at least partially gives up *the jus belli*, and which is typically the product of a treaty (the federal pact), or to refer to the latter as a constitution and which is composed of several political communities? For the above notwithstanding, Schmitt does theorize the *constitutional* form and structure of an inter-state union of states (bund) as distinctive *political form* in terms of the sovereignty problematic. This is so, despite his rejection as oxymoronic of the concept of semi-sovereign states, or of divided or pooled sovereignty.

Schmitt was clearly writing in reaction to the dominant approach both in German Staatslehre and in international law, that looked at federal constitutional forms in terms of the dichotomy mentioned above: either a confederation (staatenbund) seen as an international alliance or a federal state (bundesstaat) – a consolidated, constitutional municipal legal order with international legal standing.[183] Schmitt's interest was not in the distinction between a federal state and a unitary state – two species of the same genus (state) – for these raise no fundamental questions from his sovereignty-oriented perspective insofar as the locus of sovereignty is resolved in both of them. But he understood that federal phenomena raised new and important constitutional questions of *political form* in the international arena that escape the above binary. He thus rejected the statist paradigm informing the conceptual framework with which the debate around German federal theory of his day operated (confederation/federal state) arguing that it was motivated by polemical considerations, namely the effort to differentiate the 1871 constitution of the German Empire (a state) from the German bund of 1815 (deemed a mere confederation).[184] Schmitt's own polemical purposes notwithstanding, however, his conceptual analysis is innovative and insightful and has the merit of centering on the core constitutional issues that any regional or global federal project perforce raises.

Thus, instead of following German Staatslehre, he drew his inspiration from nineteenth-century American debates about the nature of federal union for which the issue of the locus of sovereignty was central. What interested Schmitt in these debates is that the protagonists sought to conceptualize a federal union of states as a body politic with a specific political-constitutional form, distinct from an international treaty organization and from a consolidated federal state, thus directly confronting the conceptual and political issues such a polity raises.

While he admired and drew upon the work especially of John C. Calhoun, however, Schmitt tried to avoid what has been called the "Calhounian dilemma."[185] That dilemma is presented as a stark either/or: in a federal union, either the central state must be sovereign, or the member states must be sovereign. *Tertium non datur.* What is intriguing about the Schmittian model is that it breaks with this binary while nonetheless developing a sovereignty-oriented taxonomy of political-constitutional forms which foregrounds federal union (bund) as a distinct ideal type of non-state polity. Schmitt praises Calhoun for developing the "essential concepts of a constitutional theory for a federation, with the aid of which one should recognize the distinctiveness of certain political formations."[186] Yet he explicitly criticizes Calhoun's analysis of the American federal union insofar as it presented the member states as sovereign – a claim he deemed incorrect on conceptual and not only empirical grounds. However, he also rejected the opposite position (of Webster and Lincoln among others), namely that sovereignty lay with the federal union rather than with the member states. Referring to Calhoun, he stated: "This theory . . . is incorrect, because it presents the member states as sovereign, not the federation, which is just as unfair to the distinctiveness of the federation as the opposite claim."[187]

How is Schmitt able to square the circle – i.e. to construct a non-statist, yet sovereignty-based conception of a bund? There is a deeper way to pose this question. Like the Americans prior to the Civil War, Schmitt's concern is with *political legitimacy* underlying specific constitutional forms and this is why he deems the sovereignty problematic to be central. *Indeed in the epoch of popular sovereignty, he, like the Americans before him, had to ask how it is possible to attribute a constitution to a demos, the sine qua non for legitimacy of any political form, while avoiding construal of the polity thereby constituted as the state of a single people and thus sovereign.* How can one deem member states of a political unity to be states if the federal union they construct is ascribed the *jus belli?* How can member states of a *political unity* still be sovereign, autonomous political entities, if their constitutional orders are penetrated by the constitutional order of the federation, if the latter can enforce its decisions and sanction non-compliance by member states, and if the former at least partially give up the *jus belli* within the federation? How can a bund be a political form with its own constitution imputable to a constitution-making power, a demos, if it is not a federal state?

Schmitt's concept of the federation (bund) attempts to answer these questions through the development of a tripartite taxonomy organized around the locus of sovereignty, and focused on analyzing a bund as a distinct type of polity. Accordingly, a bund constitutes a form of inter-state relations which is differentiated from an international law-based alliance or treaty organization (bundniss), and from a federal state (bundesstaat). In an international alliance (bundniss) as in any inter-state treaty organization, sovereignty is vested in the states, i.e. in the units. As such, entry into an alliance does not alter the political status of a member state or its constitution. International agreements pertain to particular state goals, like reciprocal trade arrangements, or they establish organizations, like a postal union, but these do not affect the sovereignty of the state in any profound way. Ideal-typically they remain functional agencies of states serving state purposes. Even if one considers an alliance that obligates a state to go to war, the latter's *jus belli* is contractually bound only with respect to a particular case. Thus though war involves political existence and the ultimate decisive expression of the political element, so long as the *jus belli* itself is not conclusively renounced or turned over to a third party, the constitutional order of the alliance member is not affected. Entering into an alliance is a foreign political act of which only a politically existing sovereign state is capable under international law and thus involves the exercise of an authority already presupposed in each sovereign state's constitution![188] Accordingly an alliance has no collective will or political existence in Schmitt's sense.[189] The rest of the typical features of an alliance (or of a confederation understood as an alliance) described earlier follow from this. The contract or treaty that is the legal basis of the alliance is a pure international law arrangement that does not effect a constitutional change in member states' constitutions; the jurisdiction and competences of any international organization established via an alliance are limited and delegated by the sovereign member states; if any legislative body is established it is typically a conference of the parties; and there is typically no direct effect, supremacy, right to intervene in member states, or citizenship within such an organization. The territories of the member states do not become the territory of the alliance or international organization under such contractual arrangements and the latter does not acquire sovereignty. States can exit at will assuming they fulfill their contractual obligations. Finally any change to the contractual legal order established by an alliance typically requires unanimity: this is what ensures and actualizes the contractual nature of the union.

By contrast, in a federal state, as in any state, sovereignty is vested in the center, meaning that the state as a whole is sovereign, not its component parts, however decentralized it may be. For Schmitt, as indicated, sovereignty pertains to the political self-determination of a politically organized people and to the entity they establish. Insofar as a federal state is a state, it is the political expression of a single people and rests on their constitution-making power, i.e. there is one demos that is the "constituent power" in any federal state that rests on the principle of democratic as distinct from monarchical legitimacy.[190] This means that for Schmitt the distinction between a federal and a unitary state, in which he exhibited little interest insofar as it does not pertain to the question of sovereignty, is primarily a matter of the mode of organizing a state. In a democratic constitutional federal state, the "federal" institutional dimension involves a complicated system of separation and division of powers, but this is, in Schmitt's view, really little more than the complement of liberal, rule of law principles.[191] Schmitt does grant that federal states are a distinctive type of state.[192] Nevertheless, even if it has a federal foundation etched in the constitution, even if its origin is in a federal union, once the "decision" has been taken (or facts have evolved such) that the federal polity is to be construed as the state of a politically united people (the positive decision concerning the type of political existence), its federal features become superficial. Indeed in a federal state insofar as there is only a single people (one demos to whom the constitution is ascribed), the state character of the member states is eliminated: " in a state whose type and form of political existence rests on the constitution-making will of the entire people, there can be no more than *one* political unity."[193] Member states are deprived of independent decision over their political existence and become only organizational components of a perhaps extensive legislative autonomy and self-government.[194]

Schmitt spends no time describing the internal features of federal states or what distinguishes them from unitary states: ultimately an unimportant distinction from his point of view. But it is obvious that like all states, a federal state has as its legal basis a constitution, not a treaty, its jurisdiction is original and comprehensive, its legislative body and arrangements can vary but must include representatives of individual citizens, not only of member units, its law is supreme, has direct effect, and citizenship is individualized and nationalized.[195] The center controls foreign policy, member "states" do not have independent political existence, the *jus belli*, international legal standing, or the right to make independent foreign policy, and there is no right of exit. From the sovereignty-centered perspective, this is what makes it different from a federation of states: "There is, consequently, only *one* political unity, while in every genuine federation ... a multitude of political unities continue to exist alongside the federation."[196]

What, then, are the distinctive features of a federation (bund) on this model? The last sentence already provides much of the answer. Schmitt's ideal type of a federation (bund) as a unique political form involves a mode of integration and set of relationships quite different from those obtaining in a bundniss (treaty organization under international law) or in a federal state (bundesstaat). Most crucially, he maintains that in a federal union of states (bund), the locus of sovereignty is undecided between the center and the units. "It is part of the essence of the federation, however, that the question of sovereignty between federation and member state always remains open as long as the federation as such exists alongside the member states as such."[197] In other words the distinctive feature of this constitutional political form is that the final (ultimate) decision as to which level is sovereign is deferred. Members act and interact in such a way as to avoid or resolve conflicts that would force them to conclusively confront and settle the issue. *But what can this mean and how is this conceivable in a sovereignty-centered theory?*

Schmitt defines a federation (bund) as a permanent association that rests on a free agreement and that serves the common goal of the political self-preservation of all member states.[198] However, he also maintains that the comprehensive status of each federal member in political terms is changed insofar as they enter into (and willingly construct) a new and autonomous legal and political community. Indeed he insists that entry into a federation entails a change of every member state's constitution irrespective of whether any of the words therein are altered. "[I]t is far more important that the constitution in the positive sense, in other words the concrete content of the fundamental political decisions on the entire manner of existence of the state is nevertheless essentially changed."[199] The states become transformed into members of a new political totality but they remain, nonetheless, Schmitt insists, states in the full sense of the word.

In order to understand why these assertions are not contradictory, one has to inquire into the special nature of the federal pact. Indeed, and this is one of

Schmitt's most interesting contributions to the theory of federation, the federal pact must be understood in dualist terms as must the unique type of polity and legal order it establishes. The federal pact or "bundesvertrag" is a "constitutional treaty" that creates a unique dualist order and which accommodates a dual set of goals characteristic of every federation of states: to wit to maintain the political existence of its members while creating a new political unity with its own political existence and purposes, to which they belong. In other words, what the sovereignty-oriented perspective reveals is that the foundational legal order, the political existences it relates and creates, and the purposes for which a federation is formed are all essentially and fundamentally dualistic. The dualist logic of federation is what links the international and the domestic, the external and the internal in a unique political formation.

The dual character of the "constitutional contract" at the foundation of a bund is evident from the terms: contract, constitutional. *It is through this unique form of agreement that the external is made internal without, however, entirely abolishing the equal political autonomy of member states.* The contractual (treaty) dimension pertains to the voluntary decision of each state (as sovereign) to join and become a member of the federation. This is the international law component. The constitutional dimension refers both to the product of the contract (the treaty as the federation's constitution along with the institutions it establishes such as the legislative body, courts, and so on) but also to the fact that once they join up, states are integrated into a politically comprehensive system with respect to general purposes.[200] This is why their sovereign decision to join requires domestic constitutional change. Thus this dimension escapes the "free contract" aspect, for the pact does not simply regulate discrete and definable individual relations as per an alliance or as per ordinary international treaties under international law. Accordingly the constitutional contract is called by Schmitt an "interstate *status contract*."[201] This is the internal public constitutional law component.

The constitutional contract constructs an autonomous, constitutional legal and institutional order for the organized federal polity and thereby renders internal the relevant relations among the member states whose conflicts must now be resolved peacefully through law. The law (and relations) of the federation is public and constitutional, not external or international. In other words its political and legal order is autonomous, supreme in its constitutionally specified functional domains, endowed with the competence to use its powers enumerated in the constitutional treaty, and the member states are bound by its subsequent decisions whether or not they ratify them individually. In the terms discussed above, federation law has direct effect.[202] As Schmitt puts it, the will of the federation is directly the will of every member state and even if voting is still by unanimity (though typically in a federation legislative body it is on the basis of qualified majority) federal law needs no special ratification by the individual states. Every member state and its courts are bound directly and in public law terms by the federal decision because the federal constitution is a component of its own constitution![203] Moreover, the federation may intervene in member states to enforce its law with regard to its specific functions. In this respect the internal order of the member states is no longer impermeable as they are in an alliance. Yet the constitutional orders of the states and of the federation are not merged: instead there is a composite constitutional arrangement that links them while leaving their autonomy intact.

The dual institutional make-up of a federation is also distinctive. As a political unity the federation must be represented: typically it will have an assembly of the representatives of the political unities, the member states, which form the federation, along with executive organs for administrative and enforcement work and perhaps a court to adjudicate conflicts among member states and between them and the federation over competences and the like. Representation is no insignificant matter. The federal political community thereby attains a political existence internally and externally. Schmitt insists furthermore that the federation must have a territory, consisting of the territories of the member states, and also, within or alongside these, its own territorial possessions ranging from the seat of government or, in the case of imperial federations, to external possessions. This means that the institutions and being of the federation exist *alongside* those of the member states.[204]

One of the prime purposes in federating and hence a key goal of a federation is to guarantee the political existence of each member state and thus to protect its members against the outside and from one another. The federation obtains the *jus belli* via the federal pact, typically coupled with a commitment to the welfare of all its members. This entails that internally the federation ensures civil peace: federation members permanently give up self-help and the *jus belli* vis-à-vis one another: war may not take place between federation members otherwise the federation is destroyed. This is another reason why constitutional change is involved in federating. Internally there is only federal enforcement action or execution of federal law against a recalcitrant state, not war: the former external international relations among member states thereby become internal. Insofar as the federation acquires the *jus belli* it has an independent political existence and is a subject at international law. But although a federation has *a jus belli*, this need not mean that it has an *exclusive jus belli* vis-à-vis the outside. In other words, this does not preclude the possibility that member states retain the *jus belli* vis-à-vis non-members alongside that of the federation. Schmitt states that "individual members need not be deprived of the possibility of conducting war against nonmembers."[205]

Indeed, member states retain their autonomous legal and political existence. It is the express purpose and constitutive nature of a federation that it preserves and respects their political self-determination, legal autonomy, and territory. Accordingly, from their own point of view, the member states' political existence *does not derive from*, nor does the validity of their legal systems and constitutions inhere in, the constitutional contract. *The latter is not in a hierarchical relation to the former despite its supremacy with respect to law-making within its constitutionally specified domain and despite having direct effect and even implied powers.* This autonomy is expressed in the fact that typically member states' powers are not enumerated or functionally delimited in the constitutional contract of the federation although certain prerogatives can be withdrawn from their domestic jurisdiction. Competences of this sort, however, do not pertain to sovereignty for Schmitt.[206] Within the federation the political status quo in the sense of the political existence of each state must be guaranteed and normally the guarantee of territorial integrity is part of this: no federation member can have a part of its territory taken or its political existence eliminated without its consent. The political existence (and territorial integrity) of member states in a genuine federation cannot be altered or abolished either through the ordinary legislative process or through constitutional amendment.[207] This is evidence of the contractual dimension of a federal constitutional order. These guarantees stem, according to Schmitt, from the goal of self-preservation and the concept of duration (permanence) that is essential to a federal union.[208]

> The essence of the federation resides in a dualism of political existence, in a connection between federalist togetherness and political unity, on the one hand, and in the persistence of majority, a pluralism of individual political unities, on the other.[209]

The purposes of a federation are also dualistic in this basic sense: there are the goals pertaining to the interests of the member states in maintaining their political existence and autonomy and there are the goals pertaining to the federation as a politically existing body with an interest in its own autonomy and duration, and in the welfare and security of the overall political community that it instantiates.

This is so irrespective of the fact that there can be no federation without involvement in the affairs of member states. Indeed precisely because the federation has a political existence it must have a "right of supervision" and to intervene.[210] Conflicts over competences, over implied powers, over jurisdictions are inevitable in a federation including over the competence to decide upon competence – a concept which did not interest Schmitt much insofar as it does not pertain to the issue of the locus of sovereignty itself. To be sure "competence-competence" of the federation can refer to the constitutional jurisdiction for constitutional amendment, i.e. for the revision of constitutional provisions, but this is bound by the constitution itself and thus does not ordinarily raise the sovereignty issue. Probably this is why Schmitt never directly addressed the question of the appropriate amendment rule for a federation although he did give clues regarding it. Nevertheless he was aware that it is possible to exploit the possibility of constitutional revision so as to entirely transform the political status of member states, and hence to transform a federation into a federal state.[211] It would thus seem logical that the ideal-typical amendment rule of a federation should reflect its position between a confederation and a federal state.[212] Whereas for a confederation (bundniss or staatenbund), the amending powers, the states, are outside the treaty and classically, amending the treaty requires unanimity, in the case of a federal state, the "states" are within the constitution and can be treated as organs of the federal union with respect to the federal constitution. Thus an ideal-typical federal state's constitutional amendment rule could involve the use of a federal senate but its ratification would rely on individual voters of each member state. For a federation of states the amendment rule, as for a confederation, would have to retain the states as the sources of fundamental legal change (the treaty component) but the constitutional dimension of the pact would have to entail that a qualified majority of these formally equal states (one state–one vote) would be able to bind the minority. This is a way of bringing all the states into the constitution while ensuring that they remain in some sense the authors of it. A federation thus would have, from the state's perspective, a single source of ultimate legitimacy: its constitutional authorities remain the member states.

Yet it would seem that from the perspective of the federation as a whole whose fundamental law the constitution is, amendment via a qualified majority of states (voting state by state through conventions or referenda) would mean that they are acting as the organs of the federation, on its constitutional authority. A good example of a federation amendment rule is the ratification portion of the US constitution's Article 5, the ultimate hurdle in the amendment process.[213] Today the US is a federal state, yet the US constitution has the amendment rule of a federation. Indeed Schmitt refers to Article 5's requirement that a qualified majority of states is needed for constitutional change, thus that a minority can block the change, together with its absolute entrenchment of equal votes of each state in the Senate, as indicative of the *federal* (bundish) character of the constitution, established in the period when the US polity in his view was a federal union (bund), not a federal state.[214] Ideal-typically, as already indicated, abolishing the political existence or territorial basis of member states without their consent would have to be off-limits to the amendment process: otherwise their independent political existence and thus the basic structure of the constitutional compact and the federal principle would be violated.[215] The abolition of a member state without its consent is, as already indicated, possible in a federal state for the loss of genuine political existence of the former is already the case but it is not possible in a genuine federation.

Thanks to the thesis of the dualism of political existence, Schmitt assumed his sovereignty-centered approach can avoid the "Calhounian dilemma."

As we have seen, sovereignty for Schmitt pertains to the autonomy and self-determination of a political community, a state, as to its political form and to existential questions of friend and enemy. Membership in a federation renders the external internal, the foreigner into the friend. Yet sovereignty cannot be divided or shared. Nevertheless, it is not a solution to try to banish the issue of sovereignty from a federation because, thanks to its dualistic structure, existential conflicts remain possible. Thus, in a genuine federation, Schmitt insists, "sovereignty is not absent."[216] Pace Calhoun, however, nor is it unequivocally located in the member states for this would approximate a federation too closely to an international alliance (bundniss) misconstruing its dual structure of political existences. While Calhoun was right in Schmitt's view against those who insisted that the US federal constitution could be ascribed to a united national people, insisting that the term "we the people" had to refer to "we the people of each signatory state"; while he did grasp the key conceptual meaning of the constitutional contract at the basis of the federation he was involved in; and while he explicitly acknowledged the distinctive political nature of the federal unions created both by the Articles of Confederation and by the US constitution, neither being in his view reducible to an international alliance nor equivalent to a federal state – Calhoun nevertheless was wrong to insist that sovereignty lay with the member states and must in any genuine federation.[217]

Indeed Schmitt takes the intense contestation over competences and basic issues pertaining to representation, slavery, and membership criteria for new federating states that were pervasive at the time of Calhoun's writings, together with the latter's insistence on state rights, nullification, secession, etc., and the controversy these occasioned, as proof that the locus of sovereignty in the American federation remained *undecided*.[218] The very possibility (and ultimate reality in the Civil War) of an existential conflict over these issues disproves Calhoun's thesis but also proves the relevance of the sovereignty question, or sovereignty discourse, to a bund. As already indicated, the conclusion Schmitt draws is that in a genuine federation the locus of sovereignty is undecided and so long as the federation lasts, so long as the member states and the federation exist *alongside* one another, i.e. in a non-hierarchical relationship, it is *permanently deferred*.[219] This deferral is possible so long as, in other words, the conflicts do not turn into questions of friend versus enemy. In other words, if there is sufficient political will for the federation to endure, if the existential conflict can be avoided, then parties will practice constitutional pluralism and tolerance and try to resolve conflicts so as to avoid the ultimate question of the final locus of sovereignty. This practice of deferral is itself indicative of the political will to maintain both the federation and the political integrity of its units.[220] In Schmitt's words, so long as this deferral remains possible, "neither the federation in regard to the member states nor the member state in regard to the federation *plays the sovereign*"[221] (my emphasis).

This leads Schmitt to a much more interesting taxonomy of US constitutional forms (and a richer constellation of constitutional forms of inter-
state unions in general) than the standard dichotomous approach permits.
Accordingly until 1865, when the decisive existential conflict did in fact occur,
the US was a federation of states and peoples: only afterward did the constitution change its character, and the polity turn into a federal state (post-1865
to the present day) in which the possibility of an existential conflict between
the union and its member states is permanently precluded. The federal
elements of the constitution accordingly no longer involve the question of
the independent *political* existence of the states however much they matter
when it comes to disputes over competences. That such issues as nullification
and secession could seriously come up as they did in theory (Calhoun's) and
in practice does not mean that Calhoun was right about the locus of sovereignty but rather witnesses the dualistic nature of the federation and the
absence of a decision as to the locus of sovereignty. Thus Schmitt treats the
US constitution from 1787 to 1865 as founding a federal union of states and
peoples (in the political sense of constituent powers) distinct from both a mere
international organization (bundniss or confederation in traditional parlance)
and from a federal state. It is an exemplar of a third type of political formation.

But two fundamental conceptual issues remain to be addressed. First,
given his conception of sovereignty related to the thesis of the constituent
power of a politically united people, how is such a dualism of political
existence conceivable within one political formation? Second, what are the
conditions of possibility for the postponement of the ultimate existential
question, and for the endurance of such an apparently anomalous structure?
The first is of course the fundamental question from the sovereignty/legit-
imacy perspective. As we have seen Schmitt speaks of a constitutional treaty
at the foundation of a federation. As we have also seen, every state is based
on a constitution and is a political entity of a single people, such that the
constitution must be ascribed to one demos or constitution-making power
under the legitimating principle of popular sovereignty. An alliance is based
in a treaty and references no demos but only the treaty-making powers of
states as defined by their domestic constitutions. A federation as a union of
states, however, is itself not a federal state (which for Schmitt also has one
national homogeneous demos or constituent power), yet it has a political
existence and constitutional dimension insofar as it is based on a constitutional contract. *To whom, then, is the constituent power, that pertains to the
constitutional (status-altering) dimension of the constitutional compact establishing a bund, to be ascribed?* We come now to the deepest dimension of the
Calhounian dilemma.

The answer a careful reader will discern is that according to Schmitt, the
constitution-making power in a federation is plural: it is to the peoples of
the member states that the constitutional treaty must be ascribed.

Accordingly, the federal constitutional treaty creates a union of states and peoples. It is not simply an executive agreement among diplomats (union of states as an alliance) but a constitutional commitment by politically organized demoi. In other words, the constitutional element in the constitutional treaty is not an empty legalism but rather expresses the will of politically united peoples to unite politically, to become, in Schmitt's language, friends rather than foreigners and thus members of a new political community while retaining their own distinctive political existence. Member states remain states because their peoples remain politically organized: the correct formulation would have to be that "we the peoples" not "we the people" are the demoi to whom the constitutional treaty of a federation can be ascribed and who retain this quality afterward. That is why Schmitt can maintain that member states in a federation have not lost their state character. For Schmitt, a genuine constitutional contract creating a federation is neither a governmental contract nor a contract of subordination under an existing political power or a new one but rather presupposes at least two parties that already exist and will continue to exist each of which contains internally a subject of a constitution-making power.[222] Indeed in his opening discussion of the origin of a constitution in his magnum opus, Schmitt describes two possibilities:

> A constitution arises either through one-sided political decision of the subject of the constitution-making power *or* through reciprocal agreement of several such subjects ... when several political unities and independent bearers of the constitution-making power together reach such a decision reciprocally defining their political status.[223] (my emphasis)

A genuine constitutional contract that is federal thus creates a new political unity alongside of which the internal plural constituent powers of each member state continue to exist. Again the operative term is "*alongside*":

> A new constitution originates through the federal contract. All members of the federation receive a new political comprehensive status so that the political unity of the federation as such and the political existence of the federal members exist *alongside* one another.[224] (my emphasis)

But what does this mean?

Clearly the term, "alongside," indicates that the federation also has a political existence. It certainly makes existential decisions about war and peace, friend and enemy, and has the right to intervene to ensure domestic peace and security, and homogeneity, political and otherwise. Yet, and this is crucial, Schmitt insists that the federation does not have its own constitution-making authority (constituent power) because it originates in a contract.[225] Accordingly in a genuine federation as opposed to a federal state, there is no federal demos – i.e. no general national constituent power of the citizenry to whom the federal constitution may be ascribed.

But is this analysis consistent with the thesis of the dualist nature of the federation and the non-decision regarding, and deferral of the question of sovereignty? Doesn't Schmitt slip back into the Calhounian dilemma when he locates the constituent power in the member states, insisting that in a bund a plurality of political unities continue to exist alongside the federation, and that this is what distinguishes the latter from a federal state?[226] Doesn't the denial that a federal state has its own constitution-making authority due to its contractual origin undermine the assertion that it has political existence (in Schmitt's terms) alongside the multiple political unities that are its members? If the ultimate locus of political existence is in the constitution-making power of a politically united people and their sovereign decision as to political form then either Schmitt would have to impute such a power to a demos that is the referent of the federation or deny that it has political existence alongside the member states. The deferral of the sovereignty question would then ultimately refer only to competences and hierarchy of laws, i.e. jurisdictions, not sovereignty in Schmitt's sense because there could be no real claim to it on the part of the federation if the states retain and alone have constitution-making power.

The problem stems in my view from a subtle switch on Schmitt's part from an analytical to a participant perspective. The issue is the following: the dualist conception of a federal union regarding sovereignty, legitimacy, and the relation among the several political and legal orders comprising it is conceivable from the external perspective of the observer, the theorist, not from the internal perspective of the participant. It is from this stance that the deferral of the sovereignty question and the practices of constitutional plural-ism make sense. The basic discrepancy in Schmitt's argument regarding the constituent power, however, is his unaccountable switch of perspective from a third-person analyst to that of a participant. Why? Irrespective of the prob-lems surrounding the very concept of constituent power and the metaphysics of presence that seems to dog Schmitt's version, an analytical dilemma arises, given the dualist approach he otherwise rightly pursues throughout. No argument is made as to why this power must be located in the member states in a federation, rather than in the federation as a whole, from the observer's perspective. Focusing on the contractual basis of the federation in this context is odd given Schmitt's insistence on its constitutional, comprehensive, and status-altering features. Indeed, in a genuine federation, from the participant perspective, each side could make equally good arguments: the advocate of the member state and the advocate of the federation could each insist that the constituent power has to be located on the level of their political unit. Thus Calhoun so advocated for the member states while Webster and Lincoln argued for the center. Conceptually the arguments would pertain to the creation of the federation as well as to its constitutional form and principle of legitimacy. In other words, "we the peoples" versus "we the people" are the two sides of the debate: the former insisting that the constitutional contract concluded by autonomous sovereign states and ratified by their peoples first created the federal union and that the latter did not relinquish their constituent powers: hence the right to nullify and secede.[227] The latter would have to maintain that the union in some sense already obtained (i.e. a sufficiently politically united people *in nuce* at least already existed) prior to the making of the federal pact (no parts without a whole) or that with the federal pact it has come into existence, and thus that the constitutional contract that followed can be ascribed to "we the people" as the constituent power. In other words, it could be argued that "we the people" had so constituted themselves through the act of federating whether or not the term is actually used in the constitutional contract of the federation. Both of these involve ascription or imputation and are legal and political fictions insofar as "the people(s)" are concerned so this dilemma cannot be decided on an empirical level. *It is only the theorist's perspective that perforce entails reflexivity regarding this question and would, in order to be consistent with the dualist "essence" of a federation, have to argue that a definitive answer to the locus of the constituent power, i.e. the demos/demoi to whom the constitution can be ascribed, must, like sovereignty itself, also be deferred.* In other words, to be consistent Schmitt should have maintained that the jury is out on the question of the form and locus of the constitution-making power in a federation.

But, and this is the second problem, Schmitt seems to have assumed that a federal constituent power or demos must perforce be a national one composed directly of individuals. He apparently also assumed that to speak of a federal constituent power would be perforce to speak of a federal state in which deferral of the question would be out of the question. *I argue that from the observer's perspective he should have realized that his theory of dual political existence characteristic of federal union implies the conception of a compound federal demos consisting of the demoi of the member states, as the "constituent power" of the federation from the federal perspective.* This need not imply a federal state. The compound demos of the federation consists of the combined constituent powers of the member states, but it is, nonetheless, the distinctive referent of the federation to which its constitution can be ascribed. The deferral of the locus of sovereignty between the compound demos (consisting of the now interrelated multiple demoi) of the federation and the distinct demoi of each member state would then be conceivable. Indeed this would have been the only position consistent with the rest of the theory. Schmitt implies as much in his analysis of the constitutive tensions within every federation.[228]

This brings me to the second question mentioned above. As already indicated, Schmitt insisted that as a mode of political organization a federation is inherently unstable due to its internally contradictory character. He identified three structural antinomies. First, a federation's constitutional treaty aims to preserve the autonomy of member states yet it transforms their constitutional status insofar as they are subject to its autonomous legal order, thereby diminishing their political autonomy especially regarding the *jus belli*. Thus the right of *self-preservation* of each member conflicts with the requirement to renounce self-help. Second, there is a tension between the impermeability of a sovereign legal order and the tendency of a federation to intervene to enforce its own legal order. Since any genuine federal enforcement action involves interference in "domestic affairs" and jurisdictions, it conflicts with the right of *self-determination* of every single federation member. Finally, third, the "most general antinomy is ultimately the fact that every assemblage of independent political unities must appear as a contradiction in the context of a collective unity that also exists politically."[229] The coexistence alongside one another within a unity of two types of political existence – the collective existence of the federation and the individual existence of the federation members *neither of which may subsume the other* – means that the relation among these political entities is essentially heterarchical, not hierarchical. The federation, says Schmitt, exists only in this "existential connection and in this balance."[230] This last antinomy is the basis of the most dangerous, ultimately unavoidable, and deepest instability because it means that if questions of existential importance arise both the center and the units will claim the right to decide. What, then, enables this coexistence in the first place?

Unsurprisingly Schmitt insists that for a federation to exist at all, there has to be substantive homogeneity of the population along some salient lines (religion, nationality, class, or civilization) adding that similarity of the political principle of organization of each member state (monarchical, republican, or liberal-democratic) is a further element of homogeneity. He notes that "substance resides mostly today in a national similarity of the population" and invokes Montesquieu to back up his point that opposing types of state principles and political outlook cannot exist together in a bund, conveniently ignoring the latter's acknowledgment of just that in the German federation.[231] Homogeneity resolves the three antinomies in the following way. With respect to self-preservation, homogeneity enables the federation to render the external internal, to turn the foreigner into the friend, and thus precludes the most extreme escalation of otherness (war) which would otherwise constitute a threat to one's own political existence. The possibility of enmity is continuously and conclusively excluded. "But that does not depend simply on the good will of men. The best will is impotent in regard to the concrete reality of different types of peoples and colliding interests and convictions."[232] Substantive homogeneity and the inconceivability of war among federation members is the basis for the renunciation of self-help by a member state without renouncing the will to maintain its political existence.[233]

With respect to the second antinomy the same logic is at work. Intervention violates self-determination only if interference is deemed foreign, and thus is seen as an external, alien imposition. But again, federation renders the external internal, and thus even forceful intervention by the federation in the affairs of the member state is seen as enforcement action, not as war or occupation by a foreign power thanks, again, to substantive homogeneity on which the whole setup rests. Intervention loses its foreign character.

Finally the solution to the third antinomy: the coexistence of more than one politically existing entity within an overall federal union that itself exists politically is also resolved thanks to homogeneity: "because of this substantial homogeneity, the deciding case of conflict between the federation and member states cannot emerge."[234] As indicated, sovereignty is not absent in a federation. Indeed, Schmitt argues that it is possible that the decision regarding external political existence lies with the federation while that regarding preservation of public security and order remains with the member state. But he insists that this is not a division of sovereignty because in the case of conflict that determines the question of sovereignty what is involved is the political existence as such and the decision in the individual case is always entirely attributed to one or the other: that is the simple either/or of sovereignty. Given substantive homogeneity, however, the ultimate conflict doesn't, cannot, emerge: n*either level plays the sovereign.*[235] Nevertheless although substantive homogeneity is to Schmitt the condition of possibility for a federation to exist at all, it only allows for a *temporary deferral* of the ultimate question as to where sovereignty lies. Conflict is not existentially excluded in a federation as it is in a federal state, and when it occurs over something that matters enough to both sides, power not law will decide where sovereignty lies and the federal structure will collapse. Permanence is an aspiration, but it is highly unlikely in the fragile equilibrium that is characteristic of a bund. After all it is an intermediary type of political formation.

Clearly Schmitt's stress on homogeneity is polemical, meant to indicate that an inter-state alliance like the League of Nations could never amount to a federation regardless of the will of the parties or of their legal agreements given the heterogeneity among peoples that it would inevitably entail. This holds equally for a regional group of states lacking "substantive homogeneity." Nor, apparently, can political homogeneity, especially if it is democratic, in the absence of some other substantive homogeneity supply the deficit. Indeed Schmitt insists that it is precisely the logic of democratization that undermines the federal structure of a federation by pushing it to become a (federal) national state.[236] Unlike Kelsen to whom democracy, understood as self-government, thus would suit a "decentralized" federal polity well, for Schmitt, democracy means equality understood as identity and homogeneity, and democratization is thus the vehicle of nationalization that undermines genuine federal structures. Accordingly, if a federation of democratic states is formed, then the two homogeneities, federal and democratic, would inevitably merge and unleash a dynamic of nationalization of citizenship and sovereignty so that the state of suspension and equilibrium that characterized the coexistence of the politically independent member states and the federation would be ended.[237] Instead of being the condition for the possibility of deferral of the sovereignty question and the overall dualistic and non-hierarchical structure of a federation, homogeneity turns out to undermine its raison d'être.

The flaws and contradictions in Schmitt's version of the sovereignty-centered approach can be traced to some of his dogmatic presuppositions and polemical intentions. The most glaring is the reified notion of the existential unity and will of a homogeneous, politically united people pre-existing and self-determining of its political form of existence that is at the heart of his concept of a state, of a constitution, of the constitution-making power, and of sovereignty.[238] His existential concept of sovereignty together with the friend/enemy conception of the political, imply that the political existence of a people must entail the *jus belli*. Accordingly, among the essential markers of sovereignty are not only autonomy, supremacy, and self-determination of political form, but also and above all the decision over friend and enemy, internal and external, by a unitary people willing its political existence, its way of life, and deciding to maintain its homogeneity in the political sphere. For Schmitt, the concepts of the constituent power and of popular sovereignty always meant the incarnation of the subject of power in a group, a stratum, an institution, or a person. Yet this strong conception of sovereign political existence is incompatible with the theory of bund Schmitt himself develops. How can he maintain that member states retain their political existence in this sense once they renounce the *jus belli* internally and are integrated into a federation? Perhaps they do not really renounce it. In any case this conceptual dilemma is what leads Schmitt to insist both that the decision-less federal structure based on sovereign equality or equilibrium is ultimately doomed and that in the absence of substantive homogeneity, a federation is unthinkable. This flies in the face of the historical record: one need only think of the Swiss federation to make the point about diversity or to note that the American federation as Schmitt conceived it lasted nearly 100 years. What is perforce screened out is that one of the key purposes in creating a federal structure, of unifying into a larger federal polity that is not a national state, in the first place, is the preservation of a plurality of political existences in order to protect and maintain autonomy *and diversity*. As will become clear once the existential conception of sovereignty is abandoned, the insistence on substantive homogeneity as a precondition for a lasting federation can be relaxed.

There is another, theoretical drawback associated with Schmitt's version of the sovereignty-based model of federation: it yields only one, rather substantive ideal type, a defense-oriented bund. The tight link of the idea of a federation to unions of states (and peoples) with the primary purpose of *defense* against the outside (his interpretation of the guarantee of political existence) and which thus perforce obtains the *jus belli* precludes the use of the concept for federal unions with other purposes.[239] As we have indicated, Schmitt's interest was triggered by the emergence of the League of Nations and his effort to restrict the applicability of the concept, with its correlative idea of a binding public, legal order of constitutional quality, to a very narrow range of phenomena. Moreover it is clear that Schmitt believed that the twentieth-century developments (geopolitical and military technological pressures of size) that undermine the practicality of the ideal of the sovereign nation-state would not lead to its replacement by liberal, republican, and democratic federal unions but by new imperial, hegemonic formations or what he called "grossraume" – large-scale authoritarian sovereign land-based blocs imposing homogeneity internally and capable of making the friend/enemy decision, and differentiated from one another externally along "meaningful" substantive lines.[240] The concept of federation in Schmitt's hands and in the hands of later interpreters thus becomes ultimately indistinguishable from empires or grossraume or other large-scale authoritarian political formations.

If this is where the sovereignty perspective on federation leads, why not then simply abandon the cumbersome, and allegedly anachronistic concept for the "post-Westphalian constellation" altogether? Why not develop a taxonomy of types of federations, freed from the old statist concepts *and* from the discourse of sovereignty? Schmitt took the first crucial step of construing a concept of a bund as a distinctive political formation. He was right to note the pervasive dualist structure of a federation and the principles of balance and equality inherent in it. He was also right that ideal-typically a genuine federation consists of two public powers (member state and federal), whose constitutional legal orders are imbricated in heterarchical interrelations, in which an ineradicable plurality of political existences coexist and in which political structures providing for shared rule and self-rule, along with legal structures registering independence and interdependence are institutionalized. His insights into its non-hierarchical internal organizational structure are compelling and interesting as the political analogue of the juridical theory of constitutional pluralism, as I shall argue in Chapters 5 and 6. Why not then take the next step and develop a theory of federation as a form of political unity that admits of a spectrum of subtypes without any reference to sovereignty discourse at all?

2.4   The anti-sovereignty approach: non-state federal unions

The effort to develop a theory of federation independent of sovereignty analysis on the part of several contemporary theorists inspired by the development of the European Union purports to do just that.[241] Partisans of this project are dissatisfied with what they deem to be the failure of theoretical will evidenced by the discourse of a "sui generis" political formation, and by merely descriptive analyses of its empirical hybrid character (mix of "supranational" and "intergovernmental" institutions), both of which reason with reference to the classical statist dichotomies.[242] The point is not to insist that the European Union is a hybrid (which it is) or a sui generis political formation, but rather to refine the conceptual framework so that the theoretical questions it raises can be properly posed and the type of political formation of which it is an example, conceptualized.[243] To be sure, the tendency of political science until recently has been to relegate the phenomena of federal unions of states to the dustbin of history: they allegedly "lost out" to their successful competitor, the sovereign state and the international state system. But in an epoch in which the sovereign nation-state itself is now deemed increasingly obsolete not only for geopolitical (and normative) reasons but also with respect to appropriate responses to economic globalization, and to transnational risks, the phenomenon of unions of states that are neither empires nor large states (nor grossraume) nor traditional international organizations regains its significance and attraction. Imperial hegemonic and authoritarian federations of states are of course a distinct possibility as are new imperial formations. But the possibility of a republican, liberal, and democratic response to the problem of size, argue the new theorists of federal union, is certainly worth our attention.

From this perspective it apparently makes sense to abandon the state-centric *and* the sovereignty-based perspective so as to make visible what the hegemonic focus on the sovereign state has concealed. Indeed thus far no one portrays the EU as a state, federal or otherwise, but simply declaring either that it is "more than" or a "highly integrated" form of an international organization is hardly edifying. Clearly its status as a political formation and the possible or desirable emergence of similar phenomena begs for *theorization*. But this requires theory formation: i.e. the development of concepts and ideal types that can then be used to assess emergent political formations and projects of the late twentieth and twenty-first century. In short a paradigm shift is required. Indeed, given the burgeoning and somewhat indiscriminate legalistic discourse of "constitutionalization" regarding regional and global "governance" organizations and international law, and given the dearth of reflection on political form to which such a discourse must refer, renewed theoretical reflection on federation as a relevant constitutional political form is well worth the effort. As Forsyth suggests, the EU stands between two worlds: the intra-state world and the inter-state world.[244] But there have been, historically, and there are now or may be in the future other regional, subregional and possibly supraregional political formations that may fit this bill – i.e. that are unions of states that constitute non-state polities but which differ in some key respects from one another as do *subspecies of a genus*.

In order to address the possible innovative "post-modern" twentieth- and twenty-first-century responses to the imperatives (economic, normative, and geopolitical) of size, it is time to theorize federation not simply as one substantive ultimately transitional type à la Schmitt, but as a distinct genus composed of a spectrum of subtypes and to develop a taxonomy of this form of union of states against which empirical phenomena can be assessed. With respect to republican/liberal-democratic federations, such an approach would allow one to develop a conception of the specific mode of legitimacy appropriate to such a political formation instead of measuring it against inappropriate statist ideals. The anti-sovereigntist approach means to take this further step without however plunging into the cosmopolitan discourse of multi-leveled governance that is based on the individual as the ultimate unit of a globalized world order (world citizen) whose voice and rights require direct representation and global protection. Instead the focus of the federal conception as already indicated is on polycentric, legal, and political orders: the unions it describes are, importantly, unions of states and peoples. The specific form of legitimacy of federal unions must be related back to this core structure. Whether it renders sovereignty irrelevant to the conceptualization of unions of states and peoples as this approach insists is, however, another matter and I shall argue that it does not, if we abandon the absolutist and the Schmittian conceptions. Let us first turn to the anti-sovereigntist approach to see how successful this endeavor is.

Murray Forsyth took the key step in *Unions of States*. Forsyth differentiated two taxonomies to highlight the key categories of federalism: one places *federal states* somewhere on a spectrum between federal union and unitary states, the other places *federal unions* of states on a spectrum between inter-state and intra-state relations.[245] With respect to the latter, confederation and federation appear as more or less integrated forms of unions of states, i.e. as species of the genus. For the sake of clarity, I follow Olivier Beaud, much inspired by Forsyth, in using the term federation to refer to the genus, so that one can see what all subtypes of federal unions of states have in common, and then distinguish between different subtypes of federations more or less integrated.[246] Indeed, in drawing out the theoretical implications of Forsyth's analysis Beaud does not view federation as an intermediary category between confederation and the federal state (as does Schmitt), but rather, like Forsyth, construes it as a genus of which confederation or an international alliance and federal state form two specific outer limits. The idea is to free the theory of federal union entirely of statist and sovereigntist language so that one can grasp and articulate the conceptual juridical/political/institutional specificity of these types of political formations. But in order to get this project off the ground we have to know what concept of state is operative for this approach against which the federation concept is distinguished. The issue is important because federation is understood in terms of a consensual union of (territorial) states and peoples which is not itself a state but which also perforce transforms the inter-state relations and the state character of the units once they become members.

According to both Forsyth and Beaud, a state is a compulsory union of individuals in a body politic. It is founded not on a voluntary contract among bodies politic with those equal in status to one another, as is the case of a federation, but rather, on the unilateral imposition of relations of subordination with the monopoly of command, rule, and punishment.[247] A state is thus fundamentally legislative rather than federative in Locke's sense: it makes laws for those who are unequal in status to itself rather than treaties with peers. Thus the relation of the state to those subject to its law is one of command and obedience. Indeed, sovereignty is as much an essential characteristic of the state for these thinkers as for Schmitt and Kelsen. Sovereignty is a matter of hierarchy, command, unity, indivisibility: it characterizes a public power that is unique and superior over every other power in its circle of jurisdiction and which, in relation to the outside, is independent of the law of other states. As per the traditional conception, for them, sovereignty is centered in the state and signifies hierarchy, a concentration and monopolization of political and juridical power exercised on a territory and over a population subsumed under the public power of the state which by virtue of internal sovereignty is omni-competent, and comprehensive.[248] Indeed, echoing Schmitt's definition, Forsyth maintains that the hallmark of the state with respect to the act of constitution, by which its law-making and law-applying organs are established, is that they and it represent the will of one people or nation.[249]

> By contrast, a federation is not the constituted unity of one people or nation, but a unity constituted by states – a contract between equals to act henceforth as one.[250]

Olivier Beaud agrees in part: indivisibility refers to the bearer of sovereign power, which, in a democratic state, is the people, but this contradicts the reality of a federation, which is a union of states *and peoples*.[251] This is one reason why a focus on sovereignty is deemed an obstacle to the study of federation.[252] Moreover, if sovereignty entails hierarchy, supremacy, and subordination regarding the legal and political units within a state, it means either that the legal and political orders of member states in a federation are derivative of the central constitutional political order or the reverse. Since this is precisely not the case in a federation, according to this school of thought, then the concept of sovereignty is useless in helping one understand the institutional and organizational structure of a federal union of states that is not itself a state. Indeed unlike the law of a sovereign state, federal or unitary, law and government in a federation is not omni-competent or comprehensive insofar as its reach is delimited with respect to the purposes for which it is created. It thus does not totally envelop the individual and should be understood as based on a constitutive "principle of incompleteness."[253] Indeed, federations, unlike states, must be conceptualized with respect to their purpose. Thus one cannot grasp the relations between federation and member states in statist categories like sovereignty and hierarchy. Even more important, nor can one deploy statist categories to grasp the specific form that the principle of legitimacy takes in a republican federal union.[254]

The solution, then, to the Calhounian dilemma is neither to locate sovereignty in the member states nor to locate it in the center, nor to try to come up with a concept of a non-sovereign state, nor even, as per Schmitt whose influence otherwise is acknowledged by all members of this school, to speak of deferral of the question, but rather to develop a theory of federation without reference to the statist concept of sovereignty at all.[255] Ultimately the project is to develop a juridical (and political) theory of federation without lapsing into Kelsenian monism, by reframing its core features in non-statist, non-sovereigntist terms: the dualist nature of the federal pact, the contradictory dualities inherent in the purposes of federations, the institutional character of the federation as product and the tripartite structure that ensues, the legal forms specific to it, and the implications, both juridical and political, of the transformation of independent states into members of a federation. Once this is done the spectrum of subtypes of the genus, federal union, can come into view and one can then properly specify the nature of empirical hybrids and reflect on the desirability or drawbacks of federal union.

Accordingly, and in agreement with Schmitt, the consensual and dual nature of the federal pact as a constitutional contract is a marker of the specificity of this political and constitutional form. This not only distinguishes its foundational logic from an empire and from a nation-state, it also implies the founding of a new institution that becomes a corporate political and legal entity in its own right: the federation. However, and in contrast to Schmitt and Calhoun, here the contractual dimension is interpreted in terms of a consensual covenant based on mutuality that is radically distinct from the principle of sovereignty (unilateralism and hierarchy) and which seeks to reconcile diversity in unity.[256] The federation that results from such a covenant is a union that maintains the political and legal existence of its members but it is nonetheless a political and legal unity with its own interests.

> By forming a union, therefore, states in seeking to promote their own interests by way of a treaty become part of something which has its own inner and outer, its own state-like interests. Yet this new body is not a state, it is not a union of individuals in a body politic, but a union of states in a body politic.[257]

However, again, and unlike the sovereigntist perspective of Calhoun or Schmitt, the two entities comprising the Federation are not of different natures: rather the federation in the strict sense is a community of the same nature as the communities that give birth to it.[258] Taking seriously the consensual horizontal nature of the federal pact and the reproduction of horizontal mutual relations within the federation means that the latter has to be grasped as an autonomous institution which exists in a heterarchical rather than a hierarchal relation to its members while preserving their equal status vis-à-vis one another. However, instead of the bipartite model of Schmitt which construes the federation as existing alongside its member states in order to articulate this heterarchical relation (ultimately understood in sovereignty terms as a decision-less and thus unstable structure), theorists of this approach argue that only a tripartite structural model can get at the institutional specificity and juridical structure of federal unions while avoiding statist logic.

This approach thus appropriates the core Kelsenian insight but detaches it from the centralization/decentralization frame and adapts it to an entirely different taxonomy. In the process, it provides a non-hierarchical, non-monist version of the tripartite conception by virtue of which one can grasp the structural similarity and equality among the political instances comprising a Federation. If one accepts that in a Federation, the member states and the federal organs are both autonomous and interdependent, then one must indeed have reference to a third: the global Federal ensemble that comprises both the federal organs and the member states.[259] This enables one to avoid referring to the federal organs as national organs representing a national demos; a misleading (statist) formula for a federal union of states.[260] Moreover, a non-sovereigntist but also non-monist tripartite approach accounts for the otherwise incomprehensible idea that the federation (the global ensemble) including the Federal court if there is one, must protect both the federal order and the federated orders without ipso facto being a party to the conflict. The tripartite model can and should be severed from Kelsen's dogma of international monism and from his hierarchical conception of legal order and their interrelation. Indeed the very idea and project of a federal union belies both the dogmas of hierarchy and of monism.[261] The Federation is not a state subordinating the federal and federated elements; rather it is an ensemble that entails mechanisms of inclusion and integration that allow for heterarchical relations among autonomous but interdependent legal and political orders within it. But neither can it be construed as an international organization or as a combination of international and domestic elements. Instead of speaking of international law or public domestic law in the sense of state law, to describe the relations of the Federation with the outside and the inside: one should speak of external and internal Federal law.[262] In other words, a federation involves different juridical categories than an international organization. As already indicated a Federation renders the external internal, thus it is not an inter-state organization in the international law sense (an IO). It has its own "inner" and "outer." The international law perspective on a federation is able to acknowledge this united face vis-à-vis the outside only by screening out its internal plurality and complexity and by treating it as if it were a state (a "municipal order"). This is inadequate, because it is perfectly possible *both* that a Federation is, vis-à-vis the outside, a corporate person and a subject at international law *and* that its members are co-states internally yet retain the status of sovereign states and legal subjects internationally, i.e. with respect to non-members. Moreover, because federation involves a voluntary step to a new political formation that pertains to the constitutional dimension of legal orders constructing it, and impinges on citizenship such that citizens of member states are ipso facto citizens of the federation, it must, unlike an ordinary functionally defined international organization, be understood as a union of states and peoples, rather than as a complex set of cooperative diplomatic or technical relations among sovereign states.[263]

Accordingly it seems that by dropping statist/sovereigntist categories as well as the monist centralization/decentralization model, the distinctive corporate existence of federations and of the institutional and legal relations among its component parts can come into view. The relations that obtain within a Federation between the federal and the member states' political organs and legal orders are, accordingly, characterized by "independence and interdependence" (replacing the "statist" language of shared, pooled, or suspended sovereignty). These are typically expressed in the federal constitution through institutionalized immunities and prerogatives for member units along with provisions for participating in the political legislative processes of the federal government. But interdependence also means, as Schmitt pointed out, an intrinsic connection between the constitutional orders of the federal and federated units. Indeed the legal orders within a federation are interdependent in another way: they reference one another through structures of reciprocity rather than vertical hierarchy. The principle of independence is articulated in the guarantee of the status of member states by federal law *and* the autonomy ascribed to federal institutions and federal law. But the principle of interdependence is expressed by the fact that the federal constitutional pact regulates their interrelations and, of course, by the phenomena of mutual referral and direct effect. The significance of this structure of interdependence and independence is that the two legal orders are not foreign to one another: each must recognize a part of the law of the other as part of its own law.[264] Coordinate constitutionalism, constitutional pluralism, and the practice of constitutional tolerance are concepts that express this complex relationship.

The antinomies noted by Schmitt inherent in the dual nature of the structure and goals of Federal unions of states and peoples, are not denied by the anti-sovereigntist approach: they are de-dramatized. The latter openly acknowledges the tensions between the particular goal specific to each member state of preserving its individual political existence and autonomy while creating common purposes and a common political structure (political community) in which they are members, which then has its own general purposes are inherent in every federal polity. The Federation must guarantee the prerogatives of the units while providing for internal and external security and the general welfare of each and of the whole: desiderata that can lead to conflict. Federal law protects while also potentially undermining the political identity of member states. A balancing act indeed is at issue as Schmitt rightly noted between the two conflicting aspirations, but this entails acknowledging the incomplete and imperfect fulfillment of each of them as intrinsic to federal unions:

> In effect each of the two aspirations is necessarily realized in *an incomplete way*: on one side the aspiration to remain independent, specific to the particular purpose, cannot be entirely served for belonging to a Federation imposes a limit on sovereignty (which is thus no longer sovereign). This is what is called here *the metamorphosis into a member state* . . . On the other side the unification understood by the common goal is also not complete. A Federation is limited in principle . . . because it does not have the vocation to become an omni-competent state.[265] (my translation)

Indeed, the relative weight of particular and general purposes is one of the main criteria deployed by the non-sovereigntist paradigm to establish a spectrum of types of federations. This replaces the sovereignty-based distinction between confederations and federal states: the two can now appear as subspecies at the edges of the broader genus, federal union. Accordingly, in a confederation the particular goals predominate, while in a fully fledged but still genuinely federal polity, the general ones have more weight. A federal state, however, is off the map of non-state federal unions. There is room for many subtypes and combinations in between.[266] By avoiding the emphasis on sovereignty or its deferral this approach brings into view what the latter approach screens out: a spectrum or continuum of subtypes of the overall genus of federal unions of states.

But what does the guarantee of political existence mean in an anti-sovereigntist approach? What does it mean to say that the federation is of the same nature as the political communities (member units) that comprise it? The answer lies in the way the metamorphosis of the monadic state into a member state is understood.[267] As indicated above, by entering into a federation, member states become involved not only with the federal order but also with one another as co-equal, co-members of a new political institution, the Federation.[268] They retain their political existence in the following sense: "these entities have powers of constraint over persons situated in their territory while enjoying a certain political autonomy which is, for example, authenticated by the exercise of a legislative power while the federation attains one as well."[269] In other words member states retain their political existence insofar as they continue to exercise a general comprehensive (but non-exclusive) public power over a territory and a population. This form of political existence is also, however, ascribed to the federal level: its territory is the territory of the member states and it too exercises coercive public power over the same population(s). This duality of political existence, of constitutions, of public powers, of territories, once again, is what distinguishes federalism from decentralization.[270] Note that the "S" word is scrupulously avoided: political existence is definitionally de-dramatized. It is not defined in terms of the existential question of who decides friend and enemy, or the locus of sovereignty and/or the *jus belli* (Schmitt). It is not defined in terms of the will of a homogeneous people to exist politically and, when necessary, to get rid of heterogeneity. Rather, "political existence" refers to the coexistence and mutual recognition of two public powers of constitutional quality within the same polity neither of which are sovereign states in the classic or Schmittian sense of the term.[271] Accordingly the constant internal back and forth between "centralizing" and "decentralizing" tendencies, between competing claims of jurisdiction and competence on each level and the shifting balance in the scope and reach of each level of government, is inherent in every federation. There can be no fixed federal bargain regarding the allocation of competences (implied powers can always be claimed on the federal level), no absolute impermeability among the political existences, no hierarchy, but this does not render federal polities "decision-less" or necessarily shortlived, rather it allegedly means that the sovereigntist-statist conceptual framework with its assumption of the need for an ultimate decision at some point, is irrelevant to this form of polity.[272] There is, however, one fundamental "decision" that is typically absolutely entrenched in every federal bargain and thus protected from the "pouvoir constituant dérivé" or amendment power, namely the decision for a federal political structure and the prohibition against dissolving the political existence of the member states against their will, since that is what constitutes the federal structure of the federation.

Nevertheless, the member state is transformed by its entry into a federation. Unlike "monad" states, the member state is "no longer really sovereign."[273] This is so in part because the legal relationship among member units can no longer be characterized as inter-national or inter-state even if they do not thereby become intra-state relations.[274] They are as it were, "inter-federal": the horizontal relations among members of the federation involve mutual acknowledgment and reference to one another's laws while simultaneously resting on the jealously guarded autonomy of the political/legal constitutional order of each member unit. Member states' courts must in this sense communicate with one another insofar as they do have to take account of and honor the rights of one another's citizens, as they are all members of the same overarching polity. In other words member states are "co-states" and within their federation have relations with one another that are no longer foreign, yet they are not fully internal in the way that units in a decentralized state would be. Indeed the internal/external dichotomy along with the foreign/national dichotomy derives from the statist paradigm and is inadequate to describe the complexity of inter-federal relations among states, which elude this all or nothing approach.

The phenomenon of citizenship within a federation is witness to this complexity and to the alleged irrelevance of the sovereignty paradigm. According to the latter there is an exclusive bond between sovereignty and citizenship: double nationality is treated as an exception to the norm. However in a federation, dual membership of the individual in the member unit and in the federation indicates a normal duality of legal statuses each carrying distinct sets of rights and duties.[275] In this political formation, the citizen of a member state is ipso facto a citizen of the federation and must be treated as a non-alien in other constituent states, but is not thereby a citizen of another member state.[276] They have rights in the other states by virtue of being citizens of the federation. Thus boundaries are maintained but they are not total or impermeable. In federal unions that are not federal states, typically federal citizenship is mediated by the co-states and the horizontal effects of citizenship are an expression of the reciprocal relationship among these. The important point to note here is that federal citizenship mediated in this way does not necessarily imply the existence of a federal state. If ideal-typically in the latter citizenship is conferred vertically and directly and state citizenship derives from federal citizenship and residence, in a federal union of states it is typically mediate and horizontal.[277] The shift from one to the other does not follow from the mere fact of horizontally effective federal citizenship. Here too a spectrum of possibilities and combinations comes into view ranging from weakly consolidated federal unions in which there is no independent federal (national) citizenship and a very limited range of rights accorded to non-citizen members of co-member states to an arrangement bordering on that of a federal state in which citizenship comes with birth into the territory of the federation (i.e. is national) with member state citizenship following residence, plus a wide range of federally guaranteed citizenship rights. In short, federal citizenship does not necessarily imply the existence of a unitary individualized federal people.

What, then, does the non-statist, non-sovereigntist approach have to say about the issue of constituent power or of the demos to which the constitution is ascribed and which is the basis of the legitimacy of public power? As we have seen, on the sovereignty model there can be no federal demos or people in the sense of a constituent power: the constitution-making power is ascribed exclusively to the people of each member state. But, as already indicated, this is in tension with the notion that the dualistic structure of federal unions goes "all the way down" – the sine qua non for making and deferring sovereignty claims as it were. On the anti-sovereigntist approach, a federation is a *union* of states *and peoples*. The duality of political existences within it means the doubling of the referent – "the people" – such that the demos must mean something different than what it means in a state.[278] In the latter it is a unity of individuals, in the former "the people," the federal demos, is a composite: the federal "people" is composed of peoples in the plural – a demos of demoi.[279] Thus the peoples of the member states (the citizens) can exercise a constituent power on the level of the member state by giving themselves a constitution or by changing it, but they can also do so on the federal level, by *participating* in the formation of the federal constitution through ratification of the federal pact as citizens of member co-states and hence as *co-constituents*. The constituent power, then, of the federation must be postulated as a composite or compound political community of political communities.

Here we come to what in my view is a key theoretical advance over the sovereigntist approach. Construing the federal demos as a compound one, the federal union as a union of states *and peoples* provides the conceptual basis for all the other dualisms while opening the possibility for reflection on *the distinctive type of legitimacy* specific to such polities. It also provides the conceptual underpinnings for making sense of the practice and dynamics of constitutional pluralism insofar as it puts the constitutional quality and legitimacy of the federation and the member states on an equal plane. Ideal-typically a federal union entails the preservation of member states. Their representation in a federal body (diet) on *an equal basis* along with constitutional entrenchment of their existence (no abolition of a member state or alteration of its territory without its consent) is the typical expression of this fundamental purpose. These are institutional expressions not only of the continued political existence and autonomy of member states (from their perspective) but also of the compound constitutional structure of the federation itself since it is federal constitutional law that ensures the "sovereign equality" and coordinate coexistence of co-states of the federation. Hence the typical paradox inherent in every federation: namely that the federated peoples protect their political existence by participating in the exercise of *federal* constituent (as well as constituted) power.[280] The constitution-making power of a federation is thus a mediated one: it is as members of a compound demos that they participate in constitution-making and in constitutional change.

What can we conclude from this regarding the principle of legitimacy specific to federal unions? Ideal-typically, insofar as unions of states and peoples involve a constitutional treaty, one which changes the constitutional status of states and of their citizens (turning them into member- or co-states of the federation), it should require a distinctive procedure involving the constitution-making powers (the people) of the member states at least at the stage of ratification. Instead of being an executive or diplomatic act of "the high contracting parties" as per international law for ordinary treaty-making (ratified according to normal domestic procedures by whatever constituted powers these include), the constitution-transforming step that entering into a federation entails should, ideally, be construable as an act of the constitution-making powers of the entrants into the new polity. The legitimacy of a federal constitutional contract insofar as it creates a new political union and transforms the constitutional orders of entrants requires an appropriate level of discussion, public deliberation, and distinctive procedures for ratification perhaps along the lines of the American model of conventions in member states, or, less desirable in my view, referenda. The guarantee of sovereign equality within the federation for member states is also necessary to secure the federal principle and hence the legitimacy of the constituted institutional form of the federation. An appropriate amendment rule for the federal constitution along the lines suggested above that includes the peoples of the member states in their composite form – i.e. a supermajority – of member states or state conventions for ratification of any amendment would also fit the federal form of legitimacy and the compound nature of the demos. To be sure other elements can be added to the constitutional contract without undermining these federal principles of legitimacy of a polity construed as a union of states and peoples: certainly liberal protections against federal organs (bills of rights) and against member states as well, an appropriate separation and division of powers, a requirement of a republican or democratic form of government for member states, new members, and the federation as a whole as well as other modes of representation of citizens of the federation within the federal organs are all certainly imaginable. It is not my task to go into detail here. The specific institutional forms articulated in the federal constitution would obviously vary with the degree of consolidation of the particular federation, i.e. of the subtype it constitutes, and with the dynamics of contestation between the particular and the common concerns and the practices of constitutional pluralism that ensue.

How, then, does the non-statist, non-sovereigntist approach to federation construe the relation between this political form and its specific legitimacy, to forms of government and their legitimacy criteria? My interest here is the way in which this perspective construes the relation of the federal form to the issues of homogeneity and democratic legitimacy raised by Schmitt. One of the advantages of this approach is that the issue of homogeneity is addressed in dynamic rather than static terms. Lacking the polemical thrust of Schmitt, it rightly rejects the claim that substantive homogeneity, along linguistic, ethnic, national, racial, or religious lines, is essential to a successful federation.[281] Indeed, federations whose member states have heterogeneous forms of government also have existed, although they are rare and far more fragile than those composed of member states having and required to have the same political regime: republican, democratic typically, or even (historically) monarchical. Montesquieu referred to unions between small republics and small monarchies as "républiques fédératives mixtes."[282] What is interesting is the tendency within such federations toward a rapprochement among the political regimes of the member states and of the overarching federation. A dynamic of iteration occurs through which the dominant form of government is increasingly approximated by the other units. This need not be required legally – it can occur through other mechanisms.

This sort of "homogenization" of regime type, however, is distinct from that ascribed to the logic of democratization which Schmitt deemed to be ultimately corrosive of the essence of the federal political form. If one abandons Schmitt's polemical, substantive conception of democratic equality as equivalent to identity of a homogeneous people, the referent of the discourse of popular (and state) sovereignty and constituent power, and if one looks at the historical record, then there is no essential teleology that must turn democratic federal polities into federal states ascribing their constitutional order to a unitary individualized demos. Neither the Swiss nor the Canadian federations have succumbed to this logic: instead we get the iterative duplication of the democratic political system on both levels.[283] In other words, there is a "duplication of the democratic system" in the sense that there are two spheres in which the citizens can exercise their political rights: the federal sphere and the federated sphere.[284] To be sure the transformation of the ideal-typical representative body of emergent federations, the "federal diet" – which is neither an intergovernmental conference of diplomats nor a parliament – into a bicameral parliament can be seen as a nationalizing effect of democratization. But the principle of democratic legitimacy does not inexorably undermine the federal structure of federal polities.

Nevertheless there are obvious tensions between the *federal principle of equal representation of member states* in the ideal-typical federal representative body (the "diet") and *the democratic principle* of equality based on one person–one vote, especially once a second house is created on the federal level. If combined with the project or fact of nationalization of political life, and if member states are republican and/or democratic or as they democratize, the push for at least a second house in which representation is based on population is inevitable although it is not the case that bicameralism is inherent in federal unions.[285] Nationalization plus democratization also carries pressures toward the direct election of members of both chambers extending the principle of democracy from the sphere of the member state to the federal sphere. *This shifts the principle of legitimacy of the members of the chamber from a federal one (sovereign equality of states) to a democratic one (one person–one vote).*[286] However, when this happens what is occurring is a double process: nationalization of political life in conjunction with democratization. It is not the case, however, that democratization on its own inexorably must undermine the federal principle of legitimacy in the chamber representing the states as the example of Switzerland demonstrates for there political life has not been nationalized.[287] Thus and moreover it would be wrong to argue that the federal principle of legitimacy, which secures the equality and autonomy of co-states in a federation, is anti-democratic. The two principles of legitimacy are distinct but they do have an elective affinity with one another and can be mutually reinforcing. Indeed the federal principle can, as already indicated, be seen as democracy-reinforcing in two senses: insofar as it ensures the equal representation of all member states within the federation it protects the small and the weak from control by the strong, and if member co-states are democratic, the federal principle protects the self-determination or self-government of citizens on the municipal level. Moreover, the federal principle implies equal treatment of populations of member states insofar as federal law, and the rights of federal citizens it establishes (against the federation and vis-à-vis treatment by governments of co-states of citizens of the federation), is uniform, and insofar as all powers created by or embedded in the federal constitution are regulated by it. Requiring consensus-building and the creation of compound majorities for issues relating to the federal principle of the polity and issues over which there is deep disagreement is not ipso facto anti-democratic although it does temper the simple majority principle. The relation between federal and democratic legitimacy, in other words, is complex. It varies with and depends on the degree of consolidation and nationalization of the polity and the purposes for which it is erected. Given the comprehensive nature of government on the member state level and the (de)limited role of the federal government in emergent and even in relatively consolidated federal unions that are not states, it would be wrong to argue that there is by definition a democratic deficit if the federal level does not reproduce exactly and exclusively the principle of one person–one vote within its representative organs. This misleading domestic analogy obscures the distinctive federal principle of legitimacy. On the other hand, a federal republic must perforce be a republic of republics (a republican federation): if the republican form of government is what characterizes the political regimes of the member states then a homologous form on the federal level is certainly to be expected. By republican what is meant here is a form of government characterized by the separation of powers, the rule of law, and constitutionalism, and whose powers derive directly or indirectly from the people and whose officials have a limited term of office which is based on the principle of election. But the form of election, and the nature of legitimacy on the federal level, need not ape that which exists on the level of democratic member states: for the federal level draws on a dual legitimacy: federal (i.e. the idea of sovereign equality) and republican/democratic.[288] Assuming that the federation enjoys the fundamental legitimacy that comes with a constitutional commitment to the federal constitution on the part of the constitution-making power of member states, then the degree of democratic legitimacy, direct or indirect, that is required for a federal union would vary as already indicated with the kind of purposes, extent of competences, level of consolidation, and the kind or amount of legislation and administration engaged in at the federal level.

To be sure, the "nationalization" of political life does have an elective affinity with centralization and "statization" of the federation. But, contra Schmitt, nationalization is not the inevitable result of democracy in the member states, nor does it automatically follow from the legitimating principle of popular sovereignty. Instead, one could suggest as have many theorists ranging from Montesquieu and Arendt to Olivier Beaud, that perhaps the push toward the nationalization and centralization of political life in a federation occurs at least in part due to "external" causes as when a federation succumbs to the imperial(ist) temptation.[289] On this analysis it is the imperial choice and logic that undermines the internal federal character of federations, not the democratic character of member states.[290] By introducing an altogether different sort of duality into the federal polity – asymmetry between rights and privileges of citizens who are members of federated states and those ruled by the Federal polity living in territories which are not meant to become equal co-states (members) of the federation and which have no constitutional protections against Federal power – imperial(ist) rule involves erection of central hierarchical powers and a nationalist nationalizing logic that threaten both the federal and democratic/republican character of the polity.[291] This external factor may in turn be related to the particular governmental type and institutional design of the federation, i.e. whether it is presidential or parliamentary, hegemonic or egalitarian, republican or not.[292] But if sovereign states in a system of states and imperialist tendencies have an elective affinity with one another the argument here is that federal unions and imperial structures do not. These are analytically distinct responses to the imperatives of size. This is yet another reason why this approach insists on abandoning the sovereignty perspective: In contradistinction to a state which is defined and characterized by sovereignty and internal legal and political hierarchy, federations are characterized by three different and unique principles that are apparently opposed to the hierarchical organizational logic of sovereignty: the principle of federative duality (there are two public powers in a Federation); the principle of federative parity (the two federal and federated legal orders are equal); and the principle of federative plurality (there are necessarily several member "states" in a federation).[293] In short, sovereignty is deemed irrelevant because it does not characterize the internal organizational relations among the public powers within federal unions.

2.5   Conclusion

The advantages of the anti-sovereigntist approach to the theory of federation are many. Above all, by theorizing the distinctive constitutive features of a genus of federal political formations through the device of focusing on emergent federal unions, rather than on consolidated federal states, it develops a new political paradigm or rather a new taxonomy of political forms. It allows us to think outside the boxes of both state-oriented inter-national law and reductionist statist analyses of federal unions. This approach does not work with the typical contrast between federal and unitary states, focused on the territorial allocation of power within states. It also breaks with the dichotomy that contrasts international organizations (confederations) to federal states. Unlike the Schmittian theory from which it nonetheless draws heavily, however, the anti-sovereignty approach does not deem non-state federal unions to be a unique but unstable and doomed intermediary political form between confederations and federal states. Instead it opens the possibil-ity of developing a spectrum of subtypes of federal unions as subspecies of the genus Federation. This can be used to analyze empirical variants that have cropped up throughout modern history and which are likely to pro-liferate in the future. Accordingly the variables already culled from the centralization/decentralization approach can be put to use in a framework that neither loses sight of the distinctive federal form (matrix) nor restricts it to one species of the genus (Schmitt). The subspecies of the genus of feder-ation could vary not only in terms of the predominance of particular or general purposes (Beaud) but also according to the nature of the consti-tutional treaty that founds it; the type of legislative body (from a federal board or "diet" to a bicameral parliament); the presence or absence of direct effect; the type of voting rules (unanimity, supermajority, majority); the nature of the mode of revision or amendment rule; the criteria for admitting or creating new members; the mode of acquiring citizenship within it; the prerogatives to engage in foreign policy, jurisdiction, right of exit or secession; whether or not member states also have international legal standing; the purposes for which it has been created (preservation of political autonomy of member states, ensuring peace or welfare among co-states, defense vis-à-vis the outside); degree of homogeneity of political regime, and so on.[294] If, as I believe, federation is a normatively promising way to respond to the problematic of size in the twenty-first century this is indeed an important theoretical gain. As Olivier Beaud rightly suggests, it is only on the basis of an adequate theory of federal union that one can properly pose the question as to whether the European Union is or should become a federation and what sort of legitimacy such a union requires.[295] The same holds true for other unions of states.

The other advantage of this approach is that it brings front and center the *distinctive principle of legitimacy* of federal unions both with respect to the constitution-making power and with respect to the constituted structure of the polity created. The concept of a compound federal constituent power (a federal demos of demoi) existing alongside the constituent powers of each member state, to which each constitution, the federal and that of the member state, can be ascribed, is the theoretical solution to the dilemmas and incon-sistencies plaguing Schmitt's sovereigntist analysis. By implication joining a federal union and participating in the creation of its constitutional treaty requires an act not only of the representatives of the "high contracting parties" but also of the constitution-making powers of each prospective member state and its citizenry, indicating their willingness to enter into a new political formation and to be transformed into co-states and co-citizens. This is the most fundamental basis for the political legitimacy of a federal union. But the "republican" constitution (and constitutionalism) generated by these founding acts does not entail a step into a monist legal or political order (a state). Rather it sets up the possibility for plural, coordinate, and synthetic constitutionalism, i.e. for the practices of constitutional tolerance, mutual monitoring of and by each level, mutual dialogue in further developing constitutionalist principles, and complex principles of legitimacy.[296] *Thus, ideal-typically, a federal union of states is the political form that is the analogue of the theory of constitutional pluralism.* Since the political existence of the co-states in a federation founded (or re-founded) through and referencing the demoi of each polity is not annihilated while a composite demos is created, it is possible to generate a composite set of constitutional principles at the central level compatible with if distinct in some ways from those established at the co-state level, which ensures tolerance for diversity and the dualities of political existence that characterize federations of states that are not states. The constitutionalization of what were international legal relations among the member states through such acts turns them into internal relations among co-states of a polity, a federation, with specific purposes and a specific kind of legitimacy.

Accordingly, a federation consists of two public powers (member state and federal), whose constitutional legal orders are involved in heterarchical rather than hierarchical interrelations, in which an ineradicable plurality of political existences coexist and which institutionalizes political structures providing for shared rule and self-rule, along with legal structures registering independence and interdependence. It does entail making the external internal in key respects but turning the foreign into the friend, international into internal relations and laws for specific purposes – i.e. a co-member – does not require the leveling of social or political differences. Instead it requires a form of political integration that generates solidarity and trust across such differences and plurality. Just what must be shared in order for this to occur, how much agreement and political homogeneity across the component parts is required, will vary with the purposes of the federal union. Recall that accommodation of diversity is a key feature of federal union. What matters is that on the anti-sovereigntist approach the distinctive features of this political form and logic imply that its internal tensions can be productive. Provided there is the political will to maintain the federal form of political coexistence, neither structural tensions nor substantive heterogeneity need lead to destructive instability or conflicts that force a "decision" about the locus of sovereignty that would have to mean the end of the federation. Instead, shared goals and projects, constitutional tolerance, cooperative interactions, mutual and common interests, and mechanisms of ordering and coordinating the dynamics of pluralist constitutionalism are what make a federation and its endurance possible. Constitutional integration specific to a federation does not demand homogeneity or substantive community or intimate affinity, hierarchy or monism but it does require a minimal level of solidarity, communication and dialogue, common purpose and the political will to maintain it.

However, the question still remains as to whether this new paradigm successfully dispenses with the discourse of sovereignty or whether it even should. Can one conjure away the sovereignty problematic by re-definitional fiat? And does the resolute avoidance of this concept on the level of theory with its insistence that neither the federal nor the member state level is sovereign, unnecessarily screen out possible candidates among the species of the genus, federal union of states, in which this would not be true? Certainly one can understand why this approach wants to break with the "statist paradigm" so as to theorize the distinctive character of federal unions that are not states, but it is not clear that one has to or even can entirely abandon the sovereignty concept in order to do so. For surely the question of supremacy and/or of sovereignty is intrinsic to federal union and not merely to the statist version of it.[297] This is not only because conflicts will inevitably arise over jurisdictions, competences, and competences to decide competences, or because there is no internal hierarchy, no clear-cut functional principle, and no self-evident rule of subsidiarity that can ipso facto resolve such issues.[298] Most serious is the inherent possibility of confrontation regarding the principle of political (and democratic) self-determination and constitutionalism of member states when faced with federal laws or regulations that appear to violate these principles, their own constitutional identity, and/or the very purpose of the basic federal pact. This is one key context in which the sovereignty discourse is bound to reappear. Another is in regard to the foreign relations of member states of a federal union. For if member states do retain their international legal standing independent of (or alongside) that of their federal union, if they retain the monopoly on the means of force, then it does not make sense to say that they are no longer really states or really sovereign – at most such a statement could only refer to their relations qua being co-states within the federal union and even here, abandoning sovereignty discourse is not always congruent with the object-language of the actors. Finally the thesis that the constituent power of the federation is a composite one that coexists with the constitution-making power of citizens of each state, even though it appropriately de-dramatizes and de-substantializes the Schmittian model, even though it is thereby able to reconcile diversity and political plurality within a unity that does not level or homogenize difference, does not in itself parry or resolve the supremacy or the democracy question.

If a co-state feels that its constitutional principles or identity are being violated by the Federation then the sovereignty question can re-emerge. Indeed the idea of constitutional pluralism rests on the coexistence of two demoi – the compound demos of the federation and the individual demos of (each) member state – and it presupposes that this question of supremacy is not resolved. Since democracy is bound to be more developed at the local level in a federation of democratic states, given the bounded and delimited purview of the federal level, the more consolidated the federation becomes and the more competences it assumes, the more likely it is that issues around ultimate democratic legitimacy will arise. Indeed the possibility of raising the sovereignty question with some resonance among the citizenry is inherent in the heterarchical relations among the units each of which from their own perspective can assert ultimate supremacy, constitution-making power, autonomy, self-determination, and so on. But these of course are, as Schönberger cogently acknowledges, nothing other than sovereignty formulae.[299]

Instead of dispensing with the discourse of sovereignty altogether even on the level of theory, I argue that the better solution is to abandon the classical and the Schmittian conceptions of sovereignty and to develop a revised conception which fits the object-language, the practice, and yes, the theory of federal unions. Critics of sovereignty analysis are right to argue that sovereignty does not characterize the organizational structure of federations. They are also right against the classical and Schmittian conceptions: neither organ sovereignty, nor hierarchy, nor comprehensive impermeable legal jurisdictions or political orders, nor self-evident unconditional supremacy, nor reference to a homogeneous unified people as the constituent power existing prior to and outside any legal norm, nor the ultimate decision as to friend and enemy, nor insistence on homogeneity as the condition of possibility helps much when it comes to theorizing relations within or the legitimacy of federal unions. What is required is the kind of reconceptualization and de-dramatization of sovereignty analysis I argued for in the first chapter of this book, not the premature abandonment of the concept. I thus propose a synthesis of the various approaches so that questions as to the relevance of the federal concept to a variety of regional and global orders are not prematurely foreclosed.

Assertions of sovereignty within federal unions are a way of defending constitutional integrity, political and/or democratic self-determination of each unit. But it is not necessary to understand sovereignty, constituent power, the political, or democracy, in the way Schmitt does. Sovereignty need not be defined in terms of existential unity with "volkish" overtones, or as the locus of the decision about friend and enemy. It is not necessary to reify the constitution-making power along the lines of a substantively homogeneous "people" or any metaphysics of presence regarding "the people" to whom a constitution must be ascribed in order for it to be politically legitimate.

The political need not be defined in terms of the friend/enemy relationship but rather pertains to the institution of society and of its political forms or regimes while sovereignty pertains to the idea of legal and political self-determination of a polity.[300] However, legal and political sovereignty should not be understood in a solipsistic but in a relational way. As indicated in the previous chapter, the political conception of popular sovereignty (vis-à-vis legitimacy, constituent power, the ultimate source of the constitution) must be understood *ex negativo*, i.e. such that no agent, institution, representative instance subject, or individual can embody it or put itself in the place of the people (the citizenry) or be identified with the people and that no foreign polity can determine the legal or political order of a sovereign state. Rather popular sovereignty remains an intact legitimating principle and is not usurped only if the citizenry can "act" through a variety of representative bodies and processes on the constituted and on the constituent level in addition to the strategies of influence they devise in their civil society associations and social movements.[301] Nor should sovereignty be defined in terms of any particular prerogative. My idea of changing sovereignty regimes refers to changes in what are deemed the prerogatives of sovereign polities while retaining the idea of sovereign equality of states, whether they are members of a federal union or not.

Finally, democracy need not and should not be defined in terms of homogeneity or identity. The concepts of equality (equal citizenship) and self-government (those subject to the law can construe themselves to be its authors), which are at the heart of the democratic ideal, have as their antonyms inequality and foreign imposition not difference or otherness or heterogeneity. Sameness is the opposite of difference or otherness, not inequality. The equality/difference dichotomy is based on an analytic confusion that is anything but innocent. Thus democracy does not require sameness or homogeneity in Schmitt's sense: rather it requires an operative principle of equal citizenship, acknowledgment of social division, contestation, plurality, discussion and deliberation in civil and political public spaces, accountability of public officials, and the right to have rights and in particular to have a say in government, to associate and to organize and to demand justification of any public policy or law.[302] Nor does collective identity require the banishment of otherness.[303] If, in short, one abandons Schmitt's political theology regarding the constituent power, popular and state sovereignty, representation, and democracy, one can see that nothing in the latter principle requires substantive homogeneity and that democracy can do well, indeed better, without it.[304] Thus, much that is ascribed to the sovereignty perspective in Schmitt's work (and generally) is not intrinsic to the concept but only to certain conceptions of it. Indeed, sovereignty as I have argued in the previous chapter is best understood as a negative concept, not in terms of positive powers or features of the relevant demos except as pertains to equal standing and equal right to participate in international law-making. As such, sovereignty means autonomy of a legal order vis-à-vis the outside and its internal supremacy, and political self-determination meaning non-imposition of political form or rule by outsiders or foreigner powers. Thus, abandoning the existentialist and/or Westphalian solipsistic conceptions of sovereignty does not mean we have to embrace a one-sided juridical conception focused exclusively on issues of normative hierarchy and constitutional supremacy over external norms. The legitimacy dimension remains crucial.

Indeed, the best versions of the "anti-sovereigntist" theories of federation actually contribute, inadvertently, to the task of reconceptualization. As Schönberger rightly notes, while the sovereignty question is structurally unanswerable in a federation, while it does not describe their organizational structure, it is a marker of a federal union that is not a federal state, that both the federal level and that of the member state come to describe themselves in sovereignty formulae each asserting the autonomy of their legal orders, self-determination of their political and constitutional forms and so on.[305] The concept of a federal union entails the idea that both member states and the federation have a fundamental legal and political order. Sovereignty entails non-imposition of a legal order or political regime by a foreign or external power but it does not require exclusive jurisdiction, the *jus belli*, or homogeneity. *Rather, today sovereignty as autonomy must be understood in relational, not solipsistic terms and coupled with sovereignty as participation as a peer in the decision-making institutions of supranational (federal or confederal), regional, or global legal and political orders which affect one's domestic legal and political order, both hopefully limited by accepted constitutionalist (including human rights) principles.* Indeed, it is only on the basis of such a reconceived conception of sovereignty (and sovereign equality) and dedramatized conception of constituent power, that the idea of deferral makes sense within a federation and which, as already indicated, undergirds the practice of constitutional tolerance and pluralism that such unions require. Each level asserts its autonomy and supremacy yet conditionally accepts the laws and rules of the others on the basis of its constitution: so long as the constitutional identity of the relevant political order is not undermined and so long as each participates appropriately in the compound demos that makes the laws of the whole (that of the federation). New forms of cooperative federalism in which competences are shared, rather than the older type of nineteenth-century federalism characterized by a jealous focus on exclusive jurisdictions, can be grasped from this optic and make sense with respect to non-state federal unions. *The distinctive principle of legitimacy of the federation rests on this dual reconception of sovereign equality among co-equal member states, popular sovereignty (the anti-embodiment model), and compound constitution-making power.*

I want to argue that both the sovereigntist and the anti-sovereigntist approaches too quickly prejudge the issue as to whether the genus, federation, could not also encompass a subtype that might apply to what today goes under the heading of global governance institution, one that includes all states but for partial delimited purposes. Since federal unions do not involve comprehensive, hierarchical governance or legal or institutional monism, since federations are created for specific purposes which can vary, but which perforce include the preservation of political autonomy of member states and the principle of sovereign equality, it is not clear why one cannot apply federal principles to functionally delimited public global governance institutions if the need or will arises. I believe that they could help us think through the legitimacy problematic such institutions face. As international organizations morph into global governance institutions that expand their competences on the basis of an implied powers argument, as they reinterpret their purposes (functional mission creep), as they begin to make rules and public policies backed up by sanctions that directly and at times adversely impact individuals while claiming a constitutional quality and supremacy for these policies and rules, questions of political form, issues of executive fiat, lack of accountability, and political legitimacy become pressing. The cat is already out of the bag given the proliferating demands for the (further) constitutionalization and even democratization not only of regional but also of global governance institutions. In the latter case, however, it is premature to jettison either the concept of sovereignty or of federation with respect to member states of changing international organizations. Thinking in terms of federal principles for global governance institutions does not necessarily lock one into an infeasible cosmopolitan utopia, the main reason Kant and even the most sophisticated theorists of federation (with the EU in mind) retreat from such a proposition.[306] For on the non-absolutist, non-Westphalian, and non-Schmittian conception of sovereignty informing this book, federal principles for GGIs would not mean the end of sovereignty as Kant and others presume. Nor would the loosely consolidated type of federation which a global governance institution like the UN could conceivably become, require homogeneity of political regime type for its members. The degree of political homogeneity would, to be sure, be an important variable regarding the scope of federal power, the more loosely consolidated confederacy at the one end of the spectrum perhaps imaginable for a GGI requiring much less (and carrying out fewer and more carefully delimited functions and purposes) than a more highly integrated federation at the other end of the ideal-typical spectrum. But for its supremacy claims, rights-impacting decisions, and expanding competences and prerogatives and future reform, a federal frame may be illuminating. A clear ideal type of federal union, and of subtypes, ranging from the less to the more integrated, and differentiated according to the variables discussed above would shed light on empirical hybrids and perhaps indicate a direction for appropriate reform.

Before ruling anything out, it is worth taking a closer look at the legitimacy problems faced by IOs morphing into GGIs due in part to the new purposes, functions, and the expanding interventionist scope they assume, and then rethinking the question of whether the federal principle can help in resolving some of them especially with respect to demands for constitutionalization and democratization. If the step to federal union is inappropriate on this level, it is worth being clear about why and perhaps then toning down the global constitutionalist rhetoric and interventionist enthusiasm with respect to these institutions. I turn to this issue in the following chapters. The next three chapters will take up the innovations of global governance institutions in three areas: the discourse of international human rights and humanitarian intervention, transformative occupation, and UN terrorist listing practices. I will conclude by addressing the legitimation problems these raise and propose a way to think about the changing sovereignty regime and how to reform the respective global governance institution so as to resolve the legitimation problem. If the charges of hegemonic international law, new imperial formation or con-dominium regarding the most important GGI, the UN Charter system, are to be countered, then reform either along the lines of a step toward a quasi-federal structure or retreat back to a less ambitious international organization will be necessary.

International human rights, sovereignty, and global governance: toward a new political conception

The legalization of international human rights norms and the globalization of human rights discourses challenge the way we think about sovereignty, legitimacy, and international law. The international human rights regime that began after World War Two, blossomed in the mid-1970s and took on new force after 1989 has led some cosmopolitan moral and legal theorists to conclude that the sovereignty and external legitimacy of governments should be considered contingent on their being both non-aggressive and basically just (i.e. rights-respecting).[1] A radical idea is at stake: that the "international community" may articulate moral principles and create legal rules regulating the conduct of governments toward their own populations when human rights are at issue.[2]

It is also argued that the international community has the default obligation to protect individuals and enforce basic human rights when states fail to do so or when they violate the rights of those under their authority or control.[3] The changing norms of the international system seem to be indicative of a new political culture regarding sovereignty that has shifted from one of impunity to one of responsibility and accountability.[4] The expansion of human rights law and the expectation, since the mid-1990s, that it should be backed up, in cases of grave violations, by sanctions imposed at the international level including military (humanitarian) intervention, suggest to some that the internal legitimacy of governments as well as the sovereignty of the state have become contingent on outside judgments based on cosmopolitan principles of justice.[5] From this perspective too, the rules protecting state sovereignty such as the principles of non-intervention and domestic jurisdiction enshrined in the UN Charter appear to be out of date, and the international legal and political order based on them increasingly illegitimate.[6] Accordingly those embracing this perspective advocate redefining sovereignty as the responsibility to protect (R2P) rather than as state autonomy.[7]

Indeed, it appears as if the debates over the international order today take place between two camps: "statists" who are still enchanted by sovereignty and "strong" cosmopolitan liberals who are entranced by human rights, and who applaud what they see as a shift from state-centric (consent-based) international law to an international or global legal order based on consensus, and justice to persons.[8] The latter construe the expansion and individualization of international criminal law, the coming into force of the ICC, and the development and partial merger of the international human rights regime with humanitarian law ("humanity's law") as indicative of an emergent consensus on the basic values of the "international community" that challenge atavistic rules about sovereignty, state consent, and "legalism" pervasive in the UN Charter.[9] Accordingly the old focus of international society on the security and integrity of states irrespective of the nature of their political regimes and domestic practices is and should be shifting to a human rights-oriented approach that focuses on justice to persons, construing individuals as the ultimate referent and unit of membership in the international community. In other words, "state-centrism" and the principle of the equal sovereignty of states in international law should cede to a direct focus on the individual – his or her security, dignity, and basic human rights as the subject of cosmopolitan law. International human rights law allegedly has the correct orientation insofar as it construes the individual, not the state, as the ultimate unit of moral concern and places respect for the equal dignity and worth of all individuals above state sovereignty, non-intervention, and sovereign equality, all deemed derivative principles of merely instrumental value.[10]

"Strong statists," however, insist that international law is and should remain protective of state sovereignty, domestic jurisdiction, and the principle of non-intervention. These principles are articulated in the UN Charter and membership in the UN, notably, is not conditioned on regime type.[11] They argue that Article 2(7) of the UN Charter, providing that "nothing contained in the present Charter shall authorize the United Nations to intervene in matters which are essentially within the domestic jurisdiction of any state," is hard international law next to which doctrines like humanitarian (or democratic) intervention, or the responsibility to protect are non-binding moral principles. The only permissible exceptions to such hard international law are the enforcement measures the Security Council is empowered to take, ". . . in order to maintain or restore international peace and security" under Chapter VII. Domestic rights violations do not ordinarily come under this purview. Only those domestic abuses that the Security Council determines pose such threats can trigger Chapter VII enforcement measures. Moreover, it is argued that international human rights law is designed primarily to encourage states to remedy the inadequacies of their laws and to respect the rights of their citizens and residents, not to directly empower individuals with the international legal standing to enforce their rights in global courts or to trigger coercive enforcement by states parties to the relevant treaties.[12] States remain the main subjects of international law (the law-makers) even if they are no longer the only ones but it is international organizations, not individuals, who are the newcomers to the field as legal subjects.

Indeed, as with all treaty law, human rights covenants are binding upon states parties and create legal obligations of states: every state party is obliged to every other state to carry out its undertakings and every other state has the right to have the obligation carried out. It is disputed whether such treaties create legal human rights of the individual.[13] Certainly they do not substitute human rights for the principles of state sovereignty or sovereign equality or turn domestic respect for international human rights into a condition of the international recognition of state sovereignty.[14] To be sure, the domestic perpetration of genocide, crimes against humanity, war crimes, and ethnic cleansing involve severe depredations that constitute violations of international customary and treaty law, and are now subject to the jurisdiction of the ICC.[15] But apart from the role accorded to the Security Council in the Genocide Convention, none of this is clearly within its jurisdiction.[16] Moreover the ICC has no legal jurisdiction over non-states parties and unlike the Genocide Convention, which has near-universal state endorsement, major powers including China, India, Russia, and the US are not parties to the treaty establishing the Court.

Nevertheless the "strong statist" view does seem to miss out on what is new in our contemporary constellation. For surely there has been an important transformation in what is considered to be "essentially" within the domestic jurisdiction of states, and the grave violations of human rights alluded to above no longer fit that bill. The shift at least in political culture from state impunity to responsibility to the international community and the new liability of perpetrators of such crimes, be they state officials or private persons, to international sanction is impressive. Moreover, the distinctive purpose of international human rights treaties is obscured by the strong statist perspective. Unlike ordinary multilateral treaties concluded for the sake of reciprocal exchange and mutual benefit among contracting states, human rights treaties are concluded for the purpose of protecting the basic rights of individuals irrespective of their nationality, against the state of their nationality and all other contracting states. Such treaties are interpreted in ways that limit the "margin of appreciation" of signatories and typically do not permit unilateral withdrawal. Human rights conventions thus tend to take on autonomous international meaning and weight that is not simply at the disposal of individual signatory states.[17] While strict legal enforcement is typically domestic, such treaties can and have established international or global monitoring bodies and some create *erga omnes* obligations. International human rights treaties indicate that domestic violations are potentially of international concern.[18] However, and also typically, even when an optional protocol such as that attached to the International Covenant on Civil and Political Rights (ICCPR) provides that the UN Human Rights Commission may receive and consider communications from individuals claiming to be victims of violations of any rights in the Covenant with respect to signatory states, this does not vest the Commission with the power to render a legally binding decision or provide for inter-state complaints.[19] Nor is there a global court with compulsory jurisdiction regarding human rights violations, despite the impressive proliferation of supranational courts on regional levels and in other global functional regimes. In these respects the international human rights "regime" differs substantially from other international regimes which usually are erected by states for mutual benefit and which typically establish mechanisms for the authoritative resolution of disputes, in addition to the standard mechanisms of reciprocity and, ultimately, sanctions.[20]

If the strong cosmopolitan depiction exaggerates the trends toward the individualization of international law and the apparent shift from equal sovereignty to justice to persons as the emergent basic norm of the increasingly legalized and even, allegedly, constitutionalized global order, the Westphalian premises of the strong sovereigntist approach are also unconvincing today.[21] Indeed the expanding reach of regional and global "governance" institutions that make authoritative policies and coercive rules regulating the actions of state and non-state actors seems to render the latter approach anachronistic.[22] The emergence of "global administrative space" and the apparent morphing of international organizations like the UN, or the WTO, or the EU into global or regional "governance" institutions do not really fit either model very well. Moreover, these transformations have led to debates about the legitimacy of these institutions.[23] The question is not only what role such institutions should play in fostering and/or enforcing respect for human rights domestically, but also how to ensure that they themselves are rights-respecting, accountable, and democracy-reinforcing.

I agree that the development of international human rights norms and law is indicative of a new and salutary political culture regarding sovereignty. Nonetheless, although the international legal norms and rules regarding the prerogatives of sovereign states have changed, sovereignty has not been displaced by human rights as the basic principle of the international legal order. International human rights treaties are not designed to abolish state sovereignty or to replace it with global governance and global law but to prod states to erect and commit to a common international standard and to abide by it in their domestic law and policies. Nor does the fact that grave violations by states of their own populations' basic rights is now a matter of international concern (via international treaties and transnational human rights movements) mean that sovereignty has been replaced by a new global principle of legitimacy – respect for human rights. *The thesis of this chapter is that sovereignty (and sovereign equality) and human rights are two distinct but interrelated legal principles of the same, dualistic, international political system and that both are needed to construct a more just version of that system.* The relation between these principles has shifted, indicating the emergence of *a new sovereignty regime,* but sovereign equality and the correlative principles of non-intervention, domestic jurisdiction, and self-determination *remain the default position of the international legal order although international human rights do have a new role to play.* If we see sovereignty not as a fact of state power but as a normative concept and as an international legal entitlement to political autonomy, we can view international human rights treaties as mechanisms designed to help prevent and correct injustices that may follow from the international legal ascription and distribution of sovereignty to states on the basis of efficacy alone.[24] As such, respect for international legal sovereignty, and for human rights and humanitarian law, are in a recursive relationship. But we must not fall into the conceptual trap that construes sovereignty and human rights as components of two antithetical, mutually exclusive legal regimes or world orders: the one characterized (or caricatured) as "Westphalian" (and deemed anachronistic today), the other construed as "cosmopolitan" (and seen as the desirable trend in current international legal developments and the road to a global rule of law). International human rights norms should be seen as part of a new sovereignty regime signaling changes in the prerogatives of sovereignty, setting new limits to its legitimate exercise, and indicating shifts in the understanding of what falls within the "domestic jurisdiction" of a sovereign state and what are illegitimate acts by (or tolerated by) state officials for which an agent can no longer evade responsibility by ascribing authorship to a fictional legal person.[25] In other words, we should realize that since 1945 we have been confronted with new and at times contradictory institutionalizations of both principles and that their interrelation has to be periodically readjusted.

But, in order to redeem the normative promise of both principles an additional element in the conceptualization of sovereignty alongside political autonomy and domestic supremacy has to be adequately theorized, namely, sovereignty as status and inclusion in global governance institutions.[26] Given the emergence of powerful GGIs, appropriate representation for stakeholders, well-designed procedural and substantive rules, mechanisms of accountability, responsiveness, etc., especially in those institutions whose function it is to frame criteria for assessing human rights violations and to decide about enforcement, are crucial for their legitimacy and proper functioning. Sovereignty as equal status and inclusion in GGIs is also crucial for member states in order for them to maintain their sovereign equality (within and outside such institutions) and their political autonomy. It is on the terrain of the dualistic conception that we must consider the issue of the legitimacy of these institutions.[27] The proliferation of theories and projects aiming to "constitutionalize" or "democratize," and not simply to render more efficient, these forms of governance will be the topic of Chapter 5.

This chapter will address the question of how to think about the relation between human rights and sovereign equality in the epoch of "global governance" and humanitarian intervention, construed as the enforcement by the international community of "human security rights."[28] The present chapter cuts into this problematic by analyzing some variants of an influential new approach to international human rights dubbed by its adherents the "political conception" in contradistinction to what they take to be the traditional approach. The former focuses on the alleged function that international human rights play with respect to state sovereignty in instances of grave violations; the latter focuses on the ethical/moral justification of fundamental human rights, typically derived from a teleological conception of basic interests in personal autonomy, dignity, or in well-being, ascribed to all individuals. I will argue for an alternative political conception which acknowledges the humanitarian function international human rights discourses have taken on but which argues for disaggregating this dimension from a different politics of human rights – the politics of actors who invoke the international documents and rely on strong moral arguments when declaring and claiming *their own rights* vis-à-vis the exercise of the public power first and foremost of their own state – a dimension lost in the new enthusiasm for international enforcement of the rights of others and transnational activism by international non-governmental organizations (INGOs) aimed at saving victims. I do not attempt to provide an alternative moral justification of human rights to the traditional approach, although I believe this is an important enterprise and thus do not agree with the dominant political conception's denial of the need for and possibility of a non-foundational, non-teleological, reflexive, universalistic moral approach to justification.[29]

My focus is on rethinking the relationship of the new politics of human rights to state and popular sovereignty, and to constitutionalism and democracy. We face two issues in the current context that I will address in this chapter. First, thanks in part to the merger of humanitarian and international human rights discourses, there is a disconnect between trans- or international human rights advocacy/enforcement and the activity and voice of those whose rights are violated. This invites a moralization of politics and cheating by the powerful, who engage in "humanitarian" intervention allegedly to protect the rights of victims, but always also for their own self-interested strategic purposes.[30] The alleged incompatibility of international human rights and state sovereignty plays into this dynamic. Thus the first issue is how to incorporate principles of humanitarian responsibility into international law that aim to secure respect for basic human rights without weakening Charter constraints on the use of armed force and without undermining the constitutive principle of sovereign equality. This is one aspect of the conundrum of legality and legitimacy in the contemporary context, wherein respect for human rights supplements, but does not replace, sovereign equality as a core principle of international law. The second issue is how to reconnect conceptually and practically the politics of human rights to the agency of those whose rights are at issue and to democratic politics on all levels where public power is exercised. This raises the legitimacy problematic from a different, "internal" participant perspective.

I begin by situating the emergence of the new political conception of international human rights in historical context (Section 3.1). It is important to have a sense of the changing function of the international human rights discourse since the 1990s, for the political conception emerged in reaction to this shift. But we have to go back to the beginnings in the post-1945 context and especially to the 1970s, the period in which international human rights discourse and movements "took off," to understand the significance of the shifts in the 90s. I then turn to "the traditional approach" as constructed from the perspective of the new political conception (Section 3.2). The latter is explicitly developed as an alternative to accounts of human rights that start from controversial metaphysical (natural rights) or philosophical principles and which focus on foundational arguments and moral justification. In contrast the political conception seeks to theorize and assess the historically new (since 1945) concept and practice of international human rights that avoids issues of justification. It is thus important to see how it construes and differentiates itself from the former and what it sees as its characteristic flaws. Two influential versions of the political conception and the distinctive functional relationship they articulate between sovereignty and human rights with respect to enforcement are addressed in the next sections (3.3 and 3.4). A critical assessment and alternative way to conceive of this relationship that builds on some of the insights of the political conception is then articulated (Section 3.5), and a new dualistic political conception that differentiates between human security rights and human rights proper is developed in Section 3.6. I conclude by indicating why, once one differentiates between the concept, function, and mode of enforcement of these two domains, the moral justification of human rights proper is important (to parry charges of ethnocentrism or parochialism) and yet benign (coercive intervention by outsiders is not at issue). I also suggest that rights advocates should shift the focus back to the domestic arena and the empowering and emancipatory role that human rights discourses still have to play therein when invoked by local actors, i.e. those whose rights are at issue, even though today these discourses reference international norms.

3.1   The historical background: an overview

3.1.1   The post-war revival

Before turning to the political conception of human rights, I want to situate its emergence. Human rights discourses are always polemical and ultimately unintelligible if one does not understand the political stakes in historical context. The original push to revive the concept of the rights of man and to construct a new approach occurred in the wake of atrocities committed by the great powers against civilians and prisoners of war during World War Two, generating the well-known tribunals, declarations, treaties, and covenants.[31] The idea was to erect an *international regime* that articulated the human rights of every individual, thereby indicating that how a state treats its own nationals and resident populations is now a matter of international concern.[32] This entailed a shift from the apparently discredited and ineffectual treaties aimed at protecting the rights of minorities in the interwar period in the context of nation-state-making out of the debris of the old land-based empires in continental eastern and southern Europe.[33] The rights of every individual, not only of national minorities in certain areas, were now the stuff of international declarations and treaties. While there was some attempt at a revival of justificatory theories of objective natural law or natural rights in the face of a largely discredited legal positivism, the new declarations and covenants avoided foundational rhetoric.[34]

This is one but by no means the most important difference to the classic conception of the rights of man that was the product of the famous and influential 1789 French Declaration – the progenitor and referent of modern human rights discourses for the next two centuries. The French revolutionaries who declared their rights did so in order to establish the first principles of their constitutional polity, while the international human rights declarations signed after World War Two were initially deemed peripheral to the new international legal and political order constituted through erection of the UN Charter system.[35] More significant, the French declared the rights of man *and* citizen, differentiating but also linking constitutionalism, rights, and popular sovereignty as the new legitimating principles of their polity. They saw no conflict between ". . . proclaiming the emergence of a sovereign nation of Frenchmen and announcing the rights of man at one and the same time."[36] The French Declaration located the source of sovereignty in the people (called the nation) while declaring that all men are born free and equal in rights, stating that the purpose of all political association is the preservation of the natural rights of man: liberty, property, security, and resistance to oppression but also the free communication of thoughts and opinions.[37]

Thus the French Declaration went hand-in-hand with the erection of a representative constitutional democracy. It linked the principles of liberal (universal and fundamental human rights) and republican constitutionalism (self-government under the rule of law, separation of powers) to the discourse of popular sovereignty, replacing monarchical with republican and democratic legitimating principles. Indeed the penultimate Article insisted that any society in which the guarantee of rights is not assured or the separation of powers settled has no constitution.[38] The goal in short was to move from a state based on the principle of monarchical legitimacy, absolutism, and arbitrariness of rule, to one based on democratic legitimacy and human rights, public freedom, personal liberty, and non-domination. It was this political project that fired the imagination of nineteenth-century nationalisms and why Hannah Arendt deemed the principles of equal citizenship and political freedom as central to it.[39] The rights of man were ascribed to every individual and in this sense were universalistic in thrust but the referent was the political community and the project was to establish equal citizenship in a sovereign state that is a rights-respecting democratic republic.[40] The rights of man and citizen went together.

While the Universal Declaration of Human Rights (UDHR) passed in 1948, the later ICCPR drafted to give it legal effect in 1966, and the early regional documents (the European Convention on Human Rights (ECHR)) were clearly modeled on the French Declaration – Article 1 of UDHR also declares that all human beings are born free and equal in dignity and also articulates civil and political rights – these rights are now framed as *international* human rights.[41] At the time they were declared, they were neither the product of nor did they produce a social or revolutionary movement by nationals seeking to constitutionalize or democratize their own state.[42] The politics surrounding these declarations were thus profoundly different. In the first case (the French and earlier the American) the politics involved in declaring rights were the politics of those affected and entailed their agency; in the second case it was initially the politics of state executives and diplomats involved in the founding of the UN, declaring the rights of others. The inclusion of references to human rights in the preamble and in the first Article of the Charter was, to be sure, partly a concession to pressure exerted by NGOs and smaller democracies but they succeeded thanks to the need to generate support for the new organization that not only enshrined state sovereignty but also the prerogatives and hegemony of the victors and their allies (the old great powers) in the Security Council.[43] The references to international human rights in the UN Charter were intended to be symbolic, and UDHR came into being with no legal force and no effective machinery in the UN system to back it up. It took two decades to successfully realize the promise of legalization of UDHR resulting in the promulgation of not one but two covenants neither of which came into force before 1976 and neither of which has compulsory or effective enforcement mechanisms.[44] Certainly the escalation of the Cold War made legalization of enforcement or of a human rights court a chimera and it led both sides either to ignore or to instrumentalize rights discourses and organizations once the treaties were signed in the mid-1960s.[45] Probably because they were articulated as *international* human rights, the post-war innovation, implying international concern for what was once deemed to be exclusively within the domestic jurisdiction of sovereign states, the risk that internal treatment of one's own citizens, or subject populations in the case of empires, could come under international scrutiny, and that international human rights could become genuine limitations to state prerogatives, ensured that they would be made toothless at the outset otherwise many states would not sign on at all.[46] International human rights were not intended to constitutionalize or democratize a global political system nor were they seen as an alternative to the principle of sovereign equality also enshrined in the UN Charter, although they did imply the end of absolute impunity of sovereign states regarding their domestic practices.[47]

The main exception to rhetorical or declaratory human rights documents of the immediate post-war period is the regional ECHR.[48] This convention established under the auspices of the Council of Europe was designed to be enforceable. It defined a set of civil and political rights for all persons within the jurisdiction of its member states and initially established a Commission on Human Rights to receive and review petitions and a court to try cases sent to it. The Commission could investigate a case, try to settle it, or send it to the European Court of Human Rights (ECtHR) and member states are legally bound to comply with the Court's decisions.[49] Moreover, although this Convention was also not the result of pressure from domestic social movements, as Moravcsik has convincingly argued, there was nonetheless a strong link between the creation of and concern to preserve domestic democracy and constitutionalism and the willingness to create a strong regional human rights regime on the part of member states.[50] But why would executives of democratic states delegate some of their sovereign powers to a strong regional regime and court (which acquired compulsory jurisdiction)? The answer is that they were executives of *newly (re-) established democracies* who sought to create supranational mechanisms to help lock in domestic constitutionalist and democratic institutions against the re-emergence of anti-democratic political threats.[51] The motivation behind erecting and signing on to an effective international human rights treaty regime was not to perpetuate their own personal power but to establish reliable judicial constraints on future non-democratic governments or on democratically elected ones that may seek to subvert democracy from within.[52] But the expectation was not that other states parties to the Convention would intervene militarily to enforce human rights norms. Instead, being party to such a treaty would constrain the behavior of future national governments hopefully ex ante through international controls functioning as a signaling device to trigger appropriate *domestic* responses.[53] The possible enforcement of human rights by the ECtHR could serve as a mechanism helping to strengthen domestic courts and institutions of judicial review, parliamentary legislation, and public action.[54] Indeed the idea of signing on to a strong regional human rights regime was a way to supplement and reinforce, not substitute for, the domestic institutions of constitutional democracy. Presumably such an international judicial capacity could provide a form of accountability along with incentives for domestic compliance. Enforcement by a regional court was nonetheless built into the design of this treaty regime from the beginning, as was the right to petition under certain criteria, and this involved enforceable commitments.[55] Nevertheless, this kind of international human rights treaty was the exception not the rule in the first period.

3.1.2   The second wave

A second wave of international human rights discourse and treaty-making was most strikingly associated with projects of liberation from and emancipation within the Soviet empire and with domestically led democratic transitions in Latin America in the mid-1970s and early 1980s.[56] The invocation of internationally and regionally articulated human rights agreements by local activists helped them challenge repression by their own states and/or imperial oppression.[57] Despite still being largely exhortatory insofar as the treaty law created in the 1960s and 1970s was rarely equipped with effective legal machinery for monitoring compliance or enforcement, the new legally binding international human rights covenants were an important normative referent for domestic civil society and social movement activists.[58] They helped legitimate justice-based and democracy-oriented demands for domestic political change, and were used strategically by citizen movements to claim rights against their own governments and to demand their legal and constitutional institutionalization.[59] The role of external actors was restricted to "soft" forms of intervention. Although human rights campaigns involved linkages between domestic and transnational "activists beyond borders," the emphasis was on local agency, on facilitating the emergence of internal actors, and the organization and institutionalization of their learning experiences.[60] Local activists seeking liberty, constitutionalism, and democratization invoked and contributed to international human rights discourses, while transnational INGOs helped via investigations and exposés, enabling domestic actors to shame their governments by publicizing their egregious rights violations. It is true that transnational human rights movements blossomed in this period and became increasingly influential. *Yet in this context international and domestic human rights discourses and campaigns, the idea of democratic entitlement, linkages with transnational activists, and participation in the multilateral institutions did not appear to threaten either the popular sovereignty/self-determination of citizens or the sovereignty of their states.*[61] By denouncing and resisting domestic injustice, the political agency of local actors and movements was the main vehicle for getting their states to institutionalize and respect international human rights and for giving "ethical-political" meaning to the universal principles they were invoking, their very praxis revealing that the content of basic rights would be determined domestically and politically. Struggles by those affected against old and new forms of injustice, exclusion, oppression, and marginalization informed context-relevant interpretations and selections of the locally relevant international human rights listed in the documents, and when successful, institutionalization in context-sensitive ways of basic rights securing equal citizenship and personal freedoms in domestic constitutions.[62]

In this respect there were continuities as well as discontinuities between the new politics of international human rights in the 1970s up to the mid-1980s and the politics surrounding the classic declaration of and struggles for the rights of man and citizen despite disclaimers regarding the political nature of their activism on the part especially of dissidents in the East. There, human rights activism burst onto the scene in the mid-1970s with the signing of the

Helsinki accords.[63] Dissidents and activists in East Europe and the Soviet Union, and their supporters elsewhere, adopted the discourse of human rights, framing them as a matter of deep moral principle, and denying that there was any partisan, or ideological or political transformative project behind the humanistic (even humanitarian) concerns they were raising.[64] For obvious reasons the East European and Soviet dissidents famously coupled their human rights claims with the stance of anti-politics.

Nevertheless, one of the most insightful theorists in the West (who remained on the left), who supported the new human rights discourse and mobilization in the East, Claude Lefort, was right to reject this self-interpretation. Lefort argued that the path-breaking innovation of placing their demands under the sign of human rights by the dissidents was anything but apolitical or non-partisan. In two nuanced essays he emphasized the "continuity" between the old and the new, by focusing on the pragmatic and symbolic meaning of actors declaring their rights and mobilizing around them even though the reference to international documents along with their moralistic apolitical self-description distinguishes the self-understanding of the dissidents from the earlier French revolutionaries.[65] These differences notwithstanding, Lefort convincingly argued that the practice of declaring and mobilizing around human rights involves a politics, with an elective affinity to democracy, even if one makes only "moral" claims. Declaring and mobilizing for one's rights entails more than overt pleas for a more just exercise of public power, or limits to arbitrariness, or even the rule of law – it also entails wresting the power to participate in the politically relevant discussion and decisions regarding who should be accorded which rights, whose voices should be heard, what rights people have, how these should be interpreted, and about how public power should be exercised. In so doing actors thereby instantiate and exercise the very rights to free horizontal communication, personal autonomy, and political agency – in short, the right to have rights – that they are also demanding. Speaking, assembling, and associating to declare and claim rights on the part of those affected opens up civil public spaces outside the control of power creating a new mode of access to, and conceptualization of, the public sphere and of citizenship.[66] Irrespective of whether actors frame their own rights as minimal "non-partisan" moral claims, the act of publicly declaring and demanding them and the strategy of invoking binding international human rights treaties, and hooking up with transnational actors is a way to make their own voices count, to participate in the politically crucial debates about who has rights and what rights they have and to demand accountability of state power to its own citizens. The agency of those whose rights are at stake is thus created by their own actions, and by their participation in and their taking responsibility for civic public life, which they thereby recreate.[67]

From the dynamic perspective, then, human rights are not simply the object of a declaration, an international legal document those in power can sign and ignore;

rather it is their essence to be declared by those whose rights are at stake.[68] The public activity of those citizens and persons directly affected by a particular state or regime, in declaring their own rights even while referencing international legal documents and benefiting from outside support, involves a deeply political process of struggling for freedom and of contesting the legitimacy of certain uses or structures of power.[69] The pragmatics of the practice of declaring one's rights and positioning oneself as a rights holder is the link between the civil and the political, private and public autonomy, rights and politics, and, ultimately, rights and democracy understood as the political autonomy of free and equal citizens to co-determine the laws that are to bind them.

There are nonetheless important discontinuities between the politics involved in the classic declaration of the rights of man (and citizen) and those surrounding international human rights declarations and activism. What distinguishes the second wave of post-war international human rights politics from the first elite-dominated and UN-focused discourse of diplomats and state executives is that it was adopted by grassroots movements and organizations whose transnational activism bypassed the UN machinery. But what differentiates this activism from that of the classic period was the focus of the transnational human rights activists on international exposure of suffering individuals to "world public opinion" whereby the INGOs assumed the posture of custodians of international human rights norms and law.[70] Alongside domestic activism, it is crucial to acknowledge the striking proliferation and mobilization of *transnational* human rights organizations in the form of INGOs since the 1970s, focused on the rights of others.[71] This is not to say that earlier struggles for the rights of man had no transnational dimensions: the abolitionist movement that focused on the rights of others and women's movements for the suffrage in the nineteenth and twentieth centuries that linked up domestic and transnational actors are just two obvious examples. Continuities are there but so are the discontinuities. However, one should not ignore the innovative focus of transnational mass organizations like Amnesty International and subsequent INGOs on neutrality (in the Cold War) and on the humanitarian dimension of human rights involving violations of basic *dignity* as in torture, disappearances, killings, gulags, etc. Human dignity had gained a new centrality in international human rights documents and in the 1970s it was catapulted to the center of the new transnational activism.[72] Indeed it was the transnational human rights mass organizations from Amnesty International and Human Rights Watch to the more streamlined professional Americas Watch that were the progenitors of the strategy of using "apolitical," "non-partisan" (i.e. vis-à-vis the Cold War blocs) humanitarian discourse focused on generating moral outrage (the whole world is watching) and solidarity with those whose most basic rights to human dignity were being violated and on garnering support from people and governments around the world to pressure for the alleviation of the suffering such rights violations caused.[73] These and other international NGOs and transnational movement activists took over from the early agents of legalization – the small democracies and newly independent former colonies and legal activists that were instrumental in codifying UDHR and the Convention on the Elimination of All Forms of Racial Discrimination (CERD) in the 1960s – to become the prime movers of codification in the 1970s–1980s for human rights treaties and of international pressure for domestic respect for rights.[74] Their success, however, had unintended consequences in the aftermath of the end of the Cold War.

As indicated above, in the 1970s–1980s activists beyond borders hooked up with domestic actors enabling the latter to publicize their grievances and do an end run around repressive states. Transnational activism supplemented, but did not substitute for domestic struggles for equal citizenship and constitutional democracy such that domestic actors, especially in contexts of transition, were able develop their own political agency in pressing for liberalization, democratization, and ultimately domestic constitutionalization and contextualized interpretation of their human rights.[75] But the moralistic and humanitarian rhetoric that informed human rights activism of increasingly well-funded INGOs, together with the embrace of human rights discourse in the late 1970s by a US president whose own moralistic orientation linked up with the new international campaigns, helped catapult human rights to the center of global rhetoric, and to engender a new focus of US foreign policy.[76] Many have noticed the shift of human rights discourses from a minimalist apolitical moral rhetoric to a maximalist moral utopianism in the decade prior to 1989.[77] With the collapse of the Soviet empire, the stage was thus set for human rights rhetoric to become linked not only to the new and heady discourse of global justice, global governance, global rule of law, and global constitutionalism, but also to a new interventionism on the part of states and GGIs claiming to be acting non-politically, in the name of the international community and its core values – human rights.[78]

3.1.3   Human rights and humanitarian intervention: the discourse of enforcement in the 1990s

The third wave of human rights practice and discourse differs dramatically from its predecessors. Indeed in the aftermath of the Cold War, human rights violations have been invoked as justification for the imposition of debilitating sanctions, military invasions, and authoritarian occupation administrations by multilateral organizations (NATO, UNSC) and/or states acting unilaterally under the rubric of "humanitarian" and even "democratic" intervention.[79] The focus of the transnational human rights INGOs of the previous period on dignity harms to victims caused by egregious rights violations lent itself to a merging of humanitarianism (alleviation of suffering) and human rights ideas that was turned into a moralistic interventionism in the hands of others. Discourses of good governance along with humanitarian rescue missions were wedded to international human rights rhetoric. However, the new emphasis on individual and human security in human rights discourses coupled with paternalistic interpretations of those rights in a global context where the focus is on the (coercive) enforcement of international legal norms, tends to bypass or undermine rather than enhance the political agency of domestic actors struggling against injustice.[80] The risk is that the link between the politics of human rights and democratic politics gets severed when it is foreign states, foreign activists, and global governance institutions who under the humanitarian impulse, assert and purport to enforce the human rights of victims. In the name of an external and universal standard of legitimacy – humanitarian justice to persons – an allegedly neutral standard of good governance is to be ensured and/or provided by global institutions.[81] Small wonder, then, that the effort to reformulate the doctrine of intervention for humanitarian purposes by invoking human rights rhetoric came to be linked to challenges to the very idea of sovereignty and to sovereign equality as the organizing principle of international law. Enthusiasm about the prospects of global governance and global justice guided by cosmopolitan (human rights) principles and oriented toward ensuring that all states respect them, was one motivation behind this challenge.

Indeed as indicated above, many in cosmopolitan circles embraced the idea of shifting the discussion of humanitarian intervention toward a focus on "the responsibility to protect" rather than the permissibility to intervene, on human rather than state security, and on the right of individuals to be rescued (and the duty to rescue) when their basic rights are being violated, instead of on who has the right to do the rescuing.[82] The implications for the international legal rules regulating the use of force and Charter law are serious.[83] The claim is that while the state has the primary responsibility to protect its population, if it is unwilling or unable to do so the default responsibility lies with the "international community." Thus the "legalistic" sovereignty/intervention frame (apparently too dependent on the presumption of equal sovereignty and the default principle of non-intervention) should be abandoned in favor of the "right to be rescued/responsibility to protect" frame for addressing instances of serious human rights violations. Humanitarian intervention is the concept that links humanitarian law (the law of war: rules for treatment of civilians, prisoners, etc. in wartime) with international human rights law. The "responsibility to protect" (R2P) is the doctrine devised to get around the limits allegedly posed by the principle of sovereignty and international law based on it to coercive humanitarian intervention absent an international war nexus.[84]

The R2P discourse came into vogue thanks to the influential report of the International Commission on Intervention and State Sovereignty (ICISS) set up in response to the request of then UN Secretary-General Kofi Annan and supported by the Canadian government in 2001.[85] But the initial trigger was the Kosovo crisis, which led to a push to reformulate the doctrine of intervention and to link it to international human rights violations. To be sure the ground had been prepared in the early 1990s when there had already been an unprecedented series of armed interventions for humanitarian purposes in the context of initially internal conflicts in Iraq, Somalia, Croatia, and Bosnia. But it was in the aftermath of the Rwandan genocide and the continuing crisis in the former Yugoslavia, that the push came from strong cosmopolitans focused on human rights and security (moral philosophers and international lawyers) and from the newly influential and militaristic neo-conservatives in the US during the second Clinton administration, to rethink international law and to question whether it should be reformulated so as to permit such interventions.[86]

As is well known, the 1999 NATO intervention in Kosovo was not a Security Council Chapter VII action. Indeed Kosovo was the first time since the inception of the UN Charter system that a coalition of states, acting outside the authority of that system, justified a military invasion and the violation of another state's sovereignty on a humanitarian basis.[87] President Clinton announced a new and very broad doctrine of humanitarian intervention, which proclaimed that, "... if somebody comes after innocent civilians and tries to kill them en masse because of their race, their ethnic background or their religion, it is within our power to stop it and we will stop it wherever you live."[88] This conception of humanitarian intervention, subsequently linked by Kofi Annan to the imperative of *halting gross and systematic violations of human rights*, was also very broad, insofar as it provided no criteria as to who might decide and under what circumstances such intervention is warranted or which rights violations would trigger it.[89] Indeed Annan himself articulated the dilemma this entailed: how to reconcile the imperative of halting gross violations of human rights without violating the legal principle of equal sovereignty and without erecting dangerous precedents for future interventions for self-serving purposes. Interestingly Annan, at the time Secretary-General of the UN, did not condemn the Kosovo intervention as illegal because unauthorized by the UNSC but rather, with Rwanda in mind, framed it as a wrenching moral dilemma that called for serious rethinking about sovereignty and international law.[90] Indeed, alarm expressed on the part of vulnerable states in the global South led to the creation of a commission to write an objective report to assess the Kosovo intervention, which it famously concluded was "illegal but legitimate."[91] Legitimate, because it was a humanitarian rescue but illegal because it was not authorized by the SC under Article 39. The report went on to articulate some threshold principles for a legitimate humanitarian intervention: severe violations of international human rights or humanitarian law on a sustained basis, or subjection of a civilian society to great suffering and risk due to the "failure" of their state, which entails the breakdown of governance at the level of the territorial sovereign state.[92]

The ICISS document was the result of further pressure for the development of clear and general standards that could potentially be embraced by the United Nations General Assembly (UNGA). This report did narrow down the triggers for intervention compared to the Clinton Doctrine and the Kosovo report by restricting the relevant rights violations to large-scale loss of life due to action or inaction of states and large-scale ethnic cleansing.[93] It also reiterated traditional just war doctrine, by emphasizing "just cause, right intention, proportionality and right authority," locating the latter in the UNSC. These were meant to ensure that humanitarian interventions were genuine rescue missions. Moreover the report's path-breaking concept – the responsibility to protect – included the responsibility to prevent and to rebuild as well as to react. However, although it identified the right authority as the UNSC it did not rule out other measures in "crisis" situations if the SC does not act.

While the ICISS report did not gain acceptance by the UNGA, the R2P concept was quickly interpreted by enthusiastic theorists and activists as a way to redefine sovereignty and demote it from its place in international law, thereby dethroning the non-intervention principle, the corollary of sovereign equality. Indeed, the ICISS report itself used the R2P concept to argue for a shift of criteria for the international legal recognition of a state's sovereignty from efficacy in maintaining control to the degree to which it ensures the respect for the basic rights of persons in its care. The old model focused on the capacity of a state to make authoritative decisions with regard to the people and resources within its territory and the state's ability and willingness to respect every other state's sovereignty. Thus the principles of non-intervention, domestic jurisdiction, and territorial integrity are directly associated with the concept of sovereign equality and enshrined in the UN Charter. Sovereignty meant internal supremacy and full jurisdiction/ external autonomy and equal standing. Regime type was not relevant.

But the R2P concept in the report seeks to dramatically alter not only the criteria for international recognition (by adding justice) but also the meaning of sovereignty by literally redefining it as the "responsibility" to secure basic rights. Sovereignty is not only conditioned on responsibility, it is redefined as responsibility meaning that the state's "sovereignty function" is that of protecting the safety and lives of its citizens and promotion of their welfare.[94] Accordingly sovereignty is a dual responsibility: externally to respect the sovereignty of other states and internally to respect international human rights and human security norms.[95] But this means that internally at least, sovereignty is thereby reconceived once again as a positive function – protection of the welfare, dignity, and basic rights of citizens – that can, and this is the point, be performed by others. Understood in this way – as the responsibility to protect – state sovereignty is construed as a bundle of prerogatives that is made contingent on the state's proper fulfillment of its function. Accordingly, if the state reneges it is the responsibility of the international community to step in and act in its place. As Allan Buchanan and Robert

Keohane argue, the "sovereignty bundle" can then be disaggregated: other states or coalitions of states can assume by default the traditional prerogatives of sovereignty in order to carry out the function (and duty) of protection in their role of instantiation of the international community.[96] Thus states that do not measure up to the external moral standard of what amounts to a human rights-based concept of sovereignty lose not only their legitimacy but also their international legal standing and right to political and legal autonomy (external sovereignty). They can be placed in a trustee relationship to the "international community" and accorded elements of "quasi-sovereignty" piecemeal as they resume their protective functions.[97]

Accordingly sovereignty as responsibility resolves the dilemma posed to a system of international law based on the principle of equal sovereignty and the practice of humanitarian intervention through redefinitional fiat: state sovereignty now entails the function of protection of basic human security rights including welfare, and the international legal standing of the state along with prerogatives of sovereignty are conditioned on this and can be redistributed to other actors when need be. Human rights-based sovereignty does not only trump atavistic concerns with state security: now intervention into (and occupation of) "unjust states" is to be understood as the international community's shouldering of the responsibility to protect what really matters: human security. But since the UN is still deemed by many to be a "statist organization," and since R2P goes against black letter Charter law, it is unsurprising that strong cosmopolitan liberals extract the discourse of the responsibility to protect from the UN reform project in which it was originally embedded and invoke it in order to justify unilateral humanitarian interventions or as the basis for "reform" proposals that would establish multilateral alternatives (coalitions of democratic states) to the SC's exclusive authorization mechanisms.[98]

The possibility of so interpreting the R2P doctrine inheres in the redefinition of the concept of sovereignty at its core. This differs from my discussion of the legal nature of the concept of domestic jurisdiction and the idea of redescribing the scope of what are the prerogatives of sovereign states through international law.[99] The functionalist rights-based redefinition of sovereignty as responsibility helps to undermine the default position of sovereign equality in international law and to dethrone the non-intervention principle thus eliminating the protective role they both play vis-à-vis the creation of dangerous precedents and the risks of strategic, self-serving "humanitarian" or "democratic" interventions. Indeed by merging the discourses of global justice, humanitarianism, human rights, and human security, the R2P doctrine opens a Pandora's box. It raises the chimera of global protection and external enforcement of the very wide range of international human rights in the legal documents and to all sorts of maximalist claims regarding forceful intervention. For example, the claim that a human right to democracy is crystallizing into a legal entitlement under customary international law led some cosmo-politan liberal theorists to insist that this right legitimates the use of force in pro-democratic invasions to restore or spread democracy, and to argue for the conditioning of the international legal recognition of states' sovereignty on their observance of "basic" human rights including a right to "minimal" democracy.[100] The stance of apolitical impartial humanitarian intervention under the R2P doctrine is coupled with a non-neutral conception of the regime type of states to whom sovereignty and sovereign equality will be ascribed.

All this invited charges of cultural, western, and/or liberal imperialism which in turn triggered an effort to counter-pose a "functional" and "polit-ical" to a "traditional" understanding, of human rights partly to block their instrumentalization for strategic or hegemonic purposes.[101] Theorists of the political conception seek to retreat from a maximalist position – which holds that human rights are coextensive with rights founded on a universalistic liberal, religious, or metaphysical conception of justice allegedly included in the documents – so as to parry the charges of western ethnocentrism, parochialism, and neo-imperialism.[102] Given the link between human rights and humanitarian intervention their strategy is twofold: (a) to avoid what they take to be traditional ways of approaching human rights, as a set of moral rights derived from or grounded in the correct moral theory, based on metaphysical assumptions either drawn from the natural rights tradition or from a controversial philosophical anthropology, both of which conflict with what Rawls called the fact of (reasonable) pluralism; and (b) to narrow the concept of international human rights to a "proper subset" of the extensive lists in the various international human rights documents (or of moral rights generally) in light of their function of justifying interventions by outsiders. Insofar as violations place the legitimacy of a government or state in question and can undermine its international legal standing as sovereign and open it to external intervention, the strategy is to construe the concept in terms of this function and to pare down the lists accordingly. Let us turn to the ideal-typical understanding of the traditional conception of human rights formu-lated by advocates of the political approach, in order to highlight how the political conception differentiates itself, and then look at two of its variants.

I will argue that advocates of the political conception are right to seek ways to avoid an overly broad conception of international human rights whose violation can be used to justify forceful interventions. But they err in redefin-ing the *concept* of human rights in terms of this function. They thus make a parallel mistake to those R2P theorists who seek to resolve the dilemma of sovereignty and humanitarian intervention by redefining sovereignty in func-tional terms. This time it is international human rights that are functionally redefined: the function is allegedly suspension of the sovereignty argument against intervention. While it is correct that there is now a discursive linkage between human rights and humanitarian intervention, this linkage misleads advocates of the political conception to argue that the purpose and hence the very definition of international human rights is to provide interference-justifying reasons in case of serious violations. But it is not convincing to define the concept of human rights in terms of this function.[103] Nor is it convincing to reduce the political pragmatics of claiming and demanding the institutionalization of human rights to the politics surrounding international enforcement of the treaties, whether this involves juridical, economic, or military sanctions and interventions. As we have seen, from the perspective of individuals and social movements (those affected) announcing and claiming their human rights, the politics at issue do not have as their aim eliciting international intervention and are irreducible to external enforcement of the international documents by other states or by GGIs. There are, then, at least two politics of human rights that must be differentiated.

I will thus propose an alternative dualistic political conception that tries to re-differentiate the humanitarian (external interventionist) from the social and moral dynamics involved in the domestic politics of human rights. If one differentiates between the perspectives of domestic actors asserting their human rights from the invocation by external actors of grave violations of human rights and humanitarian principles to justify international enforcement and coercive intervention by outsiders one can avoid the risks of minimalist and maximalist accounts. I will argue that maximalism in the former case is innocuous while in the latter case it is pernicious. I will suggest a conception of the R2P principle that resituates it within a UN reform project aimed at incorporating the principles of humanitarian responsibility in international law without weakening Charter constraints on the use of armed force and without undermining the constitutive principle of sovereign equality on which that law is based. This will involve a second look at the R2P principle in its contemporary form and another understanding of the relation between sovereignty and human rights.

3.2   The traditional conception of human rights

The traditional approach frames human rights as moral rights that all individuals have by virtue of being human. Accordingly, human rights are universal, have unrestricted validity, and are binding on all individuals and societies whatever their religion, tradition, or culture.[104] Although human rights can also have a juridical nature insofar as they are articulated in national constitutions and international treaties, they entail moral requirements whose force does not depend on their expression in enforceable law.[105] Human rights are deemed to be the most important among moral rights – articulating especially valuable goods or interests, particularly weighty moral concerns that all human beings have.[106] They are ascribed to all individuals equally.[107] Individuals have them irrespective of any personal merit or accomplishment or of any associative relations they have entered into. Indeed human rights are meant to protect the essential and universal features of human personhood from abuse.[108]

This approach raises the question of what the essential and universal features of human beings are that must be protected by human rights. Competing conceptions of human rights as moral rights give different answers, some constructing minimal, others maximal, lists. On the traditional approach, the point is that ordinary moral reasoning will enable us to arrive at an answer to the question of which moral norms are to be deemed a human right.[109] Here it is sufficient to indicate that the "traditional account" thus tends to trigger an effort to derive human rights from some basic feature of human beings, which is universally acknowledged to be intrinsically valuable and essential to all else which is valuable in human life.[110] Ideal-typically, traditional approaches ground human rights in an ethical conception of crucially important interests they are meant to protect, involving a substantive notion of the good from which, in one way or another, the key human rights can be derived.[111] Some come up with an agency or personhood conception of humanity while others focus on a conception of basic interests, the idea of autonomy, or intrinsic human dignity, or basic capacities.[112] There is nothing wrong with deeming personhood or agency or dignity or some other set of basic interests as of special moral significance. But as theorists of the political conception argue, any attempt to derive the content of human rights from the essentially human will lead to a list that is either overly narrow or one that is overly broad and involve controversy.[113]

One example is the attempt to construe human rights on the model of natural rights.[114] While contemporary theorists in this tradition try to give a "post-metaphysical" grounding of human rights and thus to avoid dogmatism, they nonetheless embrace what they take to be the core insight of the natural rights approach, namely that human rights are pre-political in the sense that their validity and existence does not depend on any legal or political recognition.[115] However, the contemporary natural rights model of human rights specifies this insight in a particular way giving another meaning to "pre-political," namely that human rights are the rights individuals would have in a "state of nature," i.e. independently of any institutional or contingent social relationships.[116] They are the rights that no political association can violate and still be deemed legitimate but they do not derive from the special nature of any particular form of association or institutional constellation. Accordingly, they can indeed provide independent standards for judging the justice and legitimacy of a political society but these would perforce be rather minimal – restricted to some pre-institutional account of negative liberty or bodily integrity.[117] The problem is that such an approach and indeed any very minimalist substantive account risks ending up with a list that is so restrictive as to be useless in grounding, accounting for, or

constructively criticizing contemporary human rights documents and practice. Most of the rights in the relevant documents would not pass muster as
human rights on this account: for the impulse is to conclude that any right
that is not a negative right in the above pre-political sense is not a genuine
human right.[118] But this seems to throw out the baby with the bathwater.

On the other hand, concepts of personhood, human dignity, or agency suffer
from the opposite flaw of the natural rights approach: they are too plastic and
unable on their own to provide a clear criterion for deciphering what rights are
essential for securing the "essence" of personhood, or dignity, or agency, or
basic capabilities and in what this essence consists.[119] These concepts thus
either tend to lead to maximal accounts or are unable to provide adequate
criteria for rendering their basic ground more determinate. In other words,
given the indeterminacy of such conceptions, once they become more generous
than the negative liberty approach, they have no way to stop becoming still
more so.[120] The risk is that they lead to lists of human rights that are so
comprehensive that one would be left with no principled distinction between
what human rights secure and what the conditions for having a good life are, or
between human rights and the whole of morality and/or justice.[121] Nor would
we have a way to distinguish which, among all of the rights listed in the various
human rights documents, are genuine human rights and which are missing.
Most important for the adherents of the political conception, it is argued that
such an approach abstracts away from the role that human rights discourses
play in contemporary international politics and law, courting the risk that the
philosophical enterprise becomes irrelevant or worse, too easily appropriated
by the powerful for purposes that have little to do with ensuring the liberty,
agency, integrity, capabilities, or dignity of persons.[122]

3.3   The political conception of human rights: suspending the sovereignty argument

The political conception thus starts from an account of the role international
human rights play in international discourse or politics and attempts to
articulate normative criteria for assessing them in light of their function.[123]
The point is not to give a merely descriptive analysis of what is referred to as
the "international human rights regime" but rather to start, for example as in
the case of Beitz or Raz, from the existing documents, covenants, and discursive practices these generate so as to clarify the meaning of international
human rights with respect to their aims and purposes.[124] The operative idea
is that if we continue to be distracted by the philosophical enterprise of
providing a normative foundation that grounds the concept and generates a
particular conception (set) of human rights by virtue of our humanity, we will
fail to grasp the distinctive nature, role, and purpose of international human
rights. The task of the political conception is thus not to come up with the

best moral theory that grounds an ethically correct list of human rights: indeed the political conception seeks to avoid this sort of justificatory foundational enterprise altogether.

To be clear: adherents of the political conception do not deny that there are moral rights. They do not reject the possibility or need to identify the moral standards which can be invoked in response to the question of why human rights provide reasons for action, or to explain their reason-giving force.[125] Nor are they positivistic or "legalistic" about international human rights: they do not consider it a necessary condition for the existence of a human right that it be listed in the international documents. Indeed, one purpose of the functional account is to gain a critical purchase on those that are so listed. Some advocates of the political conception do not entirely reject the enterprise of moral constructivism – a philosophical project to provide "post-metaphysical" reasons for establishing an individual interest as a moral right and ultimately as a human right.[126] And they agree that every individual has international human rights. But the point of the political conception is to reverse the order of argumentation: the first task of the theorist of international human rights is not to discover the deeper order of values from which human rights in international doctrine allegedly derive their authority so as to judge the extent to which that doctrine conforms to it. Instead the first task is to understand the function that the idea of international human rights is meant to play in the international system.[127] An understanding of this public role should constrain the content of the doctrine and thus yield a standard with which one can critically assess existing practices. In short, instead of interpreting international human rights law or practice in light of an a priori, independently intelligible and "true" moral doctrine, the political conception prescinds from stipulating the basis or nature of the ultimate moral authority of human rights.[128]

Like the first groundbreaking human rights document, UDHR, and the subsequent human rights covenants, the political conception remains silent on the question of the ultimate moral foundation of human rights. As several analysts have pointed out, UDHR does not propose any justifying theory for the rights included in the document, it simply declares certain values to be human rights.[129] As already indicated, the framers obviously understood that while they could agree (or compromise) on the content it would have been impossible to generate agreement about theoretical or normative foundations.[130] The assumption was that people in various cultures could find reasons within their own ethical traditions to support the Declaration's practical requirements. Indeed, the fact that the human rights documents refrain from foundational justifications, and that the framers agreed to disagree about such issues, is, in the view of advocates of the political conception, one of its main virtues for it allows one to parry the charge of cultural imperialism.[131] Taking its cues from this and focusing instead on the function and purpose of international human rights, the claim of the political approach is that an adequate critical conception of human rights cannot be derived from moral rights attached to one's humanity. But neither are they equivalent to the full panoply of constitutional rights of citizens in liberal democracies (or in a liberal-democratic conception of justice). That too would open the international human rights practice to the charge of western liberal parochialism. Moreover, partly for this reason, and partly due to the specific function the political conceptions assign to international human rights, no version of that conception deems genuine international human rights to be equivalent to the expansive lists in the international documents. Adequate analysis of their function instead will yield the clues as to how to determine the appropriate subset of rights that are genuinely human rights.

As in the traditional approach, human rights protect urgent or very important individual interests, against depredation by states or the failure of states to protect these interests from non-state actors in their jurisdiction. However, unlike the former, the political conception construes human rights as political also in the sense that they are special rights that one has by virtue of the distinctive features of (and risks posed by) political associations and institutions, rather than simply by virtue of one's humanity.[132] Human rights thus are not rights one has in a pre-political state of nature: rather one has them by the virtue of political association – i.e. they pertain to contingent social relationships. They are associational rights, activated by the presence of and membership in specific socio-political institutions and they impose constraints on these institutions, and on those acting in their name.[133] As Josh Cohen puts it,

> Human rights are not rights that people are endowed with independent of the conditions of social and political life, but rights that are owed by all political societies in light of basic human interests and the characteristic threats and opportunities that political societies present to those interests.[134]

What, then, is the function of international human rights? International human rights indicate that the way a state treats its own citizens is a matter of international concern.[135] They function as standards for the government of states such that their violation or the failure to fulfill them supplies a justification for remedial and/or preventive action by the world community or those acting as its agents.[136] International human rights discourses and practices thus serve to justify grounds of interference by the international community in the internal affairs of states. In short they disable the "sovereignty argument" against political or social interference, criticism, sanctions, and military intervention by outsiders in the affairs of a state.[137] Their function in international law and international relations is, then, to set limits to the domestic jurisdiction of states, and to override the non-intervention principle, if and when these rights are violated. For some, they serve as the gatekeeper for membership and standing in the international community.[138] Human rights discourses continue to play other roles, but the political conception focuses on the issues of sovereignty and intervention.

Accordingly, human rights are rights "... whose actual or anticipated violation is a (defeasible) reason for taking action against the violator in the international arena."[139] While this is a paraphrase from a recent article by Joseph Raz, theorists familiar with Rawls's *Law of Peoples* will recognize it as drawing on the most famous version of the political conception.[140] The two approaches discussed below differ from Rawls's theory yet they both follow him in distinguishing between moral and liberal constitutional rights on the one hand and international human rights on the other, reserving the latter appellation for the subset of rights whose violation may warrant coercive intrusive action by outsiders. As Rawls puts it, human rights "specify limits to a regime's internal autonomy," and set a limit to pluralism among peoples regarding membership in international society while establishing a principle of toleration and its limits in international affairs.[141]

All versions of the political conception adopt from Rawls the idea that the public role of human rights doctrine must constrain its content. To be sure different theorists of the political conception have different views on the nature of international concern and intervention this involves. Rawls, as is well known, developed his version in the form of a philosophical account of the "Law of Peoples," drawing a tight link between questions of international peace and standards for decency of domestic institutions. His political conception of human rights belongs to the public reason-based understanding of the law of peoples that both decent hierarchical and liberal peoples could embrace as the members in good standing of an international society.[142] The idea is to delineate through the concept of human rights the normative boundaries of acceptable pluralism in international affairs. Rawls offers no independent moral or philosophical ground for his conception of human rights but, instead, assumes that liberal peoples will accept them on liberal grounds and others on other grounds.[143] In this sense human rights are deemed a standard of international legitimacy, which embraces the value of toleration and reasonable pluralism. Accordingly they generate a shared basis of political justification and cooperation in an international society composed of liberal and decent peoples thus helping to achieve stability and peaceful interaction insofar as compliance guarantees the security, autonomy, and freedom from interference of its members. The important point is that human rights in the Rawlsian account function (a) so as to provide a suitable definition of limits to a government's sovereignty, (b) to articulate the conditions for membership in international society (along with non-aggression), and (c) to restrict the justifying reasons for coercive intervention or war.[144]

Rawls sought to develop rules for foreign policy of liberal and decent states in an international society of states that could avoid the charge of liberal intolerance or parochialism. His concern to acknowledge reasonable pluralism among different societies is clearly the motive behind his narrow list of human rights. They are defined strictly in terms of the rights whose violation justifies not only interference but also the denial of sovereign equality to states, indeed even the denial of membership in international society.[145]

The other versions of the political conception are influenced by Rawls's functional political approach, but differ in that they reason from the actual doctrine and discourses of international human rights and aspire to a critical fidelity to the main documents and practices. Charles Beitz develops what he calls a "practical conception" arriving at the function of international human rights from reflection on the role they are designed to play and do play in international affairs. He follows Rawls in arguing that the content of genuine human rights must be determined by their role in providing reasons for interference by outsiders in case of their violation by states. International human rights are indications that such violations will be matters of international concern, because each person is a subject of global concern irrespective of their spatial location or what polity or group one belongs to.[146] For him as well, international human rights are by definition bound up with the state system and are principles governing interference by outsiders into sovereign states. But Beitz does not define human rights with reference to or as a subset of a wider class of universal moral rights: rather they are deemed sui generis norms. Moreover, Beitz's conception of interference is not restricted to coercive intervention and thus presumably would generate a much broader list of genuine human rights than Rawls's conception did.[147] Indeed many of the examples of "interference" that he mentions such as critical public discourse, activities by INGOs, reporting and monitoring mechanisms in the major international texts, "naming and shaming," international assistance or aid and so on, have nothing to do with criteria for the recognition of states, conditions of their membership in international society, disabling of the sovereignty argument, or the suspension of the non-intervention principle which in international law refers to coercive intrusions.[148] Nevertheless, he adheres to the general approach initiated by Rawls of conceiving of human rights in terms of their function as justifying grounds of concern and interference by the international community in the internal affairs of states as the basic idea of the doctrine and of the practice he himself deems basic. For him as well, international human rights are by definition bound up with the state system and are principles governing interference by outsiders into sovereign states.[149]

The two versions of the political conception I discuss below fall somewhere in between Beitz's and Rawls's approaches. Insofar as they also focus on the practice and purpose of international human rights documents and discourses they are close to the approach of Beitz. Yet insofar as they conceptualize human rights as a subset of far more extensive lists of universal individual moral rights, reserving the appellation "human rights" to those moral rights which have the function of suspending the sovereignty argument against intervention, their approach is closer to Rawls's. Indeed they both are motivated by the same anxiety that inspired Rawls's theory: namely, that overly expansive lists of international human rights would lead to unwarranted interventions open to the charge that parochial (western-centric) liberal-democratic principles are being illegitimately used to coerce societies that have different standards of internal legitimacy or justice to conform to foreign standards. Like Rawls the concern is to do justice to reasonable pluralism, to show respect for the principles of sovereignty, sovereign equality, and self-determination, and to minimize the risk of self-serving and/or neo-imperial interventions by powerful outsiders. On the other hand, the concern is also general fidelity to the practice and the documents and this leads them to seek to include more moral rights or more rights listed in the documents as human rights than Rawls's extremely parsimonious list.

Indeed all of the advocates of the political conception assume that one cannot arrive at a conception of genuine human rights by projecting a particular domestic conception of justice onto the international arena. This is why they all revive the distinction between internal and external legitimacy. They recognize that it is wrong to equate the limits of sovereignty or the reasons for international intervention with the internal legitimacy (or justice) of governmental authority as not every action exceeding a state's legitimate authority domestically or its own or liberal standards of justice can or should justify interference by other states.[150] From an internal perspective citizens may press for a more just basic structure or a regime that includes a very broad range of rights, and assess the legitimacy of their governments accordingly. The external legitimacy of a polity or government must rest on distinct, less demanding criteria. In other words given their alleged function, international human rights are not, on any version of the political conception, equivalent to the liberal principles of justice or legitimacy that characterize liberal constitutionalist democracies. They do justify intervention but therefore must be a proper subset of the rights a liberal constitutional democracy would recognize and a smaller subset than those broad lists that are enunciated in the international documents.

How, then, can one arrive at the "proper subset" of rights that fit the requirements of the political conception?[151] What is at issue for the conceptions discussed below is identifying that set of international human rights that will justify coercive action against violators irrespective of whether a state has institutionalized the same subset in its own constitution and irrespective of whether it has incorporated any international treaty that stipulates such rights into its domestic law. To put this another way, what is at issue are the normative criteria for including some but not all of the human rights articulated in the various international rights documents or identifiable as moral rights in the proper subset.[152]

One recent version of the political conception proposes that we must go empirical as it were. Joseph Raz, as indicated above, follows Rawls in defining human rights as those rights which set limits to the sovereignty of states in that their violation provides a defeasibly sufficient ground for taking action against violators that would not otherwise be permissible or normatively available.[153] Suspension of the sovereignty argument against intervention, then, has become the dominant function in human rights practice. Raz rightly argues that sovereignty does not justify state actions but protects states from external interference.[154] Violation of human rights disables this response.[155] But which subset of rights in the broad lists in the human rights documents, not to mention the ever expanding number of moral rights claims can legitimately serve this function?[156] For Raz this is a normative question because he assumes that state sovereignty is, given the world today, a morally justified institution limiting the permissibility of outside interference in the domestic affairs of a state even when the state is in the wrong.[157] This explains both why human rights as sovereignty-limiting measures have to be justified and why international law is at fault when it recognizes as a human right something which morally speaking is not one whose violation might justify international action against a state. In short he calls for caution in giving outsiders the right to intervene.

This is also why Raz rejects the traditional approach and opts instead for a conception of human rights "without foundations." Given their function, political reflection about which rights are human rights must vary with whether intervention is warranted and feasible. One cannot arrive at an answer to this question by reasoning from the premise that human rights are moral rights possessed by everyone by virtue of their humanity. But given the variability of these empirical criteria, Raz also refrains from devising an ultra-minimal list along the lines of Rawls. Instead, he argues that ascertaining the human rights-based limits to sovereignty is contingent on two factors: the conditions within a particular society and the current nature of the international system, i.e. who is in a position to assert the limitations on that society's sovereignty. Since the international domain could be composed of self-interested intrusive bullies, or an imperial hegemon, the proper subset of genuine international human rights depends at any given time not only on the conditions within a society (urgency) but also on the likelihood of morally sound, impartial interference by outsiders.[158] Accordingly human rights lack a foundation in not being grounded in a fundamental (or universal) moral concern but depend instead on contingencies of the system of international relations.[159]

Nevertheless and somewhat contradictorily, Raz does seem to suggest that human rights are a subset of moral rights held by individuals and that ordinary moral reasoning aided by assessments of the current geopolitical context is the way to arrive at an appropriate list at any given time.

He proposes a procedure that involves three layers of argument: first, the identification of an individual interest that establishes an individual moral right; second, an argument that shows under what conditions states are duty-bound to respect or promote that moral right; and third, an argument showing that states do not enjoy immunity from interference regarding these matters.[160] Only those moral rights that pass this three-part test rise to the level of human rights.

Presumably this "empirical" approach would imply that under current conditions, there exists a very narrow range of human rights whose violation would suspend the sovereignty argument against intervention, given the fact of an unrivaled superpower that utilizes human rights discourses to justify its self-interested interventions around the globe.[161] Under these circumstances the moral principles setting limits to sovereignty will be very protective of sovereignty. Under different conditions, however, a broader set of rights including even a right to democracy could rise to the level of an international human right. That is, it could be given institutional recognition such that governments have the duty to protect the interests that such a right protects. Then the sovereignty argument would be unavailable to block military or other coercive interventions into polities that do not deliver on the democratic entitlement. What would be wrong with this outcome?

While it helpfully advocates prudence when reflecting on which moral rights should become human rights given their alleged function of neutralizing the sovereignty argument, the empirical approach does not offer a philosophically defensible substantive moral standard that would protect states from intervention whatever the nature of the international environment. Nor does it offer a procedure for determining how to or who should make the decision as to which rights rise to the level of human rights at any given time or whether the appropriate condition of the international order obtains for the rights that are so recognized. It thus cannot provide an adequate critical standard to assess current human rights practice, which was part of the point of the exercise. Moreover, despite its pretentions to be without foundations, Raz's approach is open to the charge that it is ultimately parasitic on "traditional" conceptions of human rights because it presupposes an underlying wider class of universal moral rights (or interests) of which human rights comprise the varying proper subset at any given time.[162] This implies that "au fond" the political conception cannot do without moral or ethical argumentation.[163]

3.4 The political conception and membership

The alternative is to devise an explicit substantive moral principle for determining the "proper subset." In several recent articles Josh Cohen proposes a political conception that construes human rights as entitlements that ensure the bases of membership, or inclusion into organized political society.[164]

The central idea is that a normative notion of membership requires that a political society's basic institutions, laws, and decisions are oriented to the common good and that every person's good is taken into account:[165]

> failing to give due consideration to the good of members ... is tantamount to treating them as outsiders, persons whose good can simply be dismissed in making laws and policies.[166]

The membership principle requires less than full justice, but more than a minimalist conception of human rights. It is presented as a moral standard for determining which subset of moral rights qualify as human rights that meet the three requirements of a good political conception: fidelity to a sufficient range of the rights identified by the principal documents and to their purpose, toleration of diverse polities and political cultures, and compatibility with the principle of self-determination.[167]

In tune with the other political conceptions already discussed, Cohen also defines human rights as international (his word is global) standards whose violation warrants external interference that can involve sanctions and humanitarian intervention.[168] Cohen shares the associational approach of all political conceptions: human rights are not rights people have independent of socio-political life but rather are rights owed by all political societies in light of basic human interests and characteristic threats and opportunities political societies present to those interests.[169] Unlike Raz, however, Cohen is not hesitant to deem such rights to be universal in the sense that they are owed by every political society to all individuals, although he also insists that as requirements of political morality, which do not depend on their actual expression in legal documents, they must be especially urgent.[170] In addition to universality, urgency, and fidelity, Cohen's conception is characterized by non-juridification and open-endedness, in the sense that the membership principle provides a normative way of reasoning in support of human rights not previously identified or listed in any legal document while remaining abstract enough to be open to interpretation and support by societies with a variety of conceptions of justice, political legitimacy, and the good.

The advantage this conception has over minimalist views based on a natural rights conception or on the "lowest common denominator" approach, both of which (for different reasons) tend to reduce human rights to the barest requirements of (negative) personal liberty and bodily integrity, is that it can meet the requirement of fidelity and account for the more capacious lists in the documents while providing a critical moral standard yet remaining "un-foundational" in the sense of not resting on a particular (hence parochial) ethical conception of the good.[171] In other words the membership conception of human rights is presented as an interpretation of the core moral idea behind the actual lists and international human rights practice. Accordingly international human rights identify the goods that are the requirements of membership such that due consideration is given to the common good *and* to the good of all members ensuring that those subject to a political society's regulations, laws, and policies matter, i.e. have their good taken into account. This principle operates as a threshold below which a political society can no longer invoke the sovereignty argument against interference by the international community. That interference can range from naming and shaming to coercive sanctions and military interventions. Conversely if the membership principle is respected for all those within its jurisdiction, outsiders have no right to invoke violation of their conception of human rights as a reason for interference.

The membership principle is "un-foundational" in another sense: Cohen leaves open the deeper normative reasons underlying the claim to and for membership.[172] Accordingly his approach seeks to avoid the indefensible metaphysical assumptions of natural rights theories along with the confusion of "substantive" with "justificatory minimalism" typical of empirically oriented and/or "lowest common denominator" approaches. The latter end up being tolerant in the wrong way because they accommodate the fact of pluralism uncritically in seeking to find de facto overlaps of views (substantive minimalism via another route) rather than a free-standing moral principle to which all reasonable societies commit however much they differ in other respects. "Justificatory minimalism" by contrast articulates a moral conception of international human rights without itself being based on a particular ethical or religious outlook. It is animated by the acknowledgment of "reasonable pluralism" and the need for toleration in elaborating a conception of international human rights that can gain support in "global public reason" from a variety of societies organized on the basis of a wide range of ethical conceptions of the good or religious principles. In other words the idea is to formulate a conception of human rights as an independent normative enterprise that can lead to reasonable global norms and standards acceptable to different political societies and to which they can be held accountable. The relevant public here is global, hence the concept of "global public reason."[173] The membership principle as a free-standing moral principle tailored to what is deemed to be the unifying conception and purpose underlying the key human rights documents is designed to fit that bill.

Thus, like Rawls, Cohen argues that international principles of human rights can only be understood as a "proper subset" of the rights founded on a liberal conception of justice. Although he certainly embraces a liberal conception of justice and subscribes to the liberal and democratic view that persons are free and equal and merit equal concern and respect, he assumes that this view is based on a substantive ethical outlook that represents individuals as "self-authenticating sources of valid claims" that not all societies share.[174] While this can be the basis for rights claims made within liberal, constitutional democracies, insofar as they involve a regime as well as a form of society based precisely on the conception of the equality of all persons and the immanence of authority and legitimacy principles, it cannot form the basis of international human rights claims given their function. Instead of intolerantly imposing an account of human rights predicated on the liberal conception of justice, one must develop a conception that is compatible with many ethical world-views but which has reasonable standards to which all political societies can be held.[175]

For example, Cohen argues that while justice may require democracy, democracy is not a human right. To construe democracy as a human right which could trigger sanctions if it were violated would be tantamount to generalizing legitimacy criteria from one form of society (individualist, egalitarian, democratic) and one political regime (liberal-democratic) to all polities, thus violating the principles of global public reason and toleration, vitiating the point of a political conception.[176] Because the norms of membership do not entail democracy or even liberal constitutionalism, they do not violate the value of toleration. And toleration of reasonable pluralism is what drives the attempt to come up with a political conception in the first place for the Rawlsians. Cohen repeats Rawls's assertion that toleration is crucial because it indicates respect for a political society and for the individual members of that society who ordinarily have some identification with their polity and its way of life even if they are critical of some of its practices and ethos.[177] Collective self-determination is the operative term that captures this intuition, replacing democracy and a full-blown liberal conception of justice.

Following Rawls, Cohen deems the principle of collective self-determination to be a natural correlate of the requirement to treat all citizens as members.[178] While he is careful to distinguish between collective self-determination and democracy, he maintains that the former requires a political process representative of the diverse interests and opinions of those subject to the government's laws and policies.[179] But this need not entail direct representation of individuals along the lines of one person–one vote; it can entail representation of the subgroups of which they are members. Collective self-determination is a normative requirement of any conception of human rights based on the membership principle, but less demanding than a requirement of democracy which, for Cohen, is one form of collective self-determination.[180] The prerequisites of collective self-determination include the rights of dissent and appeal, freedom of expression and conscience, and the obligation of the government to publicly justify its policies to its citizenry.[181] These are not the only human rights entailed by the membership principle, but they are indicative of the idea that human rights are norms of social and political inclusion such that all individuals count insofar as their interest and welfare are taken into account by government. The claim is that this conception of the membership principle can be met in a variety of societal types, including those based on status hierarchies, those with an official public religion, and those which do not endorse the ideal of a democratic society as an association of equal individuals.[182]

Indeed, one could analyze the capacious lists in the human rights documents as expressive of the norms of membership. But one could also question whether all the rights on these lists are required by the membership principle, namely that political society must attend to the good of all subject to its regulations. Disagreements about the scope of human rights would become disagreements about the norms of membership – about what it means to be included as a member of a political society. The requirements of membership and thus identifying international human rights are a core issue for global public reason understood as a terrain of reflection and argument among all peoples who share responsibility for interpreting its principles, monitoring, and enforcing them.[183] This idea captures Raz's intuition that given their function in suspending the sovereignty argument against intervention, the scope of human rights can vary with the nature of the international political environment: but this time the content of human rights varies with the shifting determinations of global public reason.

This is an elegant formulation of the political conception. Nevertheless it has flaws that are characteristic of all the Rawls-inspired versions of that conception. I will mention only three. First, respect for collective self-determination is the important intuition behind the reluctance to generalize parochial understandings of human rights norms as the basis for powerful outsiders (states or the Security Council) to judge the legitimacy of other societies and to suspend the non-intervention principle (the sovereignty argument) in cases of violation. But as others have pointed out, the principle of collective self-determination equivocates on the meaning of the self. Cohen, like Rawls, wishes to require that the "self" of his normative conception of collective self-determination does not refer simply to the government of a state securing its independence from, say, colonial rule but also entails its institutional responsibility to and relationship with the citizenry. This implies that the "self" is the people ruled by that government that therefore must take its interests into account. But unless "the people" are construed as a unity, like a species, it is entirely possible that a minority, minorities, or even a majority among them do not think that their interests or welfare are being properly taken into account or that their voices are being heard and appropriately responded to even in what might appear to outsiders as a decent consultation hierarchy and even if members embrace other aspects of the political culture and way of life of their society. But the political conception would have to deny both that these members have a human right to resist unequal, discriminatory, and non-democratic forms of political rule and that "interference" even in the most minimal sense of criticism or "naming and shaming" by outsiders such as non-governmental actors allied with domestic critics who invoke the norms in the international documents would be legitimate.[184] This would deprive domestic critics of a powerful normative argument, namely invoking their human right to equal concern and respect or equal dignity against discrimination and against unequal representation and lack of voice in the political system.[185]

Related to this problem is the issue of adaptive preferences. It is certainly important to respect the forms of political organization established by diverse political communities and wrong to hold them to a conception of justice that its members do not see as their own (the point of external sovereignty linked to the non-intervention principle and to a normative idea of responsive collective self-determination). But if these "preferences" are the result of domination, silencing, and political oppression, and are rejected by *some* members of the political community at issue, who challenge the inequalities or exclusions or discriminatory treatment they derive from and reinforce, then there is no convincing reason to deny the dissenters, even if they are a minority, the powerful claim that their human rights are being violated. Respect for the integrity of a political community must also involve respect for the integrity of all of its members and forced acceptance of social or political norms is incompatible with that. Internal challenges to majority interpretations and to laws deemed unjust within a society do not indicate that it is time to suspend the sovereignty argument, but they can and often do involve the invocation of human rights to equal dignity, to equal liberty and voice, to non-discrimination, and so forth. It may be that in some hierarchical polities the rigid political cultures under dominant interpretations offer little basis for an immanent critique of the domestic constitutional arrangement or policies. This is especially true of gender hierarchies inculcated in primary socialization, based on oppression and exclusions in adult life (especially denial of higher education) and backed up by traditionalist patriarchal structures and privileges in private and public law. The demands for full and equal membership that the invocation of human rights claims expresses on the part of some of those affected are, to be sure, first and foremost addressed to their own government, but by invoking international human rights standards they are able to refer now also to general standards. If their states have signed on to these international covenants, the standards are in some sense immanent rather than external, and thus rightfully invoked by domestic dissenters to hierarchical and discriminatory norms and practices. There is no reason why such dissent cannot have echoes outside the relevant polity in the discourses of outsiders willing to help publicize and provide moral support, and to name and shame governments that oppress such dissent or worse.

Second, as we have already seen, there are some internal inconsistencies with the resolute "un-foundational" stance of political conceptions of human rights. Rainer Forst provides the best counter-argument. I agree with Forst that insofar as justificatory minimalism seeks to avoid reliance on parochial ethical doctrines of the good, in fidelity with the international documents that refrain from invoking a comprehensive philosophical or religious doctrine to justify the concept or conception of human rights, the political conception is right on the mark. But this does not mean that an autonomous moral justification is not important to the practice or concept of human rights and it is indeed implausible to claim that such a justification could be "unfoundational" or "minimal" if that means agnostic regarding its foundations.[186] As Forst convincingly argues, if one seeks an independent moral argument for a normative notion of membership or of any other conception of human rights, if one means by independent a normative argument that is not reducible to a de facto overlap of existing cultures or traditions, and if it is part of a human rights-based conception of membership and collective self-determination that any conception of the rights or duties of persons as members of a polity must be justifiable to them by those empowered by it (Cohen's claim), then it is not possible to avoid a substantive moral argument about the respect owed to persons as agents to whom one owes reasons (justifications) for claims that are to bind them.[187] Indeed the normative concept of collective self-determination deployed by Cohen entails a dynamic of justification especially to those who are discriminated against, who criticize exclusions and asymmetries, otherwise there does not seem much point to insisting on this feature as central to the membership principle. The point is that this approach implicitly has a conception of the person as a moral equal worthy of the respect that mutual justification entails and thus as a bearer of human rights – which ultimately rests on a foundational argument that can and should be made explicit. Another way of putting this is that the dynamic of mutual justification implicit in the concept of collective self-determination entails the participation of all those affected in public processes of deliberation, reason-giving, debate, and so forth which implies the moral equality of all participants. Ultimately Cohen's membership principle linked to the concept of collective self-determination has the internal telos of equality and agency which he associates with democracy because the only way to determine whether or not one's good is being taken into account sufficiently is for those affected to participate in the discussion and to hear their arguments regarding legitimate ways in which they should be treated the same or differently from others.[188]

A similar argument can be made with respect to Joseph Raz's empirical account, insofar as he too deems human rights after all to be a subset of moral rights, although the proper subset is partly dependent on contextual conditions. It is not my purpose here to get into the debate of whether there is a meaningful distinction to be made, as Forst believes, between the moral and the ethical, between the right and the good, which is the basis of his argument that a moral theory of human rights must come first (prior to political constructivism), to guide and constrain the practices of any political society, to ground its internal legitimacy, and to constrain any institutional articulation of human rights in covenants and official declarations. I will return later to the distinction Forst makes between moral and political constructivism and to his reflexive construction of the relation between the two to see how this approach speaks to the political practices of declaring human rights on the part of those affected so that their agency and creativity is accounted for appropriately in theory. I turn now to a related and for the purposes of this chapter more pressing third criticism of the political conception since my aim here is not to provide a philosophical theory or justification of human rights but to address the ways in which they relate to state sovereignty.

The third objection to the political conception refers to the definition of human rights in functional terms, in particular as principles governing external intervention into states. Why should suspension of the sovereignty argument be conceived of as the main or sole function of international human rights? Why define international human rights in terms of sovereignty-suspension, i.e. in terms of the *pro tanto* justifiability of international intervention against states that commit rights violations?[189] Isn't the issue of which acts or omissions on the part of a state should be recognized as possible triggers for intervention, particularly for coercive sanctions and military intervention that constrain the principle of sovereignty, distinct from the definition of the very concept of human rights? Isn't it a logical mistake to conceive of the nature and purpose of human rights norms in this way? Yes, the very fact that there are international human rights enshrined in international covenants and declarations indicates that they are a matter of international concern. But this fact should not reify the external perspective of the outsider who observes a political structure and reflects on the grounds for intervention.[190] The internal perspective of those affected who declare and announce their human rights and whose intra-national purpose is to create a more just, more legitimate, perhaps more liberal and democratic domestic political system should be the main one although in so doing they ipso facto invoke universalistic principles.

The worry of most advocates of the political conception that the extensive lists of human rights in the various covenants and treaties could be used to justify coercive and self-serving interventions by the powerful (including attempts to impose their own conceptions of justice onto others) is a legitimate one. So is the need to disarm the sovereignty argument when it is invoked in order to protect the impunity of rulers who engage in or indirectly support grave violations of human rights. But the political conception errs insofar as it embraces the merger of humanitarian and human rights discourses as if the two are inextricable and serve the same function. They err, in other words, in embracing the enforcement model that humanitarian intervention articulates regarding grave humanitarian crises or grave rights violations as the heart of the international human rights "regime." Although the articulation of human rights in the international documents does indicate international concern, this does not require either a concept of human rights that equates them to this function or a redefinition of sovereignty and abolition of the non-intervention principle in international law in order to come into effect. Nor is that their purpose or main function. Two distinctions are in order here. First the bulk of human rights in the documents are not meant to trigger and are not equipped with international enforcement mechanisms and rightly so. Moreover, those rights whose violation could or should, defeasibly, entail coercive intervention and suspension of the sovereignty argument against international enforcement, along with related violations of humanitarian law do not require a redefinition of the concept of sovereignty or of human rights. Instead, what is required is a change in the political culture of sovereign impunity. The relevant subset of such rights tracks changes in the prevailing conception of what is legitimately within the domestic jurisdiction of a state. What is at stake here is a changing international sovereignty regime, not the redefinition of sovereignty as a set of functions or its replacement by international human rights as the new basic norm of the international system. Conversely it makes little sense to *define* human rights in terms of the function of suspending the sovereignty argument against intervention. Surely separate issues are at stake here. I thus propose to disaggregate the two discourses of international human rights and humanitarian intervention conceptually in order to focus on the second issue, namely how to devise legitimate principles and international procedures for assessing and deciding cases of international action that do indeed directly challenge the non-intervention principle and require a shift in the existing sovereignty regime. The "enforcement" function and the role of the bulk of the international human rights norms and covenants involve a distinct dynamics. What is at issue in both cases is a new sovereignty regime that takes sovereignty, sovereign equality, and human rights seriously.

From this perspective, Cohen's focus on the norms of membership is helpful. But his construal of these norms is too broad if we have in mind coercive "humanitarian" intervention and ultimately legal institutionalization of the principles regulating it. Suspension of the sovereignty argument when rights to individual dissent, free expression, appeal, and the requirement of public justification of policy are violated could amount to a green light to intervene against any authoritarian regime militarily.[191] Would this not turn Cohen's conception of membership rights into just another way, albeit less demanding than insisting on democracy, of giving the ultimate decision on the internal legitimacy of a political system to outsiders? Would not this formulation of the content and function of the membership principle have the wrong result of disabling both domestic and international criticism of discriminatory and unjust regimes while justifying military interventions in too wide a range of polities? I turn to this problem first and will point in the conclusion to a different "political conception" of the role and purpose of international human rights proper and their domestic "enforcement."

3.5 Sovereign equality and the right to have rights: rethinking the membership principle

There is a compelling intuition behind the idea of conceptualizing a subset of human rights violations that could suspend the sovereignty argument against intervention in terms of the membership principle. This together with carefully formulated principles regulating all armed conflicts, domestic or international (humanitarian law), could inform the effort to devise appropriate procedures and to reform international rules and institutions so that they can legitimately assess and decide when external action is justified.[192] But one must go about this *ex negativo*. Instead of trying to come up with a positive list of individual rights that fair membership entails, one should proceed by establishing the threshold of radical violations of the membership principle that indicate not the absence of political participation, dissent, or concern and respect, but rather, absolute non-belonging. Political membership is indeed about inclusion, and to treat some categories of citizens as no-counts, as people whose good can be completely dismissed, yet over whom the state continues to rule, is tantamount to treating them as outsiders, or as mere things. Recall that it is membership in a non-voluntary and coercive public organization – a sovereign state – that is being discussed. The question then is under what circumstances can the "international community," i.e. foreigners, determine that the membership principle is being so radically violated that harsh sanctions or military intervention may be called for, without inviting the charge of intolerance, or liberal imperial imposition? Since suspension of the sovereignty argument in international law means that humanitarian intervention is at issue, the question is what negative rules regarding membership should rise to the level of internationally sanctionable legal norms. In other words, which subset of grave violations of human rights and humanitarian principles should acquire a status that comports with the discourse of external enforcement, and suspension of the sovereignty argument regarding domestic jurisdiction, thus possibly justifying sanctions and intervention by the international community?

We already have some of the answer in existing international law. The Genocide Convention outlaws genocide and requires states to prevent and punish it, leaving it up to the Convention's parties and the UN to decide how to enforce it.[193] Thus the Security Council has the authority and obligation to prevent and punish genocide, as do all states. Moreover mass extermination, expulsions (ethnic cleansing, mass deportations), and crimes against humanity including enslavement of particular categories of its citizenry, are not deemed to be within the domestic jurisdiction of any state and are outlawed by certain treaties and customary international law.[194] They have attained the status of *jus cogens* norms meaning that no treaty concluded by states to engage in such actions will be considered valid. Such violations are certainly considered matters of international concern. However, as we have already seen, violations of the relevant humanitarian and/or human rights law do not clearly give any state or even the Security Council legal "jurisdiction" to intervene militarily in such cases: the exception being enforcement measures under Chapter VII to maintain international peace and security.[195]

I want to argue that the membership principle, as revised below, can give us a coherent normative argument for this "proper subset" without undermining the default position of equal sovereignty, domestic jurisdiction, and non-intervention in the international or the UN Charter system and without requiring minimalism regarding human rights. This version of the political conception would apply *only* to those rights violations that could justify R2P becoming what it is not now, formal international law, although that would require institutional reforms of the relevant international institutions as will be made clear below. My use of the membership principle, then, is not meant to serve as a criterion for defining international human rights generally, but only for helping to stipulate those whose violation could involve suspension of the sovereignty argument against coercive intervention. I will return further on to the separate question of how to understand the very different political function of the other international human rights in the documents (international concern, referents for domestic social movement actors, for domestic courts, for incorporation into constitutions, and for transnational solidarity) and how they may be justified. Once one distinguishes these conceptual issues, once we re-differentiate the two political functions of international human rights – humanitarian, international enforcement and intervention from above and outside; domestic invocation from below helped by transnational indications of concern and criticism and internal enforcement by the relevant institutions within a constitutional legal order – then the need to construct minimalist lists or minimalist justifications for the latter diminishes.

The negative approach to the membership principle focuses on external not internal legitimacy. By this I mean that it pertains to what I believe is already an implicit cultural shift in the conception of what should be in the "domaine reserve" of any sovereign state. In short when a state (or its proxies) indulges in what I call the four E's – (mass) extermination, expulsion, ethnic cleansing, enslavement (virtual or formal) – it forfeits the claim to be standing for and thus to be sovereign over the groups it oppresses in these radical ways. For what such policies "say" to the targeted group is "you are not one of us, you are no longer a member of this political community, you are the enemy, you as a group have no right to exist, or you as a group are so inferior that you have no right to have rights as members, we can use you and your labor but you are not persons or citizens under our (or any) law." These practices violate individual moral and human rights but they must also be understood as a politics of exclusion and of denial of membership of the relevant group in the political community that the sovereign state is supposed to represent internationally. By denying not a particular set of rights such as freedom of speech, or participation through a "decent consultation hierarchy," but the very right to have rights within the state, the government forfeits the claim to speak for and the "right to coercively rule" the groups it constitutes, excludes, and oppresses in these radical ways.[196] In other words, the government itself has abolished the political and legal relationship between the state and the targeted group that sovereignty establishes.[197] Such radical violations of the membership principle create an obvious "non-fit," to borrow Walzer's term without its cultural connotation, between those subject to sovereign power and the political community in whose name it is supposed to be exercised.[198] The principle of the sovereign equality of states need not and today does not construe this form of radical exclusion from the political community as falling within the "domaine reserve" of any state. Moral rights against mass extermination, expulsion, ethnic cleansing, and enslavement (or radical discrimination such as apartheid), thus rise to the level of the "proper subset" of human security rights that neutralize the prima facie sovereignty argument against the possibility of intervention.[199]

So understood, although membership is a substantive moral principle it is also deeply political. It presupposes both the value of and the limits to the sovereignty of states. It also signals the awareness that politics, power, and political relationships are always at stake when it comes to human rights. Framing the issue in terms of membership invites reflection on the politics of membership and exclusion, and acknowledges that the goal of such rights violations is always also the political death of a segment of the political community as well as the redefinition of the identity of that community through violence, as part of a power play by those in or seeking control of government.[200] While moral rights of victims are of course being violated, it is the political project behind the violations and the political prerogatives of sovereignty that must be addressed by this particular subset of human rights and humanitarian law discourses. By construing the membership principle and the proper subset of human security rights in this way, it becomes clear that today, at least, sovereign equality cannot be invoked to shield this kind of "redefinition" of the political community. The human rights treaties that prohibit genocide or crimes against humanity and enslavement, the humanitarian law of armed conflict that rules out ethnic cleansing, as well as crimes against humanity in all armed conflict be it domestic or international, say in effect that the radical attacks on membership of this sort should not be deemed to be within the domestic jurisdiction of states and the principle of sovereign equality will therefore not automatically shield them. Understood in this way, violation of the substantive moral principle of membership can serve as a defeasible ground for imposing sanctions and could become hard international law if appropriately institutionalized. There is a "cosmopolitan" intuition at work here that was grasped by Hannah Arendt long ago: crimes against humanity which involve any of the four E's aim not only to excise categories of people from membership in a particular domestic political community but also, ultimately, from membership in the human and, hence, international community.[201] This, apart from the obvious international consequences of, say, ethnic cleansing or expulsions that create refugees and so on, is why such violations rise to the level of serious international concern and are not considered within the purview of any sovereign.

The variants of the political conception that I have discussed try to avoid flaws associated with the traditional approach but fail to provide a convincing alternative. Their greatest weakness, apart from those already mentioned and apart from inattention to procedure, to which I shall return, is that they fail to clarify theoretically and normatively just what the restriction of the proper subset of human rights via the membership principle, or empirically, is meant to protect.[202] Gesturing toward toleration of diversity does not suffice to account for why the threshold should be so high when it comes to violations of the moral rights of persons. Although the Rawlsians mention the moral importance of state sovereignty, they do not explain this intuition. What is missing is an account of why respecting sovereignty entails respect for the members of a political community even when the latter's moral rights are violated by their own government. Without addressing this issue it is difficult to find a principled argument against foreign interventions aimed at overthrowing a tyranny, a dictatorship, or a corrupt ruling power even absent mass killing or expulsions. What is also missing from the membership model is the "right to have rights" of non-members, and the obligation of states to respect and protect them.[203] I will address each issue in turn.

Since I will propose my own versions of the political conception, let me make the argument for the political autonomy of states (sovereignty) and their universal inclusion in the key institutional embodiment of the international community: the UN. The concept of sovereign equality ideal-typically articulates the idea of political autonomy in a double sense: it helps construct the external independence of political and legal relationships within a polity by establishing domestic jurisdiction and differentiating among distinct legal and political systems, thereby securing the internal conditions of possibility for self-determination and self-government under law – i.e. for political freedom.[204] I will address the external and the internal aspects separately although they are connected.

The second half of the twentieth century witnessed an unprecedented effort to legally regulate the use of force and install a collective security regime. But it also witnessed successful assertions of political autonomy and sovereignty by states emerging out of the debris of European empires. The legal principle of sovereign equality enshrined in the UN Charter and its corollary, the principle of non-intervention, were key elements of this effort.[205] In the aftermath of decolonization when it became interpreted in light of the concept of self-determination, sovereign equality was invoked in projects to generalize the principles of political autonomy, domestic supremacy of a state's internal legal order, and non-intervention to *all* states in the international system: and to all member states in the UN (192 as of 2010). The international order thereby became more inclusive and more "legalized" than ever before. Sovereign equality morphed into the counter-concept to empire.[206]

According to this principle all sovereign states have an equal entitlement to participate in the formation of international law (as legal subjects) and to take on international obligations because they are equally holders of full international legal personality. A *principle of reciprocity* with legal effect follows from the principle of sovereign equality: all states are formally entitled to the same general rights and subject to the same general obligations. Any state claiming a right under international law has to accord all other states the same right. Moreover the ascription of sovereignty is a matter of international recognition and involves a range of cooperative practices from diplomatic relations to participation in international organizations to equal legal standing before international courts, indicating inclusion in international society (now globalized) and in the UN Charter system. *Sovereign equality is thus a relational concept.* The legal principle of sovereign equality also entails *jurisdiction*: the authority to make and enforce rules within a certain geographic area, limiting the application of external power. From the juridical perspective, *domestic jurisdiction* and *immunity* from foreign laws (autonomy) is the sine qua non for international law as it delimits legal systems from one another and thus articulates plurality. It means that states are not subject to other states' jurisdiction although the scope of acts for which state officials are accorded immunity can be restricted by international law (today restrictions concern acts of aggression, forced annexation, genocide, and other international crimes). In other words, a state is sovereign because it is normatively, legally deemed independent from any other state and recognized as such with all this entails: it is bound only by international law and by the rules of the international organizations it signs on to.

External sovereignty – independence – is matched by internal sovereignty – the domestic supremacy of the state's legal system and political institutions. By implication, internal and external sovereignty entail each other. Together they comprise the unity and indivisibility of sovereignty: domestically the indivisibility of sovereignty signifies the unity of the polity and its legal system; internationally it means the legal personality of the state, its autonomy, its ability to enter into treaties, assume obligations, etc. This does not, however, mean that the *prerogatives* associated with sovereign power must be exercised by one instance domestically (organ sovereignty), or that a sovereign state is impermeable to international law, or that its officials can hide behind the legal personality of the state when they violate it.[207] Nor does it mean that the prerogatives ascribed to sovereign states cannot be "unbundled" – delegated or ascribed to various actors or restricted by international law. But it does mean that the unity of sovereignty in the above sense of legal supremacy and political self-determination domestically and political autonomy/equal legal standing internationally cannot be "disaggregated."

It is nonetheless important to keep the internal and external perspectives analytically distinct: domestic supremacy of a legal system (necessarily linked to de facto control even though we are defining sovereignty as a norm) cannot mean, from an international law perspective, that a state's legal system is deemed supreme globally. It cannot entail the generalization of one state's perspective, ethical political principles, or institutions to the globe, however liberal, democratic, or powerful the state is. That would be to equate sovereignty with an imperial perspective. Rather one has to recall that the autonomy ascribed via the principle of sovereign equality to all states is normative and relational and involves practices of mutual recognition and membership in an international society and/or community of states. Accordingly no state is legally supreme internationally. The external sovereignty ascribed to all states by the principle of sovereign equality arises within, indeed is constitutive of a *plural* normatively egalitarian political and legal universe (international society) which can of course also involve institutionalized multilateralism: but it is one in which neither a world empire nor imperialist polities ruling over colonies or "peripheries" can or should be tolerated today. Sovereignty is a form of legal empowerment to act with legal effect that is ascribed by international law to every state: it is thus a legal institution, not a mere fact. Accordingly, the principle of sovereign equality indicates that "the rules according to which international law is interpreted, developed and changed are not the billiard balls of classical realism, but rather the table upon which the game is played."[208] Indeed, vis-à-vis the old Westphalian conception *a key change* occurred with the principle of sovereign equality: instead of seeing sovereignty as existing apart from and prior to international law – as a pre-existing political "fact" of absolute and impermeable state power, "sovereign equality" is now seen as the core rule set up by the international system itself. Moreover, this principle has always been linked with a utopian ideal of greater substantive equality in law-making – the trend toward a more inclusive international community has been accompanied by a push in that direction. It is important to note that de facto inequalities of power and privilege in the international system do not necessarily violate the legal principle of sovereignty: it remains the organizing principle so long as equal legal standing, domestic jurisdiction, sovereign immunity, reciprocity, and non-intervention apply to all states. Sovereign equality means equality before the rule, not within the rule.[209] It is a "constitutive legal fiction," an institution that structures the entire edifice of international law without ignoring the (always shifting) facts of power. But it is also the basis on which claims to actual equalization of conditions can be and are raised.

Understanding the principle of sovereign equality as a legal norm of the international community allows one to see that the prerogatives ascribed to sovereign states can change – that there can be *different sovereignty regimes*.[210] This is the way to interpret the key transformations in international law since the Second World War: sovereign states gave up their "sovereign" right to go to war, aggression and annexation became illegal, colonialism was dismantled, and "empire" became a pejorative term, deemed a violation of the principle of self-determination. Sovereign states cooperate in a multiplicity of international organizations by whose rules they are bound and to whom they delegate many functions and they accept being limited by human rights principles, renouncing absolute impermeability to international law in this domain. Sovereign states can subscribe to treaties establishing international human rights thereby altering in yet another way their own prerogatives. Since the 1990s, human rights principles codified earlier have been taken more seriously and have partly merged with humanitarian law such that genocide, ethnic cleansing, expulsion, and enslavement are not considered today to be within the domestic jurisdiction of any state. These are the new "rules" of sovereignty in the international society of states, not indications of its abolition.

From the domestic point of view sovereignty is also a relational concept: it involves a distinctive legal and political relationship between a citizenry and a state. The citizen is the referent of public power and of the constitutional principles (public law) regulating the exercise of sovereign power. From this perspective, the citizen is construed as a member of a political and legal community involved in a collective project of governing itself under law, as the discourses of collective self-determination and popular sovereignty imply. Accordingly, citizens are subjects and potentially construable as authors of the laws and political institutions under which they are governed. *Shaping these political relationships, assessing their legitimacy, involves political participation in processes and relationships that are and ought to be uniquely theirs.* This is the core normative principle expressed by the two dimensions, supremacy and autonomy, of sovereignty.

One can defend this claim without invoking the cultural arguments of communitarians and without illegitimately generalizing liberal-democratic institutional norms. But in order to do so, it is necessary to shift from the perspective of the rights-bearing moral person, and from the identity perspective of membership in a cultural community, to the political perspective of the citizen construed as a member of a political community (polity).[211] From this perspective, citizens are involved in a distinct set of political and legal relationships with one another and with their government in a discrete, bounded polity. The concept, "people," refers to citizens as legal subjects, as members (nationals of the polity), and as involved in shifting or stable majorities and minorities, but nonetheless potentially able to see themselves as "collective" authors of the laws and political institutions under which they are governed. Domestic jurisdiction and territorial integrity matter because, as already indicated, they help delimit the legal and political system of one political community from another and hence the space in which self-government under law becomes possible. The legal concept of sovereignty constructs and protects the external autonomy of the political community, as well as the internal supremacy of its legal system *and* the integrity of the ethical political practices of the citizenry including their internal debates, contestations, negotiations that shape the community's political institutions and give content to the rights articulated in domestic laws and the constitution.[212]

The sovereign territorial state remains the key locus within which such a public, authoritative, coercive legal order, with direct effect on its individual members, can be erected and enforced creating distinct associative obligations and duties.[213] It is only by virtue of a concrete public legal order that has direct effect on individuals, endowing them with actionable rights that their external liberty in the Kantian sense as well as their security, the stability of their expectations, and the preservation of their rights can be in principle guaranteed. As Kant argued, equal individual liberties first get constituted through actionable law enforceable by a legal system with jurisdiction and supremacy within a bounded territory recognized to be the domain of an identifiable political authority.[214] The state is still the primary locus of this form of legal personhood today. Sovereign equality and its correlative principles of territorial integrity, domestic jurisdiction, and non-intervention help constitute and protect such coercive yet freedom-guaranteeing legal orders. Even if a particular polity does not guarantee equal subjective rights to all members, it is within the framework of an autonomous sovereign state as a distinct legal and political order with domestic jurisdiction that such rights can be fought for, acquired, and secured.

Thus one aspect of the authoritative relationship between members of a political community and their government established by internal sovereignty involves the rules by which a state's coercive force is to be exercised over individuals construed as legal persons, subject to the law. But external sovereignty is also the precondition for the principles of autonomous collective self-government and collective self-determination (public autonomy) of a political community to be actualized. This is the correct intuition inspiring Rawls, Raz, Cohen, et al. To see what is at stake we have to reason from the horizontal perspective of a citizenry construed as legal and political consociates, who can come to see themselves as *authors*, not only subjects of the law and of their rights.[215] It is this political composite "we" perspective that allows citizens to construe the establishment of good laws, just institutions, and democracy as their common project. The process by which rights are claimed, asserted, interpreted, and institutionalized in domestic constitutions is not simply a legal one but also deeply political involving contestation among a plurality of social and political groups of citizens. Indeed, rights assertion, vigilance, and what has recently been called "editorial" control by a plurality of domestic actors is what helps create and maintain the separation of powers and the rule of law so crucial to constitutionalism.[216] The political context of such struggles is, above all, domestic even if reference to universal human rights norms and international law is made and even if local movements hook up with well-meaning transnational actors.

Accordingly, it is the members of an autonomous political community who are the distinctive audience of the legitimacy claims of its political and legal institutions because they are the subjects of these institutions. *Hence the crucial normative distinction between internal and external legitimacy: the audiences and criteria cannot be the same for insiders and outsiders.*[217] *External sovereignty protects this normatively special standing of members.* The harm to self-respect entailed by foreign coercive intervention or imposition is, from this perspective, the harm of paternalism: the denial of the capacity of members of a political community to assess for themselves the internal legitimacy of their government and laws, and to be involved in the learning processes entailed by their struggles (including the ability to compromise) to create a more inclusive political process, more just laws, and their own new interpretations of rights. What is at issue is not tolerance for cultural diversity but the value of political agency. As Michael Walzer put it, ". . . the recognition of sovereignty is the only way we have of establishing an arena within which freedom can be fought for and sometimes won."[218] Coercive intervention in contexts other than those involving the radical denials of membership discussed above becomes usurpation.[219]

By protecting the autonomy and plurality of polities and their legal systems, sovereign equality helps constitute the space in which political freedom *and* the rule of law can emerge and mutually reinforce each other. I use the word "polity" advisedly to indicate that the size and nature of the political unit can change. I have argued in the previous chapter that plurality in the international system can shift to larger territorial units in response to the pressures of size.[220] Sovereign equality could be ascribed to non-state territorial entities like the European Union, a polity in transition whose laws already have direct effect and supremacy and which may acquire even more of the attributes of a federation than it now has.[221] Sovereign equality also characterizes the relations among its member states. The point is that sovereign equality protects the plurality of the units comprising the international system and as components of non-state polities, serving as a bulwark against imperial or great power predations.

3.6   Toward a new political conception: rethinking enforcement

Even if we explicate the value of sovereignty, and the membership principle in this way, we are still open to a serious objection. Couldn't Schmittians retort that it is precisely the role of the sovereign to decide who the internal or external enemy (or friend) is, that an emergency exists, and to declare the exception? Wouldn't any attempt by outsiders, multi- or unilaterally to intervene in the name of a human rights-based interpretation of the membership principle be tantamount to usurpation? Are there really any humanitarian heroes who disinterestedly intervene or isn't it the case that he who invokes humanity wants to cheat?[222] Wouldn't the fact that an international organization (or group of powerful states within it) is entitled to make the decision that an exception exists, and engage in war ("humanitarian" or "democratic" intervention) against the government that it has declared to be criminal and whose sovereignty it violates indicate that there is a new locus of sovereign power (an imperial hegemon or a group of great powers)?[223] Do not today's human rights-based humanitarian discourses simply replace the old standard of civilization to justify the monopoly of sovereign decision-making by the powerful and serve to reintroduce hierarchy in the international system?[224] Whether it is the Security Council, a coalition of great powers, or a superpower acting unilaterally, doesn't conditioning sovereignty on the respect for however minimal a list of basic human security rights entail normalizing criteria that ultimately deny the autonomy of a state while pretending to acknowledge it? Needless to say, for a Schmittian, this decision cannot be normed.

These doubts about the politics and logic of humanitarian intervention should be taken seriously. An appropriate response to the Schmittian argument has to have three dimensions. First, pace Schmitt, sovereignty is a normative and legal category, not only a fact of power. Law and power are mutually interdependent and co-constitutive of both internal and external sovereignty, albeit in different ways. Sovereignty refers both to the public power that enacts law and the law that authorizes and constrains that power (in the double sense that it must be exercised through law and respect legal restraints, for example regarding basic rights). The paradoxical dual register of sovereignty – as politics and as law – is not a sign of its conceptual incoherence as Foucault believed, but rather the key to a dynamic process of the mutual constitution and containment of law and politics.[225] Indeed only if one reasons exclusively either from a purely decisionistic political perspective (Schmitt) or from a purely normative legal register (Kelsen) would the concept of sovereignty founder on the apparently contradictory dual claim that it always makes.[226] Recall that we are dealing with public power and public authority.[227]

Second, it is not convincing to define sovereignty in terms of a particular prerogative as does Schmitt regarding the right to war and the right to decide the exception, nor, third, to revive the myth that sovereignty cannot be legally limited or that the exception cannot be normed. Constitutionalism and sovereignty are not incompatible, despite what theorists of absolute, organ sovereignty tried to argue. Nor is it necessary to imagine the circle of constituent and constituted power as vicious. Instead here too is a dynamic that recalls the indispensable legal context of politics (constitutional government through law and the legal construction of the people) as well as the indispensable political context of law (law as expressive of, and the result of, the exercise of political power).

The same is true of external sovereignty. Sovereignty and sovereign equality are ordering concepts of the international legal system, which ascribes political autonomy, legal standing, and certain prerogatives to states. They are indicative of the plural structure of the international political system, of the way in which political communities and public power are organized and differentiated from one another. There can be different sovereignty regimes and nothing prevents sovereign states from acknowledging that certain prerogatives such as waging aggressive war or grave violations of humanitarian principles/human rights are not within the domestic jurisdiction of any state.[228] They can agree to these principles, create binding international law, and ascribe to specific organs of the international community that they constitute, the function of protecting and enforcing them in particular delimited cases of radical default thereby creating a dualist international system: based on the two legal principles of sovereign equality and human rights. *To interpret such violations in terms of the membership principle as I have above is to reject the existential Schmittian conception of sovereignty and of political identity formation by denying to any authority the prerogative to redefine the friend component of the citizenship principle through radical, violent forms of exclusion that create a condition of absolute rightlessness for categories of individuals.*

Accordingly, one could interpret the normative meaning of the universalization of the principle of sovereign equality, and the concurrent international legal importance of human security rights, as bulwarks against the creation of radical rightlessness and lawless zones either domestically or in the international system at large. This would mean that we should not buy into the ideological construction of outlaw states, which, due to the criminal activity of their governments, can be stripped of membership in international society and deprived of legal standing and coverage by international law. Instead, the concept would have to be de-dramatized: criminal or outlaw governmental officials are law-breakers subject to the sanctions and protections of international law, precisely because their states are members of international society, and of the only global governance institution legitimately entitled to decide on military sanctions, the UN. To strip a government official of immunity is to render him subject to the jurisdiction of courts, not to deprive him of a legal persona. The same principle should apply to other individuals: no person, not even those labeled "terrorist" or "unlawful enemy combatant," can be excised from membership in the global human community, categorized as rightless, and deprived of a legal persona. My interpretation would thus invoke the two legal principles of sovereign equality and human security rights against the two discursive strategies of those supporting or inadvertently playing into the hands of an imperial or great power deformation of international law – the discourse of outlaw or criminal states and of rightless terrorists or unlawful enemies.

This brings me to the second issue mentioned above: the rights of non-members: legal and illegal resident aliens, refugees, stateless persons, etc. who come under the jurisdiction of states but are not their citizens. How can we conceptualize the institutionalization of sovereign equality and human rights, of genuine political plurality and global justice that has been on the agenda since 1945, in a way that protects the autonomy, self-determination, and political freedom of and within each polity while simultaneously ensuring that everyone's right to have rights (and thus to the protection of the law) and the rule of law is accepted as a principle and ensured by all members of the international community?

If one proceeds from the perspective of sovereignty as an international legal entitlement that is distributed equally among the political communities international law recognizes as sovereign states, then it is possible to see the way in which the two *legal* principles that are co-constitutive of the current dualist international system – sovereign equality and human rights – are systematically interrelated. The first, sovereign equality as a legal principle, protects the autonomy of polities and their distinct jurisdictions constituting an inclusive international society. The second, human rights, involves the cosmopolitan moral idea that all individuals are of equal moral worth and that everyone deserves protection against grave rights violations especially by officials of authoritative coercive political and legal institutions. On the dualistic conception being used here, human rights come to possess international legal significance because they operate as mechanisms to prevent and mitigate the abuse of power and of prerogatives that follow from the ways in which sovereignty is constituted and distributed in the international legal system.[229] In other words one can view international human rights law as functioning to address injustices (distributive and otherwise) produced by the structure of an international order that ascribes sovereignty as a legal entitlement to all states on the basis of the principle of effectiveness. Accordingly, human security rights of everyone serve as a corrective to the way in which international law organizes international political reality into a legal order, i.e. the current sovereignty regime. Thus states may not intentionally create rightlessness or statelessness, nor may they exercise their sovereign jurisdiction in ways that would involve extreme violations of the rights of non-citizens who are subject to their power. The "cosmopolitan" dimension of what I call our dualistic international order thus has a global aspect, meaning that there should be no individuals or groups denied a legal persona or membership in the international community or in their respective domestic political communities, and thus that the project of creating lawless zones and rightless individuals symbolized by the Guantanamo detention center, is not within the sovereign discretion of any state.

The conception of "the proper subset" of human rights whose violation might suspend the sovereignty argument against international enforcement and sanctions should thus be restricted to what have been called the "new human security rights" indicative of a partial merger between humanitarian and human rights regimes.[230] Apart from these, I argue for the disaggregation conceptually, discursively, and normatively of the international human rights and international humanitarian legal regimes. Indeed, it is not really clear that one can speak coherently of *individual human rights* in the narrower context of human security law even if this is the language of the hybrid regime.[231] For what is at stake in these "rights" against extermination, expulsion, ethnic cleansing, and enslavement (de facto or formal) are not really individually actionable subjective rights, but a rule of law baseline against group-based persecution and oppression by states or their proxies that warns of possible sanctions, including humanitarian intervention and international prosecution for violations.[232] The legal subjectivity created by the juridification/constitutionalization on the domestic level of the rights of man and citizen empowers the individual rights holder with the choice of whether to exercise her constitutional rights and/or to sue for their enforcement. This is not the case with criminal law or with humanitarian law. In these legal domains it is the duty of the state or the authoritative international institution to enforce and act in accordance with the law at issue.

Thus, it would seem more accurate to speak of a merger of international humanitarian with international criminal law (the key post-war innovation culminating in the creation of the ICC) for the hybrid human security regime rather than of a merger of the former with human rights law even though the moral rights of individuals are of course being violated when the four E's are being perpetrated. As is well known, the idea of a "crime against humanity" was first articulated in the law of war in the Nuremberg Charter, quickly followed by the Geneva Convention's Common Article 3 pertaining to internal armed conflict.[233] The four E's were elaborated in the subsequent statutes of the ICTY and ICTR ad hoc tribunals, in the statute of the ICC and in the R2P documents that framed them partly in human rights terms, but what these statutes produced and further elaborated is comprehensible primarily in terms of international criminal and humanitarian law. These statutes use the concept of "crime against humanity" to expand the idea of "protected group"(beyond the Genocide Conventions) to include any constructed and targeted group be it political or based on race, ethnicity, or even gender, thus revealing insight into the dynamics of the membership principle discussed above. Equally important is the application of these principles to any armed conflict and indeed to any state policy irrespective of an inter-state war nexus. Teitel is thus right to see this emergent complex of human security law as constituting a new type of generalized "minority rights" regime.

I argue that it is important to clearly restrict this hybrid of humanitarian and international criminal law cum human rights discourses to the four E's given the distinctive enforcement mechanisms associated with it. Doing so would protect the independent normative status of international human rights law while opening up the space for serious reflection on the issue of the legal institutionalization of the hybrid regime of "humanity's law."[234] For, even absent the risks of over-inclusiveness, human security "rights" linked to the possibility of humanitarian intervention and other international sanctions including indictment by international courts are certainly open to political manipulation. As indicated in the introduction, the ICC is not a universalistic institution given the non-membership of the US, China, India, and Russia and despite the fact that the SC can refer or block any case to it even apparently against non-signatories. This fact together with the nexus linking the ICC to the Security Council, given the veto of the P5, also undermines its impartiality and hence its legitimacy.[235] The limits of ad hoc tribunals created by the UNSC vis-à-vis the P5 are also obvious. Thus the claim that these global enforcement institutions and practices already entail the instantiation of a global rule of law is premature.

Indeed as already indicated neither human security norms, nor the R2P concept, are black letter international law that binds or triggers Security Council action in domestic conflicts and contexts not to mention unilateral interventions by states or coalitions of states. The task before us is to foster institutional and legal reform of globalizing governance institutions so as to arrive at a global rule of law that protects *both* the sovereign equality of states and human security. If we simply abandon the principle of sovereign equality and the present rules of international law on non-intervention and collective security, we lose an important barrier to the proliferation of imperial projects and regional attempts at grossraum ordering by emerging twenty-first-century great powers.

The alternative project entails acknowledging the existence and value of what I have been calling a *dualistic* world order whose core remains the international society of states embedded within (suitably reformed) international institutions and international law but which also has important cosmopolitan elements.[236] The latter, especially *jus cogens* human security principles and individual liability of officials, should be seen as part of a *new sovereignty regime*: signaling changes in the prerogatives of sovereignty, setting new limits to its legitimate exercise, and as indicative of shifts in the cultural understanding of what falls within the "domestic jurisdiction" of a state and what are legitimate acts of state for which an agent can no longer evade responsibility.

But the only way to grasp this constellation as a dualist international regime comprised of sovereign states (international society) and global governance institutions (which are themselves importantly dualistic) with discrete functional competences, is to realize two things: (1) that a new dimension of sovereignty has emerged in the present epoch and (2) that formal legal and procedural reform of such institutions is indispensable for their legitimacy today, given their increasingly powerful intrusive new role in the international system. Only then would it make sense to claim that global governance institutions enforcing humanity law, making global regulations or global public policy decisions and state sovereignty are not in a zero-sum relationship and that participation in the former can even enhance sovereignty.[237]

Sovereign equality as an international legal entitlement has acquired a new dimension, namely the status of being a member of the international community with the right to participate in international organizations that make coercive decisions affecting all states and their citizens. Internationally sovereignty has always been a status claim and since 1945, UN membership has been perceived as a validation of sovereign status. Today it is increasingly the case that for states to realize their sovereignty (as international lawmakers, as exercisers of international political influence, and as having a say in decisions that affect their citizens) they need the status of member with the right to participate in the decision-making processes of the various international organizations and networks that regulate the international system, on fair terms. Unlike Anne-Marie Slaughter and Chayes and Chayes, however, I argue that this "new" dimension of sovereignty as status and inclusion in coercive global governance institutions, supplements but does not replace sovereignty as autonomy.[238] Indeed, the two aspects of sovereignty are interrelated, as is obvious in the case of the Security Council, which exercises the crucial functions of deciding which violations of human rights suspend the prima facie sovereignty argument, and on appropriate enforcement measures. The idea that interdependence or the proliferation of global governance institutions makes sovereignty as autonomy irrelevant is based on the false premise that sovereignty entails autarky and that it is only a matter of factual power (control) rather than normative and legal construction. Inclusion and status in global governance institutions does not render sovereignty as autonomy irrelevant or anachronistic any more than democratic institutions render rights protecting personal autonomy irrelevant in a republic.

However, given the linkage of sovereignty to participation in these institutions, we face a new task: in order to redress injustices that the legal ascription of sovereignty to states *and poorly designed global governance institutions generate*, institutional and legal reform is required. What the Rawlsian theorists of the political conception of human rights tend to ignore is the need for an institutional locus, fair procedural rules, mechanisms for accountability, and adequate voice for stakeholders, for arriving at what they like to call global public reason. Only within a universal international body with fair procedures that includes all states as members would the transfer of jurisdiction limiting a functional dimension of state sovereignty not become, cumulatively, tantamount to the abolition of sovereignty. Inclusive GGIs that create public fora for reaching understanding and cooperation, and which establish accountability mechanisms make it possible to coordinate international law with domestic approaches and thus to parry the charge of liberal imposition and to answer the Schmittian challenge. Participation under fair rules and legitimate procedures for rule-making in functionally delimited GGIs could make it possible for political communities to maintain their autonomy in establishing the particular forms that rights will take in their own communities while viewing the international community and its laws, including the articulation of the proper subset of human security violations that *may* trigger temporary suspension of the sovereignty argument against intervention, also as their own. Precisely because coercive global governance institutions are subject to hegemonic capture, legal and procedural constraints are crucial especially regarding humanitarian intervention.

I thus support the strategy of UN reform – the UN is the key universalistic world organization and it has still has global legitimacy. It thus merits serious efforts at rendering its internal procedures and structures fair, impartial, and thus more legitimate and more just.[239] In this context it is worth noting that although the original ICISS report did not gain acceptance by the UN many of its provisions along with the R2P concept reappeared in a report by the 2004 UN panel on "Threats, Challenges and Change" which was unanimously endorsed as part of the 2005 summit Outcome Document by the General Assembly.[240] That document was accepted partly because it restricted the "right authority" to use coercive means to the Security Council while further narrowing the triggers for R2P.[241] Here again the issue was how to incorporate principles of humanitarian responsibility without weakening Charter constraints on the use of armed force and without undermining the constitutive principles of sovereign equality and non-intervention. Crucially, the Summit Outcome Document reaffirms the UN Charter's prohibition of the use of force allowing only two exceptions: self-defense under Article 51 in the face of an attack or an immanent threat, and military measures authorized by the Security Council under Chapter VII. It rejects the effort to expand the conception of self-defense to include the unilateral "preventive" use of force advocated at the time by the Bush administration. Instead it reaffirms the principle of non-intervention, arguing that in a world full of perceived threats, the risk to global order is simply too great for the legality of unilateral preventive action as distinct from collectively endorsed action to be accepted.[242] Moreover the bulk of its discussion of prevention refers to non-military means such as greatly expanded foreign aid crucial to conflict prevention.[243] It also reaffirms the legal principle that Chapter VII of the UN Charter fully empowers the Security Council, and *nobody else* to authorize the use of force. Unilateral humanitarian intervention is thus rejected. Right authority is insisted upon.

Thus, in this context the concept of the responsibility to protect and the effort to articulate legal guidelines for humanitarian intervention is linked to a project of UN reform; it is not meant to provide an ideology for bypassing the UN. There are principled as well as pragmatic reasons for supporting the project to formalize UN guidelines regulating the authorization of the use of force (humanitarian intervention) in carefully circumscribed domestic cases of grave rights violations, *along with* efforts to update and expand Security Council membership and to articulate better procedures for arriving at decisions in case of Security Council deadlock.[244] The specification of the sorts of violations that won't be shielded by invocations of sovereignty must be done within an inclusive international political organization.

The debate of course continues over whether or not it is wise to legally "norm the exception." A General Assembly resolution even when unanimous does not amount to hard letter international law. There are good arguments on both sides. One side rejects formal legal reform, arguing that it is more prudent to insist on the cardinal principles of the prohibition of the use of force, and non-intervention, thereby forcing states to offer justifications to the international community when they violate existing law for "humanitarian" purposes.[245] This approach favors the strategy of "exceptional illegality": the idea is to keep the burden of proof on would-be interveners, who know they are acting illegally and that they will be subject to an ex post facto "jury-ing" process by the international community.[246] The latter may, as in the case of Kosovo, conclude that the action was "legitimate albeit illegal," or alternatively it may condemn an intervention as opportunistic, illegitimate, and illegal and subject the violator to sanctions. Keeping humanitarian interventions "exceptional" would allegedly ensure that each case was treated as unique and thus avoid setting a dangerous precedent. Supposedly this approach of "exceptional illegality" would shift the focus of inquiry to the consequences of the delict with arguments of legitimacy being seen as pleas for mitigation and entailing admission of the lack of a legal basis for intervention and special obligations to make amends for its consequences.[247]

This position is predicated on the view that it is impossible to achieve consensus on criteria of thresholds for possible intervention in the cases of grave humanitarian rights violations. It also assumes that procedural reform of the UN Security Council is not feasible given the veto.[248] But the deeper reasoning behind the "exceptional illegality" position is that it buys into the assumption that it is not possible to norm the exception: "... the circumstances in which the law may be violated are not themselves susceptible to legal regulation."[249] The effort to develop a normative regime, moreover, allegedly makes the error of assuming the possibility of an "ideal" humanitarian intervention.[250] The fear is that legalization would enable opportunistic interventions, rendering them more likely.

The problem with this position is that the genie is already out of the bottle: it is less and less convincing to use the language of "unique and exceptional circumstances" given the frequency with which humanitarian interventions have been authorized, indulged in, or called for since the 1990s.[251] Moreover, the "exceptional illegality" approach offers no solution to the lack of consistency and incoherence of the current system of Security Council authorization. That too threatens respect for the rule of law. The plasticity of the Security Council's mandate carries the risk that its criteria for designating certain domestic crises as "threats to international peace and security" will seem arbitrary. If it appears that the Security Council is asserting "Kompetenz-Kompetenz" in an area that the Charter did not provide for while exempting its own veto-wielding members from any sanctions for their own violations of "human security rights" domestically or in the aftermath of an intervention, respect for international institutions will be undermined. This is even more likely if the Council appears as a vehicle for the assertion of the particular interests of the great powers sitting on it. Indeed the absence of clear guidelines and good procedures is partly responsible for the perception that in the area of humanitarian intervention, the SC appears more as a rubber stamp to the pre-planned interventions of powerful states within it than as a disinterested agent of the international community.[252]

Worse, insistence on the impossibility and undesirability of formal legal and institutional reform invites *attempts to reform international law by stealth* – to provide exceptions for a state or a group of states to violate rules that continue to apply to all the others – precisely what the "exceptional illegality" approach seeks to forestall in the first place.[253] There are already "reform" proposals afoot that seek to gain legitimacy for "coalitions of the democratic willing" to engage in humanitarian intervention and the preventive use of force in the case of Security Council "deadlock."[254] This inegalitarian approach is packaged as an alternative to unilateralism, but it is really an attempt to do an end run around the UN.

The other side thus argues for taking the route of legal reform. It may be difficult but it certainly is not impossible to come up with thresholds that can be accepted as signaling a possible context warranting external intervention. Nor is it impossible to come up with mechanisms to ensure accountability or procedures to secure legitimacy. To be sure, one could not legally provide for all emergencies or contingencies in advance but this does not mean that general criteria and procedural rules cannot be established. Indeed if legal reform were to involve not triggers for intervention but criteria for considering its possibility, then R2P norms could play a preventive role since governments would know that their domestic actions violating the four categories of human security rights could entail suspension of the sovereignty argument against intervention.

The Summit Outcome Document was an attempt to articulate such criteria for the *legitimacy* for any authorization by the Security Council regarding humanitarian interventions.[255] This is important because it openly acknowledges the de facto shift in the conception of threats to international peace and security to include internal grave human security rights violations. In short, the Document sought to reverse the de-formalization of international law and the alarming reduction of the Security Council to a rubber stamp through haphazard uncontrolled delegations of "enforcement action" and post facto acquiescence to unauthorized unilateral actions.[256] These criteria were adopted as guidelines for the Security Council in a *formal declaratory resolution adopted by the General Assembly.* General Assembly resolutions do not qualify as international law but it is worth noting that in the 2009 summer session which considered yet another report of the Secretary-General on "Implementing the Responsibility to Protect," the great majority of states reaffirmed their commitment.[257] This, again, is not meant as a trigger for intervention but rather as an expression of key norms whose violation is to be taken as a trigger for discussion and debate about whether intervention is warranted, i.e. as guidelines for any Chapter VII action to be deemed legitimate. It also is clearly meant to foster reflection as to what the consequences of any intervention might be.

Accordingly the list contains the now standard just war criteria which should be taken into account by the Security Council when considering whether to authorize the use of military force: seriousness of threat, proper purpose, last resort, proportional means, balance of consequences, proper authority. But it is worth emphasizing that the report restricts the possibility of humanitarian military intervention to four sets of circumstances: actual or immanent genocide, large-scale ethnic cleansing, crimes against humanity, and war crimes (large-scale violations of humanitarian law).[258] By keeping the threshold high, the Panel was not only being pragmatic, it is trying to maintain intact the principle of sovereign equality, limit Security Council arbitrariness, and ward off opportunistic behavior.

Along these lines, I argue that the "seriousness of the threat" principle should be seen in political and not only in moral terms. Extermination, expulsion, enslavement, and ethnic cleansing obviously are grave injustices, but they also, as indicated above, involve a political project: the political death of a segment of the political community and the redefinition of the identity of that community through violence, as part of a power play by those in or seeking control of government. Thus to the moral calculus about humanitarian intervention I would add a "republican" political consideration: does domestic violence against a particular group make political involvement or contestation by that group impossible, and if it does, would the violence entailed by intervention (and long-term "humanitarian occupation" that follows) paralyze the political life of the polity intervened in, freeze the relations of force on the ground, or involve constitutional imposition so that the political autonomy and self-determination of the citizenry is blocked?[259] The principles of sovereign equality, self-determination, and popular sovereignty require this political assessment. Otherwise moralistic interveners invite the charges of paternalism and opportunism.[260]

The point of adding these political and legal considerations to the moral discourse associated with human security rights is to protect the political values that the principle of sovereign equality stands for. The bundle theory of sovereignty and its functionalist reduction to the responsibility to protect undermines respect for the key principle that constitutes political plurality and safeguards political autonomy along with the discrete space within which political freedom can emerge. Moreover, the sovereign state remains the main context of justice and the principle of sovereign equality helps protect weak against strong states. This is not yet an anachronism. The fiction of a global legal system in the process of being constitutionalized based on the individualistic principle of justice to persons is dangerous if it comes at the expense of the principle of sovereign equality. So is the discourse of a global rule of law if it is prematurely linked to humanitarian interventions and other global sanctions in the present context in which major powers remain exempt, partly due to the veto in the Security Council to the new rules being imposed on all the other states.

3.7 Conclusion

Today international rights talk is prey to two distortions: the inflation of their content and the deflation of their referent (the bearers of such rights). Inflation of what counts as a human right *if linked to the function of suspending the sovereignty argument* against intervention and/or international enforcement involving sanctions, invites the powerful to abuse the discourse of enforcement for strategic purposes when actually violating international law pertaining to sovereign equality.[261] It also invites the efforts of worried theorists, as we have seen, to avoid such abuse along with the risks of imposing parochial views by devising minimalist lists and justifications. Deflation in this sense and in the sense of narrowing of the circle of individuals covered by the legal persona that human rights and humanitarian law is supposed to ascribe to everyone is the second danger. The discourse of human security, improperly used, could serve both purposes. The effort on the part of some to recreate a hierarchal international society and legal system from which "outlaw," "rogue" or "criminal" states are excluded; the effort to restrict the reach of the Geneva Convention's protections and block the trend toward their expansion beyond a statist model to include partisans, guerrilla warriors fighting occupation and people involved in civil wars, by excluding persons

labeled illegal enemy combatants or terrorists are obvious examples. Both inflation and deflation can be seen as part of a neo-imperial project(s) to undermine
the integrity of international law, weaken Charter restraints against the use of
force, and to subject multilateral institutions to hegemonic capture.[262]

My response to these risks has two prongs or rather involves two sets of
distinctions. As already argued, it is crucial to distinguish between what are
now called "human security rights" – those fundamental interests that are
merged with the humanitarian and international criminal law regimes – and
the independent normative status of international human rights.[263] It is also
crucial to distinguish the enforcement mechanisms distinctive to each. Two
different "political conceptions" of human rights are appropriate here. The
first does refer to the possibility of suspension of the sovereignty argument
given grave violations although, as I argued above, extreme caution must be
exercised regarding right authority, feasibility, reflection on likely outcomes,
and the problem of mixed motives that pertain to any coercive international
enforcement. There is also the pressing need to reform the institutional
framework of the UN for the twenty-first century so that legitimate procedures for assessing cases of possible external action are devised which are
applicable and justifiable to all concerned.

The second refers to international human rights proper and to the kind of
political practice or "enforcement" these entail. Here too a political and
functional approach is useful but this pertains to the politics engaged in by
domestic actors who declare their own rights and, insofar as they invoke the
international documents and treaties, do so strategically in order to
strengthen their critique of arbitrariness and oppression in the polities and
social structures in which they live. The point is to strengthen their hand in
fostering domestic political change so as to make respect for these rights part
of the accepted criteria of the internal legitimacy of their constitutional and
political system. The participant perspective is and should be primary because
what is at stake is the local (domestic) contextualization of human rights on
the part of those affected as persons and as citizens. While international
human rights have been articulated as global public standards and aspirations,
their main function is not to serve as norms to which the international
community of states holds each country's government accountable through
reciprocity mechanisms. Rather they function as public standards of critique
to which citizens and residents, domestic rights activists, and social movement actors can refer in order to hold their own governments accountable,
especially (but not only) if these governments have signed on to the relevant
human rights treaties. This is why it is crucial to re-differentiate humanitarian
from human rights discourses and to question the rigid antithesis between
sovereignty and human rights informing so much of cosmopolitan humanitarianism: otherwise the main political function of human rights discourses as
distinct from humanity's law gets screened out.

From this internal perspective, the human rights claims of citizens and residents are today features of a domestic politics of dissent and contestation that can parry the charge of imperial imposition of external standards. This political function of domestic rights mobilization also serves as a counterweight to the deflationary project. The rights people have are the rights they declare, collectively interpret, and fight for and when domestic actors take the interpretation of their human rights (of man and/or citizen) into their own hands and put them into a local idiom their selection among the rights listed in the international documents or their introduction of new rights poses no threat to sovereignty (popular or state). The ultimate focus is the domestic constitutionalization or enforcement of human rights. Today such mobilizations are continuous with the rights-oriented movements of the 1970s and 1980s that were so important in delegitimizing dictatorship and in further democratizing democratic societies by expanding the subjects (women, children, immigrants), issues (ecology, feminism, gay rights, economic justice), and referents (states, and potentially of global governance institutions, transnational networks) of rights-based claims. The fact that international human rights treaties have been designed by diplomats, state executives, or lawyers should not obscure the equally important fact that success in getting governments to live up to their paper commitments and to respect the human rights of their constituents requires the mobilization of domestic social actors.[264] These public commitments can be powerful instruments in the hands of domestic rights claimants: by insisting that governments hold to their international legal obligations local actors seeking domestic justice and democratization, individual and collective emancipation, can develop their own political agency and interpretive power. As recent research has shown, "enforcement" of international human rights commitments is the task primarily of domestic social and political actors, not interstate pressure or intervention.[265] In this scenario, activists beyond borders can supplement but not substitute for domestic social movement and party political actors who target their own states and offer their own contextualized ethical political interpretation of the general rights principles they invoke. International concern and solidarity with domestic rights activists, although important, is not the main mechanism generating compliance. Indeed the international legalization of human rights was not based on the assumption that states would enforce human rights standards against one another and it was not designed with contractual state-to-state reciprocity in mind.[266] Accordingly,

> the true significance of the treaties has been neither in the willingness of the UN collectively to enforce them nor in the will of individual governments to do so. Rather the impact of international commitments on domestic politics has been most significant in realizing actual gains in most cases.[267]

Conversely the kinds of international concern appropriate to assisting domestic human rights struggles involve discursive interaction, political communication, and publicity, not humanitarian intervention.

When domestic actors target their own states and take the initiative by mobilizing for the "rights of man" they act politically as citizens and persons concerned with their own emancipation. At issue for them is the internal legitimacy of the political and social structure of the society in which they live. They re-link the politics of human rights to domestic democratic politics by creating publics and public spaces in which to make and debate new claims and thereby participate in deciding what rights they have. As Lefort rightly insisted this is the core political function of human rights declarations and assertions. From this perspective, the legitimating principles of popular sovereignty, democracy, and human rights although distinct are complementary. I do not deny the historical specificity of post-World War Two international human rights law and practices, of transnational human rights movements, or their importance as expressions of international concern (naming and shaming, condemnation) and as referents for domestic critique, dissent, and mobilization. As such the practice of international human rights is in key respects distinctive and discontinuous with rights discourses of previous epochs. But it is also important to recognize the continuities of contemporary human rights discourses and struggles on the part of domestic actors, with earlier human rights declarations and struggles.[268] In this regard Rainer Forst is correct to insist, following Lefort and Habermas, that human rights discourses have, since the onset of modernity, been a language of political protest, and of political emancipation closely linked to the principles of democratic legitimacy. Declaring one's rights (as distinct from insisting on privileges) involves protest against injustice, oppression, exploitation, and exclusion, demands for freedom from arbitrary social or political domination, *and* for a voice in co-determining the laws and institutions by which people will be bound.[269] The link between personal and political autonomy, civil and political rights, the rights of man and citizen is discernible in all of the major declarations from the French to UDHR.[270]

But understanding this political function of international human rights in domestic struggles does not mean that one need not reflect on the moral dimension of human rights claims or that one can or must do without efforts to develop a moral justification of the concept of human rights so as to account for their independent normative status as urgent interests requiring protection against typical threats. It is important to understand these not as higher-order ethical values or interests from which human rights claims can be derived, as per the "traditional approach," but rather as claims that participants in a discourse would have to justify to one another.[271] This has implications for the appropriate way to understand the project of moral justification.

Although providing a moral justification is not my enterprise in this chapter, I am partial to the approach of Rainer Forst regarding such a project. Forst proceeds by reflecting on the normative deep grammar of protests and struggles against injustice in which concrete demands for justification are made in the language of rights addressed, typically, to one's domestic political community in a contextualized local idiom, yet which implicitly rely on moral principles that are context-transcending. By reflecting on the communicative practice in which people assert and mutually justify their human rights claims, Forst uncovers the ideas of moral personhood, reciprocity, equal worth, and mutual respect these entail. But he also insists on the reflexive structure of the practice and hence of the meaning of declaring and claiming human rights inherent in the pragmatics of protest and emancipation framed in that language. This perforce involves the ascription to each person of the status of an agent who possesses a right to justification and to voice, regarding any exercise of social and/or public power in any context of justice: domestic, transnational, inter-national, or global. The reflexive dimension means that subjects of justification must in principle be seen as participants in the process of determining and justifying what rights they have.

Adopting Rawls's terminology, Forst thus distinguishes between moral and political constructivism, although in a more Habermasian vein both are seen as forms of discursive constructivism. On the moral level, constructivism means that the very idea of practical discourse entails that persons engaged in it must accord one another the status of equal autonomous agents entitled to and able to give reciprocally justifiable reasons for rights.[272] The practice itself entails recursively the basic moral right of justification. While denying that a concrete or "saturated" list of rights can be derived from the right to justification or from the moral constructivist approach, the latter nevertheless yields, in Forst's view, an abstract list of those basic human rights that persons who respect one another as equals with rights to justification cannot reasonably (with reasons) deny one another. This opens up a normative space for claims that secure a person's status as an agent of justification and provides a normative referent for struggles for the concrete realization of such rights. The claim is that moral constructivism uncovers only an abstract unsaturated set of rights that pertain to the standing of an agent of justification rather than a thick ethically determinate fully specified scheme of concrete regulations that a legitimate legal system must mirror. This is the way the constructivist approach seeks to parry the charge of ethnocentrism. The idea is that concrete institutionalized fully justified rights are articulated and realizable only via the practice and participation of those affected in a legally constituted political order.

Indeed, because human rights have a twofold character as general moral rights and as concrete legal rights, a distinct process of political constructivism is required. All rights, including the abstract rights yielded by moral constructivism, have to be concretely interpreted, justified, institutionalized (and fought for) within a legally constituted political order, first and foremost on the domestic level of the constitutional order of a state. While any set of juridical human rights contain the core of moral human rights it may be more extensive and moreover cannot be understood as the mere application of moral principles, for they are always the contextual product of struggle. Nor is their content prior to political justice in the sense of natural rights.[273] Political constructivism then reflects the process by which the basic rights of citizens and persons are given determinate and legally binding shape in distinct social contexts in which members make claims, struggle, engage in contestation over, deliberate and decide in common about what rights they have and about the concrete realization of their rights. This involves an autonomous discursive practice of citizens engaged in establishing a legitimate social and political order with a contextualized structure of rights. Hence there is a second level of reflexivity:

> Recursively speaking ... the point of human rights is that persons have the basic right to live in a society where they themselves are the social and political agents who determine which rights they can claim and have to recognize.[274]

This means then that there is no fixed concrete set of rights that can be determined by or derived from a moral theory independently or in advance of social struggles. It also means that what human rights we have can vary over time, and with the relevant context.

Whether Forst or others who embrace the distinction between moral and political constructivism can really escape the charge that they are deriving the most fundamental human rights from the best or correct moral theory remains an open question.[275] For as Baynes has cogently pointed out, so soon as one moves from the very abstract principle of a right to justification or the premises of communicative argumentation or the idea of the right to have rights, to a list of moral human rights these principles allegedly entail and which serves to constrain the deliberations within a political society concerned with specifying rights (political constructivist level), one invites the charge that after all one does assume that there are fixed and determinate human rights provided by the correct moral theory in advance of social struggles.[276] Much of this turns on other contested distinctions: between the right and the good, between the moral and the ethical. However one comes down on this issue, the distinctions between moral and political constructivism, between the right and the good, between universal moral principle and particularistic ethical good, are clearly part of an effort to articulate the context-transcending thrust of all struggles that invoke human rights (and not only because they are now listed in international documents) while seeking to parry the charges of parochialism or of ethnocentric ethical imperialism. Whether or not these efforts are ultimately convincing, the core intuition remains important, namely that the content and subject of human rights are open-ended and in that sense indeterminate: the subject (and new content) of human rights is whosoever asserts her rights-claims against new or old forms of oppression or newly understood forms of injustice and exclusions whenever and wherever this occurs.[277] Human rights assertions are never really only local and contextual irrespective of the historically situated nature of this discursive practice. The international human rights documents and practice are witness to this fact even if one is always able to trace their history and contextualized meanings.

Let me conclude. When it comes to the proper subset of institutionalized and enforceable international human rights – i.e. human security "rights" – whose function is to suspend the sovereignty argument, one cannot read them off the pragmatics of legitimate law-making within a constitutional democracy.[278] This won't work because the proper subset would entail rights that are articulated on the supranational level and are binding even on those states that have not included them in their law or constitutions. These are the principles states must not violate and when violated can entail suspension of the sovereignty argument against intervention. On the other hand, they cannot be read off the international legal human rights documents because the list of rights these entail is far too broad given the function at issue.[279] That is why I tried to articulate a substantive version of the political conception that links up with the empirical approach in one crucial respect: it takes into account the function of new hybrid of international humanitarian, criminal and human rights law and the related discourse of enforcement, in the current political constellation and for the foreseeable future (in a dualist system). But if in the foreseeable future it is unlikely that all states will become rights-respecting constitutional democracies and if it is not possible to read the existing human security rights and obligations as hard law, then the task of institutionalizing the proper subset of globally binding human security law remains before us. The question then becomes, by whom and how? This could be accomplished, in my view, in one of two ways. Either states in international society come together and covenant anew, making explicit and determinate the proper scope of human security principles that would be considered hard international law and whose violation thus would serve as the defeasible justification for suspending the sovereignty argument and imposing sanctions. Or this is done within the framework of the most important global organization with universal membership – the United Nations, perhaps in a special session of the General Assembly, perhaps with representatives of "civil society" being permitted to speak and influence the discussion, perhaps with a special voting procedure also involving the Security Council without any veto. The procedural and voting rules for such a project would have to be very carefully designed, to say the least.

However this is done, it is crucial in my view to cabin this domain of human security law from the rest of international human rights discourses, law, and practice. We must acknowledge the important and independent political, legitimating, and mobilizing role of international human rights accords and practices. The framing of claims against domestic injustice in the language of human rights and the ability of diverse social movements and concerned actors to invoke international legal principles agreed to by their and/or most states is a powerful tool on the strategic, symbolic, and normative level. It would be absurd to deprive domestic social movements of this important label by restricting the concept of human rights to those rights which function to suspend the sovereignty argument against intervention. Nor should one deny the importance to domestic actors, of condemnation (naming and shaming) and publicity on the part of allies in international or transnational publics.[280] These sorts of discourses and protests could inform and help generate "global public reason" about what constitutes morally legitimate governance, which could interact productively with domestic constitutional and discursive practices without undermining domestic popular or state sovereignty. But such invocations of human rights must be carefully distinguished from the subset of legal international human rights the violation of which serves to disable the sovereignty argument against coercive intervention. Moreover it must be seen as part of a domestic political practice of emancipation, not as a neutral enterprise of enforcing apolitical moral principles. Whether my distinction between two "political" conceptions and their different enforcement mechanisms and functions – one restricted to the "proper subset" of international human security rights and the other to a political conception of human rights generally – will do the trick is not certain but the need for a distinction of some kind is clear in the current context.

Sovereignty and human rights in "post-conflict" constitution-making: toward a *jus post bellum* for "interim occupations"

JEAN L. COHEN

Is there and should there be international law relevant to "post-conflict" constitution-making under foreign occupation? Should we attempt to develop a "*jus post bellum*"? In an epoch of "humanitarian" and "democratic" interventions, UN-sponsored "regime change" and "nation-building" for "failed" or "outlaw" states, and the prolonged and highly transformative foreign occupations that all of these tend to entail, this question inevitably arises. It is analytically distinct from the issues of the justice of the war itself (*jus ad bellum*) and the justice of how the war has been conducted (*jus in bellum*).[1] At issue are the principles and rules regulating "interim administrations" erected by occupying forces in the aftermath of foreign military intervention in the context of a belligerent or humanitarian occupation.[2] Such foreign administrations typically exercise full plenary powers in the "host state" ruling directly over the local population, replacing the legal authority of the former national government, and participating in political and legal "reconstruction" over a lengthy period of time. At stake, then, are not only the human rights, but also the sovereignty and self-determination of the occupied. To put it succinctly, if "post-conflict" constitution-making is to be an exercise in self-determination instead of foreign imposition, if the sovereignty of the occupied state and people is to remain intact while that state and the constitution is being reconstructed, then occupying forces must not themselves engage in expansive legislative and institutional changes that pre-empt autonomous political decision-making by the occupied regarding the nature of their political, social, and economic regime. Yet the need to replace an "ousted sovereign" involved in the grave rights violations that allegedly occasioned humanitarian (or democratic) intervention in the first place and to change rights-violating and typically undemocratic domestic laws, including the constitution, is also undeniable. How, then, can sovereign equality, self-determination, and human rights all be secured in such a context?

Apparently the relevant international law of *jus post bellum* is the law of belligerent occupation codified in two key treaties, the 1907 Hague

Regulations Respecting the Laws and Customs of War on Land and the 1949 Fourth Geneva Convention Relative to the Protection of Civilian Persons in Time of War, and in the Additional Protocols I and II 1977.[3] These treaties enshrine what is known as the "conservation principle" by prohibiting unnecessary changes in the legal, political, economic, or social institutions of the occupied territory.[4] The concepts of belligerent occupation and the conservation principle delimit the authority of the occupier administering a territory he controls by virtue of the purely factual nature of his power – which was assumed to be temporary and provisional. Indeed, the foundation of the "entire law of occupation ... is the principle of inalienability of sovereignty through the actual or threatened use of force."[5] This is what the conservationist principle "conserves," and what differentiates de facto occupation from actual annexation and/or complete and permanent control by outside powers (subjection).

This all sounds rather quaint today. It is unsurprising that the concept of belligerent occupation seemed to fall into desuetude during World War Two and in the epoch of the Cold War, with its numerous undeclared and rather transformative occupations.[6] The development of UN-administered humanitarian occupations in "failed" or deeply divided states in the 1990s, in the aftermath of the Cold War, was hardly the context in which to revive it.[7] Nevertheless, it was resuscitated, albeit reluctantly, by the US and Britain's declaration that they were occupying powers in Iraq. Additionally, Security Council Resolution 1483 expressly recognized the US and Britain as occupying powers and required them to comply with their obligations under the international law of belligerent occupation, specifically mentioning the Hague Regulations and the Fourth Geneva Convention.[8] This is quixotic given that the occupation of Iraq, like the only other self-declared occupation since World War Two, the Israeli occupation of the West Bank and Gaza since 1967, clearly promised to be a highly "transformative occupation," with no intention to respect the rules or laws of the ousted sovereign.[9] Moreover, Resolution 1483 itself appears contradictory and ambivalent, insofar as it also called for the occupying authority to "assist the people of Iraq in their efforts to reform their institutions," to "[create the] conditions in which the Iraqi people can freely determine their own political future," "[to promote] economic reconstruction and the conditions for sustainable development," and "[to promote] the protection of human rights."[10] Such "requests" hardly involve respect for the prior laws and institutions of the Iraqi state and certainly were not geared toward the restoration of the status quo ante.

Thus, we face a paradox that others have noted: if the conservation principle intrinsic to the law of belligerent occupation rules out fundamental change in political, economic, legal, and social structure by occupying powers, don't the imperatives of contemporary occupations, be they unilateral and belligerent or UN-sponsored, render it an anachronism today? If what is at stake in an occupation is the protection of human rights, regime change, and ultimately "post-conflict constitution-making," if the quality of governance is now generally a matter of international concern, shouldn't the conservationist principle be deemed moot and the law of belligerent occupation abandoned or radically reinterpreted/reformed so as to enable the occupier to institute normatively desirable political change?[11] Wouldn't it be absurd for an occupier to maintain the laws of a tyrannical or a racist regime out of respect for the "ousted sovereign"? Shouldn't concerns for human rights and democracy trump outdated conceptions of ruler sovereignty? Moreover, since the world in which the concept of belligerent occupation was devised and made sense no longer exists, isn't it anachronistic to attempt to revive or even reform it?[12] Indeed wouldn't it be absurd to apply rules designed to restrain individual states occupying a territory in the aftermath of an inter-state war prior to a peace treaty, to the humanitarian occupations under Security Council auspices often in the aftermath of civil war or ethnic cleansing or genocidal threats whose aim is regime change? Shouldn't the direction of influence be the other way around? To be sure, annexation is ruled out in cases of both belligerent and humanitarian occupation. But aren't the historical context, international community values, and premises of contemporary occupations light years away from those informing the law of belligerent occupation in a context when war was an acknowledged tool of foreign policy, exchange of populations (ethnic cleansing) an accepted normal outcome of victory, and when the nature of the domestic political regime was deemed irrelevant to international law? If it is correct to say that contemporary humanitarian occupations are premised on a legal model of the state that not only precludes annexation, changes to existing borders, or population exchanges in the aftermath of war or humanitarian intervention but also which favors a rights-respecting pluralist ideal political regime, then shouldn't the legal framework used to evaluate occupation regimes and the post-conflict constitution-making that occurs under their auspices take this collective vision of territory, individual rights, and appropriate political institutions into account?[13] Aren't all contemporary occupations perforce prolonged and transformative?

On the other hand, how can they avoid the charge of liberal imperialism if occupiers have a free hand to impose their preferred form of "liberal-democratic" constitution and institutions on a subject population? Aren't prolonged transformative and humanitarian occupations more akin to a modern form of indirect colonialism or con-dominium, respectively, than the selfless liberation they often pose as? Shouldn't we be suspicious of the revival in contemporary discourse of concepts like "shared" or "disaggregated" sovereignty and "neo-trusteeship," whether these refer to belligerent occupation or UN-sponsored, Chapter VII "transitional" administrations, given the extraordinary power administrators appropriate, when they regulate and legislate for the subject population? Absent careful legal regulation of all occupations, what would prevent the resuscitation of an informal type of mandate or trustee system that once again condones prolonged occupation and foreign control and, in the name of the "civilized" values of the international community (liberalism, democracy) treats the occupied paternalistically as wards incapable or unwilling to responsibly govern themselves?[14] In the case of UN-sponsored humanitarian occupation, can we simply ignore the asymmetries in the Security Council between the permanent five and the other members, not to mention the inordinate influence of the sole superpower since the 1990s and its efforts to create what has been called Hegemonic International Law?[15] Can we assume that the Council's new and apparently unlimited legislative role under Chapter VII is by definition exercised in the interest of the international community and leave it at that? Shouldn't we resist giving a legal imprimatur to any (non-consensual) foreign project of transformative occupation and leave the burden of proof on the occupier?[16] How can the assertion that the occupied state and population remain sovereign be convincing in the face of a foreign occupier imposing a new legal and political order acting, in short, like a sovereign dictator?[17]

I take these dilemmas seriously. Nevertheless, I will argue first that the spirit of the conservation principle, if not the letter of the law of belligerent occupation, remains relevant today and that it is well worth the effort to articulate its normative thrust in light of contemporary conditions. In particular, I will maintain that the principle of the "inalienability of sovereignty by force" remains valid, although the understanding of who the ultimate bearer of national sovereignty is, and of what prerogatives sovereignty entails, have undergone important shifts. Second, I will claim that it is advisable to acknowledge the need for reform of occupation law in light of these shifts and to articulate clear principles (purposes) and determinate rules that should guide such reform. In particular I want to argue that the sovereignty which must be conserved is that of the indigenous population rather than the ousted ruler. The Hague Regulations and Geneva Conventions remain relevant customary international law, but it is important to update them so as to develop rules adequate to contemporary understandings, conditions, and expectations. I will thus also argue that reform is crucial vis-à-vis Chapter VII humanitarian occupations. The administration of occupied territory and peoples under the auspices of a global governance institution like the UNSC must be guided and limited by clear norms and legal principles. We must, in short, navigate between the Scylla of rigid legalism regarding Hague and Geneva IV, which invites the wholesale disregard of occupation law as anachronistic or a willful misreading of it as simply enabling, and the Charybdis of overly enabling reforms in the name of human rights or "democratic regime change," which undermine the very principle that occupation law should be protecting.[18]

I will thus argue in favor of the development of a *jus post bellum* to forestall the usurpation of sovereignty and constituent power that is all too likely in the case of prolonged occupations, belligerent or humanitarian. I will begin by addressing the two major approaches to the law of occupation that my own interpretation is at odds with: the moral humanitarian and the realist/Schmittian, both of which suggest that the classic conservation principle is irrelevant today. Section 4.1 will discuss the former approach, which interprets the development of occupation law as a process of humanization guided by the increasing and salutary influence of human rights and the emergent international norm of democratic legitimacy linked to the idea of popular sovereignty, on humanitarian law. The logical implication of this approach is the expansion of the scope of the legislative, constitutional, and institutional change on the part of occupying powers in order to protect the welfare and rights of the occupied population and to secure future peace. The law of belligerent occupation and the newer Chapter VII, UN-sponsored humanitarian occupations are interpreted in that light. Section 4.2 will discuss the latter approach, which entails a historicist interpretation of the concept of belligerent occupation along with the conservation principle that argues its limited contemporary relevance because the international order and social structural conditions to which they corresponded and were functional no longer exist. It sees the revival of the discourse of belligerent occupation by revisionists seeking to use it to justify highly transformative occupations as at best naive, or at worst, suspect and self-serving on the part of the great powers. It also denies that a substantive model of the state (liberal-democratic) has or should replace earlier neutrality and agnosticism on the part of international law regarding qualification for sovereign statehood or that such a goal legitimates intrusive transformative occupation administrations. In short it rejects both the revisionist interpretation of the law of belligerent occupation to accommodate transformative unilateral occupations in the name of humanization, and the creation of a new *jus post bellum* for UN-sponsored humanitarian occupations. Given the mixed motives of every intervention and occupation, legalization would be too enabling, and play into neo-imperialist hands. In Section 4.3, I will suggest a third alternative, which grants that we are in an epoch of transformative and humanitarian occupation but argues that this is precisely why clear norms and updated legal rules that remain true to the spirit of the conservation principle are so necessary. It is possible to square the circle if we look more closely at what is at stake in the law of occupation today in light of other relevant principles of international law. Our epoch is regulated not only by human rights norms, but also by the normative legal principles of sovereign equality, self determination, non-intervention, and the strictures against aggression and annexation – these principles provide the basis on which to reconstruct the conservation principle in a compelling way. In Section 4.4, I conclude by arguing that unilateral as well as UN-sponsored humanitarian occupations should be regulated by international law, based on the principles these norms embody. I will thus counter-pose my argument to the position that seeks to update the conservation principle for belligerent occupations, but rejects its applicability to Chapter VII occupation administrations.[19] As we shall see the dualistic world order does indeed involve two distinct levels of relations: international relations among sovereign states in international society to which the law of belligerent occupation, appropriately interpreted, certainly still does and should apply; and global governance institutions whose newly expanded legislative functions and highly intrusive, dictatorial interventions in domestic legal and constitutional processes are sorely in need of legal regulation, normative guidance, and limits. I argue that sovereign equality, self-determination, and human rights should be safeguarded in all occupations. As we shall see, institutional reform of the structures and procedures of the newly active and legislative GGI, i.e. the UNSC, may be required if legitimacy is to be maintained with respect to new legal regulation.

4.1   The development of occupation law as a story of humanization

The standard humanitarian interpretation of the development of occupation law (and the law of war generally) is that its main purpose is to moderate the excesses of modern warfare and military rule, the focus being the welfare of the helpless civilian population at the mercy of a foreign army.[20] Legal rules were deemed necessary because the ousted sovereign no longer has the ability to protect the local population; and the occupier, precisely because his occupation is seen as temporary, has no interest in doing so. Indeed the international law of belligerent occupation is understood today as that branch of humanitarian law that regulates the occupation and administration of foreign territory by an entity that is not its sovereign government, either during a war or after a cease-fire.[21] The nineteenth-century trend toward the humanization of the laws of war on this reading thus spilled over into a *jus post bellum*.

4.1.1   The beginnings of the humanitarian approach

The humanitarian story begins with the first codification of the law of belligerent occupation prepared by Dr. Francis Lieber during the American Civil War in an 1863 text called "Instructions for the Government of the Armies of the United States in the Field," and issued as General Order No. 100 to Union Forces on April 24, 1863 at President Lincoln's request.[22] The Lieber Code is famous as an early attempt to humanize the conduct of modern war and it covers many topics, including treatment of prisoners, enemy property, prohibition of rape and enslavement, but a large part of the code is also devoted to belligerent occupation.[23] The original articulation of the idea behind the modern concept of "belligerent occupation" is attributed to Emmerich de Vattel, although the first usage of the concept was by a German publicist in 1844.[24] "Belligerent occupation" refers to the possession or control of territory acquired under an occupation that is deemed provisional and pending a treaty of peace, and thus involves temporary and limited prerogatives of administration rather than outright sovereignty and, by implication, a special legal status. Accordingly the concept of "belligerent occupation" was distinguished from the older "right of conquest" which ipso facto ascribed full sovereignty over conquered territory and the total subjugation of its inhabitants – absolute dominion – to the victor in a war. The latter could do as he pleased with the conquered territory and subjugated population as a corollary of his absolute sovereignty over everything that came under his control – the ruler's forces could lay waste, annex, set up a client state, cede the territory to a third state, etc. The merely temporary and limited rights of administration accorded to a military administration under the concept of belligerent occupation thus appear as an important step in the humanization of war and its aftermath, because de facto power did not immediately translate into de jure sovereignty, conquest, and subjugation. This is all the more impressive since the norms delimiting what could be done under a "belligerent occupation" developed in a context in which war was still deemed a legitimate tool of statecraft and in which annexation (pending a peace treaty) was normal practice.[25]

Although the Lieber Code referred to an "internal conflict," it was influential as a model for the national manuals of European militaries and paved the way for international codification.[26] There were attempts throughout the nineteenth century to codify an international law of belligerent occupation, starting with the 1874 Intergovernmental Conference at Brussels and culminating in the 1907 Hague Convention Respecting the Laws and Customs of War on Land, which included fifteen articles addressing belligerent occupation under the rubric "Military Authority over the Territory of the Hostile State."[27]

4.1.2   The occupier as "trustee" of the ousted sovereign

On the humanitarian reading, the distinction between belligerent occupation and conquest/subjugation, along with limits on the prerogatives of the victor during occupation (especially those articulated in Article 43) developed in reaction to the brutality and punitive practices that accompanied the dominion following from past conquests. "With the rise of standing armies and more standardized codes of conduct in the nineteenth century, efforts were made to restrain these excesses of conquest."[28] However, given assumptions about the absoluteness of a sovereign's prerogatives and his right to war, and given the fact that only states had international legal personality, it was inconceivable to attempt to limit the brutality of occupations by invoking human rights or forbidding aggressive war at this period.[29] The only way to do this was to deny full sovereignty to the occupier and to speak instead of the "authority of the legitimate power having in fact passed into the hands of the occupant," and of preserving the laws and institutions of the "ousted sovereign."[30] As already indicated, "belligerent occupation" involved the establishment of military administrative authority over the territory and subject population that was deemed temporary, provisional, and "interim" between the cessation of hostilities and the final disposition of the territory in question. In other words, occupation law according to the Hague Regulations governs the period of interregnum between the end of a war and the conclusion of a peace treaty between the contending parties. Accordingly, the occupying military authority, and the administration it set up, was placed in the position of trustee of the interests and rules of the ousted sovereign. Included among those interests were the preservation of property, basic order, and basic welfare of the civilian population.[31]

Occupation law thus protects the indigenous population, as well as the interests of the "ousted sovereign," while providing legal cover for exigencies and needs of the occupying power (security, duty to ensure the peace, and certain basic rights). This triple imperative requires a balancing of the right of the occupier to protect its forces and preserve peace, the interests of the ousted sovereign, and the humanitarian needs of the population. Accordingly, the occupier may not alter the existing form of government, upset the constitution and domestic laws of the occupied territory, or set aside the rights of the inhabitants unless absolutely required by military necessity.[32] On the other hand, it can and must set up a military administration that provides public order and security for its own forces. Such an "interim administration" is, in some respects, similar to a domestic emergency regime under military authority, but it is meant to be restrained and to maintain the status quo ante regarding the laws and institutions under which the civilian population functions.[33]

The humanization of the law of occupation was predicated on the development of the all-important distinction between citizen (civilian) and soldier that emerged in the context of the development of the modern state and the international state system. The latter institutionalized the general differentiation between public and private power (and offices), public and private property, public fiscal and monetary policies and private economic activity, and the differentiation between standing armies and private civilians. By the mid-1870s, this development reached the point where King William of Prussia could state on August 11, 1870, "I conduct war with the French soldiers, not with the French citizens."[34] As Eyal Benvenisti convincingly argues, war was seen as a match between governments and their armies, and thus civilians were left out of war and to be kept physically and economically unharmed as much as possible.[35] Given the general laissez-faire economic orientation of most states, the policy of minimal governmental intervention in the economy, and the great respect for private economic rights, the theory was advanced that just as states have little interest in regulating the economic activity of their own citizens, so occupying powers should have little interest in regulating or interfering with the economic activity and property of the occupied.[36] That is why it was possible to conceive of the occupier as trustee of the ousted sovereign and the local population: it was assumed that there was no conflict in principle between the temporarily subject population and the occupying power, once all resistance died down. Military administration of occupied territory was thus to be tamed and humanized by law: the preservation of order and security was not to involve interference with the daily lives of the civilian population. The numerous rules protecting the latter's property in the 1907 Hague Convention thus gave rise to the civil liability, in the form of compensation, of belligerents who violated them.[37] The complementary duty of the occupied population was to abide by the occupant's exercise of authority. In addition, the occupier was accorded the power to administer state property while being placed under the duty to safeguard it and refrain from destroying or depleting national resources.[38]

However, the idea of rights of conquest did not vanish entirely – it survived in the concept of "debellatio," the counter-concept to "belligerent occupation."[39] War was, as already indicated, still deemed a legitimate way to pursue national policy and full sovereignty over territory could be obtained either through a peace treaty or through the "total defeat" of an adversary – a concept entailing the complete destruction of the political and juridical institutions of the sovereign and the total disintegration of the enemy state.[40] So long as no other power continued the struggle on behalf of the defeated sovereign, occupation in such a case transfers sovereignty.

This exception to the law of belligerent occupation reveals the limits of the Hague principles from the humanitarian point of view. As Benvenisti aptly points out, it reveals that the only relevant political interests in the Article 43 regime were those of state elites, not the citizenry. Territory and sovereignty could be transferred to a victor in a war culminating in debellatio irrespective of the wishes of the local population – who, of course, were not consulted. Even in the case of belligerent occupation, the occupant was expected to privilege the interests of the "ousted sovereign" over those of the indigenous population if these diverged.[41] Moreover, of the fifteen articles on belligerent occupation, only three were related to the physical integrity of civilian persons, the rest dealt essentially with the protection of property.[42] There was no discourse of human rights informing the Hague Regulations, but only a limited and vague humanitarianism at best. Indeed, the inter-state character of the Hague Convention, and the principles of inter-elite reciprocity it enshrined, explains its deficiencies from the humanitarian point of view.

4.1.3   The resurgence of humanitarianism through Geneva I

The humanitarian spirit resurfaced with the effort to define anew the international law of occupation in reaction to atrocities committed in occupied territories during World War Two. Coming in the aftermath of the Nuremberg Charter and the 1948 Genocide Conventions, the Fourth Geneva Convention sought to create a new balance between the rights of the occupant and the need to protect civilian populations in occupied territory.[43] Given the massive internments, deportations, reprisals, hostage-taking, enslavement, and murder of civilians in occupied Europe by both the Soviets and the Nazis, the need to remedy the deficiencies of the 1907 Hague Regulations appeared self-evident. The International Committee of the Red Cross (ICRC) was accordingly charged with drawing up a revised codification of the law of belligerent occupation. The Fourth Geneva Convention, devised to supplement the Hague Regulations, thus went much further in protecting the humanitarian needs of civilians against violence.[44] Benvenisti argues that it "delineates a bill of rights for the occupied population" by giving them the legal status of "protected persons" and enumerating a specific set of rights which occupants must protect. For example, Article 27 asserts the duty of the occupier to ensure the humane treatment of "protected persons," and to respect the persons' honor, family rights, religious convictions and practices, manners, and customs, while forbidding discrimination on the basis of race, sex, political opinion, or religion.[45] The Convention protects civilians against torture or inhuman treatment, willful killing, collective punishment, reprisals, deportation, settlement of the occupier's own nationals in the occupied territory, and the subjection of that territory to the occupier's own national laws.[46] It also spells out, in detail, rules requiring the occupant to facilitate the proper working of institutions devoted to the care and education of children; it addresses labor conditions prohibiting the deliberate restriction of job opportunities in occupied territory or efforts to create unemployment or to induce locals to work for the occupier; and several articles address medical and hospital services and the maintenance of health and hygiene.[47] The fact that there is a list of human rights articulated in the Convention as well as its title reveals that the focus is now on the protection of civilian *persons* and their humanitarian treatment.[48] The Convention thus amounted to a "new constitution" for occupation administrations: "... the very decision to dedicate the Fourth Geneva Convention to persons and not to governments signified a growing awareness in international law of the idea that peoples are not merely the resources of states but rather that they are worthy of being the subjects of international norms."[49] Moreover, violation of these norms is considered a grave breach that is subject to criminal prosecution.

Indeed, Theodor Meron insists that by creating a set of affirmative duties for the occupier, who must assume active responsibility for the welfare of the population under its control, Geneva IV created a "new balance between the rights of the occupant and the rights of the population in the occupied country."[50] He agrees with Benvenisti that the Convention initiated an important shift from an emphasis on the interests of states or governments to the rights of individuals and civilian populations.[51] He emphasizes that, together with the Nuremberg Charter and the Genocide Convention, the 1949 Geneva Conventions helped shift some state-to-state aspects of international humanitarian law to individual criminal responsibility, thereby opening up the path to individual standing in international law.[52] Even though the concept of a "protected person" was initially defined within the traditional state-centric reciprocity-based approach of classic international law, and thus restricted to nationals of the occupied state, Geneva IV laid the groundwork for future developments of humanitarian law under the influence of human rights principles. This allowed humanitarian law to "go beyond the interstate level and to reach for the level of the real (or ultimate) beneficiaries of humanitarian protection, i.e. individuals and groups of individuals."[53]

4.1.4   The modern expansion of humanitarian principles

Accordingly, the subsequent development of the law of occupation, starting with the Additional Geneva Protocol I, adopted in 1977, which extended protection against reprisals to the entire civilian population, individual civilians, and civilian objects and cultural objects, is seen as a step-by-step movement beyond the inter-state paradigm to an individualized rights-based approach. The gradual expansion of the category of "protected persons" beyond nationals of the occupied state, to include *all* persons on the adverse side who fall into the hands of a party to an armed conflict, is a prime example of the salutary assimilation of occupation law to human rights law, on this view. Already under Common Article 6/6/6/7, rights were granted to "protected persons" themselves.[54] But under Article 4 of Geneva IV, the concept of "protected persons" referred only to "those who, at a given moment and in any manner whatsoever, find themselves in case of a conflict or occupation in the hands of a Party to the conflict or Occupying Power of which they are not nationals."[55] This not only excluded nationals of a neutral state and nationals of non-signatories, it also excluded civilians under military occupations resulting from internal armed conflicts such as civil wars.

The decision in the 1999 appeal of the Tadic case altered this restrictive approach by ruling that the war in the former Yugoslavia amounted to an international conflict,[56] and by embracing a flexible, substantive approach to the application of the category of protected person.[57] In short, it rejected the literal legalistic approach, which required different nationalities in order to

meet the definition of protected persons, characterizing its own approach as
follows:

> This legal approach, hinging on substantial relations more than on
> formal bonds, becomes all the more important in present-day inter-
> national armed conflicts ... [I]n modern inter-ethnic armed conflicts
> such as that in the former Yugoslavia, new States are often created during
> the conflict and ethnicity rather than nationality may become the
> grounds for allegiance ... [A]llegiance to a Party to the conflict and,
> correspondingly, control by this Party over persons in a given territory
> may be regarded as the crucial test.[58]

Moreover, the Appeals Court cited ICRC commentary to the effect that the
purpose of Geneva IV is first and foremost to protect individuals, not to serve
state interests, and thus is directed to the protection of civilians to the
maximum extent possible. Indeed, regarding Article 4 it stated:

> Its primary purpose is to ensure the safeguards afforded by the Conven-
> tion to those civilians who do not enjoy the diplomatic protection, and
> correlatively are not subject to the allegiance and control, of the State in
> whose hands they may find themselves.[59]

This individualized human rights-based approach to humanitarian law in
general, and the law of occupation in particular, is evident in Additional
Geneva Protocol II that extended protections to civilian populations in
non-international "internal" armed conflicts.[60] Accordingly, the general
principle articulated in the ICRC commentary to the Fourth Geneva Convention seems to be a generally accepted legal norm: every person in enemy hands
must have some status under international law either as a prisoner of war, and
thus covered by the Third Geneva Convention, or as a civilian, covered by the
Fourth Convention. Nobody in enemy hands can be considered outside the
law. Thus the importance of citizenship to status as a "protected person" has
diminished, the potential victim class in war crimes prosecutions has
expanded, requiring a lesser degree of intervention by other states to inter-
nationalize an internal conflict, and human rights-inspired jurisprudence
within the humanitarian framework has also expanded.[61]

It is thus unsurprising that the story of normative progress and progressive
individualization of the subject of occupation law puts the emphasis on the
affirmative duties of occupiers to actively protect human rights. Advocates are
undisturbed that this seems to require expanding the legislative powers of
administrations in occupied territories for the benefit of the civilians in their
care, especially in protracted occupations.[62] Indeed, Benvenisti criticizes the
minimalism of Geneva IV, complaining that the commands of the Convention
neither direct the occupant to treat the occupied people with standards similar
to the ones employed for its own nationals, nor require the occupant to develop
(not just maintain) the economic, social, and educational infrastructure.[63]

Accordingly, human rights advocates who invoke the humanitarian impulses of occupation law as a story of moral progress seek to ascribe the posture of benevolent custodian and trustee to occupying powers. To accomplish this goal, they seek to expand the scope of legal and legitimate action of occupying powers to ensure that post-conflict regimes are rights-respecting.[64] The affirmative obligations imposed by Geneva IV, in conjunction with other sources of international law, require respect for human rights and are invoked to justify the abrogation of laws and institutions that presumably violate the Convention, even if they pose no obstacle to maintaining order or pursuing military objections (the Hague criteria).[65] In the context of an occupation that results in "regime change," this orientation suggests that the identity of the trustee has shifted from the ousted sovereign to the civilian population. This implies a new focus on the welfare and basic rights of the civilian population, guided by the principle of "humanity."[66] Accordingly, the occupant is no longer cast as a disinterested watch-guard, but rather as an involved regulator and provider.[67] Indeed, the rise of the interventionist "welfare" state in the twentieth century allegedly generates the expectation that an occupying power, like a domestic state, should provide for basic social services and thus fulfill the requirements of good governance.[68] While Article 64 of Geneva IV and the Additional Protocols already reflected the need to relax Hague Article 43's strong bias against modifying local law, they apparently did not go far enough. Instead, they left occupiers engaged in fostering human rights and thus vulnerable to being charged with violating existing international law.

Security Council Resolution 1483, passed on May 22, 2003, recognized the US and UK forces in Iraq as occupying powers (a status they took on reluctantly), and is seen as the solution to this dilemma and as the latest and most authoritative restatement of several basic principles of contemporary occupation law.[69] On the one hand, the Resolution rescued the law of belligerent occupation from oblivion by requiring the Coalition Provisional Authority (CPA), established by the aforementioned powers, to comply fully with their obligations under international law including, in particular, the Geneva Conventions of 1949 and the Hague Regulations of 1907.[70] On the other hand, it granted a mandate allowing the occupants to promote the welfare of the Iraqi people, human rights, legal and judicial reform, and to transform the previous legal and political system so as to facilitate the establishment of institutions of representative governance.[71] The tension between the two imperatives and the ambiguity of the Resolution has led some commentators to reject any interpretation that would permit or encourage the US and UK to engage in a "transformative occupation."[72] But on the humanitarian reading, although the Resolution resurrected the law of belligerent occupation from its slumber, it did so clearly under the influence of UN-supported humanitarian interventions or peace-enforcement operations in the 1990s which involved highly transformative "state-building" processes. Indeed UN interim occupation administrations were ascribed plenary powers with no limits placed on their legislative or executive roles apart from being subject to internationally recognized human rights standards. In Kosovo and East Timor, UN Interim/Transitional Administrations were ascribed all legislative and executive authority, including the administration of justice.[73] To be sure, the latter were not unilateral belligerent occupations; they were "humanitarian occupations" involving international administrations established under the UN Security Council Chapter VII prerogatives, and thus did not come under Hague or Geneva rules. They nevertheless allegedly provided the background and context for understanding Resolution 1483 as a revision of the law of belligerent occupation in general, and the particular claim that the occupation administration in Iraq must take on a transformative hue for the sake of human rights and democratic state-building.

According to Benvenisti, the UN's reference (for the first time) to the concept of occupation in Resolution 1483 served four purposes. First, it refuted the claim that occupation as such is illegal, by reviving the applicability of the law and the neutral connotation of the doctrine.[74] If occupation does not amount to unlawful alien domination then the population is not entitled to struggle against it. Second, it reaffirmed the sovereignty and territorial integrity of Iraq, thereby indicating that the total demise of the Iraqi regime notwithstanding, total victory did not result in *debellatio*, and hence did not pass sovereignty over to the occupant.[75] This outcome was conceivable thanks to a shift in the understanding that the (Iraqi) people, not the "ousted government," were the ultimate holders of sovereignty, and were ascribed the right to freely determine their own political future and control over their own natural resources and thus to have their popular sovereignty respected. Third, the Resolution "recognizes in principle" the continued applicability of international human rights law in occupied territories in tandem with the law of occupation. Human rights law may thus complement the law of occupation on specific matters.[76] Fourth, the Resolution envisions the role of the modern occupant as a heavily involved regulator.[77] Indeed, Resolution 1483 empowers the occupant to promote economic reconstruction and to provide the conditions of sustainable development to the occupied. On this reading, humanization of occupation law is driven by increasing respect for every individual's human rights and welfare, and the law of belligerent occupation turns into the law of transformative occupation.

The ultimate logic of this trajectory is to apply the fullest possible range of human rights obligations to occupied territories.[78] However, this reading of the development of the humanitarian features of occupation law, and of Resolution 1483 as its most current restatement, would seem to render the conservation principle at the heart of that law moot.[79] Indeed getting around the prohibition on constitutional change in the occupied territory at the hands of the occupying power seemed to be precisely the point of John Yoo's argument for an expansive reading of occupation law that gives occupiers broad discretion to reform the occupied state not only so as to protect human rights but also to institutionalize constitutional democracy.[80] He specifically argued with respect to the belligerent occupation of Iraq by the US that,

> in order for the United States to fulfill its obligations [under occupation law], maintain an orderly government, and protect its national security as well as the security of its armed forces while occupying Iraq, it almost certainly will be necessary for the United States to change Iraqi Law to dismantle current Iraqi government institutions and create new ones to take their place.[81]

Indeed Yoo insisted that given Iraq's abysmal record in the area of human rights, the US cannot fulfill its obligations under Geneva IV without replacing the institutions of the Hussein regime.[82] On this extreme version of the reformist reading especially of Articles 27–34 of Geneva IV, the law of belligerent occupation itself requires the occupiers to change local laws, not only so as not to violate human rights themselves, but also to engage in constitutional and other legal changes that institutionalize rights and democracy.[83]

This is claimed despite the fact that Geneva IV is clearly humanitarian in purpose and not meant as a green light for occupiers to engage in democratic regime change or post-conflict constitution writing. As Fox has noted, it is no accident that human rights essential to political participation such as voting and freedoms of speech, press, and conscience are omitted in Geneva IV.[84] He thus contests the claim that Resolution 1483 endorsed the agenda of the CPA for transformative occupation in Iraq. Instead, the Resolution's studied ambiguity aimed to urge the CPA to make an early exit and leave a light footprint although it was ambivalent regarding the mandate to reform the previous legal system it granted the occupier on the one side, and fidelity to the conservation principle in occupation law and to the principle of Iraqi ownership of its own transformative political process, on the other.[85] Resolution 1483 gave a mandate to the CPA to transform the previous legal system to enable the Iraqi people "freely to determine their own political future and control their own natural resources ... to form a representative government based on the rule of law that affords equal rights and justice to all Iraqi citizens without regard to ethnicity, religion or gender."[86] The ultimate logic of the radical reformist version of the humanization thesis would not involve tempering the conservation principle by contemporary human rights standards but rather would permit an occupier to assume the role of sovereign dictator, impose a new constitution, rewrite civil and criminal laws, secularize public institutions, and so forth.[87] As Fox incisively puts it, "... that would not be an accommodation between humanitarian law and human rights but a full substitution of the latter for the former ... for a single occupier, it is simple cherry-picking between equally binding treaty obligations."[88] Among these obligations is the requirement that existing institutions are to be preserved meaning that an occupier may not impose its country's laws or new constitutional and fundamental economic laws on the occupied, *and* the possibly conflicting obligation that the occupier not enforce laws and institutions that violate human rights.[89] The problem with the humanization approach, taken to extremes, is that it reads one of the alternatives out of the law altogether.[90]

4.2   The realist/Schmittian reading of the law of belligerent occupation

The realist/Schmittian reading of occupation law points in the same direction, but for radically different reasons. Formulated explicitly as an alternative to the humanitarian account, which is seen as abstract, ahistorical, and either naively or cynically moralistic, the Schmittian approach insists on a structural-functional and a historicist/contextualized analysis of the law of belligerent occupation.[91] Accordingly, the real function of the law of belligerent occupation, as it developed in the aftermath of the 1815 Congress of Vienna and throughout the nineteenth century (culminating in the 1907 Hague Regulations), was to help re-found the concrete European order of sovereign states and reconstitute a *jus publicum Europaeum*.[92] The "determinate content" of the concept of belligerent occupation was tied to geopolitical and ideological interests, rather than some sort of moral humanitarianism.[93] Accordingly, the rules of belligerent occupation made possible the creation of a system of sovereign states, a European "international society," in which conflicting principles of political legitimacy (the dynastic versus the democratic) and a plurality of constitutional regimes (absolutist, liberal parliamentarian, and enlightened and unenlightened despotism, imperial and republican) could coexist.[94] They served to block the revolutionary transformation of a domestic order through intervention by another state (revolutionary wars "exporting republican liberty") or insurrection from below.[95] While the administration of the occupant ended up serving two interests – the preservation of the rights of the ousted sovereign and the humanitarian interests of the indigenous population – the occupant, as we have already noted, was always to prefer the former over the latter. Thus the very concept of belligerent occupation – the provisional, temporary, and purely de facto exercise of power by the occupant until a peace treaty legitimately and legally resolved the outcome of the dispute – was constituted in the context of and served to preserve the sovereignty of rulers and the concrete spatial order of the European sovereign state system. Neither the concept nor the law of belligerent occupation applied to colonial possessions of European powers which, by definition, were not considered sovereign states and whose "uncivilized" populations were not deemed capable of self-determination.[96]

4.2.1 The historical development according to the realist model

The socio-political context (conditions of possibility) and function of the concept and law of belligerent occupation were thus historically specific and unique. The concept takes on a functional intelligibility only in the context of late eighteenth- and nineteenth-century European politics.[97] In particular, it was developed in the aftermath of the French Revolution and Napoleonic wars which challenged the old intra-European political order by introducing transnational revolutionary movements and occupations which claimed to be liberations insofar as they replaced autocratic with republican constitutions albeit in the context of conquest and even annexation. The concomitant and new form of political identity – national republican citizenship – and new type of political movement – nationalism – linked to ideas of popular sovereignty all were, to say the least, destabilizing in the context of restoration Europe.[98] Thus,

> [b]y enjoining the occupant from changing the political order of the occupied territory, and by interdicting the legal transfer of sovereignty until the state of war was formally concluded, the legal category of belligerent occupation effectively facilitated the mediation of territorial and constitutional change . . . the negotiated concurrence . . . of the Great Powers was a practical precondition for the appropriation of territory . . . The revolutionary transformation of the domestic order of a state through the intervention of another state was effectively bracketed.[99]

So too was the legitimacy of local civilian resistance to an occupant's rules or to the preservation of the laws and institutions of the ousted sovereign. Indeed, on this reading, the conservation principle, along with the distinctions between combatant and non-combatant, and soldier and civilian, served to de-legitimize civilian struggles for regime change and resistance to occupying forces.[100] This resulted in the enabling of harsh measures against partisans and "irregular combatants."[101] Far from being an impartial trustee, the occupant under the law of belligerent occupation was clearly biased against the political interests of the subject population. It cannot be stressed too strongly that even though it was not supposed to institute a new political or legal order, the temporary administration established during a belligerent occupation was a military one, which assumed plenary (dictatorial) powers and could, in order to maintain order, not only suspend civil and political liberties, but also engage in harsh disciplinary techniques. It is right to invoke the analogy between a belligerent occupation in which the military temporarily exercises discretionary powers to maintain order, and what Schmitt called a domestic "commissarial dictatorship" – referring to the discretionary powers exercised in emergencies by the executive via the military (such as martial law), to provide security and protect the constitutional order when it appears to be under threat.[102]

4.2.2   The Schmittian reading of belligerent occupation as "outdated"

Accordingly, the concept of belligerent occupation seems anachronistic today because the international order and social structural conditions to which it was functional no longer exist. If the codification of the conservation principle in the Hague Regulations was already like the owl of Minerva in 1907, the 1949 revival of conservationist language, from this perspective, looks like a moralistic farce.[103] In the aftermath of total war plus highly transformative occupations, and in the absence of a new nomos to which it could be functional – the two blocs and the standoff of the Cold War did not constitute an order in the Schmittian sense – resurrecting the law of belligerent occupation appears absurd.[104] Neither superpower considered its interventions to be belligerent occupations, framing them instead as invitations from local political forces.[105] The Fourth Geneva Convention was written at a time when the prescriptions of the Hague Regulations had lost their authority and determinacy as the embodiment of customary international law.[106] Indeed, the long-term post-war occupations, whose very purpose was the imposition of the occupier's socio-economic and political system, plus the resurgence of partisan and guerrilla struggle, made "the preservationist principle at the heart of occupation law seem particularly anachronistic."[107] The same is true, on this analysis, of the citizen/soldier distinction and the expectation that occupations or wars end officially with the conclusion of a peace treaty between the belligerents.

To be sure, it was the weaker states at the Fourth Geneva Convention that pushed for retention of the Hague Regulations, prevailing against the wishes of the great powers, especially the US, which sought a very permissive occupation law that would legally enable transformative occupation. The former position stood for those countries at risk of being occupied; the latter position expressed the perceived lack of such a risk on the part of powerful victors.[108] However, it is also true that the 1949 resurrection of the "conservation" principle of inalienability of sovereignty through force served the Allies' geopolitical interests. Indeed, it provided the perfect legal justification for the return of Southeast Asian colonies "liberated" by the Japanese during the war to the "ousted sovereign," despite violent opposition of large segments of the local populations.[109] This, rather than any humanitarian purpose, could help explain, from the "realist" perspective, why the victors accepted the revival of the discourse of belligerent occupation. With regard to occupied

Germany and Japan, it appears that the principle of "inalienability of sovereignty through the use of force" was respected insofar as there was no attempt to annex or subjugate these territories, despite the invocation of the concept of debellatio (given their unconditional surrender) to justify liberal-democratic imposition.[110] As for the victorious invading Allied forces in Southeast Asia, the principle of inalienability of sovereignty permitted the Allies to return those colonies to the "ousted" imperial sovereign once the Japanese were defeated, under the cover of full legality. As Benvenisti tellingly notes, "invocation of the law of occupation proved useful to reoccupants who invoked it to allow military administrations" to use "wide discretionary powers against resistance, unencumbered by constitutional restraints."[111]

This rather cynical interpretation of why the powerful acquiesced to the Fourth Geneva Convention's resurrection of the conservation principle notwithstanding, on the realist/Schmittian reading, it is apparently redundant today. But this is not because the development of human rights norms, including the "human right" to popular sovereignty and national self-determination, has problematized the notion that the occupier is the trustee for the ousted sovereign government, duty bound to preserve its laws and institutions. Rather, it is because the social structural and political presuppositions for the concept of belligerent occupation to make sense have vanished. Today, we are irrevocably in the world of the regulatory state, global capital, unilateral and multilateral military interventions allegedly for "humanitarian" purposes or for the sake of "democratic regime change," and the inevitable transformative occupations that will accompany them.[112]

4.2.3 The Schmittian approach as it applies today

Nevertheless, unlike the "reformist" approaches to occupation law,[113] the Schmittian approach rejects any attempt to give a legal/conceptual imprimatur to the project of transformative occupation. The law of belligerent occupation, on this view, is inappropriate to situations in which the occupant purports to exercise the de facto power of a sovereign dictator, by transforming the state, law, and socio-economic institutions and in effect appropriating the constituent power of the domestic population even if it does so "temporarily" in the name of instituting democracy. Nevertheless, to legalize transformative occupation would be a dangerous mistake. Whether this involves vesting supreme authority in the hands of a single state and its coalition partners (unilateral occupation) or in a UN-sponsored transitional administrative authority (humanitarian occupation), legalization would de-legitimize resistance avant la lettre, thereby pre-empting the meaning of local political struggle and its outcome.[114] It would, in other words, give a green light to self-interested transformations on the part of occupiers before one had a chance to assess the legitimacy of the occupation from the point of view of the occupied.

Legalization of transformative occupation would, under such circumstances, block local self-determination and pre-empt autonomous processes of post-conflict constitution-making.

Indeed, a transformative occupation involves an inevitable paradox: before it can succeed in attaining local legitimacy for its actions, it has to subordinate (quell resistance); but the more an occupier tries to subordinate through the use of force and sheer imposition of rules and institutions, the less it appears as legitimate.[115] I would add that even if resistance is fully quashed and finally dies down, this could be a sign of a successful imperial imposition ("liberal democratization") rather than the acceptance of the changes made by the occupier as legitimate. This is especially true if the occupied have a minimal or subordinate role in the state-rebuilding and constitution-making processes.[116] This dilemma was clearly operative in the two prominent cases of unilateral occupation – that by Israel in Gaza and the West Bank, and by the US and Britain in Iraq.[117] But it is also operative in the UN-sponsored occupations. Although the latter established genuinely international governance structures, they nevertheless are not exempt from serious questions about their political selectivity, dictatorial methods, and, in some cases, paternalistic orientation to the subject population.[118] Thus, it is not a good idea to give presumptive legitimacy to transformative occupations by legalizing them avant la lettre, as it were, especially given the rather ambivalent record of such occupations.

Moreover, the Security Council, which decides on humanitarian occupations through its Chapter VII resolutions, is acting as a political, not a juridical body and the degree to which it makes its decisions as a result of genuine collective deliberation about the merits of the case – as opposed to itself being instrumentalized by powerful member states pursuing their own interests – is an open and serious question.[119] Indeed there are many who view Resolution 1483 as an example of the latter.[120] The Resolution brought the UN back after its initial refusal to acquiesce in the US invasion of Iraq, but it did so in an indeterminate and irresponsible way. Far from providing effective control or real accountability mechanisms, pace Benvenisti, Resolution 1483 failed to establish an effective independent mechanism for ensuring that the occupation Authority, to which it ascribed wide powers, could meet its obligations.[121]

> While it has been hailed for bringing the United Nations back into Iraq, Resolution 1483 leaves the UN role in post-war Iraq extremely vague and uncertain, refusing even to concede to the United Nations those tasks within its established expertise, such as verifying and supervising a free and fair election.[122]

This mode of legalizing what remains a unilateral transformative occupation is thus highly suspect. But even multilateral UN occupations initiated by the Security Council and administered under UN auspices can be instances of what is called "global hegemonic international law."[123] Here too delegation to those states able and willing to take on the task of occupation administration is hardly avoidable and there are no selfless humanitarian heroes among them.

Thus, far from taking UN transformative occupations as a sign of an emerging legal norm relevant to unilateral occupations as well, the realist/Schmittian questions the bona fides of these recent developments, reminding us of the context in which they occur: the neo-imperial efforts of the sole existing superpower and/or former and re-emerging great powers (the P5 on the Council) and their penchant for designating some polities "rogue states" deemed undeserving of full sovereign equality and open to international tutelage.[124] The current popularity of the discourse of "neo-trusteeship" and "shared sovereignty" to describe the transformational occupation regimes in those subdued rogue states is disingenuous in such a context.[125] So is the attempt to distinguish such administrations from "classical imperialism" on the grounds that they are multilateral and temporary. As Kelsen argued long ago with respect to the transformative occupation of Germany, just because a sovereign power refrains from annexation, or includes other co-administrators, or decides that its presence will be temporary, does not mean that it lacks full de facto sovereignty or that it is somehow shared with someone else.[126] The decision to co-administer, and to leave, is the sovereign's decision; certainly the occupied had no role in making this choice or in enforcing it.

Moreover, stressing the differences between *classical imperialism* and "neo-trusteeship" fails to parry the charge of neo-imperialism. James Fearon and David Laitin, for example, grant that there appears to be an analogy between classical nineteenth- and twentieth-century imperialism and the transformational occupation administrations they call neo-trusteeship: both involve strong states "taking over . . . the governance of territories where Western-style politics, economics, and administration were underdeveloped," and both invoke international legal authority (with the exception of Iraq) and in the former case, League of Nations mandates.[127] Still, these authors insist there are two "striking differences" between the models: the classical imperial model involved unilateral administrations imposed by great powers jealously monopolizing control of their imperial domains, conceived of as indefinite in duration, while the "neo-trusteeship" model involves multilateral administrations aimed at rebuilding self-supporting, but politically and economically acceptable state structures, with the intention to leave as quickly as possible.[128] This implies either that such transformative occupations are already legal and legitimate, although some tinkering may be necessary to create mechanisms to ensure efficiency and accountability, or that legal recognition of transformative occupation is desirable to accomplish those goals.

Of course, this analysis is unconvincing to those who see the imposition of state structures and constitutions by outsiders as neo-imperial and in conflict with the self-determination which is characteristic of a pluralist international system based on sovereign equality. Such imposition usurps domestic constituent power, with military bases and "advisors" left behind and the threat of re-intervention for good measure. Given the continued absence of a global nomos, that is, given the undecidability at the present time of the nature and direction of the international system, it is accordingly imperative to keep transformative occupation outside legality and within the realm of sheer facticity and power politics, where it belongs. This, at least, would place the burden of proof on the occupier to demonstrate local legitimacy and impartiality in the transformations put in place by the occupant's administration. Legalizing transformative occupation through revised and/or new occupation law would, in short, be too enabling and inevitably play into the hands of neo-imperialists. Thus, on the realist/Schmittian approach, the law of belligerent occupation is unsusceptible to updating or reform to cover transformative occupations of any sort. Because we are in an epoch without a clear nomos, the exercise of power and the projection of force by a militarily unchallenged superpower, intent on creating global hegemonic law to give it legitimacy (with the collusion of other self-interested great powers with privileged positions on the UNSC), may make transformative occupations unavoidable, but still, we should not give them legal cover.

There are two other compelling reasons, from this perspective, for challenging the reformist project of reinterpreting the law of belligerent occupation so as to use it to legitimate transformative occupations, belligerent and humanitarian. First, the historicist argument as to its origin does not quite render the conservation principle or the existing law of belligerent occupation completely anachronistic because the current dualistic world "system" still consists of an international society of sovereign states which has, in the context of decolonization (1950–65), universalized one key aspect of the 1815 nomos – the principle of the formal equality of sovereign states and the related assumption that a plurality of political regimes within international society can, does, and must coexist.[129] This is a still valid legacy of the nineteenth-century European order.[130] Thus agnosticism regarding the regimes of sovereign states, from the perspective of international law, remains and should remain in force on the realist/Schmittian view. Although the *conduct* of governments within states is subject to certain universal norms such as human rights law and international criminal law, as is the conduct of occupying authorities today (to ensure that the latter does not violate its own humanitarian and human rights obligations), this does not give an occupier a free hand to transform the entire political and legal order of a rights-violating and/or occupied state.[131] The occupier might have to retrench parts of a prior legal order if it is deeply incompatible with human rights but this does not mean that the occupier is authorized to replace it by creating an entirely new order or by imposing a new constitution. This much of the conservation principle, despite its content-indeterminacy, apparently remains in force today at least regarding belligerent occupations.

Second, construing the transformation of a territory's political order to be an objective authorized by international law would erase the line between sovereign and non-sovereign powers regarding the occupant and the occupied.[132] Thus it is wrong to read the updating of the law of belligerent occupation either along the lines of the humanization argument or through the lens of Chapter VII humanitarian occupations that seem to legitimize transformative projects by occupiers who exercise control over state reconstruction or constitution-making processes, for the sake of democratic regime change. Unless we are ready to claim that the international community has embraced a specific substantive vision of the state, and of its economic order (liberal-democratic, capitalist, and neo-liberal), and that all states which don't measure up are illegitimate and non-sovereign – a hardly convincing and rather unfeasible notion given the nature of the governments and economies of many states acknowledged as sovereign equals (including some of the most powerful such as China) – then legalization of transformative humanitarian occupations must be resisted if we are to avoid the formal reinstitution of hierarchy in the international system.[133]

We must avoid the lure of justifying sovereign dictatorships of transitional occupation administrations in the name of creating the conditions for popular sovereignty, democracy, or self-determination. When occupiers assume a prolonged and central role in post-conflict state- and constitution-making by designing and imposing, directly or indirectly, liberal-democratic constitutions (and neo-liberal capitalist economies), allegedly preparing the ground for full local self-determination, they put the domestic legitimacy of the constitutional order that they imposed permanently at risk and enter into obvious self-contradictions.[134] Indeed, the difference between this sort of claim and the rationales for maintaining dependent territories during the colonial era is hard to see, as William Bain has noted.[135] As Bhuta states:

> The proposition that international law and the law of belligerent occupation can and should be adapted to promote not just constitutional transformation but a *particular vision* of a domestic constitutional order anticipates a return to a radically more substantive concept of international order.[136]

But for both prudential and normative reasons, it is ill advised.[137]

Accordingly the law of belligerent occupation has not been transformed in the way Yoo and others claim, nor should it. Admittedly this stance involves a gap between the law of military occupation which prohibits wholesale transformation of the political and legal order in the name of implementing human rights standards or democracy, and the regulative agency of the occupier with respect to establishing a new political order to replace the old one.[138] This gap in the law is not, however, filled by Chapter VII humanitarian occupations (state- and nation-building missions) because Security Council practice does not aim or purport to transform the law of belligerent occupation.[139] Inter-state belligerent occupations are distinct from UN missions and the law regulating the former is not directly applicable to the latter despite the similarities that exist in substance between belligerent and humanitarian occupations (both entail foreign military presence, combat operations, and involvement in governance).[140] Thus the new phenomena of humanitarian occupation exist alongside and outside the legal institution of belligerent occupation. Indeed in my framework, the law of belligerent occupation pertains to the interrelations among states in the international society of states, while the phenomena of humanitarian occupation pertain to the legislative prerogatives of the supreme global governance institution in the global political system: the UN Security Council. Thus against those who deploy a single general concept of occupation and occupation law for foreign territorial administration involving the presence of armed forces, the realist/ Schmittian insists on the difference between the two, emphasizing that the latter operates on a parallel and distinct track of case-by-case authorization through Security Council resolutions.[141] This is a distinction that makes all the difference, according to Bhuta, because it allows one to question whether a legal imprimatur should be given in advance to the results of any transformative occupation. For the occupants' local authority, after all, derives from pure facticity – sheer power predominance locally – thus the legitimacy of such an occupation remains unclear.

Thus just as the law of belligerent occupation has not been reformed to permit post-conflict state- or constitution-making – transformative occupation – by an occupying state, so too no general rules of international law exist (and should not be created) to regulate/enable Chapter VII transitional administrations. A situation of *non liquet* – no law – is allegedly preferable to regulative rules which tend to enable an occupier's self-interested legislative innovations regardless of its proclaimed benevolent intentions and regardless of whether the occupier is a single state or the UNSC, a political body hardly immune to manipulation by the super- or great powers permanently serving on it.[142]

4.3   Toward a *jus post bellum* that respects sovereign equality, self-determination, and human rights: rethinking the conservation principle

I take the arguments of the humanitarians and the realists seriously, but maintain that they are symmetrically one-sided. We are indeed in a new epoch. The changes described by both approaches, however, make it urgent, in my view, to develop principles and rules to regulate *all* types of occupations, in order to block the legitimation of creeping annexation or of indirect neo-imperial control through the emergence of global hegemonic law. While the human rights and democracy-building approach to occupation law rightly seeks to update it in light of contemporary norms, it fails to take the conservation principle or the principle of sovereign equality seriously as articulating a normative idea: the political autonomy, self-determination, and equal standing of all political communities – rather than as an expression of the "non-ideal" fact that we are still in a "statist" international system.[143]

The historicist and functionalist approach of the Schmittian/realist school, on the other hand, throws out the baby with the bathwater by apparently rejecting the relevance of the law of belligerent occupation today to most contexts (because it has become abstract and indeterminate), along with any attempt at legal reform with respect to transformative humanitarian occupations. Its contemporary advocates are nonetheless parasitic on the continued force of the conservation principle at the heart of that law; as evidenced in their critique of imperial usurpation of domestic sovereignty, their embrace of the pluralist versus substantive conception of the international order, and their support of the cognate principles of sovereign equality, non-intervention, and self-determination.[144] That is, they implicitly rely on the principle of the inalienability of sovereignty by force, the heart of the concept of belligerent occupation (and of the UN Charter), when they seek to leave the "burden of proof" on the occupier and argue in favor of prohibitive as opposed to regulative rules in this area.[145] Indeed I believe their stance presupposes the interpretive shift from ruler to popular sovereignty as the referent of the conservation principle. Moreover, I argue that the discourse of sovereign equality and self-determination indicates that there is indeed a new nomos at stake since the Cold War: the one established by the UN Charter system and then reaffirmed in the Geneva Conventions, the UN Declaration on Friendly Relations, human rights law, and in the recent UN Reform Proposal of 2005.[146] To be sure, the sovereignty regime established in 1945 is in transition. The dualist nature of the international system involving international *and* cosmopolitan principles, sovereign equality *and* human rights, sovereign states *and* global governance, has undergone important shifts.[147] The most crucial one, however, is the ascription of sovereign equality to all states and the membership of all states in the key global governance institution in the political system, the UN, as well as in the global economy. The principle of sovereign equality, the rejection of colonialism, and the norms of the Charter are accepted by all states participating in the international system unlike the standoff of the Cold War epoch. The contemporary realist/Schmittian approach acknowledges this with respect to occupation law when it grants that under Geneva IV an occupying power may amend or repeal existing laws in order to ensure that it does not violate its own human rights and humanitarian law obligations.[148] This does not mean that there is consensus on the particular institutional forms of the ideal or good state or that there are no power plays in the global political system. Rather, the law of occupation is indeed hinged between neo-imperial imposition in the name of a substantive model of the good polity (liberal-democratic) and economy (neo-liberal capitalist) or the pluralistic conception of the international order of sovereign states coexisting with certain basic cosmopolitan norms to be enforced by the international community's GGIs (no annexation, no aggressive war, no ethnic cleansing, enslavement, or extermination of civilian populations, no apartheid, etc.).[149] But this is precisely why it is imperative to come up with regulative international law principles and rules adequate to the normative and structural conditions of the current epoch that provide an alternative to hegemonic international/global law and push the development of the future content of occupation law along the right track. Otherwise, when the existing but now indeterminate international law of occupation is dismissed as irrelevant to the imperatives of our contemporary epoch the neo-imperialists will reap the benefits. They will do so either by claiming moral and even legal legitimacy for their use and/or bypassing of international rules and institutions, or they will destroy the credibility of international law and institutions altogether.[150] It is possible that international legal reform may not be able to bind the superpower or the great powers permanently on the Security Council, but it is the only way to deprive them of the claim to legality and legitimacy when they impose institutions on occupied populations without their genuine participation or consent. The time is ripe to devise determinate content and appropriate interpretations for the law of belligerent occupations and for legal principles that will regulate humanitarian occupations.

Thus, the issue before us is the following: how can the "transformative aspects of occupation" required by human rights principles, in the current context, be reconciled with the spirit of the conservation principle and its core premise of the inalienability of sovereignty by force? How can the principles of sovereign equality and its cognates, self-determination and non-intervention, be reconciled with the obligation of the supreme global governance institution to secure international peace and security and to protect against the most egregious human rights abuses in domestic contexts in post-conflict situations that involve occupation administrations? How can one insist on the continued applicability of the law of occupation, yet acknowledge the changes in role ascribed to the occupant, shifts in the definition of who is the ousted sovereign, and shifts in the nature of the trustee relationship established between the two?

The circle can be squared if one takes account of two crucial changes in international law that neither the humanitarian nor the Schmittean/realist approaches acknowledge in the right way. The first involves a shift from governmental to popular sovereignty accomplished in part through a reinterpretation of the self-determination principle; the second refers to a change in the nature of the sovereignty ascribed by international law to states via the legal principle of sovereign equality enunciated in the UN Charter in 1945, and generalized as a global principle in the aftermath of decolonization.[151] Let me address each in turn.

4.3.1 Self-determination and occupation law

To put the first point succinctly: If it is no longer assumed that the ousted government is necessarily the holder of sovereignty, and if the occupying power does not claim permanent sovereignty (annexation) then it is up to the citizenry of an intact territorial state to authorize the new representative of popular sovereignty. The conservation principle can still mean that the occupier may not usurp the rights of the sovereign in occupied territory, but the sovereignty in question pertains to the citizenry and the territorial state in which they live, not to the ousted ruler. This, then, is the other "anachronistic reading" of the conservation principle that I wish to advocate.[152]

The Fourth Geneva Convention foreshadowed this move with its shift of attention from the rights of "the ousted sovereign," i.e. the governing elite, to the rights of the population. According to Benvenisti, the growing awareness in international law of the idea that peoples are not merely the resources of rulers, but rather are worthy of being subjects of international norms, created a foothold for diminishing the claim of ousted elites to return to areas they once controlled if they do not enjoy the support of the indigenous population.[153] Indeed, he argues that already in 1945, the attempt on the part of the Allies to resurrect the doctrine of debellatio in order to justify their transformative occupation was an archaism that misleadingly assimilated state and government.[154] He is right to insist that this doctrine has no place in contemporary international law which has come to recognize the principle that sovereignty lies in a people, not in a political elite.[155] The idea that sovereignty inheres in the people indicates the demise of the concept of debellatio: accordingly, "regime collapse does not extinguish the sovereignty" of the defeated state; nor does "total defeat and disintegration of the governing regime" transfer it to the occupant.[156] Thus the fall of a government has no effect whatsoever on the sovereign title over the occupied territory, which remains vested in the local population.[157] The most current restatement of law of occupation in Resolution 1483 confirms this view by reaffirming that the sovereignty and territorial integrity of the Iraqi state remains intact despite total subjugation. This indicates that sovereignty lies with the Iraqi people and not with the demised regime, stressing the right of the former to freely determine their own political future and control their own natural resources, and finally encouraging efforts by the people of Iraq to form a representative government that respects the rule of law.[158] I argue that the concept of organ and ruler sovereignty presupposed in the original theory of belligerent occupation is thereby displaced by that of inalienable state and popular sovereignty as the key assumptions informing contemporary international humanitarian law. But this does not mean that we should naively substitute "the people" for "the ruler" as the organ that bears sovereignty. Popular sovereignty is rather a principle of legitimacy than an alternative locus for exercising rule: the people cannot directly rule or govern and we should avoid myth-making in this regard.[159] Nor does it mean that a single substantive or institutional conception of a legitimate government has replaced the pluralism of international society.

The germ for this position can be found in the UN Charter, which mentions respect for the principle of self-determination of peoples as one of its purposes, but acquired practical relevance via the reassertion of that principle in the 1970 Declaration of Friendly Relations, and in the context and aftermath of decolonization.[160] It is true that in the period between the two world wars, the concept of territorially located "peoples" that qualify for self-determination had an ethno-national meaning which gave it resonance against alien and imperial domination.[161] This revival of the ethnic/substantive signification of "peoples" made little sense in the context of decolonization in Africa and elsewhere, for it was well known that the borders of ex-European colonies, retained in the process of national state-making, included a hodgepodge of cultures, languages, ethnic groups, and the like. For example, it would have been impossible to come up with any reasonable interpretation of a substantive concept of "the people," in either cultural or ethno-national terms, to describe those who were bundled together into a single state across most of Africa.[162] But the term provided a useful fiction and valuable rhetoric against foreign colonial/imperial control and its meanings were multiple and shifting. Subsequently, the concept of self-determination was insisted upon by the new states to protect their political autonomy in creating domestic political institutions, in controlling their economic resources, and in choosing political, economic, social, and cultural systems without interference by other states. Gradually it has come to be bound up with the concept of popular sovereignty, acquiring a procedural rather than a substantive connotation.[163] Today that concept is associated with the ideas of self-rule, political autonomy, and popular sovereignty. Its relevance for occupation law is complex but compelling. Indeed, "self-determination appears firmly entrenched in the corpus of international general rules in only three areas: as an anti-colonialist standard, as a ban on foreign military occupation and as a standard requiring those racial groups be given full access to government."[164]

In what follows, I shall avoid addressing the highly fraught issue of which populations merit designation as a people to whom the right of self-determination can or ought to be ascribed; it is sufficient for my purposes that the international community acknowledge a population under occupation by a foreign power in this way.[165] Once this is done, then the principle of self-determination implies that under an occupation, it is the people rather than the ousted government that is the holder of sovereignty. This facilitates acceptance of a key feature of the concept of "transformative occupations," namely that the sovereign in the deepest sense is the people, not the former "tyrannical" or "rogue" government. Clearly if the latter was tyrannical, in the true sense, i.e. if there is no "fit" between the ousted government and the citizenry, then it should not be incumbent upon the occupier either to enforce tyrannical or discriminatory laws (thereby violating other international law) or to return the ousted government to power. Thus although it is true that historically support for the normative status of self-determination pertained to its "external face," namely the right of colonial territories to choose independent statehood, the concept of self-determination always had a relation to the idea of popular sovereignty and thus an internal dimension, embedded in the idea that if the choice is independent statehood, then external interference in the domestic construction of the political order is precluded.[166]

However, this should not be taken as a green light for an occupation administration either to impose new laws and a new political/economic system, or as an invitation to outsiders to intervene militarily to depose a tyrannical regime and "give" the locals rights and democracy, or, for that matter, to dismember a territorial state.[167] Instead, the proper way to read the shift from the sovereignty of elite rulers to the sovereignty of the people is to do so in terms of the spirit of the conservation principle. Accordingly, one must update the conservation principle in light of the principle of self-determination, and insist that the inalienability of sovereignty refers to popular and state sovereignty. Regarding the latter, it means that the external sovereignty of the state cannot be alienated by force, as we have already seen. But the former means that the internal sovereignty of the people, which involves a special political and legal relationship between a population and its government, cannot be confiscated or intrusively regulated by outsiders.[168] Accordingly, the "conservation principle" requires that major transformations occurring in the context of an occupation must be accomplished by the people themselves – through their representatives, not the occupying authority. It is thus incumbent upon the latter to facilitate this process as quickly as possible, by securing order and stability and stepping back and permitting the coming together of representatives of all the segments of the population to rebuild their own legal and political institutions. It is not up to the occupiers to exclude what they consider rights-violating or anti-democratic groups from the process of state- or constitution-making.[169] Nor is it up to them to designate a specific form of representation (their version of liberal democracy) as the only valid one. To be sure, one hopes that such processes will result in representative governments that are rights-respecting, but the occupant may not seek to ensure this by usurping the constituent power of the occupied population through imposing major or irreversible reforms. Deferring sweeping, especially constitutional reforms until the emergence of an indigenous government and facilitating the setting up of a process for negotiations involving all popular forces before this comes to pass, while repealing offensive laws that are seriously rights-violating, would allow a "transformative occupation" to avoid violating the principles of the inalienability of sovereignty and of self-determination.[170] I argue that in this form, the conservation principle applies to multilateral as well as unilateral occupations.

We should be careful here, however. The shift of the concept of ousted sovereign to "the people" does imply that the latter's sovereignty is "suspended" during an occupation, until their representatives become active and form a government.[171] But this should not be taken to entail an "anti-statist" interpretation of the concept of self-determination of peoples: the legal personality of the state and its "international legal sovereignty" remains intact.[172] At issue are rather the representatives of popular sovereignty. Unless the relation between a government and the people is autonomous and intact, popular sovereignty is in abeyance. This raises innumerable issues regarding the obligations of the state during an occupation, that become pressing if that occupation is prolonged, which I cannot enter into here except to urge that the longer an occupation, the less legitimacy and legality it should enjoy under updated occupation law.[173] What is important to stress from the normative perspective is that the shift in the referent "ousted sovereign" to the people does not give *foreigners* a license to intervene militarily in order to depose a ruler and impose a "democratic" regime, nor does it permit occupiers to redesign the political or economic institutions of the occupied territory – this is a task that requires the consent and primary participation of domestic representatives of the citizenry.[174] Suspended sovereignty is not "shared" sovereignty in that sense.[175] The discourse of "rogue" or "failed" states and the new vogue of talk about disaggregated or shared sovereignty and neo-trusteeship under the international community or the major "democratic" powers must not be used to justify the imposition of a political, economic, or social regime that deprives occupied peoples of their political autonomy in the name of their so-called basic rights.

As reaffirmed in the 1970 Declaration on Friendly Relations, "Every State has an inalienable right to choose its political, economic, social and cultural systems, without interference in any form by another State."[176] Already the Geneva Conventions recognized the problem of quisling governments and outlawed sanitizing agreements with pliant local bodies put in power by occupants to further their own self-interest.[177] Nor should the shift in the referent of "the ousted sovereign" enable an occupant to question the sovereignty of the ousted power in order to reject the applicability of the Fourth Geneva Convention protections to the occupied population.[178] Rather, it means the occupier is trustee for the sovereignty of the indigenous population, and as such it must ensure that the latter has the opportunity, at the earliest possible moment and with the greatest possible scope and autonomy, to determine its own political institutions. Self-determination interpreted along these lines is thus not an invitation to disrupt the territorial integrity or national unity of a country.[179]

It is true that popular sovereignty as a presupposition of external self-determination is procedurally thin; international law requires at most a plebiscite involving the population in the yes/no choice over independent statehood, and the subsequent non-imposition of its constitutional form of government by outsiders (or former colonial powers). It is also true that as a legal principle internal self-determination is indeterminate with the exception of the stricture that a government must represent the population of the territory without systematic exclusion or discrimination against groups on the basis of race, creed, or color.[180] Accordingly an occupant can remove or require the removal of laws that discriminate on these bases as violating the principle of internal self-determination and of the idea that a government must represent the whole population.[181] Thus the argument that the law of self-determination implies popular sovereignty in an underdetermined way is correct insofar as it provides no guidance as to the form of an internal political order or political regime and no guidance as to the process of creating it.[182] Bhuta insists on this indeterminacy in order to challenge the claim that this area of international law allows occupiers to impose a specific substantive model of liberal democracy onto a subject population or to steer and control the process of post-conflict constitution-making so as to institutionalize such a model. This much is convincing. The concept of self-determination cannot be invoked to justify transformative occupation by unilateral or multiple belligerents along the lines advocated by John Yoo. But the argument that it is therefore useless with respect to devising international rules that might regulate the role of occupiers in contexts where a new internal political order has to be created does not follow from this. On the contrary, new legal rules should invoke the core principle behind the contemporary understanding of self-determination, namely that it is the popular sovereignty of the indigenous population that must be respected and thus occupiers must not be the ones determining which groups may not participate in state remaking and nation-rebuilding, or in the processes of constitution-making. In other words this indeterminacy is precisely what allows a pluralist international society to continue to exist as one in which sovereign equality applies to every polity. But this reading of the principle of self-determination is not so indeterminate that it precludes establishing legal limits on what occupiers can do in its name. The representation principle must be honored, sovereign dictatorship of occupiers avoided.

The realist argument that the realities of state-making in a post-conflict situation must be taken into account is convincing: it may indeed turn out that the groups with effective power – the guns or the numbers or the loudest voices – will tend to be included in the early stages of indigenous post-conflict state- and constitution-making and occupiers should not exclude them (or anyone else) due to their past rights-violating or undemocratic behavior or positions. Democratic legitimacy or rights-respecting litmus tests imposed from the outside are counter-productive in such contexts.[183] On the other hand post-conflict constitution-makers would be well advised to include and hear from representatives of all segments of the population in the relevant processes. Certainly the constitution-making process must be wholly indigenous even if the local population would do well to learn from the experience of other countries regarding the risks and most promising scenarios for peace and justice down the road.[184] I cannot go into these issues here. My point is to argue that the very indeterminacy of the self-determination principle and the principle of popular sovereignty now associated with it can help square the circle by permitting one to honor norms linking the pluralist idea of an international society of sovereign states to restrictions on the role of an occupier who must both avoid violating human rights and undo those laws that cause such violations, while fostering as quickly as possible the conditions within which the popular sovereign can recreate their state and representative constitutional government, facilitating, but refraining from determining, the particular processes, or outcomes. The principle the occupier has to follow is inclusiveness, but this cannot mean imposing a particular regime onto the occupied. Sovereignty is meaningless if it is restricted to the international legal sovereignty of the state: it must entail the exercise of domestic political autonomy – i.e. the autonomous decision-making of the representatives of the domestic population in post-conflict institutional design and constitution-making. While this decision-making must comply with international human rights standards in the sense that egregious forms of discrimination or worse may not be tolerated, this does not obviate the link between the societal/political autonomy principle and the law of internal self determination.[185] The conservation principle must be so understood.

4.3.2   Sovereign equality

This reinterpretation of the conservation principle in light of a proceduralized concept of self-determination conforms to the other key prong of contemporary international law, namely, the principle of sovereign equality. First enunciated in the UN Charter as a legal principle, the fundamental importance of the principle of sovereign equality was reaffirmed in the 1970 Declaration on Friendly Relations, as well as in the 2005 UN Reform Proposal, all of which insist that only if states comply fully with the requirements of this principle can the purposes of the United Nations be implemented.[186]

As already indicated, the principle of sovereign equality constitutes a plural international society in which every state has an equal standing in international law. Accordingly, all states have an equal entitlement to participate in the formation of international law (consent) and to take on international legal personality. A principle of reciprocity with legal effect follows from this: all states are formally entitled to the same general rights and are subject to the same general obligations. Any state claiming a right under international law has to accord all other states the same right. Sovereign equality is thus a relational concept. The legal principle of sovereign equality also entails jurisdiction: the authority to make and enforce rules within a certain geographic area, limiting the application of external power. From the juridical perspective, domestic jurisdiction and immunity from foreign laws (autonomy) is the sine qua non for international law as it delimits legal systems from one another and thus articulates plurality. It means that states are not subject to other states' jurisdiction. Still, it should be noted that the scope of acts for which state officials have immunity can be restricted by international law (today, restrictions concern acts of aggression, forced annexation, genocide, and other international crimes and grave human rights violations). In other words, a state is sovereign because it is normatively and legally deemed independent from any other state: it is bound only by international law.[187]

Thus the principle of sovereign equality, which ascribes political autonomy to all states equally, has the following corollaries: the principle of non-aggression, the concept of domestic jurisdiction, and the stricture against annexation or the acquisition by another state resulting from the threat or use of force. The Declaration on Friendly Relations puts all this very succinctly:

> All states enjoy sovereign equality. They have equal rights and duties and are equal members of the international community, notwithstanding differences of an economic, social, political or other nature. In particular, sovereign equality includes the following elements: (a) States are judicially equal; (b) Each State enjoys the rights inherent in full sovereignty; (c) Each State has the duty to respect the personality of other States; (d) The territorial integrity and political independence of the State are inviolable; (e) Each State has the right freely to choose and develop its political, social, economic and cultural systems; (f) Each State has the duty to comply fully and in good faith with its international obligations and to live in peace with other States.[188]

In a separate paragraph, the Declaration asserts that "The territory of a State shall not be the object of military occupation resulting from the use of force in contravention of the provisions of the Charter."[189] The many references to self-determination in the Declaration discussed above militate against the cosmopolitan-liberal anti-pluralist defense of military intervention for the purpose of regime change. It is as crucial to reassert and reinforce the principle of sovereign equality in the battle against the imperial transformation of international law as it is to retain the reinterpreted conservation principle. Indeed, as already indicated, these normative ideas complement each other.

However, it is also important to note the effect of human rights law on the conception of the prerogatives of sovereignty ascribed to states by the legal principle of the sovereign equality enunciated in the UN Charter. In short, state sovereignty is no longer deemed to be absolute – the prerogatives of sovereignty are determined by the international legal system. Sovereign states do not have the right to go to war or to annex other states. Nor are grave rights violations like genocide, ethnic cleansing, torture, crimes against humanity, or the more drastic forms of discrimination like apartheid deemed to be within their domestic jurisdiction. It is, moreover, the duty of sovereign states to comply with their international obligations, even if these were voluntarily assumed, and of course, with customary international law, *jus cogens* norms, and Security Council rulings. Human rights law is part of contemporary international law. Yet acknowledging that certain human rights norms are relevant to the law of occupation need not lead to an overly expansive interpretation of the occupant's prerogatives, thereby facilitating a neo-imperial form of "liberal-democratic" imposition through the back door that undermines the egalitarian nature of the international system. Instead, occupants must follow the spirit of the Fourth Geneva Convention in light of the international law principles just mentioned, and interpret human rights obligations as circumscribing specific acts or modes of governance, not as an invitation to comprehensive legislation by an occupier, and certainly not as a right to impose a liberal or democratic constitution. The duty to protect human rights should not become a vehicle for transforming the occupier into a sovereign dictator or an excuse for short-circuiting domestic political processes of constitution-making and state remaking.[190] Indeed, notwithstanding the human rights fundamentalists, an occupant cannot expect to institute all the human rights protections that exist in international covenants or which oblige a state acting domestically. The question of which rights an occupant must provide has yet to be seriously discussed. But in light of the principle of the inalienability of sovereignty and the general presumption against institutional and constitutional change *imposed* by outsiders, it would be a good idea to proceed cautiously, especially, but I submit, not only, in the case of a unilateral occupation. One could start with the repeal of offensive laws that require the occupant to violate well-established human rights principles, move on to the enactment of new laws tailored to particular violations in the absence of legal protection, and help facilitate the erection of supervisory institutions or review mechanisms to help prevent and sanction human rights violations.[191]

But I also want to argue for a more systematic legal reform that applies to UN-sponsored interim administrations as well as unilateral occupants. The relatively new tendency of the Security Council to indulge in legislation and to ascribe unlimited legislative and executive powers to its "peace-enforcing" transitional administrations during humanitarian occupations, in the absence of effective mechanisms of accountability or clear legal-normative guidelines, should give us pause.[192] The issue here is not the enforcement of the Hague rules or Geneva Conventions because the Security Council is not bound directly by humanitarian law, but only by the UN Charter. As already indicated, Chapters VI and VII of the Charter have been interpreted very permissively to allow the vesting of ultimate legislative authority in an agent of the Secretary-General, through SC resolutions, leading to near-dictatorial powers in refashioning the legal, political, economic, and social structure of the occupied territory. Granting such powers to the Security Council, a body meant to be political, not legislative, without any independent mechanisms to ensure it is acting responsibly, or within appropriate limits, is an alarming prospect given the nature and special powers of its hardly disinterested permanent membership. The fact that thus far, the Security Council resolutions establishing highly transformative interim administrations have failed to establish meaningful accountability mechanisms is not reassuring. Nor is the fact that UN-authorized enforcement operations, including humanitarian occupations, are not subject to the 1999 Bulletin of the Secretary-General that announced the application of international humanitarian law to UN forces involved in peacekeeping and peace enforcement operations.[193] Though both the missions erected in Kosovo and East Timor were required to report regularly to the Security Council, they were not subject to judicial review. Rather, the only check was the Ombudsperson, established to look into human right abuses and other abuses of authority, not however by the administrative forces themselves.[194]

In my view, the lack of real accountability mechanisms in the case of UNSC interim administrations and the lack of enforcement mechanisms for existing occupation law in belligerent occupations are very serious indeed.[195] But in order for this to be rectified, it is crucial to articulate a coherent principled normative and legal framework (a *jus post bellum*) for humanitarian occupations which can articulate guidelines and provide clear limits to the legislative powers of occupiers. For the deeper issue at stake is not corruption or arbitrariness of occupiers but usurpation. As already indicated, here too juridification should be guided by strong insistence on the "conservationist" principle of the inalienability of sovereignty by force, the principles of self-determination, popular sovereignty, and sovereign equality. In other words it should be clear that the goal even of a transformative humanitarian occupation should be the inclusion of all possible social forces in the country in the political bargaining process that occurs in post-conflict state remaking and constitution-making. Otherwise, expanding the Security Council's powers regarding humanitarian occupations in the name of human rights or democratic regime change, in the context of great power privilege and US predominance on the SC, is a dangerous game, opening the latter to the charge of neo-imperialism, or con-dominium, especially given the selectivity of UN-sponsored interventions. It is not enough to reinvent the discourse of trusteeship, proportionality, and accountability, for this is too laden with bad connotations from the old epoch of civilizing missions, mandates, and all the rest. What is at stake is the sovereign equality and self-determination (popular sovereignty) of the occupied polity. Any talk about limits on the powers of occupants or "consultation" between the occupied and the occupant interim administration will ring hollow without such a reform. So will the lip service regarding the sovereignty of the occupied state or people. Unless "transformative occupations" involve the quick turnover of legislative power to the genuine representatives of the indigenous population, any post-conflict constitution that emerges out of the process will appear to be imposed.

Self-determination (popular sovereignty), human rights, and the principle of sovereign equality are all at risk in prolonged and transformative occupations and none should be reduced to or sacrificed in the name of the other. Only if the conservation principle, suitably interpreted, is respected can these norms be reconciled under an occupation regime, humanitarian or belligerent. This is also the only way that sovereign equality instead of hierarchy can remain the organizing principle of international relations in international society and inform the UN Charter system of global governance.

4.3.3   The wrong approach to legal dualism

I thus strongly disagree with the argument of Fox that "state-centric" norms such as self-determination, the conservation principle, and so forth do not and should not pertain to humanitarian occupations undertaken under the auspices of a Chapter VII Security Council resolution.[196] Like Bhuta, Fox insists that the law of belligerent occupation was devised to regulate the decentralized, anarchical, highly competitive international society of sovereign states in which the latter typically act unilaterally in pursuit of their own particular interests. Fox argues that self-determination is a concept correlative to the conservation principle and important for limiting the prerogatives of a belligerent occupation administration by precluding overbroad systemic changes and sweeping constructive reforms, requiring the deferral of such transformations until the emergence of an indigenous (preferably interim) government able to undertake them.[197] He thus denies either that the new conundrum opened up with Bosnia and the occupation in Iraq, and/or SC Resolution 1483, render the conservation principle an anachronism or lend support to the "reformist" reading of humanitarian law as permitting transformative unilateral occupations. Fox strongly disagrees with those who argue that the law of belligerent occupation has shifted in favor of transformative "post-conflict" constitution-making projects by occupiers to create (impose) institutions that respect human rights and democracy (or neoliberal capitalist economies).[198] This, he argues, would violate domestic sovereignty – the political autonomy of a society which has the right to freely choose and develop its own political, social, economic, and cultural system.[199] Such an approach would, moreover, be too forgetful of the dangers of unilateralism and too enabling of self-interested belligerent occupations accomplishing in effect the goals of annexation by other means.[200]

It is also for this reason, however, that he insists on a systematic distinction between the law governing belligerent and humanitarian occupations, arguing against the idea of a single overarching concept of occupation regulated by a single set of legal norms.[201] Accordingly, the Security Council acting under Chapter VII escapes the framework of state-centric categories because its humanitarian occupations involve the agenda of collective security and peace – consensus values of the international community – rather than the agenda of a single belligerent state pursuing its self-interest. Thus, the norms regulating belligerent occupations are irrelevant to humanitarian occupation administrations acting under the auspices of Chapter VII Security Council Resolutions. The latter override the conservation principle and displace occupation law as the legal basis for any actions it prescribes.[202] Indeed humanitarian occupations are allegedly too different from belligerent occupations to come under the same law: typically the actors are not parties to the original conflict in UN-sponsored missions; the dynamics of collective decision-making in the Security Council oriented to community values and individual states oriented to self-interest differ allowing the former to escape the zero-sum competitive logic of the latter; and the notion of exclusive jurisdiction designed to safeguard national decision-making has no application to an organization that controls no territory. Most crucial, the very purpose of a humanitarian occupation is

> to end human rights violations, reform governmental institutions and restore peaceful coexistence among groups that had recently been engaged in vicious armed conflict. In this sense they are "humanitarian." The missions are social engineering projects that take international standards of human rights and governance as their blueprints. They may indeed be seen as the most far-reaching efforts at implementing those and other norms of social relations the international community has ever mounted.[203]

While, as indicated earlier, humanitarian occupations are superficially similar to belligerent occupations in that they involve military control and temporary governance by outsiders who assume ultimate legal authority without annihilating the sovereignty of the local state, they differ in that the explicit mission of the former is to create, according to Fox, a liberal-democratic order.

Note that Fox insists that humanitarian occupation is grounded in and presupposes the international community's consensus not only on peace and security but also on a new legal model of the state – i.e. a substantive conception of a liberal democracy – as the only really legitimate form of the state and as the form that is most conducive to peace and democracy. This goes well beyond the more agnostic requirement under self-determination principles that a government be representative of the population (fit).[204] Fox makes a logical argument apparently deduced from reflection on the significance of other changes in international law and from the practice of humanitarian occupations. Accordingly, the strictures against forced annexation, against forced changes to existing borders, against the achievement of homogeneity through expulsions, population exchanges, ethnic cleansing, extermination, or forcible conversion – all now incontrovertible principles of current international law – presuppose not only that internally pluralistic states are the new norm (rather than homogeneous nation-states) but also that liberal democracy has become the accepted form of regime that must be fostered or instituted by post-conflict humanitarian occupiers and constitution-makers for the sake of peace and justice.[205]

For Fox insists that it is not true that the emergence of global governance institutions and cosmopolitan principles (human rights) signals the marginalization of the sovereign state. On the contrary, the proliferation of sovereign states in the UN era as well as the commitment to their continued existence, their fixed borders, and their international legal sovereignty even when they "fail" indicates its continued importance in our epoch.[206] But Fox assumes that taken together, all of this can lead to only one conclusion: liberal democracy is the only form of the state that can be legitimately instituted in post-conflict situations.[207] Thus he makes the admittedly bold claim that "international law has now adopted liberal democracy as the preferred model of national governance."[208]

The flaws with this argumentation are relatively easy to spot. It is true that a principle of political inclusion is implicit in the international legal documents that require that a state be representative of its people, and that it does not discriminate against racial, ethnic, creedal, or national groups and so forth. But it does not follow from this either that a particular substantive form of state regime (liberal democracy) is deemed the only legitimate one or that an occupation administration may impose such a regime on the occupied! Even if the former were the acknowledged ideal by the international community (which it patently is not given the regimes of some of the key players on the Council itself not to mention of many members of the UN), that would not be sufficient to give a free hand to foreign occupiers to impose such a model onto others. The contradiction inherent in imposing a constitutional order in the name of the principle of self-determination and/or popular sovereignty is obvious.

It may be, however, that state-centric norms of international law do not and cannot apply directly to the UNSC, given that its resolutions under Chapter VII have the highest rank among international legal norms and treaties.[209] Legal rules regulating the unilateral use of force (belligerent occupation), humanitarian law, and even human rights law may indeed not be relevant for challenging, legitimating, or restricting the authority of the Council to act legislatively in the area of humanitarian occupation insofar as it has the unique authority to secure peace between and within states if domestic conflicts threaten international order. Even if self-determination, sovereign equality, and certain human rights are deemed *jus cogens* norms, Fox shows that the difficulties in applying *jus cogens* principles to limit SC discretion are manifold.[210] Nevertheless, he insists that the Council is not above the law. Rather, it is a creature of international law and necessarily situated within it, which certainly includes the principles and purposes of the UN Charter itself. However, he makes this point in order to stress that the Council has much broader authority than any single state in acting legislatively in humanitarian occupations.[211] Indeed Council-generated norms in the case of humanitarian occupation have been clearly legislative, albeit not based on state consent in the way that ordinary international law is.[212]

Thus we are faced with a rather pressing problem aptly stated by Fox toward the end of his book: "... having freed the Council from state-centric norms, is the Council then unbound by law of any kind?"[213] He correctly states that the issue is not whether the Council is a political rather than a legal body. "Rather, it is that states targeted by Council action would retain rights under state-centric rules but be unable to vindicate those rights because they would be acted upon by a body unencumbered by any reciprocal legal obligations."[214] Indeed. Moreover Fox sees that if the Council legislates regularly thereby rending the state-centric norms it supersedes worthless, the legitimacy of these norms and the Council itself will be undermined. However, he offers very little in response to this dilemma. Instead of attempting to fill the legal gap, having noticed that very few useful direct constraints exist on Council authority, he suggests indirect normative restraints, subjective and objective. The former include an (overly) optimistic understanding of the collective decision-making processes of the Council in which the collection and exchange of information and collective deliberation can generate trust. Also suggested is that in cases of Chapter VII humanitarian occupations, norms should be deemed altered only for particular states in connection with particular crises, not for everyone.[215] Apparently we are not to view the legislative action of the Council as universally legislative. That this would reintroduce hierarchy into the international system does not seem to disturb Fox. However, he does acknowledge the criticism that the Council's deliberative and collective decision-making processes have become increasingly insular and exclusionary with resolutions drafted by a few permanent members and then presented as unalterable propositions to the larger body.[216] Yet he provides no analysis of why this is so or any way to fix it. The objective element that could allegedly contribute to the legitimacy of Council action in humanitarian occupation would come from external sources such as supportive General Assembly resolutions and expressions of opinion in and by other fora that, when taken seriously, could create a positive feedback loop to Council decision-making.[217] Nothing more is offered.

I find these arguments unconvincing. The normative category question remains unanswered, for the alternatives Fox offers to state-centric law yield only very weak indirect constraints. Clearly Fox does not take the risks that particular or hegemonic or imperial interests may inform Chapter VII humanitarian occupations nearly as seriously as the risks of self-interest in belligerent occupation. He seems to think that the unique collective nature of Council goals and deliberations, assuming information is freely exchanged and deliberations are public, plus attentiveness to international public opinion (other fora) would be enough to ensure against manipulation. He seems to forget that Chapter VII occupations are typically delegated to states willing and able to undertake them and that no public political actor, including the Security Council, is innocent of self-interest and/or power aspirations. None of his proposals get at the core of the problem because the analysis does not go deep enough either with respect to the dualistic nature of the international system which Fox apparently recognizes, or with respect to the structural flaws and normative resources within the UN Charter system itself. Let me address each in turn.

As regards the first, as I have been arguing throughout this book, we are in a dualistic world order in which "state-centric" rules of international law continue to regulate the system of sovereign states alongside of which there exist global governance institutions that are the creatures of international law but which, as in the case of the UN, also function so as to enforce that law and operate under distinctive legal rules. The UNSC thus is regulated first and foremost by the UN Charter. It is worth noting, however, that the UN Charter itself enshrines the principles of sovereign equality, self-determination, domestic jurisdiction, and human rights. This means that neither single states or state coalitions nor the UNSC should act so as to undermine or eviscerate these principles. With regard to the latter, securing these principles is listed among the purposes of the Charter and the UN is to protect them for all states. As I have repeatedly argued, the understanding of what is in the domestic jurisdiction of states, and what sovereign prerogatives entail, can shift with changes in international law and in sovereignty regimes. But the concept of sovereignty cannot mean one thing for one dimension of the international system (the state-centric rules) and something entirely different for another dimension (global governance institutions) as Fox seems to imply. Sovereignty cannot mean only international legal sovereignty (intact territorial borders): it is bound up with the concept of independent statehood that cannot be disengaged from the domestic exercise of political autonomy.[218] Sovereignty thus entails domestic political and legal self-determination (especially regarding the creation of the state's form and constitutional order) and supremacy of the domestic legal order as well as its autonomy even if the former is not exclusive and the latter not untrammeled in our current sovereignty regime. It also entails, as I have argued, participation by every state as an equal in the making of international law and that includes the law of global governance institutions. The principle of sovereign equality enshrined in the UN Charter extends this status to all its members, and to all sovereign states. The Charter itself enshrines the norms of sovereign equality, self-determination, and non-intervention so there is no need to reach for state-centric norms for the principles that ought to orient humanitarian occupations under Chapter VII auspices. These principles cannot mean something totally different for the UN even though it may engage in transformative occupation whereas states involved in a belligerent occupation are forbidden to do so. What, then. can this mean?

I want to argue that the Charter principles, suitably interpreted and updated, can and should serve as functional equivalents to the conservation principle in the law of belligerent occupation in one absolutely critical respect: foreclosing the usurpation of domestic constituent power via the sovereign dictatorship of a humanitarian occupier. The risk of sovereign dictatorship should be anticipated and blocked in whatever form because it undermines the domestic legitimacy of post-conflict constitutions and blocks the crucial learning processes inherent in the necessity of political compromise for domestic political actors in post-conflict situations, if they are excluded or minor partners in constructing their own political regime. The fact that an occupation authority is international rather than unilateral, under Chapter VII auspices rather than under state-centric law is not a sufficient reason for giving a free hand to those states to whom the task of interim administration is delegated by the Council. But apart from the risk of a neo-imperial logic, from which neither the actual occupying state(s) nor the Security Council authorizing humanitarian occupation is immune, the normative ideals of self-determination and political autonomy pertain to all occupied peoples and should constrain all occupiers.

What, then, is the "transformative" role of a humanitarian occupation? The principles of popular sovereignty and self-determination that should guide and bind the Council imply that humanitarian occupation administrations also should attempt to facilitate as quickly as possible the emergence of a functioning state and interim government to take on the process of state- and constitution-making (assuming the ousted government is out of the picture and state-building as well as constitution remaking is on the agenda). Representativeness is the key here: instead of imposing a particular version of a democratic or liberal constitution, instead of choosing which domestic groups will be included in the process or favored in the outcome, the role of the transformative occupier is still in a way a negative one, i.e. to try to ensure that all social groups – the people with the guns (potential spoilers) and the representatives of all segments of the population – are included in the relevant bargaining processes. Ideally sovereign dictatorship on the part of the occupier *and* the occupied should be avoided. Thus principled normative interpretation of the UN Charter's commitment to sovereign equality, self-determination, and non-intervention should be the basis for guidelines and rules limiting the discretionary power of any occupier acting in the name of the Security Council so as to block not only corruption and arbitrariness but also and above all, the usurpation of the domestic actors' right to construct their own social and political order and to participate in the crucial learning processes that negotiating, compromising, and constitution-making involve. This is how the new "democratic norm" of the state should be understood, and not as an enabling device for sovereign dictatorship or for reintroducing hierarchy into the international system. The transformative occupier carrying out a humanitarian occupation should at most facilitate peace, inclusiveness, representative processes, and non-violation of basic human rights without prescribing a particular form of the state, constitution, or economic order.

Finally, as we shall see in the next chapter, the legitimation problem caused by the newly legislative Security Council has also arisen in other domains, and must be confronted head-on, something Fox seeks to avoid. We must not be naive regarding the logic of collective decision-making inside the Council or studiously unaware of why it tends to be less deliberative and less open the more legislative functions it takes on. I will argue that the problem is structural and that institutional reform of the Council and not only legal reform regarding its legislative acts under Chapter VII is surely on the agenda of the twenty-first century. The legitimacy of legality – of current Chapter VII actions and of any legal reform – is at stake. Surely the legitimacy deficit in this area (Council legislation vis-à-vis humanitarian occupation) has something to do with the fact that the privileges accorded to the P5 on the Council violate the very principle of sovereign equality that the Council was established to ensure in order to protect international peace and security. The lack of sovereign equality in the sense of participatory parity within the UN Charter system undermines the legitimacy in the long run of Chapter VII decisions particularly when new and expanding legislative power is asserted by the Council that directly intrudes on the principles of political autonomy, sovereign equality, and human rights.

4.4 Conclusion

It was not my task in this chapter to outline the elements of the reform of occupation law (or of the UN Charter system) but rather to articulate its normative and theoretical premises.[219] I have argued that the spirit, if not the letter, of the two prongs of the conservation principle remains valid today: the humanitarian concern for the welfare and rights of the occupied and the inalienability of sovereignty. I argue that these principles are sufficiently abstract that functional equivalents can be found for them to guide Chapter VII humanitarian occupations as well as unilateral belligerent occupations although the legal sources and actual legal rules will differ in each case. I also want to maintain that there is indeed a "nomos" at stake here: the principles of the UN Charter associated with sovereign equality, the prohibition on annexation, the negative connotation associated with empires, and the subsequent elaboration of the concept of self-determination, popular sovereignty, as well as human rights norms, are part of the dualistic world order composed of the international community's global governance institutions and a now universalized pluralistic international society which is well worth preserving. In the domain of occupation law, as in the domain of "humanitarian intervention," we face the choice between a dualistic egalitarian international society with cosmopolitan elements regulated by international law or a neo-imperial hierarchical conception of international order replete with "hegemonic international law," and even worse, the loss of legitimacy of international global institutions and law, and their replacement by "grossraum" ordering.[220] The development of a *jus post bellum* guided by the above-mentioned principles, backed up by accountability mechanisms with teeth, and regulating all occupations, might help ensure that the former has a chance against the latter.

5

Security Council activism in the "war on terror": legality and legitimacy reconsidered

Many analysts after 1989 saw a chance to realize the promise of the UN Charter and the declarations and covenants that banned aggressive war, enunciated the principles of the sovereign equality of states, the self-determination of peoples, and the human rights of all persons. The expansion of global and regional human rights regimes and their invocation by local actors (with the help of "activists beyond borders") to challenge domestic injustice and develop constitutionalism, democracy, and the rule of law, seemed to indicate that the optimism was not unfounded. References to public international law and international human rights helped empower domestic movements and coalitions of political elites seeking to create constitutional democracy, and to strengthen parliaments, courts, and the rule of law over executives and militaries. Many constitutions made in transitions from dictatorships to democracy refer directly to international human rights law. Ensuring human rights and democracy through domestic constitutionalism and the rule of law was deemed the best way to provide for human security.[1] The international human rights documents and their mention in the Charter constituted an important normative referent for progressive civil society and party political actors. As I indicated in Chapter 3, in this period (the mid-1970s to 1989), reference to international human rights, the idea of a democratic entitlement, invocation of public international law, and participation in multilateral institutions did not threaten the autonomy and sovereign equality of states or the popular sovereignty/self-determination of citizens: on the contrary it helped them institutionalize strong rights-respecting and democracy re-enforcing constitutions.

As I also argued, a shift during the late 1980s and early 1990s, oriented toward an enforcement model, has been more ambivalent. The new willingness of the Security Council (SC) to sanction grave domestic human rights breaches, and the development of supranational courts to enforce them, seemed to indicate that the basic rights of all individuals would be protected even if their own states failed to do so. These developments gave the idea of the progressive constitutionalization of international law a foothold in theoretical discussions. Non-state constitutional treaties (like that of the UN, the EU, and the WTO) began to be taken seriously as constitutions, and the articulation of the 'higher norms' (*jus cogens*) by international courts seemed to give credence to the constitutional interpretation of global law.[2] But the seemingly arbitrary redefinition of domestic rights violations as a threat to international peace and security, and the selective imposition of debilitating sanctions, military invasions, and authoritarian occupation administrations by the SC or by states acting unilaterally ("coalitions of the willing"), framed as "enforcement" of the values of the international community, gave some of us pause. Humanitarian interventions and occupations have, as we have seen, a Janus face. The enforcement model opened a "Pandora's box," and its import is becoming clear only now, in the third post-9/11 phase of the transformation of public international law.

There is a new twist associated with the current discursive frameworks of a "global war on terror" and a "global state of emergency." We are confronted with the apparent necessity of a tradeoff between human rights and human security domestically and internationally. Moreover, it seems that the global protectors of "human security," under the "responsibility to protect" (R2P) doctrine, may also undermine rights, constitutionalism, and democracy, strengthening arbitrary domestic and global executive power at the expense of parliaments, courts, and the rule of law.[3] Indeed the current form of emergency and security discourse associated with the global "war on terror" has altered the meaning of the R2P doctrine in ways that threaten constitutionalism everywhere. There is nothing new about constitutionalism and rights coming under stress in the context of war or crisis. Now, however, the threat comes not only from domestic executives (or militaries), not only from the unilateral actions of the world's "sole superpower," but also from the international institution meant to protect global security and human rights: the UN Security Council.

Given the critique of neo-imperialism and suspicions about the motives of unilateral interventions and "democratic" impositions by occupying powers, Council authorization seems like the right alternative. In the past the problem was Council stalemate and inaction. Today, however, the new forms of Council activism and legislative global governance are creating legitimation problems as we saw in the previous chapter.[4] In this chapter I argue that the Council's radical expansion of its legislative powers, particularly in pursuit of the "war on terror," threatens not only civil liberties and constitutionalism, but also the legitimacy of the UN Charter system itself. I will argue that as things now stand, the assumption by the Council of legislative powers alters the material constitution of the Charter, opening the door to a new form of hegemonic international rule and law. My focus is on legitimacy although as we shall see the legality of the new forms of Council activism is also much debated.

I will also argue that the basis of this development is the flawed hybrid structure of the UN constituted by the veto power of the five permanent members (P5) on the Council and in the amendment rule. Obviously the veto gives them unequal powers and immunities. But the veto in the Council and, more crucially, in the amendment rule also places the P5 in a unique structural relationship to what is now called the constitutional treaty and the UN Charter system. In short, they remain, in key structural respects, external to legal order created by the treaty.[5] *This structural position enables the P5's "usurpation" of the constituent authority of the international community and hides the constituent activity under the guise of a more ordinary exercise of discretionary "executive" emergency powers provided for by the Charter.*

While this structural "constitutional" design has been in place since the beginning, the "teleological" interpretation by the Council of its competence and the recent self-ascription of legislative capacity renders it increasingly threatening to the rule of law domestically and internationally. The legitimation problems generated by the Council's rights-violating legislative activity in conjunction with its "war on terror" are now leading to general debates about the existence of limits to Council competences, about the quality of the legal order constructed by the Charter, and about its very nature: i.e. whether it is a treaty, a constitution, or a constitutional treaty and whether the UNO as an international organization of states can without further ado engage in "global governance" in pursuit of cosmopolitan principles. The UN is now at the center of the global political system and new global governance functions are accruing here as elsewhere. The question is how to make these legitimate: compatible with the rule of law and constitutionalism. I will suggest that the much-discussed project of further constitutionalization is the right remedy, but a great deal depends on how it is understood. A project for correcting the flawed hybrid design of the Charter (creating a different structural position for the P5 and all other states) is crucial, but it must aim at a different type of dualism: a new sovereignty regime that places all the members of the UN in the same structural relationship to the organization formalizing the principle of sovereign equality of states in relation to the UN itself and not only with regard to the international society of states. This is a political project of constitutional reform that aims at enhancing the constitutionalist quality of the UN Charter system particularly insofar as the SC, its prime "enforcement" organ, increasingly engages in legislative and quasi-judicial global governance functions while claiming supremacy for its rulings over any other treaty or domestic laws. Such a "further" constitutionalization of the UN Charter system must, moreover, be understood in the framework of constitutional pluralism. The constitutional pluralist understanding is indispensable for preserving the principles of political autonomy expressed in the idea of sovereign equality in what remains a dualist world order. It is also crucial for protecting human rights and constitutionalism against depredations by states and by global governance institutions, in our case, the SC. Pace the happy consciousness of those who proclaimed the end of history and the worldwide triumph of liberal democracy in the early 1990s, the legitimating principles for domestic polities around the globe remain varied and the international society of states often deeply divided. We still inhabit a global pluri-verse of 193 sovereign states whose political cultures, organizational principles, conceptions of justice, and domestic legitimacy are diverse and at times in conflict with one another. Despite the increasing importance of cosmopolitan norms and global governance institutions, no project of monist global constitutionalism is feasible in such a context.

In what follows I begin by showing how the link of human rights discourse to the concepts of human security and the R2P doctrine in the "enforcement model" paved the way for the discursive shift to the current security regime (Section 5.1). I then describe this regime by analyzing three key Security Council resolutions that have constituted it – in order to pinpoint what is new and dangerous here (Section 5.2). Section 5.3 analyzes the structural features of the UN Charter system that are the enabling conditions of this transformation. The legitimation problematic this raises is then explicated (Section 5.4). An excursus on the concepts of constitution/constitutionalism comes next (Section 5.5), followed by an analysis of the constitutional quality of the UN Charter system (Section 5.6). The controversy over the recent "Kadi case" – an exemplar of the conundrum of global governance and competing constitutionalist discourses – is then analyzed (Section 5.7). This is followed by a return to the theoretical issues surrounding the concepts of internal and external constitutional and legal pluralism and the questions of political form these raise (Section 5.8). I conclude by arguing for formal legal and institutional reform and by revisiting the idea of federation in the context of the global political system (Section 5.9). I see the discourse of the constitutionalization of this area of international law as part of a political counter-project to global hegemonic international law. Against the standard monist, cosmopolitan interpretation of this counter-project (oriented to suppression of state sovereignty), however, I suggest a version of pluralist constitutionalism involving the construction of a new sovereignty regime and a re-formed UN Charter system.

5.1 The enforcement model: opening Pandora's box

During the 1990s the SC began to designate the systematic violations of human rights and humanitarian law that accompany internal armed conflict as coming under the purview of Article 39, triggering Chapter VII prerogatives.[6] While this amounted to a major shift in practice, and while Chapter VII interventions undertaken and not undertaken were criticized for being inconsistent, it would be hard to make the case that these determinations were ultra vires regarding the UN Charter or that they posed a radical challenge to public international law. The reasons are threefold: first, the Security Council did not deviate from the standard negative definition of peace; second, it consistently used a double strategy by means of which the internal humanitarian situation was regarded as a threat to regional (i.e. international) stability; and third, it addressed particular emergencies rather than proclaiming a general state of emergency or a general state of exception.[7] Moreover, there is no court within the UN system empowered to review the "constitutionality" of Security Council resolutions.

Article 39 of the Charter provides for the Security Council to determine the existence of a "threat to peace, breach of the peace, or an act of aggression" before it may impose compulsory Chapter VII coercive measures under Articles 40, 41, and 42. Since these three criteria are required in order for the Security Council resolutions to be binding, the discretion granted to it by the Charter is not unlimited. The Council has to convincingly portray the particular situations it addresses as falling within one of these categories, otherwise its Chapter VII coercive measures would not be binding on states. The Council remained within this framework throughout the 1990s even though it frequently did something unanticipated in 1945, by interpreting internal situations in these terms. What mattered is that the criteria and potential international nexus, albeit elastically interpreted, were nonetheless evoked and accepted.[8]

Yet the undeniable redefinition of what constitutes a threat to international peace and security as well as other unprecedented and expansive interpretations of its Chapter VII powers by the Council in the 1990s triggered a different approach. In addition to humanitarian intervention, innovative use of these powers included the determination of a boundary between two states, the imposition of a highly intrusive arms control and sanction regime on a state in part for domestic violations, the creation of a compensation commission and a new collective regime of state liability, and the establishment of ad hoc international criminal tribunals and interim humanitarian occupation regimes, among other things. Together with the infamous Lockerbie ruling, all this contributed to the emergence of an enforcement model with an apparent new basis and focus: global law and community values, rather than international peace per se.[9] Hence the attempt at justification through a dynamic constitutional method of interpretation. Indeed, analysts argued that dynamic interpretations of their competences by UN organs along the lines of the American constitutional doctrine of implied powers and/or the teleological method of continental Europe are appropriate for the organs of a body created by a constitutional treaty.[10] Note that such an approach to the Charter involves a subtle shift in the understanding of the structural position of the Security Council – from a political executive body established by treaty to enforce the peace and provide collective security in a crisis, to the executive organ of the international community, enforcing its global constitutional law and community values.[11] On the first model, sanctions imposed by the Council are an act of international policy, brought into play when disputes between states fail to be settled peacefully; on the second, they would amount to enforcing the principles and purposes set out in the Charter – a document with constitutional quality – as well as the fundamental interests and values of the international legal community constituted by it, whose breach would be a crime in the eyes of the community as a whole. By interpreting its powers teleologically, the SC positions itself as the chief executive of the international community, simultaneously fostering its further integration as well as the constitutional (cosmopolitan) interpretation of the Charter.[12] Yet the basis for such a role is very unclear. Unlike the constitutional treaty of, for example, the European Union, which explicitly foresees a process of legal and political integration to which the (implied) powers of its organs can be seen as related, this is not the case with the UN Charter.[13]

The constitutional approach to the teleological interpretation of its compe-tences by the Council raises the obvious question of whether its "powers of appreciation" are limitable or legally challengeable by other UN organs, such as the ICJ.[14] Indeed, early in the 1990s the question arose as to whether the UN was facing a "constitutional crisis."[15] The frequency of Chapter VII interventions into internal conflicts and other innovations regarding its competence made the language of "unique and exceptional circumstances" less and less convincing. The problems of selectivity, arbitrariness, open-ended delegations to powerful states to carry out sanctions, and rather authoritarian occupation administrations that followed, combined with the suspicion that the Council was being used as a foreign policy tool by P1, motivated the ICISS report and the UN reform project.[16] Be that as it may, my point nonetheless is that care was taken by the Council to frame its expansive reading of its powers within the discursive limits and mandate of Chapter VII, the constitutional interpretation notwithstanding.

The same cannot be said for theorists of humanitarian intervention who argue for unilateral action in the case of failure of the SC to act, nor for defenders of unlimited discretion on the part of the Council in designating internal cases of human rights violations and humanitarian crises as triggers for Chapter VII action or in delegating unlimited powers to the humanitarian occupation regimes it directly or indirectly establishes.[17] All of this has opened the door to the contemporary security paradigm, which, ironically, is so inhospitable to human rights (and to sovereign equality). The three discursive moves responsible for this opening were: first, the argument for a conception of human in lieu of state security; second, the reconceptualization of human rights in terms of security (freedom from fear and want); and third, the redefinition of sovereignty as a function – the responsibility to protect – so as to "disaggregate" it, enabling other instances of governance to take on this responsibility should the state default.[18] None of these moves, on their own, are objectionable or destructive of constitutionalism. But if rights are no longer also interpreted in terms of personal autonomy, due process, legal standing, civil and political liberties and the means to achieve these, then the distinction between human rights and the "security" provided by the intrusive regulations characteristic of global governance could be blurred.[19] Redefining sovereignty as a function instead of as a principle of autonomy is incoherent. But, more alarming, the point is to weaken the restrictions on forceful intervention and to make it incidental which instance of governance protects "human security." Indeed, by undermining respect for sovereignty as a principle of legal and political autonomy, the ideological discourse that accompanied the enforcement model paved the way for the present global security regime that is now directly threatening human rights, sovereign equality, and constitutionalism, domestically and internationally.

5.2   The new security paradigm: the Security Council starts legislating

September 11 provided the occasion for a new discourse of a global state of emergency, and the need for a permanent war on terror. On September 28, 2001, the SC adopted Resolution 1373 invoking Chapter VII powers but departing radically from its previous practice and language.[20] Resolution 1373 contains far-reaching, general obligations for states to prevent and combat terrorism.[21] States are ordered to take actions designed to prevent support for terrorists, to suppress the financing of terrorist acts, to freeze funds and other assets of any persons or entities suspected of terrorist activity or of supporting it, to strengthen border security and prevent the movement of terrorists in part by tracking migrants and refugees, and to become parties to the UN's anti-terrorism conventions and protocols.[22] Most remarkably, states are required to change their domestic laws to criminalize terrorism (and its financing) as a separate offense in national codes with harsher punishments than those attached to ordinary crimes.[23] Each nation is called upon to upgrade its legislation and executive machinery to "fight terrorism." Thus Resolution 1373 creates uniform obligations for all 193 member states of the UN, going well beyond earlier counter-terrorism conventions and protocols (sponsored by the General Assembly) binding only on those who have become parties to them.[24] The resolution established a subsidiary organ the Counter-Terrorism Committee (CTC) – a plenary committee of the Council – to monitor state compliance with the resolution.[25] All this in the absence of any definition of terrorism (this is left to the states to define) and coupled with a disavowal of responsibility to monitor the human rights violations that these requirements might entail.[26]

There was an important predecessor to this. Resolution 1267, passed by the Council in 1999, initially addressed support by the Taliban regime within Afghanistan for suspected terrorists.[27] It was expanded into a complex "smart" sanction regime adopting global measures against anyone anywhere associated with the Taliban, Osama bin Laden, or Al Qaeda.[28] The 1267

Committee was established as a subsidiary organ to monitor state compliance with Council-imposed targeted sanctions and to maintain a consolidated list of individuals and entities alleged to have the above-mentioned associations.[29] The list is updated and managed by the 1267 Committee.[30] This was the first Chapter VII regime of "smart" sanctions based on the assumption that targeting individuals is an improvement over past UN general sanction regimes that harmed innocents.

Finally, Resolution 1540, adopted in April 2004, sought to block non-state actors from acquiring WMDs.[31] It also requires states to adopt laws, this time prohibiting the acquisition or transfer of WMDs to non-state actors, and to take effective enforcement measures and institute domestic controls to prevent their proliferation. This resolution also establishes a monitoring committee.

However, Resolution 1267 and the follow-up resolutions pose the most direct threat to basic due process and property rights of those listed.[32] Any state may propose a name for the blacklist; members have 48 hours to object. The 1267 Committee operates on the basis of consensus. There are no evidentiary guidelines and very few requirements for the submitting state. A person can be placed on the list and made subject to sanctions without being given the opportunity to demonstrate that the listing is unjustified or even to know the reasons and evidence that led to their name being listed. As for delisting, this may be initiated by the state of a suspect's nationality or residence but the procedure is onerous.[33]

No court is in a position to evaluate the evidential basis on which a person or entity is placed on the list. There is no procedure for a formal appeal or review mechanism.[34] It is true that in response to the World Summit Outcome Document, which called on the Council to ensure fair and clear procedures for listing and delisting, the latter proposed minimum standards for such a regime.[35] Resolution 1730 passed in 2006 strengthened procedural safeguards to protect individual rights by establishing a focal point to receive delisting requests applying to the sanctions committees established by the Council. However, it is still the case that any Council member can block the removal of a name by veto without having to give reasons.[36]

Given the absence of legal remedies, the threat posed by this resolution to the rights to due process, the right to be heard, to property, and to freedom of movement is real. As Julia Hoffman correctly notes, the lack of access to and review of information at all stages of the process is striking.[37] Those placed on the list by state executives are to have their assets frozen and their movement restricted regardless of the fact that they have been convicted of no crime, regardless of the lack of an accepted definition of terrorism, and regardless of the absence of due process mechanisms for those listed. Moreover, the danger that the listing process will be used for political purposes by states to quell their internal opposition by framing participants as terrorists is real. Resolution

1566, passed at the request of Russia after the Beslan school massacre, set up a task force to study expanding the list of terrorist individuals and entities beyond those associated with Al Qaeda and the Taliban.[38] In short, blacklisting individuals enables domestic executives to enlist the international community on the state's side of a local conflict by invoking the Security Council resolutions that have constructed the global anti-terrorist campaign.[39]

Indeed it looks very much like the Council has arrogated to itself a judicial function in listing individuals as terrorists – by implication as global outlaws – although in doing so under Chapter VII it avoids formally making a determination of criminal activity which would warrant due process regulations and careful evaluation of evidence.[40] As one analyst puts it, blacklisting is a strange type of punishment since Council decrees lay down no prohibited activity against which the named individuals' actions or omissions are to be measured.[41] This, then, is the underside of the "individualization" of international law so celebrated by globalists. For here the direct link between public (or global) law and the individual involves a global enforcement model that undermines instead of securing their basic constitutional and/or human rights.

Moreover, Resolution 1373, and the follow-up Resolution 1540, portends an emerging Council practice involving an even more radical threat to constitutionalism on the domestic and international levels. Whereas in the 1990s the problem was the apparent arbitrariness in labeling domestic conflicts, humanitarian crises, and rights violations threats to *international* peace and security, here we encounter a different problem. There is no great stretch in construing transnational terrorism as a threat to international peace and security. However, there is indeed a very great stretch when the Security Council arrogates to itself the competence to identify not particular, but general, permanent yet amorphous threats to the existing order, and responds by legislating for the international community as a whole, thereby radically changing the way international law is made and its function. Why?

What characterized the epoch of the enforcement/security model, despite its flaws and openness to abuse, was that the powers the Council invoked were executive in character, and they were exercised in response to particular conflicts and emergencies. By their nature, sanctions were restricted by a limited purpose and time frame, whether or not specific temporal limits were stipulated.[42] Once the purpose was achieved, the mandate ended.[43] The relevant decisions of the Council were thus executive and political. They have the shape of commands relating to a specific situation, just what the Council was designed for even though the context of the situation altered from the external to the internal.

In relation to that model, Resolutions 1373 and 1540 are highly innovative in six respects: (1) They are not related to a specific threat or dispute even though they were inspired by 9/11, but rather to a vague, generally construed threat. (2) They lack any explicit or implicit time limitation. (3) The binding obligations they impose on all states are permanent. (4) Significant portions of them address generic issues and establish binding general rules of international law instead of having the status of specific decrees or commands addressed to a specific context. As several commentators have pointed out, the Security Council has started legislating.[44] If legislation is the enactment of abstract norms that are directly binding on all member states and which regulate their rights and obligations on general issues with long-term effects, irrespective of the consent of any individual state, then the SC has indeed begun to legislate. The difference with legally binding executive decisions ("measures" in the language of the Charter) that enforce the peace in a specific political crisis is clear.[45] (5) The SC arrogated to itself the competence to enact abstract norms, directly binding on member states of the UN, which are to be effective immediately and which undermine existing domestic constitutional provisions or norms that conflict with these rules thereby changing domestic constitutions. If we include Resolution 1267, the Council has thrice imposed resolutions involving substantively intrusive legal regimes that bypass the usual vehicle of community interest, the multilateral treaty. (6) The Council now resorts to its own subsidiary organs rather than to standing institutions in other relevant treaty regimes to ensure legislative success and compliance.[46]

One analyst has portrayed these developments as amounting to a new mode of exercising power by the Security Council (led by the US) that he called "global hegemonic international law."[47] Hegemony operates through non-reciprocal patron–client relations involving pledges of loyalty in exchange for security or economic benefits, replacing pacts between equals grounded in reciprocity and substituting for formal equality of states.[48] Given the veto and the advantages of permanent membership on the Council, if the P5 are in agreement, all it takes for binding action is to successfully pressure or entice four of the remaining ten non-permanent members.[49] This hegemonic form of law-making is legal under existing Charter rules: "Neither P-1 nor the other permanent members of the Council are violating the law by taking advantage of the privileges they have been granted."[50] The point is that hegemony can be exercised within multilateral institutions and via international law: it need not take the form of unilateralism or law-breaking. The exercise of hegemonic power can be collective, legal, institutional, and juris-generative, hence the appellation "global hegemonic law."[51]

A similar point is made by another insightful critic of the "global state of emergency" constructed by the SC resolutions pursuant to its anti-terror campaign.[52] As Kim Scheppele has shown, unlike earlier democracy- and rights-enhancing multilateralism, this version of global governance undermines the domestic separation of powers in favor of domestic executives and greatly strengthens the executive power of the P5 singly and as a collective body in the UN and the world at large.[53] She documents convincingly the ways in which the security regime put in place by the Council spurs and reinforces the creation of new, vague, and politically defined crimes, surveillance programs, moves toward preventive detention and aggressive interrogation by security-minded domestic forces – national executives, militaries, police, and security agencies. Their power is thereby expanded at the expense of domestic parliaments and courts while civil liberties are eviscerated. Transnational links among national executives, militaries, police, and security agencies have been extended while their relation to and control by domestic parliaments and courts have been attenuated; hardly good news for constitutionalism.[54] Many heads of states and governments are able to invoke obligatory Council resolutions to push through rights-violating domestic laws, thereby expanding their own power, justified as compliance with international law. Those states that seek to resist the Security Council's command to criminalize terrorism as a separate offense arguing that their criminal law is equipped to handle it are subject to pressure by the CTC erected to monitor national compliance.[55] Weak states are forced to comply, executives seeking to become stronger willingly play along; others committed to constitutionalism, rights and the separation of powers are pressured to conform.[56]

Scheppele's point, like Alvarez's, is that the Council does all this through the use of law. Emergency governance is not lawless; it proceeds through a plethora of rules, decrees, regulations, legal administrative measures, and international and domestic legislation.[57] It is not the absence of law, but the development of a new form of global security law and the legal pressures placed on domestic governments to comply with it that is the problem. But it is one thing to show that the Council's emergency governance involves rule-making and legislation that is technically legal, it is quite another to maintain that this is a legitimate exercise of its powers. The bodies created by the Charter are ascribed the competence to interpret their own powers to carry out their functions. The Council has the authority to enact decisions binding on all states, including non-members of the UN, to "maintain or restore international peace and security."[58] The presumption of legality for Security Council action and expansive interpretations of its powers have been the norm since the 1990s. However, critics have insisted that the Council's authority to take binding decisions under the Charter does not amount to a constitutional right for it to legislate for the world.[59] In fact, no organ of the UN was designed to be a legislature or ascribed broadly legislative functions.

One could try to invoke the concept of implied powers, and the principle of effectiveness, to justify the recent Council resolutions as the necessary exceptional response to the emergency situations created by transnational terrorism. In other words, the Council could be acting like a commissarial dictator, suspending some Charter norms, assuming plenary powers, abrogating the albeit rudimentary separation of powers and existing constitutional guarantees of due process and other human rights of suspects in the "war on terror," so as to act effectively in the face of threats to the basic order and to restore them once the threats are dealt with.[60] After all, on the treaty reading of the UN Charter, the Security Council is an emergency executive: established to identify and respond to crises, i.e. to declare the exception and to protect international peace and security. On the constitutional interpretation of the Charter, the SC was established to protect the legal order and community norms created by and articulated in the Charter. But these justifications would have to fit in the framework of the exceptional and temporary nature of police enforcement measures. It is not evident that legislative powers are required for efficacy or deducible from the concept of implied powers.[61]

Indeed in the public debates over Resolution 1540, many states expressed concern that it could become a precedent and constitute "subsequent practice" establishing general legislative powers of the Council.[62] Members of the non-aligned movement explicitly rejected a legislative role for the Council arguing that this is not a function envisaged in the Charter and that the Council is structurally inappropriate to legislate for the UN because it is not a representative body.[63] Others insisted that in principle legislative obligations such as those foreseen in the draft resolution should be established through multilateral treaties in whose elaboration all states can participate.[64]

At issue is the encroachment on the allocation of powers established by the UN Charter. By arrogating to itself the competence to legislate in this way, the Council has taken a step beyond a commissarial dictator, for it is using the discourses of a "war on terror," and emergency, not in order to protect an existing constitutional order but to institute a new one. Legislation is distinct from suspending certain rights and issuing binding decrees targeted to a specific situation, and it is not the function of a commissarial dictatorship. Moreover, in purporting to legislate for the world, the Council is apparently changing the material constitution of the Charter, engaging in an informal amendment, using the lower track of law-making and bypassing the higher track in the formal amendment rule (conflating the two tracks).[65]

What even critics fail to see, then, is that by arrogating to itself such global legislative power, the *Security Council may be exercising its legal power to make binding decisions, but it is doing something unanticipated at the founding of the UN that seems doubly illegitimate: usurping the constituent authority belonging to the international community of states and materially changing the constitutional treaty through informal amendments, both in precedent-setting ways.* In the process it is radically undermining the principle of sovereign equality, creating not only a new substantive legal regime but also a new form of hierarchical global law-making and governance. To invoke Habermas's concepts, it uses law as a medium to introduce a new form of global governance, undermining law as an institution meant to control and limit the exercise of public power by legal and constitutional norms.

5.3   The usurpation of global constituent power?

Under customary international law, all states have the equal right to partici-pate in international law-making based on consent, including making binding bilateral or multilateral treaties.[66] They are the co-authors, not only the subjects of international law. The UN Charter is a constitutional treaty, open to two different modes of interpretation. It is possible to find a legal basis for a dynamic interpretation of the Charter in the notion of "object and purpose" in the Vienna Convention on the Law of Treaties (VCLT), but on the treaty model, the teleological interpretation of their competences by the organs of the UN would still be relatively restricted.[67] The constitutional interpretation is more permissive. Yet from the perspective of the Charter as a formal constitutional document, any major change to the organizational allocation of competences, to the functions ascribed to the organs or to the organization as a whole, would have to proceed through formal amendment, via the amendment rule in the Charter.[68] Arguably, the assumption of legislative functions by the Security Council transgresses both of these readings. Given objections to a legislative role for the Council voiced by UN member states unconvinced that such powers are needed for security in the war on terror, the treaty model doesn't seem adequate, but neither does the constitutional interpretation. For by assuming the competence to legislate, the Council is not only transforming its function from enforcement and policing, it is also changing the material constitution and amending the Charter by stealth. The assumption of legislative power and its actual legislation thus have a double status: general laws are being made by an (unelected, unrepresentative) executive body and constitutional change in the allocation of powers is being perpetrated by that same body insofar as it ascribes to itself the competence and capacity to legislate for the world, thereby introducing a radically new way of global law-making.

Why do I claim that this involves constitution-making, not only legislation? After all, there is a formal amendment rule in the Charter that in principle could be invoked against such informal proceedings. As long as that rule is intact, the new legislative tract would remain just that, a legislative one. One look at the fate of the amendment rule should suffice. Articles 108 and 109 stating the procedures by which the Charter may be altered stipulate a two-thirds vote of the General Assembly including *all* the permanent members of the Security Council, thereby extending the veto of the P5 to the amendment procedure.[69] Fundamental change to the Charter and to the functions ascribed to UN organs should take place via this process. The veto presumably was meant to serve as a negative check, to block alterations unwanted by the P5. This includes blocking changes through the Charter amendment process of their own special powers on the Council or of the competences of the Council itself because the P5 can veto any proposal. However, in the current context the veto has an enabling function. Once the Security Council starts legislating, redefining its powers and function, the veto means that there is no constitutional check to such actions. Whatever informal constitutional changes the P5 manages to push through the Council cannot be undone via the amendment process, because with respect to this as well, any permanent member can veto the corrective. The P5's veto power blocks not only needed reforms the P5 don't want; it also blocks a constitutional response to informal amendments. That is why one can speak of a "usurpation" of the constituent authority of the member states – the sole entities with the authority to collectively formally change the material constitution of the Charter either via the amendment rule or via the creation of a new constitutional treaty through a convention of some sort as provided for in Article 109. There is no court authorized to decide the competence of UN organs, to police the rudimentary separation of powers, or to maintain the formal two-track structure of law-making erected by the Charter – i.e. the distinction between ordinary rule-making and constitutional change established by the amendment rule. Nor is there an effective legal or institutional remedy that could be used to undo informal amendments pushed through by the P5 in the Security Council.

We must be clear about the argument at this point. Although some critics try to claim that the Council is acting illegally when it legislates because it exceeds its ascribed competences, this is not my claim. Indeed it is very hard to make the "ultra vires" argument. Even if one maintains that the Council was never explicitly ascribed general legislative powers (i.e. the competence to enact general legal norms), and even if one argues that the particular substance of specific resolutions such as the terror listing requirements of Resolution 1267 violates textual limits on the Council's prerogatives insofar as it transgresses the principles and purposes of the Charter (which include respect for human rights), it remains the case that the Council was given very broad discretion to determine what amounts to a threat to peace and security and what measures to take not involving the use of armed force.[70] Precisely because the textual limits on the Council's powers are so vague, open-textured and scant, they provide no hard legal restrictions on the Council's choice of means and thus do not clearly render even long-term legislative enactments ultra vires. Given the lack of an independent body ascribed the power to review SC actions regarding their conformity with the Charter's principles and purposes, the charge of an illegal expansion of competences or that a specific substantive resolution is "constitutionally" invalid, is from a juridical point of view very hard to pull off.[71] Indeed as one insightful commentator has argued, the Council seems to possess the untrammeled competence to decide its own competence " . . . in both the judicial sense (because no one else can authoritatively interpret or invalidate its decisions) and in the legislative meaning (because no one can alter its competences through statute or amendment)."[72]

My argument thus pertains to legitimacy, not legality. Debates over whether there are "constitutional" limits to SC powers are significant, regardless of the difficulty of arriving at a knockdown legal answer. They indicate that the legitimacy of even technically legal action by the premier global governance institution is at risk. Why is this so?

Obviously, the condition of possibility for the radically new forms of Council activity was there since 1945. Moreover, the P5 have always been in a structurally different position than the rest of the member states in the UN. *It is the unprecedented use being made of their structural position today that creates a new legitimation problematic.* We are now in a context in which global governance is increasing and in which cosmopolitan principles and constitutionalist discourses – either as ideology or as a project to limit or reform GGIs and international law – are being taken seriously alongside the continued commitment to sovereign equality on the part of most states. The new activism of the SC – its expanding scope and new modes of exercising its powers – has opened up renewed reflection on its prerogatives and internal structure. The issue is not simply a matter of inequality – of the P5 having greater power or privileges like weighted votes or extra say in rule-making or certain immunities. Nor is it simply a matter of anachronism; correctible say, by including other twenty-first-century great powers within the privileged circle of permanent members.[73] The problem is the constitutional and structural difference of the mode of relationship of some members to the organization thanks to the amendment rule. Everyone knows that the veto in the Council exempts the P5 from having the rules they make applied to themselves. Everyone knows that there can be no enforcement of Charter principles against a permanent member or against someone they protect. Everyone also knows that the veto in the amendment rule puts the P5 in the position to block changes to their status and discretion.

But what all this actually means is that for the P5, the Charter is a treaty and the UN, a traditional international treaty organization. The P5 are external to the *constitutional* treaty and remain its "masters" in an important sense. They participate in an organization to whose rules, on the classical treaty model, they are subject, conditional on their consent. For them, the principal–agent relationship still obtains; while they do participate in a treaty organization which is a third party actor, they retain a sort of Westphalian sovereignty singly and collectively vis-à-vis that organization. Both the formal and the informal amendment rule for them is the classical amendment rule of a treaty organization: it is based on the principle of unanimity for the P5. The same is true of the ordinary "legislative" process of passing Council resolutions: their consent is required, so, for them, unanimity not qualified majority voting is the operative rule. They thus have a distinctive status compared with other UN members because they are capable of binding the others (with the consent of four non-permanent members) but cannot themselves be bound without their consent.

None of this is so for the other members of the UN. For them, the organization created via the Charter is not a classical treaty organization; it is a "global governance institution" in today's parlance. These member states are fully subject to the rules and decisions of UN organs with or without their individual consent. Decisions and resolutions of the UNGA, the ICJ, and the UNSC are taken on the basis of (variously qualified) majority vote and thus the organization is not simply their agent. Rather it is an independent institution that although created through a treaty, functions as an autonomous body and as an autonomous legal order vis-à-vis its creators. Indeed, for all non-P5 member states of the UN, the Charter is a *constitutional* treaty in the sense described in Chapter 2 of this text. For, they are also subject to an amendment rule that is not based on unanimity but on a qualified majority. Analytically such an amendment rule is more typical of a federation wherein a qualified majority of member states can amend the constitutional treaty of the organization, through a process in which each state has one vote, than it is of a classic treaty organization where every state has a veto. In such a structure, member states are within the organization, under its constitutional law and equally subject to it even though they retain their sovereignty in the sense that their legal systems are autonomous, as is the legal structure of the organization.

Thus what the formal amendment rule of the Charter constructs is a hybrid structure in which some of the member states belong to a treaty organization, while others belong to what is more akin ideal-typically to a loosely consolidated federation: their relation to the constituent treaty and to the rules made by UN organs is radically different.[74] Moreover, despite its assertion of the principle of sovereign equality, the UN Charter has formalized a hierarchy between the two types of members. The P5 are not bound by the same constitutional rules that bind the others, and they are often in a position to dictate these rules. The problem is not that member states of the organization retain their sovereignty, or that the organization is constitutionally pluralist in the sense that it constitutes an autonomous legal order yet is composed of member states whose own constitutional legal orders are also autonomous. Rather, the problem is that the formal amendment rule and the veto in the Council constructs a hierarchy within the overall hybrid nature of the organization, placing the permanent members in a position outside of the *constitutional* order created by the constituent treaty. The permanent members are able to participate in making rules and decisions that others must comply with but from which they are exempt, and to bypass the amendment rule and make material constitutional changes to which there is no legal or institutional remedy thanks to that very amendment rule and the absence of a court with constitutional review powers. The P5 can thus exercise constituent authority and revise the Charter by stealth, with the veneer of legality, if they get the requisite number of votes.[75]

5.4   The legitimation problem

Permanent membership and the veto right of the P5 in the Council was initially accepted by member states for the sake of exceptional peace enforcement. It was clear that these privileges contradicted the principle of sovereign equality articulated in Article 1 of the Charter. However, once the Council assumes a general legislative role, the threat to the principle of sovereign equality within and outside the UN system and to the basic structure of public international law becomes far more radical. The new legislative role transfers the inequality in peace and security enforcement to a much wider sphere.[76] First, it means that member states lose their right to equally participate in making international law, and to consent or make reservations or persistently object to it as they can in the multilateral treaty-making process. Article 103 of the Charter stipulates the supremacy of Charter obligations over any other international agreement. Since states must obey Council decisions, they do not have the option of opting out that exists under customary international law nor do they have any role in making it as is case in treaty law. Second, as a recent commentator on Resolutions 1373 and 1540 succinctly put it:

> The P5 effectively control the Council. Should the recent trend of targeting individuals by means of sanctions be taken up in legislation, the inequality could extend to the creation of rights and obligations of the States' nationals. The practice of equipping the primary norms with special monitoring mechanisms . . . could . . . extend the inequality further from norm creation to the monitoring phase and into enforcement.[77]

The recent legislation by the Council indeed does affect the sovereignty of most states other than the P5 insofar as their ability to participate in international law-making and to make their own domestic law autonomously is eviscerated.[78] On the other hand: "Executives in terrorist-target strong countries as well as those in terror-implicated weak states are all increasing their powers in the anti-terrorism campaign, even as more powerful states use transnational institutions to further dominate weaker ones."[79] It is, after all, executives that are behind the expansion of Council powers. These changes in the UN Charter structure and in the general system of public international law do not bode well for the rule of law or constitutionalism anywhere. If this de facto UN reform is not successfully challenged by a counter-project, then the securitizing, normalizing, regulatory techniques of administering and governing populations rehearsed in "humanitarian occupations" will be generalized to other states, carried out either by reinforced domestic executives and/or global policing agencies that ride roughshod over rights, constitutional limits, and counter-powers.[80]

This is the level on which the most serious charge of *illegitimacy* is pertinent: the rule regulating change, the amendment rule, is bypassed via informal amendment that institutes radical changes to the international legal order and the Charter itself (by turning the Council into a legislative body) which cannot be undone by a constitutional court or via formal amendment. All this is indeed juris-generative: new law and a new form of law-making have emerged. Unfortunately the new legal order that this quiet revolution seems to be ushering in is one in which a hegemonic form of global right can violate both human rights and the sovereign equality of states with apparent impunity.

The problem we face is not whether a global state of emergency can be responded to with ordinary legal methods, but whether the newly active SC can be legally limited, its legislative initiatives scaled back, the threats it poses to constitutionalism and human rights reversed, and a new dualistic sovereignty regime based on the rule of law and the principles of sovereign equality and human rights reinstituted within the UN Charter system. I am not convinced that transnational terrorism poses the kind of existential threat to the world order that could justify instituting a general state of emergency rule or the self-ascription of plenary powers on the part of the Security Council to legislate and institute a new form of global law. I am convinced, however, that part of a viable counter-project is what others have already referred to as the further constitutionalization of public international law.[81] However, much depends on how we understand this.

I see the project of the further constitutionalization of this domain of public international law as a feasible, albeit difficult to obtain, utopia. If we accept that the need for global governance is real in certain areas, and that global governance institutions are here to stay, then bringing them under the rule of law, and rendering them representative of those subject to its rules, is indispensable for their legitimacy. The UN as a global governance institution faces a triple legitimacy deficit today. On the substantive level, SC rulings that violate basic human rights undermine the legitimacy of the Council as the protector of the values of the Charter and the international community. On the procedural level, the expansion of its powers to include quasi-judicial and especially legislative functions in addition to a new unanticipated scope of executive enforcement raises serious questions about the rudimentary separation of powers and deficient system of checks and balances within the Charter structure. On the meta-procedural level, the "usurpation" of the constituent authority of member states through informal amendment, to transform the Council into a hegemonic global law-maker, whose obligatory rulings eviscerate the cardinal principle of sovereign equality in the making of public international law, undermines the credibility of the Council as an impartial agent of the international community. The hybrid structure of this organization is decreasingly legitimate. Since there are no internal legal correctives to such uncontrolled exercises of power, it also throws into doubt any normative constitutionalist reading of the Charter.

5.5   Excursus on constitution/constitutionalism

The concepts of constitution and constitutionalism are various and contested. Although associated through the modern period with the domestic legal order of states, there is no compelling reason to automatically restrict either concept to that framework.[82] Nor is it all that difficult to put some order into the multiplicity of meanings. It is important to keep the analytical question of what a constitution is or does distinct from what it should do or what is a good constitution from a normative point of view, although there is inevitable slippage because the concept of constitutional*ism* invariably evokes normative associations. I begin by reminding the reader of the Kelsenian distinction between the material and formal meanings of the concept, initially developed with reference to the domestic legal order of states.

A constitution in the material sense consists of those procedural or substantive rules that regulate the creation of general legal norms, establish organs, and delimit their powers.[83] A constitution in the formal sense is a written text that typically can be changed only through special procedures whose purpose is to render the change of these norms more difficult. The formal constitution serves to safeguard the norms determining the organs and procedure of legislation (the core features of the material constitution). Accordingly, the enactment, amendment, and annulment of constitutional laws are made more difficult than that of ordinary legislation.[84] Typically, they require a supermajority – or some other procedural mechanism that renders the formal constitution more or less rigid and accords its rules superior rank as "higher law" over the rules made by the organs established or regulated by the constitution. This creates a dualist structure that requires some body or mechanisms able to police the boundaries between the formal and the material constitution, between the modes of change specific to each.[85] However, as Kelsen points out, a formal constitution is not an essential element of a constitutional order. It is the material constitution that comprises the set of norms that establish the methods through which other norms are created, interpreted, and applied at the highest level of the legal system.[86] Normative hierarchy is a core feature of a legal system and in Kelsen's view that hierarchy culminates in (the supremacy of) the constitutional norms themselves. The chain of justification of validity and authority leads back to the constitution of the state, the ultimate positive legal "source" for validity of lower norms in the norm hierarchy.[87]

Thus far we are speaking of the concept of constitution as a blueprint for government. From this perspective, a constitution can be seen as a device for improving governmental effectiveness, an instrument that involves enabling constraints meant to serve as a medium of regulation, facilitate resolution of collective action problems, foster cooperation in matters of common interest, and enable rulers to legally pursue policy ends and/or common purposes. As an instrument of government, a constitution is to provide security, regularity, and reliability, through establishing a unified hierarchical legal system that is calculable and effective. Understood in the descriptive, empirical sense, every country has or is a constitution.[88]

But more than a blueprint for government, the concepts of a constitution – and certainly of *constitutionalism* – are freighted with normative significations. The most minimal normative meaning of "constitutionalism" denotes the commitment on the part of a political community to be governed by constitutional rules and principles.[89] A step up the ladder of normative meaning is the idea that a constitutional legal order is autonomous and, to borrow a phrase from Niklas Luhmann's followers, "structurally coupled" to the political system so that the exercise of authoritative political power proceeds through the legally determined procedures that secure the autonomy of each domain.[90] As such, constitutions help differentiate, delimit, and interrelate the legal and political systems of a polity.

From the juridical perspective, i.e. the standpoint internal to the legal system, "constitutional" refers to the assessment of the constitutionality of a particular norm with respect to its validity under the constitution. The relevant questions are whether the enacting body followed the designated procedures, whether it has the authority to enact the norm, whether the norm comports with substantive constraints articulated within the constitution, and so forth. This form of normative assessment involves the perspective of the jurist, for whom the term "constitutional" pertains to validity and "constitutionalist" to the exercise of public power through public law in accordance with prescribed constitutional norms. Accordingly, a constitution provides a comprehensive framework for the application of legal norms and for the making of new norms. It is from the internal juridical framework, higher and reflexive law, the law of law-making.

The concepts "constitution" and "constitutionalism" are also associated with meanings that enable one to assess the quality of a constitutional order from a normative point of view. Kelsen himself distinguished between what he called the legal as distinct from the political-theoretical approach to these concepts.[91] The latter, according to Kelsen, pertains not only to the norms which regulate the process of legislation but also to those norms which regulate the creation and competences of the highest executive and judicial organs, i.e. to the separation of powers. However, in Kelsen's hands these norms matter primarily insofar as they pertain to validity. An astute recent analysis interprets this distinction as a hint that there is another perspective on constitutions and constitutionalism, that, using the language of political theory, reorients us away from questions of validity toward the normative assessment of the way in which a particular constitutional order articulates, separates, and delimits the powers to create, apply, and interpret norms, among other things.[92] This political-theoretical perspective is thus focused on the quality of the legal and political order established by the constitution. Along with pragmatic assessments of efficient design, the political-theoretical approach renders evaluative questions of the justice and legitimacy of the constitutional order pertinent – both from the third person perspective and from the participant perspective of those subject to the constitutional order.

With respect to normative legitimacy, the two ideal-typical perspectives much discussed in the literature are the "liberal" and "democratic/republican" conceptions, or what are called, somewhat misleadingly, power-limiting versus power-establishing (foundational) constitutionalism. Liberal constitutionalism is accordingly associated with the idea of power limitation through mechanisms such as the articulation and protection of fundamental rights, the separation of powers, checks and balances, and so on. Liberal constitutionalism also involves the more general principle that government is limited and regulated by law (and the idea of the rule of law) and that the exercise of public power under law is for public purposes and the well-being of the individuals comprising the community.[93] A shared premise of liberal and democratic constitutionalism is that the addressees of authoritative (state) policy and rules are free and equal. That is why subjecting public power to the discipline of legal norms – to the form of law, which allegedly secures generality and impartiality – is deemed essential to the justification of power among those who conceive of one another as free and equal consociates under law.

Liberal constitutionalism also establishes some of the powers it separates, procedurally regulates, and limits by basic rights and, insofar as it requires a strong state to back it up, it enacts effective government. Nevertheless, democratic-republican constitutionalism is seen as comprehensively foundational in a distinctive sense: it involves a project to construct and ground (on an entirely new basis) a system of government, not only to shape or contractually limit a pre-existing one. Crucially, it does not acknowledge any residues of public power that are not subject to constitutional law or remain outside it or preceded it. The object, in other words, of a constitution and of constitutionalism is the establishment and exercise of public power according to a set of legal norms that owe their validity to a political decision.[94] In this model, all governmental powers derive their authority from the constitution which is supreme, and their legitimacy from the constitutive activity of the demos – the "constituent power" to whom it is imputed.[95] Thus democratic constitutionalism is not a contract between a ruler and the ruled; rather, it "defines a horizontal association of citizens by laying down the fundamental rights that free and equal founders mutually grant each other and the fundamental legal and political order under which they wish to live."[96] In the democratic model, the adoption of a constitution involves action or a series of acts ascribable

to those free and equal persons or citizens – "the people" (or their representatives) – who will be regulated by the constitution.[97] This is the democratic
version of the idea of the self-determination by a political community of its
political, legal, and constitutional forms. Constitutionalism is seen as facilitating the exercise of collective self-legislation insofar as it provides the
procedures needed to identify the popular sovereign (the demos as electorate),
for selecting its representatives, and for determining its will on a coherent
basis. Thus from the republican/democratic perspective, constitutionalism
involves more than legal reflexivity (the "higher" law of law-making) and
legal limits on the arbitrary exercise of public power (rights, separation of
powers, etc.): it entails above all political reflexivity. In other words, the
political process/procedures of constitution-making must be ascribable to
the people whose fundamental legal and political order it establishes and
whom it will regulate (those subject to the law). It must articulate the political
process/procedures through which the demos can express its opinions,
interests, and will(s), and alter even the highest laws (through conventions
or amendment rules) and which has, thus, the final say, so that it is deemed
the ultimate source of that law. The constitutional norms emanate from
political decision rather than from pre-established truth.[98] The fundamental
legitimacy of this "higher law" is thus immanent, on the democratic conception, to "will" of the people qua constituent power to whom it can
be ascribed via procedures whose quality (legitimacy) can be assessed from
this standpoint.

Taken together, liberal-democratic constitutionalism as a normative construct entails the ideal of limited collective self-government under law.
Constitutionalism is central to the legitimate exercise of public power. Constitutionalized public power, if it is to be democratic, and republican, must in
some sense be ascribable to a demos or demoi (in the case of a federation),
whose welfare, interests, opinions, and will it enables (through the institutionalization of political rights, representative political processes, as well as
civil and decisional public spheres). It somehow (through appropriate mechanisms) reflects those sources (representativeness) and is responsible and
accountable to them. This normative conception of liberal-democratic constitutionalism thus does not reify the "constituent power" or the "sovereignty" of the people: it need not buy into a Schmittian metaphysics of
presence or homogeneous unitary conception of the people and its will as a
way to do an end run around the legal order ("mere" constitutional law to
Schmitt). Instead it invokes these terms as a way to ensure that avenues exist
for the expression of people's interests, opinions, and influence and to ensure
responsiveness of public officials while blocking usurpation. It aims at
orienting coercive public power to public purposes, thereby rendering it
legitimate. The quality (legitimacy) of a constitutional order can be assessed
"politically" with reference to these criteria.

5.6   The constitutional quality of the UN Charter system

The need to rectify the legitimation deficits plaguing the UN Charter system is now pressing. Two dilemmas have to be confronted in such a project: the first is how to further constitutionalize this domain of international law, thereby creating a new form of global law that, given a world of sovereign states with vastly different characteristics, is nonetheless not imperial or "hegemonic." The second involves the necessity of binding sovereign states to a law that is autonomous with respect to their own constitutions, whose validity is not based on state consent in the classical contractual way, and which concerns in part how states treat their own populations, in addition to regulating the *jus belli*. I argue that the solution to both dilemmas lies in a reform based on a dualist conception of international/world society and a pluralist understanding of constitutionalism. International society is still a segmentally differentiated system of sovereign states but it is increasingly imbricated in a functionally differentiated world society composed of globalizing legal orders, networks, and individuals. The "further constitutionalization" of the public international law regulating the global political system has to be understood as the institutionalization of a new dualistic sovereignty regime, in which states retain their legal and political autonomy and constituent authority but within which the supranational legal order of a revised UN Charter system is also construed as autonomous *and* constrained by constitutional*ism*. This would entail bringing the P5 inside the Charter, but interpreting the transformed global constitutional order of the UN in the theoretical framework of constitutional pluralism rather than monism would acknowledge the dualist nature of the global political system. It would also entail re-institutionalizing the principles of sovereign equality and human rights to apply to this important global governance institution and not only to states. Let us recall that the principle of sovereign equality is not simply one that ensures the autonomy and equal status of sovereign states, it also is a principle of representation, such that all states can participate as equals in law-making. Once this is achieved, the proper scope of SC law-making can be addressed in the right way. But there is a prior question that requires still a bit more discussion: does any discourse of constitutionalism or constitutionalization make sense if the referent is the global political system? Is the UN Charter a constitution and if so what is it the constitution of, if there is no world state or polity?

It should be clear from my discussion in Chapter 1 and from the above, that I address the question of the status and quality of the UN Charter in the narrow sense as the constitution of the UN, and not in the global cosmopolitan sense as the constitution of world society or even in the systems-theoretical or Fassbender sense as the constitutive document of the global political subsystem.[99] But the constitutionalist discourse pertaining to the Charter involves more than the trivially true fact that it is the organizing, constitutive document of the UN Organization. The issues raised by this discourse are compelling because, as already indicated, member states have delegated very broad powers to the UN to wield over and above them. Moreover, as we have seen, the legal order of the UN is autonomous and not simply at the disposal of individual member states, indeed not even of the P5 singly or together since they cannot act using the SC without consent of other members and they are bound by the procedural rules of the Charter regulating it, although each can prevent action by that body. If constitutionalist discourse pertains to legal autonomy in this sense and to the UN as a global governance institution (given the new activism especially of the SC and its self-ascribed legislative powers) then it is important to see what this entails as distinguished from traditional discourses that refer to international treaties and international treaty organizations.[100]

It is true that the UN Charter was created through an intergovernmental process between states, and signed as a treaty. Like any typical intergovernmental organization, the bodies established by the treaty have no general legislative competence, only those delegated powers necessary to carry out their enumerated functions; their rules and decisions bind states only in certain agreed-upon domains; the domestic legal orders of the member states remain autonomous and non-derivative. Even the dispute settlement system, located in the ICJ, is state-based, voluntary, and lacks an enforcement mechanism: neither individuals nor international organizations have standing and member states can withdraw from the system. In principle, states could also exit the UN at will. These are the classic features of an international treaty organization, which has the international society of sovereign states as its referent.

However, there are important features of the Charter that escape the treaty model and make sense only on a constitutional reading. The UN Charter created a "third party actor," meant to endure indefinitely, and it defined the structure of the organization setting out the powers and functions of its organs, the rights and duties of its members.[101] It serves as a *constitutional treaty* in both the material and formal sense of the word. As a material constitution, the Charter involves a set of substantive norms (sovereign equality, human rights, peaceful settlement of disputes, domestic jurisdiction, self-determination, etc.) as well as procedural and institutional norms that establish organs and delimit their powers, including primary and secondary rules. As a formal constitution, the Charter is a solemn written document that may be changed only under the observation of special prescriptions. In an unprecedented step for international organizations at the time, the founding member states decided not only to create an institution with the power to decide the legality of the use of force; they also opted for majoritarianism in the amendment rule and in ordinary decision-making processes, qualified in the ways already described.[102] The supermajority required for amending the constitution establishes its formal character, its relative rigidity, and its superior rank vis-à-vis the rules its organs make. This was a radical break with the standard unanimity principle for treaty organizations.[103] Moreover, the Charter established an autonomous legal order that it asserted to be supreme in the event of a conflict with other treaty obligations of the members.[104] This legal order delimits the terms of membership, and the organization has acquired many new members since it was created. It has as its referent the international community of states it helped transform and construct into an integrated legal community with community interests, purposes, and values.[105] On the constitutional reading it is this legal community that the organs of the UN are supposed to represent.[106] By implication, the constituent units are legally subordinated to their new creation: its rules apply to them irrespective of their continuing consent. The constitutional treaty thus changed the status of sovereign states qua members. This is the meaning of an autonomous legal order of constitutional quality.

To be sure, as we have also seen, the constitutionalist dimension of the UN Charter is at best rudimentary in the well-rehearsed respects: there is no court with compulsory jurisdiction to police the formal constitution or enforce the material one, there isn't an adequate separation of powers or system of internal checks and balances, there are no real protections for basic rights, no global court of human rights, no compulsory dispute settlement system, no mechanisms to ensure accountability, etc. Nor is there any convincing way to assert supremacy of the Charter over *jus cogens* norms or its "incorporation" of general international law despite the fact that Article 103 indicates that obligations of a state under that charter trump other international obligations.[107] *Thus the constitutionalist reading has to be seen as aspirational.*

The greatest impediment to the constitutionalist reading, however, is not its rudimentary character; it is the weakness of the Charter with respect to a third dimension of the meaning of constitution, the normative one, without which the other two would be uninteresting. In other words, constitution in the political-theoretical, normative sense entails constitutionalism: meaning at the very least that the powers and governing bodies established in the constitutional legal order are regulated and limited by it. *There can be no space for holders of public power constituted by a constitutional document to somehow still stand outside the legal order it creates.*[108] The point of the constitutionalization of public power is to place it under law and subject it to legal limits. The qualitative concept of constitutionalism also means that certain substantive values, including human rights, the rule of law, and the exercise of public power for public purposes and the community's well-being, inform and orient a particular institutional order.[109] It is on this normative level that the constitutionalist nature of the Charter falls short, for the permanent members of the Security Council are absolute in the old-fashioned sense thanks to the peculiar hybrid structure of the UN established by virtue of the veto in the Council and in respect of amendment.

One can hardly call such a structure constitutionalist in the democratic foundational sense because despite the rhetoric of the preamble, the peoples regulated by the UN Charter had no say in its construction and have no role in the law-making its organs engage in. I discuss below the loss of output legitimacy with respect to terror-listing practices and the constitutionalist counter-reactions on the part of the EU and other actors. This loss is the tip of the iceberg of the legitimacy problematic, however, for the deeper issue is the threat to input or process legitimacy, once the SC engages in global governance, undertakes legislative initiatives, and passes resolutions directly and adversely impacting individuals and their rights. In short, the new forms global governance and constitutionalist discourse (higher law, supremacy) invite the charge of liberal and democratic legitimacy deficits.

Maybe one can make the case that according to the VCLT the Council does technically have the competence to interpret its own competence regarding the necessary measures to accomplish its purpose (international peace and security) under the constitutional *treaty* (the Charter) that established it. Perhaps legislation is such a "measure." Be that as it may, at the very least one must conclude that the design of the Charter as a *constitutional* treaty is deeply flawed, and seriously deficient from a qualitative constitutionalist perspective.[110]

5.7 The Kadi case and the conundrum of global governance

Indeed, the recent groundbreaking Kadi 1 judgment by the European Court of Justice seems to indicate as much.[111] The dynamics and the debates over this case show that courts have to confront the serious legitimacy issues raised by the new global governance functions adopted by the Council particularly when they apparently lead to the violation of rights guaranteed by domestic and/or regional constitutional legal orders. In Kadi 1, the overriding legal obligations of the international system were invoked by the SC to strengthen, not to limit executive discretion, in ways that eviscerate domestic democratic and constitutionalist controls and the rights of individuals. It is thus illustrative of the legitimation problematic and the dilemmas of constitutionalist discourse with regard to global governance.

The case addressed the listing of Yassin Kadi, a Saudi national, as a terrorist by the special sanctions committee established by the Security Council in Resolution 1267 adopted under Chapter VII of the UN Charter. At issue was the EU's compliance with the resolution by freezing his assets within the European Community (EC). (The case took place before the further consolidation of older EC structures within the EU, hence the references to the Community below.) Since the EU acts for member states in the area of foreign policy, even though neither it nor the EC is a party to the Charter, it passed the relevant implementing regulations.[112] The EU Council and Commission argued they had no choice but to implement binding Chapter VII resolutions without alteration and without review. Kadi sued, maintaining he was wrongly identified and – absent any way to legally challenge the listing under international law – that his rights to a fair hearing, to judicial remedy, and to property, all enshrined in the European Community's legal order, were violated by the Community's implementing regulation.

The case thus involved a confrontation between the legal orders of the EU, its member states, and international law. The efficacy of highest norms in the international legal system was at issue: Article 103 of the UN Charter that asserts its supremacy over all other treaties or obligations of states, and the binding status of Chapter VII resolutions.[113] The conundrum is the following: states presume they are legally compelled to implement Chapter VII resolutions without alteration or review. They can thus disclaim responsibility for and deny the reviewability of their own implementing measures. But the measures at issue directly impact individuals and impinge on their basic rights. They thus have no redress against arbitrary, biased, or politically motivated listing by states' executives via the Council and then domestically. Listed individuals are potentially placed into a legal black hole.

In response, two EU courts took up the challenge, but they reached opposite conclusions. What is of interest is the conceptual basis for their reasoning, as it latches onto *the very dichotomy* with which I opened this book in Chapter 1: monist constitutionalism versus legal pluralism (construed as a contemporary version of dualism). In my view, most commentators have (mis-)read and either defended or criticized these decisions on similar grounds. I will summarize, offer a different kind of reasoning, and point to a way to resolve the legitimacy problems highlighted by the case, from the perspective of constitutional pluralism.

5.7.1   The cosmopolitan constitutionalist analysis of the Court of First Instance (the primacy of globalizing public international law)

The first court to hear Kadi's case was the Court of First Instance (CFI).[114] Citing Article 103, it argued that the obligations of member states under the UN Charter prevail over other obligations of domestic or international law, including those under the EC treaties and the European Convention on Human Rights and Fundamental Freedoms.[115] It found that it had no authority to review the contested Security Council regulation or to indirectly review its resolutions to assess their conformity with fundamental rights as protected by the Community legal order.[116] Yet the Court then went on to assert its jurisdiction to assess the lawfulness of Security Council resolutions with regard to *jus cogens* – a body of higher rules of public international law binding, so it claimed, on all subjects including the bodies of the United

Nations.[117] Reminiscent of *Marbury v. Madison* in the American constitutional tradition, the court asserted its jurisdiction to conduct such review (indirectly reviewing the Security Council itself), even if it went on to determine that no *jus cogens* rights were violated in this particular case.[118]

According to one commentator, the judgment represents a picture of a regional organization at once faithful and subordinate to – yet simultaneously constituting itself as an independent check upon – the powers exercised in the name of the international community under the UN Charter.[119] Accordingly, the assertion of *jus cogens* was intended to demonstrate deference to the international legal order and subordination of EU treaty law to the higher law of that order to which it belongs. In short, the court positioned itself as an organ of the international legal system under a single global hierarchy of public international law.

This so-called *dédoublement fonctionelle* of the Court – as an organ both of the European legal order *and* of the globalized international legal order – was a striking move.[120] It treated the legal order coupled to the global political system as if it already constituted a unified, monist, and hierarchical system with higher norms of constitutional quality, binding all other domestic legal orders or treaty organizations, deemed to be integrated parts of that order.[121] In this respect it indirectly confronts the Security Council's step into a legislative role and the concomitant direct impact of its legislative resolutions on individuals and states; it placed itself on the same constitutional plane. I see the "Marbury" move as a classic exercise in "political justice" – an attempt through adjudication to foster the further integration/constitutionalization of the international legal order, and to assert the Court's own power within such a system.[122] At the same time, the Court appeared to be a good citizen of the international legal system.

One problem with this move, apart from the fact that it gave no relief to Kadi, is that if other courts followed this reasoning they would reduce the constitutional standards for global governance institutions to a minimum, for very few international norms have or are likely to attain a *jus cogens* status. The Court designated the right to a fair hearing, to judicial process, and to property as *jus cogens* norms but denied that they had been arbitrarily violated in this case, given the humanitarian exceptions the 1267 invocation allows, and given the security considerations at issue.[123] The generous reading of *jus cogens* rights was complemented by a stingy application. Given debates over which norms have the status of *jus cogens*, and given the fact that no court can simply decide this on its own, this was a startling and much criticized move.[124]

There are two additional problems – conceptual and normative – with this approach to the relations among legal orders. First, the Court reasoned from a standpoint of a systemic (UN-centered) hierarchical global constitutionalism that does not yet exist. Second, by treating the EU as an ordinary international treaty organization, subordinate to and fully permeable by the higher norms and rules of public international law, it ignored and even tended to undermine the constitutional quality and unique political form of the legal-political order of the European Union that does in fact exist.

To act as if the EU and by implication domestic courts of other countries are already organs of a cosmopolitan legal order and global legal-political community whose core values and institutional structure are already constitutionalized and thus directly binding on all actors is a paradigmatic example of "symbolic constitutionalism" – the invocation of the normative plus that constitutionalist discourse carries in an inappropriate context, thereby cloaking power relations in universalistic garb. This approach undermines the link between the courts of a particular political community and both domestic political processes and internal constitutionalist structures – along with the legitimacy those courts enjoy flowing from them – in the name of a higher legitimacy that in my view is lacking. This is especially disturbing in the case of polities enjoying democratic legitimacy. Such an approach prevents autonomous courts from undoing the constitutionalism- and democracy-eviscerating effects of global governance described above. In short, the structure of the global legal-political system at present does not warrant such deference when it comes to Security Council legislative resolutions that directly impact individuals and violate their most basic due process rights. Contrary to the CFI's approach, it is not up to a domestic or regional court to produce the missing legitimacy.

On the other hand, the autonomous, constitutional and constitutionalist status of the EU legal order within the European Union has been insisted upon by the ECJ for years and has been accepted by member states.[125] The complex dynamic that simultaneously distinguishes and integrates the legal order of the EU with those of member states internally has been analyzed by many from the internal perspective. Surely the fact that it is an integrated legal order in which the validity of EU law also means immediate validity within member states' national legal orders (direct effect) makes this a distinctive legal and political formation. However, as others have noted, the constitutionalist integrity of the Union also has perforce an external dimension that entails its autonomy and self-determination internationally.[126]

5.7.2   The "sovereigntist" analysis of the ECJ: the primacy of domestic constitutionalism and the revival of dualism?

The ECJ took the opposite approach from the CFI and proceeded with its review in light of the fundamental rights guarantees found among the general principles of EC law, and determined that Kadi's rights to be heard, and to effective due process, were violated. The Court annulled the relevant regulations.[127]

The arguments the Grand Chamber of the ECJ deployed in favor of review were based on a constitutionalist understanding of the nature of the EC and its relation to international law. Instead of treating it as just another international treaty organization – porous and subordinate to the binding dictates of the Security Council – the Court construed the EC's legal order as an autonomous one of constitutionalist quality.[128] Accordingly, the EC is based on the rule of law, equipped with a complete system of legal remedies and procedures such that neither member states nor its own organs can avoid review of the conformity of their acts with its "constitutional charter."[129] The Court rejected the idea that an international treaty – the UN Charter – could affect the internal constitutional allocation of powers, the autonomy of the EC legal system, or its core constitutional principles (which include fundamental rights) in any way.[130] It thus rested its case squarely on the internal requirements of the integrity of the EC's legal order construed as distinct and independent from public international law and asserted the primacy and autonomy of its core constitutional principles.[131] The Court held national and EC executives responsible for the implementing legislation and itself capable of reviewing that legislation when basic rights and the fundamental principles of EC constitutionalism are at issue.

The Court insisted that "obligations imposed by an international agreement cannot have the effect of prejudicing the constitutional principles of the EC Treaty."[132] From this internal perspective, the ECJ reinvents itself as a domestic constitutional court, taking yet another step in fostering the evolution of the supremacy and direct effect of the constitutionalist European legal order with respect to its member states.

On the external axis, the Court solidified the autonomous status of the European legal order by treating it as one of constitutional(-ist) quality whose completeness and integrity preclude unreviewable intrusion by the international legal order or by any international agreement of member states that affects the fundamental principles of that order. Indeed it went so far as to argue that, even if the obligations imposed by the UN Charter were to be seen as part of a hierarchy of norms within the EC legal order, they would be secondary in rank to the EC's constitutional principles.[133] Clearly, the Court assumed an asymmetry in the nature of the distinct legal (and political) orders involved.

Unlike the approach of the CFI, the Grand Chamber did not reason as if a monist global public international legal order of constitutional quality already exists, whose highest norms and institutions can claim unconditional supremacy with respect to its member states or regional orders. It seemed to opt instead for a classical dualist stance, insofar as it rested its case squarely on the internal requirements of integrity of the European constitutional legal order – and asserted the primacy and autonomy of European constitutional law over public international law.

This decision has been hailed by some as a victory for human rights against executive predation justified in the name of global security and the war on terror.[134] But others have criticized it for its alleged revival of classical dualist (today, legal pluralist) arguments regarding the relation among legal orders.[135] The Court's reasoning appears sovereigntist in the old-fashioned sense.[136] Its allegedly inward-looking stance and "dualist" logic is seen as bad international citizenship coming at a high price: it impugns the EU's image as a law-abiding international actor, and it dims the prospects that this regional order and its courts might play a role in building a global constitutionalism of shared values and principles via inter-institutional dialogue.[137] By eschewing direct engagement with the international legal order, the decision allegedly fails to come to grips with the innovations in global governance in a constructive way and instead takes a parochial stance sealing off the European order from the rest of the international system.[138] It thus allegedly exacerbates the legitimacy problematic at the heart of that system in which the EU is, despite its dualist pretensions, nonetheless situated.[139] Others defending the dualist strand of the decision argue that it is not the responsibility of a constitutionally based jurisdiction to instruct the institutions of other entities whether or not they adhere to their own legal standards.[140]

All of these assessments obviously draw on (and are trapped in) the dichotomy described in Chapter 1 of this book: either there is a single (monist) international legal order of constitutional quality to whose higher norms and decisions the EU and member states must defer, or one embraces the dualist/legal pluralist stance and protects one's own constitutionalist values come what may. Neither approach offers much help in resolving the legitimacy problems at issue. Is there another way to consider the matter?

5.7.3   The case for constitutional pluralism

There is, and it was articulated by then Advocate General Miguel Poiares Maduro in his opinion delivered to the ECJ upon Kadi's appeal of the CFI's judgment.[141] It was Maduro's argument, adopted by the Grand Chamber, that the appropriate way to address the relation between the international system and the EC is to proceed from the assumption that the latter is an autonomous legal order "beholden to" but "distinct from" public international law.[142] He thus insisted that the primary obligation of the ECJ, the constitutional court of the EC, is to enforce its constitutional law.

But fully aware of the interdependence and increased communication among the plurality of globalizing legal orders in the international system, and of the potential external impact of an ECJ decision, Maduro's opinion was not purely inward-looking. It articulated a strategic, communicative stance with respect to the outside while denying that non-compliance would amount to judicial review of Security Council resolutions or entail extra-systemic jurisdiction on the part of the EU.[143] Maduro noted the presumption that the EC wants to honor its international commitments and insisted that his analysis does not mean that the EC's "municipal" legal order and the international legal order pass by each other "like ships in the night."[144] It explicitly addressed the deficiencies of the Security Council processes in its legislative initiatives and resolutions involving targeted sanctions, noting that annulment of the implementing legislation in the EU could have a positive political consequence of prodding the United Nations, in the face of likely other legal challenges and threats of non-compliance, to respect the basic human rights principles of due process.[145] But the legal effects of an ECJ ruling would remain confined to the EC.[146]

While Maduro's reasoning obviously influenced the ECJ, it was clearly informed by the premises of a constitutional pluralist analysis, rather than a cosmopolitan monist or a sovereigntist dualist one. Though his opinion ultimately reached a conclusion similar to that of the Grand Chamber, due to its distinctive underlying conceptual framework, it was more open to dialogue with the international legal system and to spurring its further constitutionalization – without, however, sacrificing the rights of the plaintiff. However, it is also clear that Maduro understood that the necessary institutional preconditions for a viable constitutional pluralist relationship among the EU's legal order, the globalizing international legal order in general, and that of the UN Charter system in particular are lacking at present.[147] Hence the hopes that reform on the international level might follow from a challenge by the ECJ to the validity of the measures implementing the rights-violating resolutions of the Security Council.[148]

Throughout his opinion Maduro refers to the treaties constituting the EC as its basic "constitutional charter" – one that constituted an autonomous legal and political community, an approach followed by the ECJ. The Community's constitutional treaties, unlike the intergovernmental European human rights convention, have founded a *legal and political order* in which states and individuals have immediate rights and obligations. The direct effect of EC legislation also distinguishes it from the legal and political order established by the Convention. The complex polity that is the EU is thus deemed by Maduro to be different in kind from the organization constituted by the ECHR. The latter is an international law treaty "designed to operate primarily as an interstate agreement that creates obligations between the contracting Parties at the international level." It is not a "constitutional charter" that constitutes and articulates the law of a polity.[149] In Maduro's words, this means that the ECJ is designed to be and has a duty to act as the constitutional court of the "municipal" legal order or *polity* of transnational dimensions – that is, the EC as regards its jurisdiction *ratione personae* and as regards the relationship of the autonomous legal system of the Community to public international law.[150] It was Maduro's argument, also adopted by the

Court, that the "constitutional charter" of the EC established a complete system of legal remedies and procedures designed to enable the ECJ to review the legality of acts of the institutions of the Community and that its constitutional treaty and its law thus enjoy the same autonomy as any municipal legal order.[151]

This sounds like a classical dualist interpretation of the relation between the autonomous "municipal" legal order of the EC and international law, indistinguishable from the one ultimately put forth by the ECJ. However, Maduro's argument is more nuanced than this and rests on a different conceptual framework. Unlike the latter, Maduro articulated a conditional, alternative conceivable relationship between the EC legal order and that of the United Nations. He argued that neither Article 103 nor Chapter VII Security Council resolutions preclude EC courts from reviewing domestic implementing measures to assess their conformity with fundamental rights, *so long as* the United Nations does not provide a mechanism of independent judicial review that guarantees compliance with fundamental rights.[152]

Had there been a genuine and effective mechanism of judicial control by an independent tribunal at the level of the United Nations, this might have released the EC from the obligation to provide for judicial control of implementing measures that apply within the EC legal order.[153] However, as the system governing the functioning of the United Nations *now* stands, the only option available to individuals who seek access to an independent tribunal so as to gain adequate protection of their fundamental rights is to challenge domestic implementing measures before a domestic court.[154] Under these circumstances, the relationship between international law and the EC legal order must be governed by the EC legal order itself, "and international law can permeate that legal order only under the conditions set by the constitutional principles of the Community."[155] This stance is itself premised on the assumption that the human rights at issue – due process rights, rights to a fair hearing, property rights – are not idiosyncratic features of a single jurisdiction. They are universal, as the relevant international human rights documents and the UN Charter indicate: thus it is incumbent on all legal orders to institutionalize and protect them in the appropriate manner.[156] At the present time, however, given the fact that neither the global political system generally nor the UN Charter system in particular is sufficiently integrated or adequately constitutionalized, given the absence of legal remedies on these levels, unquestioning deference to the international legal order(s) is unwarranted.

The Advocate General clearly meant to evoke the well-known "Solange" jurisprudence of the German Federal Constitutional Court (GFCC) that conditions the supremacy of EU law on the degree to which it secures an equivalent respect for fundamental constitutional rights to that which exists in the domestic constitutions of member states.[157] In the case that became known as "Solange 1," the GFCC famously reserved for German courts the right to review EC acts for their conformity with the German Basic Law (*Grundgesetz*) so long as the integration process has not progressed so far that Community law also receives a catalogue of fundamental rights.[158] This prompted the ECJ and the European Community/EU to institutionalize and show greater respect for individual rights, a development which the German Constitutional Court later acknowledged in its Solange II decision. In that judgment it indicated that it would no longer review European measures so long as rights continued to be effectively ensured at the European level. It did not, however, renounce its ultimate authority regarding fundamental rights or the ultimate supremacy of the German constitution.[159] The logic of this jurisprudence was to foster the highest level of individual rights and constitutionalist, rule of law protections within all the relevant legal orders. While some fear that the "constitutional pluralist" approach this jurisprudence apparently initiated is dangerously centrifugal and dissociative, others have pointed to the dialogic dimension it opens up among the relevant legal actors and its integrative potential.[160] At issue is the threat to the uniformity of law and implementation of EU or UN resolutions posed by insistence on domestic constitutional supremacy, on the one hand, and the threat to fundamental constitutionalist principles if unconditional hierarchy were accepted, on the other. But if reference is to the highest level of protection of human rights that are acknowledged in the relevant legal orders, then the judicial suspension of an external legal obligation is not solipsistic but rather meant to trigger an equivalent level of protection among the relevant interconnected but not hierarchically related legal orders and to initiate dialogue among the respective judicial organs.[161]

As I indicated in Chapter 1 of this book, the theory of constitutional pluralism was developed to account for this dialogic mutually accommodating practice of constitutional tolerance and cooperation among autonomous legal orders and organs (courts) within the overarching shared legal order of the EU.[162] The "Solange" approach is theorized as a dynamic process that involves conflict and contestation (the pluralist dimension) but also initiates dialogue and cooperation among legal actors and organs with a view toward fostering reciprocity and legal resolution on the basis of shared constitutionalist (basic rights, rule of law) standards that are or should be common to all jurisdictions (the constitutionalist dimension). It is also predicated on sovereign equality among the member states of the Union. Accordingly it fosters an integrative and reflexive, not a dissociative logic based on parochial understandings. Indeed this dialogic interpretation of constitutional pluralism is "juris-generative."

This is not the approach of a dualist or of a traditional sovereigntist. However, any attempt to analogize the ECJ's Kadi decision with the "Solange" jurisprudence of the GFCC, is, nonetheless, premature.[163] For what Maduro's argumentation and the decision of the ECJ (which did not use the Solange language) indicate is that in the absence of an appropriate interlocutor – an international court with jurisdiction to review Security Council legislation and enforce human rights – a conflict between the two legal orders could hardly be avoided or resolved through constitutional toleration or judicial comity.[164] Human rights exist in the Charter system and in the international legal order generally. What is missing, among other things, is an appropriate independent body (court), which could serve as an interlocutor for domestic or EU courts. The absence of a suitable dialogue partner on the international level is one reason why the Solange logic cannot simply be ratcheted up to the next level.

By implication, the theory and practice of constitutional pluralism as developed within the EU (where national courts can and do double as EU courts, dialogue with and cite the ECJ and one another) that characterizes the relations among the autonomous yet interconnected legal orders of the member states and the EU legal order is not yet applicable or appropriate to the globalizing international political system. The legal order of the UN Charter system is neither sufficiently integrated with national legal orders or with that of the EU – there is no direct effect operative between them – nor is it adequately constitutionalized for the kind of deference especially by domestic constitutional courts to supranational bodies that Solange II, still conditionally, accepts. Until it is, the primary obligation of the constitutional court of an autonomous legal order is to protect the latter's own liberal-democratic constitutionalist principles if the effect of a norm or act under international law severely conflicts with those principles. To do so, however, is not to indulge in idiosyncratic solipsistic behavior or to exit the international system. Rather, given the likelihood (and reality today) of other legal challenges and instances of non-compliance in the name of constitutionalism and human rights being triggered by this decision, it may well foster a general political debate and a constitutionalist response on the international level.

To be sure, no regional or domestic court can declare a resolution of the Security Council invalid, or legally null and void for all member states. But every member state of the UN can declare implementation of a resolution impossible within its own territory as can a regional organization such as the ECJ did in Kadi 1, thus indirectly reviewing the Council's legislative decisions. After all, members of the UN are sovereign states in the international system and thus their non-compliance, as well as the non-compliance of a regional constitutional order like the EU, remains the most significant "external" check on the arbitrariness and overreaching of the UNSC, the key organ of what remains in key respects an international organization created by states.[165] This feature pertains to the legitimacy dimension of the analysis. The aim, however, of the analysis of the Advocate General and the decision of the ECJ in Kadi 1 was both to protect constitutionalist principles enshrined in the EU legal order and its member states, *and* to incite the further respect for human rights and perhaps even trigger the further constitutionalization of the international legal order of the UN Charter system. The hope is that this would better protect international human rights and other constitutionalist (rule of law) principles put at risk by the highest executive body in the international system – the UN Security Council – made up, after all, of state executives focused on security rather than human rights, as the relevant resolutions indicate.

Indeed, the ECJ's decision did address the Security Council insofar as it indicated what would be necessary in order for a court of a constitutionalist, rights-respecting rule of law system to accept the supremacy and direct impact on individuals of the Security Council's acts. Both the ECJ and the Advocate General noted the presumption that the EU wants to honor its international commitments.[166] But given that the CTC and the 1267 Committee created by the Security Council are bodies coordinating security-oriented executives, designed precisely to bypass domestic constitutional due process provisions and limit judicial review, this "dialogue" is different in kind from what occurs between constitutional courts situated within an encompassing legal order of constitutional quality.[167]

5.8 Internal and external pluralism: the issue of political form

The distinction between the "internal constitutional" and "external legal" pluralism made by Maduro in a different context is helpful for reflection on the legitimacy basis for the juridical and political practice of constitutional pluralism.[168] Internal constitutional pluralism refers to a plurality of constitutional orders and sources internal to an overarching legal (and political) order without a determinate hierarchical relationship among them. It involves the coexistence of several political communities *within* a specific overarching political community of communities each of which has its own legal order of constitutional quality. As indicated in Chapter 1, the EU is the key referent of the discourse and practice of internal constitutional pluralism.[169] As argued above, its multiple autonomous constitutional orders, sites of norm creation, and power coexist within an overarching order of orders, coordinated, according to this theory, in a "heterarchical" manner. The internal legal pluralism of the EU thus involves a plurality of constitutional sources whose interrelation cannot be analyzed in monist or dualist terms.

To be sure, it is part of the dynamics of internal constitutional pluralism that each constitutional legal order sees itself as autonomous and supreme. From the internal legal/normative perspective of the constitutional order of each member state, the reason why the rules of the EU are directly effective, enforced, and supreme is ultimately that the member state's constitutional order has accepted its rule-making capacity and supremacy given the appropriate provisos. From the perspective of the autonomous constitutional legal order of the EU, however, its own rules are supreme in its relevant domain and that is why they are directly binding on and effective in national courts. The internal perspective of each is perforce, initially at least, "monist." But from the external sociological or theoretical perspective, these are legally, indeed constitutionally interconnected albeit distinct constitutional orders in a dynamic non-hierarchical relationship with one another. *Reflexivity* on the part of participants allows for a dynamic understanding of the non-hierarchical, yet not disorderly, legal relationship among the legal orders informed by an ethic of political responsibility and constitutional toler-ance.[170] In other words, the legal actors (courts, jurists) are themselves aware of the complex interrelation among the legal systems they are involved in and that their interpretations regarding legal answers (what the law is) must take this into account. They adopt the Hartian "internal attitude" toward the community's legal order and to their own. This is the way to meet the objections of those who believe constitutional pluralism is oxymoronic and incompatible with legality because law is 'intrinsically monistic,' and thus precludes negotiation with others regarding ultimate authority by a supreme juridical instance.[171] Reflexivity means that juridical actors in the EU know their legal systems are imbricated: and that these legal orders must be seen as simultaneously open and closed to one another.[172]

In such a context – where constitutional pluralism is internal to a legal order supported by its own political community – the various courts inside that community see themselves as bound *both* by their particular legal order and by the broader legal order in which they are also situated.[173] When they have to double as organs of the international community and as organs of the member state, courts have a serious responsibility. The duty of a domestic court within a transnational *polity* such as the EU is to frame arguments that challenge an EU law or decision in general terms, invoking substantive norms that are held also to be applicable on the general level even while referring to the autonomy of its own legal order.[174] The duty of the highest court of the Union, correspondingly, is to so interpret norms such that they mesh with the best composite understanding of rights and constitutionalist principles among its member states.[175] However, these legal relationships and "obliga-tions" are based on an underlying political legitimacy, not only on inter-judicial cooperation and coordination.

Clearly this approach – and the very ideas of constitutional tolerance and internal constitutional pluralism – is predicated on a background political culture of mutual accommodation and compromise. Thus as the response to Solange I indicates, the political actors of the EU developed a rights-based legal order that comports with the key foundational elements of normative orders of the member states, adjusting to the liberal and republican constitu-tionalist principles their various constitutions require.[176] But it is important to see that this political achievement is itself predicated on a political reality:

membership within and commitment to a discrete, overarching political community of communities. The distinctive political form of the EU is not named by Maduro in his advisory opinion. But his deployment of the international law concept of a "municipal order" of transnational dimensions is certainly more evocative of the concept of a federation of states than it is of an international treaty organization.[177] Of course, as others have pointed out, the European Union is a complex hybrid – a union of states composed of institutional arrangements partly typical of international organizations and partly typical of federal states; it has constitutional arrangements typical of federations of states and/or of confederations (depending on one's taxonomy); and a level of material integration evocative of a federal state.[178] The EU has an autonomous legal order and a Court charged with policing its boundaries and judging the "constitutionality" of measures taken by its organs. Whatever our assessment of the constitutionalist quality of the hybrid structure that is the EU and whatever are its legitimation problems, the EU is certainly not a state. Nor, however, is it an ordinary international organization with the usual meaning. One can point to the broad scope of issues and objects under its purview, its dense organizational structure comprising all the branches of government typical of a state, and the intensity of effects its operations and law directly and indirectly have on member states and citizens, as well as the complex net of legal norms and the status of the treaties constituting the EU as higher law, as indications of this lack of fit with the category of international organization.[179]

However, it is also clear that the EU receives its legal foundation from its member states, which remain masters of the treaties, and that its legal order is not the expression of the self-determination of "the people" about the form and substance of their political union that, on some analyses, are typical of the modern state.[180] Thus, reasoning from this political perspective it appears to some analysts that the EU's legal order is not a constitution in the full modern sense: republican, democratic, or even liberal (Grimm). Others who analyze the EU as a highly integrated international organization (de Witte) or as a complex hybrid (Weiler) also deny that it has a constitution (the former) because it is not a federal state, or insist that it already has a constitution (the latter) but understand that term in a legalistic and relative narrow sense (treaties as constitutive documents of the Union) and argue against any new constitutional project because that would apparently undermine the sovereignty of member states and mutual tolerance between them and the legal and political order of the EU that exists within this functioning hybrid.[181] They too fear that the step toward constitutionalization would entail the step toward a federal state, which may end up as a lose/lose proposition: i.e. a loss of the genuine achievements of constitutionalism on the domestic level and the failure to compensate for these on the level of a federal European superstate.

For my purposes, two conceptual points are worth emphasizing here. First, what makes the stance and practice of internal constitutional pluralism conceivable in this context is the distinctive character of the EU, which (however complex and hybrid its actual institutional and behavioral aspects are) *renders the external internal*: relations among member states of the EU with respect to EU law, institutions, and public policies are understandable not as international but as internal relations. The treaties constituting the EU do have constitutional quality in many respects and constitute today an autonomous legal and political order integrated with domestic legal orders and bound up with a political project of forming an "ever closer" union among the peoples of Europe. Indeed, I agree with Maduro's most recent formulation:

> we can conceive of the EU and national legal orders as autonomous but part of the same European legal system. For those practicing law in Europe, this European legal system implies a commitment to both legal orders and imposes an obligation to accommodate and integrate their respective claims.[182]

This entails construing constitutional pluralism in the EU as a pluralism of constitutional claims of authority within an overarching legal order rather than as a simple pluralism of legal orders (EU and national).

But this does not mean that one would have to construe the EU as a federal *state* or that the political community subtending the legal community of the EU is a supranational demos composed directly of individuals. Rather, it means that the political community is composed of multiple political communities, or multiple demoi.[183] Understanding themselves and acting as members of an overarching legal and political union of states and as involved in a common project toward an ever closer union, in addition to the requirement that all member states be constitutional democracies, constitutes the political context in which internal constitutional pluralism in Maduro's sense is possible and productive instead of disintegrative.[184]

Second, for this all to make sense, however, I argue that one would have to analyze the EU from the lens of federal theory and break with the dichotomous political and legal framework that the international law term "municipal" carries with it. Accordingly the overarching legal order within which national and EU legal orders are situated would be that of the Federation, as conceptualized in Chapter 2. As we have seen, I contend that *ideal-typically* the political formation to which constitutional pluralism is the appropriate legal analogue is neither a state (not even a federal state) nor an international treaty organization but a union of states combining international and domestic legal features in a complex structure that is found to greater or lesser degrees in all federal unions.[185] The binary choice between monism and dualism, between domestic and international, and between treaty and constitution is transcended in such a structure. My point is not to argue that the EU already is a federation today or that member states have committed themselves to the creation of a federal union – that was, for some, the project of the failed constitutional moment of 2004.[186] Instead my point is that one should make use of the taxonomy developed in Chapter 2 to assess the distinctive features of the complex hybrid that the EU is today, in order to think through the vicissitudes of constitutional pluralist discourses and practices regarding it as well as legitimacy problems peculiar to the specific form of this Union and what to do about them. Reasoning from the lens of federation theory, in other words, would allow for a clear (comparative) assessment of the structure, logic, and possible paths of development for this specific political formation without cabin-ing it in a statist discourse that is inappropriate to it or renouncing theoretical reflection by deeming it "sui generis." The theoretical framework of federation theory could shed new light on debates over legitimation problems and dysfunctional institutional features of this and other unions (including, I shall argue, the UN Organization) engaging in regional or global governance, and suggest a range of alternatives screened out by the statist perspective.[187]

For those who remain wed to the statist model, however (most notably Dieter Grimm and Martin Loughlin), any discourse of constitutionalism (including constitutional pluralism) for non-state orders including even the EU is inappropriate at present and inadvisable for the future, unless one intends thereby to turn the EU into a federal state.[188] Reasoning from a qualitative, normative constitutionalist perspective, Grimm correctly insists that the discourse of constitutionalism is distinct from and more demanding than that of the juridification or legalization of public power. He also grants that of all the extant "international organizations" the EU comes closest to the five features of a modern constitution genetically linked to the modern state that constitute its normative "achievement."[189] Nevertheless, there are important deficiencies in the hybrid organization that is the EU in his view that vitiate any meaningful constitutionalist discourse with respect to it as things now stand. Most crucial is the fact that (a) "... the Treaties are not an expression of the self-determination of a people or a society about the form and substance of their political union," and (b) "... the EU does not decide upon its own legal foundation."[190] Both of these deficiencies mean that the treaties constituting the Union do not and cannot enjoy the democratic legitimacy or core structural features that characterize a constitution. With respect to the latter the key test is the amendment rule: "... if the amendment power remains in the hands of the member states and is exercised in the manner of treaties, the transition from treaty to constitution has not taken place."[191] Needless to say, this step has not occurred because the amendment rule for the treaties is based on the principle of unanimity rather than qualified majority. Sovereign equality does describe the relation among member states of the EU, unlike the UN, but insofar as each state has a veto the former remains a treaty organization rather than a constitutionalist polity. Since it is not the result of a process wherein the subjects of the legal order, the people, are construable as a demos determining its own form of political existence, the EU also lacks on the deepest level the democratic legitimacy that characterizes each of its member states and which today goes hand-in-hand with constitutionalism in his view.

Indeed, according to Grimm, the EU faces the following distressing conundrum: the more the EU intervenes in and takes over functions of its member states, the more it undermines the loci of the real achievements of democratic constitutionalism. But, he insists, the solution of "constitutionalization" of the EU, unless the step were taken to turn it into a fully fledged federal state, cannot compensate for the loss of importance and relevance of state level democratic constitutionalism and democratic legitimacy.[192] Only a step to a federal state would give the EU (via its federal demos), the power of self-determination (even if the member states retain a share in the decision of the new entity as they do in most federal states), and only then would its legal foundation turn into a constitution.[193] In this sense the EU is an appropriate object of constitutionalization discourse because it has reached the point (internal political homogeneity and integration) where such a step is conceivable. However, Grimm is not at all convinced that the step to a federal state and formal democratization of the EU would be accompanied by a gain in "substantive democracy" or that a European demos exists (or would come to exist) to whom the constitution of such a state could be ascribed. He thus prefers to abandon constitutionalist discourse altogether for the supranational domain, with respect to the EU or any other object.[194] Indeed according to Grimm it is wrong to distinguish between two types of constitutions – the liberal (rule of law) type and the democratic/republican type – as equally realizing the achievement of constitutionalism. Only a synthetic liberal-democratic constitution is capable of fulfilling the highest expectations of constitutionalism and any discourse that settles for less cheapens the meaning of constitution.[195] Thus the discourse of internal constitutional pluralism referencing a political and legal community that is not a state has no place in this approach.

It should be immediately striking to the reader that this analysis remains trapped in the binaries of the statist paradigm discussed in Chapter 2. It screens out entirely the third alternative that this book began with, namely the ideal type of a federal union of states that is not itself a state (with a broad spectrum of more or less integrated forms) and thus fails to adequately assess the unique features of the discourse and theory of constitutional pluralism vis-à-vis legality and legitimacy pertaining to federal unions of states. Without going into detail so as to avoid repetition with respect to Chapter 2, a federal union that is not a state ideal-typically is constituted by a constitutional treaty with an amendment rule that includes the states under a qualified majority structure. The states remain the sources of constitutional change but are within and under the constitutional treaty of the Union because, unlike the amendment rule of an international organization, the majority can bind the minority. However, unlike the ideal-typical amendment rule of a federal state, the majority that binds is not 51 percent of the citizenry of the federal union: there is no second track involving individualized voting (one person–one vote) alongside voting by state as in a federal senate, the typical dual structure of a federal state's rule for constitutional change. Recall that a federal union of states that is not a state would have, as I argued in Chapter 2, a compound demos composed of the demoi (constituent powers) of each member state, based on the principle of sovereign equality such that no single state (or subgroup of states) has the power to determine the political form or legal foundation or scope of the federation. Conceptually such a federal union is not a state although its legal foundation has constitutional quality and its powers of self-determination do exist, albeit in a restricted form. It thus does not undermine democratic legitimacy within member states and it has its own distinctive form of legitimacy (sovereign equality internally, thus equal standing and voice within) that is indeed constitutionalist.

The constitutive dualistic structure of federal unions discussed in Chapter 2 and the all-important deferral of the sovereignty question internally means that the member states are not outside the constitutional treaty that creates the federal union, but nor are they non-sovereign subordinate entities. Instead, sovereignty does not describe the everyday relations among the units within the Union and much of the practice of constitutional pluralism, cooperation, communication, and conditional deference among the units aims at avoidance: i.e. to prevent the sovereignty question from arising. Constitutional pluralism is the theoretical stance that fits this sort of constitutional politics. It presupposes a dual commitment to the political community created by the federal constitutional treaty and to the distinct autonomous political communities to whom member states' constitutions are ascribed. In international society, however, member states remain autonomous sovereign states.

Grimm is right: the EU as it now exists is a potential object of constitutionalization if one thinks of its range of competences, its increasing comprehensive scope, the density of its structure, the intensity of its effects on individual citizens, and so forth. He is also right that the step to constitutionalization in the future would have to involve a political act whereby the member states agree to give up their power to determine singly (each with a veto) the legal foundation of the EU. But he is wrong to assume this would have to mean that the latter thereby would become a federal state. Instead it could mean making the commitment explicitly to become a federation: a non-state federal union of states.[196] Thus far this explicit political commitment has not been made by the "demoi" of the member states of the EU. But, given its internal political homogeneity (all member states are and are required to be liberal constitutional democracies), if the political will were there, the democratic legitimacy of the EU could be greatly enhanced were an appropriate political process to be set up that would enable such a transition. Depending on the content of the new constitutional treaty/federal constitution, and the relations it establishes with member states, the democratic legitimacy of the latter would not be undermined but most likely strengthened insofar as mechanisms to prevent executive discretion at the expense of parliaments and courts could be established for all levels. Such political commitment to the Union's "further constitutionalization" would also ground the practice of internal constitutional pluralism more firmly in political legitimacy. This would be the normative plus of such a step: citizens, and their representatives, in addition to judicial actors, would thenceforth alter their internal perspective of their legal and political order to include the claims of the supranational or federal legal order as also their own. Thus if members (peoples) of the EU were to decide to take the step to a closer union, i.e. to embrace the idea of federation and a federal constitutional treaty with an appropriate amendment rule, explicitly through a special procedure of discussion, deliberation, and ratification perhaps through state conventions, then the referent of internal constitutional pluralist discourse would be even more securely and legitimately in place because political and not only legal actors would be committed to it.[197] The theoretical point here is that constitutionalization in this political sense of re-founding, i.e. creation of a new constitutional treaty ratified by the demoi of member states, would not ipso facto turn the Union into a federal state. But it would constitute a new *constitutional* treaty henceforth ascribable to a "new" compound demos comprised of the multiple demoi of the member states as a composite constituent power preferably with an amendment rule in which the majority (of demoi) can bind henceforth the minority.

The federal lens thus provides a way to respond to those who criticize the discourse of constitutionalization on the supranational level as apolitical legalism, while taking into account the important link between a constitution and a political community (a politically constituted people).[198] This link need not, as in the case of a state, be territorially bounded: in a federal political community composed of political communities (peoples), as we have seen, borders are constitutively open to extension and porous to the citizens of co-states.

This would not have to mean that the constitutional claim of the Federation would be identical to that of member states. As already indicated in Chapter 2, the former's constitutionalism need not involve comprehensiveness regarding competences or functional scope. As Grimm rightly argues in my view, domestic or national political communities remain the best forum for democratic constitutionalism. But as others have also pointed out, a federal union can also contribute to the realization of certain democratic values such as helping national democracies to collectively regain control over transnational processes, expanding the myopic scope of national democracies to include ex ante consideration of the impact of their decisions on those affected in member states and to control for negative externalities by giving voice to those concerned, and by providing for the protection of minority rights and avenues for minority voices at the federal level that might otherwise be ignored domestically.[199] Constitutional pluralism typical of a federation adds the division of powers and legal orders to the pluralism traditionally associated with state-level democratic constitutionalism, namely, the separation of powers and the pluralism of interpretations of law and of instances authorized to make these interpretations. This is standard fare for a federal constitutional order. Once we abandon the ideas of apex and organ sovereignty, it becomes evident that modern democratic constitutionalism is intrinsically pluralist thanks to its principle of legitimacy, which precludes locating sovereignty in any single constituted instance and which institutes a circular process regarded as the final authoritative locus of law-making.[200]

Given the highly integrated although perhaps increasingly dysfunctional hybrid nature of the EU, the internal constitutional pluralist frame makes sense right now, although the quality and legitimacy of the EU "constitution" could surely be improved. Certainly the constitutional pluralist frame is the most helpful in theorizing the fact that national courts are now tied both to the national and the EU legal orders and are thus part of a European legal system composed of both the EU and national legal orders.[201] Yet, every empirical political formation is a hybrid of some sort. As already indicated above, the legitimacy of the Union would certainly be enhanced for its citizens if a path to political self-determination opened up, such that they could see themselves as the authors (qua composite demoi, constituent powers) of the political and legal order whose subjects they already are. Even without such a step, the discourse of internal constitutional pluralism helps make sense of the communicative practices of courts and other actors within the Union and is no more inappropriate than the discourse of international law associated with treaty organizations.

However, the same stance is inappropriate in a context of the external pluralism characteristic of the global political system in general and the UN Charter system in particular, at this time. There is increased juridification of the international political system and the emergence of a new layer and a new form of law: so-called humanity law that brings together the humanitarian law of war, and human rights law focused on persons and peoples rather than sovereignty and states.[202] Nevertheless, and despite increased communication and coordination among the proliferating juridical actors and legal orders on the world scene, there is no order of orders supported by commitment to a

new global political community, there is little democratic legitimacy underlying the Charter system, the latter has no Court that is an appropriate
interlocutor regarding constitutional questions, and there is surely no democratic conditionality for membership. Heterogeneity characterizes the political regimes of member states. International human rights law lacks the
efficacy of and does not serve the same function as fundamental rights
protection within the EU. The SC's "enforcement" of humanity law is selective
and its own terror-listing practices undermine important human rights and
constitutionalist principles. Given the absence of a Court within the UN
Charter system able to compulsorily rule on constitutionality of acts of UN
organs, or to review measures that violate individual rights, the discourse of
internal constitutional pluralism or even the rule of law makes little sense for
this domain. Here we confront external legal pluralism, not internal constitutional pluralism. In such a context, domestic constitutional courts are
bound by the particular constitutional order of the political community
which has directly delegated competence to them for constitutional review
and from which they derive their legitimacy. Of course, in an increasingly
interdependent world, different legal orders will have to endeavor to accommodate each other's jurisdictional claims and judicial coordination among
existing supranational courts and tribunals can be rights- and democracy-
reinforcing – as witnessed by the cascading impact of the Kadi case.

Accordingly, "unilateral" non-implementation of Security Council "law" by
a constitutional court is justifiable as a right of resistance when the former
imposes decisions that are manifestly inimical to the principles of domestic or
regional constitutionalist systems as well as the substantive values (human
rights) articulated by the UN Charter itself and international law generally
(in human rights treaties or customary international law). By explicitly
referring to the deficiencies in the international legal system from a constitutionalist perspective, the Kadi 1 judgment clearly meant to prod the relevant
actors to create due process remedies when targeting sanctions directly on
individuals. The aim was obviously not to undermine the international legal
system but to foster its further "constitutionalization" in light of its own
universalistic rule of law principles. The strategic point of the Advocate
General's opinion and of the overall judgment is that a mutually beneficial
cooperative, dialogic, positive-sum game among domestic, regional, and
international orders could (only) become possible with the further constitutionalization of the international legal system – but this would have to mean
the creation of the appropriate new institutions and the redesign of existing
ones within the UN Charter system.

This, however, is a political project: it is not a task for technocrats or legal
experts or courts on their own. A very modest beginning is the creation by the
Security Council in Resolution 1904 (2009) of an ombudsperson to examine
requests from individuals and entities to be taken off the sanctions list: clearly a

response to the increasing reluctance of states to put new names on the list and to the proliferating court challenges to listings. But the power of the ombudsperson falls quite short of an independent review mechanism and there is still no body that can order people or entities to be removed from the terrorist list.

5.9   Conclusion

Nevertheless, and pace Grimm and other skeptics, I argue that the UN Charter system is also an appropriate object for "further constitutionalization" albeit in a different way and to a different extent than regional unions like the EU. The UN Charter is not a world constitution and not only because it does not aggregate all public power exercised on the global level or enjoy anything approximating the comprehensive, concentrated public power of the modern state.[203] The project of constitutionalization of the UN Charter system should not aim at this. Nor should one understand this project as a way to substitute and compensate for the loss of comprehensiveness of state constitutional orders regarding the exercise of public power in their territories and their apparent diminution, from a global perspective, to the status of being partial orders.[204] It is true that today public power and state power are no longer congruent, and that the validity of acts of public authority in states' territory that do not emanate from the state seems to decrease the constitutional legitimacy and limitation of public power as things now stand.[205] It is also true that certain sovereign rights were delegated to the UN so as to create the system of collective security and peace in part because the problem-solving capacity of an international organization surpasses that of single states and transitory alliances. Nonetheless it is a mistake to view the project of constitutionalizing the UN Charter system in terms of an alternative, substitute, or functional equivalent for domestic (democratic) constitutionalism. Instead one must view this project as a way to undo and block the constitutionalism-eviscerating and democracy-undermining effects of the legislative initiatives engaged in by the UN's increasingly activist central enforcement organ, ascribable in part to its flawed institutional design. There may be no substitute on the global level for the normative achievements of democratic constitutionalism on the level of the modern state. But the Charter is the constitutive treaty of the UN Charter system and as such its constitutional quality can surely be improved so as to reinforce rather than undermine domestic (and regional) constitutionalism and the rule of law everywhere. Moreover, insofar as it engages in global governance, insofar as the Charter is deemed a *constitutional* treaty, then the legitimacy of its supremacy claims will increasingly depend on reforms that improve its constitutional quality so that member states can come to see its legal order also as their own in which they have equal standing and voice, and hence to see it as normatively and not only factually legally binding.

It is indeed the case that there is no going back to the Westphalian model of comprehensive and absolute state sovereignty. Nor would that be desirable. However, it is also true that "Public power stands in need of legitimation and limitation regardless of the power-holder."[206] The task before us is thus to imagine a project of constitutionalization of the UN Charter system that undoes the zero-sum dynamic involved in the conundrum aptly identified by Grimm, namely that:

> National constitutions will not regain their capacity to legitimize and regulate comprehensively the public power that takes effect within the territory of the state. The regulation of internationally exercised public power is expanding, but remains a legalization unable to live up to the standard of constitutionalism. Whoever invokes constitutionalism in this connection uses a thin notion of constitutionalism with its democratic element always left out.[207]

I contend that an appropriate reform of the UN Charter system could mediate between these two dynamics and help turn global governance into a positive-sum game for sovereign states in which collective action problems can get resolved without cheapening the meaning of constitutionalism, or destroying the quality and efficacy of domestic democracy. To see this, one has to reason outside the straitjacket of the statist paradigm.

The first step is to undo the features of global governance that strengthen executive discretion at the expense of constitutionalism and democratic and/ or constitutionalism-protecting (legislatures, courts respectively) bodies. This, however, requires a constitutionalist reform of the UN Charter system itself. As we have seen, from the perspective of constitutionalism, the UN Charter system is obviously deficient in the power-limiting sense and in need of some type of a two-pronged (re-)foundational reform: no residues of public power behind the law should remain untouched (requiring transformation of the quasi-absolutist powers of the Security Council's permanent members) and the organs established by the Charter should be adequately regulated by it. Clearly, this would have to entail elimination of the hybrid structure of the UN – a relic of World War Two – by abolishing at least the veto of the permanent five in the amendment rule, thereby extending the two-thirds supermajority threshold to all the members of the General Assembly.[208] This would be a "democratizing" move insofar as it would vindicate the principle of sovereign equality enunciated in the Charter within the UN itself, thus eliminating the worst aspects of legalized hierarchy in the system. The dramatic new legislative role of the Council should be scaled back, as this is not an appropriate organ for global law-making. In addition, the constitutionalization would have to involve creation of a global court(s) with jurisdiction to review rights-violating resolutions that are legislative in character and directly and adversely affect individuals – possibly through some sort of preliminary reference procedure. Some body or mechanism to police the (ideally reformed) dualist constitutional structure established within the UN Charter system is also crucial, especially as it assumes more governance functions.

Such a constitutionalist transformation, were it to occur through the amendment rule of the existing Charter, or through some other appropriate process, could be understood in the republican foundational tradition as an act of political self-determination, ascribable to "we the peoples" of the member states of the United Nations. But the dimensions of that model relevant on the global level are not the idea of revolutionary founding, or the exercise of the "constituent power," as the will of a united and individual-ized global citizenry (a world demos), or as the establishment of a full congruity between the subjects and the authors of global law. The reconsti-tuted albeit still functionally delimited UN Charter system and its key global governance institution would not thereby become a monist constitutional legal or political order or a global state. The dualism between the international society of states and the functionally differentiated world society and inter-national community would still be reflected in the UN Charter system through its reformed constitutional treaty. Its constitutionalization and its relation to the constitutions of member states (and regional polities like the EU) would have to be understood in constitutional pluralist, not monist, terms.

It is debatable whether it makes sense to use the terminology and imaginary of federation for such a project regarding a global functional organization. What is being imagined, to be sure, is a form of political organization in which the members are states (politically organized peoples) rather than individuals but which binds actors on the basis of supermajority rather than unanimity rules of decision-making and amendment, and also clearly depends on the cooperation of the autonomous polities that are its members. But it is questionable how much integration of the global political system is desirable – surely it is not a feasible project for it to approximate the degree of integration warranted by a polity in formation like the EU. The heterogeneity of political regimes of member states precludes this, as does the problem of size. If federal theory were deemed to be appropriate, then given the political-institutional heterogeneity among its member states, only a thin con-federal structure regulating a narrow range of subject matters would be apposite. In other words, one would have to situate such a reformed UN Organization at the lower end of the federation spectrum in terms of ideal types (i.e. as a confederation). What matters is that all actors would be under law, and unlike in the current UN Charter system, that a legal response would be possible to any informal amendment, or violation of the rules, principles, and purposes of the Charter that the powerful might attempt to make. But what also matters is that by so applying the principles of sovereign equality to the

UN system itself, such a re-foundational reform could render it more legitimate internationally and help block Council initiatives that tend to be constitutionalism-eviscerating and rights-violating by ensuring, formally at least, that those making the rules are also subject to them. Only this would warrant deference of the so-called Solange II type attitude toward the supremacy claims regarding global law produced by the UNSC.

Given the degree of heterogeneity of political regimes in the world today and for the foreseeable future, the "legislative" role of such a body would have to be minimal. Freedom for individuals in such a constitutional legal order would be secured not through expansion of the list of human rights that become hard enforceable (by global institutions) cosmopolitan law but by blocking the constitution-eviscerating effects of an overly intrusive and legislative central instance, while the transformations of global political culture and of the political culture and institutional structure of each state in a more public-regarding and rights-respecting direction have time to occur. This form of constitutionalization would not eviscerate really existing domestic democracies and thus need not be construed as an inferior alternative from the democratic perspective: rather it should be seen as a benign way to legitimate and limit the exercise of global power alongside and in conjunction with the public power exercised by sovereign states.

In order to conceive of this project as a third path, one would have to abandon the legal monism of the Kelsenian school and embrace the concept of constitutional pluralism for this domain as well. In other words, the relations between a constitutionalist UN Charter system and the constitutions of member states and regional polities would have to be seen as "heterarchical," not hierarchical: they would all be autonomous legal orders interrelating in specified ways and supremacy would be conditional on respect for constitutionalist principles. To the degree to which the relevant actors acquire the consciousness that their polities are part of a regional and global political system in whose just basic structure they wish to participate, help preserve, and improve, they can gain the requisite reflexivity to develop what theorists of constitutional pluralism have called "constitutional tolerance."[209] Constitutional pluralism in this sense would provide a safeguard against hegemonic law-making from the center. Again, this is a long-term project.

Such constitutionalist reforms would not create a cosmopolitan world order. Instead the outcome would be a new sovereignty regime in which member states of "global governance" institutions like the UN retain their legal autonomy and constituent authority but the supranational legal order of such institutions would also be construed as autonomous and of constitutional quality with important (rights-reinforcing) cosmopolitan elements that constrain its members and organs. Along with the legal pluralists, I agree that although some functional equivalents for democracy are possible on the global level (accountability mechanisms, avenues of influence for civil society, communication about best practices, non-decisional parliaments, and so on), they could never amount to the kind of representative and individualized electoral participation possible on the level of the state or even in a regional federal union. Grimm is right: on the global level constitutionalization is no match for the achievements of democratic constitutionalism on the level of the state. This is reason enough to value the autonomy of different national, regional, and international political orders and the concomitant legal pluralism. The international society of sovereign states should thus continue to exist alongside the international community of member states within the UN Charter system. On the other hand, the global constitutionalists are right to look to the further constitutionalization of international law regulating global governance institutions, and to the cooperation of domestic, regional, and international courts in fostering such a project, but the outcome must not be imagined as a monistic cosmopolitan global legal order that dispenses with state sovereignty and the process must involve more than legal self-reflection.

The basic idea, then, is to acknowledge that autonomous legal orders of constitutional quality can exist in the global political system – of sovereign states and of the key global governance institution within it – and that the latter's claims to autonomy, supremacy, and constitutional quality can coexist alongside the continuing claims of states. Mutual cooperation and dialogue across legal orders, adequate receptors for influence within them to human rights and other concerns, and a legal-political ethic of responsibility should inform the efforts to handle competing claims and to cooperatively further develop the constitutionalist character of all the legal orders involved. Collisions and conflict, as the legal pluralists rightly note, can lead to reflexivity and cooperation; tension need not end in the fragmentation of either legal system, for none of them is self-referentially closed – they are open systems. I repeat: the integrity of a legal system requires that each new legal decision is coherent with previous ones; so long as the participants share a commitment to the project of maintaining and improving a global legal-political order of constitutional quality, integrity is not impossible even given heterogeneity and diversity. Indeed the stance of constitutional pluralism would create the condition of possibility for constitutionalist-minded courts and domestic legislatures to cooperate in salutary ways for all of us.

To put this in political-theoretical terms: the task is to create a new sovereignty regime in which internal and external sovereignty are more congruent vis-à-vis constitutionalism. We have already seen that important changes have been made regarding what is deemed to be legitimately within the domestic jurisdiction of sovereign states and thus that since 1945 we are already living in a new sovereignty regime. Theoretical clarity regarding this, however, has been lacking. So I return to this issue once more.

In the "Westphalian" system, once the absolutist model of organ sovereignty was dropped, internal sovereignty, as we have seen in Chapter 1, was deemed quite compatible with liberal, republican, and ultimately democratic constitutionalism.[210] Public power was to be regulated by public law. The separation of powers, rule of law, and democratic legitimacy linked the legal and political sovereignty of the state to the sovereignty of the people as the ultimate source of authority and constitutional norms. Thus the internal powers of the sovereign state could be exercised by various instances of government (i.e. institutionally disaggregated), and considered to be delegated and subject to the rule of law and the democratic "exercise" of popular sovereignty through representative institutions. The liberal-democratic constitutional state thereby became construed as a domain of justice, law, freedom, and internal self-determination while the unified sovereignty of the polity inhered in the political community as a whole.[211] Indeed internal public power and the "right to rule" came to be seen as the artifact of the constitution such that its exercise under law became the precondition for its legitimacy. As we have seen, on the republican foundational conception (shared by many liberal constitutionalists as well) modern constitutionalism does not limit pre-existing power holders but rather constitutes the basis for the legitimate exercise of public power as such.[212]

However, on the Westphalian model, external sovereignty was still construed, even by liberal and republican constitutionalists, along the lines of organ sovereignty.[213] That is, from the external perspective, the state was deemed to be in an international state of nature requiring a unitary sovereign representative personifying its power, jurisdiction, and authority vis-à-vis other sovereign states (and non-sovereign entities). External equal sovereignty in the system of states (along with imperial/ist power exercised over non-sovereign dominions) thus retained key features of absolutist theory and practice including the assumption that in the international domain the sovereign state was *legibus solutus*, subject only to "natural law" and to those positive legal rules to which it consents and only so long as it continues to do so. Once legal positivism replaced natural law as the dominant paradigm in the mid-nineteenth century, the rules of public international law binding sovereigns were restricted to treaties and customs with many avenues for exemption and objection. The internal exercise of jurisdiction by the sovereign state remained a "black box" to outside powers or any international actors. Sovereignty, it was assumed, had be comprehensive not only vis-à-vis internal contenders but also vis-à-vis external powers. Constitutionalism thus had no place or application in such a context.

The constitutionalization of the public power wielded by the most important global governance institution, the UN, and especially its key organ, the Security Council, could finally lay to rest the old absolutist conception of external sovereignty (reproduced for the P5 on the Council) while helping to block new forms of hegemonic international law and/or con-dominium by great or super-powerful states exempting themselves from the rules that apply to all the others. It would end the extreme asymmetry between the external and internal dimensions of state sovereignty (under law versus above the law) without abolishing it altogether. To be sure, this "low-intensity" constitutionalization of the UN Charter system would not render external and internal sovereignty fully congruent because democratic legitimacy and constitutionalism on the domestic and global levels must perforce differ in institutional form and scope. But a positive-sum game can emerge in a new dualistic sovereignty regime based on the reconceptualization and generalization of the concepts of sovereign equality, self-determination, and autonomy described in this book. Constitutionalization along the lines indicated above would relegate the "state of nature" paradigm of international relations to the dustbin of history. If one makes use of federal theory as per Chapter 2, this reconceptualization of sovereignty could resolve the problem that plagued international political theorists since Kant: i.e. how to imagine a political and legal order composed of sovereign states which itself is not only not lawless, but constitutionalist in its structure and dynamics.[214] So long as public power exercised within the sovereign state and with respect to it is itself under constitutionalist mechanisms, then the loss of comprehensive jurisdiction by the latter need not mean its loss of democratic legitimacy, sovereignty, or efficacy if the state is a democratic one. Participation as a sovereign equal within the UN Charter system or any other GGI enhances rather than undermines such efficacy. Sovereign equality within the UN system could reinforce the rhetorical strength of domestic level democratic constitutionalism, given that according to Freedom House Reports approximately 119 out of 192 states could be described and describe themselves as electoral democracies, regardless of the fragility of democracy in many of them. So long as a state retains its autonomy in international society, this participation would not undermine its sovereignty either.

Accordingly it is perfectly conceivable that a state can give up the *jus belli* (except for self-defense), accept that all states are bound by certain enforceable human rights norms, and even open up its territory to jurisdiction by a functionally delimited supranational legal order, and still be sovereign. Sovereignty, I repeat, entails the supremacy of a legal order and the autonomy/self-determination of a political community regarding its political form.[215] From the internal perspective, the state is sovereign so long as there is an autonomous self-determined political relationship between the government and the citizenry, and so long as its legal order is supreme. The sovereign domestic constitutional legal order can delegate competences and even accept the primacy of rules made in the appropriately designated manner by a supranational organization in certain domains, since it is the capacity of the sovereign domestic legal order to make such delegations and to accept such decisions particularly if it has a role in making them. From its internal perspective, the domestic legal order remains supreme and retains interpretive

autonomy over jurisdiction and over issues of compatibility of external decisions with its internal constitutional legal order. In the constitutionalized UN
Charter system, states are sovereign equals, and outside it they are equal
sovereign members of international society: i.e. they participate in GGIs and
retain their autonomy. This is the meaning of a dualistic world order. But,
as I have argued throughout, internal autonomy need not be tightly coupled
to exclusivity of jurisdiction. It is certainly possible to conceive of autonomy
and sovereignty without comprehensive territorial exclusivity.[216] The development of a constitutionalist functionally delimited, supranational quasi-
federal legal order can thus supplement and overlap without abolishing the
autonomy of segmentally differentiated territorial sovereign states.[217] Domestic constitutionalist, democratic legitimacy would not be undermined if all
public power exercised within the territory of a state is regulated by public law
and comports with constitutionalist principles and if sovereign equality
means that every state has equal standing and voice in the deliberations and
decision-making within global governance institutions.

   Were the political decision to be made to alter the constitutional treaty of
the UN (the Charter) by abolishing the veto of the P5 in the amendment rule
and conceivably in the Council, their status would change, such that they
become equal co-states of the UN system. But even if the constituent authority of all member states were given legal form in the amendment rule, and the
UN was acknowledged to be a quasi-federation, their equal sovereignty and
autonomy would remain intact and the former would remain functionally
delimited.[218] The stance of constitutional pluralism reveals that each autonomous legal order sees itself as supreme in terms of validity: each has its own
grundnorm in the sense that the basic constitutional norms and legal sources
are not derived from any higher legal system. There is no need for the kind of
homogeneity Schmitt insists upon, but only for an overlapping consensus on
the basic purposes, functions, values, and procedures articulated in the
reformed constitutional treaty.[219] There is also no reason why it cannot be
global in scope despite the cultural and institutional diversity of member
states. As already indicated, constitutional pluralism would be the appropriate
analogue of the concept of sovereign equality in a constitutionalist UN
Charter system and of a new sovereignty regime. It means that within a
constitutional treaty organization, both the supranational legal order and
the constitutional orders of the member states are autonomous, and neither
is comprehensive in jurisdiction although the former must be functionally
delimited. They can coexist so long as the self-determination of all the
political communities is respected as well as the basic principles of the
overarching legal order vis-à-vis what is considered to be within the domestic
jurisdiction of states, and what is not, etc. If one adds the feature that while a
reformed UN Charter system would continue to have the monopoly of
legitimacy to determine the use of force internationally, member states would

continue to retain the right to self-defense as well as the actual forces, then it is clear that we are speaking of a dualist structure and a new sovereignty regime.

Finally, there is the obvious question: why adopt the stance of constitutional pluralism and propose the relevance of federal theory or retain sovereignty discourse for such a project? There is a normative and a strategic answer to this question. As already indicated, we should understand sovereignty as a negative concept involving supremacy of a domestic legal order and autonomy in the political sense of self-determination (non-imposition by foreigners) by a political community of its political regime and constitutional order. External sovereignty has the positive dimension of equality of standing and equal right to participate in international law-making. Accordingly, sovereignty protects the special relationship between a citizenry and its government and the possibility of basing this relationship on principles of constitutionalism and democracy. The principle of sovereign equality accords this status to all states. A federal union, even the least integrated con-federal arrangement, provides for collective action, problem-solving, and rule-making on the supranational level but it protects and is based on the legal and political autonomy (sovereignty) of member states. Low-intensity constitutionalism is possible on the global level without democracy-disabling tradeoffs, if one thinks in such federal terms.[220] Thus for those wed to republican political principles and democratic aspirations, the constitutional pluralist approach is the best way to protect domestic democratic achievements in a context of global governance. Because it would require political commitment and action, the charge of legalism made against constitutionalization discourses would not be compelling.[221] Indeed the example of a rights- and constitutionalism-respecting global governance institution could help build a global political culture on which domestic actors seeking to create or improve domestic democratic and constitutionalist institutions could draw.

~

Conclusion

The UNSC now engages in global governance tasks that go beyond its traditional functions including humanitarian interventions, the erection of highly transformative interim administrations of occupied territories, the imposition of sanctions directly targeting individuals (some of which violate their basic rights) in its pursuit of the "war on terror," and the issuing of binding resolutions that are legislative and quasi-judicial in form. These practices are Janus-faced: while in some instances they prevent or help rectify humanitarian disasters and protect human rights, in others they lead to the evisceration of the rule of law and constitutionalism on all levels of the international political system, and undermine the foundational Charter principles of sovereign equality and human rights.

In response to the danger that a new form of hegemonic international law and new forms of hierarchical rule – con-dominium inside the UN Charter system, new imperial formations alongside it – are taking shape, I have argued for low-intensity constitutionalization as a way to steer the evolution of the universal GGI in the international political system in a normatively more attractive direction. The internal dualist structure of the UN as a constitutional treaty organization should be retained. But it must be reformed so as to bring it into line with the rule of law and to rectify some of its worst hierarchical features. Constitutional reform along the lines I have suggested would help ensure that the rules and decisions made by the SC, its key organ, and the actions it sponsors are rights-respecting. It would also create the possibility of a legal assessment of and response to ultra vires resolutions. Insofar as further constitutionalization would revitalize the principle of sovereign equality internal to the UN qua global governance institution, the latter would attain a greater degree of "democratic" legitimacy with respect to its right to rule in its designated domains because all states would have equal standing and a voice within the inclusive organization and all would be under its rules. This could, recursively, shore up sovereign equality in the international society of states, counteracting the spillover effects of hierarchy that now occur thanks to the newly expansive governance role of the UNSC. Shifts regarding which prerogatives are considered to be in the domestic jurisdiction of states, what powers or competences are delegated to the SC and other UN bodies, which domestic rights violations can defeasibly trigger suspension of the sovereignty argument against authorized intervention, etc., could be debated by sovereign equals and lead, when appropriate, to legitimate global legal rules. Clear principles regulating humanitarian occupation could also be devised. Legality would in short be realigned with legitimacy on this level of global governance.

I have argued in this book that a new dualistic sovereignty regime that constructs a normatively appropriate interconnection between human rights, political autonomy, and constitutionalized global governance, understood in the theoretical framework of constitutional pluralism, still has a chance. I have focused on the global political subsystem of world society and in particular, on the UN Charter system. I have argued that the quality of the UN constitutional treaty certainly can be assessed from the perspective of constitutionalist normative principles and that it comes up short in this regard. Given its new global governance functions, activism, and legislative initiatives, constitutional reform is desirable. I have also argued that this should be understood in the frame of constitutional pluralism meaning that the sovereignty and autonomy of member states within a suitably reformed UN Charter system would remain intact: the UN constitutional treaty and its further development cannot be understood through a monist frame. I do not consider the UN Charter to be the constitution of the world system as a whole or a subsystem of some other de-centered world constitution. I have not addressed the much more contentious claim made by some that constitutionalism pertains to the relations among the various GGIs, IOs, and other entities within contemporary global regulatory space, because it seems clear to me that these relations must be understood in terms of legal pluralism, not global constitutionalism or constitutional pluralism as I have distinguished these terms.[1] The discourse of constitutionalism pertaining to IOs morphing into GGIs such as the UN allows us to leverage its normative language in assessing and seeking to reform a universal political institution of great importance. The discourse of constitutional pluralism, and even of federation, though aspirational in this context, could help us to see that this is a political and not only juridical project and that it need not place sovereignty or sovereign equality at risk.

However, since reform of the veto is so difficult, limits to Council misbehavior must first come from other constitutionalist orders, assuming the political will and legal ingenuity is available. At present and in the foreseeable future, the only constitutional sources of legal limits on the SC absent a formal amendment of the amendment rule that abolishes the veto are those in existing liberal-democratic constitutionalist polities that see themselves, and are seen, as autonomous. By revealing that legitimacy will be lost when rights, constitutionalism, and the rule of law are undermined, the strategic retreat to quasi-dualism by courts like the ECJ and/or a "Solange threat" of the sort articulated by the Advocate General in the Kadi case could have a recursive effect, in the long run contributing to the development of the political will to revise offending SC resolutions.[2] This is one way to break the vicious circle of discretionary self-aggrandizing global and domestic executive powers mutually reinforcing one another at the expense of constitutionalism, rights, democracy, and political autonomy everywhere. But even greater political will and political as distinct from legal action is needed to bring about institutional reforms at the international level that scale back Council "usurpation" and amend the Charter amendment rule, introducing more effective separation of powers and checks and balance mechanisms and a more integrated international political community.

One final word on the implications of this project for democracy and democratic legitimacy is necessary before closing. This book rejects the absolutist political-theological conception of sovereignty that has informed advocates and critics of both global constitutionalism and sovereigntist/statist alternatives. The conception of sovereignty that I defend retains the core meaning of a unified legal order supreme and autonomous in its domestic (territorial) domain and the idea of self-determination by the political community of its political form of existence. But the holistic conception of constitution that went hand-in-hand with the modern "Westphalian" international system of sovereign states is historically contingent.[3] We have learned that the sovereignty of the state does not preclude domestic constitutionalism, that popular sovereignty does not require a homogeneous people but can go together with a pluralist *and* egalitarian society and a liberal-democratic regime. Now it is time to realize that domestic sovereignty need not be comprehensive – other international or global jurisdictions can be effective in the state's territory – and that external sovereignty need not be absolutist – it can go together with positive international and global law. A sovereign state can delegate many functions to supranational institutions and be open to external observation and legal regulation regarding, for example, international criminal and human rights law so long as it enjoys sovereign equality and participates in determining these. It is time, in other words to abandon the absolutist conception of external sovereignty and its claim to exclusive internal jurisdiction over persons, territory, or subject matter, along with the deceptive metaphor of an international state of nature, both criticized by Kelsen long ago.

We should not, however, throw out the baby (autonomous self-determining political/legal communities organized into states) with the bathwater (solipsistic bellicose, *legibus solutus* sovereign states in an allegedly atomistic lawless international system of states). Understanding external sovereignty in the latter way tends to foster anti-constitutionalist organ sovereignty domestically.[4] Instead of abandoning sovereignty discourse altogether it is more advisable to rethink external sovereignty in terms that fit the new constellation of globalization, global governance, and globalizing international law, including the globalization of the international system of sovereign states. Sovereignty is indeed an international legal entitlement, and recognition of sovereign statehood today (presumably based on effectiveness) is not only the bilateral prerogative of every single sovereign state in international society: it is also a crucial function of the UN – an increasingly important GGI in this regard. Sovereignty as participation on an equal status basis within GGIs is becoming as important as sovereignty as autonomy. Given all of the above, and in light of its new functions, the further constitutionalization of the UN Charter system is crucial today. In order to see how this can be conceptually compatible with our best understanding of democratic constitutionalism gleaned from developments on the level of the state, we need to reflect one more time, briefly, on the conceptual relation between democracy and constitutionalism and avoid reductionist analyses.

In the last chapter I indicated how further constitutionalization of the architecture of the UN Charter could counter the constitutionalist- and democracy-eviscerating effects of some of its contemporary forms of global governance. I meant to show that, on the empirical level, given appropriate reforms, globalization need not be in a zero-sum relation with the democratic constitutional state. But this entails two theoretical claims: that it is possible (a) not only to sever constitutionalism from the state, but also (b) to distinguish it conceptually from democracy while acknowledging their deep interrelation, and thus to have a project for the constitutionalization of the global domain of public power that does not require the same kinds of individualized electoral institutions or identical forms of democratic legitimacy that have come to be identified with state level democratic constitutionalism. I acknowledge the great achievements of modern democratically rooted constitutionalism. But, I argue that if we do not buy into a reductionist analysis that equates democracy with constitutionalism, saying in effect no constitutionalism without democracy, we can come to realize that it is possible to apply the idea of constitutionalism to the suprastate domain without demeaning the normative weight of either and without denying their deeper interrelationship that moral philosophy has revealed.[5] While I cannot go into the philosophical analysis necessary to vindicate this claim here, let me close by briefly explaining what I mean.

I have already argued that the exercise of public power requires limitation and legitimation no matter which institution exercises it. I have analyzed the legitimacy problems generated by the apparently legally unlimited exercise of certain forms of power by the UNSC.[6] Constitutionalism and democracy met these requirements regarding the establishment and exercise of public power on the level of the modern state in a mutually reinforcing way. To be sure, on the empirico-historical level these involved distinct processes and projects. But today they are seen as mutually reinforcing and predicated on the same deep moral philosophical premises, whatever tensions may exist between them on the normative or institutional level.[7] I agree with Neil Walker that while modern conceptions of democracy and constitutionalism share the underlying "social imaginary" of individuality, egalitarianism, constructivism, and progressivism and thus refer back to the same modern moral order nevertheless they are analytically distinct.[8] Theirs is thus a "double relationship" of mutual support and mutual tension regardless of their necessary interrelation.[9] I also agree that constitutionalism (the rule of law, limited government under law, etc.) and democracy (self-rule or self-government by the people's representatives) are incomplete ideals in two senses: (a) insofar as both are unavoidably, no matter the empirical approximation on any level, a vérité à faire always open to a better institutionalization and (b) insofar as both are necessary to help "complete" or realize each other.[10] It is true that placing public power under public law and other features of constitutionalization always raises the legitimacy question from the political perspective and that democratic legitimacy does not on its own resolve the rule of law question of the appropriate design, necessary limits to, and place of non- (but not anti-) democratic public instances (e.g. courts) in a democratic polity.

Thus it is as much of a conceptual mistake to assimilate constitutionalism to democracy as it is to radically separate them. Once this is accepted, one can get beyond the "two dominant but opposing understandings of the new forms of post-national constitutionalism."[11] The first rejects the discourse of supra- or post-national constitutionalism because of its weak democratic credentials and attenuated link to the democratic state (presupposing the assimilationist view of their interrelation); the second embraces the discourse of supra- or post-national constitutionalism denying that its thin democratic credentials pose a problem so long as human rights are respected.[12] Both approaches are one-sided and inadequate on conceptual and normative grounds. As Habermas has argued, constitutionalism and democracy, human rights and popular sovereignty are based on co-original and co-equal ideals, namely the symbiotic relationship between private and public autonomy.[13] These ideals can neither be reduced to each other nor deemed irrelevant to either project. They do indeed normatively presuppose each other. Nevertheless, this correct thesis of their normative, pragmatic, and logical mutual relatedness does not obviate the fact that these are distinct on the empirical and even the normative level. Even though I do not believe that today we can have a democratic polity that is not constitutionalist, the reverse is not equally true.

The conclusion I draw from this thin philosophical sketch is that their deep normative co-equivalence and shared "social imaginary" notwithstanding, constitutionalization and democratization are distinct processes which may occur at different times and which are open to a variety of institutional embodiments. The link between them cannot be entirely severed even at the global level lest each loses its normative compelling character. But we must not model our expectations regarding either process on the rather recent though to be sure normatively compelling synthesis that now seems to be self-evident on the level of the contemporary democratic constitutional state. Thus on the level of key global governance institutions, I have focused on "low-intensity" constitutionalization although I have identified some of the democratizing moves even this apparently minimalist approach would have to entail (a constitutional reform ascribable to the constituent powers of the member states of the UN Charter system that includes abolition of the veto of the P5 at least in the amendment rule, internal vindication of the principles of sovereign equality, due process and separation of power reforms, and creation of a court able to police that separation and so forth). I mean to indicate by this that there is always a legitimacy claim tied to the project of constitutionalization. Efforts to contain and channel public power (at least since the onset of modernity) should be seen today as proto-democratic.[14] The hope is that a constitutionalist and more egalitarian political structure in the premier global governance institution would not only undo and block the evisceration of domestic constitutionalism by SC resolutions, but also help foster indirectly, by example, the development of a rights- and democracy-respecting political culture globally and in all member states.

From the standpoint of the ideal of the democratic constitutional state, these constitutionalizing and democratizing steps may appear to be very minimal. I do not mean to suggest that one should abandon more radical democratic utopian aspirations for global governance institutions, for even if they are infeasible now, they may help us realize and expand what is indeed possible and become more feasible in the future.[15] Thus I do not accept the minimalist stance that severs constitutionalism as a means of civilizing politics through legal restraints entirely from issues of democratic legitimacy. The cat is out of the bag with respect to the moral presuppositions of equality, individuality, and constructivism in our late modern world, and thus questions of democratic legitimacy will inevitably recur regarding supranational constitutionalism, eliciting different politics and different answers over time. The social dynamics of making claims, challenging given institutionalizations and structures that appear unjust or insufficiently accountable, inclusive, or representative of stakeholders (those subject to decisions and rules) that we associate with democratic contestation are inevitable once the discourse of constitutionalization is applied to any domain. Demands for justification of the exercise of global public (and private) power will continue to arise. As we have seen in Chapter 3, this pertains also to the dynamics of human rights claims, interpretations, and to interventions justified in their name. The question of the political legitimacy of any rights-based decision or interpretation at the international level and the politics this involves cannot be conjured away by invoking the universality of the value underlying it or by deploying the apparently neutral language of rights-based global constitutionalist rhetoric.[16] As one astute analyst puts it, human rights discourse cannot render obsolete, "... a connection between the always necessarily political nature of the decision-making that takes place at the international level and a political community capable of legitimating it."[17] As I have been arguing throughout this book, the connection between legal and political community and the question of political form is unavoidable once the discourse of constitution/constitutionalism/constitutionalization arises.

However, nor do I mean to suggest that democratizing constitutionalist reforms that alter, redesign, or re-found GGIs on the global level can substitute for democracy on the level of the state. My point is that we are very far even from a situation in which the international legal order could be analogized to the internal legal order even of a regional polity like the European Union in which internal constitutional pluralism, direct effect – immediate validity of EU legal norms – and their conditional supremacy (Solange II tactics) make sense, thanks to the homology of political forms (all legal orders within the transnational legal order of the EU are required to be liberal constitutional democracies) and the political commitment to integration. International heterogeneity with respect to legitimating principles precludes this for now, democratizing trends notwithstanding. It is not, however, for me to exclude such a development in the future for the global political system. For the time being, however, low-intensity constitutionalization may be as good as it gets.

NOTES

Introduction

1 Of fifty-seven armed conflicts fought in 1990–2005, only four were between states: Eritrea–Ethiopia; India–Pakistan; Iraq–Kuwait; Iraq–US and allies. G. H. Fox, *Humanitarian Occupation* (Cambridge University Press, 2008), p. 5.

2 Hedley Bull, *The Anarchical Society*, 3rd edn. (Basingstoke: Palgrave Macmillan, 2002).

3 J. Goldstein, M. Kahler, R. O. Keohane, and A.-M. Slaughter, "Introduction: Legalization and World Politics," in J. Goldstein, M. Kahler, R. O. Keohane, and A.-M. Slaughter (eds.), *Legalization and World Politics* (Cambridge, MA: MIT Press, 2001), pp. 1–15; G. Teubner, "Societal Constitutionalism: Alternatives to State-Centered Constitutional Theory?" in C. Joerges, I. Sand, and G. Teubner (eds.), *Transnational Governance and Constitutionalism* (Portland, OR and Oxford: Hart Publishing, 2004), pp. 3–28; A.-M. Slaughter, *A New World Order* (Princeton University Press, 2004).

4 Slaughter, *A New World Order*.

5 See Chapter 5 for discussion of the concept of global governance institution.

6 See Chapters 1 and 5 for citations and a discussion of this literature.

7 The focus of this book is on legal and political, rather than economic or technological globalization although the latter provides the backdrop. The shift from international to global law-making and the emergence of global governance will be analyzed with respect to the new "human security" regime and the new roles acquired by the key "governance" institution in the global political system – the UN Security Council – since the 1990s.

8 See Chapters 3–5. For the concept of humanitarian occupation, see Fox, *Humanitarian Occupation*, pp. 2–4.

9 R. O. Keohane, "Political Authority After Intervention: Gradations in Sovereignty," in J. L. Holzgrefe and Robert O. Keohane (eds.), *Humanitarian Intervention: Ethical, Legal, and Political Dilemmas* (Cambridge University Press, 2003), pp. 275–298; S. D. Krasner, "Rebuilding Democracy After Conflict: The Case for Shared Sovereignty," *Journal of Democracy*, 16 (2005), 60–83; S. D. Krasner, "Sharing Sovereignty: New Institutions for Collapsed and Failing States," *International Security*, 29 (2004), 85–120. On neo-trusteeship see J. D. Fearon and D. D. Laitin, "Neo-Trusteeship and the Problem of Weak States," *International Security*, 28 (2004), 5–43.

10 The R2P doctrine was first articulated in ICISS, *The Responsibility to Protect: Report of the International Commission on Intervention and State Sovereignty* (Ottawa: International Development Research Centre, 2001). It was reaffirmed in United Nations, *A More Secure World: Our Shared Responsibility*, Report of the Secretary-General's High-level Panel on Threats, Challenges and Change (New York: United Nations, 2004), www.un.org/secureworld.

11 See A. Anghie, *Imperialism, Sovereignty and the Making of International Law* (Cambridge University Press, 2004); M. Hardt and A. Negri, *Empire* (Cambridge, MA: Harvard

University Press, 2000); N. Krisch, "Imperial International Law," Global Law Working Papers (2004), available at http://eprints.lse.ac.uk/id/eprint/13215; J. L. Cohen, "Sovereign Equality Versus Imperial Right: The Battle Over the New World Order," *Constellations*, 13 (2006), 485–505.

12 M. Koskenniemi, *The Gentle Civilizer of Nations* (Cambridge University Press, 2001), pp. 494–517.

13 On the imperialist concept of quasi-sovereignty see L. Benton, *A Search for Sovereignty: Law and Geography in European Empires, 1400–1900* (Cambridge University Press, 2010), pp. 222–301. See also G. W. Gong, *The Standard of "Civilization" in International Society* (Oxford: Clarendon Press, 1984).

14 On the distinction between segmental and functional differentiation see N. Luhmann, *The Differentiation of Society* (New York: Columbia University Press, 1981). For the systems-theoretical concept of "world society" see N. Luhmann, "The World Society as a Social System," *International Journal of General Systems*, 8 (1982), 13–138; and Teubner, "Societal Constitutionalism."

15 On the concept of changing sovereignty regimes see D. Philpott, *Revolutions in Sovereignty: How Ideas Shaped Modern International Relations* (Princeton University Press, 2001).

16 These issues are addressed in Chapters 2 and 4

17 See H. L. A. Hart, *The Concept of Law* (Oxford University Press, 1961) for a brilliant critique of this conception.

18 These depend on international law but at the very least a sovereign state has the prerogative to participate in international law-making by customary international law or treaties and to participate in international organizations that make law. It also has the right to self-defense, although this is limited by the UN Charter principles.

19 C. Schmitt, *The Nomos of the Earth in the International Law of the* Jus Publicum Europaeum (New York: Telos Press, 2003).

20 The original source is N. MacCormick, "The Maastricht-Urteil: Sovereignty Now," *European Law Journal*, 1 (1995), 259–266. For a superb discussion, see N. Walker, "The Idea of Constitutional Pluralism," *Modern Law Review*, 65 (2002), 317–359.

21 M. Forsyth, *Unions of States: The Theory and Practice of Confederation* (New York: Holmes & Meier, 1981), is one of the first to do such a retrieval.

22 On the distinction between "coming-together" and "holding-together" federalism, describing different types of federal states, see A. Stepan, J. L. Linz, and Y. Yadav, *Crafting State-Nations: India and Other Multinational Democracies* (Baltimore, MD: Johns Hopkins University Press, 2011), pp. 1–38.

23 *Ibid.*

24 O. Beaud, *Théorie de la fédération* (Paris: Presses Universitaires de France, 2007).

25 C. Schmitt, *Constitutional Theory* (Durham, NC: Duke University Press, 2008), pp. 379–408.

26 Beaud, *Théorie de la fédération.*

27 See United Nations, A More Secure World.

28 R. G. Teitel, *Humanity's Law* (Oxford University Press, 2011).

29 See ICISS, *The Responsibility to Protect.*

30 Human dignity seems to be replacing autonomy as the intrinsically valuable core in every person that is protected by human rights.

31 P. Macklem, "Humanitarian Intervention and the Distribution of Sovereignty in International Law," *Ethics and International Affairs*, 22 (2008), 369–393.

32 E. Benvenisti, *The International Law of Occupation* (Princeton University Press, 1993), p. 5.

33 European Court of Justice, Joined Cases C-402/05 P and C-415/05P 2008. Case T-315/01 *Kadi v. Council and Commission* (2005) ECR II-36649 (Kadi CFI); and Case T-306/01 *Yusuf and Al Barakaat International Foundation v. Council and Commission* (2005)

ECR II-3353 *Yassin Abdullah Kadi and Al Barakaat International Foundation* v. *Council of the European Union and Commission of the European Communities*, September 2008.

34 Walker, "The Idea of Constitutional Pluralism"; M. P. Maduro, "Contrapunctual Law: Europe's Constitutional Pluralism in Action," in N. Walker (ed.), *Sovereignty in Transition: Essays in European Law* (Oxford: Hart Publishing, 2003), pp. 501–539; and J. H. H. Weiler, "On the Power of the Word: Europe's Constitutional Iconography," *International Journal of Constitutional Law*, 3 (2005), 173–190. For a critique see J. B. Cruz, "The Legacy of the Maastricht-Urteil and the Pluralist Movement," EUI Working Papers, RSCAS 2007/13.

35 The term "low-intensity constitutionalism" comes from M. Maduro, "The Importance of Being Called a Constitution: Constitutional Authority and the Authority of Constitutionalism," *International Journal of Constitutional Law*, 3 (2005), 332–356.

Chapter 1 Sovereignty in the context of globalization: a constitutional pluralist approach

1 Freedom House Report, *Democracy's Century: A Survey of Global Political Change in the 20th Century* (New York: Freedom House, 1999), describing 119 out of 192 states as electoral democracies.

2 On the universalization of sovereign state as a political form, see D. Armitage, "The Contagion of Sovereignty: Declarations of Independence since 1776," *South African Historical Journal*, 52 (2005), 1–18.

3 On the distinction between segmental and functional differentiation, see N. Luhmann, *The Differentiation of Society* (New York: Columbia University Press, 1981). For the systems-theoretical concept of "world society," see N. Luhmann, "The World Society as a Social System," *International Journal of General Systems*, 8 (1982), 131–138, and G. Teubner, "Societal Constitutionalism: Alternatives to State-Centered Constitutional Theory?" in C. Joerges, I. Sand, and G. Teubner (eds.), *Transnational Governance and Constitutionalism* (Portland, OR and Oxford: Hart Publishing, 2004), pp. 3–28.

4 "Global governance institution" (GGI) is a vague but useful term to indicate a new form of global regulation and rule-making that raises distinctive legitimacy problems. See Allan Buchanan and Robert Keohane, "The Legitimacy of Global Governance Institutions," *Ethics and International Affairs*, 20 (2006), 405–437.

5 There are centered and de-centered versions of the constitutionalist approach. For a version that sees the global constitution of the world system centered in the UN Charter system, see B. Fassbender, "The United Nations Charter as Constitution of the International Community," *The Columbia Journal of Transnational Law*, 36 (1998), 529–619. For a neo-Kelsenian de-centered version, see A. Fischer-Lescano, *Globalverfassung: Die Geltungsbegründung der Menschenrechte* (Weilerswist: Velbrück Wissenschaft, 2005). For two essay volumes that include a variety of approaches, see R. J. Macdonald and D. M. Johnston (eds.), *Towards World Constitutionalism: Issues in the Legal Ordering of the World Community* (Boston: Brill, 2005) and J. Klabbers, A. Peters, and G. Ulfstein, *The Constitutionalization of International Law* (Oxford University Press, 2009). See also the new journal *Global Constitutionalism* (Cambridge University Press, 2011).

6 The principle of *jus cogens* was asserted in the Vienna Convention on the Law of Treaties 1969 and invoked by the ICTY. See the Vienna Convention on the Law of Treaties, Article 53. *Jus cogens* norms are peremptory international legal norms from which no derogation is possible and in violation of which a treaty will be deemed void. The candidates for *jus cogens* norms with higher law status are the prohibitions against genocide, torture, ethnic cleansing, enslavement, disappearances, and crimes against humanity. See D. Shelton, "Normative Hierarchy in International Law," *American Journal of International Law*, 100 (2006), 291–323.

7 See A. Fischer-Lescano, "Constitutional Rights–Constitutional Fights: Human Rights and the Global Legal System" (unpublished); and Fischer-Lescano, *Globalverfassung: Die Geltungsbegründung der Menschenrechte*. There is much debate on all of this and the relation between *jus cogens* norms and human rights law has not been determined. See F. Moneta, "State Immunity for International Crimes: The Case of Germany versus Italy before the ICJ," www.haguejusticeportal.net (2009), indicating that violations of human rights norms even if these would nullify a treaty do not necessarily invoke *jus cogens* principles. See also H. Brunkhorst, "Die Globale Rechtsrevolution. Von der Evolution der Verfassungsrevolution zur Revolution der Verfassungsevolution?" in R. Christensen and B. Pieroth (eds.), *Rechtstheorie in rechtspraktischer Absicht* (Berlin: Duncker & Humblot/FS Müller, 2008), pp. 9–34.

8 K. Alter, "Delegating to International Courts: Self-Binding vs. Other-Binding Delegation," *Law and Contemporary Problems*, 71 (2008), 37–76.

9 Fischer-Lescano, *Globalverfassung: Die Geltungsbegründung der Menschenrechte*.

10 *Ibid.* See also Teubner, "Societal Constitutionalism."

11 By legal cosmopolitans I mean legal theorists who argue for the shift from international to global law with special place for individual rights. See N. Feldman, "Cosmopolitan Law?" *Yale Law Journal*, 116 (2007), 1024–1070. There is great overlap with global constitutionalists, and the main point for all of them is that the individual becomes the referent of global legal norms, and that global law is not based exclusively on state consent as is international law. For the concept of moral cosmopolitanism, see T. Pogge, "Cosmopolitanism," in R. Goodin, P. Pettit, and T. Pogge (eds.), *A Companion to Contemporary Political Philosophy*, 2nd edn. (Oxford: Blackwell, 2007), pp. 312–331.

12 This suspicion is not identical to the realist challenge that assumes power, not law is what matters in the international system. For a discussion, see J. L. Cohen, "Whose Sovereignty? Empire Versus International Law," *Ethics and International Affairs*, 18 (2004), 1–24 (pp. 2–5).

13 W. B. Gallie, "Essentially Contested Concepts," *Proceedings of the Aristotelian Society*, 56 (1955), 167–198.

14 Individuals are subjects in international criminal law, humanitarian law, and human rights law. But what this means is contested. Individuals have a hard time suing in an international court. Indeed, the individualization thesis regarding individuals as subjects of international law with full legal standing able to sue in court is overblown. In part it depends on the regime. Individuals can sue in the ECtHR but not in the ICJ. See Moneta, "State Immunity for International Crimes."

15 J. Weiler, "The Geology of International Law: Governance, Democracy and Legitimacy," *Volkerrecht/Heidelberg Journal of International Law*, 64 (2004), 547–562.

16 In this chapter, I concentrate on reconceptualizing sovereignty. In Chapter 3, I will address its normative thrust and why it is worth preserving in discourse and in practice.

17 Thus I do not address the concept of global constitutionalism in terms of the relations among the various GGIs in world society or the relations among the different legal regimes proliferating therein. When I refer to the global political system and its legalization, I have in mind the transformations of the UN Charter system and the related human rights regime.

18 I use the term "centralization" in the Kelsenian sense of the introduction of a hierarchy of both legal norms and institutions (courts). National and international law form part of the same single legal system (monist) in which there is normative hierarchy and international courts able to provide legal remedies such that the subject of international law includes individuals as bearers of legal rights and legal duties. Individualization, hierarchy, and centralization entail one another for the Kelsenian. As is well known,

Kelsen famously argued for an international criminal court (among others) and compulsory jurisdiction as a step toward legal centralization.

19 Here I give an ideal-typical model of the absolutist conception of sovereignty.

20 J. Bodin, *On Sovereignty: Four Chapters from the Six Books of the Commonwealth*, ed. J. Franklin (Cambridge University Press, 1992). For a superb critical analysis of Bodin's theory of sovereignty, see J. Franklin, *Jean Bodin and the Rise of Absolutist Theory* (Cambridge University Press, 1973).

21 A century after Bodin wrote, Thomas Hobbes developed his own theory of absolutist sovereignty oriented to the crucial function of providing internal peace and security. Both developed their absolutist conception of sovereignty in the aftermath of religious civil wars. T. Hobbes, *Leviathan* (New York: Bobbs-Merrill, 1958).

22 The best-known nineteenth-century theorist of the command theory of law is J. Austin, *The Province of Jurisprudence Determined*, ed. W. E. Rumble (Cambridge University Press, 1995).

23 *Ibid.* On the concept of organ sovereignty, see R. Carré de Malberg, *Contribution à la théorie générale de l'état* (Paris: Dalloz, 2004) pp. 69–88.

24 Nevertheless it is, at least according to Bodin, limited by higher, natural law, which it does not create. Bodin, *On Sovereignty*, pp. 31–32. See Carré de Malberg, *Contribution à la théorie générale de l'état*, p. 78.

25 See notes 26–28 supra.

26 Accordingly, international law has no "direct effect" (i.e. is not immediately binding on domestic courts). Even where it does, it is because the domestic constitution stipulates as much, otherwise international law has to be "incorporated" – passed by the domestic legislature to be binding on state actors. Nor does international law directly confer rights on individuals that obligate domestic courts.

27 See O. Gierke, *Natural Law and the Theory of Society 1500–1800*, trans. E. Barker (Boston: Beacon Press, 2010), pp. 36–198, for a superb discussion of the absolutist conception and the constitutionalist alternative.

28 H. Bull, *The Anarchical Society*, 3rd edn. (Basingstoke: Palgrave Macmillan, 2002). For a critique of Bull, see E. Keane, *Beyond the Anarchical Society: Grotius, Colonialism and World Order in International Politics* (Cambridge University Press, 2002). See also C. Schmitt, *The Nomos of the Earth in the International Law of the Jus Publicum Europaeum* (New York: Telos Press, 2003); A. Anghie, *Imperialism, Sovereignty and the Making of International Law* (Cambridge University Press, 2004), pp. 46–65, for an analysis of the role the concept of international society played in denying non-European states sovereignty and equal standing in international law.

29 Anghie, *Imperialism, Sovereignty and the Making of International Law*; Schmitt, *The Nomos of the Earth*.

30 B. Fassbender, "Sovereignty and Constitutionalism in International Law," in N. Walker (ed.), *Sovereignty in Transition: Essays in European Law* (Oxford: Hart Publishing, 2003), pp. 115–144 (p. 119).

31 G. Jellinek, *Allgemeine Staatslehre* (Bad Homberg: Hermann Gentner Verlag, 1960), pp. 435–504; H. Kelsen, *General Theory of Law and the State* (Cambridge, MA: Harvard University Press, 1945), pp. 328–390; H. Kelsen, *Das Problem der Souveränität und die Theorie des Völkerrechts* (Tübingen: Mohr, 1928); Carré de Malberg, *Contribution à la théorie générale de l'état*; H. L. A. Hart, *The Concept of Law* (Oxford University Press, 1961), pp. 49–77.

32 Advocates like Carl Schmitt and critics like Hannah Arendt of the concept of popular sovereignty both buy into this mistaken idea. A. Arato and J. L. Cohen, "Banishing the Sovereign? Internal and External Sovereignty in Arendt," *Constellations*, 16 (2009), 307–330.

33 For a systematic critique of this position, see Hart, *The Concept of Law*, pp. 49–77.

34 Apex sovereignty is only one possible form of regime. The rest depends on the nature of the constitutional order in place. The US constitution for example has a version of the separation of powers that lets Congress strip the Supreme Court and federal courts of jurisdiction along with a rather rigid but nevertheless clear amendment rule that allows other organs to overturn a Supreme Court or Congressional or Executive ruling. In short, there is no single institutional locus, higher than all the rest, that ultimately decides what the law is – "sovereignty" circulates in such an order although the state is nonetheless sovereign domestically and internationally.

35 Jellinek, *Allgemeine Staatslehre*, unlike Kelsen, has a two-sided theory of the state: one side refers to the legal juridical order, the other to the sociological dimension of power and organization.

36 Jellinek, *Allgemeine Staatslehre*, pp. 435–504; Kelsen, *General Theory of Law and the State*, pp. 328–390; Kelsen, *Das Problem der Souveränität und die Theorie des Völkerrechts*.

37 As H. L. A. Hart argued in his famous critique of the command theory of law and of indispensability of ruler and organ sovereignty to the unity of a legal order, it is the legal and constitutional rules that establish the powers and prerogatives of state organs and the locus of supreme power within a state and not the reverse. See Hart, *The Concept of Law*. Kelsen makes a similar point (and made it first) regarding sovereign prerogatives of states in the international field: these derive from the rules of international law not from some "essence" of sovereignty. Kelsen, *General Theory of Law and the State*, pp. 327–390. To be sure, Carl Schmitt challenged the legalistic redefinition of sovereignty and ridiculed the Kelsenian reduction of the state to the domestic legal system. He sought to replace the absolutist model based on the omnipotence of organ sovereignty, the "wrong political theology," with a better one, focused on the exception and the sovereign as he who decides the exception, analogized with the miracle in theology. Schmitt's shift from the absolutist, monarchical model to popular sovereignty thus resurrects the core of the idea of organ sovereignty rejected by the legal theorists discussed here. He construes popular sovereignty in a populist way that treats the people as a macro-subject, as a unity based on some shared substantive characteristic (ascribed to them), endowed with a will that can and indeed must be embodied in a sovereign representative (insofar as the people cannot act) particularly in cases of emergency. Schmitt's existential conception of sovereignty revives the idea of organ sovereignty in emergencies, linking it to the concept of sovereign dictatorship in which the separation of powers, basic rights, and other law and democratic procedures limiting the exercise of sovereign power are all suspended. He thus revives the old incarnation model of Hobbes in a new form. In *Constitutional Theory* (Durham, NC: Duke University Press, 2008), this theory of internal sovereignty became quite nuanced splitting into the theory of the constituent power and its sovereign representative. But there the concept of constituent power became the new locus for political theological myth-making. See A. Arato, "Multi-track Constitutionalism Beyond Carl Schmitt," *Constellations*, 18 (2011), 324–351. While I reject Schmitt's existential conception, it is worth noting that the discourse of popular sovereignty does involve ideas of political self-determination and legitimacy that escape Kelsen's legalistic analysis. However, the political conception of sovereignty (vis-à-vis legitimacy, constituent power, the ultimate source of the constitution, etc.) must be understood *ex negativo*, i.e. such that no agent, institution, subject, or individual can embody it, or put itself in the place of the people, and no foreign power can determine the legal or political order of a sovereign state. See Chapter 2 for more on Schmitt's sovereignty concept.

38 Hart, *The Concept of Law*, pp. 49–77.

39 Bodin, *On Sovereignty*.

40 Hart, *The Concept of Law*, pp. 49–77.
41 Kelsen, *Das Problem der Souveränität und die Theorie des Völkerrechts*, p. 53.
42 *Ibid.*, p. 320: "Die Souveränität Vorstellung freilich muss radikal verdrängt werden." That was in 1927. In later work, Kelsen decided to retain the concept, redefining it to mean simply that states are subject to public international law but not legally constrained by other states. Kelsen, *General Theory of Law and the State*, pp. 383–385. Finally, in 1944 he substituted the concept of sovereign equality for that of sovereignty. H. Kelsen, "The Principle of Sovereign Equality of States as a Basis for International Organization," *Yale Law Journal*, 53 (1944), 207–220.
43 Kelsen thus breaks with Jellinek's *Zwei-Seiten Lehre*, which viewed the state from a sociological perspective in terms of its organizational structure as well as from a legal perspective, but he agrees with the latter's critique of organ sovereignty. See Jellinek, *Allgemeine Staatslehre*, pp. 435–504. For a brilliant critique of organ sovereignty that challenges the notion that popular sovereignty can be embodied in an organ of the state (posing as the sovereign representative of the people), see Carré de Malberg, *Contribution à la théorie générale de l'état*, pp. 69–88.
44 Kelsen, *General Theory of Law and the State*, p. 384.
45 Kelsen engaged in a relentless critique of sociological realism regarding the state's monopoly of legitimate force, which he ascribed rather unfairly given the predicate "legitimate" to Max Weber's conception. For a good discussion, see A. Somek, "Kelsen Lives," *European Journal of International Law*, 18 (2007), 409–451 (pp. 436–438).
46 Austin, *The Province of Jurisprudence Determined*.
47 Kelsen, *General Theory of Law and the State*, p. 32.
48 While the overall legal order must be effective, it is not part of the concept of law that every legal norm must be effective or obeyed. Obviously, unlawful behavior occurs and does not undermine the validity of the relevant norm. *Ibid.*, p. 23.
49 *Ibid.*, p. 372.
50 *Ibid.*, p. 21.
51 *Ibid.*, p. 110. Kelsen sharply differentiates the realm of fact from the realm of norm, ought from is, validity from facility.
52 The "grundnorm" is a transcendental postulate, not a substantive norm. Its function in Kelsen's theory is to secure legal normativity and legal autonomy, and to free the foundational validity of law from extrinsic considerations: politics, religion, natural law, religion, and other transcendent points of view as well as to protect it from political instrumentalism. This entails a strict separation of legality from legitimacy issues and serves to conjure away the issue of the political origins of legal systems or of the "constituent power" from the concern of the jurist focused on validity. For a critical assessment that insists on the natural law-like quality of the concept of the basic norm, see J. Raz, "Kelsen's Theory of the Basic Norm," in *The Authority of Law: Essays on Law and Morality*, 2nd edn. (Oxford University Press, 2009), pp. 122–145.
53 Kelsen, *General Theory of Law and the State*, p. 367.
54 *Ibid.*, p. 111.
55 *Ibid.*, p. 116.
56 *Ibid.*
57 *Ibid.*, p. 121.
58 This use of the terms "monism" and "dualism" should not be confused with ordinary international law usage. For a clarification of the distinction, see N. Walker, "Late Sovereignty in the European Union," in Walker (ed.), *Sovereignty in Transition*, pp. 3–32, note 23. Kelsen refers to the two versions of monism (state-centered and international law-centered), i.e. the unity of national and international law, as an "epistemological postulate." Kelsen, *General Theory of Law and the State*, p. 373.

59 *Ibid.*, p. 363.
60 *Ibid.*, p. 384.
61 *Ibid.*, pp. 381–386.
62 *Ibid.*, p. 387.
63 *Ibid.*, p. 385.
64 *Ibid.*, p. 387. On idealizations endemic to the monist and the dualist perspectives, see Somek, "Kelsen Lives," pp. 431–432.
65 Kelsen, *General Theory of Law and the State*, p. 388. This is an example of one of Kelsen's own unnecessary idealizations. Somek, "Kelsen Lives."
66 Kelsen, *General Theory of Law and the State*, p. 349.
67 *Ibid.*
68 Moreover, even though states are the creators of international law through treaties and custom, these are law-creating facts thanks to the legal principles of positive international law that they presuppose.
69 Kelsen, *General Theory of Law and the State*, p. 381.
70 *Ibid.*, pp. 369–370.
71 *Ibid.*, p. 368.
72 *Ibid.*, p. 373. Thus, the inferior orders (state domestic legal orders) from the perspective of the superior order can be conceived of as partial orders within the superior total order.
73 *Ibid.*, p. 385.
74 *Ibid.*, p. 387.
75 *Ibid.*, p. 373.
76 *Ibid.*, pp. 343–349, 365.
77 *Ibid.*, pp. 343–348.
78 *Ibid.*
79 See Somek, "Kelsen Lives," pp. 418–419.
80 Kelsen, *General Theory of Law and the State*, p. 348. Somek does not take notice of this important statement of Kelsen's.
81 *Ibid.*, pp. 371–372.
82 *Ibid.*, pp. 371–380.
83 *Ibid.*, pp. 374–375.
84 I am paraphrasing Somek, "Kelsen Lives," p. 425.
85 *Ibid.*, p. 423.
86 Kelsen, *General Theory of Law and the State*, p. 388.
87 Political legitimacy or the political context of law is, to the theorist reasoning from the perspective of internal legal validity, irrelevant. If the order is efficacious, then legal validity can be analyzed while screening out considerations of political legitimacy – the "pure theory's" point. However, the political context of law and of legitimacy does matter to the theory in one key respect: regarding the requirement of efficacy. Kelsen restricts the concept of the state to the valid legal order; nevertheless legal enactment that creates institutions is not sufficient to create a state absent *effective* power, manifested in the successful capacity to dominate a territory and population, and thereby enforce commands. For power to be effective, it has to be sociologically legitimate in the Weberian sense – involving a claim to legitimacy that is accepted. Facticity (sociological legitimacy in this sense of effective stable power) and normativity come together around the basic norm in the form of an empirico-transcendental couplet. I am paraphrasing from N. Bhuta, "New Modes and Orders: The Difficulties of a Jus Post Bellum of Constitutional Transformation" *University of Toronto Law Journal*, 63 (2010), 799–854. Kelsen's ignoring of issues of legitimacy leads him to deny any relevance to the legal theorist of the difference between coups d'état, revolutions,

and radical yet legal transformations, and indeed to regard, from the international legal monist perspective, revolutionary change of domestic constitutions as "amendments" insofar as domestic basic norms are only relative – a patent absurdity in my view. See Kelsen, *General Theory of Law and the State*, pp. 117, 219–221.

88 For a more appropriate epistemological approach to the problem of sovereignty that does not reproduce Schmittian political theology, anathema to Kelsen, see J. Derrida, *Rogues: Two Essays on Reason* (Stanford University Press, 2005).

89 Hart, *The Concept of Law*, pp. 9, 30, 55–56, 234. On the influence of Wittgenstein's linguistic turn on Hart's epistemology, see N. Lacey, *A Life of H. L. A. Hart: The Nightmare and the Noble Dream* (Oxford University Press, 2004). Hart was concerned primarily with the internal attitude of jurists as his examples show in determining what the law is and which law is supreme. But the internal attitude of the citizenry matters as well for legitimacy.

90 H. L. A. Hart, "Kelsen's Doctrine of the Unity of Law," in *Essays in Jurisprudence and Philosophy* (Oxford: Clarendon Press, 1983), pp. 309–343.

91 See Somek, "Kelsen Lives," pp. 426–429, for a rebuttal of Hart's critique of Kelsen.

92 For this view on international law, see Hart, *The Concept of Law*, pp. 208–231.

93 Hart, "Kelsen's Doctrine of the Unity of Law."

94 *Ibid.*; but see Anghie, *Imperialism, Sovereignty and the Making of International Law*, pp. 46–65, for an analysis that argues that these criteria did not determine recognition as a sovereign state but, rather, the "criterion of civilization" mediating membership in international society played that role. See also G. Gong, *The Standard of "Civilization" in International Society* (Oxford: Clarendon Press, 1984).

95 Hart, "Kelsen's Doctrine of the Unity of Law"; and Somek, "Kelsen Lives," p. 427.

96 Kelsen, *General Theory of Law and the State*, p. 350.

97 Hart, "Kelsen's Doctrine of the Unity of Law," p. 322.

98 *Ibid.*, p. 319.

99 *Ibid.*, p. 338. In other words, the criterion of membership of laws in a single system is independent of and indeed presupposed when we apply the notion of one law deriving validity from another.

100 Hart, *The Concept of Law*, p. 104. Joseph Raz also adopts this position from Hart. See Raz, "Kelsen's Theory of the Basic Norm"; and Raz, *The Authority of Law*, pp. 128–129. Raz goes even further, arguing that there is a circularity in Kelsen's position: if the basic norm serves the function of identifying the unity and normativity of a legal system, insofar as the identity and unity of the legal system depends on the possibility of relating all laws back to one chain of validity, then it cannot really help in identifying the legal system because, in order to identify the legal system, one can only identify the basic norm of a legal system after the identity of the legal system has been established. Moreover, Raz argues, using the example in England of customary and posited constitutional law, that there is nothing in the theory to prevent two legal systems from applying to the same territory.

101 Kelsen would of course reply that the authority of courts to decide in case of conflict between national and domestic norms which norm to apply derives from the decentralized character of one overarching monistic global legal system. But this flies in the face of the sociological realism (efficacy) and issues of legitimacy that I have raised above and which Hart's Soviet Union example articulates.

102 Kelsen, *General Theory of Law and the State*, p. 363; cited in Hart, "Kelsen's Doctrine of the Unity of Law," p. 322.

103 Somek, "Kelsen Lives," p. 429.

104 *Ibid.*

105 Hart, *The Concept of Law*, pp. 26–48. Secondary rules do not tend to have sanctions attached to them but primary rules, e.g. of criminal law, certainly do.

106 The term "constitutional tolerance" comes from J. Weiler, "On the Power of the Word: Europe's Constitutional Iconography," *International Journal of Constitutional Law*, 3 (2005), 184–190. See also M. P. Maduro, "Sovereignty in Europe: The European Court of Justice and the Creation of a European Political Community," in M. Volcansek and J. Stack, Jr. (eds.), *Courts Crossing Borders: Blurring the Lines of Sovereignty* (Durham, NC: Carolina Academic Press, 2005), pp. 43–61 (pp. 50–52, 55–58).

107 As late as 1949, Kelsen wrote: "however strange it may seem – most theories of international law do not share this monistic view. International law and national law are, in their opinion, two separate, mutually independent legal orders that regulate quite different matters and have quite different sources." Kelsen, *General Theory of Law and the State*, p. 383.

108 Most regarded the UN and its organs, especially the Security Council and the General Assembly, as political bodies, the Charter as a treaty, and member states as sovereign, even though they gave up the *jus belli* with one crucial exception: self-defense.

109 A.-M. Slaughter and W. Burke-White, "An International Constitutional Moment," *Harvard International Law Journal*, 43 (2003), 1–21. For a critique, see A. Fischer-Lescano, "Redefining Sovereignty via International Constitutional Moments?" in M. E. O'Connell, M. Bothe, and N. Ronzitti (eds.), *Redefining Sovereignty: The Use of Force After the End of the Cold War* (Ardsley, NY: Transnational Publishers, 2005), pp. 335–364.

110 Fassbender, "The United Nations Charter as Constitution of the International Community," p. 579; B. Fassbender, "'We the Peoples of the United Nations': Constituent Power and Constitutional Form in International Law," in M. Loughlin and N. Walker (eds.), *The Paradox of Constitutionalism* (Oxford University Press, 2007), pp. 269–290 (p. 288), refers to the founding of the UN Charter as a constitutional moment in the history of the international community, and views the Charter as a constitutional document, not simply an international treaty, that reorganized the world community for the benefit of succeeding generations.

111 On discourse of international society, see Bull, *The Anarchical Society*. On the concept of international community, see E. Kwakwa, "The International Community, International Law, and the United States: Three in One, Two against One, or One and the Same?," A. Paulus, "The Influence of the United States on the Concept of the 'International Community,'" and M. Koskenniemi, S. Ratner, and V. Rittberger, "Comments on Chapters 1 and 2," all in M. Byers and G. Nolte (eds.), *United States Hegemony and the Foundations of International Law* (Cambridge University Press, 2003), pp. 25–56, 57–90, 91–116.

112 Or "civilized." Armitage, "The Contagion of Sovereignty"; Gong, *The Standard of "Civilization" in International Society.*

113 United Nations, *The United Nations Universal Declaration of Human Rights* (New York: UN, 1948); United Nations, *International Covenant on Economic, Social and Cultural Rights* (New York: UN, 1966).

114 Fassbender, "The United Nations Charter as Constitution of the International Community," p. 579; but see also Fischer-Lescano, *Globalverfassung: Die Geltungsbegründung der Menschenrechte*. Nevertheless, it is not settled whether *jus cogens* principles established in the Vienna Convention on the Law of Treaties and reasserted by the ICTY go beyond treaty rules or which range of human rights norms are involved.

115 ICISS, *The Responsibility to Protect: Report of the International Commission on Intervention and State Sovereignty* (Ottawa: International Development Research Centre, 2001); and United Nations, A More Secure World: Our Shared Responsibility, Report of the

Secretary-General's High-level Panel on Threats, Challenges and Change (New York: United Nations, 2004), www.un.org/secureworld.

116 Slaughter and Burke-White, "An International Constitutional Moment." This misunderstands the concept, "grundnorm," insofar as it is a transcendental postulate not a substantive principle.

117 G. H. Fox, *Humanitarian Occupation* (Cambridge University Press, 2008). S. Talmon, "The Security Council as World Legislature," *American Journal of International Law*, 99 (2005), 175–193; and P. Szasz, "The Security Council Starts Legislating," *American Journal of International Law*, 96 (2002), 901–905, both of whom are enthusiasts of this development.

118 Fox, *Humanitarian Occupation*.

119 K. W. Abbott, R. O. Keohane, A. Moravcsik, A.-M. Slaughter, and D. Snidal, "The Concept of Legalization," in R. O. Keohane, *Power and Governance in a Partially Globalized World* (New York: Routledge, 2002), pp. 132–151.

120 Alter, "Delegating to International Courts", discussing delegation to international courts and the effects of IC rulings on state sovereignty, but arguing that sovereignty remains strong and an important component of the international system.

121 Progress to Kelsen means individualization and centralization in the sense that courts, global, trans-, and national, now apply and enforce international law. Domestic courts can also act as such agents as, for example, they do in the EU vis-à-vis the European Community.

122 For a discussion of contemporary legal pluralists and the relevant citations, see Section 1.5 below.

123 I am paraphrasing M. Koskenniemi, "The Fate of Public International Law: Between Technique and Politics," *Modern Law Review*, 70 (2007), 1–30 (p. 23). See also K. Günther, "Legal Pluralism or Uniform Concept of Law: Globalization as a Problem of Legal Theory," *NoFo*, 5 (2008), 5–21.

124 M. Koskenniemi, "Constitutionalism as Mindset: Reflections on Kantian Themes about International Law and Globalization," *Theoretical Inquiries in Law*, 8 (2007), 9–36 (p. 13); "Fragmentation of International Law. Problems caused by the Diversification and Expansion of International Law," Report of the Study Group of the International Law Commission finalized by Martti Koskenniemi A/CN4/L.682 (13 April 2006) (Analytical Report); and Günther, "Legal Pluralism or Uniform Concept of Law," pp. 5–15.

125 Koskenniemi, "Constitutionalism as Mindset," 13.

126 See Chapter 5.

127 The terms of the debate are even accepted by its critics. See Koskenniemi, "Constitutionalism as Mindset."

128 On cosmopolitan pluralism, see M. Kumm, "Who is the Final Arbiter of Constitutionality in Europe?" *Common Market Law Review*, 36 (1999), 509–514; and M. Kumm, "The Cosmopolitan Turn in Constitutionalism: On the Relationship between Constitutionalism in and beyond the State," in J. L. Dunoff and J. P. Trachtman (eds.), *Ruling the World? Constitutionalism, International Law and Global Governance* (Cambridge University Press, 2009), pp. 258–324 (p. 291). On systems-theoretical versions of constitutional pluralism, see Teubner, "Societal Constitutionalism"; and Fischer-Lescano, *Globalverfassung: Die Geltungsbegründung der Menschenrechte*.

129 A recent collection is Klabbers, Peters, and Ulfstein, *The Constitutionalization of International Law*; see also the new journal *Global Constitutionalism*.

130 Fassbender, "Sovereignty and Constitutionalism in International Law."

131 *Ibid.*, pp. 134–141.

132 Kelsen, "The Principle of Sovereign Equality of States," p. 208. This piece was a reflection on the Moscow conference of October 1943 that preceded the San Francisco conference founding the UN. Kelsen argued for an international court with compulsory jurisdiction, as something that states would not deem undermining of their legal sovereignty. He believed that without a compulsory international court, the step to an effective international legal system would fail, and no real guarantees for collective security and peace would exist since there would be no binding way to settle disputes peacefully. He argued that compulsory jurisdiction of an international court would not abolish sovereign equality but only put an end to settling conflicts by means of force.

133 Fassbender, "Sovereignty and Constitutionalism in International Law," p. 212.

134 *Ibid.*, p. 209.

135 *Ibid.*, pp. 211–212.

136 On the origins of the doctrine of international community, see Fassbender, "The United Nations Charter as Constitution of the International Community," footnote 14; and "'We the Peoples of the United Nations,'" p. 272.

137 Fassbender, "The United Nations Charter as Constitution of the International Community," 564.

138 Fassbender, "Sovereignty and Constitutionalism in International Law," p. 130.

139 A. Somek, "From the Rule of Law to the Constitutionalist Makeover: Changing European Conceptions of Public International Law," University of Iowa Legal Studies Research Paper No. 09–25 (2009), p. 36.

140 Somek, "Kelsen Lives," p. 426. Somek, however, rejects the constitutionalist discourse for international or global law.

141 See E. Wet, "The International Constitutional Order," *International Comparative Law Quarterly,* 55 (2006), 51–76; A. Verdross, *Die Verfassung der Völkerrechtsgemeinschaft* (Vienna: J. Springer, 1926); C. Tomuschat, "International Law: Ensuring the Survival of Mankind on the Eve of a New Century: The Hague General Course on Public International Law," *Revue des Cours,* 281 (1999), 9–438; and B. Simma, "From Bilateralism to Community Interest in International Law," *Recueil des cours,* 250 (1994), 217–384, for a sampling of those who argue for an international community based in shared, now constitutionalized values. Fischer-Lescano, *Globalverfassung: Die Geltungsbegründung der Menschenrechte,* and Fassbender represent the de-centered and centered versions respectively. See below. For collections of essays on global constitutionalism, see Macdonald and Johnston (eds.), *Towards World Constitutionalism;* C. Joerges and E. U. Petersman (eds.), *Constitutionalism, Multilevel Trade Governance and Social Regulation* (Oxford: Hart Publishing, 2006); and Klabbers, Peters, and Ulfstein, *The Constitutionalization of International Law.* See also the introduction in Fassbender, "The United Nations Charter as Constitution of the International Community."

142 Kumm, "The Cosmopolitan Turn in Constitutionalism," p. 291.

143 Fassbender, "The United Nations Charter as Constitution of the International Community," p. 560.

144 Kumm, "The Cosmopolitan Turn in Constitutionalism," note 138, pp. 290–295.

145 But see Koskenniemi's critique of this stance in "The Fate of Public International Law," p. 18.

146 Fassbender, "The United Nations Charter as Constitution of the International Community"; and "'We the Peoples of the United Nations,'" p. 281. I will address the issue of whether the Charter is a treaty, a constitution, or a constitutional treaty in Chapter 5.

147 Fassbender, "'We the Peoples of the United Nations,'" p. 282.

148 Fassbender, "The United Nations Charter as Constitution of the International Community," p. 585; and "'We the Peoples of the United Nations,'" p. 283.

149 Fassbender, "Sovereignty and Constitutionalism in International Law," especially p. 131.

150 *Ibid.*, p. 135, on the relation of general international law as subordinate to Charter law. See also Fassbender, "The United Nations Charter as Constitution of the International Community," p. 587.

151 As for the relation to the disputed category of *jus cogens* norms, Fassbender argues that only decisions consistent with *jus cogens* can create obligations under Article 103, the supremacy clause of the Charter. Fassbender, "The United Nations Charter as Constitution of the International Community," pp. 590–591; so there has to be a symmetry of peremptory norms and constitutional obligations arising under the Charter.

152 Insofar as there are now effective organs of the international community thanks to the constitutional character of the Charter, this replaces the category of *erga omnes* obligations originally introduced to give states unaffected by a breach of rules a legal interest in their protection. Now the organs of the UN can order performance of obligations *erga omnes*, although individual states still have a role to play in ensuring compliance. Fassbender, "The United Nations Charter as Constitution of the International Community," p. 592. At present only the prohibition of aggression and arguably grave violations of human rights can be enforced by a community organ. According to Fassbender, *erga omnes* obligations are an interim phenomenon of an international community in the process of being constitutionalized.

153 Fassbender, "'We the Peoples of the United Nations,'" pp. 288–289.

154 *Ibid.*

155 I will return to this in Chapter 4.

156 UN Charter, Chapter XVIII, Article 108.

157 H. Kelsen, *The Law of the United Nations: A Critical Analysis of its Fundamental Problems* (London: Stevens and Sons, 1950), p. 7; cited in Fassbender, "'We the Peoples of the United Nations,'" p. 288.

158 Fassbender, "'We the Peoples of the United Nations,'" p. 289. Fassbender cites as examples the US Articles of Confederation, the US Constitution of 1787, and the German Confederations of 1815 and 1920. I will return to the issue of federation in Chapter 2. Suffice it to say that federation need not require a monist hierarchical analysis of global constitutionalism, but fits much better with constitutional pluralism.

159 *Ibid.*, p. 289.

160 Walker, "Late Sovereignty in the European Union," pp. 10–14.

161 I will argue for a combination of a power-limiting and foundational understanding of the project of global constitutionalism, understood in the frame of constitutional pluralism and as a project for instituting a new sovereignty regime in Chapter 5.

162 See Chapters 2 and 5.

163 Teubner, "Societal Constitutionalism"; Fischer-Lescano, "Constitutional Rights–Constitutional Fights"; and Fischer-Lescano, *Globalverfassung: Die Geltungsbegründung der Menschenrechte.*

164 Teubner, "Societal Constitutionalism."

165 For a critique, see J. L. Cohen, "Whose Sovereignty?" pp. 11–17. For a critique of the systems-theoretical approach to law, see J. L. Cohen, "The Debate Over the Reflexive Paradigm," in *Regulating Intimacy: A New Legal Paradigm* (Princeton University Press, 2002), pp. 151–179.

166 Cohen, "Whose Sovereignty?" It is important to stress that Teubner and Fischer-Lescano are constitutionalists with respect to each global subsystem, but pluralists regarding the relations among them. G. Teubner, "Global Bukowina: Legal Pluralism in the World Society," in G. Teubner (ed.), *Global Law Without a State* (Brookfield, VT: Dartmouth Publishing Group, 1997), pp. 3–15; A. Fischer-Lescano and G. Teubner,

"Regime Collisions: The Vain Search for Unity in the Fragmentation of Global Law," *Michigan Journal of International Law*, 25 (2004), 999–1046; and A. Fischer-Lescano and G. Teubner, *Regime-Kollisionen: Zur Fragmentierung des globalen Rechts* (Frankfurt am Main: Suhrkamp, 2006).

167 Teubner, "Societal Constitutionalism" and "Global Bukowina: Legal Pluralism in the World Society."

168 Teubner, "Global Bukowina: Legal Pluralism in the World Society"; also Fischer-Lescano, *Globalverfassung: Die Geltungsbegründung der Menschenrechte.*

169 Teubner, "Societal Constitutionalism."

170 However, it does not guarantee nor is it oriented to the usual purposes of power-limiting constitutionalism, namely the orientation of public power to public purposes and the common good. On the distinction between power-limiting and foundational constitutionalism, see C. Mollers, "The Politics of Law and the Law of Politics," in E. O. Eriksen, J. E. Fossum, and A. J. Menendez (eds.), *Developing a Constitution for Europe* (New York: Routledge, 2004), pp. 128–139.

171 N. Luhmann, *Grundrechte als Institution: ein Beitrag zur politischen Soziologie* (Berlin: Duncker & Humblot, 1999). Rights ensure limits to the internal systemic logic of any one subsystem vis-à-vis imperial tendencies toward the others.

172 Fischer-Lescano and Teubner, "Regime Collisions."

173 A.-M. Slaughter, "A Global Community of Courts," *Harvard International Law Review*, 44 (2003), 191–219.

174 See Chapter 3 for my discussion of the responsibility to protect (R2P) doctrine embraced by the UN.

175 *Jus cogens* norms cited in the 1969 Vienna Convention on the Law of Treaties. See Shelton, "Normative Hierarchy in International Law," p. 309. The Vienna Convention treaty referred to the rules of *jus cogens* as the heart of an international constitution and as rules "accepted and recognized by the international community of States as a whole ... from which no derogation is permitted and which can be modified only by subsequent norm[s] of general international law having the same character." ICTY invoked their human rights character in its *jus cogens* arguments (the prohibitions on genocide, slavery, trading in human beings, torture, aggression). See the Vienna Convention on the Law of Treaties, Article 53.

176 Fassbender, "'We the Peoples of the United Nations,'" p. 279.

177 Fischer-Lescano and Teubner, "Regime Collisions."

178 Kumm, "The Cosmopolitan Turn in Constitutionalism."

179 Fischer-Lescano, "Constitutional Rights–Constitutional Fights" p. 12.

180 The focus is validity or, as will become clear regarding Kumm, morality/justice. Political legitimacy, however, involves a different perspective. Unlike Schmitt, however, I do not believe that considerations of legitimacy in general and democratic legitimacy in particular require a new political theology, populism, or political instrumentalism regarding law.

181 The term is coined by Matthias Kumm; see Kumm, "Who is the Final Arbiter of Constitutionality in Europe?" and "The Cosmopolitan Turn in Constitutionalism," pp. 262, 268. Kumm's fascinating work is not easy to locate thus I will discuss it twice: under the constitutionalist approach and when I discuss the pluralist approach. Systems theorists purport not to be engaging in normative moral or political theory.

182 *Ibid.*

183 *Ibid.*, p. 268.

184 *Ibid.*

185 *Ibid.*, pp. 291, 278.

186 A. Somek, "Monism: A Tale of the Undead," University of Iowa Legal Studies Research Paper No. 10–22 (2010).

187 Kumm, "The Cosmopolitan Turn in Constitutionalism," pp. 263–264. For a critique of the concept of subsidiarity, see D. Elazar, "The United States and the European Union: Models for Their Epochs," in K. Nicolaidis and R. Howse (eds.), *The Federal Vision: Legitimacy and Levels of Governance in the United States and European Union* (Oxford University Press, 2001), pp. 31–53 (pp. 42–46).

188 See J. B. Cruz, "The Legacy of the Maastricht-Urteil and the Pluralist Movement," EUI Working Papers (RSCAS 2007/13), available at www.eui.eu/RCSAC/Publications. The EU is a hybrid. There are debates over whether it is a highly integrated international organization or a weakly integrated federation. See Chapter 2 for a discussion of the concept, federation.

189 R. Hirschel, *Towards Juristocracy: The Origins and Consequences of the New Constitutionalism* (Cambridge, MA: Harvard University Press, 2004).

190 M. Kumm, "The Jurisprudence of Constitutional Conflict: Constitutional Supremacy in Europe Before and After the Constitutional Treaty," *European Law Journal*, 11 (2005), 262–307.

191 Kumm's position regarding sovereignty is clearly influenced by the seminal article of N. MacCormick, "The Maastricht-Urteil: Sovereignty Now," *European Law Journal*, 1 (1995), 259–266, which linked the practice of constitutional pluralism to the absence of sovereignty in the EU order.

192 See Chapter 2.

193 Indeed legal pluralism emerged initially as a challenge to the state's claim of legal sovereignty as the monopoly of law-making capacity. See B. Z. Tamanaha, "Understanding Legal Pluralism: Past to Present, Local to Global," *Sydney Law Review*, 30 (2008), 375–411. See also B. de Sousa Santos, *Toward a New Legal Common Sense: Law, Globalization and Emancipation* (London: Butterworths, 2002).

194 Tamanaha, "Understanding Legal Pluralism."

195 With or without a constituent power: it would mean empire or at least the emergence of new imperial formations.

196 See especially P. S. Berman, "Global Legal Pluralism," *Southern Carolina Law Review*, 80 (2007), 1155–1238 (p. 1236); N. Krisch, "The Pluralism of Global Administrative Law," *European Journal of International Law*, 17 (2006), 247–278; N. Krisch, *Beyond Constitutionalism: The Case for Pluralism in Post-National Law* (Oxford University Press, 2010), especially Chapters 2 and 3, pp. 27–109; and P. S. Berman, "The New Legal Pluralism," *Annual Review of Law and Social Science*, 5 (2009), 225–242.

197 Tamanaha, "Understanding Legal Pluralism," pp. 375–385.

198 This claim draws on critical anthropological studies. For an overview of earlier pluralist literature, see Berman, "The New Legal Pluralism." For an early exemplar, see E. Ehrlich, *Grundlegung der Soziologie des Rechts* (Munich and Leipzig: Duncker & Humblot, 1913) for the argument that independent customary law can be more important than state law, based on a study of a province, Bukowina, in the east of the Hapsburg empire; and S. F. Moore, "Law and Social Change: The Semi-Autonomous Social Field as an Appropriate Subject for Study," *Law and Society Review*, 7 (1973), 719–746, arguing that law is not only internally pluralistic but embedded in other social fields and their normative systems such as customs, religion, etc. Teubner's "Global Bukowina: Legal Pluralism in the World Society," p. 315, draws on these claims and applies them to the twenty-first century's global world system. However, unlike the cultural anthropological approaches, the systems theorist insists on the distinctiveness of the legal medium and legal code vis-à-vis other normative systems and, indeed, seeks to shield that code from the "imperialisms" of other subsystems.

199 For an analysis of legal pluralist origins of the western legal tradition that similarly castigates the leveling and homogenizing thrust of the sovereignty paradigm see H. J. Berman, *Law and Revolution* (Cambridge, MA: Harvard University Press, 1983).

200 Tamanaha, "Understanding Legal Pluralism," pp. 83–84; Teubner, "Global Bukowina: Legal Pluralism in the World Society."

201 S. E. Merry, "Legal Pluralism," *Law and Society Review*, 22 (1988), 869–896. See also J. Griffiths, "What is Legal Pluralism?" *Journal of Legal Pluralism and Unofficial Law*, 50 (1986), 1–55, surveying theories of legal pluralism at the time. For recent discussions of legal pluralism within empires, see K. Barkey, *Empire of Difference: The Ottomans in Comparative Perspective* (Cambridge University Press, 2008); and L. Benton, *A Search for Sovereignty: Law and Geography in European Empires, 1400–1900* (Cambridge University Press, 2010).

202 This is not the case for global legal pluralists of the systems-theoretical bent. As already indicated, with respect to the legal order internal to each legal system, they are neo-Kelsenian constitutionalists but pluralist regarding the relations between the globalized functional subsystems of world society.

203 B. de Sousa Santos, *Toward a New Common Sense: Law, Science and Politics in the Paradigmatic Transition* (New York: Routledge, 1995), p. 114.

204 *Ibid.*, p. 473.

205 This stance distinguishes legal pluralists from classical dualists as well, insofar as the latter assume the impermeability of distinct legal orders while contemporary legal pluralists assume hybridity, porousness, and overlap of normative orders. Again, this is not true of the systems theorists. See Koskenniemi's critique that charges them with simply ratcheting up the billiard ball model of sovereign states to the global level of functionally differentiated (hermetically sealed) global subsystems in "The Fate of Public International Law," pp. 22–24. Insofar as systems-theoretical legal pluralists identify institutional orders on the global level (regimes) with subsystems and their rationality they are guilty of a category mistake: collapsing an analytic logic with a concrete institutional order.

206 Sousa Santos, *Toward a New Common Sense*. See also the discussion in Günther, "Legal Pluralism or Uniform Concept of Law."

207 I count among the strong legal pluralists N. Krisch, P. S. Berman, and D. Kennedy, "One, Two, Three, Many Legal Orders: Legal Pluralism and the Cosmopolitan Dream," *New York University Review of Law & Social Change*, 31 (2007), 641–659.

208 *Ibid.*

209 Krisch, *Beyond Constitutionalism*, p. 12. Krisch is aware of theories of constitutional pluralism but chooses to ignore them for the sake of the dichotomy between constitutionalism and pluralism that he buys into.

210 *Ibid.* Hence the constitutionalist mechanisms such as federalism, consociationalism, local autonomy, and so forth that accommodate diversity, not to mention multicultural jurisdiction are not feasible for the global order. This is correct as things now stand but, as I will show, can change. There are indeed political preconditions for this sort of constitutionalist vocabulary and techniques or their functional equivalents to apply to the global domain. But the latter need not take the form of a state for this to become plausible. The error informing this dismissive analysis is the construal of federation as entailing a federal state.

211 *Ibid.*, pp. 21, 22; Berman, "Global Legal Pluralism," 1229–1238; Sousa Santos, *Toward a New Common Sense*.

212 Krisch, "The Pluralism of Global Administrative Law"; and *Beyond Constitutionalism*, p. 13.

213 Among the soft legal pluralists, see A. V. Bogdandy, "Pluralism, Direct Effect and the Ultimate Say: On the Relationship Between International and Domestic Constitutional Law," *International Journal of Constitutional Law*, 6 (2008), 397–413; M. Delmas-Marty, *Towards a Truly Common Law: Europe as a Laboratory for Legal Pluralism* (Cambridge University Press, 1994); M. Delmas-Marty, *Le pluralisme ordonné* (Paris: Editions du Seuil, 2006); W. Burke-White, "International Legal Pluralism," *Michigan Journal of International Law*, 25 (2004), 963–979; and according to his own self-interpretation, M. Kumm, "The Legitimacy of International Law: A Constitutionalist Analysis," *European Journal of International Law*, 15 (2004), 907–931; and, in some respects, Kumm, "Who is the Final Arbiter of Constitutionality in Europe?"; G. de Búrca, "The EU, The European Court of Justice and the International Legal Order After Kadi," *Harvard International Law Journal*, 51 (2009), 1–49. Accordingly, Kumm straddles the line between soft pluralism and de-centered constitutionalism and thus is considered to be a "soft" pluralist. Despite his pluralist rhetoric, however, and given his stance on sovereignty and on the unity of national and international legal orders, he does seem to fit more into the global constitutionalist camp, as per my argument above.

214 Kumm, "The Legitimacy of International Law." See also S. Besson, "How International is the European Legal Order?" *NoFo*, 5 (2008), 50–70; and S Besson, "Theorizing the Sources of International Law," in S. Besson and J. Tasoulias (eds.), *The Philosophy of International Law* (Oxford University Press, 2010), pp. 163–187.

215 Burke-White, "International Legal Pluralism"; A.-M. Slaughter, *A New World Order* (Princeton University Press, 2004).

216 I will argue that they do not. See below and Chapter 5.

217 C. Offe, "Governance: An Empty Signifier?" *Constellations*, 16 (2009), 550–562.

218 Günther, "Legal Pluralism," pp. 15–16.

219 J. Habermas, "Law as Medium and Law as Institution," in G. Teubner (ed.), *Dilemmas of Law in the Welfare State* (Berlin: Walter de Gruyter, 1985), pp. 203–220.

220 *Ibid.* But Klaus Günther is guilty of what Somek calls an idealization by reading too much extrinsic normativity into the legal medium, for he assumes democratic legitimacy is intrinsic to the concept of law.

221 *Ibid.*

222 Somek, "Kelsen Lives," p. 429.

223 Günther, "Legal Pluralism," pp. 16–18. This gets at the internal normativity of the legal medium and why it is compelling beyond its ability to sanction, i.e. why its commands can be deemed different from the commands of a gunman. See also Raz, "Kelsen's Theory of the Basic Norm" for a discussion of the kind of justified normativity his theory entails.

224 Günther, "Legal Pluralism."

225 I follow Neil Walker on this point. N. Walker, "The Idea of Constitutional Pluralism," *Modern Law Review*, 65 (2002), 317–359, and "Late Sovereignty in the European Union."

226 Walker, "The Idea of Constitutional Pluralism."

227 See Chapter 5 for a discussion of the distinction between the EU and the UN as political formations now and in the future.

228 But, as we shall see, there is no need to assume that the global legal/political formation should or could develop in the same way as a regional political formation like the EU. Differences in degrees of integration, desirable and actual, and in degrees of heterogeneity would indicate different approximations of the various ideal types of political formations appropriate for the praxis of constitutional pluralism. See the next chapter and Chapter 5. Every empirical order is of course a hybrid vis-à-vis an ideal type.

229 Pace Martin Loughlin who argues that it is. See M. Loughlin, "What is Constitutional-ism?" in P. Dobner and M. Loughlin (eds.), *The Twilight of Constitutionalism?* (Oxford University Press, 2010), pp. 47–72.

230 Walker, "Late Sovereignty in the European Union," p. 15. Here we must distinguish between delegation of competences, division of competences, efficacy, and the con-fused idea of divided sovereignty. Efficacy is always a vérité à faire, and as indicated earlier, competences can be distributed, as per the separation of powers in a consti-tutional republic or the division of powers in a federal state. None of this means that sovereignty itself is divided.

231 Walker, "Late Sovereignty in the European Union."

232 *Ibid.*, pp. 10, 17. Neil Walker rightly states that sovereignty is still a central part of the "object-language" of the domestic constitutional law of states and hence should not be abandoned on the level of meta-language of theorists.

233 *Ibid.*, p. 10, for the distinction between object-language of actors and participants and meta-language of theorists.

234 Indeed ascriptions of sovereignty can also be ways to limit and render public power responsible.

235 Walker, "Late Sovereignty in the European Union," p. 10.

236 *Ibid.*, p. 17. This can, of course, change. However, deferral may be as good as it gets and need not be seen as transitional to a state-like structure.

237 From this perspective, see also Walker, "The Idea of Constitutional Pluralism" for an early and excellent discussion of the concept.

238 Walker, "Late Sovereignty in the European Union," p. 28. See also M. Loughlin, "Ten Tenets of Sovereignty," in Walker (ed.), *Sovereignty in Transition*, pp. 55–86.

239 Walker, "Late Sovereignty in the European Union," p. 28.

240 Krassner understood Westphalian sovereignty to involve the exclusion of external political actors from the political structures of a territorial state, and international sovereignty as indicative of a state's capacity to control flows across borders. Internal or "domestic" sovereignty involved the actual ability of political authorities to control process inside their borders. See S. D. Krassner, *Sovereignty: Organized Hypocrisy* (Princeton University Press, 1999), pp. 3–42.

241 Walker, "Late Sovereignty in the European Union," p. 28.

242 I will be addressing constitutionalization not of the entire world system but of the UN Charter legal and political system: where I differ from Fassbender and others is (a) that I do think the constitutionalization of this system is a project not a fait accompli and (b) that I view it through the lens of constitutional pluralism not monism.

243 Its quality as autonomous does not endow it with constitutional quality. Nor would constitutionalization of the international or global legal order attached to the global political system define its relation to domestic legal orders: this, as per the theory of constitutional pluralism, could remain open. As an autonomous legal order, the UN Charter system has its own legal sources and determines the validity and rank of norms within globalizing international law. Constitutionalization entails hierarchization of international legal sources to match developing hierarchies of norms (e.g. Article 103 of the UN Charter). But this would still be from the internal legal perspective of that legal order. Besson, "How International is the European Legal Order?" pp. 54–55.

244 See Chapter 5 for details.

245 On the need to reform this amendment rule, see J. L. Cohen, "A Global State of Emergency or the Further Constitutionalisation of International Law: A Pluralist Approach," *Constellations*, 15 (2008), 456–484; and Chapter 4.

246 Assuming we want to undo, challenge, or avoid and provide an alternative to the route of empire or new imperial formations.

247 The originator of this concept is Neil MacCormick, "Beyond the Sovereign State," *Modern Law Review*, 56 (1993), 1–18, and "The Maastricht-Urteil: Sovereignty Now." MacCormick changed his position regarding sovereignty in his later work, *Questioning Sovereignty: Law, State, and Nation in the European Commonwealth* (Oxford University Press, 1999).

248 M. P. Maduro, "Courts and Pluralism: Essay on a Theory of Judicial Adjudication in the Context of Legal and Constitutional Pluralism," in Dunoff and Trachtman (eds.), *Ruling the World?* pp. 356–361.

249 There is a debate about the nature of the EU: i.e. whether it is an international organization or "something more," but I cannot get into this here. I follow the logic of Maduro's argument (*ibid.*), which indicates how one would have to construe the EU (i.e. as a polity) for constitutional pluralism to be fully realized and democratically legitimate. But Maduro does not spell this out. He treats the EU as if it were already a polity of the requisite sort, i.e. a federation. I discuss Maduro's position in greater detail in Chapter 5. See Chapter 2 for a discussion of the concept of federation that is, I argue, the analogue of the theory of constitutional pluralism. Cruz, "The Legacy of the Maastricht-Urteil and the Pluralist Movement," is suggestive in this regard for he too argues that if courts take an internal point of view when operating within the scope of European Union law, and acknowledge it has its own rule of recognition, then they are acting as if the Treaty is a federal constitutional pact and as if national constitutions have mutated implicitly when the treaty was adopted. In this case European Union law would supersede national law, including the constitution, within the scope of Union law as defined by the ECJ, leaving intact the supremacy of the constitution outside it. Indeed. However, a commitment to the EU as a federation has not occurred in its member states. Nevertheless, this does not obviate Neil Walker's constructivist position that sees constitutional pluralism as the best descriptor of existing EU legal practice while aspiring to a future thicker sense of trans-systemic constitutional normativity that acceptance of a documentary federal constitution on the EU level would entail. The point is that such a step would obviously involve and help create greater commitment to the EU project and political community without, however, entailing monist constitutionalism. N. Walker, "Constitutionalism and Pluralism in the Global Context," forthcoming in M. Avbelj and J. Komarek (eds.), *Constitutional Pluralism in the European Union and Beyond* (Oxford: Hart Publishing, 2012), note 25. The other side is represented by B. de Witte, "The European Union as an International Legal Experiment," in G. de Búrca (ed.), *The Worlds of European Constitutionalism* (Cambridge University Press, 2011), pp. 19–56; draft version for the workshop, The EU Between Constitutionalism and International Law, New York University, October 5–6, 2008.

250 See J. E. Fossum and A. J. Menendez, *The Constitution's Gift: A Constitutional Theory for a Democratic European Union* (New York: Rowman & Littlefield, 2011) for a discussion of the kind of constitutional synthesis EU constitutionalism entails vis-à-vis constitutions of member states.

251 MacCormick, "The Maastricht-Urteil: Sovereignty Now," p. 265.

252 *Ibid.*

253 *Ibid.*

254 For an excellent theoretical elaboration, see Walker, "The Theory of Constitutional Pluralism"; J. Weiler, *The Constitution of Europe: "Do the New Clothes Have an Emperor?" and Other Essays on European Integration* (Cambridge University Press, 1999); M. P. Maduro, "Contrapunctual Law: Europe's Constitutional Pluralism in Action," in Walker (ed.), *Sovereignty in Transition*, pp. 501–538; and M. P. Maduro, "Sovereignty in Europe: The European Court of Justice and the Creation of a European

Political Community," in Volcansek and Stack, Jr. (eds.), *Courts Crossing Borders*, pp. 43–61. For a critique of some versions of the constitutional pluralist approach, see Cruz, "The Legacy of the Maastricht-Urteil and the Pluralist Movement."

255 I am paraphrasing Walker, "Constitutionalism and Pluralism in Global Context," pp. 9–11.

256 *Ibid.*, pp. 11–12.

257 Walker, "Late Sovereignty in the European Union," 18.

258 Maduro, "Contrapunctual Law."

259 Maduro makes this point for the EU. *Ibid.*, pp. 525, 527–528; but this goes for political as well as legal actors. The legal theorists focus only on the legal actors; too narrow a set in my view.

260 Weiler, "On the Power of the Word"; Weiler calls this "constitutional tolerance" with respect to the EU.

261 Walker, "Late Sovereignty in the European Union"; Maduro, "Contrapunctual Law," p. 530.

262 Kumm, "The Legitimacy of International Law"; Besson, "How International is the European Legal Order?" endnote 31.

263 See Chapter 5.

264 *Ibid.*

265 See Chapter 3 and J. L. Cohen, "Rethinking Human Rights, Democracy and Sovereignty in the Age of Globalization," *Political Theory*, 36 (2008), 578–606.

266 The concept of informal constitutional moments is pernicious insofar as it deflects efforts to use or reform the formal amendment rule in a constitution or constitutional treaty.

267 See United Nations, A More Secure World.

268 A. Chayes and A. H. Chayes, *The New Sovereignty: Compliance with International Regulatory Agreements* (Cambridge, MA: Harvard University Press, 1998), p. 27; A.-M. Slaughter, "Security, Solidarity and Sovereignty: The Grand Theme of UN Reform," *American Journal of International Law*, 99 (2005), 619–631 (pp. 627–630).

269 See Chapter 4.

270 See Chapter 4.

271 See T. Endicott, "The Logic of Freedom and Power," in Besson and Tasioulis (eds.), *The Philosophy of International Law*, pp. 245–260, and my reply in the same volume, J. L. Cohen, "Sovereignty in the Context of Globalization: A Constitutional Pluralist Perspective," pp. 261–282.

272 In the process, learning to compromise and engage in cooperative politics that reinforces whatever degree of democracy and justice they establish. See Cohen, "Rethinking Rights, Democracy and Sovereignty."

273 See Chapters 5 and 6.

Chapter 2 Constitutionalism and political form: rethinking federation

1 On the universalization of sovereign statehood, see D. Armitage, "The Contagion of Sovereignty: Declarations of Independence Since 1776," *South African Historical Journal*, 52 (2005), 1–18. See also D. Armitage, *Declarations of Independence: A Global History* (Cambridge, MA: Harvard University Press, 2007).

2 T. Fazal, *State Death: The Politics and Geography of Conquest, Occupation, and Annexation* (Princeton University Press, 2008).

3 Hannah Arendt pointed out the dilemmas regarding the ideal of the homogeneous nation-state long ago in *The Origins of Totalitarianism* (New York: Harcourt, 1994), pp. 11–54, 158–184, 267–304.

4 On the concept of state-nation, see A. Stepan, J. J. Linz, and Y. Yadov, *Crafting State-Nations: India and Other Multinational Democracies* (Baltimore, MD: Johns Hopkins University Press, 2011), pp. 1–38.

5 See O. Hintze, *The Historical Essays of Otto Hintze* (Oxford University Press, 1989); and H. Spruyt, *The Sovereign State and Its Competitors* (Princeton University Press, 1994) for the historical point. See Arendt, *Origins of Totalitarianism*, pp. 269–270, arguing that modern power conditions make national sovereignty a mockery except for giant states; and C. Schmitt, *The Nomos of the Earth in the International Law of the* Jus Publicum Europaeum (New York: Telos Press, 2003), pp. 295–322, 351–355, for the contemporary diagnosis.

6 M. Hardt and A. Negri, *Empire* (Cambridge, MA: Harvard University Press, 2000).

7 D. Held and D. Archibugi, *Cosmopolitan Democracy: An Agenda for a New World Order* (Cambridge: Polity Press, 1995); D. J. Elazar *Exploring Federalism* (Tuscaloosa, AL: University of Alabama Press, 1987).

8 K. Nicolaidis and R. Howse (eds.), *The Federal Vision: Legitimacy and Levels of Governance in the United States and the European Union* (Oxford University Press, 2001); O. Beaud, *Théorie de la fédération* (Paris: Presses Universitaires de France, 2007).

9 See below, Section 2.1 of this chapter.

10 Hannah Arendt construed federation as the alternative to sovereignty. H. Arendt, *On Revolution* (New York: Penguin, 1965), pp. 159–160, 259–260. For a critique, see A. Arato and J. L. Cohen, "Banishing the Sovereign? Internal and Eternal Sovereignty in Arendt," in S. Benhabib (ed.), *Politics in Dark Times: Encounters with Hannah Arendt* (Cambridge University Press, 2010), pp. 137–171. See also Elazar, *Exploring Federalism*, pp. 34–36; M. Forsyth, *Unions of States: The Theory and Practice of Confederation* (New York: Holmes & Meier, 1981), p. 6, discussing and rejecting world federalism.

11 Elazar, *Exploring Federalism*, pp. 34–40, 64.

12 See Forsyth, *Unions of States*, pp. 379–408; Beaud, *Théorie de la fédération*; C. Schönberger, "Die Europäische Union als Bund," *Archiv des öffentlichen Rechts*, 129 (2004), 81–120.

13 Beaud, *Théorie de la fédération*.

14 J. Bohman, *Democracy Across Borders: From Dêmos to Dêmoi* (Cambridge, MA: MIT Press, 2002).

15 R. Goodin, "Global Democracy: In the Beginning," *International Theory*, 2 (2010), 175–209.

16 For a critique of the concept of governance, see C. Offe, "Governance: An Empty Signifier?" *Constellations*, 16 (2009), 550–562.

17 Goodin, "Global Democracy: In the Beginning"; A. Buchanan and R. Keohane, "The Legitimacy of Global Governance Institutions," *Ethics & International Affairs*, 20 (2006), 405–437; A. Buchanan, "The Legitimacy of International Law," in S. Besson and J. Tasioulis (eds.), *The Philosophy of International Law* (Oxford University Press, 2010), pp. 79–96; P. Pettit, "Legitimate International Institutions: A Neo-Republican Perspective," in Besson and Tasioulis (eds.), *The Philosophy of International Law*, pp. 119–138.

18 I thus differ from Anne-Marie Slaughter, *A New World Order* (Princeton University Press, 2004), who sees transnational governance as involving the demise of state sovereignty and the emergence of a "disaggregated" world order.

19 By political form, I do not mean regime or type of government. Political form refers to the issue of whether a polity is a state, an empire, an international organization, a confederation, a federation of states, a federal state, and so on. Regime type refers to whether the government is a democracy, an aristocracy, a monarchy, a dictatorship, a republic, and so forth.

20 H. Kelsen, *General Theory of Law and the State* (Cambridge, MA: Harvard University Press, 1945), pp. 303–328. This approach is taken up by W. H. Riker, *Federalism: Origin, Operation, Significance* (Boston: Little, Brown, 1964); and K. Wheare, *Federal Government* (New York: Oxford University Press, 1964).

21 See Elazar, *Exploring Federalism*, pp. 33–79, for a discussion of contrasting models and a critique of the approach to federalism as a matter of decentralization.

22 Schmitt's model as developed in *Constitutional Theory*, pp. 379–408, is sovereignty-centered. The models developed by Forsyth, *Unions of States*, and Beaud, *Théorie de la fédération*, are not sovereignty-centered.

23 On the concept of ideal type see M. Weber, *Economy and Society*, 2 vols. (Berkeley, CA: University of California Press, 1978), vol. I, pp. 4–24.

24 *Ibid.*, pp. 54–56, defines the state as a means, not in terms of ends or purposes; but see Beaud, *Théorie de la fédération*, Chapter 8, pp. 273 and following, for a critical discussion of Georg Jellinek's and Max Weber's approach.

25 The literature is enormous. For an overview, see A. Follesdal, "Federalism," in E. N. Zalta (ed.), *The Stanford Encyclopedia of Philosophy* (2010), available at www.plato.stanford. edu; Elazar, *Exploring Federalism*, pp. 1–79; Forsyth, *Unions of States*, pp. 33–79; A. Amar, "Five Views of Federalism: 'Converse-1983' in Context," *Vanderbilt Law Review* 47 (1994), 1229–1249.

26 Beaud, *Théorie de la fédération*, pp. 101–183, 261–284; Schmitt, *Constitutional Theory*, pp. 383–388; Elazar, *Exploring Federalism*, p. 5.

27 My focus is thus on what is now called in the literature "coming together federalism" rather than "holding together federalism" that pertains to multinational federal states. I also focus on federations in *statu nascendi*. For the distinction between these, see Stepan, Linz, and Yadov, *Crafting State-Nations*. My interest is in the theory of federations that begin as voluntary associations of independent and equal states and which have a conception of constituent state citizenship, thus not those polities emerging from decolonization that don't have such a conception or which are in an inherently unequal relation to a former colonial power (e.g. the Commonwealth) or in movements toward the decentralization of a unitary state (Spain, Belgium). For a comparative analysis, see C. Schönberger, *Unionsbürger: Europas föderales Bürgerrecht in vergleichender Sicht* (Tübingen: Mohr Siebeck, 2005).

28 Elazar, *Exploring Federalism*, p. 16, on the idea of shared rule and self-rule. See Beaud, *Théorie de la fédération*, pp. 261–329 on the idea of dual purposes of federations.

29 Elazar, *Exploring Federalism*, pp. 5, 97; Forsyth, *Unions of States*, p. 1; Beaud, *Théorie de la fédération*, pp. 321–344.

30 It is possible that member states retain their international legal standing as sovereign states with respect to non-members alongside the legal standing of their federal union. This depends on the degree of integration and the type of federal union that is constructed.

31 Forsyth, *Unions of States*, pp. 1–72; Elazar, *Exploring Federalism*, pp. 1–32.

32 Forsyth, *Unions of States*; Spruyt, *The Sovereign State and Its Competitors*, pp. 109–180. My focus here is sovereign state-making and the system of states, but it is worth recalling that this process also involved competition for overseas dominions, control over trade routes, and so forth.

33 C. Tilly, "War Making and State Making as Organized Crime," in P. B. Evans, D. Rueschemeyer, and T. Skocpol (eds.), *Bringing the State Back In* (Cambridge University Press, 1985), pp. 169–191.

34 Hintze, *Historical Essays*.

35 For an analysis of this "underside" of European state-making and the conundrums of imperial sovereignty, see L. Benton, *A Search for Sovereignty: Law and Geography in European Empires, 1400–1900* (Cambridge University Press, 2010).

36 Spruyt, *The Sovereign State and Its Competitors*; Forsyth, *Unions of States: The Theory and Practice of Confederation*, pp.17–72.

37 Forsyth, *Unions of States*; Schmitt, *Constitutional Theory*.

38 *Ibid.* and D. Elazar, "The United States and the European Union: Models for Their Epochs," in Nicolaidis and Howse (eds.), *The Federal Vision*, pp. 31–53 (pp. 32–34), discussing the alternative approach of federal union of the protestant, Althusias versus that of the catholic Bodin. A much earlier discussion can be found in Otto Gierke, *Natural Law and the Theory of Society 1500–1800*, trans. E. Barker (Boston: Beacon Press, 2010), pp. 45–47, 50–53, 70–79, 164–165.

39 Jean Bodin, *Six Books of the Commonwealth*, originally published in 1576, is the classic source along with Thomas Hobbes, *Leviathan* (1651), of the absolutist concept of sovereignty attached to the developing theory of the state first in France, then in England. Johannes Althusias's *Politics*, originally published in 1603, is the source of the constitutionalist theory of (popular) sovereignty and the beginning of a line of federal thinking which was developed more consistently and systematically by Samuel von Pufendorf in a body of works culminating in *The Law of Nature and Nations* (1729), which may be said to be the first sustained theoretical analysis of the nature of a confederation of states. See Forsyth, *Unions of States*, pp. 74–85.

40 J. Madison, A. Hamilton, and J. Jay, *The Federalist Papers*, ed. C. Rossiter (New York: Penguin Classics, 2003), especially Nos. 14, 28, 48, 51 on the principle of representation together with the federal principle as permitting a republic to grow larger with no loss in liberty. See J. C. Calhoun, *Union and Liberty* (Indianapolis, IN: Liberty Fund, 1992) for a fully fledged theory of "con-federal" union of independent polities that creates a polity, rests on a constitutional contract, yet does not create a nation. Finally, see also Schmitt, *Constitutional Theory*, Part IV, for a highly influential discussion. Needless to say, I do not embrace either Calhoun's pro-slavery, anti-nationalist motivations, or the contemporary states' rights revival of much of his rhetoric on the part of the American "Tea Party," nor, for that matter, Schmitt's disparaging assessment of the federal unions and his preference for "grossraume." See also Forsyth, *Unions of States*, pp. 73–160.

41 Spruyt, *The Sovereign State and Its Competitors*, pp. 153–194; Elazar, "The United States and the European Union," p. 34.

42 Hardt and Negri, *Empire*, pp. 160–218.

43 Arendt, *On Revolution*, pp. 159–160; Hardt and Negri, *Empire*, pp. 163–164. Arendt, however, does not construe the federal form as imperial. Hardt and Negri thus criticize her for uncritically celebrating American federalism and for construing the second logic as a non-imperial, federal logic. See Arato and Cohen, "Banishing the Sovereign?" (in Benhabib (ed.), *Politics in Dark Times*) for a more nuanced analysis of Arendt, American sovereignty, and federation.

44 Arendt, *The Origins of Totalitarianism*, pp. 123–266, argues that imperialist forms of rule and legal arrangements that erect a dual set of state institutions – one under rule of law and separation of powers-based republican constitutionalism, the other designed to govern imperial subjects – tend ultimately to destroy the republican constitution of the "mother country." Montesquieu made a similar point regarding republics that become empires. Montesquieu, *The Spirit of the Laws*, Book IX; Hardt and Negri, *Empire*, pp. 166–167, elide these distinctions. On the concept of the dual state see E. Fraenkel, *The Dual State: A Contribution to the Theory of Dictatorship* (Oxford University Press, 1941).

45 Hardt and Negri, *Empire*, pp. 166–182.

46 A. Anghie, *Imperialism, Sovereignty, and the Making of International Law* (Cambridge University Press, 2004), pp. 81 and following, notes that the problem of how polities that possessed and yet did not possess sovereignty fit within a schema pairing degrees of civilization with graduated membership in international society was never resolved.

His thesis is that membership in international society based on criteria of civilization was determinative in allocation of sovereignty. But this, I will argue below, is inapposite to federal unions in which there is equality, and in which the issue of degrees of civilization is irrelevant. See also G. Gong, *The Standard of "Civilization" in International Society* (Oxford: Clarendon Press, 1984).

47 Benton, *A Search for Sovereignty*, p. 238 (my parenthetical additions).

48 *Ibid.*, p. 239.

49 Albeit for a different historical period. *Ibid.*, pp. 236–299.

50 Montesquieu, *The Spirit of the Laws*, Book XI; Madison, Hamilton, and Jay, *The Federalist Papers*, ed. Rossiter, Nos. 1–10.

51 Arendt, *Origins of Totalitarianism*, pp. 123–266.

52 Hintze, *Historical Essays*; and Spruyt, *The Sovereign State and Its Competitors*, pp. 78–109. But unlike Hintze, who argues the competitive advantage of size, or Tilly, "War and State Making as Organized Crime," and C. Tilly (ed.), *The Formation of National States in Western Europe* (Princeton University Press, 1975), who focuses on war-making, Spruyt's claim is that the issue of credible commitments led the sovereign state to win out as a political form over its competitors.

53 The issue of distinguishing between legal regulation of European colonists, legal subjects of empires, and indigenous overseas populations was an old one that plagued imperial legal and political theorists ever since the fifteenth century. See Benton, *A Search for Sovereignty* for a thorough discussion.

54 Gong, *The Standard of "Civilization" in International Society*; Benton, *A Search for Sovereignty*, arguing that imperial rule was law-based and rulers were obsessed with law but that the indeterminacy inherent in imperial legal subjectivity always left the door open to "political" solutions to legal conundrums.

55 M. Mamdani, *Citizen and Subject: Contemporary Africa and the Legacy of Late Colonialism* (Princeton University Press, 1996).

56 For a taxonomy comparing empires to territorial states, see Spruyt, *The Sovereign State and Its Competitors*, pp. 34–58; and M. Doyle, *Empires* (Ithaca, NY: Cornell University Press, 1986), pp. 30–51, for a useful political/institutional definition of empire.

57 Hardt and Negri, *Empire*, pp. 182–204.

58 Doyle, *Empires*, pp. 82–104.

59 Montesquieu, *The Spirit of the Laws*, Book XI, section 19, p. 180. Such was the distribution of the three powers in Rome. But they were far from being thus distributed in the provinces. Liberty prevailed in the center and tyranny in the extreme parts.

60 Montesquieu, *The Spirit of the Laws*, Book XI, section 19.

61 *Ibid.* Montesquieu's is thus one of the first theories of imperial blowback. For a contemporary discussion, see C. Johnson, *Blowback: The Costs and Consequences of American Empire* (New York: Henry Holt & Co., 2004).

62 *Ibid.*, p. 180.

63 Hardt and Negri, *Empire*, p. 168.

64 Arendt, *Origins of Totalitarianism*, pp. xix, 124–135; and *On Revolution*, pp. 159–160, on distinction between expansion and extension. There can of course be imperial and asymmetrical federations. The latter in my view suffer from normative deficit compared with the sovereign equality that obtains in symmetric federations and thus are *à faute de mieux* typically engaged in for the sake of holding together federal states.

65 The racist basis of this should be obvious. See L. Benton, "Colonial Enclaves and the Problem of Quasi-Sovereignty," in *A Search for Sovereignty*, pp. 222–278. See also A. Rana, *The Two Faces of American Freedom* (Cambridge University Press, 2010). Hardt and Negri, *Empire*, pp. 176–179, do argue that the US had an imperialist phase, but during and after the Cold War the US shifted to empire in their sense.

66 Law, jurisdiction, and rule rather than territory and fixed borders are the basis of imperial sovereignty. Benton, *A Search for Sovereignty*, pp. 281, 288–299. However, state-making first under absolute monarchs and then in the nineteenth century under constitutional monarchies and republics, and the system of states in Europe did link territory to sovereignty more fundamentally. The outcome was a mix of territorially based imperialist sovereign states.

67 For a thorough discussion of all aspects and debates regarding the questionable constitutional bases of this kind of expansion, one indeed that challenges its constitutionality insisting that the constitution and rights under it should govern new territories and citizens, see G. Lawson and G. Seidman, *The Constitution of Empire: Territorial Expansion and American Legal History* (New Haven, CT: Yale University Press, 2004).

68 Hintze, *Historical Essays*, Conclusion; and J. Alvarez, *International Organizations as Lawmakers* (Oxford University Press, 2005), pp. 199–217, discussing hegemonic international law.

69 Beaud, *Théorie de la fédération*, pp. 253–258, on the conceptual structure of imperial federation, in particular of the US type.

70 Theorists of the European Union are already engaging in this enterprise. Forsyth, *Unions of States*; Beaud, *Théorie de la fédération*; Schönberger, "Die Europäische Union als Bund." For others, see the contributors to Nicolaidis and Howse (eds.), *The Federal Vision*.

71 I return to the conceptual distinction between network form and the interactive constitutional pluralism of a matrix structure ideal-typical of federations, presented by Elazar, *Exploring Federalism*, pp. 33–42, after discussing Kelsen's power pyramid taxonomy.

72 Montesquieu, *The Spirit of the Laws*, Book IX, section 1.

73 Citing Montesquieu, *The Spirit of the Laws*, Book IX, Chapter 1 in Madison, Hamilton, and Jay, *The Federalist Papers*, ed. Rossiter, No. 9, p. 69.

74 Montesquieu, *The Spirit of the Laws*, Book IX, section 1: "As this government is composed of petty republics, it enjoys the internal happiness of each; and with regard to its external situation, by means of the association, it possesses all the advantages of large monarchies."

75 *Ibid.*

76 He states: "Liberty is a right of doing whatever the laws permit, and if a citizen could do what they forbid he would be no longer possessed of liberty, because all his fellow-citizens would have the same power." Montesquieu, *The Spirit of the Laws*, Book XI.

77 P. Pettit, *Republicanism: A Theory of Freedom and Government* (Oxford University Press, 1997).

78 Montesquieu, *The Spirit of the Laws*, Book IX, section 2.

79 *Ibid.*

80 I. Kant, "To Perpetual Peace: A Philosophical Sketch," in *Perpetual Peace and Other Essays* (New York: Hackett, 1983), pp. 107–143, follows this line of argument.

81 See Federalist No. 51 in Madison, Hamilton, and Jay, *The Federalist Papers*, ed. Rossiter.

82 But see N. Urbinati, *Representative Democracy* (University of Chicago Press, 2006) for an argument that representation is a way to make democracy thrive in larger polities. This of course tracks the argument in *The Federalist Papers*.

83 Rousseau agreed with Montesquieu that there is a link between (con)federation and republicanism. See his reflections in the Abstract of the Abbé de Saint-Pierre's *A Project for Perpetual Peace* in J. J. Rousseau, *A Project for Perpetual Peace*, trans. C. I. C. de Saint-Pierre (London: R. Boden-Sanderson, 1927); and Forsyth, *Unions of States*, pp. 85–95, discussing Rousseau's conception of a non-state federation.

84 Kelsen, *General Theory of Law and the State*, p. 312.

85 Elazar, *Exploring Federalism*, pp. 99–104; D. Halberstam, "Subsidiarity and Integration: Three Principles of Federalism in Europe and America," p. 1. pdf 2010 ms on file with author.

86 J. S. Mill, *Considerations on Representative Government* (London: Parker, Son, and Bourn, 1861).

87 Kelsen, *General Theory of Law and the State*, pp. 311–312.

88 Halberstam, "Subsidiarity and Integration," pp. 1–4.

89 The distinction is Amar's, "Five Views of Federalism," p. 1234. He labels the first a "progressive," the second a "populist" defense of federalism.

90 *Ibid.*

91 Elazar, *Exploring Federalism*, p. 2.

92 *Ibid.*, p. 263; and for minorities to disappear.

93 See G. Gerstle, "Federalism in America: Beyond the Tea Partiers," *Dissent*, 57 (2010), 29–36. This is a form of regulation of self-regulation. To be sure, it depends on the constellation of power: if local elites combine at the federal level in legislatures or courts can block rights enhancing federal legislation as was evident during the Jim Crow period in the US and regarding personal law and morals legislation until the 1960s.

94 This is a mistaken assumption shared by both Arendt and Elazar. The idea of popular sovereignty does not require the Jacobin state or organ sovereignty, as H. L. A. Hart, *The Concept of Law* (Oxford University Press, 1961), and R. Carré de Malberg, *Contribution à la théorie générale de l'état* (Paris: Dalloz, 2004) both demonstrated. Like Arendt, Elazar, *Exploring Federalism*, p. 41, mistakenly assumes that the Americans, unlike the French, removed sovereignty from the state and lodged it with the people, thus allowing for federal government, power sharing, and delegation. But the Americans did not remove sovereignty from the state. See Arato and Cohen, "Banishing the Sovereign?" in Benhabib (ed.), *Politics in Dark Times*.

95 Elazar, *Exploring Federalism*, p. 53.

96 *Ibid.*

97 Kelsen, *General Theory of Law and the State*, p. 312.

98 *Ibid.*

99 Halberstam, "Subsidiarity and Integration," p. 1.

100 For a discussion of compound majoritarianism, see Madison, Hamilton, and Jay, *The Federalist Papers*, ed. Rossiter, No. 51, written by Madison. See also A. Lijphart, "Consociation and Federation: Conceptual and Empirical Links," *Canadian Journal of Political Science*, 12 (1979), 499–515, and the discussion in Elazar, *Exploring Federalism*, pp. 19–26.

101 This is the case for the US, with its constitutional requirement of a republican form of government for member states, and the EU's requirement of liberal democracy for its adherents.

102 Amar, "Five Views of Federalism," pp. 1236–1237. This can pertain to coming-together as well as holding-together federalism.

103 A. Lijphart, "Non-Majoritarian Democracy: A Comparison of Federal and Consociational Themes," *Publius: The Journal of Federalism*, 15 (1985), 3–15.

104 *Ibid.*

105 I borrow this term from A. Shachar, *Multicultural Jurisdiction* (Cambridge University Press, 2010). For my critique, see J. L. Cohen, "The Politics and Risks of the New Legal Pluralism in the Domain of Intimacy," *International Journal of Constitutional Law* 10/2, forthcoming 2012.

106 Cohen, "The Politics and Risks of the New Legal Pluralism," arguing against creation of multicultural jurisdictions for religious groups in consolidated liberal democracies.

For critiques of existing versions in South Africa, India, and Israel, see H. Irving, *Gender and the Constitution* (Cambridge University Press, 2008), p. 21; S. Hassim, *Women's Organizations and Democracy in South Africa* (Scottsville: University of KwaZulu Natal Press, 2006); M. C. Nussbaum, "India, Sex Equality, and Constitutional Law," and S. Jagwanth and C. Murray, "No Nation Can Be Free When One Half of It Is Enslaved: Constitutional Equality for Women in South Africa," both in B. Baines and R. Rubio-Martin (eds.), *The Gender of Constitutional Jurisprudence* (Cambridge University Press, 2004), pp. 174–204, 230–255; F. Agnes, *Law and Gender Inequality* (New Delhi: Oxford University Press, 1999); P. E. Andrews, "Who's Afraid of Polygamy? Exploring the Boundaries of Family, Equality, and Custom in South Africa," *Utah Law Review*, 11 (2009), 351–379; Y. Sezgin, "How to Integrate Universal Human Rights into Customary and Religious Legal Systems?" *Journal of Legal Pluralism*, 60 (2010), 5–40.

107 Hence my reservations with respect to the "democratic" arguments of Stepan, Linz, and Yadav, *Crafting State-Nations*, for asymmetrical federalism in multinational states they call "state-nation." I believe that the federal principle of legitimacy (sovereign equality) and democratic norms (political equality and equality of individual rights) speak in favor of symmetric federal arrangements that do not privilege any particular territorially concentrated group with special group rights and that do not reify ethnic, religious, racial, or other substantive divisions among the population. As a pragmatic consideration asymmetric federalism may help hold a federal state together but the price can be high: ethnic or religious or linguistic identities get politicized, indeed, frozen, and equality of rights and equal citizenship undermined.

108 A. Spektorowski, "Carl Schmitt: Republican Citizenship, Repression of Libel Rights and Multi-Polarity," in Y. Peled, N. Lewin-Epstein, G. Mundlak, and J. Cohen (eds.), *Democratic Citizenship and War* (London: Routledge, 2011), pp. 13–30.

109 Elazar, *Exploring Federalism*, p. 6, for a list of varieties and various approaches. In what follows I refrain from the standard comparative analysis of federal states and focus on theoretical approaches to unions of states.

110 Kelsen, *General Theory of Law and the State*. pp. 303–327. See Forsyth, *Unions of States*, pp. 146–147, for a discussion of historical figures in this tradition, including Laband and Jellinek up to Carl Friedrich. See also the discussion in Elazar who includes Wheare and Riker in this list. Elazar, *Exploring Federalism*, pp. 149, 155.

111 Jellinek already criticized Kelsen for this. See G. Jellinek, *Die Lehre der Staatenverbindungen* (Agram: L. Hartman, 1885), p. 15, cited in Beaud, *Théorie de la fédération*, p. 91. This denies that there is any qualitative break from an intra-state to the inter-state worlds and downplays the distinctiveness of federal union.

112 Elazar, *Exploring Federalism*, sees the distinctiveness of the federal model against the power pyramid conception of Wheare and Kelsen but discusses federalism primarily in the context of state forms and varieties of federal states.

113 Schmitt's theory of federation in *Constitutional Theory* aimed at the League of Nations; Forsyth's theory in *Unions of States* referenced the EU (as a federation focused on economic welfare).

114 Forsyth, *Unions of States*, is the contemporary originator of this theoretical path along with Beaud, *Théorie de la fédération* and Schönberger, "Die Europäische Union als Bund," all of whom return to federal theory in light of developments in the EU.

115 Beaud, *Théorie de la fédération*, pp. 92–97.

116 Schönberger, "Die Europäische Union als Bund," 83; Forsyth, *Unions of States*, pp. 1–16.

117 Beaud, *Théorie de la fédération*, p. 92, provides the most compelling theoretical argument in this regard.

118 As indicated in the introduction to this chapter, there can be more or less integrated federations ranging from confederations to a form that nearly approximates a federal state. If we consider federal union a genus then one can construct ideal subtypes in terms of many of the variables Kelsen operated with and in terms of the degree of internal political homogeneity and integration.

119 Beaud rejects the use of the concept, federation, for global governance institutions. I think he prematurely prejudges this issue. He is forced to this view because he banishes the concept of sovereignty from his analysis, not seeing that a state can be sovereign in its relations even though sovereignty does not describe the interactions between the state and the federal union it is a member of. This idea informs the concept of dualistic sovereignty regime I developed in Chapter 1.

120 Kelsen, *General Theory of Law and the State*, p. 316.

121 Hamilton in Federalist No. 15 in Madison, Hamilton, and Jay, *The Federalist Papers*, ed. Rossiter, p. 103, referring to shared or dual sovereignty as "the political monster of an *imperium in imperio*," arguing for full subordination of the parts to the center, in No. 9; while Madison tried to square the circle by referring to the American federation created by the 1787 constitution as a mix of national and federal principles in Nos. 39–40.

122 See the excellent discussion in Beaud, *Théorie de la fédération*, pp. 146–147.

123 Kelsen, *General Theory of Law and the State*, p. 304.

124 *Ibid.*, pp. 310–324.

125 *Ibid.*, p. 310.

126 *Ibid.*, pp. 303–324

127 *Ibid.*, p. 317.

128 *Ibid.*, p. 324.

129 *Ibid.*, pp. 317, 322–323.

130 *Ibid.*, p. 318.

131 That is, imperfect decentralization. *Ibid.*, p. 313.

132 *Ibid.*, p. 318.

133 This despite the fact that Kelsen elsewhere seemed to grasp that the federal orders are based on coordination mechanisms rather than hierarchy. See the discussion in Beaud, *Théorie de la fédération*, pp. 144–153. See also H. Kelsen, "Die Bundesexekution. Ein Beitrag zur Theorie und Praxis des Bundesstaates," in *Festgabe für Fritz Fleiner* (Tübingen: Geburtstag, 1927), pp. 127 and 130, cited in Schönberger, "Die Europäische Union als Bund," p. 98, footnote 58.

134 *Ibid.* See Forsyth, *Unions of States*, pp. 144–145 for a discussion of others in the German *staatslehre* tradition who develop a tripartite model.

135 Kelsen, *General Theory of Law and the State*, p. 317. To simplify matters, I will follow Beaud, *Théorie de la fédération*, p. 92, and capitalize the F when speaking of the total Federal political community that encompasses the federation of states and each member state.

136 Forsyth, *Unions of States*, pp. 18–31.

137 Lawson and Seidman, *The Constitution of Empire*, thoroughly probe the constitutional issues raised regarding the acquisition especially of territories never intended to become members of the US federation.

138 *Ibid.*, for a thorough mining of this issue vis-à-vis the US federal constitution.

139 See Chapter 1.

140 Kelsen, *General Theory of Law and the State*, pp. 325–328.

141 See Beaud, *Théorie de la fédération*, p. 149.

142 It is no accident that Kelsen's discussion of the international legal community follows directly after his chapter on federation and confederacy, which concludes

with a discussion of national law as a relatively centralized legal order vis-à-vis the relatively decentralized international legal order and the denial of any absolute borderline between national and international law. *General Theory of Law and the State*, pp. 35–328.

143 See my discussion in Chapter 1.

144 Kelsen, *General Theory of Law and the State*, pp. 316–324.

145 *Ibid.*, p. 322.

146 *Ibid.*, p. 320.

147 *Ibid.*, pp. 316–317.

148 *Ibid.*, p. 319.

149 *Ibid.*

150 *Ibid.*, p. 323.

151 Schönberger, "Die Europäische Union als Bund," pp. 88–91.

152 Elazar, *Exploring Federalism*, pp. 5–79.

153 *Ibid.* What follows draws heavily from Elazar.

154 *Ibid.*, pp. 5–6.

155 So far as I know the first to theorize the idea of a constitutional compact was J. C. Calhoun, "A Discourse on the Constitution and Government of the United States," in Calhoun, *Union and Liberty*, pp. 79–284. Schmitt appropriated this idea in *Constitutional Theory*, pp. 385–386.

156 Elazar, *Exploring Federalism*, p. 6. A federation thus entails the kind of sovereignty discussed by A. Chayes and A. H. Chayes: i.e. sovereignty as participation in decision-making bodies of global governance institutions. See A. Chayes and A. H. Chayes, *The New Sovereignty: Compliance with International Regulatory Agreements* (Cambridge, MA: Harvard University Press, 1995).

157 Elazar, *Exploring Federalism*, p. 36.

158 *Ibid.*, pp. 34, 75. This is symbolized by the fact that true federal systems do not have capitals but rather, seats of government. A capital is a top of a pyramid while a seat is a place of assembly. Thus, Washington DC has no federal vote or representation in the US senate but having become a capital indicates a shift in political form.

159 *Ibid.*, p. 64.

160 *Ibid.*, p. 67. Beaud, *Théorie de la fédération*, pp. 365–385, assumes a federation requires political homogeneity regarding political form, additionally arguing that a republic is the political form best suited for a federation. The German federation of the early nineteenth century was thus an anomaly in his view. See pp. 385–422.

161 Elazar, *Exploring Federalism*, p. 40.

162 *Ibid.*, p. 17.

163 *Ibid.*, p. 41.

164 *Ibid.*

165 This of course was hotly debated by Calhoun, "A Discourse on the Constitution and Government of the United States," pp. 92–102, and the authors of the Federalist Papers, Madison, Hamilton, and Jay, *The Federalist Papers*, ed. Rossiter, Nos. 15, 39–40.

166 See the discussion in Forsyth, *Unions of States*, pp. 133–134. Indeed none of the protagonists in the debates prior to the Civil War over whether the central government was sovereign referred to the US as a "federal state": their concern was to clarify the nature of the differences between the old Confederation and the new Federal Union instituted with the constitution's ratification in 1789. As Forsyth reminds us, for them the word "state" denoted the parts of the union. On the other hand, the Federal polity was certainly deemed a state under international law and only it, not member states, could make treaties or engage in foreign policy.

167 Beaud, *Théorie de la fédération*, pp. 67–100; and Schönberger, "Die Europäische Union als Bund," pp. 91–98.
168 His most theoretically compelling discussion is in *Constitutional Theory*, pp. 381–407. See also C. Schmitt, *Die Kernfrage des Völkerbundes* (Berlin: Dümmler, 1926). See Forsyth, *Unions of States*, pp. 132–159, for a discussion situating Schmitt's work in the historical context of contemporary German debates.
169 Schmitt, *Constitutional Theory*, pp. 395, 400–401.
170 Schmitt published *Die Kernfrage des Völkerbundes* in 1926, two years before the publication of the *Constitutional Theory*, in which he analyzed the nature of the League, and the danger that such a fake "universal" *bund*, really a tool of western great powers, holds for other states insofar as it claims the right to intervene to punish violators of the norms of the "international community."
171 C. Schmitt, *The Concept of the Political* (University of Chicago Press, 1996), p. 54.
172 Schmitt, *The Nomos of the Earth*, pp. 67–79.
173 Schmitt, *Constitutional Theory*, p. 381.
174 *Ibid.*, p. 381.
175 *Ibid.*, pp. 75–80.
176 *Ibid.*, p. 405. There can be only one people in a state, including a federal state, since a state is defined as the existential expression of a politically united people.
177 *Ibid.*, p. 382.
178 C. Schmitt, *Political Theology: Four Chapters on the Concept of Sovereignty* (University of Chicago Press, 2005).
179 Early modern antagonists of monarchical and absolutist principles of legitimacy and state forms defended by Bodin and Hobbes invoked the principle of popular sovereignty understood as a principle of legitimacy that would block the emergence of organ sovereignty and of the unitary state. See Gierke, *Natural Law and the Theory of Society*, pp. 40–92.
180 C. Schmitt, *The Crisis of Parliamentary Democracy* (Cambridge, MA: MIT Press, 1986).
181 Yet the ultimate political theological thrust of his earlier theory of sovereignty in *Political Theology* remains. I reject Schmitt's existential conception, but it is worth noting that democratic legitimacy and the discourse of popular and state sovereignty does involve a dimension of political self-determination that escapes Kelsen's legalistic analysis. For a theory of democracy and sovereignty that rejects political theology, see J. Derrida, *Rogues: Two Essays on Reason* (Stanford University Press, 2005).
182 Schmitt, *Constitutional Theory*, p. 383.
183 *Ibid.*, pp. 366–367. Schmitt rejects the distinction between a *bundesstaat* (federal state) and *staatenbund* (confederation) as too simplistic. He distinguished a *bund* (federation) from both a mere alliance (*bündniss* or *allianz*) and from a *staatenbund* confederation and from a *bundesstaat*.
184 *Ibid.*, p. 385. See also the discussion in Forsyth, *Unions of States*.
185 Beaud, *Théorie de la fédération*, pp. 58–66. But Schmitt believed that all political concepts are polemical, as he famously stated in Schmitt, *The Concept of the Political*, p. 30. So too, then, is his sovereignty and *bund* concept.
186 Schmitt, *Constitutional Theory*, p. 391.
187 *Ibid.*
188 *Ibid.*, p. 383.
189 *Ibid.*, p. 388.
190 *Ibid.*, p. 405.
191 *Ibid.*
192 *Ibid.*, pp. 405–407.
193 *Ibid.*, p. 405.

194 *Ibid.*, p. 392. Here the centralization/decentralization logic of Kelsen and the issues of constitutional jurisdictions and dispersal of powers play out, but they do not pertain in Schmitt's view to deeper issues of political form or sovereignty.

195 *Ibid.*, pp. 405–406.

196 *Ibid.*, p. 405.

197 *Ibid.*, p. 390.

198 *Ibid.*, pp. 382–384.

199 *Ibid.*, p. 384.

200 *Ibid.*, p. 385.

201 *Ibid.*

202 *Ibid.*, p. 401.

203 *Ibid.*

204 *Ibid.*, p. 388. This term "alongside" plays several crucial roles in Schmitt's analysis as will become clear.

205 *Ibid.*, p. 388.

206 For Schmitt, sovereignty is not a competence, and not even the competence to define competences is a sovereignty issue unless it raises existential questions regarding political form and identity. Either the concept of the competence to decide competences (jurisdictions) as such has nothing to do with sovereignty, or it is a slogan for sovereign power which has nothing to do with competence. *Ibid.*, p. 403.

207 *Ibid.*, p. 387.

208 *Ibid.*, p. 386.

209 *Ibid.*, p. 389.

210 *Ibid.*, p. 387.

211 *Ibid.*, pp. 402–403.

212 Schmitt did not clearly specify the amendment rule for a *bund*. But he did gesture toward a formula in *Constitutional Theory*, p. 149, indicating that the federal character of a federation can be preserved by the requirement of a majority of states, simple or qualified, for a change in the federal constitution or by a requirement that the minority can block the change. I am indebted to Andrew Arato for pointing this out and for clarifying the issues in this paragraph.

213 US Constitution, Article 5 states that ratification of an amendment to the constitution requires three fourths of the states by their conventions or state legislatures.

214 Schmitt, *Constitutional Theory*, pp. 149, 153–154. He refers to a federal legislative procedure as distinct from a contractual change of the federal contract as indicative of a "transition" phase in which the federal character of the federation is preserved.

215 *Ibid.*, p. 152. Only the constituent power can change the basic structure.

216 *Ibid.*, p. 395.

217 *Ibid.*, pp. 390–393.

218 *Ibid.*, p. 391.

219 *Ibid.*, p. 389.

220 See Chapters 1 and 4.

221 *Ibid.*, p. 395.

222 *Ibid.*, p. 113.

223 *Ibid.*, p. 96.

224 *Ibid.*, p. 114.

225 "Every federation has such a political existence with an independent *jus belli*. The federation, on the other hand, does not have its own constitution-making power because it rests on a contract. Conditional jurisdiction for revisions of the federation order is not constitution-making authority." *Ibid.*, p. 396.

226 *Ibid.*, p. 405. Schmitt clearly did not embrace the Madisonian solution of a dual, i.e. national and federal, character to a federation.
227 Calhoun, "A Discourse on the Constitution and Government of the United States," pp. 79–284.
228 Schmitt, *Constitutional Theory*, p. 392.
229 *Ibid.*, p. 390.
230 *Ibid.*, pp. 388–389.
231 *Ibid.*, p. 393.
232 *Ibid.*, p. 394.
233 *Ibid.*
234 *Ibid.*, p. 395.
235 *Ibid.*
236 *Ibid.*, pp. 404–405.
237 *Ibid.* and Forsyth, *Unions of States*, p. 155.
238 See Derrida, *Rogues*, for a masterful philosophical critique of Schmitt's epistemology that subtends these political views.
239 Hence Forsyth rejects this approach, since he sees the EU as an economic federation and it lacks the *jus belli*. Forsyth, *Unions of States*, pp. 160–187.
240 Schmitt, *The* Nomos *of the Earth*.
241 The main source of inspiration for this school is Forsyth, *Unions of States*, p. 7. Those on whom he exerted a clear and explicitly acknowledged influence include Beaud, *Théorie de la fédération*; K. Nicolaidis, "The New Constitution as European Demoi-cracy?" *Critical Review of International Social and Political Philosophy*, 7 (2004), 76–93; and Schönberger, "Die Europäische Union als Bund," among others.
242 Forsyth, *Unions of States*, p. 5. Also Schönberger, "Die Europäische Union als Bund," p. 85.
243 Schönberger, "Die Europäische Union als Bund," p. 83.
244 Forsyth, *Unions of States*, p. 15.
245 *Ibid.*, p. 7. His term for the genus was confederation.
246 Beaud, *Théorie de la fédération*, pp. 20, 92.
247 Forsyth, *Unions of States*, p. 14; Beaud, *Théorie de la fédération*, p. 116.
248 Beaud, *Théorie de la fédération*, p. 40.
249 Forsyth, *Unions of States*, p. 14.
250 Ibid., pp. 15–16.
251 Beaud, *Théorie de la fédération*, p. 41.
252 *Ibid.*, pp. 43, 59.
253 *Ibid.*, p. 65.
254 *Ibid.*, pp. 363, 381.
255 *Ibid.*, pp. 43–48.
256 *Ibid.*, pp. 116, 110.
257 Forsyth, *Unions of States*, p. 7.
258 Beaud, *Théorie de la fédération*, p. 103.
259 *Ibid.*, p. 139. This is an epistemological postulate. I will now follow Beaud and use the capital F to refer to the overall Federation comprised of co-states and the federal order and the whole.
260 *Ibid.*, p. 140. The court of the Federation is not a *parti pris* representing the federation against the states. Instead it serves to protect the entire global order which is the Federation.
261 *Ibid.*, p. 150.
262 *Ibid.*, p. 95.
263 *Ibid.*, pp. 271 and 191.

264 *Ibid.*, p. 191.
265 *Ibid.*, p. 280.
266 *Ibid.*, p. 282.
267 *Ibid.*, pp. 201–231.
268 *Ibid.*, p. 202. Forsyth, *Unions of States*, p. 7.
269 Beaud, *Théorie de la fédération*, p. 204.
270 *Ibid.*, p. 333.
271 *Ibid.*, p. 204.
272 Nicolaidis and Howse (eds.), *The Federal Vision*, pp. 1–27.
273 Beaud, *Théorie de la fédération*, p. 321.
274 Forsyth, *Unions of States*, pp. 7, 207; and Beaud, *Théorie de la fédération*, pp. 206, 231.
275 See Schönberger, *Unionsbürger*; and Beaud, *Théorie de la fédération*, p. 221.
276 Schönberger, *Unionsbürger*, pp. 114–115. Typically, this includes rights of freedom of movement, residence, non-discrimination, and treatment as a non-alien.
277 *Ibid.* See also Beaud, *Théorie de la fédération*, p. 229. Typically, in a federal state, for example the US after the Civil War, citizenship is vertically created, i.e. federal citizenship is conferred immediately as a primary status and state citizenship is automatically granted to a federal citizen who takes up residence in a member state.
278 Beaud, *Théorie de la fédération*, p. 340.
279 This is a compound demos at the federal level. The federal union thus has a constituent power which is not an aggregation, and its structure is multicentered not multileveled. These are important distinctions that differentiate Beaud's analysis not only from cosmopolitan pluralists like Kumm, but also from Nicolaidis, "The New Constitution as European Demoi-cracy?" and from Bohman, *Democracy Across Borders*.
280 Beaud, *Théorie de la fédération*, p. 341. I see this as an example of the new sovereignty Chayes and Chayes discuss in *The New Sovereignty*.
281 The Swiss federation was and is not ethnically homogeneous. Rather, its federation serves to preserve diversity.
282 Montesquieu, *The Spirit of the Laws*, Book X.
283 Beaud, *Théorie de la fédération*, p. 335.
284 *Ibid.*, p. 335.
285 *Ibid.*, pp. 357–361; and Forsyth cited by Beaud, footnote 3, p. 357.
286 *Ibid.*, p. 363.
287 *Ibid.*
288 In the next chapter, I will argue for sovereign equality and human rights as the two principles of legitimacy that do or should regulate GGIs and all federations.
289 Beaud, *Théorie de la fédération*, p. 425.
290 *Ibid.*, pp. 256–258.
291 *Ibid.*, p. 425.
292 I draw on A. Arato for the link between a weak domestic presidency and the imperial temptation in US Constitutionalism. See Arato and Cohen, "Banishing the Sovereign?" in Benhabib (ed.), *Politics in Dark Times*.
293 Beaud, *Théorie de la fédération*, p. 424.
294 *Ibid.*, pp. 71–83.
295 I do not follow him in foreclosing the applicability of a subgenus of the federal ideal type to GGIs, particularly to the UN Charter system, as will become clear in Chapters 5 and 6.
296 On the idea of constitutional synthesis, see J. E. Fossum and A. J. Menendez, *The Constitution's Gift: A Constitutional Theory for a Democratic European Union* (Lanham, MD: Rowman & Littlefield, 2011).
297 See "Introduction," in Nicolaidis and Howse (eds.), *The Federal Vision*, pp. 17–18.

298 *Ibid.* See Elazar, "The United States and the European Union," pp. 45–46 for a critique of the concept of subsidiarity as implying a concession to hierarchy.
299 Schönberger, "Die Europäische Union als Bund," pp. 108–109.
300 See Chapter 1.
301 J. L. Cohen and A. Arato, *Civil Society and Political Theory* (Cambridge, MA: MIT Press), pp. 492–563.
302 C. Lefort, *The Political Forms of Modern Society* (Cambridge, MA: MIT Press, 1986) and Cohen and Arato, *Civil Society and Political Theory.*
303 Derrida, *Rogues,* demystifies this only apparently inexorable logic of identity relied upon by Schmitt.
304 C. Lefort, "Permanence of the Theologico-Political?" in *Democracy and Political Theory* (Minneapolis: University of Minnesota Press, 1988), pp. 213–255.
305 Schönberger, "Die Europäische Union als Bund," pp. 107–109.
306 Forsyth, *Unions of States*; Beaud, *Théorie de la fédération*; and Kant, "To Perpetual Peace: A Philosophical Sketch."

Chapter 3 International human rights, sovereignty, and global governance: toward a new political conception

1 A. Buchanan, *Justice, Legitimacy, and Self-Determination* (New York: Oxford University Press, 2004); T. Pogge, "Priorities of Global Justice," in T. Pogge (ed.), *Global Justice* (Oxford: Blackwell, 2001), pp. 6–23; and T. Pogge, *World Poverty and Human Rights* (Cambridge University Press, 2002).
2 On the concept of international community, see E. Kwakwa, "The International Community, International Law and the United States: Three in One, Two against One, or One and the Same?" and A. Paulus, "The Influence of the United States on the Concept of the 'International Community,'" both in M. Byers and G. Nolte (eds.), *United States Hegemony and the Foundations of International Law* (Cambridge University Press, 2003), pp. 25–56, 57–90.
3 ICISS, *The Responsibility to Protect: Report of the International Commission on Intervention and State Sovereignty* (Ottawa: International Development Research Centre, 2001). For debates over whether this responsibility includes a democratic entitlement, see G. H. Fox and B. R. Roth, *Democratic Governance and International Law* (Cambridge University Press, 2000).
4 For an argument linking R2P to international human rights law, and not only to humanitarian law, see D. Gierycz, "The Responsibility to Protect: A Legal and Rights-Based Perspective," in *Responsibility to Protect,* NUPI Report No. 5 (Oslo: Norwegian Institute of International Affairs, 2008). The ICISS report makes a similar linkage.
5 Buchanan, *Justice, Legitimacy, and Self-Determination*; A. Buchanan and R. Keohane, "The Preventive Use of Force: A Cosmopolitan Institutional Proposal," *Ethics & International Affairs,* 18 (2004), 1–22.
6 Article 2(7) of the UN Charter states that "nothing contained in the present Charter shall authorize the United Nations to intervene in matters which are essentially within the domestic jurisdiction of any state." United Nations, *Charter of the United Nations* (New York: UN, 1945), Article 2 (7).
7 See ICISS, *The Responsibility to Protect.*
8 For a discussion of the statist versus cosmopolitan approach, see R. Forst, "Towards a Critical Theory of Transnational Justice," in Pogge (ed.), *Global Justice,* pp. 169–203. The most forceful statist position developed subsequently is that of T. Nagel, "The Problem of Global Justice," *Philosophy and Public Affairs,* 33 (2005), 113–147. For a critique, see

J. Cohen and C. Sabel, "Extra Republicam Nulla Justitia?" *Philosophy and Public Affairs*, 34 (2006), 147–175.

9 See the Rome Statute of the International Criminal Court, available at untreaty.un.org/cod/icc/statute/romefra.htm; R. Teitel, "Humanity's Law: Rule of Law for the New Global Politics," *Cornell International Law Journal*, 33 (2002), 355–387. R. Teitel, *Humanity's Law* (New York: Oxford University Press, 2011).

10 T. Pogge "Cosmopolitanism and Sovereignty," *Ethics*, 103 (1992), 48–75 (pp. 48–49).

11 The only requirement for membership is that a state be peace-loving and willing to comply with UN purposes and international legal obligations; it need not be based on principles of popular sovereignty, democracy, or liberal constitutionalism.

12 The European Convention on Human Rights, which came into force in 1953, has the strongest individualized compulsory international human rights regime next to the EU, where individuals can indeed petition the Court (unlike the more universal international treaties associated with the UN, which were not designed to be enforceable). See A. Moravcsik, "The Origin of Human Rights Regimes: Democratic Delegation in Postwar Europe," *International Organization*, 54 (2000), 217–252 (p. 218).

13 Unlike legal rights, domestically which do empower individuals to be law-makers and legal subjects, international human rights do not. A particular treaty may empower individuals to petition. The ECJ is in this respect a special case. Generally, when domestic institutions fail the individual, international law and institutions do not provide these rights. See L. Henkin, G. Neuman, D. F. Orentlicher, and D. W. Leebron, *Human Rights* (New York: Foundation Press University Casebook, 1999), pp. 302–306. Unlike domestic constitutions, human rights treaties do not operate directly to provide individuals with remedies. They do obligate states parties, and, under customary international law, human rights obligations are considered *erga omnes*, applying to all states, but individuals are ultimately third party beneficiaries, objects, not subjects of rights in the sense of being legal subjects at international law.

14 Not even Louis Henkin, one of the strongest critics of sovereignty discourse, claims this. L. Henkin, "The 'S' Word: Sovereignty, Globalization and Human Rights, Et Cetera," *Fordham Law Review*, 68 (1999), 1–14.

15 As is perhaps severe racial discrimination amounting to apartheid. See the Rome Statute of the International Criminal Court.

16 L. F. Damrosch, L. Henkin, R. C. Pugh, O. Schachter, and H. Smit (eds.), *International Law* (St. Paul, MN: West Group, 2001), pp. 990–1004. Article 1 of the genocide convention requires all states to prevent and punish genocide, but it leaves interpretation of genocide to the ICJ (Article 9), and it leaves decisions over how to enforce it to the states parties or to the UN. United Nations, *Convention on the Prevention and Punishment of the Crime of Genocide* (New York: UN, 1948).

17 *Ibid.*

18 C. Beitz, *The Idea of Human Rights* (Oxford University Press, 2009), p. 1.

19 Henkin et al., *Human Rights*, p. 499, list the provisions. The Optional Protocol to the Covenant merely authorized the Committee to forward its views to the party concerned. The rules vis-à-vis the new Human Rights Council established in 2006 to replace the Human Rights Commission are not very different in this regard. See P. Alston, "Reconceiving the UN Human Rights Regime: Challenges Confronting the New Human Rights Council," *Melbourne Journal of International Law*, 7 (2006), 185–224.

20 Beitz, *The Idea of Human Rights*, pp. 43–44, is right, international human rights practice is comprised of two dimensions: aspirational and legal inter-state rules.

21 Individuals are subject to international law, but are not the subjects in the sense of law-makers.

22 See J. Alvarez, *International Organizations as Law-makers* (Oxford University Press, 2005); A.-M. Slaughter, *A New World Order* (Princeton University Press, 2004); and G. Teubner (ed.), *Global Law Without a State* (Brookfield, VT: Dartmouth Publishing Group, 1997).

23 B. Kingsbury, N. Krisch, and R. B. Stewart, "The Emergence of Global Administrative Law," *Law and Contemporary Problems*, 68 (2005), 15–61; T. Pogge, "Creating Supra-National Institutions Democratically: Reflections on the European Union's 'Democratic Deficit,'" *The Journal of Political Philosophy*, 5 (1997), 163–182. A. Buchanan and R. Keohane, "The Legitimacy of Global Governance Institutions," *Ethics and International Affairs*, 20 (2006), 405–437.

24 P. Macklem, "What is International Human Rights Law? Three Applications of a Distributive Account," *McGill Law Journal*, 52 (2007), 575–604; and P. Macklem, "Humanitarian Intervention and the Distribution of Sovereignty in International Law," *Ethics and International Affairs*, 22 (2008), 369–393. I do not agree with Macklem's cosmopolitan approach even though I am influenced by some of his formulations.

25 State sovereignty is relational and entails an international legal entitlement in this sense: an international society of sovereign states involves mutual recognition of one another as sovereign, i.e. as politically autonomous and self-determining, and it involves international legal recognition of each sovereign polity as an actor with equal standing to participate in international law-making (treaties, custom, etc.). While power or efficacy has always been one component of such recognition, it has never been the only one. Moreover, while states collectively decide just what the prerogatives of sovereignty entail, the international legal sovereignty regime they erect can change over time and, thus, what was once deemed a sovereign prerogative might no longer be one. This is clearly the case with the right to war, to annexation, and grave human rights violations. It is also true regarding sovereign immunity of state officials when they engage in or sponsor grave violation of humanitarian or human rights law.

26 A. Chayes and A. Chayes, *The New Sovereignty: Compliance with International Regulatory Agreements* (Cambridge, MA: Harvard University Press, 1998).

27 See Buchanan and Keohane, "The Legitimacy of Global Governance Institutions," for a different proposal.

28 M. Kaldor, *Human Security: Reflections on Globalization* (Cambridge: Polity Press, 2007); and R. Teitel, "Humanity Law: A New Interpretive Lens on the International Sphere," *Fordham Law Review*, 77 (2008), 667–702.

29 For such attempts see for example R. Forst, "The Justification of Human Rights and the Basic Right of Justification: A Reflexive Approach," *Ethics*, 120 (2010), 711–740; and Seyla Benhabib, *The Rights of Others: Aliens, Residents, and Citizens* (Cambridge University Press, 2004) pp. 129–169.

30 There is an enormous literature on this. For a balanced volume, see T. Nardin and M. S. Williams (eds.), *Humanitarian Intervention: NOMOS XLVII* (New York University Press, 2006). See in particular T. Pogge, "Moralizing Humanitarian Intervention: Why Jurying Fails and How Law Can Work," pp. 158–187, arguing that there are no humanitarian heroes among states or pure motives when it comes to states intervening militarily in other states; and P. Mehta, "From State Sovereignty to Human Security (Via Institutions?)," pp. 259–285. For a very strong critique from the postcolonial perspective, see M. Mamdani, *Saviors and Survivors: Darfur, Politics, and the War on Terror* (New York: Pantheon, 2009); and M. Mamdani, "Responsibility to Protect or Right to Punish?" *Journal of Intervention and Statebuilding*, 4 (2010), 53–67. For a response, see S. Benhabib, "Claiming Rights Across Borders: International Human Rights and Democratic Sovereignty," *American Political Science Review*, 102 (2009), 691–704.

31 The United Nations, *The United Nations Universal Declaration of Human Rights* (New York: UN, 1948). See J. Morsink, *The Universal Declaration of Human Rights: Origins, Drafting and Intent* (Philadelphia: University of Pennsylvania Press, 1999), p. 109; S. Moyn, *The Last Utopia: Human Rights in History* (Cambridge, MA: Harvard University Press, 2010), pp. 1–84; and B. Simmons, *Mobilizing for Human Rights: International Law in Domestic Politics* (Cambridge University Press, 2009), pp. 23–25.

32 Simmons, *Mobilizing for Human Rights*.

33 On the shift from the discourse of minority to human rights, see M. Mazower, "The Strange Triumph of Human Rights, 1933–1950," *The Historical Journal*, 47 (2004), 379–398.

34 Beitz, *The Idea of Human Rights*, Chapter 1; Moyn, *The Last Utopia*, p. 67, discussing Jacques Maritain's statement regarding the drafting of UDHR: "... we agree about the rights but on condition that no one asks us why." This is what Cass Sunstein called an "incompletely theorized agreement," i.e. the drafters refrained from the attempt to find and agree on a single overarching ground or theoretical justification for human rights and thus made it possible for states to sign on using different rationales (and interpretations) for the concept of human rights, the concept of human dignity placed at their core, and for the list of rights that was included. C. Sunstein, *Legal Reasoning and Political Conflict* (New York: Oxford University Press, 1996).

35 Moyn, *The Last Utopia*, p. 82.

36 *Ibid.*, p. 28. However, Moyn seems to lose the important distinction between the idea of the rights of man as the civil rights that every citizen has in the French polity, and a more universalistic principle articulating the rights every individual has as a person and which should be acknowledged by every polity and every other human being.

37 Déclaration des Droits de l'Homme et du Citoyen (1789) Articles 1, 2, 3, 11.

38 *Ibid.*, Article 16.

39 H. Arendt, *The Origins of Totalitarianism* (New York: Harcourt, 1994), pp. 123–147, 267–302.

40 For a critical discussion, see J. L. Cohen, "Rights, Citizenship, and the Modern Form of the Social: Dilemmas of Arendtian Republicanism," *Constellations*, 3 (1996), 164–189.

41 United Nations, *International Covenant on Civil and Political Rights*, December 19, 1966, 999 U.N.T.S. 171 (entered into force March 23, 1976) (New York: UN, 1966); United Nations, *The United Nations Universal Declaration of Human Rights*.

42 Moyn, *The Last Utopia*, pp. 44–84 stresses this point. But see also Simmons, *Mobilizing for Human Rights*, p. 40, for an argument that focuses on the significance of the treaties for domestic politics after their coming into force. For an analysis of the politics that went into the drafting of the UDHR see Morsink, *The Universal Declaration of Human Rights*.

43 Moyn, *The Last Utopia*, pp. 47, 61.

44 United Nations, *International Covenant on Civil and Political Rights*; United Nations, *International Covenant on Economic, Social and Cultural Rights*, 993 U.N.T.S. 3 (entered into force January 3, 1976) (New York: UN, 1966).

45 Y. Dezalay and B. Garth, "From the Cold War to Kosovo: The Rise and Renewal of the Field of International Human Rights," *Annual Review of Law and Social Science*, 2 (2006), 231–255.

46 Moyn, *The Last Utopia*, p. 82. Recall that this was the period of segregation in the US.

47 The Universal Declaration of Human Rights, adopted in 1948, is non-binding, and does not condition UN membership on its adoption by present or future member states. The 1966 UN Covenants on civil and political and social rights lack provisions for enforcement and adjudication.

Reservations to human rights treaties are profound and widespread. Indeed, the CEDAW (Convention for the Elimination of Discrimination against Women), adopted and opened for signature, ratification, and accession by the UNGA Resolution 34/180 on December 18, 1979, entry into force September 3, 1981, has more reservations than any treaty. See Simmons, *Mobilizing for Human Rights*, pp. 202–255, arguing nonetheless that it has had salutary effects on women's rights. Even when a country ratifies a UN human rights treaty agreeing to respect the rights the treaty covers, it does not necessarily agree to make them directly enforceable in domestic courts. That would require implementing legislation. J. Nickel, "Human Rights," in E. N. Zalta (ed.), *The Stanford Encyclopedia of Philosophy* (2010), available at www.plato.stanford.edu. The Convention on the Elimination of All Forms of Racial Discrimination entered into force in 1969.

48 European Convention on Human Rights, signed November 4, 1950 (entered into force September 3, 1953).

49 Two optional clauses subsequently adopted by all member states permit individual and state-to-state petitions and compulsory jurisdiction of the Court. Many European governments have incorporated it directly or indirectly into domestic law and compliance is consistently high. Moravcsik, "The Origin of Human Rights Regimes," p. 218.

50 *Ibid.*

51 *Ibid.*, pp. 218–249.

52 *Ibid.*, p. 228. This is thus different from the argument of R. Hirschl, *Towards Juristocracy: The Origins and Consequences of the New Constitutionalism* (Cambridge, MA: Harvard University Press, 2004).

53 Moravcsik, "The Origin of Human Rights Regimes," p. 238.

54 *Ibid.*

55 *Ibid.*, p. 281. Nevertheless the ECtHR rulings, unlike those of the ECJ, do not have direct effect.

56 M. E. Keck and K. Sikkink, *Activists beyond Borders: Advocacy Networks in International Politics* (Ithaca, NY: Cornell University Press, 2007), pp. 88–92, noting the central place of Chile in this.

57 Moyn, *The Last Utopia*, pp. 121–175; J. Laber, *The Courage of Strangers: Coming of Age with the Human Rights Movement* (New York: Public Affairs, 2002). But Moyn also insists that anti-colonialism laws was not a human rights movement, pp. 84–119: an argument contested by R. Blackburn, "Reclaiming Human Rights," *New Left Review*, 69 (2011), 126–138.

58 For example, CEDAW; the Convention Against Torture (1987); and the Convention on the Rights of the Child (1990). The Helsinki Final Act 1975 made human rights compliance a legitimate concern of diplomacy in conferences for security and cooperation in Europe.

59 Realist international relations arguments deem signing international rights treaties as "cheap talk" entailing few risks and often no intention to comply. O. Hathaway, "Do Human Rights Treaties Make a Difference?" *Yale Law Journal*, 111 (2002), 1935–2042; and L. Keith, "The United Nations International Covenant on Civil and Political Rights: Does it Make a Difference in Human Rights Behavior?" *Journal of Peace Research*, 36 (1999), 95–118. But see Simmons, *Mobilizing for Human Rights*, p. 201, for a counterargument. Accordingly, a binding international legal human rights treaty ratified by one's own government creates a political opportunity and, depending on the costs, an important symbolic referent for domestic rights activists.

60 Keck and Sikkink, *Activists beyond Borders*, stress the role of transnational advocacy networks and alliances that do an end run around highly repressive states by hooking up with domestic actors and providing resources for them. The focus is on publicity of local violations and claims and the "boomerang" effect from local to global back to local

change. This is not a legal model of external enforcement. Beth Simmons stresses the focus of domestic actors in getting their governments to live up to their treaty obligations also emphasizing that it is primarily domestic actors who get compliance even if they have outside help. Simmons, *Mobilizing for Human Rights*, pp. 154, 372. Globalized enforcement is a chimera, but the importance of the treaties is not.

61 T. M. Franck first asserted the idea of a democratic entitlement in international law in "The Emerging Right to Democratic Governance," *American Journal of International Law*, 86 (1992), 46–91. Yet he explicitly rejected the idea that such a right could justify pro-democratic invasions.

62 This is certainly true of CEDAW, the beneficiary of women's movements within and across states that arose in the mid-1960s and flourished in the 1970s, forming a "second wave," cresting in 1985, the final year of the United Nations Decade for Women. The women's movement was at its height between 1965 and 1985, the epoch of détente and before the emergence of religious traditionalism and challenges to secular nationalism. Simmons, *Mobilizing for Human Rights*, pp. 202–255. Thus, there was a window of opportunity for elaboration of international norms of equality for women, spurred on by feminists domestically and pushing internationally.

63 Moyn, *The Last Utopia*, pp. 149–173. For the association of East European dissidents with the discourse of anti-politics, see pp. 170–172. See also J. L. Cohen and A. Arato, *Civil Society and Political Theory* (Cambridge, MA: MIT Press, 1992), pp. 29–82.

64 *Ibid.*

65 C. Lefort, "Politics and Human Rights," in C. Lefort, *The Political Forms of Modern Society* (Cambridge, MA: MIT Press, 1986), pp. 239–272; and "Human Rights and the Welfare State," in C. Lefort, *Democracy and Political Theory* (Minneapolis: University of Minnesota Press, 1988), pp. 21–44.

66 Lefort, "Politics and Human Rights," pp. 241–244, assessing the Eastern European dissidents' practice in these terms.

67 *Ibid.* All of this is intolerable to "totalitarian" or autocratic regimes, which abrogate precisely these rights (of conscience, assembly, speech, association, petition, etc.) the minute they manage to consolidate their power. Such regimes can neither tolerate the autonomous socio-political practice of domestic dissidents and activists, nor can they accept the indeterminacy of who might claim the rights of man and citizen and of what might be claimed that is constitutive of human rights activism.

68 *Ibid.*, p. 257.

69 In this regard, there is a link between human rights and democracy according to Lefort, insofar as both are indeterminate and constitute two different ways of creating and acting within public spaces. See also J. Habermas, *Between Facts and Norms* (Cambridge: Polity Press, 1996), pp. 82–131, for an argument regarding the co-equivalence and links between human rights and popular sovereignty.

70 Paraphrasing Moyn, *The Last Utopia*, pp. 129–146. This is true especially of Amnesty International in 1975.

71 For a list, see Dezalay and Garth, "From the Cold War to Kosovo."

72 C. McCrudden, "Human Dignity and Judicial Interpretation of Human Rights," *European Journal of International Law*, 19 (2008), 655–724.

73 *Ibid.* See also Moyn, *The Last Utopia*, p. 130; Simmons, *Mobilizing for Human Rights*, pp. 23–56.

74 Simmons, *Mobilizing for Human Rights*, p. 49.

75 Keck and Sikkink, *Activists beyond Borders*; Simmons, *Mobilizing for Human Rights*, p. 372.

76 Dezalay and Garth, "From the Cold War to Kosovo," p. 250; Moyn, *The Last Utopia*, p. 155.

77 M. Ignatieff, *Human Rights as Politics, Human Rights as Idolatry* (Princeton University Press, 2001).
78 Human rights appear as a neutral language beyond and above politics based on an alleged global consensus.
79 For a discussion of the trajectory, see S. Wertheim, "A Solution from Hell: The United States and the Rise of Humanitarian Interventionism, 1991–2003," *Journal of Genocide Research*, 12 (2010), 149–172.
80 ICISS, *The Responsibility to Protect*, pp. 14–17.
81 J. R. Wallach, "Human Rights as an Ethics of Power," in R. A. Wilson (ed.), *Human Rights and the War on Terror* (Cambridge University Press, 2005), pp. 108–137.

A caveat: At issue here is not the so-called "paradox of rights" whereby legal rights appear to empower and free the individual legal subject but also serve as the medium by which the administrative apparatuses regulate and coerce these very subjects, thereby turning them into sites of "governance." All law backed by sanctions entails coercion, as the most casual reader of Hobbes will note, but law is the condition of possibility of subjective freedom and of realizing the principle of equal liberty, as any reader of Kant should also know. Law is also the medium through which collective self-government, political autonomy, democracy, and the accountability of political power become possible in the modern world, which is why democratic theorists from Rousseau to Arendt and Habermas have insisted that popular sovereignty or public freedom has to be exercised within a constitutional framework that allows the subjects of law to understand themselves as its authors. The duality of law as "institution," constituting legal persons to whom freedom and political equality are ascribed, and law as the "medium" that constitutes subjects as objects of rule and the vehicle through which administrative apparatuses penetrate the life world, is a phenomenon that has been discussed in great detail by many including Habermas, Foucault, and myself with Andrew Arato. Habermas, *Between Facts and Norms*; M. Foucault, "Governmentality," in G. Burchell, C. Gordon, and P. Miller (eds.), *The Foucault Effect: Studies in Governmentality* (Hemel Hempstead: Harvester Wheatsheaf, 1991), pp. 87–104; and Cohen and Arato, *Civil Society and Political Theory*.

A clue as to where the weight of a legal right will lie – freedom-enhancing or disempowering – is whether the subjects of rights have a say in determining which rights they have, in interpreting the meaning of the content of rights, and in which respects they are to be treated equally. This is an unending process involving both legal adjudication and struggle, but it presupposes the priority of the internal addressees of the law in determining the political legitimacy of any given set of rights. In other words, the interpretation of rights involves an ethical-political process in which the addressees, members of the political community, must have a say or their political autonomy is undermined. Legal rights and the politics of rights are thus part of the complex relation between law and power. This by no means implies that the politics of rights is the only politics. But it does mean that the dualism of the legal medium cannot be wished away, and that there is no viable alternative to government through law, or to the legal articulation of basic rights and the struggles over the interpretation of such rights. Accordingly, a one-sided critique of rights as simply sites of governmentality and subjectivation is as naive as a one-sided defense of rights as simply freedom-guaranteeing.

The issue that we confront on the international level is somewhat different. What is at stake is the shift from one form of rights discourse and practice to another. The first involved domestic actors fighting for the transition from dictatorship to democracy and/or for liberation from foreign rule, in which invocation of human rights standards articulated in international documents played a role, but in which domestic actors were the authors and interpreters of the rights they were asserting. The second involves the invocation of human rights "law" by powerful outsiders – states – that, in the name of the "international community," intervene in domestic conflicts, impose severe sanctions, and even new legal systems in the context of onerous occupation regimes. Here, the problem is not that the legal medium is the vehicle of "governmentality," but rather that the nature of the international law in question is ambiguous: many human rights documents entail "soft," deformalized law, and their binding legal character is disputed. Those pushing an imperial project are happy with soft, indeterminate law since it gives them the leeway to invoke moral principles to legitimate intervention; others want hard human rights law. This opens up the question as to which rights should acquire the status of hard international law, and how to democratize the process of making this decision, the subject of this chapter.

82 See the articles by K. Tan, "The Duty to Protect," and C. Bagnoli, "Humanitarian Intervention as a Perfect Duty: A Kantian Argument," in Nardin and Williams (eds.), *Humanitarian Intervention: NOMOS XLVII*, pp. 84–116 and 117–142.

83 UN Charter Chapter VII Article 39, and international law generally, outlaws intervention through use of force with one exception: enforcement measures ordered by the Security Council under Chapter VII. United Nations, *Charter of the United Nations*.

84 Humanitarian intervention has to be linked by the Security Council to threats to international peace and security. The R2P doctrine articulated in the ICISS report and, later, in the 2005 UN Summit Outcome Document, which won the unanimous assent of member states, tries to get around this restriction. United Nations, General Assembly, *World Summit Outcome* (New York: UN, 2005). Available at www.un.org/summit2005/documents.html; ICISS, *The Responsibility to Protect*.

85 This was triggered by concern over the NATO intervention in Kosovo and by more general attempts of Kofi Annan and others to wrestle with the questions surrounding humanitarian intervention given the assault on national sovereignty it entails. ICISS, *The Responsibility to Protect*, p. vii. A careful reader can see tensions in the report between strong cosmopolitans willing to abandon entirely the discourse of sovereignty and others seeking to articulate a new sovereignty regime.

86 Wertheim, "A Solution from Hell," pp. 159–160.

87 N. Wheeler, "Humanitarian Intervention After Kosovo: Emergent Norm, Moral Duty or the Coming of Anarchy?" *International Affairs*, 77 (2001), 113–128.

88 M. Doyle, "International Ethics and the Responsibility to Protect," *International Studies Review*, 13 (2011), 72–84.

89 K. Annan, "Reflections on Intervention," in K. Annan, *The Question of Intervention: Statements by the Secretary-General* (New York: United Nations Department of Public Information, 1999), p. 4. Clearly disturbed by the failure to act in the Rwandan genocide, Annan articulated some concern for the possibility of a dangerous precedent by NATO but he did not oppose the Kosovo war; rather, human rights became the central discourse and source of legitimacy for the intervention there and Annan endorsed humanitarian intervention.

90 See the discussion in Doyle, "International Ethics and the Responsibility to Protect."

91 This was not a legal intervention in that it was not a Chapter VII Article 39 Security Council action but an action by NATO. It was dubbed illegal but legitimate subsequently by many. See A. Bellamy, "Kosovo and the Advent of Sovereignty as Responsibility," *Journal of Intervention and Statebuilding*, 3 (2009), 163–184. But see also D. Zolo's critique in "Humanitarian Militarism?" in S. Besson and J. Tasioulas (eds.), *The Philosophy of International Law* (Oxford University Press, 2010), pp. 549–568.

92 Doyle, "International Ethics and the Responsibility to Protect."

93 *Ibid.*

94 ICISS, *The Responsibility to Protect*, p. 13.

95 *Ibid.*, p. 8.

96 Buchanan, *Justice, Legitimacy, and Self-Determination*, pp. 280–288; R. O. Keohane, "Political Authority After Intervention: Gradations in Sovereignty," in J. Holzgrefe and R. O. Keohane (eds.), *Humanitarian Intervention: Ethical, Legal and Political Dilemmas* (Cambridge University Press, 2003), pp. 275–282.

97 I do not endorse this discourse or approach. For a critical analysis of the legal concept of quasi-sovereignty, see L. Benton, *A Search for Sovereignty: Law and Geography in European Empires, 1400–1900* (Cambridge University Press, 2009), pp. 222–278.

98 Buchanan and Keohane, "The Preventive Use of Force."

99 I will return to this issue in the conclusion of this chapter.

100 M. Reisman, "Sovereignty and Human Rights in Contemporary International Law," and M. Byers and S. Chesterman, "You the People: Pro Democratic Intervention in International Law," both in G. H. Fox and B. R. Roth (eds.), *Democratic Governance and International Law* (Cambridge University Press, 2000), pp. 239–258 and 259–292. Simmons rightly rejects this use of the discourse of human rights in *Mobilizing for Human Rights*, pp. 14–18. See also F. Teson, "The Liberal Case for Humanitarian Intervention," in Holzgrefe and Keohane (eds.), *Humanitarian Intervention*, pp. 93–129, arguing that, since all borders are the serendipitous result of past violence and other morally irrelevant historical facts, they have no basic right to non-intervention.

101 Zolo, "Humanitarian Militarism?"; and Mamdani, *Saviors and Survivors*.

102 J. Rawls, *The Law of Peoples* (Cambridge, MA: Harvard University Press, 1999); Ignatieff, *Human Rights as Politics, Human Rights as Idolatry*; Beitz, *The Idea of Human Rights*; J. Cohen, "Minimalism about Human Rights: The Most We Can Hope For?" *The Journal of Political Philosophy*, 12 (2004), 190–213; J. Cohen, "Is There a Human Right to Democracy?" in C. Sypnowich (ed.), *The Egalitarian Conscience: Essays in Honor of G. A. Cohen* (Oxford University Press, 2006), pp. 226–248; and J. Raz, "Human Rights Without Foundations," in Besson and Tasioulas (eds.), *The Philosophy of International Law*, pp. 321–338, among others.

103 Beitz, *The Idea of Human Rights*, does not interpret the function as narrowly as Raz, as we shall see, but nonetheless gives a functionalist definition of human rights. For critiques of the functionalist redefinition of human rights, see K. Baynes, "Discourse Ethics and the Political Conception of Human Rights," *Ethics & Global Politics*, 2 (2009), 1–22; J. Griffin, "Human Rights and the Autonomy of International Law," in Besson and Tasioulas (eds.), *The Philosophy of International Law*, pp. 339–357; and Forst, "The Justification of Human Rights."

104 Whether there is a traditional approach, and whom it fits, is contested. See Griffin, "Human Rights and the Autonomy of International Law." I discuss here the political conception's ideal type of the traditional approach. Included are theorists such as A. Gewirth, *Human Rights* (University of Chicago Press, 1982) and J. Donnelly, *Universal Human Rights* (Ithaca, NY: Cornell University Press, 2003).

105 As such they have a "Janus face" insofar as they are capable of moral and legal justification. J. Habermas, "Kant's Idea of Perpetual Peace with the Benefit of 200 Years' Hindsight," in K. Baynes and M. Lutz-Bachmann (eds.), *Perpetual Peace: Essays on Kant's Cosmopolitan Idea* (Cambridge, MA: Harvard University Press, 1997), pp. 113–154. See also Forst, "The Justification of Human Rights," p. 711.

106 Nickel, "Human Rights"; and T. Pogge, "Human Rights and Human Responsibilities," in A. Kuper (ed.), *Global Responsibilities: Who Must Deliver on Human Rights?* (London: Routledge, 2005), pp. 3–35.

107 Pogge, "Human Rights and Human Responsibilities."

108 For a critique, see J. L. Cohen, *Regulating Intimacy: A New Legal Paradigm* (Princeton University Press, 2002), pp. 97–101.

109 J. Tasioulis, "Are Human Rights Essentially Triggers for Intervention?" *Philosophy Compass*, 4 (2009), 938–950.

110 Raz, "Human Rights Without Foundations," p. 323, lists four features of the traditional approach that he ascribes to Alan Gewirth and James Griffin, among others. See Griffin's reply to Raz, "Human Rights and the Autonomy of International Law."

111 The most interesting recent example is J. Griffin, *On Human Rights* (Oxford University Press, 2008), pp. 32–33, who argues that the core value protected by human rights is our normative agency – the precondition for deliberating, assessing, choosing, and acting to make what we see as a good life for ourselves. Thus, human rights are derived from the high value we attach to our personhood as individuals with a higher order interest in choosing and pursuing the good. He does insist that to make this conception of agency determinate, one would have to consider practicalities: aspects of human nature and society that help us figure out what is necessary to secure our agency goods and to justify obligations of others. Nonetheless, the ultimate foundation is an ethical conception of agency as the good. For a critique of Griffin's ethical conception, see Forst, "The Justification of Human Rights and the Basic Right of Justification," pp. 720–726.

112 For two distinct agency views, see Gewirth, *Human Rights*; and Griffin, *On Human Rights*. For a basic interest view, see J. Finnis, *Natural Law and Natural Rights* (Oxford: Clarendon Press, 1980); and J. Raz, *The Morality of Freedom* (Oxford University Press, 1988). For a natural rights-based view of human rights, see A. J. Simmons, "Human Rights and World Citizenship: The Universality of Human Rights in Kant and Locke," in A. J. Simmons, *Justification and Legitimacy: Essays on Rights and Obligations* (Cambridge University Press, 2000), pp. 179–196. For a capabilities account, see M. Nussbaum, "Human Rights Theory: Capabilities and Human Rights," *Fordham Law Review*, 66 (1997), 273–300; M. Nussbaum, "Capabilities and Human Rights," in P. De Greiff and C. P. Cronin (eds.), *Global Justice and Transnational Politics* (Cambridge, MA: MIT Press, 2002), pp. 117–149; and A. Sen, "Elements of a Theory of Human Rights," *Philosophy and Public Affairs*, 32 (2004), 315–356. For a "will theory" approach, see H. L. A. Hart, "Are There Any Natural Rights?" *Philosophical Review*, 64 (1955), 175–191. For a dignity view, see Forst, "The Justification of Human Rights and the Basic Right of Justification," pp. 721–722, who tries to cash this out not as ethical but as deontological and reflexive on the practice of human rights claimants.

113 Cohen, "Is There a Human Right to Democracy?"

114 M. Cranston, *What are Human Rights?* (London: Bodley Head, 1973); and M. Cranston, "Are There Any Human Rights?" *Daedalus*, 12 (1983), 1–17.

115 See the discussion in Baynes, "Discourse Ethics and the Political Conception of Human Rights."

116 Beitz, "Naturalistic Theories," in Beitz, *The Idea of Human Rights*, pp. 48–72.

117 Cranston, "Are There Any Human Rights?"

118 James Griffin, "Discrepancies Between the Best Philosophical Account of Human Rights and the International Documents," *Proceedings of the Aristotelian Society*, 101 (2001), 1–28; and Griffin, *On Human Rights*, Chapter 11. A favorite target is UDHR Article 24 listing a right to "periodic holidays with pay."

119 Raz, "Human Rights Without Foundations," pp. 322–327.

120 I am paraphrasing James Griffin on Raz's characterization of his work. James Griffin, "Human Rights and the Autonomy of International Law," p. 347.

121 Raz, "Human Rights Without Foundations."

122 For an attempt to develop a philosophical account of human rights that does not seek to derive them from a basic ground but which does seek to provide moral justification for human rights, see Forst, "The Justification of Human Rights and the Basic Right of Justification."

123 As I see it, there are really two broad subgroups within the political conception. One group, which includes among others the early work of Charles Beitz and Thomas Pogge, is focused on issues of global distributive justice, and rejects natural right theories (Beitz) and traditional interactional theories of moral rights in favor of a political conception because they assume the latter will vindicate claims to socio-economic rights (included in documents such as the ICESCR and in UDHR) as genuine human rights and generate rights claims to global institutions. They hope to get arguments for global economic justice off the ground through a rights-based approach. They thus seek to avoid the minimalism and/or statism of the traditional approach. The problem is that they tend to elide the difference between global justice and human rights disclaimers to the contrary notwithstanding. The second group, which includes authors such as the later Beitz, Rawls, Raz, and Joshua Cohen, is focused more directly on the political implications (and function) of international human rights doctrine and practice – i.e. on issues of sovereignty, intervention, imposition, toleration, pluralism, and so on. This group seeks to navigate between minimalist and maximal approaches. It involves an internal critique of the maximalist versions of political and other conceptions that equate human rights with justice. But it supports a range of interventions for causes that fall short of the lack of full justice or full domestic democratic legitimacy. This chapter is concerned exclusively with the arguments of the latter group and their implications for international law. It does not engage in the debate over global distributive justice and human rights.

124 On distinctiveness of this "regime," see Beitz, *The Idea of Human Rights*, p. 43.

125 *Ibid.*, p. 105.

126 Raz, "Human Rights Without Foundations, pp. 334–337. But see Griffin, "Human Rights and the Autonomy of International Law," p. 351, arguing that the political conception of Raz is self-contradictory.

127 Beitz, *The Idea of Human Rights*, p. 8. But see Forst for the reverse argument reading the moral foundational principles from the intersubjective practice of asserting human rights. "The Justification of Human Rights and the Basic Right of Justification."

128 Beitz, *The Idea of Human Rights*, pp. 103–104.

129 Ignatieff, *Human Rights as Politics, Human Rights as Idolatry*; Beitz, *The Idea of Human Rights*, p. 8.

130 See M. A. Glendon, *A World Made New: Eleanor Roosevelt and the Universal Declaration of Human Rights* (New York: Random House, 2001), Chapter 3; and Moyn, *The Last Utopia*, citing Maritain.

131 Ignatieff, *Human Rights as Politics, Human Rights as Idolatry*, p. 88. To those schooled in Rawls, this, however, is distinct from the latter's idea of overlapping consensus. Ignatieff's approach is rather empirical, or a "lowest common denominator" model more akin to the idea of a modus vivendi among existing views. Thus it involves a substantive rather than justificatory minimalism. For the distinction, see Cohen, "Minimalism about Human Rights."

132 However, international human rights are not grounded in some action of the rights holder, such as a promise, nor in desert or transactions they have entered into.

133 Raz, "Human Rights Without Foundations," p. 12; Pogge, "Cosmopolitanism and Sovereignty," p. 179.

134 Cohen, "Is There a Human Right to Democracy?" p. 232. For all theorists of the political conception, human rights are standards to which political societies can

reasonably be held, indicating when they are appropriately subject to external criticism or interference.

135 Beitz, *The Idea of Human Rights*, p. 13.

136 *Ibid.*, pp. 13, 31–32.

137 Raz, "Human Rights Without Foundations," pp. 328–329; Cohen, "Is There a Human Right to Democracy?" p. 234. Cohen states here that ". . . human rights standards are urgent standards of political morality whose violation warrants external reproach (and in extreme cases sanctions and intervention)."

138 For Rawls, *The Law of Peoples*; Buchanan, *Justice, Legitimacy, and Self-Determination.*

139 Raz, "Human Rights Without Foundations," p. 328. By "defeasible," Raz means that the violation of human rights is not an automatic trigger to sanctions but opens up the discursive space for considering appropriate responses, including military intervention, on the part of the international community.

140 Rawls, *The Law of Peoples.*

141 *Ibid.*, pp. 79–80.

142 The concept *public reason* refers to principles and norms that all members of the society of peoples can share. Human rights are a component of such norms. This is not a matter of self-interested bargaining, but commitment to shared principles and laws based on them including intervention.

143 Forst, "The Justification of Human Rights and the Basic Right of Justification," p. 714.

144 Rawls, *The Law of Peoples*, pp. 27, 65, 78–81.

145 *Ibid.*, p. 65. Rawls's list includes only rights to life, to the means of subsistence, personal liberty including liberty of conscience but not equal liberty, personal property, formal equality or equal treatment under the law. Thus, he argues that they cannot be rejected as peculiarly liberal or special to the western tradition.

146 Beitz, *The Idea of Human Rights*, p. 1.

147 *Ibid.*, pp. 102–117, criticizes Rawls for leaving out much too much of the practice of international human rights from his conception.

148 *Ibid.*, p. 107.

149 Like the other political conceptions, this definition creates the following dilemma: If a claim does not generate international concern, then does this mean it would not be a human right? Why restrict human rights to international concern? Some domestic struggles and rights claims may not rise to that level but should this mean that human rights are not involved?

150 Raz, "Human Rights Without Foundations." This is also obviously Rawls's thesis in *The Law of Peoples*. Raz believes that Rawls is guilty of eliding the difference between internal and external legitimacy insofar as Rawls regards human rights as the necessary minimal conditions for a system of social cooperation. For him, human rights thus determine the internal legitimacy of a regime and the obligation of its members to obey its laws, and the external legitimacy of a regime insofar as their violation supplies reasons for international non-recognition of the sovereignty of the state (its inclusion in the society of peoples), and for external intervention. Raz rightly, in my view, argues that whether or not a state has full internal legitimacy in the eyes of its members is a different issue as to whether foreigners have a sufficient reason for coercively intervening in a state.

151 I do not discuss Rawls's answer as many have analyzed it. Rawls, *The Law of Peoples*, pp. 68 and 78–83. For a summary of the criticisms of Rawls's view, see Nickel "Human Rights," pp. 5–6.

152 Rawls never articulated a justification for the normative status of the rights he singles out from the Universal Declaration as the "proper subset" in *The Law of Peoples*. For Rawlsians, the discussion focuses on the proper subset of moral rights, which set

external limits to the sovereign will of peoples but presumably will form part of the "law" of peoples, or binding international law.

153 Raz, "Human Rights Without Foundations," p. 328.

154 *Ibid.*, pp. 328, 330. Sovereignty is the counterpart of rightful intervention. He correctly argues against confusing the limits of external sovereignty with the limits of legitimate authority. Sovereignty limits the right of outsiders to interfere in domestic jurisdiction of a state, it does not determine the criteria of legitimate authority internally or the morality of an authority's actions.

155 *Ibid.*, p. 328

156 *Ibid.*, p. 322.

157 *Ibid.*, p. 328.

158 *Ibid.*, p. 331.

159 *Ibid.*, p. 336. He also claims that they need not be universal (p. 332). Other theorists of the political conception differ on this point. See Cohen, "Is There a Human Right to Democracy?" p. 229.

160 Raz, "Human Rights Without Foundations," p. 336.

161 *Ibid.*, p. 331. He mentions domination of a superpower over its rivals and client states.

162 Tasioulis, "Are Human Rights Essentially Triggers for Intervention?"

163 Griffin, "Human Rights and the Autonomy of International Law"; and Forst, "The Justification of Human Rights and the Basic Right of Justification."

164 Cohen, "Is There a Human Right to Democracy?" p. 235. Cohen proposes as a "substantive normative thesis" that political conception and doctrines count as reasonable within global public reasons only if they accept the norms of membership, although this does not entail endorsing the liberal idea of society as an association of equals.

165 *Ibid.*, pp. 237–238. This is a gloss on Rawls's concept of system of cooperation.

166 *Ibid.*, pp. 238–239.

167 *Ibid.*, p. 230.

168 *Ibid.*, p. 234; Cohen, "Minimalism about Human Rights," p. 194.

169 Cohen, "Is There a Human Right to Democracy?" p. 232.

170 *Ibid.*, p. 230.

171 Cohen, "Minimalism about Human Rights," p. 199.

172 *Ibid.*, p. 199. See the discussion in Forst, "The Justification of Human Rights and the Basic Right of Justification," p. 716.

173 Cohen, "Is There a Human Right to Democracy?" p. 236, defines global public reason as global in its reach, applying to all political societies, and in its agent as the common reason of all peoples who share responsibility for interpreting its principles, and monitoring and enforcing them.

174 Cohen, "Minimalism about Human Rights," pp. 206–207, citing Rawls.

175 *Ibid.*, p. 207.

176 Cohen, "Is There a Human Right to Democracy?" pp. 239–242. I have argued in a similar vein in J. L. Cohen, "Whose Sovereignty? Empire Versus International Law," *Ethics and International Affairs*, 18 (2004), 1–24.

177 Cohen, "Is There a Human Right to Democracy?" p. 235. Cohen cites Rawls's argument that the costs of intolerance include lapsing into contempt on the one side, bitterness and resentment on the other. See Rawls, *The Law of Peoples*, p. 62.

178 Cohen, "Is There a Human Right to Democracy?" p. 238.

179 *Ibid.*, p. 233. Accordingly, collective self-determination need not involve equal representation and it can assign special weight to interests of some social groups. This is a gloss on Rawls's concept of "decent hierarchical societies."

180 *Ibid.*, p. 233.

181 *Ibid.*
182 Or of gender equality.
183 Cohen, "Is There a Human Right to Democracy?" pp. 236–238.
184 Forst, "The Justification of Human Rights and the Basic Right of Justification," p. 730. In short, this involves toleration for the wrong reasons.
185 *Ibid.*, p. 730.
186 *Ibid.*, pp. 730–732.
187 *Ibid.*
188 Habermas, *Between Facts and Norms*, pp. 409–426.
189 Tasioulis, "Are Human Rights Essentially Triggers for Intervention?"
190 Forst, "The Justification of Human Rights and the Basic Right of Justification," p. 727.
191 While he does not say much about intervention, Cohen implies that violation of these rights and the internal principle of self-determination, as he construes it, would be tantamount to a defeasible reason for sanctions by the international community. I think this is too permissive.
192 See 1949 Geneva Convention for the Amelioration of the Condition of the Wounded and Sick in Armed Forces in the Field, Article 3, available at www.umn.edu/humanrts/instree/y1gcacws.htm. Here, the Convention incorporates armed conflict not of "an international character" into the lexicon of the Law of War.
193 Genocide Convention, and the ICC statute defining and outlawing crimes against humanity, ethnic cleansing, and severe forms of discrimination that amount to enslavement. See United Nations, *Convention on the Prevention and Punishment of the Crime of Genocide*; and the Rome Statute of the International Criminal Court. My purpose is to provide a systematic justification for the proper subset and for restricting legal collective sanctions that suspend the sovereignty argument to this subset.
194 See Teitel, "Humanity's Law: Rule of Law for the New Global Politics."
195 Doyle, "International Ethics and the Responsibility to Protect," arguing that R2P is not yet black letter law. He correctly notes that the ICC has jurisdiction for certain grave crimes when states parties do not prosecute them domestically, and that the UN can establish ad hoc, mixed tribunals and so on. But this does not quite entail universal jurisdiction: the US, China, India, and Russia are not parties to the treaty establishing the ICC, and the Security Council can block cases if it is handling a related issue. See the Rome Statute of the International Criminal Court.
196 The term "right to have rights" comes from Hannah Arendt. She meant the right to be a member, a citizen of a polity, and she believed that citizenship status constructs natural persons into rights holders, with legal standing and a legal persona. However, the "right" to have rights is a universal moral right, pertaining to all human beings. It is open to a cosmopolitan interpretation such that non-citizens in any polity, residents, aliens, and even illegal aliens also have international human rights. Her interpretation of the idea of a crime against humanity is framed in terms of a universalistic membership principle: i.e. every individual and group must be deemed a member of the human group, humanity. See Arendt, *Origins of Totalitarianism*, pp. 267–304, 252–279; H. Arendt, *Eichmann in Jerusalem: A Report on the Banality of Evil* (New York: Penguin, 1994), pp. 253–279; Cohen, "Rights, Citizenship, and the Modern Form of the Social"; and Benhabib, *The Rights of Others*, for a cosmopolitan reading of Arendt.
197 Sovereignty entails an authoritative political and legal relationship between a government and a citizenry within a bounded territory.
198 M. Walzer, "The Moral Standing of States," *Philosophy and Public Affairs*, 9 (1980), 209–229. Walzer offers communitarian, rights-based, and republican arguments in defense of the moral standing of states. One can make the point without buying into

the communitarian argument, without accepting his defense of unilateralism, or his version of just war theory.

199 As Teitel insightfully notes in "Humanity's Law: Rule of Law for the New Global Politics," p. 377, these new norms amount to a universalized minorities regime, but one I would argue without ethnic connotations. In other words, they rest on a conception of crimes against humanity as per the Rome Statute of the ICC that involves persecution against any identifiable group or collectivity on political, racial, national, ethnic, cultural, religious, gender grounds. See the Rome Statute of the International Criminal Court, Article 7.

200 As per the friend/enemy version of the sovereignty concept defended by C. Schmitt in *Political Theology: Four Chapters on the Concept of Sovereignty* (University of Chicago Press, 2005).

201 Arendt, *Eichmann in Jerusalem*, pp. 253–279. Thus, she wanted an International Court with universal, compulsory jurisdiction to try such crimes.

202 Inattention to procedure is serious, as it opens the door to unilateralism and diverts attention from the appropriate institutional design (reform) of the international organization making the relevant decisions. J. L. Cohen, "Sovereign Equality Versus Imperial Right: The Battle Over the New World Order," *Constellations*, 13 (2006), 485–505.

203 It follows from the universalistic scope of Arendt's concept – all human beings have the right to have rights – that there should be legal protections for the basic human rights of residents and aliens, regardless of their citizenship status.

204 See Cohen, "Sovereign Equality Versus Imperial Right," pp. 491–494, for a discussion of the concept of sovereign equality and its normative thrust.

205 Originally it also enshrined empire insofar as sovereignty, acknowledged by the Charter, included imperial sovereignty over colonies. See M. Mazower, *No Enchanted Place: The End of Empire and the Ideological Origins of the United Nations* (Princeton University Press, 2008).

206 Cohen, "Whose Sovereignty? Empire Versus International Law." See also B. Kingsbury, "Sovereignty and Inequality," *European Journal of International Law*, 9 (1998), 599–625.

207 See Chapter 1 of this book.

208 M. Byers and S. Chesterman, "Changing the Rules About Rules? Unilateral Humanitarian Intervention and the Future of International Law," in Holzgrefe and Keohane (eds.), *Humanitarian Intervention*, pp. 177–203 (p. 196).

209 M. Cosnard, "Sovereign Equality – 'The *Wimbledon* Sails On,'" in Byers and Nolte (eds.), *United States Hegemony and the Foundations of International Law*, pp. 117–134, p. 122. However, see Chapter 5 for an argument that there is, in the flawed UN Charter system, no equality before the rule between the P5 and other members. See also N. Krisch, "More Equal Than the Rest? Hierarchy, Equality, and US Predominance in International Law," in Byers and Nolte (eds.), *United States Hegemony and the Foundations of International Law*, pp. 135–175.

210 D. Philpott, *Revolutions in Sovereignty: How Ideas Shaped Modern International Relations* (Princeton University Press, 2001), for the concept of changing sovereignty regime.

211 J. L. Cohen, "Changing Paradigms of Citizenship and the Exclusiveness of the Demos," *International Sociology*, 14 (1999), 245–268, for a discussion of the analytic of the citizenship principle.

212 "Ethical-political" refers to the question of how we (a particular group) want to live as a particular political community (the good) as distinct from the moral question of what is right for all. See J. Habermas, *Justification and Application: Remarks on Discourse Ethics* (Cambridge, MA: MIT Press, 1993), Chapter 1.

213 Nagel, "The Problem of Global Justice." But Nagel's account is deeply Hobbesian regarding international relations, and he fails to adequately address issues of global governance and globalizing international law.

214 I. Kant, *The Metaphysics of Morals* (Cambridge University Press, 2000).

215 Habermas, *Between Facts and Norms*, Chapter 3.

216 See P. Pettit, "Democracy, National and International," *The Monist*, 89 (2006), 301–324.

217 See Walzer, "The Moral Standing of States."

218 *Ibid.*, p. 214.

219 *Ibid.* Especially when it involves the imposition of laws or a new constitution by outsiders. J. L. Cohen, "The Role of International Law in Post-Conflict Constitution-Making: Toward a *Jus Post Bellum* for 'Interim Occupations,'" *New York Law Review*, 51 (2007), 497–532. See Chapter 4 of this book

220 Cohen, "Whose Sovereignty? Empire Versus International Law."

221 On the international law definition, a "state" has a territory, a people, effective internal governance, and the ability to conduct foreign relations with other states. Restatement of the Foreign Relations Law of the United States, Third, Section 201 (1996) cited in Alvarez, *International Organizations as Law-makers*, p. 15.

222 C. Schmitt, *The Concept of the Political* (University of Chicago Press, 1996).

223 See P. Chatterjee, "Empire and Nation Revisited: Fifty Years After Bandung," *Inter-Asia Cultural Studies*, 6 (2005), 487–496.

224 G. W. Gong, *The Standard of "Civilization" in International Society* (Oxford: Clarendon Press, 1984). On the concept of hierarchy in international law, see G. Simpson, *Great Powers and Outlaw States: Unequal Sovereigns in the Internal Legal Order* (Cambridge University Press, 2004).

225 Foucault, "Governmentality." I am quoting from Neil Walker, "Late Sovereignty in the European Union," in N. Walker (ed.), *Sovereignty in Transition: Essays in European Law* (Oxford: Hart Publishing, 2003), pp. 3–32 (pp. 19–20).

226 Walker, "Late Sovereignty in the European Union."

227 *Ibid.*, p. 20.

228 Cohen, "Sovereign Equality Versus Imperial Right."

229 I am paraphrasing from Macklem, "What is International Human Rights Law?"

230 Teitel, "Humanity's Law: Rule of Law for the New Global Politics," pp. 376–377.

231 *Ibid.*, p. 377.

232 *Ibid.* and Teitel, *Humanity's Law*

233 Teitel, "Humanity's Law," p. 377.

234 *Ibid.*, p. 380.

235 Rome Statute of the International Criminal Court (UN Doc. A/Conf. 183/9), 1999–2002.

236 See Cohen, "Whose Sovereignty? Empire Versus International Law," pp. 19–24.

237 See R. O. Keohane, S. Macedo, and A. Moravcsik, "Democracy-Enhancing Multilateralism," *International Organization*, 63 (2009), 1–31. Nevertheless, the problem of democracy-eviscerating multilateralism is also serious. See K. L. Scheppele, "The International State of Emergency: Challenges to Constitutionalism after September 11," paper presented at the Yale Legal Theory Workshop, Princeton University (2006).

238 Chayes and Chayes, *The New Sovereignty*, p. 27; A.-M. Slaughter, "Security, Solidarity, and Sovereignty: The Grand Theme of UN Reform," *American Journal of International Law*, 99 (2005), 619–631.

239 See Chapter 5.

240 See United Nations, A More Secure World: Our Shared Responsibility, Report of the Secretary-General's High-level Panel on Threats, Challenges and Change (New York: United Nations, 2004), www.un.org/secureworld. 192 member states have signed it.

241 This is narrowed to four: genocide, war crimes, ethnic cleansing, and crimes against humanity. *Ibid.*, paragraphs 138–139.

242 *Ibid.*

243 This focus is reaffirmed in the Secretary-General's Report, which describes what the UN could do to prevent R2P violations and to rebuild with the consent of the relevant state. United Nations, *Secretary-General's Report: Implementing the Responsibility to Protect* (New York: UN, 2009).

244 The High Commission suggests reviving the Uniting for Peace proposal of Butros Ghali, to resort to the General Assembly in case of Security Council deadlock or abuse of the veto. It rejects outright any resort to "coalitions of the willing."

245 S. Chesterman, *Just War or Just Peace? Humanitarian Intervention and International Law* (Oxford University Press, 2002), p. 231. See also Byers and Chesterman, "Changing the Rules About Rules," pp. 199–201.

246 *Ibid.*, pp. 199–200. On the debate over Thomas Franck's theory of jurying, see T. Franck, "Legality and Legitimacy in Humanitarian Intervention," in Nardin and Williams (eds.), *Humanitarian Intervention: NOMOS XLVII*, pp. 143–157; B. D. Lepard, "Jurying Humanitarian Intervention and the Ethical Principle of Open-Minded Consultation," in Nardin and Williams (eds.), *Humanitarian Intervention: NOMOS XLVII*, pp. 217–243; and Pogge, "Moralizing Humanitarian Intervention: Why Jurying Fails and How Law Can Work," in the same volume.

247 On mitigation, see T. Franck, "Interpretation and Change in the Law of Humanitarian Intervention," in Holzgrefe and Keohane (eds.), *Humanitarian Intervention*, pp. 204–31.

248 Chesterman, *Just War or Just Peace?* pp. 228–99.

249 *Ibid.*, p. 230. Unless one buys into a Schmittian conception of sovereignty, I see no logical reason why one cannot develop mechanisms and principles to regulate humanitarian intervention while keeping intact the general prohibition against forceful intervention.

250 *Ibid.*

251 L. F. Damrosch (ed.), *Enforcing Restraint: Collective Intervention in Internal Conflicts* (New York: Council on Foreign Relations Press, 1993), cites a range of triggers for Chapter VII determinations of threats to peace including genocide, ethnic cleansing, war crimes (Former Republic of Yugoslavia, Iraq, Liberia), violations of ceasefires (Former Republic of Yugoslavia, Liberia, Cambodia), collapse of civil order (Liberia, Somalia), and coups against democratic governments (Haiti). Needless to say, twenty-first-century interventions have expanded the list. See Doyle, "International Ethics and the Responsibility to Protect."

252 Chesterman, *Just War or Just Peace?* pp. 162–218.

253 Byers and Chesterman, "Changing the Rules About Rules," p. 197.

254 Buchanan and Keohane, "The Preventive Use of Force," pp. 16–22.

255 United Nations, A More Secure World.

256 Chesterman, *Just War or Just Peace?* pp. 162–218.

257 United Nations, *Secretary-General's Report: Implementing the Responsibility to Protect*; Doyle, "International Ethics and the Responsibility to Protect."

258 United Nations, A More Secure World, paragraphs 138–139.

259 See A. Arato, *Constitution Making Under Occupation: The Politics of Imposed Revolution in Iraq* (New York: Columbia University Press, 2009), for a critical analysis from this perspective of the intervention and occupation administration in Iraq.

260 See Chapter 4 of this book.

261 Another form of "inflation" occurs if political goals and projects are framed exclusively in human rights terms. See Moyn, *The Last Utopia*, pp. 212–230.

262 See T. Evans, *The Politics of Human Rights: A Global Perspective* (London: Pluto Press, 2005), Chapter 2; and D. Kennedy, *The Dark Side of Virtue: Reassessing International Humanitarianism* (Princeton University Press, 2004), pp. 3–36.

263 Teitel, "Humanity's Law: Rule of Law for the New Global Politics," p. 380.

264 Simmons, *Mobilizing for Human Rights*, p. 373. Indeed, it was thanks primarily to the efforts of non-state actors that support was gained for the proliferating treaties that elaborated UDHR and made its obligations legally binding.

265 Simmons, *Mobilizing for Human Rights*.

266 *Ibid.*, pp. 372–373.

267 *Ibid.*, p. 55.

268 Moyn's *The Last Utopia* underestimates the continuities on the moral justificatory level and on the level of claim-making among all fundamental rights discourses whether these appear as the rights of man, civil rights, or international human rights. See Blackburn, "Reclaiming Human Rights," challenging Moyn's historical record and arguing for greater continuity among rights discourses than Moyn grants.

269 Forst, "The Justification of Human Rights and the Basic Right of Justification," pp. 716–718, 729. See also Cohen and Arato, *Civil Society and Political Theory.*

270 Forst, "The Justification of Human Rights and the Basic Right of Justification," p. 718.

271 *Ibid.*, p. 736.

272 *Ibid.*, p. 735.

273 Habermas, "Kant's Idea of Perpetual Peace with the Benefit of 200 Years' Hindsight."

274 Forst, "The Justification of Human Rights and the Basic Right of Justification," p. 757.

275 Baynes, "Discourse Ethics and the Political Conception of Human Rights," pp. 3–6, for a critical assessment of the Forst/Habermas/Benhabib approach.

276 *Ibid.*, p. 6.

277 Lefort, "Politics and Human Rights."

278 Habermas, *Between Facts and Norms*, pp. 82–131.

279 Habermas is right: international human rights have an ambiguous status today because they do not yet have full legal weight; and he is also right to suggest/hope that the current situation is a transient one. Yet I disagree with his suggestion, repeated by Thomas Pogge, that one can identify Article 28 of the Universal Declaration as a source that could establish the legal status of the proper subset of such rights. J. Habermas, "Remarks on Legitimation Through Human Rights," *Philosophy and Social Criticism*, 24 (1998), 157–171 (pp. 160–161); and Pogge, "Human Rights and Human Responsibilities."

280 Nothing said in this chapter would preclude states from condemning tyranny or dictatorship and using their foreign policy to influence such governments to respect human rights and transition to democracy. Such influence, however, may not entail military intervention.

Chapter 4 Sovereignty and human rights in "post-conflict" constitution-making: toward a *jus post bellum* for "interim occupations"

1 *Jus ad bellum* deals with the justice of the decision to go to war; *jus in bello* deals with the justice of conduct of the battles. *Jus post bellum* should deal with justice after the war. See M. Walzer, *Arguing About War* (New Haven, CT: Yale University Press, 2004), p. xiii. I am concerned primarily with the legitimacy of post-war occupation and issues of international legal regulation of occupation regimes raise. My analysis thus shifts the emphasis of just war theory from moral philosophy to legal and political theory.

2 I restrict my analysis to non-consensual occupations. National sovereignty is not placed into question if intervention is consensual; for example, when foreign lawyers or advisors

are invited to monitor elections or advise on the drafting of constitutions, as in Eastern European transitions and in South Africa, or following of UN Chapter VI actions as in Cambodia and El Salvador, at the invitation of those states. In such cases, success is due in part to legitimacy, generated by real participation by domestic actors and a real process of self-determination. K. Boon, "Legislative Reform in Post-Conflict Zones: Jus Post Bellum and the Contemporary Occupant's Law-Making Powers," *McGill Law Journal*, 50 (2005), 285–326 (p. 288). I find helpful Benvenisti's definition of occupation as ". . . the effective control of a power (be it one or more states or an international organization, such as the United Nations) over a territory to which that power has no sovereign title, without the volition of the sovereign of that territory." E. Benvenisti, *The International Law of Occupation* (Princeton University Press, 2004), p. 4. This covers occupations following upon unilateral humanitarian interventions as well as UNSC-sponsored Chapter VII peace enforcement missions that involve full international governance. Nevertheless the distinction between belligerent (unilateral or multilateral coalitions of the willing) and humanitarian (UNSC-sponsored under Chapter VII of the Charter) occupation is important, as G. H. Fox has argued in *Humanitarian Occupation* (Cambridge University Press, 2008), p. 4; they draw on different legal sources, have different aims, and thus legal rules regulating them will differ. Fox defines humanitarian occupation, as ". . . the assumption of governing authority over a state or a portion thereof, by an international actor for the express purpose of creating a liberal, democratic order."

3 Technically, Hague and Geneva rules regarding belligerent occupation are deemed part of *jus in bellum*, a core aspect of humanitarian law, or the law of war, but I will refer to them as part of *jus post bellum* also in order to cover cases of occupation even if no full-scale war occurred and even if a war ends without a peace treaty. Hague Regulations Respecting the Laws and Customs of War on Land, October 18, 1907 [hereinafter 1907 Hague Convention]; Convention IV Relative to the Protection of Civilian Persons in Time of War (Geneva, Switzerland, 1949) [hereinafter Fourth Geneva Convention].

4 Occupation law prohibits the acquisition of sovereignty over the occupied territory (no annexation) and it accordingly also requires occupiers to respect the laws in force "unless absolutely prevented" from so doing. This is the "conservation principle" meant to prevent creeping annexation through imposition of a legal and political regime of the occupier or a quisling government. Hague Regulations Respecting the Laws and Customs of War on Land, Article 43; Convention IV Relative to the Protection of Civilian Persons in Time of War, Article 64.

5 Benvenisti, *The International Law of Occupation*, p. 5.

6 *Ibid.*, pp. 59–184.

7 UN Security Council-sponsored interim administrations are deemed not subject to the law of belligerent occupation, which was designed to regulate inter-state relations. See Fox, *Humanitarian Occupation*, pp. 218–250.

8 United Nations, *Security Council Resolution 1483* (New York: UN, 2003), paragraph 5, available at www.un.org/documents/scres. ("Calls upon all concerned to comply fully with their obligations under international law, including in particular the Geneva Conventions of 1949 and the Hague Regulations of 1907.") Resolutions 1483 and 1511 did not authorize this occupation by the "coalitional provisional authority" (CPA), but they acknowledged it and insisted that the authority remain bound by the Geneva Conventions. In addition, these resolutions charged the CPA with duties that go beyond the Geneva Conventions, such as establishing and administering a development fund for Iraq. See D. J. Scheffer, "Beyond Occupation Law," *American Journal of International Law*, 97 (2003), 842–859 (pp. 845–846).

9 Indeed one of the stated war aims was regime change. G. H. Fox, "The Occupation of Iraq," *Georgetown Journal of International Law*, 36 (2005), 195–297 (p. 196). Israel is

the other contemporary power that acknowledges it is engaged in an occupation, but it grants only the de jure relevance of the Hague Regulations. It claims that the Fourth Geneva Convention's humanitarian provisions will be applied de facto, but that otherwise they do not apply to its occupation of Palestinian territory of the West Bank and Gaza. See Benvenisti, *The International Law of Occupation*, note 2, pp. 104–108. See also, A. Imseis, "On the Fourth Geneva Convention and the Occupied Palestinian Territory," *Harvard International Law Journal*, 44 (2003), 65–138 (pp. 136–137).

10 The United Nations, Security Council Resolution 1483, note 7, paragraph 5.

11 J. Yoo (Visiting Fellow, American Enterprise Institute Professor of Law, University of California at Berkeley), "Iraqi Reconstruction and the Law of Occupation: Hearing on Constitutionalism, Human Rights and the Rule of Law in Iraq Before the Subcommittee on the Constitution, Senate Subcommittee on the Judiciary" (2003). Yoo reinterprets the Hague Regulations as enabling of transformative occupations. He argues that occupiers have the discretion to dismantle institutions posing a threat to international peace and security, to institutionalize democracy and human rights protections, to dismantle existing institutions of a state (Iraq under the CPA), and to create new ones. Others argue that the law of belligerent occupation is an anachronism today but should not be reformed to accommodate transformative projects of occupiers. See Scheffer, "Beyond Occupation Law," note 7; N. Bhuta, "The Antinomies of Transformative Occupation," *European Journal of International Law*, 16 (2005), 721–740.

12 Bhuta, "The Antinomies of Transformative Occupation," 734–737.

13 T. M. Fazal, "State Death in the International System," *International Organization*, 58 (2004), 311–344. See also Fox, *Humanitarian Occupation*, pp. 12–13.

14 Since decolonization, the UN trusteeship system established in 1945 is basically defunct, so it is unsurprising that the Secretary-General has recommended deletion of the Trusteeship Council from the Charter. See The Secretary-General, *In Larger Freedom: Towards Development, Security and Human Rights for All*, paragraph 218, delivered to the United Nations General Assembly (2005).

15 On shared sovereignty, see R. O. Keohane, "Political Authority After Intervention: Gradations in Sovereignty," in J. L. Holzgrefe and R. O. Keohane (eds.), *Humanitarian Intervention: Ethical, Legal, and Political Dilemmas* (Cambridge University Press, 2003), pp. 275–298; S. D. Krasner, "Rebuilding Democracy After Conflict: The Case for Shared Sovereignty," *Journal of Democracy*, 16 (2005), 60–83; S. D. Krasner, "Sharing Sovereignty: New Institutions for Collapsed and Failing States," *International Security*, 29 (2004), 85–120. On neo-trusteeship, see J. D. Fearon and D. D. Laitin, "Neotrusteeship and the Problem of Weak States," *International Security*, 29 (2004), 5–43. On the concept of Hegemonic International Law, see D. F. Vagts, "Hegemonic International Law," *American Journal of International Law*, 95 (2001), 843–848; and J. E. Alvarez, "Hegemonic International Law Revisited," *American Journal of International Law*, 97 (2003), 873–888, stating that hegemonic international law jettisons the formal equality of states, replacing pacts between equals grounded in reciprocity with patron–client relationships in which clients pledge loyalty to the hegemon in exchange for security or economic sustenance). Hegemonic international law is characterized by indeterminate rules whose vagueness benefits primarily the hegemon, fostering recurrent projections of military force, and interventions in the internal affairs of other nations. Elsewhere I have referred to this phenomenon as "imperial law." J. L. Cohen, "Whose Sovereignty? Empire Versus International Law," *Ethics and International Affairs*, 18 (2004), 1–24.

16 See Bhuta, "The Antinomies of Transformative Occupation," p. 740.

17 A sovereign dictator uses plenary power to impose a new order, not to preserve an old one.

18 For an example of such a willful misreading, see Yoo, "Iraqi Reconstruction and the Law of Occupation."

19 That is the position of Fox, *Humanitarian Occupation.*
20 For the classic statement, see T. Meron, "The Humanization of Humanitarian Law," *American Journal of International Law,* 94 (2000), 239–278.
21 *Ibid.,* p. 239; Meron makes much of the fact that the law of war today is now called "humanitarian law," stressing the impact of human rights principles.
22 Known as the Lieber Code, it is cited in D. Graber, *The Development of the Law of Belligerent Occupation 1863–1914: A Historical Survey* (New York: Columbia University Press, 1949).
23 See Meron, "The Humanization of Humanitarian Law," p. 245, note 22.
24 See Graber, *The Development of the Law of Belligerent Occupation.* Vattel asserted that "possession acquired under occupation was not definite until the treaty of peace."
25 Benvenisti, *The International Law of Occupation,* p. 27.
26 See A. Roberts and R. Guelff (eds.), *Documents of the Laws of War* (Oxford University Press, 2000), p. 12; see also Imseis, "On the Fourth Geneva Convention and the Occupied Palestinian Territory," pp. 87–88. The national military manuals of the Netherlands in 1871, France in 1877, Serbia in 1882, Spain in 1882, Portugal in 1890, and Italy in 1896 all drew on the Lieber Code.
27 1907 Hague Convention in Roberts and Guelff (eds.), *Documents of the Laws of War,* note 3. For this history, see Graber, *The Development of the Law of Belligerent Occupation,* pp. 1–34, cited in Imseis, "On the Fourth Geneva Convention and the Occupied Palestinian Territory," pp. 85–88.
28 Fox, "The Occupation of Iraq," p. 229. Meron, Benvenisti, and Imseis all can be characterized as partisans of the humanitarian reading. Fox actually differs from these thinkers by wishing to limit the application of human rights law to humanitarian law. Graber, *The Development of the Law of Belligerent Occupation,* pp. 54–63.
29 Fox, "The Occupation of Iraq," pp. 229–230.
30 *Ibid.,* p. 235.
31 Benvenisti, *The International Law of Occupation,* p. 6.
32 Fox, "The Occupation of Iraq," pp. 236–237.
33 See Bhuta, "The Antinomies of Transformative Occupation," pp. 727–729, analogizing a belligerent occupation to that of a "commissarial dictatorship," where a "dictator" is granted emergency powers in order to preserve the existing constitutional system.
34 E. Benvenisti, "The Security Council and the Law on Occupation: Resolution 1483 on Iraq in Historical Perspective," *Israeli Defense Force Law Review,* 1 (2003), 19–38.
35 See Benvenisti, *The International Law of Occupation,* p. 27.
36 *Ibid.*
37 Imseis, "On the Fourth Geneva Convention and the Occupied Palestinian Territory," p. 89.
38 1907 Hague Convention, Article 55.
39 Benvenisti, *The International Law of Occupation,* pp. 28–29; S. Korman, *The Right of Conquest: The Acquisition of Territory by Force in International Law and Practice* (Oxford University Press, 1996), pp. 221–222.
40 *Ibid.,* p. 27.
41 Benvenisti, *The International Law of Occupation,* pp. 30–31.
42 Meron, "The Humanization of Humanitarian Law," p. 246.
43 Imseis, "On the Fourth Geneva Convention and the Occupied Palestinian Territory," p. 89; Meron, "The Humanization of Humanitarian Law," p. 246.
44 Convention IV Relative to the Protection of Civilian Persons in Time of War (Geneva, Switzerland, 1949).
45 *Ibid.*
46 *Ibid.*

47 *Ibid.*, Articles 50–59.

48 Convention IV Relative to the Protection of Civilian Persons in Time of War; Benvenisti, *The International Law of Occupation*, p. 104.

49 *Ibid.*, p. 106.

50 Meron, "The Humanization of Humanitarian Law," p. 246.

51 *Ibid.*, p. 240.

52 *Ibid.*, pp. 243, 257, where Meron admits that the Fourth Geneva Convention remained faithful to the traditional state-centric reciprocity-based approach, but subsequent developments, via the impact of human rights norms, shifted to a focus on all individuals.

53 *Ibid.*, p. 246.

54 *Ibid.*, p. 252.

55 International Committee of the Red Cross, "Commentary On The Geneva Convention (IV) Relative to the Protection of Civilian Persons In Time of War" (1958), cited in Meron, "The Humanization of Humanitarian Law," p. 258.

56 *Prosecutor v. Dusko Tadic*, International Criminal Tribunal for the Former Yugoslavia (1999), paragraph 87.

57 *Ibid.*, paragraphs 164–165, cited in Meron, "The Humanization of Humanitarian Law," p. 259.

58 *Prosecutor v. Dusko Tadic*, paragraph 166, cited in Meron, "The Humanization of Humanitarian Law," p. 260.

59 *Prosecutor v. Dusko Tadic*, paragraph 168.

60 Protocol Additional to the Geneva Conventions of 1949 (Protocol II) (Geneva, Switzerland, 1977).

61 For a discussion of recent practice by states and international tribunals see Fox, *Humanitarian Occupation*, pp. 226–268. Nonetheless, Fox insists – and I agree with him – that human rights law and humanitarian law are not identical; although it is Meron's thesis that these concepts are merging.

62 But see A. Roberts, "Prolonged Military Occupation: The Israeli-Occupied Territories since 1967," *American Journal of International Law*, 84 (1990), 44–103, discussing counter-arguments.

63 Benvenisti, *The International Law of Occupation*, p. 105. The danger is that this could lead to stagnation which would be unfair and unjust in a prolonged occupation.

64 D. Kretzmer, *The Occupation of Justice: The Supreme Court of Israel and the Occupied Territories* (Albany, NY: State University of New York Press, 2002), cited in Fox, "The Occupation of Iraq," pp. 238–239.

65 For a counter-argument, see Fox, "The Occupation of Iraq," pp. 228–242, note 8.

66 *Ibid.*, pp. 270–271.

67 Benvenisti, "The Security Council and the Law on Occupation," p. 29.

68 *Ibid.*, p. 23.

69 Benvenisti, *The International Law of Occupation*, pp. x–xi.

70 The United Nations, Security Council Resolution 1483, paragraph 5.

71 *Ibid.*, paragraph 8.

72 See generally Fox, "The Occupation of Iraq," p. 8.

73 Thus the "Special Representative" of the UN Interim Administration Mission in Kosovo (UNMIK) could declare that "[a]ll legislative and executive authority with respect to Kosovo, including the administration of the judiciary, is vested in UNMIK and is exercised by the Special Representative of the Secretary-General." The Special Representative of the Secretary-General, *On the Authority of the Interim Administration in Kosovo* (New York: UN, 1999). Similar language is used for the United Nations Transitional Administration in East Timor. See The Special Representative of the Secretary-General,

On the Authority of the Transitional Administration in East Timor (New York: UN, 1999). On this topic, Benvenisti says that had the law of occupation applied here, these occupations would have made fewer mistakes. Benvenisti, *The International Law of Occupation*, p. xvii. For a nuanced analysis of the conundrums of sovereignty and trusteeship in East Timor, see Fox, *Humanitarian Occupation*, pp. 103–106.

74 Benvenisti, *The International Law of Occupation*, p. xi.

75 Benvenisti, "The Security Council and the Law on Occupation," p. 36.

76 Benvenisti, *The International Law of Occupation*, p. xi.

77 *Ibid.*

78 This, and not the usurpation of domestic sovereignty, seems to be the goal of Benvenisti, most likely with Israel's occupation of Palestinian territories in mind.

79 Fox, "The Occupation of Iraq," pp. 246–247. Indeed, from the perspective of substantive contemporary human rights standards, one could justify the imposition of a new constitution on a defeated polity, wholly rewriting its civil and criminal laws, restructuring the judicial system, and imposing a new political structure. This, of course, would leave human rights fundamentalists at a loss when it comes to their own embrace of the principle of self-determination, and at a loss over how to distinguish imperial from autonomous democratization.

80 Yoo, "Iraqi Reconstruction and the Law of Occupation."

81 Published version of his testimony reprinted as J. Yoo, "Iraqi Reconstruction and the Law of Occupation," *Journal of International Law & Policy*, 11 (2004), 7–22.

82 *Ibid.*, p. 21.

83 *Ibid.*, pp. 20–21.

84 Fox, *Humanitarian Occupation*, p. 243.

85 *Ibid.*, pp. 263–272. For a brilliant analysis, see also A. Arato, *Constitution Making Under Occupation: The Politics of Imposed Revolution in Iraq* (New York: Columbia University Press, 2009).

86 Benvenisti, *The International Law of Occupation*, p. xi, citing the text of the Resolution.

87 Fox, *Humanitarian Occupation*, p. 246, arguing against this interpretation of the law of belligerent occupation.

88 *Ibid.*

89 Fox rightly notes that tempering the conservation principle with human rights considerations and with the imperative that the occupation administration itself does not violate international human rights law could be accomplished by repeal of offensive laws without replacement legislation. *Ibid.*, p. 247.

90 *Ibid.*, p. 241. Fox denies that Resolution 1483 indicated the demise of the conservation principle. See also Fox, *Humanitarian Occupation*, pp. 263–270.

91 C. Schmitt, *The Nomos of the Earth in the International Law of the Jus Publicum Europaeum* (New York: Telos Press, 2003), pp. 207–209; Bhuta, "The Antinomies of Transformative Occupation," pp. 723–726.

92 Bhuta, "The Antinomies of Transformative Occupation," p. 723. For Schmitt's discussion of *jus publicum Europaeum* on which Bhuta clearly relies, see Schmitt, *The Nomos of the Earth*, pp. 140–213.

93 Bhuta, "The Antinomies of Transformative Occupation," p. 723. Of course, the law of belligerent occupation did not apply beyond Europe. It applied only to European states and their land wars with one another. See Schmitt, *The Nomos of the Earth*, pp. 42–49, for the concept of concrete order on which Bhuta draws. For the concept of "nomos," see *ibid.*, pp. 336–350.

94 Bhuta, "The Antinomies of Transformative Occupation," pp. 730–731.

95 *Ibid.*, p. 723.

96 *Ibid.*, pp. 729–730.

97 *Ibid.*, p. 732.
98 *Ibid.*, pp. 730–732.
99 *Ibid.*, p. 732.
100 These distinctions were both predicated on the historically specific differentiation between public and private power, property, and armed conflicts described above.
101 Bhuta, "The Antinomies of Transformative Occupation," p. 733.
102 According to Schmitt, a commissarial dictator exercises discretionary power to preserve a constitutional order against internal or external threats, while a sovereign dictator exercises unlimited constituent power for an indeterminate period to create a new constitutional order. This is analogized by Bhuta to the distinction between belligerent and transformative occupation. Bhuta, "The Antinomies of Transformative Occupation," pp. 724, 728, citing C. Schmitt, *Die Diktatur: von den Anfängen des modernen Souveränitätsgedankens bis zum proletarischen Klassenkampf* (Berlin: Duncker & Humblot, 1994).
103 G. W. F. Hegel, *The Philosophy of Right*, trans. T. M. Knox (Oxford University Press, 1967). The phrase implies that the legal articulation of the rules of belligerent occupation occurred only after the reality that subtends it has fully come into existence. In this case, its moment was already almost past as the emergence of total war only seven years later indicated.
104 The first total war of the twentieth century was World War One. The transformative occupations I am referring to after World War Two are in Germany and Japan by the Allies, and in occupied Eastern Europe and East Germany by the Soviets. Benvenisti argues that the law of belligerent occupation was basically disregarded in the epoch of two blocs. Bhuta, following Schmitt, argues that there was no nomos at that time since there was no single spatial order within which competing principles of legitimacy could be, or had to be, mediated. Thus the law of occupation was redundant. Bhuta, "The Antinomies of Transformative Occupation," p. 734; Schmitt, *The Nomos of the Earth*, pp. 351–355.
105 Bhuta, "The Antinomies of Transformative Occupation."
106 Benvenisti, *The International Law of Occupation*, pp. 96–97.
107 Bhuta, "The Antinomies of Transformative Occupation," p. 734. "Whoever occupies a territory also imposes on it his own social system ... as far as his army can reach" (quoting Stalin).
108 Benvenisti, *The International Law of Occupation*, p. 103.
109 *Ibid.*, p. 97.
110 *Ibid.*
111 *Ibid.*, p. 152.
112 Bhuta, "The Antinomies of Transformative Occupation," p. 733, citing J. Stone, *Legal Controls of International Conflict* (New York: Rinehart, 1954). Insurgencies, total war, guerrilla war, "terrorist" actions, et al. also undermine the civilian/soldier distinction crucial to the concept of belligerent occupation.
113 These "reformist" approaches attempt to construe occupation law as enabling from the beginning, or interpret Resolution 1483 as updating it in order to legitimatize/legalize post-Cold War transformative occupations in the name of human rights principles (including the "right to popular sovereignty").
114 Benvenisti, *The International Law of Occupation*, pp. xi, 187, discussing the illegitimacy of resistance to a legal belligerent occupation.
115 Bhuta, "The Antinomies of Transformative Occupation," p. 739.
116 This is certainly the case for the governing council in Iraq. See Arato, *Constitution Making Under Occupation*; Fox, "The Occupation of Iraq."
117 Fox, "The Occupation of Iraq," for a discussion of the ways in which the CPA in Iraq violated occupation law with its excessively transformative occupation.

118 Benvenisti, *The International Law of Occupation*, pp. xvi–xvii. See also Fearon and Laitin, "Neo-Trusteeship and the Problem of Weak States," pp. 14–24.

119 Fox does not question the impartiality of the UN occupations. But see Alvarez, "Hegemonic International Law Revisited," pp. 874–882. J. Quigley, "The United Nations Security Council: Promethean Protector or Helpless Hostage?" *Texas International Law Journal*, 35 (2000), 129–172, criticizing Fox's position.

120 Bhuta, "The Antinomies of Transformative Occupation," p. 735, note 10; Alvarez, "Hegemonic International Law Revisited," pp. 883–886; Fox, "The Occupation of Iraq," pp. 202–205.

121 See Alvarez, "Hegemonic International Law Revisited," pp. 882–883.

122 *Ibid.*, p. 883, note 50, arguing that the provision for a UN special representative, with "independent responsibilities," to work with the Authority is a studied effort to avoid any of the usual trigger words for UN involvement in election supervision, thereby according the authority very wide latitude in administrating in Iraq and deciding its future.

123 *Ibid.*, p. 888. "Global HIL is more insidious, as it provides legal cover and shared blame."

124 See J. L. Cohen, "Sovereign Equality Versus Imperial Right: The Battle Over the New World Order," *Constellations*, 13 (2006), 485–505 (p. 494). See also Bhuta, "The Antinomies of Transformative Occupation," p. 736; Cohen, "Whose Sovereignty? Empire Versus International Law," p. 24.

125 Fearon and Laitin, "Neo-Trusteeship and the Problem of Weak States," p. 7; Keohane, "Political Authority After Intervention"; Krasner, "Rebuilding Democracy After Conflict: The Case for Shared Sovereignty"; Krasner, "Sharing Sovereignty: New Institutions for Collapsed and Failing States."

126 H. Kelsen, "The Legal Status of Germany According to the Declaration of Berlin," *American Journal of International Law*, 39 (1945), 518–526.

127 Fearon and Laitin, "Neo-Trusteeship and the Problem of Weak States," p. 12.

128 *Ibid.*, p. 13. Although they use the term "post modern imperialism," the thrust of their argument is that these occupations are not imperial at all.

129 N. Bhuta, "New Modes and Orders: The Difficulties of a Jus Post Bellum of Constitutional Transformation," *University of Toronto Law Journal*, 60 (2010), 99–854 (p. 803).

130 Bhuta, "The Antinomies of Transformative Occupation," p. 740.

131 Bhuta, "New Modes and Orders," pp. 803, 824.

132 *Ibid.*, p. 825.

133 *Ibid.*, p. 803.

134 *Ibid.*, pp. 803–804. He cites Scheffer, "Beyond Occupation Law," p. 850, and H. Perritt, Jr., "Structures and Standards of Political Trusteeship," *UCLA Journal of International Law and Foreign Affairs*, 8 (2004), 385–472, as proponents of post-conflict democracy-building who base their arguments on the claim that fostering popular sovereignty will remove the causes of violence. See also A. Roberts, "Transformative Military Occupation: Applying the Laws of War and Human Rights," *American Journal of International Law*, 100 (2006), 580–622, for the argument that occupying powers can justify such intrusive transformative policies not only as an important part of a human rights package but also as a means of hastening the end of an occupation.

135 W. Bain, *Between Anarchy and Society: Trusteeship and the Obligation of Power* (Oxford University Press, 2003), p. 162, cited in Bhuta, "New Modes and Orders," p. 804, note 26.

136 Bhuta, "New Modes and Orders," p. 803.

137 *Ibid.*

138 In Iraq the CPA helped destroy the Iraqi state by its policies of de-baathification and its destruction of the army and it then purported to actively engage in state and nation rebuilding and constitution-making. Arato, *Constitution Making Under Occupation.*

139 Bhuta, "New Modes and Orders," p. 825.

140 Ibid., pp. 825–826, citing Fox, "The Occupation of Iraq," p. 195. But humanitarian occupations typically occur in domestic post-conflict contexts, there is no expectation of an international peace treaty among the internal belligerents, and the occupier is typically not one of the belligerents. Internal peace and security is the goal of such occupations and thus the means may differ from belligerent occupations. However, fostering the inclusion of representatives of all the key segments of the population need not entail the position of a specific model of liberal democracy.

141 Bhuta "New Modes and Orders," p. 825, note 131, citing G. T. Harris, "The Era of Multilateral Occupation," *Berkeley Journal of International Law,* 24 (2006), 1–78.

142 Bhuta, "New Modes and Orders," pp. 824, 849–850.

143 They thus have much in common with contemporary cosmopolitan liberals. For a critique of the cosmopolitan neo-Kantian theory behind this position and of cosmopolitan liberalism, see Alvarez, "Hegemonic International Law Revisited," p. 884, and G. Simpson, *Great Powers and Outlaw States: Unequal Sovereigns in the International Legal Order* (Cambridge University Press, 2004); Alvarez, "Hegemonic International Law Revisited," p. 884, note 12.

144 Bhuta, "The Antinomies of Transformative Occupation," p. 740.

145 Bhuta, "New Modes and Orders," pp. 824–825.

146 See United Nations, A More Secure World: Our Shared Responsibility, Report of the Secretary-General's High-level Panel on Threats, Challenges and Change (New York: United Nations, 2004), www.un.org/secureworld; Cohen, "Sovereign Equality Versus Imperial Right: The Battle Over the New World Order," p. 494.

147 See Chapter 1 of this book.

148 Bhuta, "New Modes and Orders," p. 824.

149 Bhuta, "The Antinomies of Transformative Occupation," p. 740.

150 This oscillation was most evident in the international behavior of the then Bush administration and its chosen UN representative, John Bolton.

151 United Nations, *Charter of the United Nations* (New York: UN, 1945), Article 2, paragraph 1.

152 Bhuta "The Antinomies of Transformative Occupation," p. 734, advocates the first anachronism.

153 Benvenisti, *The International Law of Occupation,* p. 106.

154 *Ibid.,* pp. 94–95.

155 *Ibid.,* p. 95.

156 *Ibid.,* p. xi.

157 *Ibid.*

158 United Nations, *Security Council Resolution 1483* (New York: UN, 2003), paragraphs 4 and 9, note 7; see also Benvenisti, *The International Law of Occupation,* p. xi.

159 See Chapter 3 discussing Schmitt's political theology regarding popular sovereignty. We should also avoid a reified and overly dramatic conception of constituent power. I use the term here to indicate that domestic representatives of the domestic population, rather than foreigners, are the ones who should be involved in constitution-making processes.

160 United Nations, *Charter of the United Nations,* Article 2, paragraph 1; United Nations, *Declaration On Principles of International Law Concerning Friendly Relations and Co-operation Among States in Accordance with the Charter of the United Nations* (New York: UN, 1970) stating that "the subjection of peoples to alien subjugation, domination

and exploitation constitutes ... a denial of fundamental human rights," and that "[b]y virtue of the principle of equal rights and self-determination of peoples enshrined in the Charter of the United Nations, all people have the right to freely determine their political status and freely pursue their economic, social and cultural development."

161 This was also one of the meanings Wilson gave to the concept. Wilson at times used the concept to mean the consent of the population to territorial change or changes of sovereignty over them and the idea that governments should be based on consent of the governed. See Bhuta, "New Modes and Orders," p. 810.

162 D. Makinson, "Rights of Peoples: Point of View of a Logician," in J. Crawford (ed.), *The Rights of Peoples* (Oxford: Clarendon Press, 1992), pp. 69–92 (p. 74).

163 The substantive connotation of "people" cannot be dispensed with, but its source can shift, thus permitting multicultural and multinational sovereign federal "nation-states" to exist without contradiction or even conflict.

164 A. Cassese, *Self-Determination of Peoples: A Legal Reappraisal* (Cambridge University Press, 1999), p. 319.

165 This is the case with Iraq and the Palestinians under occupation. The first time the UN recognized a population as a people deserving self-determination and used this to trump the sovereignty claim by the state in which it was located was in the case of Bangladesh. See Benvenisti, *The International Law of Occupation*, pp. 173–177, discussing this issue.

166 Bhuta, "New Modes and Orders," pp. 811–12; Fox *Humanitarian Occupation*, pp. 207–208.

167 The 1970 Declaration on Friendly Relations anticipated this gambit and thus reaffirmed the non-intervention principle strictly forbidding the organization, forma-tion, assistance, or incitement of subversive activity toward the violent overthrow of the regime of another state for any reason. United Nations, *Declaration On Principles of International Law Concerning Friendly Relations and Co-operation Among States in Accordance with the Charter of the United Nations*, p. 124.

168 On sovereignty as involving a political relationship see M. Loughlin, "Ten Tenets of Sovereignty," in N. Walker (ed.), *Sovereignty in Transition: Essays in European Law* (Oxford: Hart Publishing, 2003), pp. 55–86.

169 Arato, *Constitution Making Under Occupation*.

170 See generally Fox, "The Occupation of Iraq," p. 250, note 59.

171 On the concept of suspended sovereignty, which I prefer to the oxymoron "shared sovereignty," see generally A. Yannis, "The Concept of Suspended Sovereignty in International Law and Its Implications in International Politics," *European Journal of International Law*, 13 (2002), 1037–1052. However, I disagree that this term means that the concept of sovereignty is no longer relevant. I prefer to insist on a reinterpreted conservation principle involving popular sovereignty, self-determination, and the international legal sovereignty of the occupied state as remaining intact.

172 But see R. Falk, "The Rights of Peoples (In Particular Indigenous Peoples)," in Crawford (ed.), *The Rights of Peoples*, pp. 17–37. Here I differ with Falk, not on the substance of the issue of what sorts of autonomy rights indigenous peoples should have, or what kinds of international representation, but on abandoning the discourse of state sovereignty. I believe that the concept of state sovereignty is indispensable for the concept of popular sovereignty – it provides the space within which the latter can be exercised.

173 See generally Roberts, "Prolonged Military Occupation," p. 58. Even Benvenisti grants that if an occupant is recalcitrant and holds out in bad faith against or during negotiations, using its control of occupied territory as leverage, the occupation should be regarded as illegal, and measures aimed at the occupants' own interest should be

void; such a position is no different from outright annexation. Benvenisti, *The International Law of Occupation*, p. 216, note 2.

174 I. Brownlie, "The Rights of Peoples in Modern International Law," in Crawford (ed.), *The Rights of Peoples*, pp. 1–16 (pp. 5, 11–12), denying that the principle of self-determination trumps the principle of non-intervention.

175 If the concept of "shared sovereignty" makes any sense, it does so in the context of participation by equals within a broader institutional and legal framework like the EU. It becomes pure ideology when applied to an occupation regime. I thus reject the use of this concept made by Keohane and Krasner. Keohane, "Political Authority After Intervention"; Krasner, "Rebuilding Democracy After Conflict: The Case for Shared Sovereignty"; Krasner, "Sharing Sovereignty: New Institutions for Collapsed and Failing States."

176 United Nations, *Declaration On Principles of International Law Concerning Friendly Relations and Co-operation Among States in Accordance with the Charter of the United Nations*, p. 123.

177 See Fox, "The Occupation of Iraq," p. 295, arguing that the Iraqi Governing Council set up by the CPA in Iraq was just such a body whose "consent" to radical institutional reform was not autonomous. Neither the CPA nor Resolution 1483 provided any mechanisms by which the Security Council could disapprove CPA actions. This sets a bad, dangerous, and clearly failing precedent.

178 As in the case of Israel vis-à-vis the occupied Palestinian territories. See Imseis, "On the Fourth Geneva Convention," pp. 92–96, note 8, stating that Israel was a high contracting party, signed the Fourth Geneva Convention, and originally intended to apply it to the occupied Palestinian territories after the June 1967 war. It subsequently altered its position in October 1967 stating that it would apply the "humanitarian" provisions de facto, but that it was not de jure bound by Geneva IV because of the "missing reversioner" theory – the absence of a legitimate ousted sovereign. According to this argument, Jordan and Egypt were the ousted rulers of the territories, but they were not lawful sovereigns as a result of their unlawful aggression against Israel in 1948. Accordingly, that territory was not a territory of a high contracting party under Common Article 2, and Israel's control over it was the result of a defensive conquest. Imseis argues that this is unconvincing. Quoting W. T. Mallison and S. V. Mallison, *The Palestine Problem in International Law and World Order* (Harlow: Longman, 1986), p. 257, Imseis points out that "if humanitarian law were to be interpreted so that its application were made contingent upon acceptance by the belligerent occupant of the justness and non-aggressive character of the war aims of its opponent, it is clear this law would never be applied" (at p. 96). For a detailed presentation and rebuttal of this argument, see Mallison and Mallison, *The Palestine Problem*, at p. 16. See also Richard Falk, "The Relevance of International Law to Palestinian Rights in the West Bank and Gaza," in *Legal Defense of the Intifada*, *Harvard International Law Journal*, 32 (1991), 129–157.

179 See United Nations, *Declaration on the Granting of Independence to Colonial Countries and Peoples* (New York: UN, 1960). "The subjection of peoples to alien subjugation, domination and exploitation constitutes a denial of fundamental human right ... [a]ny attempt aimed at the partial or total disruption of the national unity and the territorial integrity of a country is incompatible with the purposes and principles of the Charter of the United Nations."

180 United Nations, *Declaration On Principles of International Law Concerning Friendly Relations and Co-operation Among States in Accordance with the Charter of the United Nations*, pp. 123–124, stating that "Nothing in the foregoing paragraphs shall be construed as authorizing or encouraging any action which would dismember or

impair, totally or in part, the territorial integrity or political unity of sovereign and independent states conducting themselves in compliance with the principle of equal rights and self-determination of peoples as described above and thus possessed of a government representing the whole people belonging to the territory without distinction as to race, creed or color."

181 International legal responsibility of the state also requires that obligations assumed must be by rulers with some tangible connection to the state's citizens, i.e. that the government in question must be representative. Fox, *Humanitarian Occupation*, p. 208.

182 Bhuta, "New Modes and Orders," p. 831.

183 Arato, *Constitution Making Under Occupation*; and Bhuta, "New Modes and Orders," pp. 831, 850–854.

184 Arato, *Constitution Making Under Occupation*, especially pp. 59–99 for his discussion of a new paradigm of a "post-sovereign" two-stage model of constitution-making that has emerged in the post-1989 era within deeply divided societies.

185 Fox, *Humanitarian Occupation*, pp. 247–248.

186 United Nations, *Declaration On Principles of International Law Concerning Friendly Relations and Co-operation Among States in Accordance with the Charter of the United Nations*, pp. 123–124; United Nations, A More Secure World, note 117.

187 For a full discussion, see M. Byers, *Custom, Power and the Power of Rules: International Relations and Customary International Law* (Cambridge University Press, 1999), pp. 53–125. See also Cohen, "Sovereign Equality Versus Imperial Right: The Battle Over the New World Order," p. 108.

188 United Nations, *Declaration On Principles of International Law Concerning Friendly Relations and Co-operation Among States in Accordance with the Charter of the United Nations*, p. 124.

189 *Ibid.*, p. 123.

190 Fox, "The Occupation of Iraq," p. 276, rightly insisting on the "affirmative value in some domestic norms and institutions emerging from the politics of a post-occupation society," especially regarding "political architecture, legal policy," and socio-economic structure.

191 *Ibid.*, p. 277. See also Fox, *Humanitarian Occupation*, pp. 246–247.

192 See P. C. Szasz, "The Security Council Starts Legislating," *American Journal of International Law*, 96 (2002), 901–905 (p. 902). "Under Charter Articles 25 and 48(1), the Security Council can adopt decisions binding on UN members" but the assumption was that these would refer to particular conflicts or situations, imposed for a limited purpose. While decisions of the Council generally cannot be considered as establishing new laws, several portions of Resolution 1373 are closer to laws than decrees. See Szasz, "The Security Council Starts Legislating," p. 902, noting provisions of Resolution 1373, such as designed actions against financing or supporting terrorist activities). See United Nations, *Security Council Resolution 1373* (New York: UN, 2001). This is a qualitatively different activity and enterprise for the UN. The same is true of its relatively new (since the 1990s) and unprecedented "peace-enforcement" activities, especially in Kosovo with the creation of UNMIK and East Timor with the creation of UNTAET. See Boon, "Legislative Reform in Post-Conflict Zones," pp. 311–318, for a discussion of the extent of the executive and legislative mandate of these interim administrations.

193 See The Secretary-General, *Secretary-General's Bulletin on Observance by United Nations Forces of International Humanitarian Law* (New York: UN, 1999); see Roberts and Guelff (eds.), *Documents of the Laws of War*, pp. 721–730.

194 See Boon, "Legislative Reform in Post-Conflict Zones," p. 320.

195 *Ibid.*, pp. 322–326; see also Fearon and Laitin, "Neo-Trusteeship and the Problem of Weak States," pp. 14–43, discussing the Brahimi report and the need for reform.

196 Fox, *Humanitarian Occupation*, pp. 274–288.

197 *Ibid.*, pp. 246–248.

198 *Ibid.*, p. 263; and see endnote 173 arguing against Benvenisti, "The Security Council and the Law on Occupation."

199 Fox, *Humanitarian Occupation*, p. 247 citing the UN Declaration on Friendly Relations.

200 *Ibid.*, pp. 200, 271.

201 *Ibid.*, pp. 218–304.

202 *Ibid.*, p. 263.

203 *Ibid.*, pp. 3–4.

204 *Ibid.*, pp. 12–13.

205 *Ibid.*, pp. 115–141.

206 *Ibid.*, pp. 149–150.

207 *Ibid.*, pp. 152–153.

208 *Ibid.*, pp. 154–157. Fox invokes the UN role in promoting democracy, in election monitoring, and statements by various regional associations form the OAS to the EU, the Commonwealth, and the Constitutive Act of the African Union (2000) as indicative of a normative regime to that effect.

209 *Ibid.*, pp. 211–216.

210 *Ibid.* See also the discussion, p. 210 and footnote 125 regarding *jus cogens* limits on the Security Council.

211 *Ibid.*, pp. 291, 295, note 94.

212 *Ibid.*, p. 291. Fox notes that: "States normally accept legal obligations only after a process of deliberation prior to signing treaties or opining [or not] on nascent customary norms and have the right to alter or reserve from aspects of emerging rules. Council legislation is quick, offers no chance to non-Council members to partially opt out or alter the rules, and yet is universally binding." As I argue in Chapter 5, few states ratifying the Charter believed this latter scenario would supplant the former even under limited circumstances. On the legitimation problems this causes, see Chapter 5 of this text and S. Talmon, "The Security Council as World Legislature," *American Journal of International Law*, 99 (2005), 175–193.

213 Fox, *Humanitarian Occupation*, p. 294.

214 *Ibid.*, p. 295.

215 *Ibid.*, p. 297.

216 *Ibid.*, p. 299, citing W. M. Reisman, "The Constitutional Crisis in the United Nations," *American Journal of International Law*, 87 (1993), 83–100 (p. 86).

217 Fox, *Humanitarian Occupation*, p. 300.

218 As Fox himself notes, *ibid.*, pp. 207–247.

219 See Chapter 5.

220 See Cohen, "Whose Sovereignty? Empire Versus International Law," pp. 22–23, note 10. Neither a "return" to a Westphalian international state system nor a leap into a cosmopolitan world order without the sovereign state is on the immediate agenda today.

Chapter 5   Security Council activism in the "war on terror": legality and legitimacy reconsidered

1 Scheppele argues that countries that used international law to entrench domestic constitutional protections of human rights before September 11 have been more resistant to rights-violating international pressure afterward. K. L. Scheppele, "The International State of Emergency: Challenges to Constitutionalism After September 11," paper presented at the Yale Legal Theory Workshop, Princeton University (2006). Andrew

Moravcsik shows that governments of newly established democracies (or with new liberal-democratic constitutions) seek reciprocally binding and entrenched international human rights obligations, to strengthen domestic parliaments and independent courts against executives and military elites. They hope to "lock in" the domestic political status quo – constitutional democracy and the rule of law – against their non-democratic opponents. A. Moravcsik, "The Origin of Human Rights Regimes: Democratic Delegation in Postwar Europe," *International Organization*, 54 (2000), 217–252.

2 *Jus cogens* norms are peremptory international legal norms from which no derogation is possible and in violation of which a treaty will not be deemed void. The candidates for *jus cogens* higher law status are the prohibitions against genocide, torture, ethnic cleansing, and enslavement, disappearances, and crimes against humanity. See D. Shelton, "Normative Hierarchy in International Law," *American Journal of International Law*, 100 (2006), 291–323.

3 The R2P doctrine was first articulated in ICISS, *The Responsibility to Protect: Report of the International Commission on Intervention and State Sovereignty* (Ottawa: International Development Research Centre, 2001). It was designed to shift the burden of proof from those intervening for alleged humanitarian purposes on to governments failing to protect the security of citizens against domestic state and non-state actors. This discursive and practical shift was reaffirmed in the *Report of the High-level Panel on Threats, Challenges and Change*, submitted in 2004. See Chapter 3 of United Nations, A More Secure World: Our Shared Responsibility, Report of the Secretary-General's High-level Panel on Threats, Challenges and Change (New York: United Nations, 2004), www.un.org/secureworld.

4 The first putatively legislative resolutions came in 1993 and 1994 when, acting under Chapter VII in response to atrocities in the Balkan wars and internal armed conflict in Rwanda, the Council established two international tribunals, the ICTY and the ICTR, for the prosecution of individuals responsible for committing "international crimes." The resolutions were made binding upon all states, and every state was ordered to take any measures necessary under its domestic law to implement the provisions of the resolutions and the statutes establishing the tribunals. Although it did not thereby invent individual responsibility, the Council went beyond the precedents of Nuremberg and Tokyo, in legislating a wide set of international criminal legal norms (including for the first time, rape) applicable in non-strictly international conflicts. These instances of legislative activity together with those discussed in the previous chapter and the ones discussed below amount to an important innovation and expansion of Security Council competence.

5 They remain masters of the treaty. Charter law applies to them but their veto in the Council and the amendment rule makes their consent pivotal to any effective application of or change of Charter norms.

6 United Nations, *Charter of the United Nations* (New York: UN, 1945), Article 39.

7 E. de Wet, *The Chapter VII Powers of the United Nations Security Council* (Oxford: Hart Publishing, 2004), pp. 133–177.

8 *Ibid.*

9 See the discussion in P. M. Dupuy, "The Constitutional Dimension of the Charter of the United Nations Revisited," *Max Planck Yearbook of International Law*, 1 (1997), 1–33. See also P. Szasz, "The Security Council Starts Legislating," *American Journal of International Law*, 96 (2002), 901–905.

10 Dupuy, "The Constitutional Dimension of the Charter of the United Nations Revisited," and B. Fassbender, "The United Nations Charter as Constitution of the International Community," *Columbia Journal of Transnational Law*, 36 (1998), 529–616.

11 Dupuy, "The Constitutional Dimension of the Charter of the United Nations Revisited."

12 *Ibid.*

13 De Wet, *The Chapter VII Powers of the United Nations Security Council*, p. 111, on the fundamental difference between the EU and the UN. Even within the EU the constitutionalizing role of the ECJ has been much criticized, and the latter's character as a polity (with its own legal order of constitutional quality) as distinct from being an international treaty organization with derived powers is still debated.

14 T. Franck, "The Powers of Appreciation: Who is the Ultimate Guardian of UN Legality?" *International Journal of Constitutional Law*, 86 (1992), 519–523. See also Szasz, "The Security Council Starts Legislating."

15 W. M. Reisman, "The Constitutional Crisis in the United Nations," *International Journal of Constitutional Law*, 87 (1993), 83–100. For a rebuttal, see Dupuy, "The Constitutional Dimension of the Charter of the United Nations Revisited."

16 P1 is the United States. ICISS, *The Responsibility to Protect*, and United Nations, A More Secure World.

17 For political theorists in this group, see J. L. Cohen, "Sovereign Equality Versus Imperial Right: The Battle Over the New World Order," *Constellations*, 13 (2006), 485–505. For the legal theorists in this group see De Wet, *The Chapter VII Powers of the United Nations Security Council*, pp. 136–138.

18 See S. Alkire, *A Conceptual Framework for Human Security*, Working Paper 2, Centre for Research on Inequality, Human Security, and Ethnicity, Queen Elizabeth House, Oxford University (2003); and the report of the Commission on Human Security, *Human Security Now: Protecting and Empowering People* (New York: Commission on Human Security, 2003), 97.

19 For Foucauldians this is the slippage of human rights from "law to norm." Human rights thereby become the vehicle for biopolitical "governmentality." See H. M. Jaeger, "UN Reform and Global Governmentality" (unpublished manuscript). While this analysis is quite revealing about the nature of one project of global governance, it is unable to articulate a counter-project other than sheer resistance. I try to do just that.

20 Security Council Resolution 1373 of September 28, 2001. Prior to this, the topic of international terrorism was handled by the General Assembly's Sixth (legal) Committee which had worked on several multilateral conventions on terrorism. E. Rosand, "Security Council Resolution 1373, the Counter-Terrorism Committee, and the Fight Against Terrorism," *International Journal of Constitutional Law*, 97 (2003), 333–341, footnote 5 (p. 333), for a list of terrorism conventions adopted by the Assembly.

21 See A. Marschik, "Legislative Powers of the Security Council," in R. Macdonald and D. Johnston (eds.), *Towards World Constitutionalism: Issues in the Legal Ordering of the World Community* (Boston: Brill, 2005), pp. 431–492.

22 United Nations, Security Council Resolution 1373.

23 *Ibid.*

24 Rosand, "Security Council Resolution 1373, the Counter-Terrorism Committee, and the Fight Against Terrorism," p. 334.

25 *Ibid.*, pp. 334–338; Szasz, "The Security Council Starts Legislating," p. 902.

26 K. Scheppele, "The International State of Emergency," paper presented at the Victoria Colloquium on Political, Social, and Legal Theory, University of Victoria, January 26, 2007; Rosand, "Security Council Resolution 1373, the Counter-Terrorism Committee, and the Fight Against Terrorism," p. 340.

27 United Nations, Security Council Resolution 1267 of October 15, 1999.

28 E. Rosand, "The Security Council's Efforts to Monitor the Implementation of Al Qaeda/Taliban Sanctions," *International Journal of Constitutional Law*, 98 (2004), 747–758. See

Marschik, "Legislative Powers of the Security Council," p. 471, footnote 64, for a listing the subsequent resolutions creating the most complex sanction regime of the UN.

29 United Nations, Security Council Resolution 1333 (2000) of December 19, 2000.

30 United Nations, Security Council Resolution 1390 (2002) of January 16, 2002, updating resolutions 1267 and 1333 providing that the Committee keeps the lists updated.

31 United Nations, Security Council Resolution 1540 (2004) of April 28, 2004.

32 See J. Hoffman, "Terrorism Blacklisting: Putting European Human Rights Guarantees to the Test," *Constellations*, 15 (2008), 543–560; and Marschik, "Legislative Powers of the Security Council."

33 *Ibid.* See also S. Chesterman, *The UN Security Council and the Rule of Law*, Final Report and Recommendations from the Austrian Initiative (2004–2008), pp. 16–19.

34 *Ibid.* Another resolution passed in 2006 stipulates that the Secretariat inform states of residence or nationality within two weeks of listing and that these states are asked to inform the listed person or entity. United Nations, Security Council Resolution 1735 (2006).

35 United Nations, General Assembly, *World Summit Outcome* (New York: UN, 2005). Available at www.un.org/summit2005/documents.html.

36 Hence the Austrian Initiative and the final report of Chesterman, *The UN Security Council and the Rule of Law*.

37 Hoffman, "Terrorism Blacklisting: Putting European Human Rights Guarantees to the Test."

38 Scheppele, "The International State of Emergency: Challenges to Constitutionalism After September 11," p. 56.

39 I am paraphrasing from Scheppele's excellent analysis. *Ibid.*, pp. 56–57.

40 I. Cameron, "UN Targeted Sanctions, Legal Safeguards and the European Convention on Human Rights," *New Jersey Journal of International Law*, 72 (2003), 159–214.

41 I. Cameron, *The ECHR, Due Process and UN Security Council Counter-Terrorism Sanctions*, Report to the Council of Europe, June 2, 2006, p. 10. Available at www.coe.int.

42 Szasz, "The Security Council Starts Legislating," p. 902.

43 This is not true for humanitarian interventions that end in "humanitarian occupations." While these are targeted to specific crises in specific states, all too often the mandates of the occupiers or "peace enforcers" are open-ended. See the previous chapter. The administrations are highly legislative and transformative. See G. H. Fox, *Humanitarian Occupation* (Cambridge University Press, 2008).

44 Szasz, "The Security Council Starts Legislating." See also S. Talmon, "The Security Council as World Legislature," *International Journal of Constitutional Law*, 99 (2005), 175–193, for a discussion of the pros and cons.

45 Marschik, "The Legislative Powers of the Security Council," p. 461.

46 See J. Alvarez, "Hegemonic International Law Revisited," *American Journal of International Law*, 97 (2003), 873–888, much of which is reprinted in J. Alvarez, *International Organizations as Law-makers* (New York: Oxford University Press, 2006), pp. 199–217.

47 *Ibid.*

48 *Ibid.*, p. 199.

49 The US usually gets what it wants but not always, as the failure to get Security Council go-ahead to invade Iraq revealed most clearly.

50 Alvarez, *International Organizations as Law-makers*, p. 216.

51 *Ibid.*, p. 199.

52 Scheppele, "The International State of Emergency" (2007).

53 See R. O. Keohane, S. Macdeo, and A. Moravcsik, "Democracy-Enhancing Multilateralism," *International Organization*, 63 (2009), 1–31.

54 Scheppele, "The International State of Emergency" (2007), pp. 4–5.
55 *Ibid.*, pp. 20–21.
56 *Ibid.*, pp. 8–11.
57 *Ibid.*, p. 50.
58 United Nations, *Charter of the United Nations*, Articles 25, 39, and 48.
59 Alvarez, *International Organizations as Law-makers*, p. 194. De Wet, *The Chapter VII Powers of the United Nations Security Council*, p. 137.
60 On the concept of commissarial dictator, see C. Schmitt, *Die Diktatur: von den Anfängen des modernen Souveränitätsgedankens bis zum proletarischen Klassenkampf* (Berlin: Duncker & Humblot, 1994) and *Verfassungslehrer* (Munich and Leipzig: Duncker & Humblot, 1928).
61 Marschik, "Legislative Powers of the Security Council," pp. 463–4.
62 *Ibid.*, pp. 476–840.
63 *Ibid.*
64 *Ibid.*
65 The teleological interpretation is inapposite. Unlike the example of the EU in which the powers of the organs are related to a process of legal and political integration explicitly foreseen in its constituent treaties, there is no such anticipation of an ever closer union in the Charter. De Wet, *The Chapter VII Powers of the United Nations Security Council*, p. 111. Yet I am unconvinced that informal amendments by the ECJ (working hand-in-hand with the relevant executives) are desirable or legitimate.
66 They can also opt out of customary international law by being a persistent objector. See M. Byers, *Custom, Power and the Power of Rules: International Relations and Customary International Law* (Cambridge University Press, 1999).
67 M. Rama-Montaldo, "Contribution of the General Assembly to the Constitutional Development and Interpretation of the United Nations Charter," in Macdonald and Johnston (eds.), *Towards World Constitutionalism*, pp. 504–513.
68 B. Fassbender, *UN Security Council Reform and the Right of Veto: A Constitutional Perspective* (Boston: Kluwer Law International, 1998), pp. 98–159.
69 United Nations, *Charter of the United Nations*, Articles 108 and 109. These two provisions, despite the fact that one is framed as an amendment rule while the second is framed as a constitutional convention rule which would presumably allow for far-reaching changes, both have the same procedural requirements.
70 United Nations, *Charter of the United Nations*, Article 41.
71 For an argument that the UNSC does not have the competence to legislate, see De Wet, *The Chapter VII Powers of the United Nations Security Council*, pp. 348–351. For an argument that these resolutions transgress the substantive limit of the Charter that requires SC resolutions to be in conformity with its principles and purposes, see Franck, "The Powers of Appreciation: Who is the Ultimate Guardian of UN Legality?" p. 520. J. Arato, "The Concept of Constitution and Constitutionalism Beyond the State: Two Perspectives on the Material Constitution of the United Nations," *International Journal of Constitutional Law*, 10 (2012, forthcoming), section 3.2 (ms on file with author). But see Judge Lauterpacht's 1993 opinion in the Genocide case arguing with respect to *jus cogens* that the Charter's trumping power over inconsistent treaties by virtue of Article 103 cannot – as a matter of simple hierarchy of norms – extend to a conflict between a Security Council resolution and *jus cogens*. "Indeed, one only has to state the opposite proposition thus: that a Security Council resolution may even require participation in genocide for its unacceptability to be apparent." Genocide case, 1993 ICJ at 441. Lauterpacht, however, did not declare any Security Council resolution violating *jus cogens* to be void and legally ineffective.

72 Arato, "The Concept of Constitution and Constitutionalism Beyond the State," section 3.2, p. 23, citing J. H. H. Weiler, "The Autonomy of the Community Legal Order," in Weiler, *The Constitution of Europe* (Cambridge University Press, 1999), p. 312, on the legislative and judicial meanings of Kompetenz-Kompetenz.

73 See K. Dervis, *A Better Globalization: Legitimacy, Governance and Reform* (Washington, DC: Center for Global Development, 2005).

74 It is important to recall that the genus federation can have many subspecies varying by degree of integration and consolidation.

75 Use of an informal amendment process to change minor things, and to adapt Council powers to contemporary challenges is one thing; it is quite another to change the "basic structure" of the Charter and of international law-making through such means.

76 Marschik, "Legislative Powers of the Security Council," p. 486.

77 *Ibid.* See also M. Koskenniemi, "The Police in the Temple, Order, Justice and the UN: A Dialectical View," *European Journal of International Law*, 6 (1995), 338–348.

78 Scheppele, "International State of Emergency" (2007), pp. 1–30, 59–72. The effect on domestic sovereignty pertains to the transformation of each country's domestic constitution insofar as the latter protects due process rights and constitutionalism, by strengthening domestic executives and policing agencies bent on capitalizing on Council commands to expand their own power and eviscerate the domestic separation of powers and constitutional protections for basic rights.

79 *Ibid.*, p. 11.

80 Fox, *Humanitarian Occupation.*

81 J. Habermas, "Does the Constitutionalisation of International Law Still Have a Chance?" in J. Habermas, *The Divided West*, ed. and trans. C Cronin (Cambridge, MA: Polity Press, 2008), pp. 115–193.

82 On pre-modern meanings of the term constitution, see C. McIlwain, *Constitutionalism: Ancient and Modern* (Ithaca, NY: Cornell University Press, 1958). For the most compelling argument against applying the modern usage to supranational organizations or global or transnational arrangements, see D. Grimm, "The Achievement of Constitutionalism and its Prospects in a Changed World," in P. Dobner and M. Loughlin (eds.), *The Twilight of Constitutionalism?* (Oxford University Press, 2010), pp. 3–23. For responses, see U. R. Preuss, "Disconnecting Constitutions from Statehood: Is Global Constitutionalism a Viable Concept?" in Dobner and Loughlin (eds.), *The Twilight of Constitutionalism?* pp. 23–47; N. Walker, "Beyond the Holistic Constitution?" in Dobner and Loughlin (eds.), *The Twilight of Constitutionalism?* pp. 291–309; and N. Walker, "Taking Constitutionalism beyond the State," *Political Studies*, 56 (2008), 519–543. See also Chapter 2 of this book on federation and constitutionalism for an alternative to Grimm's statist approach.

83 H. Kelsen, *General Theory of Law and the State* (Cambridge, MA: Harvard University Press, 1945).

84 *Ibid.*

85 Kelsen argued that formal entrenchment is incomplete absent a body other than the legislature able to engage in constitutional review and to declare legislative acts invalid or ultra vires. Kelsen, *General Theory of Law and the State*, pp. 155–157 and 262–263. Otherwise a legislative norm could only be challenged politically not juridically.

86 *Ibid.*, p. 258, note 8.

87 Kelsen assumes that a legal *system* must be characterized by strict unity and hierarchy in the structure of validity claims – all norms whose validity may be traced back to one and the same basic norm form a legal system (the grundnorm, understood as a transcendental postulate).

88 Prior to the modern period in Europe higher law was typically regarded as of divine origin or "natural" – i.e. fundamental laws political powers could not dispose of.

89 A. S. Sweet, "Constitutionalism, Legal Pluralism and International Relations," *Indiana Journal of Global Legal Studies*, 16 (2009), 626–667.

90 N. Luhmann, *Law as a Social System* (Oxford University Press, 2004), pp. 381–422; G. Teubner, "Societal Constitutionalism: Alternatives to State-Centered Constitutional Theory?" in C. Joerges, I. Sand, and G. Teubner (eds.), *Transnational Governance and Constitutionalism* (Portland, OR: Hart Publishing, 2004), pp. 3–28; and G. Teubner, "Global Bukowina: Legal Pluralism in the World Society," in G. Teubner (ed.), *Global Law Without a State* (Brookfield, VT: Dartmouth Publishing Group, 1997), pp. 3–15.

91 Kelsen, *General Theory of Law and the State*, p. 259. I thank Julian Arato for pointing this out to me. See Arato, "The Concept of Constitution and Constitutionalism Beyond the State," section 2.2, p. 13.

92 Arato, "The Concept of Constitution and Constitutionalism Beyond the State."

93 C. Mollers, "The Politics of Law and the Law of Politics: Two Constitutional Traditions in Europe," in E. O. Eriksen, J. E. Fossum, and A. J. Menendez (eds.), *Developing a Constitution for Europe* (London: Routledge, 2004), pp. 128–139.

94 Grimm, "The Achievement of Constitutionalism and its Prospects in a Changed World," p. 16. His conception of constitution is thus holistic and comprehensive.

95 *Ibid.* Modern republican and democratic constitutionalism invoke popular sovereignty and impute the constitution to the people or demos construed as the source of the higher law qualities and of constitutional dualism.

96 Habermas, *The Divided West*, p. 131.

97 This need not entail a Schmittian conception of constituent power. For an analysis of democratic constitution-making that avoids mythologizing the sovereign people as a macro subject, see A. Arato, "Post-Sovereign Constitution-Making and its Pathology in Iraq," *New York Law School Law Review*, 51 (2006–2007), 535–555.

98 Grimm, "The Achievement of Constitutionalism and its Prospects in a Changed World," p. 8.

99 See Chapter 1 of this book.

100 For a superb text on contemporary international organization, see Alvarez, *International Organizations as Law-makers*.

101 Fassbender, *UN Security Council Reform and the Right of Veto*, pp. 63–159; and B. Sloan, "The United Nations Charter as a Constitution," *Pace Yearbook of International Law*, 1 (1989), 61–126.

102 Grimm, "The Achievement of Constitutionalism and its Prospects in a Changed World."

103 *Ibid.*, p. 11.

104 United Nations, *Charter of the United Nations*, Article 103, is the "supremacy clause." It states that in the event of a conflict between the obligations of the members of the United Nations under the present Charter and their obligations under any other international treaty agreement, their obligations under the present Charter shall prevail.

105 On the doctrine of international community, see E. Kwakwa, "The International Community, International Law and the United States: Three in One, Two against One, or One and the Same?," A. Paulus, "The Influence of the United States on the Concept of the 'International Community,'" and M. Koskenniemi, S. Ratner, and V. Rittberger, "Comments on Chapters 1 and 2," all in M. Byers and G. Nolte (eds.), *United States Hegemony and the Foundations of International Law* (Cambridge University Press, 2003), pp. 25–56, 57–90, 91–116.

106 This, however, does not make the UN Charter the constitution of international society or of the world.
107 Fox, *Humanitarian Occupation*, pp. 205–216, for a discussion of the *jus cogens* claim and the difficulties with it.
108 D. Grimm, "Integration by Constitution," *International Journal of Constitutional Law*, 3 (2005), 193–208.
109 J. H. H. Weiler, "On the Power of the Word: Europe's Constitutional Iconography," *International Journal of Constitutional Law*, 3 (2005), 184–190. For some radical democratic theorists, a normative conception of a constitution requires full democratic legitimacy (equal representation of all affected) in the process of creating and adopting the constitutional text. It also must establish procedural norms for law-making that enable democratic politics along with protection of basic rights. See H. Brunkhorst, "A Polity Without a State? European Constitutionalism Between Evolution and Revolution," *International Journal of Constitutional Law*, 3 (2005), 88–106. I believe we have to settle for a less demanding concept of legitimacy for the global political system at this time.
110 I am unconvinced that one can blur the meaning of "measure" and "law-making" – i.e. classic executive vs. legislative functions – and the Charter provides only for measures under Chapter VII
111 European Court of Justice, Joined Cases C-402/05 P and C-415/05P 2008. Case T-315/01 *Kadi* v. *Council and Commission* (2005) ECR II-36649 (Kadi CFI); and Case T-306/01 *Yusuf and Al Barakaat International Foundation* v. *Council and Commission* (2005) ECR II-3353 *Yassin Abdullah Kadi and Al Barakaat International Foundation* v. *Council of the European Union and Commission of the European Communities*, September 2008.
112 See EC Reg. 467/00, and later EC Reg. 881/02, which replaced it. The EC/EU is not bound directly by the Charter under international law but it is under EC law. The Council of the European Union acting under the common Foreign and Security Policy provisions of the EU treaty adopted a series of common positions calling for EC measures to freeze the assets of those listed by the UN Sanctions Committee. The EC passed a series of regulations including EC Reg. 467/00, and later EC Reg. 881/02 which replaced it, freezing the assets of the listed individuals and groups throughout the territory of the EU. This included Kadi and Al Barakaat, a Swedish organization connected to a Somali financial network.
113 See the discussion in G. de Búrca, "The EU, the European Court of Justice and the International Legal Order after Kadi," *Harvard International Law Journal*, 51 (2009), 1–49.
114 *Kadi* v. *Council and Commission*, Case T-315/01, ECR II-3649 (Court of First Instance of the European Union, September 21, 2005); and *Yusuf and Al Barakaat International Foundation* v. *Council and Commission*, T-306/01, ECR II-3533 (Court of First Instance of the European Union, September 21, 2005).
115 *Kadi 1* (CFI), paragraph 159.
116 *Ibid.*, paragraphs 218–225.
117 *Ibid.*, paragraph 226.
118 *Marbury* v. *Madison*, 5 US 137 (US Supreme Court 1803), in which the US Supreme Court ascribed to itself the competence of judicial review while not overturning the contested regulation at issue.
119 De Búrca, "The EU, the European Court of Justice, and the International Legal Order after Kadi."
120 G. Scelle, "Le phénomène juridique du dédoublement fonctionnel," in W. Schätzel and H. J. Schlochauer (eds.), *Rechtsfragen der Internationalen Organisation: Festschrift für H. Wehberg* (Frankfurt am Main: Klostermann, 1956), pp. 324–342. See also G. Scelle,

"Le droit constitutionnel international," in *Mélanges R. Carré de Malberg* (Paris: Sirey, 1933), pp. 501–516.

121 The Court of First Instance noted that member states cannot circumvent their international legal obligations by creating another treaty organization such as the EC to do what they are not permitted to do and that this is expressly recognized in the treaty itself. *Kadi 1* (CFI), paragraphs 195–196.

122 O. Kirchheimer, *Political Justice: The Use of Legal Procedure for Political Ends* (Princeton University Press, 1961).

123 *Kadi 1* (CFI), paragraphs 242–252.

124 See D. Halberstam and E. Stein, "The United Nations, the European Union and the King of Sweden: Economic Sanctions and Individual Rights in a Plural World Order," *Common Market Law Review*, 46 (2009), 13–72.

125 Since the 1960s the ECJ has insisted that the legal order of the EU is autonomous. See *Costa* v. *ENEL*, Case 6–64, ECR 585 (European Court of Justice 1964), and *Van Gend en Loos* v. *Nederlandse Administratie der Belastingen*, Case 26–62, ECR 1 (European Court of Justice 1963).

126 Halberstam and Stein, "The United Nations, the European Union and the King of Sweden," p. 26.

127 EC Reg. 881/02 let the EU Council maintain the effects (listing and freezing of assets) for three months to allow a possibility to remedy the infringements found. Kadi's name was subsequently put back on the blacklist only a few months after it was removed by the ECJ.

128 *Kadi 1* (ECJ), paragraph 281.

129 *Ibid.*

130 *Ibid.*, paragraphs 281 and 316–317.

131 *Ibid.*, paragraphs 285 and 304. The Court also disclaimed any jurisdiction to review, even indirectly, the actions of the Security Council and did not rule on the legality of the Security Council resolutions themselves.

132 *Ibid.*, paragraph 285.

133 *Ibid.*, paragraphs 288 and 309.

134 S. Griller, "International Law, Human Rights and the Community's Autonomous Legal Order," *European Constitutional Law Review*, 4 (2008), 528–553.

135 De Búrca, "The EU, the European Court of Justice, and the International Legal Order after Kadi."

136 *Ibid.* De Búrca compared its reasoning to the arrogant stance of the United States in Medellin. I think this is an unconvincing comparison and an ungenerous reading of the decision. In the absence of a credible dialogue partner in the form of a court on the international level with the appropriate compulsory jurisdiction, the ECJ's reasoning makes sense.

137 *Ibid.*, and Halberstam and Stein, "The United Nations, the European Union and the King of Sweden."

138 De Búrca, "The EU, the European Court of Justice, and the International Legal Order after Kadi," pp. 31–32.

139 *Ibid.*, and Halberstam and Stein, "The United Nations, the European Union and the King of Sweden," p. 64.

140 M. Kumm, remarks, panel discussion on the Kadi judgment, New York University School of Law, New York, September 17, 2008. He also denies it is their duty to construct a global *ordre publique*.

141 For the original and so far as I know first argument to the effect that Maduro's opinion must be understood within the framework of constitutional pluralism rather than according to the dualist/monist divide, see J. L. Cohen, "A Global State of Emergency

or the Further Constitutionalisation of International Law: A Pluralist Approach," *Constellations*, 15 (2008), 456–484.

142 Opinion of Advocate General Poiares Maduro, *Yassin Abdullah Kadi and Al Barakaat International Foundation* v. *Council of the European Union and Commission of the European Communities*, Joined Cases C-402/05 P and C-415/05 P delivered January 16, 2008, paragraph 37.

143 *Ibid.*, paragraph 39. See also Cohen, "Global State of Emergency or the Further Constitutionalisation of International Law: A Pluralist Approach," 477.

144 Opinion of Advocate General Poiares Maduro, paragraph 22.

145 *Ibid.*, paragraph 38.

146 *Ibid.*, paragraph 39.

147 At issue is the shifting between external theoretical and internal participant perspectives. See Cohen, "Global State of Emergency or the Further Constitutionalisation of International Law: A Pluralist Approach," p. 473.

148 Minimally understood reform would entail that all SC resolutions respect due process norms for individuals placed on terror lists. I argue below for deeper "constitutional" reform of the Charter.

149 Opinion of Advocate General Poiares Maduro, paragraph 37.

150 The word "municipal" is somewhat misleading. I would prefer "federal" or "quasi-federal." This point that the EU is some sort of polity is even more convincing given that the EC now has international legal personality as per the Lisbon Treaty.

151 Opinion of Advocate General Poiares Maduro, paragraphs 22 and 23–25.

152 *Ibid.*, paragraphs 51–54.

153 *Ibid.*, paragraph 54.

154 *Ibid.*, paragraph 38.

155 *Ibid.*.

156 It is true that Maduro does not explicitly invoke customary international human rights or the UN Charter; but constitutional pluralism can involve this idea. J. A. Frowein, "Fundamental Human Rights as a Vehicle of Legal Integration in Europe," in M. Cappelletti, M. Seccombe, and J. Weiler (eds.), *Integration Through Law: Europe and the American Federal Experience* (Brussels: Walter de Gruyter, 1986), pp. 300–344 (p. 302).

157 Opinion of Advocate General Poiares Maduro, paragraph 19. In the case that became known as Solange I, *Internationale Handelsgesellschaft MbH* v. *Einfuhr- und Vorratsstelle für Getreide und Futtermittel*, 37 BVerfGE 271 CMLR 540 (German Federal Constitutional Court, May 29, 1974).

158 *Internationale Handelsgesellschaft MbH* v. *Einfuhr- und Vorratsstelle für Getreide und Futtermittel*, 37 BVerfGE 271 CMLR 540.

159 Solange II or BVerfG, 2 BvR 197/83 1986. Indeed in its subsequent Maastricht decision (2BrV2134/92, 2BrV2159/92) (English translation), 33 ILM 388 (1994) the GCC reasserted this principle along with its intention to strictly enforce the "principle of conferral" that demands a parliamentary ratification vote for any change of European primary law even when the treaties do not require it. Thus it will entertain ultra vires complaints charging that an EU measure transgressed the parameters of delegation.

160 N. MacCormick, *Questioning Sovereignty: Law, State, and Nation in the European Commonwealth* (Oxford University Press, 1999); N. Walker, "The Idea of Constitutional Pluralism," *Modern Law Review*, 65 (2002), 317–359; and M. P. Maduro, "Contrapunctual Law: Europe's Constitutional Pluralism in Action," in N. Walker (ed.), *Sovereignty in Transition: Essays in European Law* (Oxford: Hart Publishing, 2003), pp. 501–538.

161 W. T. Eijsbouts and L. Besselink, "The Law of Laws – Overcoming Pluralism," *European Constitutional Law Review*, 4 (2008), 395–398. For a theory of constitutional synthesis

along these lines see J. E. Fossum and A. J. Menendez, *The Constitution's Gift: A Constitutional Theory for a Democratic European Union* (New York: Rowman & Littlefield, 2011).

162 Frowein, "Fundamental Human Rights as a Vehicle of Legal Integration in Europe." See also J. H. Weiler, *The Constitution of Europe: "Do the New Clothes Have an Emperor?" and Other Essays on European Integration* (Oxford University Press, 1999).

163 See Halberstam and Stein, "The United Nations, the European Union and the King of Sweden," p. 68. While one could analogize the attempt to trigger the creation of a dialogue partner and equivalent rights protections on the international level to Solange I, the "Solange II" approach which entails the willingness of a constitutional court to refrain from review on the assumption that there is a comparable level of rights protection and constitutionalism on the level of the relevant overarching political community is clearly inapposite. The conditions required for this kind of internal constitutional pluralism do not yet exist in the international community.

164 Opinion of Advocate General Poiares Maduro, paragraph 54.

165 While no state can invalidate a Council resolution, states can declare its implementation impossible within their own territory as can a regional organization. See Arato, "The Concept of Constitution and Constitutionalism Beyond the State," p. 28. If many states do so then clearly the legitimacy of the legislative resolution would be placed in question.

166 The ECJ stressed the Community's obligations under international law. *Kadi 1* (ECJ), paragraphs 290–297.

167 E. Benvenisti, "Reclaiming Democracy: The Strategic Uses of Foreign and International Law by National Courts," *American Journal of International Law*, 102 (2008), 241–274.

168 M. P. Maduro, "Courts and Pluralism: Essay on a Theory of Judicial Adjudication in the Context of Legal and Constitutional Pluralism," in J. Dunoff and J. Trachtman (eds.), *Ruling the World? Constitutionalism, International Law and Global Governance* (Cambridge University Press, 2009), pp. 356–379. See the discussion in Chapter 1 of this book.

169 *Ibid.*, pp. 356–358.

170 On the ethic of political responsibility, grounded in commitment to the constitutional "acquis," and to the ongoing political project of European Union, see Walker, "The Idea of Constitutional Pluralism," pp. 337–348; and Weiler, "On the Power of the Word," advocating constitutional tolerance.

171 A. Somek, "Monism: A Tale of the Undead," University of Iowa Legal Studies Research Paper No. 10–22 (2010), p. 42; K. Günther, "Legal Pluralism or Uniform Concept of Law: Globalization as a Problem of Legal Theory," *NoFo*, 5 (2008), 5–21; and J. B. Cruz, "The Legacy of the Maastricht-Urteil and the Pluralist Movement," *European Law Journal*, 14 (2008), 389–422.

172 M. P. Maduro, "Three Claims of Constitutional Pluralism," working draft, http://cosmopolis.wzb.eu/content/program/conkey_Maduro_Three-Claims-of-Pluralism.pdf, pp. 25–28.

173 Maduro, "Courts and Pluralism," pp. 374–379.

174 *Ibid.*, and Eijsbouts and Besselink, "The Law of Laws – Overcoming Pluralism," p. 397.

175 Fossum and Menendez, *The Constitution's Gift*. See also A. J. Menendez, "From Constitutional Pluralism to a Pluralistic Constitution?" RECON Online Working Paper 2011/02 January 2011 www.reconproject.eu/projectweb/portalproject/RECONWorkingPapers.html

176 Fossum and Menendez, *The Constitution's Gift*, pp. 45–77, for their theory of constitutional synthesis. As analyzed by Fossum and Menendez with respect to the EU, however, constitutional synthesis presupposes basic political homogeneity of member

states' constitutional principles – i.e. liberal, democratic, and republican political regimes are required for all even though political cultural differences may mean that rights interpretations or democratic regimes may differ across states.

177 Maduro sees the treaties establishing the Community as an agreement not merely between states but between the peoples of Europe and refers to it as a "basic constitutional charter." All of these terms are more evocative of a federation than of an international organization. Opinion of Advocate General Poiares Maduro, paragraphs 21 and 37.

178 See Weiler, *The Constitution of Europe*, for the argument regarding the hybrid character of the European Union. According to the ECJ, the EU is a sui generis organization: Opinion 1/91, Draft Treaty on the Establishment of a European Economic Area (EEA), ECR I-6079 (European Court of Justice, 1991), paragraph 21. It is a new legal order (of international law) because it is autonomous and integrated into national legal orders. The EU legal order determines its own validity and sources autonomously.

179 Grimm, "The Achievement of Constitutionalism and its Prospects in a Changed World," p. 18. How to designate the political form of the existing EU ultimately boils down to a choice of ideal-typical taxonomic frameworks.

180 *Ibid.*

181 *Ibid.*, pp. 17–24; B. de Witte, "The European Union as an International Legal Experiment," paper drafted for the workshop The EU Between Constitutionalism and International Law, New York University, October 2008; B. de Witte, "The European Union as an International Legal Experiment," in G. de Búrca (ed.), *The Worlds of European Constitutionalism* (Cambridge University Press, 2011), pp. 19–56. See also D. Grimm, "Treaty or Constitution? The Legal Basis of the European Union After Maastricht," in Eriksen, Fossum, and Menendez (eds.), *Developing a Constitution for Europe*, pp. 69–87; and J. Habermas, "Why Europe Needs a Constitution," *New Left Review*, 11 (2001), 5–26, arguing against Grimm.

182 Maduro, "Three Claims of Constitutional Pluralism."

183 On the concept of "demoicracy," see K. Nicolaidis, "The Federal Vision Beyond the Federal State: Conclusion," in K. Nicolaidis and R. Howse (eds.), *The Federal Vision: Legitimacy and Levels of Governance in the United States and European Union* (Oxford University Press, 2001), pp. 439–482.

184 This is not to say that there is no democratic deficit in the EU or that reforms are not required of its hybrid structure as a "quasi-" federation or complex international organization.

185 See Chapter 2. See also M. Forsyth, *Unions of States: The Theory and Practice of Federation* (New York: Holmes & Meier, 1981); C. Schönberger, "Die Europäische Union als Bund," *Archiv des Öffentlichen Rechts*, 129 (2004), 81–120; and O. Beaud, *Théorie de la fédération* (Paris: Presses Universitaires de France, 2007).

186 Even in that 2004 project, as Grimm notes, the failed constitutional treaty did not provide for a changed amendment rule (from unanimity) that would have turned the treaty into a constitution and created a federal state with the power of self-determination. Grimm, "The Achievement of Constitutionalism and its Prospects in a Changed World," p. 19.

187 See Chapter 2 and the discussion in Forsyth, *Unions of States*, and Beaud, *Théorie de la fédération.*

188 Grimm, "The Achievement of Constitutionalism and its Prospects in a Changed World," pp. 18–19; M. Loughlin, "What is Constitutionalism?" in Dobner and Loughlin (eds.), *The Twilight of Constitutionalism?* pp. 47–72.

189 Grimm, "The Achievement of Constitutionalism and its Prospects in a Changed World," pp. 8–9. According to Grimm, these include: (1) The constitution is a set of

legal norms which owe their validity to a political decision rather than to pre-established truth. (2) The purpose of these norms is to regulate the establishment and exercise of public power as opposed to a mere modification of pre-existing public power dimensions. (3) The regulation is comprehensive in the sense that no extra constitutional bearers of public power and no extra constitutional ways and means to exercise this power are recognized. (4) Constitutional law finds its origin with the people as the only legitimate source of power. The constitution is attributed to the people and binds the government, while it regulates law-making by the government that binds the people (reflexivity). (5) Constitutional law is higher law.

190 Grimm, "The Achievement of Constitutionalism and its Prospects in a Changed World," p. 18.

191 *Ibid.*, p. 19.

192 *Ibid.*, pp. 19–21.

193 *Ibid.*, p. 19.

194 *Ibid.*, pp. 19–24.

195 *Ibid.*, p. 9.

196 This need not entail giving the Union enforcement mechanisms such as a monopoly over the means of legitimate force, nor need it entail a new federal system of courts: although all of this is possible and would depend on the new federal constitutional treaty.

197 See the dissertation manuscript of A. Domeyer on file with the author.

198 For the critique of supranational constitutionalism as legalism see Loughlin, "What is Constitutionalism?" For a response to both Grimm and Loughlin that defends the idea of constitutionalism beyond the state if linked to a concept of the people rather than to territoriality, see Preuss, "Disconnecting Constitutions from Statehood."

199 Maduro, "Three Claims of Constitutional Pluralism," pp. 15–16, describing the advantages of constitutional pluralism. See also Chapter 2.

200 In a well-ordered constitutional democracy, the legislature, the courts, and the executive all are instances of legal interpretation and given an appropriate amendment rule, even the highest court's interpretation can be "overruled" if the appropriate composite majority is attained. This is the core idea of the separation of powers and democratic constitutionalism as intrinsically pluralistic albeit assuming a unified legal order and a bounded political space.

201 Maduro, "Three Claims of Constitutional Pluralism," p. 9.

202 R. G. Teitel, "Humanity's Law: Rule of Law for the New Global Politics," *Cornell International Law Journal*, 35 (2002), 355–387.

203 Grimm, "The Achievement of Constitutionalism and its Prospects in a Changed World," p. 20.

204 *Ibid.*, p. 16.

205 *Ibid.*

206 *Ibid.*, p. 17.

207 *Ibid.*, p. 22.

208 Perhaps with some form of double voting system. See Dervis, *A Better Globalization.*

209 Weiler, "On the Power of the Word."

210 This also required dropping the absolutist "embodiment" model with respect to the people in discourses of popular sovereignty either as a stratum as in the theory of mixed government or as the assembled whole as in Rousseauian natural law theories. For a fascinating discussion of the condition of possibility of reconciling sovereignty and constitutionalism, see O. Gierke, *Natural Law and the Theory of Society 1500–1800,* trans. E. Barker (Boston: Beacon Press, 2010), pp. 149–153.

211 While this meant the end of mixed government it did not ipso facto mean homogeneity or the absence of socio-economic divisions along class lines or of cultural plurality on the terrain of the sovereign state or within civil society. Rather, social plurality became the condition of possibility for both liberal and democratic politics.

212 This understanding informs the liberal Locke as much as it does the republican Montesquieu, and combinations thereof as, for example, the political writings of Kant and the American federalists.

213 See A. Arato and J. L. Cohen, "Banishing the Sovereign? Internal and External Sovereignty in Arendt," *Constellations*, 16 (2009), 307–330.

214 Kant remained a prisoner of the statist paradigm insofar as he could imagine a juridical constitutional world order only in the form of a cosmopolitan world state. Kant linked legal order and constitution too tightly to the state concept. That is why he did not construe the order of a federal union that he advocated first for Europe and then for the world as establishing a *rechtliche* or constitutional condition because the member states would still be sovereign. I. Kant, "Idea for a Universal History with Practical Intent" and "Perpetual Peace: A Philosophical Sketch," in H. S. Reiss (ed.), *Kant: Political Writings* (Cambridge University Press, 1991), pp. 41–54 and 93–131.

215 As such, sovereignty is a negative concept. This is not Schmitt's conception of sovereignty but my own.

216 N. Walker, "Late Sovereignty in the European Union," in Walker (ed.), *Sovereignty in Transition*, pp. 3–32 (p. 23).

217 *Ibid.*, pp. 31–32.

218 *Ibid.*

219 It is true that the extent of legislation possible in a federal union would vary with the degree of homogeneity of regime types.

220 For the concept of low-intensity constitutionalism, see M. P. Maduro, "The Importance of Being Called a Constitution: Constitutional Authority and the Authority of Constitutionalism," *International Journal of Constitutional Law*, 3 (2005), 332–356.

221 A. Somek, "Kelsen Lives," *European Journal of International Law*, 18 (2007), 436–438.

Conclusion

1 For a recent argument defending the idea of constitutional linkages among the islands of constitutionality in global space see N. Walker, "Constitutionalism and Pluralism in the Global Context," RECON Online Working Paper 2010/03, www.reconproject.eu Go to Publications/RECON Working Papers. I agree with Gunther Teubner that "in the sea of globality there are only islands of constitutionality." G. Teubner, "Constitutionalising Polycontexturality," *Social and Legal Studies*, 19 (2010), 1–25, cited in Walker, "Constitutionalism and Pluralism in the Global Context," p. 11.

2 S. Besson, "European Legal Pluralism after Kadi," *European Constitutional Law Review*, 5 (2009), 237–264.

3 See N. Walker, "Beyond the Holistic Constitution?" in P. Dobner and M. Loughlin (eds.), *The Twilight of Constitutionalism?* (Oxford University Press, 2010), pp. 291–308.

4 A. Arato and J. L. Cohen, "Banishing the Sovereign? Internal and External Sovereignty in Arendt," *Constellations*, 16 (2009), 307–330.

5 J. Habermas, "Constitutional Democracy: A Paradoxical Union of Contradictory Principles?" *Political Theory*, 29 (2001), 766–781.

6 D. Grimm, "The Achievements of Constitutionalism and its Prospects in a Changed World," in Dobner and Loughlin (eds.), *The Twilight of Constitutionalism?* pp. 3–22 (p. 17).

7 N. Walker, "Constitutionalism and the Incompleteness of Democracy: An Iterative Relationship," *Rechtsfilosofie & Rechtstheorie*, 39 (2010), 206–233 (pp. 231–233).

8 *Ibid.* Individualism means here that individuals are the ultimate units of moral concern. Egalitarianism applies this to every individual. Constructivism means that we ascribe our institutions, laws, and political and legal arrangements to our own efforts at design and to our own decisions and actions whatever "path-dependence" they may have with past arrangements. Political legitimacy is thus immanent not transcendent; democratic constitutionalism is grounded on "secular" principles in this sense rather than on meta-social guarantees. On the concept of the social imaginary see C. Castoriadis, *The Imaginary Institution of Society* (Cambridge, MA: MIT Press, 1987). See also C. Taylor, *Modern Social Imaginaries* (Durham: Duke University Press, 2004), p. 3.

9 Constitutionalism accordingly realizes, supplements, and qualifies democracy and vice versa. Admittedly Walker relies heavily on Habermas ("Constitutional Democracy") for the distinction between them and the thesis of their normative co-equivalence and symbiotic relationship. He differs in stressing their tension on the normative level. Walker, "Constitutionalism and the Incompleteness of Democracy," p. 212. But see the critique by S. Rummens, "The Co-originality of Law and Democracy in the Moral Horizon of Modernity," *Rechtsfilosofie & Rechtstheorie*, 39 (2010), 256–266, and Walker's reply to this, N. Walker, "Reply to Four Critics," in the same volume, 281–286.

10 For my use of the term constitutionalism see Chapter 5.

11 Walker, "Constitutionalism and the Incompleteness of Democracy," p. 207.

12 See *ibid.*, pp. 207, 213, and footnote 25, for a list of theorists fitting into each category.

13 Habermas, "Constitutional Democracy."

14 L. Besselink, "The Globalizing turn in the Relationship Between Constitutionalism and Democracy," *Rechtsfilosophie & Rechtstheorie*, 39 (2010), 234–254, citing the monarchomach and much of the subsequent social contract literature challenging absolutist conceptions of internal ruler sovereignty on the level of the state.

15 G. de Búrca, "Developing Democracy Beyond the State," *Columbia Journal of Transnational Law*, 46 (2009), 101–158, for a typology of the relevant approaches to supranational democracy.

16 See Chapter 3 of this book. See also M. Goodwin, "Plugging the Legitimacy Gap? The Ubiquity of Human Rights and the Rhetoric of Global Constitutionalism," *Rechtsfilosofie & Rechtstheorie*, 39 (2010), 245–255.

17 *Ibid.*, p. 246.

BIBLIOGRAPHY

Books and book chapters

Abbott, K. O. W., Keohane, R., Moravcsik, A., Slaughter, A.-M., and Snidal, D., "The Concept of Legalization," in R. O. Keohane, *Power and Governance in a Partially Globalized World* (New York: Routledge, 2002), pp. 132–151.

Agnes, F., *Law and Gender Inequality* (New Delhi: Oxford University Press, 1999).

Alvarez, J., *International Organizations as Law-makers* (Oxford University Press, 2005).

Anghie, A., *Imperialism, Sovereignty and the Making of International Law* (Cambridge University Press, 2004).

Annan, K., "Reflections on Intervention," in K. Annan, *The Question of Intervention: Statements by the Secretary-General* (New York: United Nations Department of Public Information, 1999).

Arato, A., *Constitution Making Under Occupation: The Politics of Imposed Revolution in Iraq* (New York: Columbia University Press, 2009).

Arato, A. and Cohen, J. L., "Banishing the Sovereign? Internal and Eternal Sovereignty in Arendt," in S. Benhabib (ed.), *Politics in Dark Times: Encounters with Hannah Arendt* (Cambridge University Press, 2010), pp. 137–171.

Arendt, H., *Eichmann in Jerusalem: A Report on the Banality of Evil* (New York: Penguin, 1994).

The Origins of Totalitarianism (New York: Harcourt, 1994).

Armitage, D., *Declarations of Independence: A Global History* (Cambridge, MA: Harvard University Press, 2007).

Austin, J., *The Province of Jurisprudence Determined*, ed. W. E. Rumble (Cambridge University Press, 1995).

Bagnoli, C., "Humanitarian Intervention as a Perfect Duty: A Kantian Argument," in T. Nardin and M. S. Williams (eds.), *Humanitarian Intervention: NOMOS XLVII* (New York University Press, 2006), pp. 117–142.

Bain, W., *Between Anarchy and Society: Trusteeship and the Obligation of Power* (Oxford University Press, 2003).

Barkey, K., *Empire of Difference: The Ottomans in Comparative Perspective* (Cambridge University Press, 2008).

Beaud, O., *Théorie de la fédération* (Paris: Presses Universitaires de France, 2007).

Beitz, C., *The Idea of Human Rights* (Oxford University Press, 2009).

Benhabib, S., *The Rights of Others: Aliens, Residents, and Citizens* (Cambridge University Press, 2004).

Benton, L., *A Search for Sovereignty: Law and Geography in European Empires, 1400–1900* (Cambridge University Press, 2010).

Benvenisti, E., *The International Law of Occupation* (Princeton University Press, 2004).

Berman, H. J., *Law and Revolution* (Cambridge, MA: Harvard University Press, 1983).

Besson, S., "Theorizing the Sources of International Law," in S. Besson and J. Tasoulias (eds.), *The Philosophy of International Law* (Oxford University Press, 2010), pp. 163–187.

Bodin, J., *On Sovereignty: Four Chapters from the Six Books of the Commonwealth*, ed. J. Franklin (Cambridge University Press, 1992).

Bohman, J., *Democracy Across Borders: From Dêmos to Dêmoi* (Cambridge, MA: MIT Press, 2010).

Brownlie, I., "The Rights of Peoples in Modern International Law," in J. Crawford (ed.), *The Rights of Peoples* (Oxford: Clarendon Press, 1992), pp. 1–16.

Brunkhorst, H., "Die Globale Rechtsrevolution. Von der Evolution der Verfassungsrevolution zur Revolution der Verfassungsevolution?" in R. Christensen and B. Pieroth (eds.), *Rechtstheorie in rechtspraktischer Absicht* (Berlin: Duncker & Humblot/FS Müller, 2008), pp. 9–34.

Buchanan, A., *Justice, Legitimacy, and Self-Determination* (New York: Oxford University Press, 2004).

"The Legitimacy of International Law," in S. Besson and J. Tasioulis (eds.), *The Philosophy of International Law* (Oxford University Press, 2010), pp. 79–96.

Bull, H., *The Anarchical Society*, 3rd edn. (Basingstoke: Palgrave Macmillan, 2002).

Byers, M., *Custom, Power and the Power of Rules: International Relations and Customary International Law* (Cambridge University Press, 1999).

Byers, M. and Chesterman, S., "Changing the Rules About Rules? Unilateral Humanitarian Intervention and the Future of International Law," in J. Holzgrefe and R. O. Keohane (eds.), *Humanitarian Intervention: Ethical, Legal and Political Dilemmas* (Cambridge University Press, 2003), pp. 177–203.

"'You the People': Pro-Democratic Intervention in International Law," in G. H. Fox and B. R. Roth (eds.), *Democratic Governance and International Law* (Cambridge University Press, 2000), pp. 259–292.

Calhoun, J. C., *Union and Liberty* (Indianapolis, IN: Liberty Fund, 1992).

Carré de Malberg, R., *Contribution à la théorie générale de l'état* (Paris: Dalloz, 2004).

Cassese, A., *Self-Determination of Peoples: A Legal Reappraisal* (Cambridge University Press, 1999).

Castoriadis, C., *The Imaginary Institution of Society* (Cambridge, MA: MIT Press, 1987).

Chayes, A. and Chayes, A. H., *The New Sovereignty: Compliance with International Regulatory Agreements* (Cambridge, MA: Harvard University Press, 1998).

Chesterman, S., *Just War or Just Peace? Humanitarian Intervention and International Law* (Oxford University Press, 2002).

Cohen J., "Is There a Human Right to Democracy?" in C. Sypnowich (ed.), *The Egalitarian Conscience: Essays in Honor of G. A. Cohen* (Oxford University Press, 2006), pp. 226–248.

Cohen, J. L., "The Debate Over the Reflexive Paradigm," in J. L. Cohen, *Regulating Intimacy: A New Legal Paradigm* (Princeton University Press, 2002), pp. 151–179.

Regulating Intimacy: A New Legal Paradigm (Princeton University Press, 2002).

"Sovereignty in the Context of Globalization: A Constitutional Pluralist Perspective," in S. Besson and J. Tasoulias (eds.), *The Philosophy of International Law* (Oxford University Press, 2010), pp. 261–282.

Cohen, J. L. and Arato, A., *Civil Society and Political Theory* (Cambridge, MA: MIT Press, 1992).

Cosnard, M., "Sovereign Equality – 'The *Wimbledon* Sails On,'" in M. Byers and G. Nolte (eds.), *United States Hegemony and the Foundations of International Law* (Cambridge University Press, 2003), pp. 117–134.

Cranston, M., *What are Human Rights?* (London: Bodley Head, 1973).

Damrosch, L. F. (ed.), *Enforcing Restraint: Collective Intervention in Internal Conflicts* (New York: Council on Foreign Relations Press, 1993).

Damrosch, L. F., Henkin, L., Pugh, R. C., Schachter, O., and Smit, H. (eds.), *International Law* (St. Paul, MN: West Group, 2001).

de Wet, E., *The Chapter VII Powers of the United Nations Security Council* (Oxford: Hart Publishing, 2004).

de Witte, B., "The European Union as an International Legal Experiment," in G. de Búrca (ed.), *The Worlds of European Constitutionalism* (Cambridge University Press, 2011), pp. 19–56.

Delmas-Marty, M., *Le pluralisme ordonné* (Paris: Editions du Seuil, 2006).

Towards a Truly Common Law: Europe as a Laboratory for Legal Pluralism (Cambridge University Press, 1994).

Derrida, J., *Rogues: Two Essays on Reason* (Stanford University Press, 2005).

Dervis, K., *A Better Globalization: Legitimacy, Governance and Reform* (Washington, DC: Center for Global Development, 2005).

Donnelly, J., *Universal Human Rights* (Ithaca, NY: Cornell University Press, 2003).

Doyle, M., *Empires* (Ithaca, NY: Cornell University Press, 1986).

Ehrlich, E., *Grundlegung der Soziologie des Rechts* (Munich and Leipzig: Duncker & Humblot, 1913).

Elazar, D. J., *Exploring Federalism* (Tuscaloosa, AL: University of Alabama Press, 1987).

"The United States and the European Union: Models for Their Epochs," in K. Nicolaidis and R. Howse (eds.), *The Federal Vision: Legitimacy and Levels of Governance in the United States and the European Union* (Oxford University Press, 2001), pp. 31–53.

Endicott, T., "The Logic of Freedom and Power," in S. Besson and J. Tasoulias (eds.), *The Philosophy of International Law* (Oxford University Press, 2010), pp. 245–260.

Evans, T., *The Politics of Human Rights: A Global Perspective* (London: Pluto Press, 2005).

Falk, R., "The Rights of Peoples (In Particular Indigenous Peoples)," in J. Crawford (ed.), *The Rights of Peoples* (Oxford: Clarendon Press, 1992), pp. 17–37.

Fassbender, B., "Sovereignty and Constitutionalism in International Law," in N. Walker (ed.), *Sovereignty in Transition: Essays in European Law* (Oxford: Hart Publishing, 2003), pp. 115–144.

UN Security Council Reform and the Right of Veto: A Constitutional Perspective (Boston: Kluwer Law International, 1998).

"'We the Peoples of the United Nations': Constituent Power and Constitutional Form in International Law," in M. Loughlin and N. Walker (eds.), *The Paradox of Constitutionalism: Constituent Power and Constitutional Form* (Oxford University Press, 2007), pp. 269–290.

Fazal, T., *State Death: The Politics and Geography of Conquest, Occupation, and Annexation* (Princeton University Press, 2008).

Finnis, J., *Natural Law and Natural Rights* (Oxford: Clarendon Press, 1980).

Fischer-Lescano, A., *Globalverfassung: Die Geltungsbegründung der Menschenrechte* (Weilerswist: Velbrück Wissenschaft, 2005).

"Redefining Sovereignty via International Constitutional Moments?" in M. E. O'Connell, M. Bothe, and N. Ronzitti (eds.), *Redefining Sovereignty: The Use of Force After the End of the Cold War* (Ardsley, NY: Transnational Publishers, 2005), pp. 335–364.

Fischer-Lescano, A. and Teubner, G., *Regime-Kollisionen: Zur Fragmentierung des globalen Rechts* (Frankfurt am Main: Suhrkamp, 2006).

Forst, R., "Towards a Critical Theory of Transnational Justice," in T. Pogge (ed.), *Global Justice* (Oxford: Blackwell, 2001), pp. 169–203.

Forsyth, M., *Unions of States: The Theory and Practice of Confederation* (New York: Holmes & Meier, 1981).

Fossum, J. E. and Menendez, A. J., *The Constitution's Gift: A Constitutional Theory for a Democratic European Union* (New York: Rowman & Littlefield, 2011).

Foucault, M., "Governmentality," in G. Burchell, C. Gordon, and P. Miller (eds.), *The Foucault Effect: Studies in Governmentality* (Hemel Hempstead: Harvester Wheatsheaf, 1991), pp. 87–104.

Fox, G. H., *Humanitarian Occupation* (Cambridge University Press, 2008).

Fox, G. H. and Roth, B. R., *Democratic Governance and International Law* (Cambridge University Press, 2000).

Fraenkel, E., *The Dual State: A Contribution to the Theory of Dictatorship* (Oxford University Press, 1941).

Franck, T., "Interpretation and Change in the Law of Humanitarian Intervention," in J. Holzgrefe and R. O. Keohane (eds.), *Humanitarian Intervention: Ethical, Legal and Political Dilemmas* (Cambridge University Press, 2003), pp. 204–31.

"Legality and Legitimacy in Humanitarian Intervention," in T. Nardin and M. S. Williams (eds.), *Humanitarian Intervention: NOMOS XLVII* (New York University Press), pp. 143–157.

Franklin, J., *Jean Bodin and the Rise of Absolutist Theory* (Cambridge University Press, 1973).

Frowein, J. A., "Fundamental Human Rights as a Vehicle of Legal Integration in Europe," in M. Cappelletti, M. Seccombe, and J. Weiler (eds.), *Integration Through Law: Europe and the American Federal Experience* (Brussels: Walter de Gruyter, 1986), vol. I, Book 3, pp. 300–344.

Gewirth, A., *Human Rights* (University of Chicago Press, 1982).

Gierke, O., *Natural Law and the Theory of Society 1500–1800*, trans. E. Barker (Boston: Beacon Press, 2010).

Glendon, M. A., *A World Made New: Eleanor Roosevelt and the Universal Declaration of Human Rights* (New York: Random House, 2001).

Goldstein, J., Kahler, M., Keohane R. O., and Slaughter, A.-M., "Introduction: Legalization and World Politics," in J. Goldstein, M. Kahler, R. O. Keohane, and A.-M. Slaughter (eds.), *Legalization and World Politics* (Cambridge, MA: MIT Press, 2001), pp. 1–15.

Gong, G. W., *The Standard of "Civilization" in International Society* (Oxford: Clarendon Press, 1984).

Graber, D., *The Development of the Law of Belligerent Occupation 1863–1914: A Historical Survey* (New York: Columbia University Press, 1949).

Griffin, J., "Human Rights and the Autonomy of International Law," in S. Besson and J. Tasioulis (eds.), *The Philosophy of International Law* (Oxford University Press, 2010), pp. 339–357.

On Human Rights (Oxford University Press, 2008).

Grimm, D., "The Achievement of Constitutionalism and its Prospects in a Changed World," in P. Dobner and M. Loughlin (eds.), *The Twilight of Constitutionalism?* (Oxford University Press, 2010), pp. 3–22.

"Treaty or Constitution? The Legal Basis of the European Union After Maastricht," in E. O. Eriksen, J. E. Fossum, and A. J. Menendez (eds.), *Developing a Constitution for Europe* (New York: Routledge, 2004), pp. 69–87.

Habermas, J., *Between Facts and Norms* (Cambridge: Polity Press, 1996).

"Does the Constitutionalisation of International Law Still Have a Chance?" in J. Habermas, *The Divided West*, ed. and trans. C. Cronin (Cambridge University Press, 2006), pp. 115–193.

Justification and Application: Remarks on Discourse Ethics (Cambridge, MA: MIT Press, 1993).

"Kant's Idea of Perpetual Peace with the Benefit of 200 Years' Hindsight," in K. Baynes and M. Lutz-Bachmann (eds.), *Perpetual Peace: Essays on Kant's Cosmopolitan Idea* (Cambridge, MA: Harvard University Press, 1997), pp. 113–154.

"Law as Medium and Law as Institution," in G. Teubner (ed.), *Dilemmas of Law in the Welfare State* (Berlin: Walter de Gruyter, 1985), pp. 203–220.

Hardt, M. and Negri, A., *Empire* (Cambridge, MA: Harvard University Press, 2000).

Hart, H. L. A., *The Concept of Law* (Oxford University Press, 1961).

"Kelsen's Doctrine of the Unity of Law," in H. L. A. Hart, *Essays in Jurisprudence and Philosophy* (Oxford: Clarendon Press, 1983), pp. 309–343.

Hassim, S., *Women's Organizations and Democracy in South Africa* (Scottsville: University of KwaZulu Natal Press, 2006).

Hegel, G. W. F., *The Philosophy of Right*, trans. T. M. Knox (Oxford University Press, 1967).

Held, D. and Archibugi, D., *Cosmopolitan Democracy: An Agenda for a New World Order* (Cambridge: Polity Press, 1995).

Henkin, L., Neuman, G., Orentlicher, D. F., and Leebron, D. W., *Human Rights* (New York: Foundation Press University Casebook, 1999).

Hintze, O., *The Historical Essays of Otto Hintze* (Oxford University Press, 1989).

Hirschel, R., *Towards Juristocracy: The Origins and Consequences of the New Constitutionalism* (Cambridge, MA: Harvard University Press, 2004).

Hobbes, T., *Leviathan* (New York: Bobbs-Merrill, 1958).

Howse, R., "Introduction," in K. Nicolaidis and R. Howse (eds.), *The Federal Vision: Legitimacy and Levels of Governance in the United States and the European Union* (Oxford University Press, 2011), pp. 1–28.

Ignatieff, M., *Human Rights as Politics, Human Rights as Idolatry* (Princeton University Press, 2001).

Irving, H., *Gender and the Constitution* (Cambridge University Press, 2008).

Jagwanth, S. and Murray, C., "No Nation Can Be Free When One Half of It Is Enslaved: Constitutional Equality for Women in South Africa," in B. Baines and R. Rubio-Martin (eds.), *The Gender of Constitutional Jurisprudence* (Cambridge University Press, 2004), pp. 230–255.

Jellinek, G., *Allgemeine Staatslehre* (Bad Homburg: Hermann Gentner Verlag, 1960). *Die Lehre der Staatenverbindungen* (Agram: L. Hartman, 1885).

Joerges, C. and Petersman, E. U. (eds.), *Constitutionalism, Multilevel Trade Governance and Social Regulation* (Oxford: Hart Publishing, 2006).

Johnson, C., *Blowback: The Costs and Consequences of American Empire* (New York: Henry Holt & Co., 2004).

Kaldor, M., *Human Security: Reflections on Globalization* (Cambridge: Polity Press, 2007).

Kant, I., "Idea for a Universal History with Practical Intent" and "Perpetual Peace: A Philosophical Sketch," in H. S. Reiss (ed.), *Kant: Political Writings* (Cambridge University Press, 1991), pp. 41–54, 93–131.

The Metaphysics of Morals (Cambridge University Press, 2000).

"To Perpetual Peace: A Philosophical Sketch," in *Perpetual Peace and Other Essays* (New York: Hackett, 1983), pp. 107–143.

Keane, E., *Beyond the Anarchical Society: Grotius, Colonialism and World Order in International Politics* (Cambridge University Press, 2002).

Keck, M. E. and Sikkink, K., *Activists beyond Borders: Advocacy Networks in International Politics* (Ithaca, NY: Cornell University Press, 2007).

Kelsen, H., *Das Problem der Souveränität und die Theorie des Völkerrechts* (Tübingen: Mohr, 1928).

General Theory of Law and the State (Cambridge, MA: Harvard University Press, 1945).

The Law of the United Nations: A Critical Analysis of its Fundamental Problems (London: Stevens and Sons, 1950).

Kennedy, D., *The Dark Side of Virtue: Reassessing International Humanitarianism* (Princeton University Press, 2004).

Keohane, R. O., "Political Authority After Intervention: Gradations in Sovereignty," in J. Holzgrefe and R. O. Keohane (eds.), *Humanitarian Intervention: Ethical, Legal and Political Dilemmas* (Cambridge University Press, 2003), pp. 275–298.

Kirchheimer, O., *Political Justice: The Use of Legal Procedure for Political Ends* (Princeton University Press, 1961).

Klabbers, J., Peters, A., and Ulfstein, G., *The Constitutionalization of International Law* (Oxford University Press, 2009).

Korman, S., *The Right of Conquest: The Acquisition of Territory by Force in International Law and Practice* (Oxford University Press, 1996).

Koskenniemi, M., *The Gentle Civilizer of Nations* (Cambridge University Press, 2001).

Koskenniemi, M., Ratner, S., and Rittberger, V., "Comments on Chapters 1 and 2," in M. Byers and G. Nolte (eds.), *United States Hegemony and the Foundations of International Law* (Cambridge University Press, 2003), pp. 91–116.

Krasner, S. D., *Sovereignty: Organized Hypocrisy* (Princeton University Press, 1999).

Kretzmer, D., *The Occupation of Justice: The Supreme Court of Israel and the Occupied Territories* (Albany, NY: State University of New York Press, 2002).

Krisch, N., *Beyond Constitutionalism: The Case for Pluralism in Post-National Law* (Oxford University Press, 2010).

"More Equal Than the Rest? Hierarchy, Equality, and US Predominance in International Law," in M. Byers and G. Nolte (eds.), *United States Hegemony and the Foundations of International Law* (Cambridge University Press, 2003), pp. 135–175.

Kumm, M., "The Cosmopolitan Turn in Constitutionalism: On the Relationship between Constitutionalism in and beyond the State," in J. L. Dunoff and J. P. Trachtman (eds.), *Ruling the World? Constitutionalism,*

International Law and Global Governance (Cambridge University Press, 2009), pp. 258–324.

Kwakwa, E., "The International Community, International Law and the United States: Three in One, Two against One, or One and the Same?" in M. Byers and G. Nolte (eds.), *United States Hegemony and the Foundations of International Law* (Cambridge University Press, 2003), pp. 25–56.

Laber, J., *The Courage of Strangers: Coming of Age with the Human Rights Movement* (New York: Public Affairs, 2002).

A Life of H. L. A. Hart: The Nightmare and the Noble Dream (Oxford University Press, 2004).

Lawson, G. and Seidman, G., *The Constitution of Empire: Territorial Expansion and American Legal History* (New Haven, CT: Yale University Press, 2004).

Lefort, C., "Human Rights and the Welfare State," in C. Lefort, *Democracy and Political Theory* (Minneapolis: University of Minnesota Press, 1988), pp. 21–44.

"Permanence of the Theologico-Political?" in *Democracy and Political Theory* (Minneapolis: University of Minnesota Press, 1988), pp. 213–255.

"Politics and Human Rights," in C. Lefort, *The Political Forms of Modern Society* (Cambridge, MA: MIT Press, 1986), pp. 239–272.

Lepard, B. D., "Jurying Humanitarian Intervention and the Ethical Principle of Open-Minded Consultation," in T. Nardin and M. S. Williams (eds.), *Humanitarian Intervention: NOMOS XLVII* (New York University Press), pp. 217–243.

Loughlin, M., "Ten Tenets of Sovereignty," in N. Walker (ed.), *Sovereignty in Transition: Essays in European Law* (Oxford: Hart Publishing, 2003), pp. 55–86.

"What is Constitutionalism?" in P. Dobner and M. Loughlin (eds.), *The Twilight of Constitutionalism?* (Oxford University Press, 2010), pp. 47–72.

Luhmann, N., *The Differentiation of Society* (New York: Columbia University Press, 1981).

Grundrechte als Institution: ein Beitrag zur politischen Soziologie (Berlin: Duncker & Humblot, 1999).

Law as a Social System (Oxford University Press, 2004).

MacCormick, N., *Questioning Sovereignty: Law, State and Nation in the European Commonwealth* (Oxford University Press, 1999).

Macdonald, R. J. and Johnston, D. M. (eds.), *Towards World Constitutionalism: Issues in the Legal Ordering of the World Community* (Boston: Brill, 2005).

Madison, J., Hamilton, A., and Jay, J., *The Federalist Papers*, ed. C. Rossiter (New York: Penguin Classics, 2003).

Maduro, M. P., "Contrapunctual Law: Europe's Constitutional Pluralism in Action," in N. Walker (ed.), *Sovereignty in Transition: Essays in European Law* (Oxford: Hart Publishing, 2003), pp. 501–538.

"Courts and Pluralism: Essay on a Theory of Judicial Adjudication in the Context of Legal and Constitutional Pluralism," in J. L. Dunoff and

J. P. Trachtman (eds.), *Ruling the World? Constitutionalism, International Law, and Global Governance* (Cambridge University Press, 2009), pp. 356–379.

"Sovereignty in Europe: The European Court of Justice and the Creation of a European Political Community," in M. Volcansek and J. Stack, Jr. (eds.), *Courts Crossing Borders: Blurring the Lines of Sovereignty* (Durham, NC: Carolina Academic Press, 2005), pp. 43–61.

Makinson, D., "Rights of Peoples: Point of View of a Logician," in J. Crawford (ed.), *The Rights of Peoples* (Oxford: Clarendon Press, 1992), pp. 69–92.

Mallison, W. T. and Mallison, S. V., *The Palestine Problem in International Law and World Order* (Harlow: Longman, 1986).

Mamdani, M., *Citizen and Subject: Contemporary Africa and the Legacy of Late Colonialism* (Princeton University Press, 1996).

Saviors and Survivors: Darfur, Politics, and the War on Terror (New York: Pantheon, 2009).

Marschik, A., "Legislative Powers of the Security Council," in R. Macdonald and D. Johnston (eds.), *Towards World Constitutionalism: Issues in the Legal Ordering of the World Community* (Boston: Brill, 2005), pp. 431–492.

Mazower, M., *No Enchanted Place: The End of Empire and the Ideological Origins of the United Nations* (Princeton University Press, 2008).

McIlwain, C., *Constitutionalism: Ancient and Modern* (Ithaca, NY: Cornell University Press, 1958).

Mill, J. S., *Considerations on Representative Government* (London: Parker, Son, and Bourn, 1861).

Mollers, C., "The Politics of Law and the Law of Politics," in E. O. Eriksen, J. E. Fossum, and A. J. Menendez (eds.), *Developing a Constitution for Europe* (New York: Routledge, 2004), pp. 128–139.

Morsink, J., *The Universal Declaration of Human Rights: Origins, Drafting and Intent* (Philadelphia: University of Pennsylvania Press, 1999).

Moyn, S., *The Last Utopia: Human Rights in History* (Cambridge, MA: Harvard University Press, 2010).

Nardin, T., and Williams, M. S. (eds.), *Humanitarian Intervention: NOMOS XLVII* (New York University Press, 2006).

Nicolaidis, K., "The Federal Vision Beyond the Federal State: Conclusion," in K. Nicolaidis and R. Howse (eds.), *The Federal Vision: Legitimacy and Levels of Governance in the United States and European Union* (Oxford University Press, 2001), pp. 439–482.

Nicolaidis, K. and Howse, R. (eds.), *The Federal Vision: Legitimacy and Levels of Governance in the United States and the European Union* (Oxford University Press, 2001).

Nussbaum, M., "Capabilities and Human Rights," in P. De Greiff and C. P. Cronin (eds.), *Global Justice and Transnational Politics* (Cambridge, MA: MIT Press, 2002), pp. 117–149.

"India, Sex Equality, and Constitutional Law," in B. Baines and R. Rubio-Martin (eds.), *The Gender of Constitutional Jurisprudence* (Cambridge University Press, 2004), pp. 174–204.

Paulus, A., "The Influence of the United States on the Concept of the 'International Community,'" in M. Byers and G. Nolte (eds.), *United States Hegemony and the Foundations of International Law* (Cambridge University Press, 2003), pp. 57–90.

Pettit, P., "Legitimate International Institutions: A Neo-Republican Perspective," in S. Besson and J. Tasioulis (eds.), *The Philosophy of International Law* (Oxford University Press, 2010), pp. 119–138.

Republicanism: A Theory of Freedom and Government (Oxford University Press, 1997).

Philpott, D., *Revolutions in Sovereignty: How Ideas Shaped Modern International Relations* (Princeton University Press, 2001).

Pogge, T., "Cosmopolitanism," in R. Goodin, P. Pettit, and T. Pogge (eds.), *A Companion to Contemporary Political Philosophy*, 2nd edn. (Oxford: Blackwell, 2007), pp. 312–331.

"Human Rights and Human Responsibilities," in A. Kuper (ed.), *Global Responsibilities: Who Must Deliver on Human Rights?* (London: Routledge, 2005), pp. 3–35.

"Priorities of Global Justice," in T. Pogge (ed.), *Global Justice* (Oxford: Blackwell, 2001), pp. 6–23.

World Poverty and Human Rights (Cambridge University Press, 2002).

Preuss, U. R., "Disconnecting Constitutions from Statehood: Is Global Constitutionalism a Viable Concept?" in P. Dobner and M. Loughlin (eds.), *The Twilight of Constitutionalism?* (Oxford University Press, 2010), pp. 23–47.

Rama-Montaldo, M., "Contribution of the General Assembly to the Constitutional Development and Interpretation of the United Nations Charter," in R. Macdonald and D. Johnston (eds.), *Towards World Constitutionalism: Issues in the Legal Ordering of the World Community* (Boston: Brill, 2005), pp. 504–513.

Rana, A., *The Two Faces of American Freedom* (Cambridge University Press, 2010).

Rawls, J., *The Law of Peoples* (Cambridge, MA: Harvard University Press, 1999).

Raz, J., *The Authority of Law: Essays on Law and Morality* (Oxford University Press, 2009).

"Human Rights Without Foundations," in S. Besson and J. Tasioulas (eds.), *The Philosophy of International Law* (Oxford University Press, 2010), pp. 321–338.

"Kelsen's Theory of the Basic Norm," in J. Raz, *The Authority of Law: Essays on Law and Morality*, 2nd edn. (Oxford: Clarendon Press, 2009), pp. 122–145.

The Morality of Freedom (Oxford University Press, 1988).

Reisman, M., "Sovereignty and Human Rights in Contemporary International Law," in G. H. Fox and B. R. Roth (eds.), *Democratic Governance and International Law* (Cambridge University Press, 2000), pp. 239–258.

Riker, W. H., *Federalism: Origin, Operation, Significance* (Boston, MA: Little, Brown, 1964).

Roberts, A. and Guelff, R. (eds.), *Documents of the Laws of War* (Oxford University Press, 2000).

Rousseau, J. J., *A Project for Perpetual Peace*, trans. C. I. C. de Saint-Pierre (London: R. Boden-Sanderson, 1927).

Scelle, G., "Le droit constitutionnel international," in Mélanges, R. *Carré de Malberg* (Paris: Sirey, 1933), pp. 501–516.

"Le phénomène juridique du dédoublement fonctionnel," in W. Schätzel and H. J. Schlochauer (eds.), *Rechtsfragen der Internationalen Organisation: Festschrift für H. Wehberg* (Frankfurt am Main: Klostermann, 1956), pp. 324–342.

Schmitt, C., *The Concept of the Political* (University of Chicago Press, 1996).

Constitutional Theory (Durham, NC: Duke University Press, 2008).

The Crisis of Parliamentary Democracy (Cambridge, MA: MIT Press, 1986).

Die Diktatur: von den Anfängen des modernen Souveränitätsgedankens bis zum proletarischen Klassenkampf (Berlin: Duncker & Humblot, 1994).

Die Kernfrage des Völkerbundes (Berlin: Dümmler, 1926).

The Nomos of the Earth in the International Law of the Jus Publicum Europaeum (New York: Telos Press, 2003).

Political Theology: Four Chapters on the Concept of Sovereignty (University of Chicago Press, 2005).

Verfassungslehrer (Munich and Leipzig: Duncker & Humblot, 1928).

Schönberger, C., *Unionsbürger: Europas föderales Bürgerrecht in vergleichender Sicht* (Tübingen, Mohr-Siebeck, 2005).

Shachar, A., *Multicultural Jurisdiction* (Cambridge University Press, 2010).

Simmons, A. J., "Human Rights and World Citizenship: The Universality of Human Rights in Kant and Locke," in A. J. Simmons, *Justification and Legitimacy: Essays on Rights and Obligations* (Cambridge University Press, 2000), pp. 179–196.

Simmons, B., *Mobilizing for Human Rights: International Law in Domestic Politics* (Cambridge University Press, 2009).

Simpson, G., *Great Powers and Outlaw States: Unequal Sovereigns in the Internal Legal Order* (Cambridge University Press, 2004).

Slaughter, A.-M., *A New World Order* (Princeton University Press, 2004).

Sousa Santos, B. de, *Toward a New Common Sense: Law, Science and Politics in the Paradigmatic Transition* (New York: Routledge, 1995).

Toward a New Legal Common Sense: Law, Globalization and Emancipation (London: Butterworths, 2002).

Spektorowski, A., "Carl Schmitt: Republican Citizenship, Repression of Libel Rights and Multi-Polarity," in Y. Peled, N. Lewin-Epstein, G. Mundlak, and J. Cohen (eds.), *Democratic Citizenship and War* (London: Routledge, 2011), pp. 13–30.

Spruyt, H., *The Sovereign State and Its Competitors* (Princeton University Press, 1994).

Stepan, A., Linz, J. J., and Yadav, Y., *Crafting State-Nations: India and Other Multinational Democracies* (Baltimore, MD: Johns Hopkins University Press, 2011).

Stone, J., *Legal Controls of International Conflict* (New York: Rinehart, 1954).

Sunstein, C., *Legal Reasoning and Political Conflict* (New York: Oxford University Press, 1996).

Tan, K., "The Duty to Protect," in T. Nardin and M. S. Williams (eds.), *Humanitarian Intervention: NOMOS XLVII* (New York University Press, 2006), pp. 84–116.

Taylor, C., *Modern Social Imaginaries* (Durham, NC: Duke University Press, 2004).

Teitel, R., *Humanity's Law* (Oxford University Press, 2011).

Teson, F., "The Liberal Case for Humanitarian Intervention," in J. L. Holzgrefe and R. O. Keohane (eds.), *Humanitarian Intervention: Ethical, Legal, and Political Dilemmas* (Cambridge University Press, 2003), pp. 93–129.

Teubner, G., "Global Bukowina: Legal Pluralism in the World Society," in G. Teubner (ed.), *Global Law Without a State* (Brookfield, VT: Dartmouth Publishing Group, 1997), pp. 3–15.

(ed.), *Global Law Without a State* (Brookfield, VT: Dartmouth Publishing Group, 1997).

"Societal Constitutionalism: Alternatives to State-Centered Constitutional Theory?" in C. Joerges, I. Sand, and G. Teubner (eds.), *Transnational Governance and Constitutionalism* (Portland, OR and Oxford: Hart Publishing, 2004), pp. 3–28.

Tilly, C. (ed.), *The Formation of National States in Western Europe* (Princeton University Press, 1975).

"War Making and State Making as Organized Crime," in P. B. Evans, D. Rueschemeyer, and T. Skocpol (eds.), *Bringing the State Back In* (Cambridge University Press, 1985), pp. 169–191.

Tully, J., *Public Philosophy in a New Key, Volume II: Imperialism and Civic Freedom* (Cambridge University Press, 2008).

Urbinati, N., *Representative Democracy* (University of Chicago Press, 2006).

Verdross, A., *Die Verfassung der Völkerrechtsgemeinschaft* (Vienna: J. Springer, 1926).

Walker, N., "Beyond the Holistic Constitution?" in P. Dobner and M. Loughlin (eds.), *The Twilight of Constitutionalism?* (Oxford University Press, 2010), pp. 291–308.

"Constitutionalism and Pluralism in the Global Context," forthcoming in M. Avbelj and J. Komarek (eds.), *Constitutional Pluralism in the European Union and Beyond* (Oxford: Hart Publishing, 2012).

"Late Sovereignty in the European Union," in N. Walker (ed.), *Sovereignty in Transition: Essays in European Law* (Oxford: Hart Publishing, 2003), pp. 3–32.

Wallach, J. R., "Human Rights as an Ethics of Power," in R. A. Wilson (ed.), *Human Rights and the War on Terror* (Cambridge University Press, 2005), pp. 108–137.

Walzer, M., *Arguing About War* (New Haven, CT: Yale University Press, 2004).

Weber, M., *Economy and Society*, 2 vols. (Berkeley, CA: University of California Press, 1978).

Weiler, J. H., *The Constitution of Europe: "Do the New Clothes Have an Emperor?" and Other Essays on European Integration* (Oxford University Press, 1999).

"Federalism without a Constitution: The Principle of Constitutional Tolerance," in K. Nicolaidis and R. Howse (eds.), *The Federal Vision: Legitimacy and Levels of Governance in the United States and European Union* (Oxford University Press, 2001), pp. 54–70.

Wheare, K., *Federal Government* (New York: Oxford University Press, 1964).

Zolo, D., "Humanitarian Militarism?" in S. Besson and J. Tasioulas (eds.), *The Philosophy of International Law* (Oxford University Press, 2010).

Articles

Alston, P., "Reconceiving the UN Human Rights Regime: Challenges Confronting the New Human Rights Council," *Melbourne Journal of International Law*, 7 (2006), 185–224.

Alter, K., "Delegating to International Courts: Self-Binding vs. Other-Binding Delegation," *Law and Contemporary Problems*, 71 (2008), 37–76.

Alvarez, J. E., "Hegemonic International Law Revisited," *American Journal of International Law*, 97 (2003), 873–888.

Amar, A., "Five Views of Federalism: 'Converse-1983' in Context," *Vanderbilt Law Review* 47 (1994), 1229–1249.

Andrews, P. E., "Who's Afraid of Polygamy? Exploring the Boundaries of Family, Equality, and Custom in South Africa," *Utah Law Review*, 11 (2009), 351–379.

Arato, A., "Multi-track Constitutionalism Beyond Carl Schmitt," *Constellations*, 18 (2011), 324–351.

"Post-Sovereign Constitution-Making and its Pathology in Iraq," *New York Law School Law Review*, 51 (2006–2007), 535–555.

Arato, A. and Cohen, J. L., "Banishing the Sovereign? Internal and External Sovereignty in Arendt," *Constellations*, 16 (2009), 307–330.

Arato, J., "The Concept of Constitution and Constitutionalism Beyond the State: Two Perspectives on the Material Constitution of the United Nations," *International Journal of Constitutional Law*, 10 (2012, forthcoming).

Armitage, D., "The Contagion of Sovereignty: Declarations of Independence since 1776," *South African Historical Journal*, 52 (2005), 1–18.

Baynes, K., "Discourse Ethics and the Political Conception of Human Rights," *Ethics & Global Politics*, 2 (2009), 1–22.

Bellamy, A., "Kosovo and the Advent of Sovereignty as Responsibility," *Journal of Intervention and Statebuilding*, 3 (2009), 163–184.

Benhabib, S., "Claiming Rights Across Borders: International Human Rights and Democratic Sovereignty," *American Political Science Review*, 102 (2009), 691–704.

Benvenisti, E., "Reclaiming Democracy: The Strategic Uses of Foreign and International Law by National Courts," *American Journal of International Law*, 102 (2008), 241–274.

"The Security Council and the Law on Occupation: Resolution 1483 on Iraq in Historical Perspective," *Israeli Defense Force Law Review*, 1 (2003), 19–38.

Berman, P. S., "Global Legal Pluralism," *Southern Carolina Law Review*, 80 (2007), 1155–1238.

"The New Legal Pluralism," *Annual Review of Law and Social Science*, 5 (2009), 225–242.

Besselink, L., "The Globalizing Turn in the Relationship Between Constitutional-ism and Democracy," *Rechtsfilosophie & Rechtstheorie*, 39 (2010), 234–254.

Besson, S., "European Legal Pluralism after Kadi," *European Constitutional Law Review*, 5 (2009), 237–264.

"How International is the European Legal Order?" *NoFo*, 5 (2008), 50–70.

Bhuta, N., "The Antinomies of Transformative Occupation," *European Journal of International Law*, 16 (2005), 721–740.

"New Modes and Orders: Is a Jus Post Bellum of Constitutional Transform-ation Possible or Desirable?" *University of Toronto Law Journal*, 63 (2010), 99–854.

Blackburn, R., "Reclaiming Human Rights," *New Left Review*, 69 (2011), 126–138.

Bogdandy, A. V., "Pluralism, Direct Effect and the Ultimate Say: On the Relation-ship Between International and Domestic Constitutional Law," *International Journal of Constitutional Law*, 6 (2008), 397–413.

Boon, K., "Legislative Reform in Post-Conflict Zones: Jus Post Bellum and the Contemporary Occupant's Law-Making Powers," *McGill Law Journal*, 50 (2005), 285–326.

Brunkhorst, H., "A Polity Without a State? European Constitutionalism Between Evolution and Revolution," *International Journal of Constitutional Law*, 3 (2005), 88–106.

Buchanan, A. and Keohane, R., "The Legitimacy of Global Governance Insti-tutions," *Ethics and International Affairs*, 20 (2006), 405–437.

"The Preventive Use of Force: A Cosmopolitan Institutional Proposal," *Ethics & International Affairs*, 18 (2004), 1–22.

Burke-White, W., "International Legal Pluralism," *Michigan Journal of Inter-national Law*, 25 (2004), 963–979.

Cameron, I., "UN Targeted Sanctions, Legal Safeguards and the European Convention on Human Rights," *New Jersey Journal of International Law*, 72 (2003), 159–214.

Chatterjee, P., "Empire and Nation Revisited: Fifty Years After Bandung," *Inter-Asia Cultural Studies*, 6 (2005), 487–496.

Cohen, J., "Minimalism about Human Rights: The Most We Can Hope For?" *Journal of Political Philosophy*, 12 (2004), 190–213.

Cohen, J. and Sabel, C., "Extra Rempublicam Nulla Justitia?" *Philosophy and Public Affairs*, 34 (2006), 147–175.

"Global Democracy," *New York University Journal of International Law and Politics*, 37 (2005), 763–797.

Cohen, J. L., "Changing Paradigms of Citizenship and the Exclusiveness of the Demos," *International Sociology*, 14 (1999), 245–268.

"A Global State of Emergency or the Further Constitutionalisation of International Law: A Pluralist Approach," *Constellations*, 15 (2008), 456–484.

"The Politics and Risks of the New Legal Pluralism in the Domain of Intimacy," *International Journal of Constitutional Law* 10/2 (2012).

"Rethinking Human Rights, Democracy and Sovereignty in the Age of Globalization," *Political Theory*, 36 (2008), 578–606.

"Rights, Citizenship, and the Modern Form of the Social: Dilemmas of Arendtian Republicanism," *Constellations*, 3 (1996), 164–189.

"The Role of International Law in Post-Conflict Constitution-Making: Toward a *Jus Post Bellum* for 'Interim Occupations,'" *New York Law Review*, 51 (2007), 497–532.

"Sovereign Equality Versus Imperial Right: The Battle Over the New World Order," *Constellations*, 13 (2006), 485–505.

"Whose Sovereignty? Empire Versus International Law," *Ethics and International Affairs*, 18 (2004), 1–24.

Cranston, M., "Are There Any Human Rights?" *Dadaelus*, 12 (1983), 1–17.

Cruz, J. B., "The Legacy of the Maastricht-Urteil and the Pluralist Movement," *European Law Journal*, 14 (2008), 389–422.

de Búrca, G., "Developing Democracy Beyond the State," *Columbia Journal of Transnational Law*, 46 (2008), 101–158.

"The EU, the European Court of Justice and the International Legal Order after Kadi," *Harvard International Law Journal*, 51 (2009), 1–49.

Dezalay, Y. and Garth, B., "From the Cold War to Kosovo: The Rise and Renewal of the Field of International Human Rights," *Annual Review of Law and Social Science*, 2 (2006), pp. 231–255.

Doyle, M., "International Ethics and the Responsibility to Protect," *International Studies Review*, 13 (2011), 72–84.

Dupuy, P. M., "The Constitutional Dimension of the Charter of the United Nations Revisited," *Max Planck Yearbook of International Law* (1997), 1–33.

Eijsbouts, W. T. and Besselink, L., "The Law of Laws – Overcoming Pluralism," *European Constitutional Law Review*, 4 (2008), 395–398.

Falk, R., "The Relevance of International Law to Palestinian Rights in the West Bank and Gaza: In Legal Defense of the Intifada," *Harvard International Law Journal*, 32 (1991), 129–157.

Fassbender, B., "The United Nations Charter as Constitution of the International Community," *Columbia Journal of Transnational Law*, 36 (1998), 529–619.

Fazal, T. M., "State Death in the International System," *International Organization*, 58 (2004), 311–344.

Fearon, J. D. and Laitin, D. D., "Neo-Trusteeship and the Problem of Weak States," *International Security*, 28 (2004), 5–43.

Feldman, N., "Cosmopolitan Law?" *Yale Law Journal*, 116 (2007), 1024–1070.

Fischer-Lescano, A. and Teubner, G., "Regime Collisions: The Vain Search for Unity in the Fragmentation of Global Law," *Michigan Journal of International Law*, 25 (2004), 999–1046.

Forst, R., "The Justification of Human Rights and the Basic Right of Justification: A Reflexive Approach," *Ethics*, 120 (2010), 711–740.

Fox, G. H., "The Occupation of Iraq," *Georgetown Journal of International Law*, 36 (2005), 195–297.

Franck, T. M., "The Emerging Right to Democratic Governance," *American Journal of International Law*, 86 (1992), 46–91.

"The Powers of Appreciation: Who is the Ultimate Guardian of UN Legality?" *International Journal of Constitutional Law*, 86 (1992), 519–523.

Gallie, W. B., "Essentially Contested Concepts," *Proceedings of the Aristotelian Society*, 56 (1955), 167–198.

Gerstle, G., "Federalism in America: Beyond the Tea Partiers," *Dissent*, 57 (2010), 29–36.

Goodin, R., "Global Democracy: In the Beginning," *International Theory*, 2 (2010), 175–209.

Goodwin, M., "Plugging the Legitimacy Gap? The Ubiquity of Human Rights and the Rhetoric of Global Constitutionalism," *Rechtsfilosofie & Rechtstheorie*, 39 (2010), 245–255.

Griffin, J., "Discrepancies Between the Best Philosophical Account of Human Rights and the International Documents," *Proceedings of the Aristotelian Society*, 101 (2001), 1–28.

Griffiths, J., "What is Legal Pluralism?" *Journal of Legal Pluralism and Unofficial Law*, 50 (1986), 1–55.

Griller, S., "International Law, Human Rights and the Community's Autonomous Legal Order," *European Constitutional Law Review*, 4 (2008), 528–553.

Grimm, D., "Integration by Constitution," *International Journal of Constitutional Law*, 3 (2005), 193–208.

Günther, K., "Legal Pluralism or Uniform Concept of Law: Globalization as a Problem of Legal Theory," *NoFo*, 5 (2008), 5–21.

Habermas, J., "Constitutional Democracy: A Paradoxical Union of Contradictory Principles?" *Political Theory*, 29 (2001), 766–781.

"Remarks on Legitimation Through Human Rights," *Philosophy and Social Criticism*, 24 (1998), 157–171.

"Why Europe Needs a Constitution," *New Left Review*, 11 (2001), 5–26.

Halberstam, D. and Stein, E., "The United Nations, the European Union and the King of Sweden: Economic Sanctions and Individual Rights in a Plural World Order," *Common Market Law Review*, 46 (2009), 13–72.

Harris, G. T., "The Era of Multilateral Occupation," *Berkeley Journal of International Law*, 24 (2006), 1–78.

Hart, H. L. A., "Are There Any Natural Rights?" *Philosophical Review*, 64 (1955), 175–191.

Hathaway, O., "Do Human Rights Treaties Make a Difference?" *Yale Law Journal*, 111 (2002), 1935–2042.

Henkin, L., "The 'S' Word: Sovereignty, Globalization and Human Rights, Et Cetera," *Fordham Law Review*, 68 (1999), 1–14.

Hoffman, J., "Terrorism Blacklisting: Putting European Human Rights Guarantees to the Test," *Constellations*, 15 (2008), 543–560.

Ignatieff, M., "The Burden," *New York Times Magazine*, 5 January 2003, 22.

Imseis, A., "On the Fourth Geneva Convention and the Occupied Palestinian Territory," *Harvard International Law Journal*, 44 (2003), 65–138.

Keith, L., "The United Nations International Covenant on Civil and Political Rights: Does it Make a Difference in Human Rights Behavior?" *Journal of Peace Research*, 36 (1999), 95–118.

Kelsen, H., "The Legal Status of Germany According to the Declaration of Berlin," *American Journal of International Law*, 39 (1945), 518–526.

"The Principle of Sovereign Equality of States as a Basis for International Organization," *Yale Law Journal*, 53 (1944), 207–220.

Keohane, R. O., Macedo, S., and Moravcsik, A., "Democracy-Enhancing Multilateralism," *International Organization*, 63 (2009), 1–31.

Kingsbury, B., "Sovereignty and Inequality," *European Journal of International Law*, 9 (1998), 599–625.

Kingsbury, B., Krisch, N., and Stewart, R. B., "The Emergence of Global Administrative Law," *Law and Contemporary Problems*, 68 (2005), 15–61.

Koskenniemi, M., "Constitutionalism as Mindset: Reflections on Kantian Themes about International Law and Globalization," *Theoretical Inquiries in Law*, 8 (2007), 9–36.

"The Fate of Public International Law: Between Technique and Politics," *Modern Law Review*, 70 (2007), 1–30.

"The Police in the Temple, Order, Justice and the UN: A Dialectical View," *European Journal of International Law*, 6 (1995), 338–348.

Krasner, S. D., "Rebuilding Democracy After Conflict: The Case for Shared Sovereignty," *Journal of Democracy*, 16 (2005), 60–83.

"Sharing Sovereignty: New Institutions for Collapsed and Failing States," *International Security*, 29 (2004), 85–120.

Krisch, N., "The Pluralism of Global Administrative Law," *European Journal of International Law*, 17 (2006), 247–278.

Krisch, N., Berman, P. S., and Kennedy, D., "One, Two, Three, Many Legal Orders: Legal Pluralism and the Cosmopolitan Dream," *New York University Review of Law & Social Change*, 31 (2007), 641–659.

Kumm, M., "The Jurisprudence of Constitutional Conflict: Constitutional Supremacy in Europe Before and After the Constitutional Treaty," *European Law Journal*, 11 (2005), 262–307.

"The Legitimacy of International Law: A Constitutionalist Analysis," *European Journal of International Law*, 15 (2004), 907–931.

"Who is the Final Arbiter of Constitutionality in Europe?" *Common Market Law Review*, 36 (1999), 509–514.

Lijphart, A., "Consociation and Federation: Conceptual and Empirical Links," *Canadian Journal of Political Science*, 12 (1979), 499–515.

"Non-Majoritarian Democracy: A Comparison of Federal and Consociational Themes," *Publius: The Journal of Federalism*, 15 (1985), 3–15.

Luhmann, N., "The World Society as a Social System," *International Journal of General Systems*, 8 (1982), 131–138.

MacCormick, N., "Beyond the Sovereign State," *Modern Law Review*, 56 (1993), 1–18.

"The Maastricht-Urteil: Sovereignty Now," *European Law Journal*, 1 (1995), 259–266.

Macklem, P., "Humanitarian Intervention and the Distribution of Sovereignty in International Law," *Ethics and International Affairs*, 22 (2008), 369–393.

"What is International Human Rights Law? Three Applications of a Distributive Account," *McGill Law Journal*, 52 (2007), 575–604.

Maduro, M. P., "The Importance of Being Called a Constitution: Constitutional Authority and the Authority of Constitutionalism," *International Journal of Constitutional Law*, 3 (2005), 332–356.

Mamdani, M., "Responsibility to Protect or the Right to Punish?" *Journal of Intervention and Statebuilding*, 4 (2010), 53–67.

Mazower, M., "The Strange Triumph of Human Rights, 1933–1950," *The Historical Journal*, 47 (2004), 379–398.

McCrudden, C., "Human Dignity and Judicial Interpretation of Human Rights," *European Journal of International Law*, 19 (2008), 655–724.

Meron, T., "The Humanization of Humanitarian Law," *American Journal of International Law*, 94 (2000), 239–278.

Merry, S. E., "Legal Pluralism," *Law and Society Review*, 22 (1988), 869–896.

Moore, S. F., "Law and Social Change: The Semi-Autonomous Social Field as an Appropriate Subject for Study," *Law and Society Review*, 7 (1973), 719–746.

Moravcsik, A., "The Origin of Human Rights Regimes: Democratic Delegation in Postwar Europe," *International Organization*, 54 (2000), 217–252.

Nagel, T., "The Problem of Global Justice," *Philosophy and Public Affairs*, 33 (2005), 113–147.

Nickel, J., Human Rights, in E. N. Zalta (ed.), *The Stanford Encyclopedia of Philosophy* (2010), available at www.plato.stanford.edu.

Nicolaidis, K., "The New Constitution as European Demoi-cracy?" *Critical Review of International Social and Political Philosophy*, 7 (2004), 76–93.

Nussbaum, M., "Human Rights Theory: Capabilities and Human Rights," *Fordham Law Review*, 66 (1997), 273–300.

Offe, C., "Governance: An Empty Signifier?" *Constellations*, 16 (2009), 550–562.

Perritt, Jr., H., "Structures and Standards of Political Trusteeship," *UCLA Journal of International Law and Foreign Affairs*, 8 (2004), 385–472.

Pettit, P., "Democracy, National and International," *The Monist*, 89 (2006), 301–324.

Philpott, D., "Usurping the Sovereignty of Sovereignty," *World Politics*, 53 (2001), 297–324.

Pogge, T., "Cosmopolitanism and Sovereignty," *Ethics*, 103 (1992), 48–75.

"Creating Supra-National Institutions Democratically: Reflections on the European Union's 'Democratic Deficit,'" *The Journal of Political Philosophy*, 5 (1997), 163–182.

Quigley, J., "The United Nations Security Council: Promethean Protector or Helpless Hostage?" *Texas International Law Journal*, 35 (2000), 129–172.

Reisman, W. M., "The Constitutional Crisis in the United Nations," *International Journal of Constitutional Law*, 87 (1993), 83–100.

"The Revival of Empire," special section in *Ethics & International Affairs*, 17 (2003), 34–98.

Roberts, A., "Prolonged Military Occupation: The Israeli-Occupied Territories since 1967," *American Journal of International Law*, 84 (1990), 44–103.

"Transformative Military Occupation: Applying the Laws of War and Human Rights," *American Journal of International Law*, 100 (2006), 580–622.

Rosand, E., "Security Council Resolution 1373, the Counter-Terrorism Committee, and the Fight Against Terrorism," *International Journal of Constitutional Law*, 97 (2003), 333–341.

"The Security Council's Efforts to Monitor the Implementation of Al Qaeda/Taliban Sanctions," *International Journal of Constitutional Law*, 98 (2004), 747–758.

Rummens, S., "The Co-originality of Law and Democracy in the Moral Horizon of Modernity," *Rechtsfilosofie & Rechtstheorie*, 39 (2010), 256–266.

Scheffer, D. J., "Beyond Occupation Law," *American Journal of International Law*, 97 (2003), 842–859. Reprinted in *Future Implications of the Iraq Conflict*, selections from the *American Journal of International Law* (Washington, DC: American Society of International Law, Jan. 2004), pp. 130–147.

Schönberger, C., "Die Europäische Union als Bund," *Archiv des öffentlichen Rechts*, 129 (2004), 81–120.

Sen, A., "Elements of a Theory of Human Rights," *Philosophy and Public Affairs*, 32 (2004), 315–356.

Sezgin, Y., "How to Integrate Universal Human Rights into Customary and Religious Legal Systems?" *Journal of Legal Pluralism*, 60 (2010), 5–40.

Shelton, D., "Normative Hierarchy in International Law," *American Journal of International Law*, 100 (2006), 291–323.

Simma, B., "From Bilateralism to Community Interest in International Law," *Recueil des cours*, 250 (1994), 217–384.

Slaughter, A.-M., "A Global Community of Courts," *Harvard International Law Review*, 44 (2003), 191–219.

"Security, Solidarity, and Sovereignty: The Grand Theme of UN Reform," *American Journal of International Law*, 99 (2005), 619–631.

Slaughter, A.-M. and Burke-White, W., "An International Constitutional Moment," *Harvard International Law Journal*, 43 (2003), 1–21.

Sloan, B., "The United Nations Charter as a Constitution," *Pace Yearbook of International Law*, 1 (1989), 61–126.

Somek, A., "Kelsen Lives," *European Journal of International Law*, 18 (2007), 409–451.

Stoler, A., "On Degrees of Imperial Sovereignty," *Public Culture*, 18 (2006), 125–146.

Sweet, A. S., "Constitutionalism, Legal Pluralism and International Relations," *Indiana Journal of Global Legal Studies*, 16 (2009), 626–667.

Szasz, P., "The Security Council Starts Legislating," *American Journal of International Law*, 96 (2002), 901–905.

Talmon, S., "The Security Council as World Legislature," *American Journal of International Law*, 99 (2005), 175–193.

Tamanaha, B. Z., "Understanding Legal Pluralism: Past to Present, Local to Global," *Sydney Law Review*, 30 (2008), 375–411.

Tasioulis, J., "Are Human Rights Essentially Triggers for Intervention?" *Philosophy Compass*, 4 (2009), 938–950.

Teitel, R. G., "Humanity Law: A New Interpretive Lens on the International Sphere," *Fordham Law Review*, 77 (2008), 667–702.

"Humanity's Law: Rule of Law for the New Global Politics," *Cornell International Law Journal*, 35 (2002), 355–387.

Teubner, G., "Constitutionalising Polycontexturality," *Social and Legal Studies*, 19 (2010), 1–25.

Tomuschat, C., "International Law: Ensuring the Survival of Mankind on the Eve of a New Century: The Hague General Course on Public International Law," *Revue des Cours*, 281 (1999), 9–438.

Vagts, D. F., "Hegemonic International Law," *American Journal of International Law*, 95 (2001), 843–848.

Walker, N., "Constitutionalism and the Incompleteness of Democracy: An Iterative Relationship," *Rechtsfilosofie & Rechtstheorie*, 39 (2010), 206–233.

"The Idea of Constitutional Pluralism," *Modern Law Review*, 65 (2002), 317–359.

"Reply to Four Critics," *Rechtsfilosofie & Rechtstheorie*, 39 (2010), 281–286.

"Taking Constitutionalism Beyond the State," *Political Studies*, 56 (2008), 519–543.

Walzer, M., "The Moral Standing of States," *Philosophy and Public Affairs*, 9 (1980), 209–229.

Weiler, J. H., "The Geology of International Law: Governance, Democracy and Legitimacy," *Volkerrecht/Heidelberg Journal of International Law*, 64 (2004), 547–562.

"On the Power of the Word: Europe's Constitutional Iconography," *International Journal of Constitutional Law*, 3 (2005), 184–187.

Wertheim, S., "A Solution from Hell: The United States and the Rise of Humanitarian Interventionism, 1991–2003," *Journal of Genocide Research*, 12 (2010), 149–172.

Wet, E., "The International Constitutional Order," *International Comparative Law Quarterly*, 55 (2006), 51–76.

Wheeler, N., "Humanitarian Intervention After Kosovo: Emergent Norm, Moral Duty or the Coming of Anarchy?" *International Affairs*, 77 (2001), 113–128.

Yannis, A., "The Concept of Suspended Sovereignty in International Law and Its Implications in International Politics," *European Journal of International Law*, 13 (2002), 1037–1052.

Yoo, J., "Iraqi Reconstruction and the Law of Occupation," *Journal of International Law & Policy*, 11 (2004) 7–22.

Reports

Alkire, S., *A Conceptual Framework for Human Security*. Working Paper 2, Centre for Research on Inequality, Human Security, and Ethnicity, Queen Elizabeth House, Oxford University (2003).

Cameron, I., *The ECHR, Due Process and UN Security Council Counter-Terrorism Sanctions*. Report to the Council of Europe, 2 June 2006, available at www.coe.int

Chesterman, S., *The UN Security Council and the Rule of Law*. Final Report and Recommendations from the Austrian Initiative (2004–2008).

Commission on Human Security, *Human Security Now: Protecting and Empowering People* (New York: Commission on Human Security, 2003).

Convention IV *Relative to the Protection of Civilian Persons in Time of War* (Geneva, Switzerland, 1949).

"Fragmentation of International Law. Problems caused by the Diversification and Expansion of International Law." Report of the Study Group of the International Law Commission finalized by Martti Koskenniemi A/CN4/L.682 (13 April 2006) (Analytical Report).

Freedom House Report, *Democracy's Century: A Survey of Global Political Change in the 20th Century* (New York: Freedom House, 1999).

Gierycz, D., "The Responsibility to Protect: A Legal and Rights-Based Perspective," in *Responsibility to Protect*, NUPI Report No. 5 (Oslo: Norwegian Institute of International Affairs, 2008).

Hague Regulations Respecting the Laws and Customs of War on Land, 18 October 1907.

ICISS, *The Responsibility to Protect: Report of the International Commission on Intervention and State Sovereignty* (Ottawa: International Development Research Centre, 2001).

International Committee of the Red Cross, *Commentary On The Geneva Convention (IV) Relative to the Protection of Civilian Persons In Time of War* (1958).

The Secretary-General, *In Larger Freedom: Towards Development, Security and Human Rights for All,* delivered to the United Nations General Assembly (2005).

Secretary-General's Bulletin on Observance by United Nations Forces of International Humanitarian Law (New York: UN, 1999).

The Special Representative of the Secretary-General, *On the Authority of the Interim Administration in Kosovo* (New York: UN, 1999).

On the Authority of the Transitional Administration in East Timor (New York: UN, 1999).

United Nations, A More Secure World: Our Shared Responsibility, Report of the Secretary-General's High-level Panel on Threats, Challenges and Change (New York: United Nations, 2004), www.un.org/secureworld.

Secretary-General's Report: Implementing the Responsibility to Protect (New York: UN, 2009).

Official documents

Déclaration des Droits de l'Homme et du Citoyen (1789).

Geneva Convention for the Amelioration of the Condition of the Wounded and Sick in Armed Forces in the Field (1949), available at www.umn.edu/humanrts/instree/y1gcacws.htm

Hague Regulations Respecting the Laws and Customs of War on Land, October 18, 1907.

Protocol Additional to the Geneva Conventions of 1949 (Protocol II) (Geneva, Switzerland, 1977).

Rome Statute of the International Criminal Court, available at untreaty.un.org/cod/icc/statute/romefra.htm

UNICEF, *Convention on the Rights of the Child,* adopted and opened for signature, ratification and accession by General Assembly resolution 44/25 of November 20, 1989, entry into force September, 2 1990, in accordance with article 49.

United Nations, *Charter of the United Nations* (New York: UN, 1945).

Convention on the Prevention and Punishment of the Crime of Genocide (New York: UN, 1948).

Convention Against Torture, adopted and opened for signature, ratification, and accession by General Assembly resolution 39/46 of December 10, 1984 entry into force 26 June 1987, in accordance with article 27 (1).

Declaration On Principles of International Law Concerning Friendly Relations and Co-operation Among States in Accordance with the Charter of the United Nations (New York: UN, 1970).

General Assembly, *World Summit Outcome* (New York: UN, 2005), available at www.un.org/summit2005/documents.html

International Covenant on Civil and Political Rights (New York: UN, 1966).

International Covenant on Economic, Social and Cultural Rights (New York: UN, 1966).

Security Council Resolution 1333 of December 19, 2000 (New York: UN, 2000).

Security Council Resolution 1373 (New York: UN, 2001).

Security Council Resolution 1390 of January 16, 2002 (New York: UN, 2002).

Security Council Resolution 1483 (New York: UN, 2003), available at www.un. org/documents/scres

Security Council Resolution 1540 of April 28, 2004 (New York: UN, 2004).

The United Nations Universal Declaration of Human Rights (New York: UN, 1948).

Vienna Convention on the Law of Treaties (1969).

Other sources

Case T-306/01 *Yusuf and Al Barakaat International Foundation v. Council and Commission (2005) ECR II-3353 Yassin Abdullah Kadi and Al Barakaat International Foundation v. Council of the European Union and Commission of the European Communities*, September 2008.

Case T-315/01 *Kadi v. Council and Commission* (2005) ECR II-36649 (Kadi CFI).

Costa v. ENEL, ECR 585 (European Court of Justice 1964).

Cruz, J. B., "The Legacy of the Maastricht-Urteil and the Pluralist Movement," EUI Working Papers, RSCAS 2007/13.

de Witte, B., "*The European Union as an International Legal Experiment*," paper drafted for the workshop on *The EU Between Constitutionalism and International Law*, New York University, October 2008. European Court of Justice, Joined Cases C-402/05 P and C-415/05P 2008.

Jaeger, H. M., "UN Reform and Global Governmentality" (unpublished manuscript).

Krisch, N., "Imperial International Law" (2004), available at http://eprints.lse.ac.uk/id/eprint/13215

Marbury v. Madison, 5 US 137 (US Supreme Court 1803).

Menendez, A. J., "From Constitutional Pluralism to a Pluralistic Constitution?" RECON Online Working Paper 2011/02 January 2011, www.reconproject. eu/projectweb/portalproject/RECONWorkingPapers.html

Moneta, F., "State Immunity for International Crimes: The Case of Germany versus Italy before the ICJ" (2009), available at www.haguejusticeportal.net

Opinion 1/91, *Draft Treaty on the Establishment of a European Economic Area (EEA)*, ECR I-6079 (European Court of Justice, 1991).

Opinion of Advocate General Poiares Maduro, *Yassin Abdullah Kadi and Al Barakaat International Foundation v. Council of the European Union and Commission of the European Communities*, Joined Cases C-402/05 P and C-415/05 P, delivered January 16, 2008.

Prosecutor v. *Dusko Tadic*, International Criminal Tribunal for the Former Yugoslavia (1999).

Scheppele, K., "The International State of Emergency," paper presented at the Victoria Colloquium on Political, Social, and Legal Theory, University of Victoria, January 26, 2007.

Scheppele, K. L., "The International State of Emergency: Challenges to Constitutionalism after September 11," paper presented to the Yale Legal Theory Workshop, Princeton University (2006).

Somek, A., "From the Rule of Law to the Constitutionalist Makeover: Changing European Conceptions of Public International Law," University of Iowa Legal Studies Research Paper No. 09–25 (2009).

"Monism: A Tale of the Undead," University of Iowa Legal Studies Research Paper No. 10–22 (2010).

Van Gend en Loos v. *Nederlandse Administratie der Belastingen*, ECR 1 (European Court of Justice 1963).

Yoo, J., "Iraqi Reconstruction and the Law of Occupation: Hearing on Constitutionalism, Human Rights and the Rule of Law in Iraq Before the Subcommittee on the Constitution," Senate Subcommittee on the Judiciary (2003).

INDEX

accountability, 62, 65, 75, 84, 213
Afghanistan, 272
alliances, 121, 129
Alvarez, José, 351, 379, 384, 385, 392, 393, 395
America
  Civil War, 228
  constitutional form, 90
  federation, 93, 135
  imperialism, 94
  popular sovereignty, 114, 128
  theorizing of federation, 89, 114, 120
Annan, Kofi, 173, 174
annexation, principle against, 255
Arato, Andrew, 332, 347, 349, 352, 357, 359, 366, 376, 382, 388, 395, 399
Arato, Julian, 366, 394, 395
Arendt, Hannah, 166, 198
authority, 9, 31, 33, 56, 284
  competing claims to, 72
  and sovereignty, 26
autonomy, 43, 48, 74, 200, 218, 259
  and constitutional quality, 75
  external claims to, 28
  and federation, 93
  of the global legal system, 46
  and legitimacy, 204
  and self-determination, 10, 15, 67
  and sovereign equality, 201

Bain, William, 245
Beaud, Olivier, 106, 138, 139, 151
Beitz, Charles, 184
Benton, Lauren, 90
Benvenisti, Eyal, 230, 231, 232, 234, 236, 241, 249

Berman, P. S., 341, 342
Bhuta, N., 245, 246, 253
Buchanan, Allan, 175

Calhoun, J. C., 89, 120, 128, 131, 140
Calhounian dilemma, 120, 127, 129, 131, 140
centralization and decentralization, 105
Chayes, A., 210
Chayes, A. H., 210
citizenship, 92, 319
  and federation, 110
  and human rights, 170
  as membership of a political community, 202
  principle of equal, 166
civilians and soldiers, 230, 239
coalitions, 100, 174, 213
Cohen, Jean L., 330, 339, 347, 349, 352, 359
Cohen, Josh, 187–191, 193, 195, 371, 372, 373
collective security, 42, 199
command theory of law, 27, 31
communication, 62, 73, 307
competences, allocation of, 57, 63, 66
confederation, 109, 127, 143
  and autonomy, 110
  and citizenship, 110
  competence in, 110
  direct effect within, 110
  executive functions in, 110
  jurisdiction in, 110
  legal basis of, 109
  legislative body of, 109
  relationships of member states, 110

humanitarian intervention, 3
  Clinton Doctrine, 174, 175
  criteria for, 195, 197, 212
  and domestic politics, 178
  and "exceptional illegality," 212, 213
  and human rights, 14, 159, 164,
    172, 173
  and international human rights
    discourse, 182, 195
  motivation for, 227
  politics of, 205
  regulation of, 7, 212, 214
  and sovereignty, 173, 196
  theory of, 271
  triggers for, 194
humanitarian occupations, 3, 7, 16,
  17, 223–389
  and democracy, 260
  guidelines for, 225, 264
  humanization of the law of, 227
  interim administration of, 230
  and law of belligerent occupation, 259
  legitimacy of, 264
  need for reform of the law, 226
  purpose of, 227, 259, 263
  regulation of, 223, 228
  and representation, 264
humanity, agency or personhood
  conception of, 179, 180, 219

ICISS Report, 14, 173, 175
imperialism, 44, 60, 81, 89, 91, 209, 243
  features of, 91
  and federalism, 108
  and humanitarian intervention, 177
  and the imperative of size, 89,
    93, 103
  liberal, 17, 225
  and neo-trusteeship, 243
  universal empire, 91
implied powers, 276
inclusion, principle of, 260
International Commission on
  Intervention and State
  Sovereignty, 14, 173, 175, 211, 271
International Committee of the Red
  Cross, 232
  and the Fourth Geneva Convention,
    234

international community, 3, 42, 43,
  47, 315
  enforcement of its values, 267
  exclusion from, 206, 207
  institutionalized, 63
  and the membership principle,
    196, 199
  regulatory role of, 159
  responsibility to protect, 159
  rights of non-members, 207
  and UN Security Council
    legislation, 277
  values of, 17
International Court of Justice, 55, 75,
  281, 289
international courts, 22, 25, 43, 54, 266
  and *jus cogens* norms, 266
International Criminal Court, 53, 55,
  75, 208, 209
  jurisdiction of, 161
  and the UN Security Council, 209
international criminal law, 221
international human rights, 16,
  159–377 *see also* human rights
  and constitutional rights, 183
  and contingencies in international
    relations, 186
  definition of, 178
  empirical approach to, 187
  enforcement of, 164, 176, 216,
    217, 221
  functions of, 216, 218
  and human security rights, 216
  institutionalization of, 221
  in international politics and law,
    180, 181
  justificatory minimalism and, 189
  and legitimacy, 185
  membership principle, 189
  and moral rights, 183
  and non-interference, 184
  normative criteria for assessing, 180
  and pluralism, 185
  political conception of, 163, 165,
    178, 180–187
  politics of, 169
  practical conception of, 184
  role and purpose of, 180, 182, 183,
    184, 197